MODERN CRITICAL THO

Modern Critical Thought

An Anthology of Theorists Writing on Theorists

Edited by Drew Milne

Blackwell
Publishing

350 Main Street, Malden, MA 02148-5020, USA
108 Cowley Road, Oxford OX4 1JF, UK
550 Swanston Street, Carlton, Victoria 3053, Australia

First published 2003 by Blackwell Publishing Ltd

Library of Congress Cataloging-in-Publication Data has been applied for.

ISBN 0-631-22058-5 (hardback); ISBN 0-631-22059-3 (paperback)

A catalogue record for this title is available from the British Library.

Set in 10.5/12.5pt Bembo
by Kolam Information Services Pvt. Ltd, Pondicherry, India
Printed and bound in the United Kingdom
by MPG Books Ltd, Bodmin, Cornwall

For further information on
Blackwell Publishing, visit our website:
http://www.blackwellpublishing.com

Contents

Acknowledgements

The editor and publishers gratefully acknowledge the following for permission to reproduce copyright material:

1. Lukács on Marx:
Georg Lukács, 'The Phenomenon of Reification' (1922), from 'Reification and the Consciousness of the Proletariat', *History and Class Consciousness*, trans. Rodney Livingstone (London: Merlin Press, 1971), pp. 83–110.

2. Heidegger on Nietzsche:
'The Eternal Recurrence of the Same and the Will to Power' (pp. 161–183), from *Nietzsche, Volume III: The Will to Power as Knowledge and as Metaphysics* by Martin Heidegger and translated by David Farrell Krell (San Francisco: Harper & Row, 1987). Copyright © 1987 by Harper & Row, Publishers, Inc.

3. Adorno on Freud:
Theodor Adorno, 'Sociology and Psychology' (1955), trans. Irving N. Wohlfarth, *New Left Review*, 47 (1967), pp. 79–97.

4. Merleau-Ponty on Lukács:
Maurice Merleau-Ponty, '"Western" Marxism' (1953–4), *Adventures of the Dialectic* (1955), trans. Joseph Bien (Evanston, Illinois: Northwestern University Press, 1973), pp. 30–58. Reproduced by permission of Northwestern University Press and Editions Gallimard.

5. Marcuse on Sartre:
Herbert Marcuse, 'Sartre's Existentialism' (1948), *Studies in Critical Philosophy*, trans. Joris De Bres (London: New Left Books, 1972), pp. 159–190 (paperback edition retitled *From Luther to Popper* (London: Verso, 1983)).

6. Levinas on Husserl:
Emmanuel Levinas, 'Reflections on Phenomenological "Technique"' (1959), *Discovering Existence with Husserl*, trans. Richard A. Cohen and Michael B. Smith (Evanston, Illinois: Northwestern University Press, 1998), pp. 91–102.

7. Gadamer on Heidegger:
Hans-Georg Gadamer, 'Heidegger's Later Philosophy' (1960), *Philosophical Hermeneutics*, trans. David E. Linge (Berkeley and Los Angeles: University of California Press, 1976), pp. 213–228.

8. Deleuze on Nietzsche and Kant:
Gilles Deleuze, 'Critique', *Nietzsche and Philosophy* (1962), trans. Hugh Tomlinson (London: Athlone, 1984), pp. 73–94.

9. Althusser on Marx:
Louis Althusser, 'From *Capital* to Marx's Philosophy' (1968), *Reading Capital*, trans. Ben Brewster (London: Verso, 1970), pp. 13–34.

10. Derrida on Lévi-Strauss:
Jacques Derrida, 'Structure, Sign and Play in the Discourse of the Human Sciences' (1966), *Writing and Difference*, trans. Alan Bass (London: Routledge and Kegan Paul, 1978), pp. 278–293. Reproduced with permission of the Taylor and Francis Group and the University of Chicago Press.

11. Foucault on Derrida:
Michel Foucault, 'My Body, This Paper, This Fire' (1972), trans. Geoff Bennington, *Aesthetics, Method, and Epistemology: Essential Works of Foucault*, vol. 2, ed. James D. Faubion (London: Allen Lane/Penguin, 1998), pp. 393–417. Reproduced by permission of Penguin Books Ltd. Excerpts from Jacques Derrida, *Writing and Difference*, trans. Alan Bass (London: Routledge and Kegan Paul, 1978), reproduced with permission of the Taylor and Francis Group and the University of Chicago Press.

12. Habermas on Benjamin:
Jürgen Habermas, 'Walter Benjamin: Consciousness-Raising or Rescuing Critique' (1972), trans. Frederick Lawrence, *Philosophical-Political Profiles* (Cambridge, MA: MIT, 1983), pp. 129–163.

13. Rose on Lacan:
Jacqueline Rose, 'Feminine Sexuality: Jacques Lacan and the *École Freudienne*', *Sexuality in the Field of Vision* (London: Verso, 1986), pp. 52–81.

14. Bhabha on Fanon:
Homi Bhabha, 'Interrogating Identity: Frantz Fanon and the Postcolonial Prerogative', *The Location of Culture* (London: Routledge, 1994), pp. 40–65.

15. Butler on Kristeva and Foucault:
Judith Butler, *Gender Trouble* (London: Routledge, 1990), pp. 79–94. Reprinted with permission of the Taylor and Francis Group.

16. Žižek on Žižek:
Slavoj Žižek, 'Holding the Place', from Judith Butler, Ernesto Laclau and Slavoj Žižek, *Contingency, Hegemony, Universality: Contemporary Dialogues on the Left* (London: Verso, 2000), pp. 308–329.

The publishers apologize for any errors or omissions in the above list and would be grateful to be notified of any corrections that should be incorporated in the next edition or reprint of this book.

Introduction: Criticism and/or Critique

Anyone interested in modern critical thought is faced with the difficulty of knowing how to negotiate its daunting range and complexity. Where to begin? The question could hardly be simpler and yet for any modern thinker the options appear endless and, more worryingly, groundless. Anyone engaged in a specific intellectual activity is likely to feel the force of suspicions that answers to more general questions have been assumed without justification. Reflecting on such assumptions appears to be a self-critical virtue, while scepticism has become an essential dynamic of modern thought. Self-critical reflection also prompts recognition of the historical traditions and contingencies that make up modern thought. Historical continuities undermine the claims of innovation, while contingency masks the blindness of mediation and repetition. To read Judith Butler or Slavoj Žižek it is necessary to have a smattering of Hegel and Lacan, perhaps also of Kant, Marx, Nietzsche and Freud, but it is quickly apparent that smatterings are uncritical. This anthology focuses on twentieth-century thinkers who have been influential across a number of disciplines and critical approaches, as well as providing retrospective surveys of key sources in the history of modern thought. Although many of these thinkers have the status of necessary reading, they are difficult to read. Much of modern critical thought is engaged in dialogues with previous thinkers, such as Kant, Marx, Nietzsche and Freud, whose controversial legacies rule out easy consensus. This anthology provides an introduction to the way modern thought develops such dialogues through shared and conflictual conversations.

The dialogues of modern critical thought inevitably involve disagreements and different approaches to critical reading. To read particular thinkers requires some knowledge of the shared conversation of critical ideas. It has nevertheless been common to isolate thinkers from the traditions with which they engage. Isolating names and 'isms' is obviously reductive but surprisingly common. Reductive labels appear to be a necessary simplification in the market of contemporary ideas, but there is more to critical thought than the branding of positions and the commodification of intellectual 'stars'. When the quantity of publication is so great, it becomes necessary to discern quality; and quality does not come neatly packaged but requires comparative criticism.

A focus on one critic or theorist can be a useful starting point, but the critical moment more often takes place between thinkers and across different intellectual paradigms.

A defining feature of intellectual modernity is the recognition that no one philosopher or thinker can master the totality of what is known and thought. Hegel was perhaps the last to try with any success. The extraordinary erudition of subsequent thinkers such as Marx, Max Weber or Walter Benjamin is often won at the cost of encyclopedic oeuvres that remain fascinatingly incomplete. The dangers of selecting one figure as an idol are evident from the forms of dogmatism associated with Marx and Freud, but the dangers of misunderstanding are no less critical when Adorno, Derrida, Butler or Žižek are read in isolation or treated as singular authorities. Their work opens out through readings of others without providing self-contained oeuvres. Rather than being grounded in foundational claims or first principles, critical articulation through earlier traditions is constitutive of modern critique. Another distinctive feature of modern thought is the increased awareness of thinking's dependence on language and writing. Many influential forms of modern thought also offer new ways of developing critique through reading. This helps to explain the importance of critical reading and the way critical thinking rests on the texts it criticizes.

It is, accordingly, important to grasp modern critical thought's processes of exchange, dialogue and conversation. Modern European philosophy – or what is sometimes called 'continental' philosophy[1] – looms large, but modern critical thought also breaks with traditional conceptions of philosophy. What counts as philosophy in one tradition of thought or academic context may be dismissed as non-philosophical or philosophically trivial in another. Defensive denial or negation is constitutive of many border disputes. As Merleau-Ponty puts it, 'True philosophy scoffs at philosophy, since it is aphilosophical.'[2] Many of the most important modern thinkers – Kierkegaard, Marx, Nietzsche and Freud and their successors – resist thinking of their work as philosophy, indeed are critical of philosophy and suggest the necessity of crossing philosophy's borders. Habermas is as much a critical social theorist as he is a philosopher. Derrida transgresses differences between philosophical and rhetorical or literary argument. Foucault offers radical new ways of thinking historically. Žižek finds as much intellectual grist and ideological provocation in a Hitchcock movie as in the thought of Hegel or Lacan. Philosophy remains important, reconfigured in dialogue with disciplines and social questions that go beyond the traditional problems of philosophy. It can seem as if modern academic disciplines are nevertheless designed to make it difficult to study key modern thinkers in their own right and in the spirit of their critical projects. An interest in Marxism or psychoanalysis, for example, informs many approaches and disciplines, from economics and business studies to psychology, cultural studies and nursing, but there are not many university departments of Marxism or psychoanalysis. The inter-disciplinary range of modern critical thought prompts reflection on the limits of disciplines and what might come after philosophy.[3]

Recent developments in critical thought dissolve boundaries between philosophy and critical theory, between continental and analytic philosophy, between sociology and cultural studies, and so on. This anthology suggests ways in which influential thinkers prefigure this dissolution by developing a critical awareness of thought's conditions of possibility. Approaches such as Marxism, feminism or psychoanalysis, for example, are informed by critiques of philosophy, but are more concerned to develop new critical practices. The attempt to combine theory and practice so as to change the world through knowledge is influenced above all by the way Marx politicized differentiations between pure reason and practical reason. The search for critically informed practices is also constitutive of modern critical projects with emancipatory intentions, including psychoanalysis.[4] Sartre's existentialism and Butler's conceptions of gender seek to change the way we think about who we are and imply new ways of living. Similarly, Deleuze and Foucault could be described as philosophers, but their work is as much concerned with changing the way we think about social practices and institutions. The traditions of critical theory which extend from Western Marxism and the Frankfurt School to post-structuralism, postcolonial discourse and queer theory, are engaged in critical dialogues with philosophical traditions, but are concerned with problems distinct from those conventionally associated with philosophy. To the dismay of conceptual purists, recent critical theorists such as Bhabha, Butler and Žižek appropriate and transform the already unstable conceptual vocabularies of Derrida, Foucault and Lacan to generate new spaces of theory.

'Theory' has come to stand as the quickest description of the way argument has been redefined across different intellectual movements and disciplines. Against the fashion to line up the playful postmodern French side of, say, Derrida or Deleuze, against the earnest German modernism of, say, Gadamer or Habermas, the important arguments involve critical translations across linguistic boundaries. Marxism, psychoanalysis, phenomenology and post-structuralism all involve hybrids of German and French thought, and are mediated by their English-language reception. A peculiarity of 'theory' in the English-speaking world is the importance given to French thought, and the neglect of the German sources of such thought. This anthology suggests some of the dialogues between German and French thought, as well as representing work which crosses national and linguistic boundaries in the new hybrid spaces of theory.

Literary 'theory' often adopts a relation to texts which is uncritical in its imaginative use of ideas and thus transgresses the limits of critical self-reflection.[5] The language of 'theory' can make it hard to recognize the traditions of philosophical argument from which terms and concepts are borrowed. The difference between literary theory and critical theory is made all the more ambiguous by the use of 'critical theory' to describe the work of the Frankfurt School associated with Adorno, Benjamin, Marcuse and Habermas. It is not, for example, obvious from the title of *The Handbook of Critical Theory* that what is offered is a handbook to Frankfurt School thought.[6] My own selection of essays surveys Frankfurt School critical theory, phenomenology and post-structuralism, as well as approaches associated with theory in literary and cultural studies. *The Norton Anthology of Theory and Criticism*, by contrast, focuses on a literary conception of theory, offering an eclectic array of poetics, rhetoric and literary criticism from Plato to the present.[7] Eclecticism makes it hard to see the decisive ways in which theory breaks with earlier traditions of literary criticism and the ways in which modern critical thought breaks down boundaries between the languages of different disciplines.

The resulting difficulties include disagreements not just about what is meant by particular terms, but about the more diffuse process of borrowing across traditions of thought. Ideas from linguistics have influenced anthropology; psychoanalysis has been important for Marxism and for feminism; ways of reading Nietzsche have changed perceptions of power and sexuality, and so on. The impact of structural linguistics on a range of different fields, from child psychology to semiotics and ideology-critique, was sufficiently diffuse to give rise to the perception of a structuralist moment in intellectual work as a whole. If Saussure and Lévi-Strauss are the presiding influences on structuralism, the range of those associated with structuralism includes Althusser, Lacan, Foucault, Derrida, Kristeva and Deleuze.[8] These thinkers could also be read as critics of structuralist methodology, participating in the dissolution of structuralism which became known as post-structuralism. What such 'moments' reveal is not so much a specific set of shared ideas, but horizons of interpretation which constitute and divide the dialogues of modern thought.[9] Post-structuralism is subject to 'logics of disintegration'[10] in which the critical legitimacy of any stable post-structuralist paradigm is brought into crisis. Work in the wake of post-structuralism, such as Butler's and Bhabha's, is important for gender studies and postcolonial discourse, but the theoretical impetus of their work deconstructs the categories according to which such studies ground themselves. Their work, as with many of those in this anthology, is situated between critical paradigms, questioning the essentialism and uncritically empirical organization of disciplines and practices. More generally, borrowing from one discipline or tradition to illuminate another has become an important way in which new areas of thought are developed, but cross-fertilization creates plenty of room for muddle and confusion.

This anthology, accordingly, develops a different approach to the need for critical introductions. Many of those thinkers most in need of introductory explication are at their most accessible and revealing when introducing the thought of their precursors and rivals. Forced to provide brief introductions to the work of others, many critical thinkers provide succinct accounts of influences on their own work. Rather than providing generalized or unfocused overviews, such introductions reveal priorities and key areas of difference. While such introductions are not impartial, the differences of interpretation involved are themselves critical. Reviews and expositions help to highlight tensions or difficulties in the work of a thinker, while also contextualizing the relation between two thinkers. A reader seeking a quick guide to Nietzsche or Heidegger might stumble unthinkingly through encyclopedia entries or beginner's guides. But a reader analysing Heidegger's introductory lectures on Nietzsche can begin to grasp aspects of Nietzsche's thought and its impact on Heidegger's thought. As well as providing a critical introduction to Nietzsche, Heidegger's Nietzsche also provides one of the most helpful introductions to the thought of Heidegger and a point of comparison for other thinkers informed by Nietzsche, such as Derrida, Foucault and Deleuze. Similarly, a reader relying on one interpretation of Marx or Freud will encounter difficulties, but a reader who can recognize the processes of interpretation, appropriation and critical translation has begun to enter the conversation of modern thought. Given that so much of modern critical thought develops through critical readings, there is enhanced interest in reading through such processes.

Along such lines, this anthology selects essays, lectures, interventions and critical reviews which provide critical introductions to thinkers from Marx to the present. These essays are chosen to introduce key figures in modern thought, but also to serve as introductions to the thinker writing the essay: an essay by Gadamer on Heidegger serves to introduce both Heidegger and Gadamer. Essays on writers appearing earlier in the anthology build into overlapping conversations and arguments. This allows the anthology to be used for different kinds of reading and teaching, while also providing a representative survey and introduction to modern thought. The organization of the anthology also suggests how critical thinking has developed as a practice of critical reading across the boundaries and labels of more conventional introductory patterns, across differences in French and German thought, or across differences between Marxism and psychoanalysis. Each essay is introduced by some contextualization of the thinkers in dialogue, sketching lines of influence and areas of disagreement, along with suggestions for further reading. For reasons already suggested, these brief introductions need to be read sceptically as guides rather than as critical representations. The rest of this introduction provides orientation for the anthology as a whole, sketching some of the different meanings of critique and outlining some important intellectual sources and problems.

In different forms, critique is the shared core of most current theoretical work, serving as the central way in which theoretical practices are legitimated. There is, however, little agreement as to what is meant by critique or how it might differ from criticism, and one function of critique is to criticize the functions criticism is made to serve.[11] This anthology focuses on twentieth-century thought, but the modern coming together of criticism, critical reading and critique can be traced back to Kant, who made the term 'critique' and its practice central to modern thought. In the preface to the *Critique of Pure Reason* (1781), Kant suggests that: 'Our age is, in especial degree, the age of criticism, and to criticism everything must submit.'[12] The German term for criticism here is *Kritik*, often also translated as 'critique'. Kant could also be translated as describing his age as the age of critique. The difference between criticism and critique has never become firmly established in English usage, although there is a largely unexamined assumption that criticism is the more modest, nit-picking activity as opposed to the more philosophical pretensions of critique. Indeed, the cluster of associated terms in English usage still owes something to the coming together of English criticism, French *critique* and German *Kritik*, the latter a translation from French to German.[13] A measure of this process of translation is the extent to which it can sound awkward to use 'critique' as a verb, as in: *I've had enough of being critiqued, stop critiquing me!* To some ears, the verb here should be 'criticize', as in: *I've had enough of being criticized, stop criticizing me!* This difference between 'critique' as a noun and as a verb owes something to French and German resonances of *critique* / *Kritik* overlapping with the verb 'criticize', and hints at profound interconnections between English, French and German thought.

Amid European dialogue, the age of critique epitomized by Kant is that of enlightened reason subjecting religion, ethics and aesthetic judgement to rigorous and independent scrutiny. The assertion that everything should submit to critique asserts the autonomous authority of free and public examination in the court of reason. Kant's critique is not just a critique of the books or systems of reason, but a critique of the faculty of reason itself. The double genitive in the title of the *Critique of Pure Reason* indicates an important ambiguity: reason is both the subject and the object of critique. Kant delimits the epistemological conditions by which the subject of knowledge, the knower, knows the object, or the known. The critique of reason's conditions of possibility marks out Kant's conception of critique as a new philosophical reflexivity: the self-critique of enlightenment. Critique develops the practice of criticizing the ideas and writings of others into self-critical reflection. Although the critique of pure reason dominates the architecture of Kant's thought, his critical philosophy includes critiques of practical reason and aesthetic judgement, differentiating epistemology, ethics and aesthetics. Critique, for Kant, is also a practice of writing and of publicizing his thought through writing. Willi Goetschel argues that, for Kant, critical theory and critical thought imply the necessity of considering the limits of writing, and of turning the written discourse of reason into the medium of critical self-reflection.[14]

The word 'critique' derives from the Greek *krinein*, used with reference to separating, judging and deciding, modes which continue to be active in the work of book reviewers and literary critics. In this sense, 'critique' even now refers to modes of literary criticism, not least those of grammarians and philologists.[15] It would be possible, for example, to understand the American reception of Derridean deconstruction not in terms of philosophical critique, but as the radicalization of literary criticism,[16] a critical turn exemplified by the work of Paul de Man. Such developments in modes of philosophical reading combine different conceptions of criticism and critique. Interpretation and hermeneutics have become important, moreover, not just for textual scholars but for reflections on reading and language central to the work of Heidegger, Gadamer, Levinas, Habermas and Derrida. For such thinkers, and for modern critical thought more generally, understanding through interpretation is not another 'method' of investigation separable from natural or 'hard' sciences, but a necessary dimension of understanding as such.[17] Indeed, from Marx to Žižek, the characteristic presentations of modern critical thought combine philosophical critique with critical 'readings' of the texts of predecessors and contemporaries.

The possibility of combining philosophical critique with literary or textual criticism is already implicit in Kant's age of critique. Within the emergence of modern thought, however, different writing practices associated with the history of literary and textual criticism are subject to new social functions and forms of professionalization and commercialization. Raymond Williams, for example, argues against the social or professional generalization associated with criticism: '**criticism** becomes ideological not only when it assumes the position of the *consumer* but also when it masks this position by a succession of abstractions of its real terms of response (as *judgement, taste, cultivation, discrimination, sensibility; disinterested, qualified, rigorous* and so on).'[18] This list sketches key battlegrounds in the history of literary criticism, with Williams indicating his own preference for a cultural critique of criticism. Critiques of literary scholarship, philology and textual criticism can be traced back through the social distinctions and divisions of labour in eighteenth-century textual criticism. Simon Jarvis, for example, concludes one historical account of such developments by arguing, against the terms suggested by Williams, that 'professionalism in historical scholarship and its concomitant division of intellectual labour is neither a set of mistaken opinions nor a delusory worldview'.[19] The professionalization of textual criticism leaves criticism torn between the commercial market and the demands of professional rationalization associated with academic work in universities. Commodification and professionalization mean that criticism either embraces humanistic amateurism or develops the professional legitimacy of scholarly specialisms and their narrower social relevance.[20] Within the general division of intellectual labour, there is, accordingly, an ongoing struggle for intellectual freedom and for the free exchange and publication of ideas in a republic of letters.

Where modern critical thought has to struggle with the pressures of commercial trivialization and academic institutionalization, much of the energy in eighteenth-century thought was directed against the authorities of church and state, particularly those authorities that restricted freedom of intellectual expression. While the practices of criticism and critique are subject to logics of professional rationalization and modernization specific to individual disciplines, such practices are also associated with public reasoning and the reflexively self-critical work of secular discussion. Religious and political dogmas were particular targets for criticism, even if only implicitly. Comparative studies in the history of religion have the capacity to suggest critiques of Christian faith and generate new kinds of intellectual freedom. Commenting on the impact of J. G. Frazer's *The Golden Bough* (1890–1915), for example, Jane Harrison records how 'A cultured policeman, a member of the Working Men's College, . . . said to me, "I used to believe everything they told me, but, thank God, I read the *Golden Bough*, and I've been a free-thinker ever since".'[21] It is easy to forget that such intellectual freedoms are comparatively recent, especially in states of emergency which call for uncritical solidarity.

The new kinds of public discussion and exchange associated with eighteenth-century criticism and critique ranged from essays on miscellaneous subjects in journals and critical surveys, most notably Diderot's *Encyclopédie* (1751–1772), to the more philosophically systematic writing exemplified by Kant. Kant exemplifies the enlightenment culture of criticism, becoming one of the few philosophers whose work remains influential across analytic and continental philosophy.[22] Kant suggests how enlightenment and critique are linked in the assertion of reason's autonomy and its ability to legislate for itself rather than being beholden to the external authorities of church, party or state. The critical activity of the enlightenment implied a secular republic of letters developed through the publication of debates, a model of intellectual exchange that still informs contemporary thought.[23] Critique, for Kant, negotiates the difference between dogmatism and scepticism, and, as he puts it at the end of the *Critique of Pure Reason*: 'The critical path alone is still open.'[24] This means revealing the conditions that make any knowledge possible and recognizing the limits of reason's powers. In 'An Answer to the Question: What is Enlightenment?' Kant writes that: 'Have courage to make use of your *own* understanding! is thus the motto of enlightenment.'[25] Foucault draws out one of the implications of Kant's text: the moment of enlightenment when humanity reasons without subjecting itself to authority is the moment when critique becomes necessary. If Kantian critique analyses the limits of reason, Foucault suggests a new turn: 'The point, in brief, is to transform the critique conducted in the form of necessary limitation into a practical critique that takes the form of a possible transgression.'[26] A consequence of this shift, for Foucault, is that critique no longer involves the search for formal structures with universal value, but rather develops as a genealogical investigation into the historical conditions of contemporary thought and action. The philosophical attitude associated with enlightenment critique is translated into the labour of diverse inquiries. The move from necessary limitation to possible transgressions informs Foucault's interest in discourses such as madness, medicine and sexuality which unsettle the boundaries of reason.

Almost all subsequent traditions of critical thought involve such reference back to Kantian critique. Kant's account of how our phenomenal experience is structured by intellectual categories which are the conditions of the possibility of this experience continues to influence traditions of phenomenological inquiry. The work of Husserl, Heidegger, Gadamer, Merleau-Ponty and Levinas, for example, can be understood as radical attempts to rethink Kant. The intellectual background for phenomenology was formed by the various schools of neo-Kantianism in the second half of the nineteenth century, which were also a spur for sociology in the work of Durkheim and Weber and for what became Western Marxism.[27] Gillian Rose's critical survey of neo-Kantianism suggests that the attempt to break with neo-Kantianism through Durkheim's meta-critique is shared by Dilthey, Heidegger, Mannheim, Benjamin and Gadamer, and by what she sees as the neo-Kantian Marxism of Lukács and Adorno.[28]

Many thinkers have taken issue with formalist, ahistorical or metaphysical features in Kant's account of the system of concepts which constitute *a priori* knowledge, suggesting that Kant neglects the social, historical and ontological conditions of experience. Rose describes how a modified type of Kantian argument can change the problem of *a priori* knowledge into the problem of the sociological preconditions of experience: 'when it is argued that it is society or culture which confers objective validity on social facts or values, then the argument acquires a metacritical or "quasi-transcendental" structure.'[29] While Kant's 'transcendental' deduction of intuition, space and time as conditions of the possibility of knowledge remains controversial, Kant's thought reverberates beyond conflicting interpretations of his work. As Willi Goetschel puts it: 'Following Kant, every form of critique finds itself always already having to refer back to its ground- and sourcebook, the *Critique of Pure Reason*. A purely conceptual theory is not capable of accounting for an influence of this scope.'[30] Kant's influence can in part be explained by the rhetoric of Kantian critique, despite Kant's notoriously rebarbative prose. A more plausible explanation of Kant's influence lies in the way his critiques suggest the possibility of developing critique beyond epistemology, ethics and aesthetics into the critique of society.

Reference back to Kant and neo-Kantian argument is a continual recourse for more recent thinkers such as Habermas and Derrida, but for very different purposes, in part because Kant remains central to conflicts between sociology and philosophy in modern critical theory. This also reflects the way that Kant's critiques point beyond pure philosophy into practical philosophy, morality and politics. The attempt to find regula-tive principles with which to guide moral action and aesthetic judgement has become a shared critical orientation in political and social thought. Regulative principles suggest ways of criticizing the irrationality of particular arguments, practices and social arrange-ments. Critique metamorphoses into a more general quality of argument, mediating criticisms which subject particular claims, practices or institutions to scrutiny, and the more systematic claims of philosophical critique. Echoes of Kant can be heard in titles such as Sartre's *Critique of Dialectical Reason*, Sloterdijk's *Critique of Cynical Reason* or Spivak's *A Critique of Postcolonial Reason*.[31] The object criticized can range from bureaucracy and the cult of personality, to postmodern cynicism and child labour in Bangladesh. Such books exemplify the tensions between rationally self-legislating critique and criticisms of particular forms of irrationality and injustice.[32]

The meaning of critique in modern thought is, then, more extended than in Kant's work. Kant's conception of the freedom to make public use of one's reason in all matters nevertheless implies a critique of political restrictions and distortions. The autonomous exercise of practical reason also suggests a new freedom of moral action with political consequences, suggestions evident in Kant's political writings.[33] After Kant, the politics of critique motivates the emancipatory projects of critical sociology to develop accounts of the social conditions of rationality and ways of making society more rational. Indeed, an important feature of modern critical thought is scepticism towards the forms of scientific reason which do not recognize the limits of their assumed rationality. Industrial technology, for example, may seem eminently rational and efficient, but understood critically it is irrational in its inability to see the environmental and social conditions which make it possible. To recognize that technology's conditions are not autonomous but dependent on natural, historical and social conditions is to develop a critical sociology of reason, or a metacritique of scientific rationality. Sociological critique of Kant informs many of the Marxist thinkers included in this anthology, from Lukács to Žižek, while different critical renegotiations of Kant also inform Nietzsche's thought and the reinterpretations of Nietzsche offered by Heidegger and Deleuze.

The political implications of Kantian critique find their most radical translation in Marx, a translation of critique important even for those who are hostile to Marxism. The word 'critique' figures prominently in the titles of almost all of Marx's major works, from his early critiques of Hegel, through to *A Contribution to the Critique of Political Economy* (1859) and *Capital: A Critique of Political Economy* (1867). Despite the prominence of the word 'critique' in the writings of Marx, it is surprisingly difficult to pin down what Marx means by critique. There is scant evidence that Marx intends a developed analogy with Kant's conception of critique, though there have been attempts to find affinities between Kant and Marx.[34] In *The Holy Family, or Critique of Critical Critique* (1845), Marx and Engels launched a polemical attack on the high-flown intricacy of the dialectics of Critical Criticism, a rebuke which prefigures the abuse of dialectical critique within Marxism itself. *The Holy Family* is eloquently rude about the uncritical qualities of Bruno Bauer and others: 'Critical Criticism makes criticism, as a predicate and activity of man, into a subject apart, criticism which relates itself to itself and is therefore *Critical Criticism.*'[35] The sarcastic and pejorative doubling up in the term 'critical criticism' suggests scepticism about the uses and abuses of critique understood as a self-sufficient methodology. Beyond the critical practice of polemic and a judgemental torrent of disagreements, however, it is hard to see why Marx and Engels continue to use 'critique' to describe their own approach. Marx rejects the conception of critique suggested by critical philosophy, seeking to overcome philosophy through what the theses on Feuerbach call revolutionary practice and practical–critical activity.[36] Put in loosely Kantian terms, Marx's conception of critique seeks to reveal capitalism's conditions of possibility by delimiting the scientific claims of political economy.

The claim that Marx's later work involves an epistemological break with philosophy and the inauguration of a science of critique and scientific criticism is central to Althusserian Marxism. Althusser identifies the development of a new, more scientific method of critical reading in the mature work of Marx.[37] In *Capital*, Marx integrates the recognition of oversights and inconsistencies in political economy through a new conception of the object or terrain of social reality that is the condition of possibility for the discourse of political economy. Marx, accordingly, provides both an immanent critique of political economy and a symptomatic reading which provides a more 'scientific' framing of political economy. This theorization of critical reading informs the Althusserian re-reading of the symptomatic presence and absence of the anthropological, humanist and Hegelian residues in Marx's later, more scientific work. The extent to which Marx ever made a clean, scientific break is nevertheless murky. There is a continuing sense, especially in Marx's account of the fetishism of the commodity, picked up by Lukács in *History and Class Consciousness*, that the anti-metaphysical scientificity of *Capital* intends a critique of the metaphysical illusions produced by capitalism. Whatever the rhetoric, the possibility of articulating a science of metaphysics allies Marx to the problems of Hegelian philosophy. If Marx claims to overcome metaphysics, to go beyond philosophy, his practice of criticism struggles to legitimate its conception of critique scientifically and as something more than an immanent critique of the discourse of political economy.

The point of critical practice for Marx is to realize the truth of philosophy, abandoning the attempt to stand above the social conflicts which constitute philosophical experience. The young Marx claimed that: 'the critic can take his cue from every existing form of theoretical and practical consciousness and from this ideal and final goal implicit in the *actual* forms of existing reality he can deduce a true reality.'[38] This conception animates Marx's subsequent thought, and is characteristic of many modern forms of critical thought, but leaves open critical thought's scientific objectivity. *Capital* offers a politically motivated critique of the way capitalism conceals its role in structuring human existence, but it remains ambiguous whether Marx understands capitalism as a historically contingent mode of production or as a necessary, even logical condition of the possibility of socialism. Michel Henry suggests that:

> from Kant to Marx, the transcendental question shifts; it is no longer an interrogation concerning the essential possibility of science, in this case of political economy, but one that concerns first of all the reality which comes to be the object of this science, the 'economy' now understood in its relation to praxis and to the fundamental modes of its actual realization.[39]

Marx, however, has been more influential as a critic of capitalism who seeks to describe the conditions of the possibility of radical social change. The decisive difference in the Marxist conception of critique is the relative indifference to epistemology and traditional philosophical questions, in favour of a critique of society with practical, indeed revolutionary intentions. The attempt to reconfigure the ends of philosophy in a radical new conception of thought's relation to society also informs the critical relation to Kant in the thought of Hegel and Nietzsche. Insofar as both Hegel and Nietzsche offer a less explicit vocabulary of critique, the prevalence of the term in Marx's work helps to explain the subsequent diffusion of the term beyond the models of Kantian critique. To the extent that Marx's approach to critique is politically motivated, however, it remains difficult to delimit the scientificity of Marxist critique.

Marx refuses to ground his critique transcendentally or outside the immanent, historical development of capital, and yet seeks to articulate the possibility of socialism as that which transcends capitalism. The critical task of *Capital* is to demystify the pseudo-scientific 'laws' of political economy. Marx shows that such laws are not natural but historical, providing an account of how capitalism's contradictions condition the possibilities of revolutionary transformation. As Marx concedes, however, the presentation of his dialectical method, which shows the life of economics reflected back in ideas, 'may appear as if we have before us an *a priori* construction'.[40] He wants to avoid giving the impression that the logic of capital is a logic of ideas, as if the development of capital were the external working out of the idea of capital. The way he presents his scientific research nevertheless risks suggesting that his dialectical method either provides a Kantian account of the *a priori* conditions of capital or is guilty of Hegelian sophistry. Marx famously declared that he had stood Hegel on his head, inverting Hegel 'in order to discover the rational kernel within the mystical shell',[41] but this polemical quip leaves a lot to be explained. What, for example, does Marx mean when he claims that his dialectical method is the 'opposite' of Hegel's?

> For Hegel, the process of thinking, which he even transforms into an independent subject, under the name of 'the Idea', is the creator of the real world, and the real world is only the external appearance of the idea. With me the reverse is true: the ideal is nothing but the material world reflected in the mind of man, and translated into forms of thought.[42]

The meaning of critique may have Kantian resonances, but Marx owes a more important intellectual debt to Hegel and to Hegel's critique of Kant. Marx's optimistic claim that demystified dialectical thought is essentially 'critical and revolutionary' prefigures the way Marxist critique oscillates between Kant, Hegel and Marx. The philosophical opportunism of such oscillations has been a key focus for those who continue to wrestle with the possibilities of critical dialectic, while also motivating those who reject dialectics.

More germane than Kant to an understanding of what Marx means by critique is Marx's reception of Hegel and the conception of critique developed by the young Hegelians.[43] The meaning of critique for Hegel, however, is no less difficult to specify, though it is widely recognized that the critique of Kant is central to Hegel's work. Although the young Hegel announced his work in the journal he produced with Schelling as 'critical philosophy',[44] Hegel's mature work does not describe his approach as critique and is markedly reluctant to use the term. In one sense, Hegel's whole work amounts to a critique of Kant, but in another sense he transforms critique into a different kind of thinking.[45] Hegel attacks the Kantian separation of the subject and object of knowledge, and of pure and practical reason. He radicalizes critical inquiry as the immanent critique of the way knowledge develops out of the recognition of its own contradictions. Hegel's phenomenological account of the experience of consciousness is self-critical, harnassing the power of sceptical reflection to recognize and overcome the limits and divisions of subjectivity and objectivity. Hegel thus provides a critique of the epistemological enterprise which dominates modern philosophy from Descartes onwards.

Hegel's importance for modern critical thought, however, lies less in the strictly philosophical dimensions of his thinking, than in the way his critique of philosophy becomes a model for subsequent critiques of religion, law, politics and economics. Hegelian thought displaces epistemology and brings philosophy up against a different set of limits. Garbis Kortian describes the way Hegel seeks to overcome the opposition of the knower and the known as the 'metacritical' dissolution of epistemology.[46] Rather than providing a critique of knowledge claims so as to ground knowledge in a secure foundation by revealing the transcendental conditions of all possible knowledge, Hegel retraces the experience of thought as a self-critical and sceptical journey which is both historical and logical. Critique in Hegel's thought combines immanent critique with metacritical reflection. This combination is constitutive of dialectics, but it is central to Hegel's thought that dialectics is not a method or some external 'standpoint' or detached perspective. The knower and the known cannot be separated formally.

Marx's critique of Hegel's dialectical 'method' nevertheless accuses Hegel of developing a dialectic of pure thought which idealizes the power of logic and its abstraction from the material conditions of thought. For Marx, thought does not develop immanently out of its contradictions but reflects social antagonisms. In this sense, Marx's dialectical method involves a version of Hegelian metacritique, showing how thought and consciousness cannot legislate for their relation to the historical and material conditions of social being. In effect, Marx and Marxism develop a metacritical conception of the social and political unconscious. Marx's practice as critical reader of the texts of political economy nevertheless puts less emphasis on the metacritique of knowledge, than on the immanent critique of scientific attempts to describe political economy. This practice of immanent critique works less as a critique of fundamental grounds than as a way of testing particular knowledge claims, probing the inconsistencies, contradictions and aporia within both texts and reality. The key difference is in the way Marx's reading seeks to tease out contradictions which are ideological, rooted in the social and political distortions of thought rather than in the pure conditions of thought's abstractions.

The tension between Hegelian metacritique and Marx's immanent critique of political economy is fundamental to the development of the Critical Theory of the Frankfurt School and the work of Adorno, Marcuse and Habermas.[47] This tension can be seen in Max Horkheimer's essay 'Traditional and Critical Theory', a key essay in the definition of the critical programme of the Frankfurt School. Horkheimer defines critical activity as a 'human activity which has society itself for its object', citing the dialectical critique of political economy as a model.[48] The task is to develop the Marxist model into a theory of society which is critical of dogmatic forms of Marxism, revisiting aspects of philosophy Marx wrongly thought he had transcended, though the exact terms of the implicit critique of Marx remain somewhat obscure. Frankfurt School critical theory seeks to develop the emancipatory dimension of the Marxist project without regressing to dogmatic conceptions of science or retreating into foundational philosophy. As Habermas later puts it: 'Through its reflection on the conditions of its own appearance, critique is to be distinguished both from science and from philosophy. The sciences ignore the constitution of their objects and understand their subject matter in an objectivistic way. Philosophy, conversely, is too ontologically sure of its origin as a first principle.'[49] Critique seeks to transcend modern divisions of thought by developing critical theories of society with practical consequences.

Rather than seeking critical models through which to change society, the modern 'division of labour'[50] requires individual thinkers to work with specific problems and methodologies, recognizing the limitations imposed on any individual thinker and the errors that inevitably follow from impressionistic generalization. Modernity also requires individuals to think critically about the limited assumptions constitutive of a discipline's blinkered specificity. To use an example on which Hegel expends a surprising amount of effort, someone who imagined themselves an expert in the 'science' of phrenology – reading bumps on the skull as signs of psychological character – might fail to recognize the irrationality of their discipline.[51] Hegel's critique of phrenology provides a model for the critique of ideology in other pseudo-sciences of psychological divination, such as graphology and astrology.[52] The extent to which science can be uncritical and unscientific is also shown by the discourse of madness,[53] and, more recently, by modern theories about the genetic determination of psychology. Ideas about smart genes, gay genes, criminal genes, and so forth, suggest that uncritical confusions of nature and culture are rife in disciplines which claim to be scientific. A critique of gene theory, unlike a critique of phrenology or astrology, requires a more scientific account of the limits of genetic determination. Knowing the limits of such a science also requires a critical understanding of other factors of social and cultural determination that might make someone an intelligent, homosexual criminal. Recognizing critical differences between substantive new knowledge claims and ideological representation crosses boundaries that separate science from society.

It remains debatable whether politicized accounts of psychology such as Marxist and feminist appropriations of psychoanalysis can be both scientific and self-critical.[54] A similar crux emerges in the way Marx develops Feuerbach's critique of religion's inverted and distorted picture of reality into a critique of political economy.[55] The difference between religious ideology and the more general critique of ideology as a representation of conflicts between the means and relations of production has ramifications throughout Marx's work. Critical accounts of psychology, religion, gender and race show that the claims of modern thought to be scientific often depend on the uncritical acceptance and generalization of a particular approach. Social sciences, though usually more aware of the social determination of what is meant by 'science', are no less vulnerable to critiques of their pseudo-objectivity.[56] Such difficulties give rise to reflexively self-critical forms of social science, or critical sociology,[57] as well as radical challenges to sociology's neo-Kantianism.[58] The intellectual division of labour forces critical thought to recognize the necessity of working within received paradigms while reflecting on the limits of such paradigms. Critique seeks, accordingly, to delimit the claims of scientific reason.

In the light of the historical disasters of fascism and Stalinism, Horkheimer and Adorno develop the project of critical theory with a profound scepticism regarding the values of positivism, rationality and science inherited by Western society from the enlightenment. The critique of modernity also runs through the work of Husserl and Heidegger into Foucault, Deleuze and Derrida. Against Marx's enlightenment enthusiasm for the ideas of progress and science, Horkheimer's and Adorno's *Dialectic of Enlightenment* returns to the philosophical critique of enlightenment broached by Hegel and Nietzsche, reinterpreting enlightenment's self-deluding mythology of reason through Weber, Lukács and Freud. Critical reflection on the extent to which philosophy cannot be transcended as Marx thought, leads to metacritiques of modern philosophy and modern scientific rationality. Adorno, for example, restates the Hegelian metacritique of epistemology in his critique of Husserl and in the development of what Adorno later called 'negative dialectics'.[59] In the preface to *Negative Dialectics*, Adorno states that his thought seeks to free dialectics from affirmative traits, while stringently seeking 'to transcend the official separation of pure philosophy and the substantive or formally scientific realm'.[60] Put differently, Adorno attempts to develop a dialectical critique of the modern divisions of intellectual labour, without attempting to coerce the negativity

of critical reflection into positive results. His investigations into ideological contradictions and philosophical problems are developed immanently without providing a way of
grounding critique methodologically. Part of the difficulty, however, is the way Adorno's determination to think against the grain of modern rationality and the modern
division of labour risks relying too heavily on playing off one set of metacritical
assumptions against another. Critics of Adorno, such as Habermas, have suggested
that Adorno's thinking relies on an undifferentiated and reductive conception of
modernity, leaving critique in a self-referential mode of performative contradiction
which neglects the possibilities of social-scientific theoretical revision.[61] Put differently,
attempts to negotiate a space for emancipatory critique between philosophy and science
look increasingly utopian within the social scientific understanding of the modern
divisions of intellectual labour.

To the traditions of modern critical thought associated with continental philosophy,
the challenge of dialectical critique seems no less marginal. Of the thinkers represented
in this anthology, Husserl, Heidegger, Gadamer, Sartre, Merleau-Ponty and Levinas are
perhaps most closely allied with the traditions of continental philosophy associated with
phenomenology and existentialism. In different ways, each of these thinkers engages
with questions of experience, language, historicity, interpretation, politics and religion
which are not exclusively philosophical. Although Husserl remains a common point of
reference, subsequent traditions of phenomenology differentiate themselves in ways that
do not allow a meaningful summary of their shared philosophical project.[62] Conceived
as a response to the crisis of philosophy, phenomenology is torn between scientific
inquiries into the observable phenomena of experience and philosophical reflection on
the possibility of such experiences. Husserlian phenomenology describes the objects of
experience as they are intended or intuited through systematic investigations into
conscious mental processes. Heidegger's thought develops as a critique of Husserl's
emphasis on intentional consciousness. After Husserl's death, phenomenology metamorphoses into a range of hybrid inquiries, ranging from Heidegger's fundamental
reformulation of philosophy and language, to compounds of existentialism and Marxism.[63] The critique of Husserlian phenomenology is also pivotal in the work of Levinas
and Derrida. The traditions of phenomenology are often rather tentative in describing
their investigations as critiques, in part because phenomenological investigations are
often open-ended and aporetic. Phenomenology nevertheless suggests radical critiques
of the way thought's conditions of possibility are occluded or obscured by science,
technology and psychology.

Although ignored or dismissed by the analytic traditions that dominate anglo-saxon
philosophy departments, phenomenological and existential thinkers have been fundamental for developments in social psychology, poetics, hermeneutics, literary criticism,
ethics, religious thought and political theory. One explanation for their influence is less
the truth of their claims and propositions than their ability to suggest new problems,
new ways of reading and new approaches to experience incompatible with existing
paradigms of thought. Philosophy is only one of the contributory sources of modern
critical thought, and insofar as philosophy can be embodied in the rhetoric of writing,
philosophy shares the conversations of writing with other forms of discourse. Aspects of
phenomenological thought and existentialism can be traced back, for example, to the
restless authorship of Søren Kierkegaard. The writings of Kierkegaard, like those of

Nietzsche, resist being reduced to a series of philosophical truth claims or arguments, in part because of the way their thinking is stylized as a rhetoric of writing.[64] Kierkegaard poses questions of experience, ethics and religion, rather than providing a stable philosophy, and in ways which have had a dynamic but often obscure influence on intellectual history.[65]

Freud's thought has been more influential, but very few of Freud's most suggestive ideas, including such central hypotheses as the Oedipus complex, the death drive and even the unconscious, are susceptible of scientific proof or propositional defence. Despite the difficulty of providing philosophical or scientific legitimation, Freud has nevertheless informed a range of different practices, including clinical psychoanalysis, as well as changing the way even those who do not believe in his ideas think about human consciousness. A metacritical conception of knowledge is implicit in Freud's approach to the interpretation of the unconscious. Attempts to combine Marx's sociological metacritique with Freud's metacritique of the individual inform the thought of Adorno, Marcuse and Habermas, while psychoanalytic models of interpretation have also influenced Althusser, Lacan, Derrida and Žižek.[66] Freud might not be thought of as a philosopher or critic, but his work has nevertheless transformed the critical understanding of thought, self-reflection and the ideology of subjectivity.[67] As Connerton puts it, 'Without explicitly invoking the idea of a critique, Freud proposed what was in effect a new procedure of critical reflection.'[68]

Freud's work also plays an important role in the breaks with phenomenology associated with structuralism and post-structuralism, often in surprising ways. Jacqueline Rose provides one of the most incisive, feminist accounts of Lacan's re-reading of Freud in the light of structuralism. The dialogue between psychoanalysis and post-structuralism continues to inform the work of recent critical theorists such as Bhabha, Butler and Žižek, but Lacan's influence is also an acknowledged influence on Althusser's re-reading of Marx.[69] Beyond Marx, such processes of symptomatic reading have informed critical theory more generally, becoming a fundamental method in cultural and literary studies. In a characteristically awkward process of critical reading, Lacan's reading of Freud draws on structuralist linguistics and structural anthropology, to suggest new modes of critical reading. These new modes also involve the reinterpretation of Freudian interpretation. The resulting models of critical reading are then read back into Marx, and from Marx back into the critique of contemporary ideology. A measure of the difficulty arising from such borrowings is the way in which Žižek's post-Marxist critique of ideology weaves between Lacanian and Althusserian models of interpretation, using a re-reading of Hegel which goes against the grain of Althusser's resistance to Hegelian Marxism.

The chain of influence connecting Freud, Saussure, Althusser, Marx, Lacan, Hegel and Žižek is only one instance of ways in which models of critical reading can be translated. Such chains appear inconsistent if too much pressure is put on methodology rather than on the processes of intellectual dissemination developed through critical reading. Lucien Goldmann suggests, for example, that there are important affinities between Lukács and Heidegger, despite what seem to be profound incompatibilities. He finds references to reification in Heidegger's *Being and Time* which he reads as allusions to Lukács' *History and Class Consciousness*.[70] Heidegger in turn was an important teacher and influence on thinkers such as Herbert Marcuse and Jürgen Habermas and in ways that cross the apparent dividing lines between Heidegger and Western Marxism.[71] Indeed, it seems likely that polemical exaggerations of differences disguise the way important problems are shared.

What emerges from the difficulties imposed by chains of influence is the importance of recognizing that there is more to critical reading than sustained scepticism or careful philological reconstruction of such chains. Just as importantly, critical reading needs to identify shared problems animating otherwise very different conceptual terms and apparently divergent intellectual traditions. At the more local level, exposition often moves between the voice of the text being read and the voice of the writer producing the reading through modes of ventriloquism which break down the difference between the subjects and objects of critique. The effects generated range from implicit allusions to a more general use of free indirect style. Alain Badiou illustrates the problem in his critical reading of Deleuze by asking: 'If I read, for example: "force among forces, man does not fold the forces that compose him without the outside folding itself, and creating a Self within man" (*Foucault*, p. 114), is this really a statement of Foucault's? Or is it already an interpretation? Or is it quite simply a thesis of Deleuze's, for we recognize in these lines his reading of Nietzsche ... '[72] The difficulty is compounded by the diminished echoes of translation across German, French and English, but the critical task for Badiou's reader is to focus the relative importance of parts of the Deleuze-Foucault-Nietzsche composite in question.

Nietzsche often figures in such unstable composite theoretical constellations. It is possible to trace a German reception of Nietzsche through Heidegger and Karl Jaspers which has in turn influenced French Nietzscheanism from Deleuze to Derrida.[73] Such chains of influence are better understood as rhetorics of critique dramatizing differences and similarities by suggesting family trees or genealogies of argument. Jürgen Habermas, for example, is critical of Nietzsche's influence, which he identifies with the neo-conservative trends of postmodernism. He sketches Nietzsche's critique of modernity as an influence on Foucault's dissolution of singular historical metanarratives into a plurality of discontinuous islands of discourse, offering what Habermas calls 'the outline of a *transcendental historicism* at once inherited and going beyond Nietzsche's critique of historicism'.[74] Whereas Heidegger and Derrida develop Nietzsche's critique of reason through the destruction or deconstruction of metaphysics, Foucault's critique of reason does so through the destruction of historicism and historiography and through a radicalized conception of 'power'. Habermas's critical characterization of Foucault has generated a debate which reveals productive differences.[75] Habermas's critique of Foucault is developed, however, not so much as an immanent critique as a synoptic critical overview, providing a critical translation of underlying assumptions in Foucault's work into Habermas's own terms. This manoeuvre is comparable with the way Habermas positions his work at some distance from earlier Frankfurt School theorists. Such positioning, like Habermas's reconstruction of Walter Benjamin included in this anthology, exemplifies the critical strategy of second-generation Frankfurt School theorists.

Foucault's own description of his approach to Nietzsche suggests greater affinities between Foucault and earlier Frankfurt School critical theorists such as Adorno. For Foucault, Nietzsche suggests a genealogical approach which resists the linear narrative of 'history' and rejects the use of metahistorical ideals as tools of analysis. The model for genealogical critique is provided by Nietzsche's *Genealogy of Morals*, which re-evaluates historical ideas of progress and emancipation, suggesting a critical relation to enlightenment values.[76] Knowledge, according to this Nietzschean model of genealogical critique, is revealed not as a narrative of progressive freedom but as enslavement to the instinctive violence of the will to knowledge. Foucault suggests the need for critical reflection on the way intellectual history reveals practices and discourses of power rather than the grand narratives proudly abstracted from history by science and philosophy. The critique of grand historical narratives finds its most influential representation in Lyotard's account of postmodernism.[77] Despite Foucault's critique of historicism, Foucault's work has been influential on the resulting emphasis on the study of discrete constellations of discourse and power in what has become known as 'new historicism'.[78] Foucault's account of sexuality's genealogical conditions of possibility has also informed theories of sexual dissidence and 'queer theory'.[79] Foucault's own work, however, negotiates differences between philosophy, science and history, a negotiation which offers a new conception of critique as genealogical reflection with practical and ethical consequences. Foucault's response to Derrida's critique of Foucault's *Madness and Civilization* exemplifies problems in the metaphysical and metacritical assumptions at work in their differences. The more symptomatic difficulty revealed by Foucault's influence, which informs the work of Bhabha and Butler, is the tension between the philosophical dimensions of critique and the looser sense of critique as a political-critical practice.

Derrida's work puts more emphasis on the philosophical difficulties of reflexive thought and the philosophical entailments of writing practices. He has often distanced 'deconstruction' from 'critique', suggesting that deconstruction owes more to the genealogical approach suggested by Nietzsche and Heidegger than to Kantian or Marxist critique. Despite such disclaimers, deconstruction suggests critiques of the metaphysical assumptions in philosophical and non-philosophical writings. As with Hegel, Marx and Nietzsche, the impulse to define the word 'critique' is foreign to the way such words are developed within Derrida's work. Questioned about the relation between deconstruction and critique, Derrida suggests that:

> The *critical* idea, which I believe must never be renounced, has a history and presuppositions whose deconstructive analysis is also necessary. In the style of the Enlightenment, of Kant, or of Marx, but also in the sense of evaluation (esthetic or literary), *critique* supposes judgement, voluntary judgement between two terms; it attaches to the idea of *krinein* or of *krisis* a certain negativity. To say that all this is deconstructible does not amount to disqualifying, negating, disavowing, or surpassing it, of doing the *critique of critique* (the way people wrote critiques of the Kantian critique as soon as it appeared), but of thinking its possibility from another border, from the genealogy of judgement, will, consciousness or activity, the binary structure, and so forth.[80]

Characteristically, this passage suggests a practice which claims not to be critical or metacritical but which seeks to affirm a genealogy which honours and deconstructs Kantian and Marxian critique. Insofar as Derrida develops a different mode of critical practice, his approach emphasizes the conceptual, metaphysical or ontological presuppositions at work in different discourses. Derrida's way of questioning the grounds of texts without seeking new critical foundations exemplifies the scepticism of modern

thought and its oscillation between quasi-transcendental claims and historical concretization. Much of the uncritical energy of modern thought reduces critique to the
relativism of sceptical historicization. More conceptually sophisticated traditions of
thought are more critical of historical thought's conditions of possibility. The more
difficult task is to develop the critique of reason both historically and conceptually.

Such difficulties emerge in *Contingency, Hegemony, Universality*. Judith Butler questions the Kantian oppositions between quasi-transcendental claims and historical
examples in Žižek's appropriation of Hegel.[81] Ernesto Laclau, similarly, points to 'the
widespread feeling that neither a radical historicism nor a fully fledged transcendental-
ism' is viable to explain the way '*quasi*-transcendentalism' has been postulated.[82] What
emerges, however, is the need for a historical or genealogical account of the emergence
of 'quasi-transcendental' arguments in contemporary theory, and for critical reflection
on the way such arguments are deployed. The term 'quasi-transcendental' appears
earlier in Adorno's account of the way Walter Benjamin thinks through tradition.[83]
Geoff Bennington puts the complication of the empirical and the transcendental
marked by the prefix 'quasi-' at the heart of Derridean deconstruction, and the current
fashion for the term probably reflects the currency of the term in Derrida's work.[84]
Just as 'post' seems to function in a number of contemporary compounds – post-
structuralism, post-modernism, post-colonialism, post-Marxism, post-theory – without
clarifying the shifts involved, so 'quasi' seems to evade critical definition. Thus Butler
observes of quasi-transcendental formulations of sexual difference that: 'The "quasi"-
that precedes the transcendental is meant to ameliorate the harshness of this effect, but it
also sidesteps the question: what sense of transcendental is in use here?'[85] If sexual
difference is determined by 'quasi-transcendental' conditions of possibility which
cannot be changed historically, then such a theory of sexual difference effectively
prescribes the limits of possible sexual arrangements. Žižek's attempt to answer such
questions concludes the selection of essays in this anthology, but it is clear that the
complexity of the conceptual vocabularies involved exemplifies the ongoing attempt to
develop critical separations between pure and practical reason. In different ways, the
quasi-transcendental is a symptom of the difficulty of breaking with the traditions of
critique generated by Kant and Marx. To be post-critical is to be uncritical: the critical
path alone remains open.

NOTES

1 For a survey of 'continental' philosophy, see *The Edinburgh Encyclopedia of Continental Philosophy*, ed.
   Simon Glendinning (Edinburgh: Edinburgh University Press, 1999).
2 Maurice Merleau-Ponty, 'Philosophy and Non-philosophy since Hegel', trans. Hugh J. Silverman,
   Philosophy and Non-Philosophy since Merleau-Ponty, ed. Hugh J. Silverman (New York: Routledge,
   1988), pp. 9–83 (p. 9).
3 See, for example, *After Philosophy: End or Transformation?* eds. Kenneth Baynes, James Bohman and
   Thomas McCarthy (Cambridge, MA: MIT, 1987).
4 See Jürgen Habermas, *Theory and Practice*, trans. John Viertel (London: Heinemann, 1974); and *Knowledge and Human Interests*, trans. Jeremy J. Shapiro, 2nd edition (London: Heinemann, 1978).
5 The key critical text in the dissemination of 'literary theory' remains Terry Eagleton, *Literary Theory: An
   Introduction*, 2nd edition (Oxford: Blackwell, 1996); see also *Marxist Literary Theory: A Reader*, eds. Terry
   Eagleton and Drew Milne (Oxford: Blackwell, 1996).
6 *The Handbook of Critical Theory*, ed. David M. Rasmussen (Oxford: Blackwell, 1996).

7   *The Norton Anthology of Theory and Criticism*, ed. Vincent B. Leitch (New York: W. W. Norton & Co., 2001).

8   On the 'structuralist invasion' see Gary Gutting, *French Philosophy in the Twentieth Century* (Cambridge: Cambridge University Press, 2001); for a critique of Althusser's structuralism, see André Glucksmann, 'A Ventriloquist Structuralism', *Western Marxism: A Critical Reader*, edited by New Left Review (London: New Left Books, 1977), pp. 282–314.

9   See *The Languages of Criticism and the Sciences of Man: The Structuralist Controversy*, eds. Richard Macksey and Eugenio Donato (Baltimore: Johns Hopkins University Press, 1970).

10 Peter Dews, *Logics of Disintegration* (London: Verso, 1987).

11 Drew Milne, ' "The Function of Criticism": A Polemical History', *Parataxis: Modernism and Modern Writing*, 1 (Spring, 1991), 30–50.

12 Immanuel Kant, *Critique of Pure Reason*, trans. Norman Kemp Smith (London: Macmillan, 1964), p. 9 (Axi.n.).

13 On the genesis of modern 'critique', see Paul Connerton, *The Tragedy of Enlightenment: An Essay on the Frankfurt School* (Cambridge: Cambridge University Press, 1980), pp. 17–26.

14 Willi Goetschel, *Constituting Critique: Kant's Writing as Critical Praxis*, trans. Eric Schwab (Durham, NC and London: Duke University Press, 1994), p. 4.

15 On German literary and aesthetic criticism after Kant, see Walter Benjamin, 'The Concept of Criticism in German Romanticism', *Walter Benjamin: Selected Writings*, volume 1, *1913–1926*, eds. Marcus Bullock and Michael W. Jennings (Cambridge, MA: Belknap / Harvard University Press, 1996), pp. 116–200.

16 See, for example, Harold Bloom, Paul de Man, Jacques Derrida, Geoffrey H. Hartman and J. Hillis Miller, *Deconstruction and Criticism* (London: Routledge and Kegan Paul, 1979).

17 On critical thought and philosophical hermeneutics see Hans-Georg Gadamer, *Truth and Method* (London: Sheed and Ward, 1979); and *The Hermeneutics Reader*, ed. Kurt Mueller-Vollmer (Oxford: Blackwell, 1986).

18 Raymond Williams, 'Criticism', *Keywords: A Vocabulary of Culture and Society*, revised edition (London: Fontana, 1983), pp. 85–6 (p. 86).

19 Simon Jarvis, *Scholars and Gentlemen: Shakespearian Textual Criticism and Representations of Scholarly Labour, 1725–1765* (Oxford: Clarendon, 1995), p. 189.

20 Terry Eagleton, *The Function of Criticism: From The Spectator to Post-Structuralism* (London: Verso, 1984).

21 Jane Harrison, 'Preface to the Second Edition' (1927), *Themis: A Study of the Social Origins of Greek Religion* (London: Merlin, 1963), p. viii.

22 For a sketch of the differences, see Simon Glendinning, 'What is Continental Philosophy?', *The Edinburgh Encyclopedia of Continental Philosophy*, pp. 3–20. See also Michael Dummett, *Origins of Analytical Philosophy* (London: Duckworth, 1993).

23 See Jürgen Habermas, *The Structural Transformation of the Public Sphere*, trans. Thomas Burger (Cambridge: Polity, 1989); Alex Honneth, Thomas McCarthy, Claus Offe and Albrecht Wellmer, eds., *Cultural-Political Interventions in the Unfinished Project of Enlightenment*, trans. Barbara Fultner (Cambridge, MA: MIT, 1992).

24 Kant, *Critique of Pure Reason*, p. 704 (A855/B883).

25 Immanuel Kant, 'An Answer to the Question: What is Enlightenment?', *Practical Philosophy*, trans. Mary J. Gregor, ed. Allen Wood (Cambridge: Cambridge University Press, 1996), pp. 15–22 (p. 17).

26 Michel Foucault, 'What is Enlightenment?', *The Foucault Reader*, ed. Paul Rabinow (Harmondsworth: Penguin, 1986), pp. 32–50 (p. 45).

27 *Western Marxism*, edited by New Left Review.

28 Gillian Rose, 'The Antinomies of Sociological Reason', *Hegel Contra Sociology* (London: Athlone, 1981), pp. 1–47.

29 Rose, *Hegel Contra Sociology*, p. 14.

30 Goetschel, *Constituting Critique*, p. 143.

31 Jean-Paul Sartre, *Critique of Dialectical Reason*, trans. Alan Sheridan-Smith (London: New Left Books, 1976); Peter Sloterdijk, *Critique of Cynical Reason*, trans. Michael Eldred (London: Verso, 1988); and Gayatri Chakravorty Spivak, *A Critique of Postcolonial Reason* (Cambridge, MA: Harvard University Press, 1999).

32 Compare the debates in *Feminism as Critique*, eds. Seyla Benhabib and Drucilla Cornell (Minneapolis: University of Minnesota Press, 1987).

33 *Kant's Political Writings*, ed. Hans Reiss, trans. H. B. Nisbet (Cambridge: Cambridge University Press, 1970).

34 See, for example, Martin Barker, 'Kant as a Problem for Marxism', *Radical Philosophy Reader*, eds. Roy Edgley and Richard Osborne (London: Verso, 1985), pp. 3–17; Lucio Colletti, 'Kant, Hegel and Marx', *Marxism and Hegel*, trans. Lawrence Garner (London: New Left Books, 1973), pp. 113–38; and Dick Howard, *From Marx to Kant*, 2nd edition (Basingstoke: Macmillan, 1993).

35 Karl Marx and Frederick Engels, *The Holy Family, Collected Works*, vol. 4 (London: Lawrence & Wishart, 1975), pp. 1–211 (p. 21).

36 Karl Marx, 'Concerning Feuerbach', *Early Writings*, trans. Rodney Livingstone and Gregor Benton (Harmondsworth: Penguin / New Left Review, 1975), pp. 421–3.

37 Louis Althusser, *For Marx*, trans. Ben Brewster (London: Allen Lane, 1969); and, with Etienne Balibar, *Reading Capital*, trans. Ben Brewster (London: New Left Books, 1970).

38 Karl Marx, *Early Writings*, p. 209.

39 Michel Henry, *Marx: A Philosophy of Human Reality*, trans. Kathleen McLaughlin (Bloomington: Indiana University Press, 1983), p. 191.

40 Karl Marx, 'Preface to the Second Edition', *Capital: A Critique of Political Economy*, vol. 1, trans. Ben Fowkes (Harmondsworth: Penguin / New Left Review, 1976), p. 102.

41 Marx, *Capital*, p. 103.

42 Marx, *Capital*, p. 102.

43 See *The Young Hegelians: An Anthology*, ed. Lawrence S. Stepelevich (Cambridge: Cambridge University Press, 1983); Warren Breckman, *Marx, the Young Hegelians, and the Origins of Radical Social Theory* (Cambridge: Cambridge University Press, 1999); and Terry Pinkard, *German Philosophy 1760–1860: The Legacy of Idealism* (Cambridge: Cambridge University Press, 2002).

44 See *Between Kant and Hegel: Texts in the Development of Post-Kantian Idealism*, trans. with introductions by Georg di Giovanni and H. S. Harris (Indianapolis/Cambridge: Hackett, 2000).

45 See Pinkard, *German Philosophy 1760–1860*.

46 Garbis Kortian, *Metacritique: The Philosophical Argument of Jürgen Habermas*, trans. John Raffan (Cambridge: Cambridge University Press, 1980), p. 34.

47 Martin Jay, *The Dialectical Imagination: A History of the Frankfurt School and the Institute of Social Research, 1923–1950* (Boston and Toronto: Little, Brown and Company, 1973); and Rolf Wiggershaus, *The Frankfurt School*, trans. Michael Robertson (Cambridge: Polity, 1994).

48 Max Horkheimer, 'Traditional and Critical Theory', *Critical Theory* (New York: Continuum, 1972), p. 206. See also Max Horkheimer, *Between Philosophy and Social Science*, trans. G. Frederick Hunter, Matthew S. Kramer and John Torpey (Cambridge, MA: MIT, 1995); *On Max Horkheimer*, eds. Seyla Benhabib, Wolfgang Bonß and John McCole (Cambridge, MA: MIT, 1993).

49 Jürgen Habermas, *Theory and Practice*, quoted in Garbis Kortian, *Metacritique*, p. 47.

50 The classic account is Emile Durkheim, *The Division of Labor in Society*, trans. George Simpson (London: Collier-Macmillan, 1933); see also Alfred Sohn-Rethel, 'Mental and Manual Labour in Marxism', *Situating Marx*, eds. Paul Walton and Stuart Hall (London: Human Context, n.d.), pp. 44–71.

51 G. W. F. Hegel, *Phenomenology of Spirit*, trans. A. V. Miller (Oxford: Oxford University Press, 1977), pp. 185–210.

52 See T. W. Adorno, *The Stars Down to Earth and Other Essays on the Irrational in Culture*, ed. Stephen Crook (London: Routledge, 1994); and Slavoj Žižek, *The Sublime Object of Ideology* (London: Verso, 1989), pp. 207–9.

53 See, for example, Michel Foucault, *Madness and Civilization*, trans. Richard Howard (London: Tavistock, 1967).

54 See Louis Althusser, *Philosophy and the Spontaneous Philosophy of the Scientist*, ed. Gregory Elliott (London: Verso, 1990); and Juliet Mitchell, *Psychoanalysis and Feminism* (London: Allen Lane, 1974).

55 See Shlomo Avineri, *The Social & Political Thought of Karl Marx* (Cambridge: Cambridge University Press, 1968); and Breckman, *Marx, the Young Hegelians, and the Origins of Radical Social Theory*.

56 See Theodor W. Adorno and others, *The Positivist Dispute in German Sociology*, trans. Glyn Adey and David Frisby (London: Heinemann, 1976).

57   Paul Connerton, ed., *Critical Sociology* (Harmondsworth: Penguin, 1976).

58   Gillian Rose, *Hegel Contra Sociology*.

59   Theodor W. Adorno, *Against Epistemology: A Metacritique*, trans. Willis Domingo (Oxford: Blackwell, 1982); *Negative Dialectics*, trans. E. B. Ashton (London: Routledge & Kegan Paul, 1973).

60   Adorno, *Negative Dialectics*, p. xx.

61   Jürgen Habermas, 'The Entwinement of Myth and Enlightenment: Max Horkheimer and Theodor Adorno', *The Philosophical Discourse of Modernity*, trans. Frederick Lawrence (Cambridge: Polity, 1987), pp. 106–30.

62   For an introduction to phenomenology, see Edmund Husserl, *Phenomenology and the Crisis of Philosophy*, trans. Quentin Lauer (New York: Harper and Row, 1965). See also Herbert Spiegelberg, *The Phenomenological Movement*, 2 vols. (The Hague: Nijhoff, 1960); and *The Phenomenology Reader*, eds. Tim Mooney and Dermot Moran (London: Routledge, 2002).

63   See *The Debate Between Sartre and Mereleau-Ponty*, ed. Jon Stewart (Evanston, IL: Northwestern University Press, 1998); Cristina Lafont, *Heidegger, Language and World-Disclosure*, trans. Graham Harman (Cambridge: Cambridge University Press, 2000); Herbert Marcuse, *Hegel's Ontology and the Theory of Historicity*, trans. Seyla Benhabib (Cambridge, MA: MIT, 1987); Trân Duc Thao, *Phenomenology and Dialectical Materialism*, trans. Daniel J. Herman and Donald V. Morano, ed. Robert S. Cohen (Dordrecht: Reidel, 1986); and Karel Kosík, *Dialectics of the Concrete*, trans. Karel Kovanda and James Schmidt (Dordrecht: Reidel, 1976).

64   On Nietzsche's rhetoric, see Paul de Man, *Allegories of Reading* (New Haven: Yale University Press, 1979).

65   On Kierkegaard's authorship, see Theodor W. Adorno, *Kierkegaard*, trans. Robert Hullot-Kentor (Minneapolis: University of Minnesota Press, 1989); and Gillian Rose, *The Broken Middle* (Oxford: Blackwell, 1992).

66   See Joel Whitebook, *Perversion and Utopia: A Study in Psychoanalysis and Critical Theory* (Cambridge, MA: MIT, 1995); *Mapping Ideology*, ed. Slavoj Žižek (London: Verso, 1994); and Žižek, *The Sublime Object of Ideology*.

67   For philosophical critiques of Freud see Herbert Marcuse, *Eros and Civilization* (Boston: Beacon, 1955/6); Paul Ricoeur, *Freud and Philosophy*, trans. Denis Savage (New Haven: Yale University Press, 1970); Luce Irigaray, *Speculum of the Other Woman*, trans. Gillian C. Gill (Ithaca, NY: Cornell University Press, 1985); Jacques Derrida, *The Post-Card*, trans. Alan Bass (Chicago: University of Chicago Press, 1987); and Michel Henry, *The Genealogy of Psychoanalysis*, trans. Douglas Brick (Stanford, CA: Stanford University Press, 1993).

68   Paul Connerton, *The Tragedy of Enlightenment*, p. 25.

69   Louis Althusser and Etienne Balibar, *Reading Capital*, p. 16n.

70   Lucien Goldmann, *Lukács and Heidegger*, trans. William Q. Boelhower (London: Routledge, 1977).

71   See, for example, Richard Wolin, *Heidegger's Children: Hannah Arendt, Karl Lowith, Hans Jonas and Herbert Marcuse* (Princeton: Princeton University Press, 2001).

72   Alain Badiou, *Deleuze: The Clamor of Being*, trans. Louise Burchill (Minneapolis: University of Minnesota Press, 2000), p. 13.

73   Along with readings of Nietzsche by Heidegger and Deleuze in this anthology, see Karl Jaspers, *Nietzsche*, trans. Charles F. Wallraff and Frederick J. Schmitz (Tucson: University of Arizona Press, 1965); and *The New Nietzsche: Contemporary Styles of Interpretation*, ed. David B. Allison (Cambridge, MA: 1985).

74   Habermas, 'The Critique of Reason as an Unmasking of the Human Sciences: Michel Foucault', *The Philosophical Discourse of Modernity*, pp. 238–65 (p. 252).

75   *Critique and Power: Recasting the Foucault/Habermas Debate*, ed. Michael Kelly (Cambridge, MA: MIT, 1994).

76   Michel Foucault, 'Nietzsche, Genealogy, History', from *The Foucault Reader*, pp. 76–100.

77   Jean-François Lyotard, *The Postmodern Condition: A Report on Knowledge*, trans. Geoff Bennington and Brian Massumi (Minneapolis: University of Minnesota Press, 1984).

78   For representations of 'new historicism' see Marjorie Levinson, Marilyn Butler, Jerome McGann and Paul Hamilton, *Rethinking Historicism* (Oxford: Blackwell, 1989); *The New Historicism*, ed. H. Aram Veeser (London: Routledge, 1989); *The New Historicism Reader*, ed. H. Aram Veeser (London:

Routledge, 1994); Catherine Gallagher and Stephen Greenblatt, *Practicing New Historicism* (Chicago: University of Chicago Press, 2000).

79   See, for example, Jonathan Dollimore, *Sexual Dissidence* (Oxford: Oxford University Press, 1991); and Steven Seidman, *Queer Theory / Sociology* (Oxford: Blackwell, 1996).

80   Jacques Derrida, *Points: Interview, 1974–1994*, ed. Elizabeth Weber, trans. Peggy Kamuf and others (Stanford, CA: Stanford University Press, 1995), p. 357.

81   Judith Butler, Ernesto Laclau and Slavoj Žižek, *Contingency, Hegemony, Universality: Contemporary Dialogues on the Left* (London: Verso, 2000), pp. 6–7.

82   *Contingency, Hegemony, Universality*, pp. 8–9.

83   Adorno, *Negative Dialectics*, p. 54.

84   Geoff Bennington and Jacques Derrida, *Jacques Derrida*, trans. Geoff Bennington (Chicago: University of Chicago Press, 1993).

85   *Contingency, Hegemony, Universality*, p. 147.

1
Lukács on Marx

Georg Lukács (1885–1971) is the most important figure in twentieth-century Marxist critical theory. A friend of Georg Simmel, Max Weber and Ernst Bloch, his thought emerged out of the neo-Kantian schools of German thought and an early interest in Søren Kierkegaard and Nietzsche. His pre-Marxist literary essays, notably *Soul and Form* (1910) and *The Theory of the Novel* (1916), along with his later essays on literary realism, influenced literary critics such as Walter Benjamin, Lucien Goldmann, Raymond Williams and Frederic Jameson. His central contribution to Marxist thought is the collection of essays known as *History and Class Consciousness* (1923). These studies in Marxist dialectics renew the Marxist dialogue with Hegel and offer a new philosophical understanding of key concepts such as commodity fetishism, alienation and reification.

'The Phenomenon of Reification' is from the central essay 'Reification and the Consciousness of the Proletariat'. Lukács combines his exposition of Marx with Max Weber's conceptions of rationalization and bureaucracy, reconstruing the kernel of Marx's conception of the commodity structure of modern capitalism. Having set out the phenomenon of reification, Lukács goes on to argue that modern, 'bourgeois' critical philosophy is rooted in this phenomenon rather than critical of it. *History and Class Consciousness* develops such claims as a critique of Kant. According to Lukács, the formalism of Kantian critique can be overcome only through the transformation of philosophy into revolutionary praxis.

History and Class Consciousness seeks a revolutionary strategy to overcome reification through proletarian class consciousness. This positions Lukács within the dynamic response to the Russian revolution and at the centre of debates about the revolutionary tradition within what is sometimes called 'classical' Marxism. Although his book *Lenin* (1924) argues for the importance of Lenin, placing Lukács within Marxist-Leninism, *History and Class Consciousness* was attacked by the Stalinist forces of Leninist orthodoxy. *History and Class Consciousness* prefigures the discovery and publication of Marx's 1844 *Economic and Philosophical Manuscripts*, which reveal a more Hegelian dimension to the work of the young Marx. This discovery helped to make *History and Class Consciousness*, along with the work of Karl Korsch, an important influence on currents of Hegelian Marxism developed against the grain of Stalinist orthodoxy. Working within severe constraints, Lukács diverted his theoretical energies into socialist literary criticism, although *The Young Hegel* (1948) is of considerable interest in relation to *History and Class Consciousness*, not least in the way Lukács works out the philosophical history of 'alienation'. Lukács' later works nevertheless lack the critical originality of *History and Class Consciousness*. Indeed, Adorno quipped that *The Destruction of Reason* (1962) manifested the destruction of Lukács' own reason. Lukács, in turn, was self-critical of his earlier work, describing how coming to read Marx's early manuscripts shattered the theoretical foundations of *History and Class Consciousness*. Lukács also criticized the residues of Hegelian idealism and subject–object dialectics in his own work. He argued that in *History and Class Consciousness* he had over-extended the concept of political praxis; underestimated the importance of labour; and wrongly equated alienation with objectification. Lukács' early exposition of Marx nevertheless provides one of the most acute introductions to Marx's thought.

Despite being rejected by its author and suppressed by supposedly orthodox Marxists, *History and Class Consciousness* became a seminal text. In *Lukács and Heidegger* (1973), Lucien Goldmann observed that references to the 'reification of consciousness' in *Being and Time* (1927) suggest that Heidegger's thought was in dialogue with Lukács. *History and Class Consciousness* was a more direct influence on Theodor Adorno, Max Horkheimer, Herbert Marcuse and what became known as Frankfurt School critical theory. More generally, although Lukács himself sided with Eastern European Marxism, *History and Class Consciousness* is the seminal text within Western Marxism, and an important influence on the dialogue between existentialism and Marxism. Merleau-Ponty's critique of Lukács appears later in this anthology; resistance to Lukács' conception of dialectic and socialist humanism also motivates the anti-Hegelianism of Louis Althusser and Gilles Deleuze. In the mid-1920s Lukács wrote a fascinating document which has only recently been unearthed in Moscow archives and published in translation as *A Defence of* History and Class Consciousness: *Tailism and the Dialectic* (2000).

FURTHER READING

Primary works

Georg Lukács, *History and Class Consciousness*, trans. Rodney Livingstone (London: Merlin Press, 1971); nb. Lukács' self-critique in 'Preface to the New Edition' (1967), pp. ix–xlvii; *The Destruction of Reason*, trans. Peter Palmer (London: Merlin, 1980); *Goethe & His Age*, trans. Robert Anchor (London: Merlin, 1968); *A Defence of* History and Class Consciousness: *Tailism and the Dialectic*, trans. Esther Leslie (London: Verso, 2000), with postface by Slavoj Žižek; *Record of a Life* (London: Verso, 1983); *The Theory of the Novel*, trans. Anna Bostock (London: Merlin, 1971); *Soul and Form*, trans. Anna Bostock (London: Merlin, 1974); *Selected Correspondence, 1902–1920: Dialogues with*

Weber, Simmel, Buber, Mannheim, and Others, ed. Judith Marcus and Zoltán Tar (New York: Columbia University Press, 1986).

Secondary works

Perry Anderson, *Considerations on Western Marxism* (London: New Left Books, 1976).

Andrew Arato and Paul Breines, *The Young Lukács and the Origins of Western Marxism* (London: Pluto, 1979).

Eva L. Corredor, ed., *Lukács After Communism* (Durham, NC: Duke University Press, 1997).

Andrew Feenberg, *Lukács, Marx and the Sources of Critical Theory* (New York: Oxford University Press, 1986).

Mary Gluck, *Georg Lukács and His Generation, 1900–1918* (Cambridge, MA: Harvard University Press, 1985).

Lucien Goldmann, *Lukács and Heidegger: Towards a New Philosophy*, trans. William B. Boelhower (London: Routledge, 1977).

Agnes Heller, ed., *Lukács Revalued* (Oxford: Blackwell, 1983).

Axel Honneth, 'A Fragmented World: On the Implicit Relevance of Lukács' Early Work', *The Fragmented World of the Social: Essays in Social and Political Philosophy*, ed. Charles W. Wright (Albany: SUNY, 1995), pp. 50–60.

Fredric Jameson, *Marxism and Form* (Princeton: Princeton University Press, 1971).

Gareth Steadman Jones, 'The Marxism of the Early Lukács', *Western Marxism: A Critical Reader*, ed. New Left Review (London: Verso, 1977), pp. 11–60.

Arpad Kadarkay, *Georg Lukács: Life, Thought, and Politics* (Oxford: Blackwell, 1991).

Arpad Kadarkay, ed., *The Lukács Reader* (Oxford: Blackwell, 1995).

Michael Löwy, *Georg Lukács: From Romanticism to Bolshevism*, trans. Patrick Camiller (London: New Left Books, 1979).

Michael Löwy, 'Lukács and Stalinism', *Western Marxism: A Critical Reader*, ed. New Left Review (London: Verso, 1977), pp. 61–82.

Maurice Merleau-Ponty, *Adventures of the Dialectic*, trans. Joseph Bien (London: Heinemann, 1974).

István Mészáros, ed., *Aspects of History and Class Consciousness* (London: Routledge and Kegan Paul, 1971).

István Mészáros, *Lukács' Concept of Dialectic* (London: Merlin, 1972).

Tom Rockmore, ed., *Lukács Today: Essays in Marxist Philosophy* (Dordrecht: Reidel, 1988).

Galin Tihanov, *The Master and the Slave: Lukács, Bakhtin, and the Ideas of Their Time* (Oxford: Clarendon, 2000).

Georg Lukács, 'The Phenomenon of Reification' (1922), from 'Reification and the Consciousness of the Proletariat', *History and Class Consciousness*, trans. Rodney Livingstone (London: Merlin Press, 1971), pp. 83–110.

> *To be radical is to go to the root of the matter. For man, however, the root is man himself.*
> Marx: *Critique of Hegel's Philosophy of Right*

It is no accident that Marx should have begun with an analysis of commodities when, in the two great works of his mature period, he set out to portray capitalist society in its totality and to lay bare its fundamental nature. For at this stage in the history of mankind there is no problem that does not ultimately lead back to that question and there is no solution that could not be found in the solution to the riddle of commodity-*structure*. Of course the problem can only be discussed with this degree of generality if it achieves the depth and breadth to be found in Marx's own analyses. That is to say, the problem of commodities must not be considered in isolation or even regarded as the central problem in economics, but as the central, structural problem of capitalist society in all its aspects. Only in this case can the structure of commodity-relations be made to yield a model of all the objective forms of bourgeois society together with all the subjective forms corresponding to them.

The Phenomenon of Reification

1

The essence of commodity-structure has often been pointed out. Its basis is that a relation between people takes on the character of a thing and thus acquires a 'phantom objectivity', an autonomy that seems so strictly rational and all-embracing as to conceal every trace of its fundamental nature: the relation between people. It is beyond the scope of this essay to discuss the central importance of this problem for economics itself. Nor shall we consider its implications for the economic doctrines of the vulgar Marxists which follow from their abandonment of this starting-point.

Our intention here is to *base* ourselves on Marx's economic analyses and to proceed from there to a discusssion of the problems growing out of the fetish character of commodities, both as an objective form and also as a subjective stance corresponding to it. Only by understanding this can we obtain a clear insight into the ideological problems of capitalism and its downfall.

Before tackling the problem itself we must be quite clear in our minds that commodity fetishism is a *specific* problem of our age, the age of modern capitalism. Commodity exchange and the corresponding subjective and objective commodity relations existed, as we know, when society was still very primitive. What is at issue *here*, however, is the question: how far is commodity exchange together with its structural consequences able to influence the *total* outer and inner life of society? Thus the extent to which such exchange is the dominant form of metabolic change in a society cannot simply be treated in quantitative terms – as would harmonise with the modern modes of thought already eroded by the reifying effects of the dominant commodity form. The distinction between a society where this form is dominant, permeating every expression of life, and a society where it only makes an episodic appearance is essentially one of quality. For depending on which is the case, all the subjective and objective phenomena in the societies concerned are objectified in qualitatively different ways.

Marx lays great stress on the essentially episodic appearance of the commodity form in primitive societies: "Direct barter, the original natural form of exchange, represents rather the beginning of the transformation of use-values into commodities, than that of commodities into money. Exchange value has as yet no form of its own, but is still directly bound up with use-value. This is manifested in two ways. Production, in its entire organisation, aims at the creation of use-values and not of exchange values, and it is only when their supply exceeds the measure of consumption that use-values cease to be use-values, and become means of exchange, i.e. commodities. At the same time, they become commodities only within the limits of being direct use-values distributed at opposite poles, so that the commodities to be exchanged by their possessors must be use-values to both – each commodity to its non-possessor. As a matter of fact, the exchange of commodities originates not within the primitive communities, but where they end, on their borders at the few points where they come in contact with other communities. That is where barter begins, and from here it strikes back into the interior of the community, decomposing it."[1] We note that the observation about the disintegrating effect of a commodity exchange directed in upon itself clearly shows the qualitative change engendered by the dominance of commodities.

However, even when commodities have this impact on the internal structure of a society, this does not suffice to make them constitutive of that society. To achieve that it would be necessary – as we emphasized above – for the commodity structure to penetrate society in all its aspects and to remould it in its own image. It is not enough merely to establish an external link with independent processes concerned with the production of exchange values. The qualitative difference between the commodity as one form among many regulating the metabolism of human society and the commodity as the universal structuring principle has effects over and above the fact that the commodity relation as an isolated phenomenon exerts a negative influence at best on the structure and organisation of society. The distinction also has repercussions upon the nature and validity of the category itself. Where the commodity is universal it manifests itself differently from the commodity as a particular, isolated, non-dominant phenomenon.

The fact that the boundaries lack sharp definition must not be allowed to blur the qualitative nature of the decisive distinction. The situation where commodity exchange is not dominant has been defined by Marx as follows: "The quantitative ratio in which products are exchanged is at first quite arbitrary. They assume the form of commodities inasmuch as they are exchangeables, i.e. expressions of one and the same third. Continued exchange and more regular reproduction for exchange reduces this arbitrariness more and more. But at first not for the producer and consumer, but for their go-between, the merchant, who compares money-prices and pockets the difference. It is through his own movements that he establishes equivalence. Merchant's capital is originally merely the intervening movement between extremes which it does not control and between premises which it does not create."[2]

And *this* development of the commodity to the point where it becomes the dominant form in society did not take place until the advent of modern capitalism. Hence it is not to be wondered at that the personal nature of economic relations was still understood clearly on occasion at the start of capitalist development, but that as the process advanced and forms became more complex and less direct, it became increasingly difficult and rare to find anyone penetrating the veil of reification. Marx sees the matter in this way: "In preceding forms of society this economic mystification arose principally with respect to money and interest-bearing capital. In the nature of things it is excluded, in the first place, where production for the use-value, for immediate personal requirements, predominates; and secondly, where slavery or serfdom form the broad foundation of social production, as in antiquity and during the Middle Ages. Here, the domination of the producers by the conditions of production is concealed by the relations of dominion and servitude which appear and are evident as the direct motive power of the process of production."[3]

The commodity can only be understood in its undistorted essence when it becomes the universal category of society as a whole. Only in this context does the reification produced by commodity relations assume decisive importance both for the objective evolution of society and for the stance adopted by men towards it. Only then does the commodity become crucial for the subjugation of men's consciousness to the forms in which this reification finds expression and for their attempts to comprehend the process or to rebel against its disastrous effects and liberate themselves from servitude to the 'second nature' so created.

Marx describes the basic phenomenon of reification as follows: "A commodity is therefore a mysterious thing, simply because in it the social character of men's labour appears to them as an objective character stamped upon the product of that labour; because the relation of the producers to the sum total of their own labour is presented to them as a social relation, existing not between themselves, but between the products of their labour. This is the reason why the products of labour become commodities, social things whose qualities are at the same time perceptible and imperceptible by the senses. . . . It is only a definite social relation between men that assumes, in their eyes, the fantastic form of a relation between things."[4]

What is of central importance here is that because of this situation a man's own activity, his own labour becomes something objective and independent of him, something that controls him by virtue of an autonomy alien to man. There is both an objective and a subjective side to this phenomenon. *Objectively* a world of objects and relations between things springs into being (the world of commodities and their movements on the market). The laws governing these objects are indeed gradually discovered by man, but even so they confront him as invisible forces that generate their own power. The individual can use his knowledge of these laws to his own advantage, but he is not able to modify the process by his own activity. *Subjectively* – where the market economy has been fully developed – a man's activity becomes estranged from himself, it turns into a commodity which, subject to the non-human objectivity of the natural laws of society, must go its own way independently of man just like any consumer article. "What is characteristic of the capitalist age," says Marx, "is that in the eyes of the labourer himself labour-power assumes the form of a commodity belonging to him. On the other hand it is only at this moment that the commodity form of the products of labour becomes general."[5]

Thus the universality of the commodity form is responsible both objectively and subjectively for the abstraction of the human labour incorporated in commodities. (On the other hand, this universality becomes historically possible because this process of abstraction has been completed.) *Objectively*, in so far as the commodity form facilitates the equal exchange of qualitatively different objects, it can only exist if that formal equality is in fact recognised – at any rate in *this* relation, which indeed confers upon them their commodity nature. *Subjectively*, this formal equality of human labour in the abstract is not only the common factor to which the various commodities are reduced; it also becomes the real principle governing the actual production of commodities.

Clearly, it cannot be our aim here to describe even in outline the growth of the modern process of labour, of the isolated, 'free' labourer and of the division of labour. Here we need only establish that labour, abstract, equal, comparable labour, measurable with increasing precision according to the time socially necessary for its accomplishment, the labour of the capitalist division of labour existing both as the presupposition and the product of capitalist production, is born only in the course of the development of the capitalist system. Only then does it become a category of society influencing decisively the objective form of things and people in the society thus emerging, their relation to nature and the possible relations of men to each other.[6]

If we follow the path taken by labour in its development from the handicrafts via co-operation and manufacture to machine industry we can see a continuous trend towards greater rationalisation, the progressive elimination of the qualitative, human and individual attributes of the worker. On the one hand, the process of labour is progressively broken down into abstract, rational, specialised operations so that the worker loses contact with the finished product and his work is reduced to the mechanical repetition of a specialised set of actions. On the other hand, the period of time necessary for work to be accomplished (which forms the basis of rational calculation) is converted, as mechanisation and rationalisation are intensified, from a merely empirical average figure to an objectively calculable work-stint that confronts the worker as a fixed and established reality. With the modern 'psychological' analysis of the work-process (in Taylorism) this rational mechanisation extends right into the worker's 'soul': even his psychological attributes are separated from his total personality and placed in opposition to it so as to facilitate their integration into specialised rational systems and their reduction to statistically viable concepts.[7]

We are concerned above all with the *principle* at work here: the principle of rationalisation based on what is and *can be calculated*. The chief changes undergone by the subject and object of the economic process are as follows: (1) in the first place, the mathematical analysis of work-processes denotes a break with the organic, irrational and qualitatively determined unity of the product. Rationalisation in the sense of being able to predict with ever greater precision all the results to be achieved is only to be acquired by the exact breakdown of every complex into its elements and by the study of the special laws governing production. Accordingly it must declare war on the organic manufacture of whole products based on the *traditional amalgam of empirical experiences of work*: rationalisation is unthinkable without specialisation.[8]

The finished article ceases to be the object of the work-process. The latter turns into the objective synthesis of rationalised special systems whose unity is determined by pure calculation and which must therefore seem to be arbitrarily connected with each other. This destroys the organic necessity with which inter-related special operations are unified in the end-product. The unity of a product as a *commodity* no longer coincides with its unity as a use-value: as society becomes more radically capitalistic the increasing technical autonomy of the special operations involved in production is expressed also, as an economic autonomy, as the growing relativisation of the commodity character of a product at the various stages of production.[9] It is thus possible to separate forcibly the production of a use-value in time and space. This goes hand in hand with the union in time and space of special operations that are related to a set of heterogeneous use-values.

(2) In the second place, this fragmentation of the object of production necessarily entails the fragmentation of its subject. In consequence of the rationalisation of the work-process the human qualities and idiosyncrasies of the worker appear increasingly as *mere sources of error* when contrasted with these abstract special laws functioning according to rational predictions. Neither objectively nor in his relation to his work does man appear as the authentic master of the process; on the contrary, he is a mechanical part incorporated into a mechanical system. He finds it already pre-existing and self-sufficient, it functions independently of him and he has to conform to its laws whether he likes it or not.[10] As labour is progressively rationalised and mechanised his lack of will is reinforced by the way in which his activity becomes less and less active and more and more *contemplative*.[11] The contemplative stance adopted towards a process mechanically conforming to fixed laws and enacted independently of man's consciousness and impervious to human intervention, i.e. a perfectly closed system, must likewise transform the basic categories of man's immediate attitude to the world: it reduces space and time to a common denominator and degrades time to the dimension of space.

Marx puts it thus: "Through the subordination of man to the machine the situation arises in which men are effaced by their labour; in which the pendulum of the clock has become as accurate a measure of the relative activity of two workers as it is of the speed of two locomotives. Therefore, we should not say that one man's hour is worth another man's hour, but rather that one man during an hour is worth just as much as another man during an hour. Time is everything, man is nothing; he is at the most the incarnation of time. Quality no longer matters. Quantity alone decides everything: hour for hour, day for day...."[12]

Thus time sheds its qualitative, variable, flowing nature; it freezes into an exactly delimited, quantifiable continuum filled with quantifiable 'things' (the reified, mechanically objectified 'performance' of the worker, wholly separated from his total human personality): in short, it becomes space.[13] In this environment where time is transformed into abstract, exactly measurable, physical space, an environment at once the cause and effect of the scientifically and mechanically fragmented and specialised production of the object of labour, the subjects of labour must likewise be rationally fragmented. On the one hand, the objectification of their labour-power into something opposed to their total personality (a process already accomplished with the sale of that labour-power as a commodity) is now made into the permanent ineluctable reality of their daily life. Here, too, the personality can do no more than look on helplessly while its own existence is reduced to an isolated particle and fed into an alien system. On the other hand, the mechanical disintegration of the process of production into its components also destroys those bonds that had bound individuals to a community in the days when production was still 'organic'. In this respect, too, mechanisation makes of them isolated abstract atoms whose work no longer brings them together directly and organically; it becomes mediated to an increasing extent exclusively by the abstract laws of the mechanism which imprisons them.

The internal organisation of a factory could not possibly have such an effect – even within the factory itself – were it not for the fact that it contained in concentrated form the whole structure of capitalist society. Oppression and an exploitation that knows no bounds and scorns every human dignity were known even to pre-capitalist ages. So too was mass production with mechanical, standardised labour, as we can see, for instance, with canal construction in Egypt and Asia Minor and the mines in Rome.[14] But mass projects of this type could never be *rationally mechanised*; they remained isolated phenomena within a community that organised its production on a different ('natural') basis and which therefore lived a different life. The slaves subjected to this exploitation, therefore, stood outside what was thought of as 'human' society and even the greatest and noblest thinkers of the time were unable to consider their fate as that of human beings.

As the commodity becomes universally dominant, this situation changes radically and qualitatively. The fate of the worker becomes the fate of society as a whole; indeed, this fate must become universal as otherwise industrialisation could not develop in this direction. For it depends on the emergence of the 'free' worker who is freely able to take his labour-power to market and offer it for sale as a commodity 'belonging' to him, a thing that he 'possesses'.

While this process is still incomplete the methods used to extract surplus labour are, it is true, more obviously brutal than in the later, more highly developed phase, but the process of reification of work and hence also of the consciousness of the worker is much less advanced. Reification requires that a society should learn to satisfy all its needs in terms of commodity exchange. The separation of the producer from his means of production, the dissolution and destruction of all 'natural' production units, etc., and all the social and economic conditions necessary for the emergence of modern capitalism tend to replace 'natural' relations which exhibit human relations more plainly by rationally reified relations. "The social relations between individuals in the performance of their labour," Marx observes with reference to pre-capitalist societies, "appear at all events as their own personal relations, and are not disguised under the shape of social relations between the products of labour."[15]

But this implies that the principle of rational mechanisation and calculability must embrace every aspect of life. Consumer articles no longer appear as the products of an organic process within a community (as for example in a village community). They now appear, on the one hand, as abstract members of a species identical by definition with its other members and, on the other hand, as isolated objects the possession or non-possession of which depends on rational calculations. Only when the whole life of society is thus fragmented into the isolated acts of commodity exchange can the 'free' worker come into being; at the same time his fate becomes the typical fate of the whole society.

Of course, this isolation and fragmentation is only apparent. The movement of commodities on the market, the birth of their value, in a word, the real framework of every rational calculation is not merely subject to strict laws but also presupposes the strict ordering of all that happens. The atomisation of the individual is, then, only the reflex in consciousness of the fact that the 'natural laws' of capitalist production have been extended to cover every manifestation of life in society; that – for the first time in history – the whole of society is subjected, or tends to be subjected, to a unified economic process, and that the fate of every member of society is determined by unified laws. (By contrast, the organic unities of pre-capitalist societies organised their metabolism largely in independence of each other.)

However, if this atomisation is only an illusion it is a necessary one. That is to say, the immediate, practical as well as intellectual confrontation of the individual with society, the immediate production and reproduction of life – in which for the individual the commodity structure of all 'things' and their obedience to 'natural laws' is found to exist already in a finished form, as something immutably given – could only take place in the form of rational and isolated acts of exchange between isolated commodity owners. As emphasised above, the worker, too, must present himself as the 'owner' of his labour-power, as if it were a commodity. His specific situation is defined by the fact that his labour-power is his only possession. His fate is typical of society as a whole in that this self-objectification, this transformation of a human function into a commodity reveals in all its starkness the dehumanised and dehumanising function of the commodity relation.

2

This rational objectification conceals above all the immediate – qualitative and material – character of things as things. When use-values appear universally as commodities they acquire a new objectivity, a new substantiality which they did not possess in an age of episodic exchange and which destroys their original and authentic substantiality. As Marx observes: "Private property *alienates* not only the individuality of men, but also of things. The ground and the earth have nothing to do with ground-rent, machines have nothing to do with profit. For the landowner ground and earth mean nothing but ground-rent; he lets his land to tenants and receives the rent – a quality which the ground can lose without losing any of its inherent qualities such as its fertility; it is a quality whose magnitude and indeed existence depends on social relations that are created and abolished without any intervention by the landowner. Likewise with the machine."[16]

Thus even the individual object which man confronts directly, either as producer or consumer, is distorted in its objectivity by its commodity character. If that can happen then it is evident that this process will be intensified in proportion as the relations which man establishes with objects as objects of the life process are mediated in the course of his social activity. It is obviously not possible here to give an analysis of the whole economic structure of capitalism. It must suffice to point out that modern capitalism does not content itself with transforming the relations of production in accordance with its own needs. It also integrates into its own system those forms of primitive capitalism that led an isolated existence in pre-capitalist times, divorced from production; it converts them into members of the henceforth unified process of radical capitalism. (Cf. merchant capital, the role of money as a hoard or as finance capital, etc.)

These forms of capital are objectively subordinated, it is true, to the real life-process of capitalism, the extraction of surplus value in the course of production. They are, therefore, only to be explained in terms of the nature of industrial capitalism itself. But in the minds of people in bourgeois society they constitute the pure, authentic, unadulterated forms of capital. In them the relations between men that lie hidden in the immediate commodity relation, as well as the relations between men and the objects that should really gratify their needs, have faded to the point where they can be neither recognised nor even perceived.

For that very reason the reified mind has come to regard them as the true represen-tatives of his societal existence. The commodity character of the commodity, the abstract, quantitative mode of calculability shows itself here in its purest form: the reified mind necessarily sees it as the form in which its own authentic immediacy becomes manifest and – as reified consciousness – does not even attempt to transcend it. On the contrary, it is concerned to make it permanent by 'scientifically deepening' the laws at work. Just as the capitalist system continuously produces and reproduces itself economically on higher and higher levels, the structure of reification progressively sinks more deeply, more fatefully and more definitively into the consciousness of man. Marx often describes this potentiation of reification in incisive fashion. One example must suffice here: "In interest-bearing capital, therefore, this automatic fetish, self-expanding value, money generating money, is brought out in its pure state and in this form it no longer bears the birth-marks of its origin. The social relation is consummated in the relation of a thing, of money, to itself. Instead of the actual transformation of money into capital, we see here only form without content. . . . It becomes a property of money to generate value and yield interest, much as it is an attribute of pear trees to bear pears. And the money-lender sells his money as just such an interest-bearing thing. But that is not all. The actually functioning capital, as we have seen, presents itself in such a light that it seems to yield interest not as functioning capital, but as capital in itself, as money-capital. This, too, becomes distorted. While interest is only a portion of the profit, i.e. of the surplus value, which the functioning capitalist squeezes out of the labourer, it appears now, on the contrary, as though interest were the typical product of capital, the primary matter, and profit, in the shape of profit of enterprise, were a mere accessory and by-product of the process of reproduction. Thus we get a fetish form of capital, and the conception of fetish capital. In M-M' we have the meaningless form of capital, the perversion and objectification of production relations in their highest degree, the interest-bearing form, the simple form of capital, in which it antecedes its own process of reproduction. It is the capacity of money, or of a commodity, to expand its own value independently of reproduction – which is a mystification of capital in its most flagrant form. For vulgar political economy, which seeks to represent capital as an independent source of value, of value creation, this form is naturally a veritable find, a form in which the source of profit is no longer discernible, and in which the result of the capitalist process of production – divorced from the process – acquires an independent existence."[17]

Just as the economic theory of capitalism remains stuck fast in its self-created immediacy, the same thing happens to bourgeois attempts to comprehend the ideological phenomenon of reification. Even thinkers who have no desire to deny or obscure its existence and who are more or less clear in their own minds about its humanly destructive consequences remain on the surface and make no attempt to advance beyond its objectively most derivative forms, the forms furthest from the real life-process of capitalism, i.e. the most external and vacuous forms, to the basic phenomenon of reification itself.

Indeed, they divorce these empty manifestations from their real capitalist foundation and make them independent and permanent by regarding them as the timeless model of human relations in general. (This can be seen most clearly in Simmel's book, *The Philosophy of Money*, a very interesting and perceptive work in matters of detail.) They offer no more than a description of this "enchanted, perverted, topsy-turvy world, in which Monsieur Le Capital and Madame La Terre do their ghost-walking as social characters and at the same time as mere things."[18] But they do not go further than a description and their 'deepening' of the problem runs in circles around the eternal manifestations of reification.

The divorce of the phenomena of reification from their economic bases and from the vantage point from which alone they can be understood, is facilitated by the fact that the [capitalist] process of transformation must embrace every manifestation of the life of society if the preconditions for the complete self-realisation of capitalist production are to be fulfilled.

Thus capitalism has created a form for the state and a system of law corresponding to its needs and harmonising with its own structure. The structural similarity is so great that no truly perceptive historian of modern capitalism could fail to notice it. Max Weber, for instance, gives this description of the basic lines of this development: "Both are, rather, quite similar in their fundamental nature. Viewed sociologically, a 'business-concern' is the modern state; the same holds good for a factory: and this, precisely, is what is specific to it historically. And, likewise, the power relations in a business are also of the same kind. The relative independence of the artisan (or cottage craftsman), of the landowning peasant, the owner of a benefice, the knight and vassal was based on the fact that he himself owned the tools, supplies, financial resources or weapons with the aid of which he fulfilled his economic, political or military function and from which he lived while this duty was being discharged. Similarly, the hierarchic dependence of the worker, the clerk, the technical assistant, the assistant in an academic institute *and* the civil servant and soldier has a comparable basis: namely that the tools, supplies and financial resources essential both for the business-concern and for economic survival are in the hands, in the one case, of the entrepreneur and, in the other case, of the political master."[19]

He rounds off this account – very pertinently – with an analysis of the cause and the social implications of this phenomenon: "The modern capitalist concern is based inwardly above all on *calculation*. It requires for its survival a system of justice and an administration whose workings can be *rationally calculated*, at least in principle, according to fixed general laws, just as the probable performance of a *machine* can be calculated. It is as little able to tolerate the dispensing of justice according to the judge's sense of fair play *in individual cases* or any other irrational means or principles of administering the law . . . as it is able to endure a patriarchal administration that obeys the dictates of its own caprice, or sense of mercy and, for the rest, proceeds in accordance with an inviolable and sacrosanct, but irrational tradition. . . . What is specific to modern capitalism as distinct from the age-old capitalist forms of acquisition is that the strictly rational *organisation of work* on the basis of *rational technology* did not come into being *anywhere* within such irrationally constituted political systems nor could it have done so. For these modern businesses with their fixed capital and their exact calculations are much too sensitive to legal and administrative irrationalities. They could only come into being in the bureaucratic state with its rational laws where . . . the judge is more or less an automatic statute-dispensing machine in which you insert the files together with the necessary costs and dues at the top, whereupon he will eject the judgment together with the more or less cogent reasons for it at the bottom: that is to say, where the judge's behaviour is on the whole *predictable*."

The process we see here is closely related both in its motivation and in its effects to the economic process outlined above. Here, too, there is a breach with the empirical and irrational methods of administration and dispensing justice based on traditions tailored, subjectively, to the requirements of men in action, and, objectively, to those of the concrete matter in hand. There arises a rational systematisation of all statutes regulating life, which represents, or at least tends towards a closed system applicable to all possible and imaginable cases. Whether this system is arrived at in a purely logical manner, as an exercise in pure legal dogma or interpretation of the law, or whether the judge is given the task of filling the 'gaps' left in the laws, is immaterial for our attempt to understand the *structure* of modern legal reality. In either case the legal system is formally capable of being generalised so as to relate to every possible situation in life and it is susceptible to prediction and calculation. Even Roman Law, which comes closest to these developments while remaining, in modern terms, within the framework of pre-capitalist legal patterns, does not in this respect go beyond the empirical, the concrete and the traditional. The purely systematic categories which were necessary before a judicial system could become universally applicable arose only in modern times.[20]

It requires no further explanation to realise that the need to systematise and to abandon empiricism, tradition and material dependence was the need for exact calculation.[21] However, this same need requires that the legal system should confront the individual events of social existence as something permanently established and exactly defined, i.e. as a rigid system. Of course, this produces an uninterrupted series of conflicts between the unceasingly revolutionary forces of the capitalist economy and the rigid legal system. But this only results in new codifications; and despite these the new system is forced to preserve the fixed, change-resistant structure of the old system.

This is the source of the – apparently – paradoxical situation whereby the 'law' of primitive societies, which has scarcely altered in hundreds or sometimes even thousands of years, can be flexible and irrational in character, renewing itself with every new legal decision, while modern law, caught up in the continuous turmoil of change, should appear rigid, static and fixed. But the paradox dissolves when we realise that it arises only because the same situation has been regarded from two different points of view: on the one hand, from that of the historian (who stands 'outside' the actual process) and, on the other, from that of someone who experiences the effects of the social order in question upon his consciousness.

With the aid of this insight we can see clearly how the antagonism between the traditional and empirical craftsmanship and the scientific and rational factory is repeated in another sphere of activity. At every single stage of its development, the ceaselessly revolutionary techniques of modern production turn a rigid and immobile face towards the individual producer. Whereas the objectively relatively stable, traditional craft production preserves in the minds of its individual practitioners the appearance of something flexible, something constantly renewing itself, something produced by the producers.

In the process we witness, illuminatingly, how here, too, the *contemplative* nature of man under capitalism makes its appearance. For the essence of rational calculation is based ultimately upon the recognition and the inclusion in one's calculations of the inevitable chain of cause and effect in certain events – independently of individual 'caprice'. In consequence, man's activity does not go beyond the correct calculation of the possible outcome of the sequence of events (the 'laws' of which he finds 'ready-made'), and beyond the adroit evasion of disruptive 'accidents' by means of protective devices and preventive measures (which are based in their turn on the recognition and application of similar laws). Very often it will confine itself to working out the probable effects of such 'laws' without making the attempt to intervene in the process by bringing other 'laws' to bear. (As in insurance schemes, etc.)

The more closely we scrutinise this situation and the better we are able to close our minds to the bourgeois legends of the 'creativity' of the exponents of the capitalist age, the more obvious it becomes that we are witnessing in all behaviour of this sort the structural analogue to the behaviour of the worker *vis-à-vis* the machine he serves and observes, and whose functions he controls while he contemplates it. The 'creative' element can be seen to depend at best on whether these 'laws' are applied in a – relatively – independent way or in a wholly subservient one. That is to say, it depends on the degree to which the contemplative stance is repudiated. The distinction between a worker faced with a particular machine, the entrepreneur faced with a given type of mechanical development, the technologist faced with the state of science and the profitability of its application to technology, is purely quantitative; it does not directly entail *any qualitative difference in the structure of consciousness.*

Only in this context can the problem of modern bureaucracy be properly understood. Bureaucracy implies the adjustment of one's way of life, mode of work and hence of consciousness, to the general socio-economic premises of the capitalist economy, similar to that which we have observed in the case of the worker in particular business concerns. The formal standardisation of justice, the state, the civil service, etc., signifies objectively and factually a comparable reduction of all social functions to their elements, a comparable search for the rational formal laws of these carefully segregated partial systems. Subjectively, the divorce between work and the individual capacities and needs of the worker produces comparable effects upon consciousness. This results in an inhuman, standardised division of labour analogous to that which we have found in industry on the technological and mechanical plane.[22]

It is not only a question of the completely mechanical, 'mindless' work of the lower echelons of the bureaucracy which bears such an extraordinarily close resemblance to operating a machine and which indeed often surpasses it in sterility and uniformity. It is also a question, on the one hand, of the way in which objectively all issues are subjected to an increasingly *formal* and standardised treatment and in which there is an ever-increasing remoteness from the qualitative and material essence of the 'things' to which bureaucratic activity pertains. On the other hand, there is an even more monstrous intensification of the one-sided specialisation which represents such a violation of man's humanity. Marx's comment on factory work that "the individual, himself divided, is transformed into the automatic mechanism of a partial labour" and is thus "crippled to the point of abnormality" is relevant here too. And it becomes all the more clear, the more elevated, advanced and 'intellectual' is the attainment exacted by the division of labour.

The split between the worker's labour-power and his personality, its metamorphosis into a thing, an object that he sells on the market is repeated here too. But with the difference that not every mental faculty is suppressed by mechanisation; only one faculty (or complex of faculties) is detached from the whole personality and placed in opposition to it, becoming a thing, a commodity. But the basic phenomenon remains the same even though both the means by which society instills such abilities and their material and 'moral' exchange value are fundamentally different from labour-power (not forgetting, of course, the many connecting links and nuances).

The specific type of bureaucratic 'conscientiousness' and impartiality, the individual bureaucrat's inevitable total subjection to a system of relations between the things to which he is exposed, the idea that it is precisely his 'honour' and his 'sense of responsibility' that exact this total submission,[23] all this points to the fact that the division of labour which in the case of Taylorism invaded the psyche, here invades the realm of ethics. Far from weakening the reified structure of consciousness, this actually strengthens it. For as long as the fate of the worker still appears to be an individual fate (as in the case of the slave in antiquity), the life of the ruling classes is still free to assume quite different forms. Not until the rise of capitalism was a unified economic structure, and hence a – formally – unified structure of consciousness that embraced the whole society, brought into being. This unity expressed itself in the fact that the problems of consciousness arising from wage-labour were repeated in the ruling class in a refined and spiritualised, but, for that very reason, more intensified form. The specialised 'virtuoso', the vendor of his objectified and reified faculties does not just become the [passive] observer of society; he also lapses into a contemplative attitude vis-à-vis the workings of his own objectified and reified faculties. (It is not possible here even to outline the way in which modern administration and law assume the characteristics of the factory as we noted above rather than those of the handicrafts.) This phenomenon can be seen at its most grotesque in journalism. Here it is precisely subjectivity itself, knowledge, temperament and powers of expression that are reduced to an abstract mechanism functioning autonomously and divorced both from the personality of their 'owner' and from the material and concrete nature of the subject matter in hand. The journalist's 'lack of convictions', the prostitution of his experiences and beliefs is comprehensible only as the apogee of capitalist reification.[24]

The transformation of the commodity relation into a thing of 'ghostly objectivity' cannot therefore content itself with the reduction of all objects for the gratification of human needs to commodities. It stamps its imprint upon the whole consciousness of man; his qualities and abilities are no longer an organic part of his personality, they are things which he can 'own' or 'dispose of' like the various objects of the external world. And there is no natural form in which human relations can be cast, no way in which man can bring his physical and psychic 'qualities' into play without their being subjected increasingly to this reifying process. We need only think of marriage, and without troubling to point to the developments of the nineteenth century we can remind ourselves of the way in which Kant, for example, described the situation with the naïvely cynical frankness peculiar to great thinkers.

"Sexual community", he says, "is the reciprocal use made by one person of the sexual organs and faculties of another . . . marriage . . . is the union of two people of different sexes with a view to the mutual possession of each other's sexual attributes for the duration of their lives."[25]

This rationalisation of the world appears to be complete, it seems to penetrate the very depths of man's physical and psychic nature. It is limited, however, by its own formalism. That is to say, the rationalisation of isolated aspects of life results in the creation of – formal – laws. All these things do join together into what seems to the superficial observer to constitute a unified system of general 'laws'. But the disregard of the concrete aspects of the subject matter of these laws, upon which disregard of their authority as laws is based, makes itself felt in the incoherence of the system in fact. This incoherence becomes particularly egregious in periods of crisis. At such times we can see how the immediate continuity between two partial systems is disrupted and their independence from and adventitious connection with each other is suddenly forced into the consciousness of everyone. It is for this reason that Engels is able to define the 'natural laws' of capitalist society as the laws of chance.[26]

On closer examination the structure of a crisis is seen to be no more than a heightening of the degree and intensity of the daily life of bourgeois society. In its unthinking, mundane reality *that* life seems firmly held together by 'natural laws'; yet it can experience a sudden dislocation because the bonds uniting its various elements and partial systems are a chance affair even at their most normal. So that the pretence that society is regulated by 'eternal, iron' laws which branch off into the different special laws applying to particular areas is finally revealed for what it is: a pretence. The true structure of society appears rather in the independent, rationalised and formal partial laws whose links with each other are of necessity purely formal (i.e. their formal interdependence can be formally systematised), while as far as concrete realities are concerned they can only establish fortuitous connections.

On closer inspection this kind of connection can be discovered even in purely economic phenomena. Thus Marx points out – and the cases referred to here are intended only as an indication of the methodological factors involved, not as a substantive treatment of the problems themselves – that "the conditions of direct exploitation [of the labourer], and those of realising surplus-value, are not identical. They diverge not only in place and time, but also logically."[27] Thus there exists "an accidental rather than a necessary connection between the total amount of social labour applied to a social article" and "the volume whereby society seeks to satisfy the want gratified by the article in question."[28] These are no more than random instances. It is evident that the whole structure of capitalist production rests on the interaction between a necessity subject to strict laws in all isolated phenomena and the relative irrationality of the total process. "Division of labour within the workshop implies the undisputed authority of the capitalist over men, who are but parts of a mechanism that belongs to him. The division of labour within society brings into contact independent commodity-producers who acknowledge no other authority than that of competition, of the coercion exerted by the pressure of their mutual interests."[29]

The capitalist process of rationalisation based on private economic calculation requires that every manifestation of life shall exhibit this very interaction between details which are subject to laws and a totality ruled by chance. It presupposes a society so structured. It produces and reproduces this structure in so far as it takes possession of society. This has its foundation already in the nature of speculative calculation, i.e. the economic practice of commodity owners at the stage where the exchange of commodities has become universal. Competition between the different owners of commodities would not be feasible if there were an exact, rational, systematic mode of functioning for the whole of society to correspond to the rationality of isolated phenomena. If a rational calculation is to be possible the commodity owner must be in possession of the laws regulating every detail of his production. The chances of exploitation, the laws of the 'market' must likewise be rational in the sense that they must be calculable according to the laws of probability. But they must not be governed by a law in the sense in which 'laws' govern individual phenomena; they must not under any circumstances be rationally organised through and through. This does not mean, of course, that there can be no 'law' governing the whole. But such a 'law' would have to be the 'unconscious' product of the activity of the different commodity owners acting independently of one another, i.e. a law of mutually interacting 'coincidences' rather than one of truly rational organisation. Furthermore, such a law must not merely impose itself despite the wishes of individuals, it may *not even be fully and adequately knowable*. For the complete knowledge of the whole would vouchsafe the knower a monopoly that would amount to the virtual abolition of the capitalist economy.

This irrationality, this – highly problematic – 'systematisation' of the whole which diverges *qualitatively and in principle* from the laws regulating the parts, is more than just a postulate, a presupposition essential to the workings of a capitalist economy. It is at the same time the product of the capitalist division of labour. It has already been pointed out that the division of labour disrupts every organically unified process of work and life and breaks it down into its components. This enables the artificially isolated partial functions to be performed in the most rational manner by 'specialists' who are specially adapted mentally and physically for the purpose. This has the effect of making these partial functions autonomous and so they tend to develop through their own momentum and in accordance with their own special laws independently of the other partial functions of society (or that part of the society to which they belong).

As the division of labour becomes more pronounced and more rational, this tendency naturally increases in proportion. For the more highly developed it is, the more powerful become the claims to status and the professional interests of the 'specialists' who are the living embodiments of such tendencies. And this centrifugal movement is not confined to aspects of a particular sector. It is even more in evidence when we consider the great spheres of activity created by the division of labour. Engels describes this process with regard to the relation between economics and laws: "Similarly with law. As soon as the new division of labour which creates *professional lawyers* becomes necessary, another new and independent sphere is opened up which, for all its essential dependence on production and trade, still has also a special capacity for reacting upon these spheres. In a modern state, law must not only correspond to the general economic condition and be its expression, but must also be an *internally coherent expression* which does not, owing to inner contradictions, reduce itself to nought. And in order to achieve this, the faithful reflection of economic conditions suffers increasingly...."[30] It is hardly necessary to supplement this with examples of the inbreeding and the interdepartmental conflicts of the civil service (consider the independence of the military apparatus from the civil administration), or of the academic faculties, etc.

3

The specialisation of skills leads to the destruction of every image of the whole. And as, despite this, the need to grasp the whole – at least cognitively – cannot die out, we find that science, which is likewise based on specialisation and thus caught up in the same immediacy, is criticised for having torn the real world into shreds and having lost its vision of the whole. In reply to allegations that "the various factors are not treated as a whole" Marx retorts that this criticism is levelled "as though it were the text-books that impress this separation upon life and not life upon the text-books".[31] Even though this criticism deserves refutation in its naïve form it becomes comprehensible when we look for a moment from the outside, i.e. from a vantage point other than that of a reified consciousness, at the activity of modern science which is both sociologically and methodologically necessary and for that reason 'comprehensible'. Such a look will reveal (without constituting a 'criticism') that the more intricate a modern science becomes and the better it understands itself methodologically, the more resolutely it will turn its back on the ontological problems of its own sphere of influence and eliminate them from the realm where it has achieved some insight. The more highly developed it becomes and the more scientific, the more it will become a formally closed system of partial laws. It will then find that the world lying beyond its confines, and in particular the material base which it is its task to understand, *its own concrete underlying reality* lies, methodologically and in principle, *beyond its grasp*.

Marx acutely summed up this situation with reference to economics when he declared that "use-value as such lies outside the sphere of investigation of political economy".[32] It would be a mistake to suppose that certain analytical devices – such as we find in the 'Theory of Marginal Utility' – might show the way out of this impasse. It is possible to set aside objective laws governing the production and movement of commodities which regulate the market and 'subjective' modes of behaviour on it and to make the attempt to start from 'subjective' behaviour on the market. But this simply shifts the question from the main issue to more and more derivative and reified stages without negating the formalism of the method and the elimination from the outset of the concrete material underlying it. The formal act of exchange which constitutes the basic fact for the theory of marginal utility likewise suppresses use-value as use-value and establishes a relation of concrete equality between concretely unequal and indeed incomparable objects. It is this that creates the impasse.

Thus the subject of the exchange is just as abstract, formal and reified as its object. The limits of this abstract and formal method are revealed in the fact that its chosen goal is an abstract system of 'laws' that focuses on the theory of marginal utility just as much as classical economics had done. But the formal abstraction of these 'laws' transforms economics into a closed partial system. And this in turn is unable to penetrate its own material substratum, nor can it advance from there to an understanding of society in its entirety and so it is compelled to view that substratum as an immutable, eternal 'datum'. Science is thereby debarred from comprehending the development and the demise, the social character of its own material base, no less than the range of possible attitudes towards it and the nature of its own formal system.

Here, once again, we can clearly observe the close interaction between a class and the scientific method that arises from the attempt to conceptualise the social character of that class together with its laws and needs. It has often been pointed out – in these pages and elsewhere – that the problem that forms the ultimate barrier to the economic thought of the bourgeoisie is the crisis. If we now – in the full awareness of our own one-sidedness – consider this question from a purely methodological point of view, we see that it is the very success with which the economy is totally rationalised and transformed into an abstract and mathematically orientated system of formal 'laws' that creates the methodological barrier to understanding the phenomenon of crisis. In moments of crisis the qualitative existence of the 'things' that lead their lives beyond the purview of economics as misunderstood and neglected things-in-themselves, as use-values, suddenly becomes the decisive factor. (Suddenly, that is, for reified, rational thought.) Or rather: these 'laws' fail to function and the reified mind is unable to perceive a pattern in this 'chaos'.

This failure is characteristic not merely of classical economics (which regarded crises as 'passing', 'accidental' disturbances), but of bourgeois economics *in toto*. The incomprehensibility and irrationality of crises is indeed a consequence of the class situation and interests of the bourgeoisie but it follows equally from their approach to economics. (There is no need to spell out the fact that for us these are both merely aspects of the same dialectical unity.) This consequence follows with such inevitability that Tugan-Baranovsky, for example, attempts in his theory to draw the necessary conclusions from a century of crises by excluding consumption from economics entirely and founding a 'pure' economics based only on production. The source of crises (whose existence cannot be denied) is then found to lie in incongruities between the various elements of production, i.e. in purely quantitative factors. Hilferding puts his finger on the fallacy underlying all such explanations: "They operate only with economic concepts such as capital, profit, accumulation, etc., and believe that they possess the solution to the problem when they have discovered the quantitative relations on the basis of which either simple and expanded reproduction is possible, or else there are disturbances. They overlook the fact that there are qualitative conditions attached to these quantitative relations, that it is not merely a question of units of value which can easily be compared with each other but also use-values of a definite kind which must fulfil a definite function in production and consumption. Further, they are oblivious of the fact that in the analysis of the process of reproduction more is involved than just aspects of capital in general, so that it is not enough to say that an excess or a deficit of industrial capital can be 'balanced' by an appropriate amount of money-capital. Nor is it a matter of fixed or circulating capital, but rather of machines, raw materials, labour-power of a quite definite (technically defined) sort, if disruptions are to be avoided."[33]

Marx has often demonstrated convincingly how inadequate the 'laws' of bourgeois economics are to the task of explaining the true movement of economic activity *in toto*. He has made it clear that this limitation lies in the – methodologically inevitable – failure to comprehend use-value and real consumption. "Within certain limits, the process of reproduction may take place on the same or on an increased scale even when the commodities expelled from it have not really entered individual or productive consumption. The consumption of commodities is not included in the cycle of the capital from which they originated. For instance, as soon as the yarn is sold the cycle of the capital-value represented by the yarn may begin anew, regardless of what may next become of the sold yarn. So long as the product is sold, everything is taking its regular course from the standpoint of the capitalist producer. The cycle of the capital-value he is identified with is not interrupted. And if this process is expanded – which includes increased productive consumption of the means of production – this reproduction of capital may be accompanied by increased individual consumption (hence demand) on the part of the labourers, since this process is initiated and effected by productive consumption. Thus the production of surplus-value, and with it the individual consumption of the capitalist, may increase, the entire process of reproduction may be in a flourishing condition, and yet a large part of the commodities may have entered into consumption only in appearance, while in reality they may still remain unsold in the hands of dealers, may in fact still be lying in the market."[34]

It must be emphasised that this inability to penetrate to the real material substratum of science is not the fault of individuals. It is rather something that becomes all the more apparent the more science has advanced and the more consistently it functions – from the point of view of its own premises. It is therefore no accident, as Rosa Luxemburg has convincingly shown,[35] that the great, if also often primitive, faulty and inexact synoptic view of economic life to be found in Quesnay's "Tableau Economique", disappears progressively as the – formal – process of conceptualisation becomes increasingly exact in the course of its development from Adam Smith to Ricardo. For Ricardo the process of the total reproduction of capital (where this problem cannot be avoided) is no longer a central issue.

In jurisprudence this situation emerges with even greater clarity and simplicity – because there is a more conscious reification at work. If only because the question of whether the qualitative content can be understood by means of a rational, calculating approach is no longer seen in terms of a rivalry between two principles within the same sphere (as was the case with use-value and exchange value in economics), but rather, right from the start, as a question of form versus content. The conflict revolving around natural law, and the whole revolutionary period of the bourgeoisie was based on the assumption that the formal equality and universality of the law (and hence its rationality) was able at the same time to determine its content. This was expressed in the assault on the varied and picturesque medley of privileges dating back to the Middle Ages and also in the attack on the Divine Right of Kings. The revolutionary bourgeois class refused to admit that a legal relationship had a *valid* foundation merely because it existed *in fact*. "Burn your laws and make new ones!" Voltaire counselled; "Whence can new laws be obtained? From Reason!"[36]

The war waged against the revolutionary bourgeoisie, say, at the time of the French Revolution, was dominated to such an extent by this idea that it was inevitable that the natural law of the bourgeoisie could only be opposed by yet another natural law (see Burke and also Stahl). Only after the bourgeoisie had gained at least a partial victory did a 'critical' and a 'historical' view begin to emerge in both camps. Its essence can be summarised as the belief that the content of law is something purely factual and hence not to be comprehended by the formal categories of jurisprudence. Of the tenets of natural law the only one to survive was the idea of the unbroken continuity of the formal system of law; significantly, Bergbohm uses an image borrowed from physics, that of a 'juridical vacuum', to describe everything not regulated by law.[37]

Nevertheless, the cohesion of these laws is purely formal: *what* they express, "the content of legal institutions is never of a legal character, but always political and economic".[38] With this the primitive, cynically sceptical campaign against natural law that was launched by the 'Kantian' Hugo at the end of the eighteenth century, acquired 'scientific' status. Hugo established the juridical basis of slavery, among other things, by arguing that it "had been the law of the land for thousands of years and was acknowledged by millions of cultivated people".[39] In this naïvely cynical frankness the pattern which is to become increasingly characteristic of law in bourgeois society stands clearly revealed. When Jellinek describes the contents of law as metajuristic, when 'critical' jurists locate the study of the contents of law in history, sociology and politics what they are doing is, in the last analysis, just what Hugo had demanded: they are systematically abandoning the attempt to ground law in reason and to give it a rational content; law is henceforth to be regarded as a formal calculus with the aid of which the legal consequences of particular actions (*rebus sic stantibus*) can be determined as exactly as possible.

However, this view transforms the process by which law comes into being and passes away into something as incomprehensible to the jurist as crises had been to the political economist. With regard to the origins of law the perceptive 'critical' jurist Kelsen observes: "It is the great *mystery* of law and of the state that is consummated with the enactment of laws and for this reason it may be permissible to employ inadequate images in elucidating its nature."[40] Or in other words: "It is symptomatic of the nature of law that a norm may be legitimate even if its origins are iniquitous. That is another way of saying that the legitimate origin of a law cannot be written into the concept of law as one of its conditions."[41] This epistemological clarification could also be a factual one and could thereby lead to an advance in knowledge. To achieve this, however, the other disciplines into which the problem of the origins of law had been diverted would really have to propose a genuine solution to it. But also it would be essential really to penetrate the nature of a legal system which serves purely as a means of calculating the effects of actions and of rationally imposing modes of action relevant to a particular class. In that event the real, material substratum of the law would at one stroke become visible and comprehensible. But neither condition can be fulfilled. The law maintains its close relationship with the 'eternal values'. This gives birth, in the shape of a philosophy of law to an impoverished and formalistic re-edition of natural law (Stammler). Meanwhile, the real basis for the development of law, a change in the power relations between the classes, becomes hazy and vanishes into the sciences that study it, sciences which – in conformity with the modes of thought current in bourgeois society – generate the same problems of transcending their material substratum as we have seen in jurisprudence and economics.

The manner in which this transcendence is conceived shows how vain was the hope that a comprehensive discipline, like philosophy, might yet achieve that overall knowledge which the particular sciences have so conspicuously renounced by turning away from the material substratum of their conceptual apparatus. Such a synthesis would only be possible if philosophy were able to change its approach radically and concentrate on the concrete material totality of what can and should be known. Only then would it be able to break through the barriers erected by a formalism that has degenerated into a state of complete fragmentation. But this would presuppose an awareness of the causes, the genesis and the necessity of this formalism; moreover, it would not be enough to unite the special sciences mechanically: they would have to be transformed inwardly by an inwardly synthesising philosophical method. It is evident that the philosophy of bourgeois society is incapable of this. Not that the desire for synthesis is absent; nor can it be maintained that the best people have welcomed with open arms a mechanical existence hostile to life and a scientific formalism alien to it. *But a radical change in outlook is not feasible on the soil of bourgeois society.* Philosophy can attempt to assemble the whole of knowledge encyclopaedically (see Wundt). Or it may radically question the value of formal knowledge for a 'living life' (see irrationalist philosophies from Hamann to

Bergson). But these episodic trends lie to one side of the main philosophical tradition. The latter acknowledges as given and necessary the results and achievements of the special sciences and assigns to philosophy the task of exhibiting and justifying the grounds for regarding as valid the concepts so constructed.

Thus philosophy stands in the same relation to the special sciences as they do with respect to empirical reality. The formalistic conceptualisation of the special sciences become for philosophy an immutably given substratum and this signals the final and despairing renunciation of every attempt to cast light on the reification that lies at the root of this formalism. The reified world appears henceforth quite definitively – and in philosophy, under the spotlight of 'criticism' it is potentiated still further – as the only possible world, the only conceptually accessible, comprehensible world vouchsafed to us humans. Whether this gives rise to ecstasy, resignation or despair, whether we search for a path leading to 'life' via irrational mystical experience, this will do absolutely nothing to modify the situation as it is in fact.

By confining itself to the study of the 'possible conditions' of the validity of the forms in which its underlying existence is manifested, modern bourgeois thought bars its own way to a clear view of the problems bearing on the birth and death of these forms, and on their real essence and substratum. Its perspicacity finds itself increasingly in the situation of that legendary 'critic' in India who was confronted with the ancient story according to which the world rests upon an elephant. He unleashed the 'critical' question: upon what does the elephant rest? On receiving the answer that the elephant stands on a tortoise 'criticism' declared itself satisfied. It is obvious that even if he had continued to press apparently 'critical' questions, he could only have elicited a third miraculous animal. He would not have been able to discover the solution to the real question.

NOTES

1 Karl Marx, *A Contribution to the Critique of Political Economy*, trans. N. I. Stone (London: Kegan & Paul, 1904), p. 53.
2 Karl Marx, *Capital: A Critique of Political Economy*, ed. F. Engels, trans. Samuel Moore and Edward Aveling (London: Lawrence & Wishart, 1959), 3 vols., vol. III, p. 324.
3 *Capital* III, p. 810.
4 *Capital* I, p. 72. On this antagonism cf. the purely economic distinction between the exchange of goods in terms of their value and the exchange in terms of their cost of production. *Capital* III, p. 174.
5 *Capital* I, p. 170.
6 Cf. *Capital* I, pp. 322, 345.
7 This whole process is described systematically and historically in *Capital* I. The facts themselves can also be found in the writings of bourgeois economists like Bücher, Sombart, A. Weber and Gottl among others – although for the most part they are not seen in connection with the problem of reification.
8 *Capital* I, p. 384.
9 *Capital* I, p. 355 (note).
10 That this should appear so is fully justified from the point of view of the *individual* consciousness. As far as class is concerned we would point out that this subjugation is the product of a lengthy struggle which enters upon a new stage with the organisation of the proletariat into a class – but on a higher plane and with different weapons.
11 *Capital* I, pp. 374–6, 423–4, 460, etc. It goes without saying that this 'contemplation' can be more demanding and demoralising than 'active' labour. But we cannot discuss this further here.
12 Karl Marx, *The Poverty of Philosophy* (London: Lawrence & Wishart, 1956), pp. 58–9.

13 *Capital* I, p. 344.

14 Cf. Friedrich von Gottl-Ottlilienfeld, *Wirtschaft und Technik*, Grundriss der Sozialökonomik, 2 vols., vol. II, pp. 234ff.

15 *Capital* I, p. 77.

16 This refers above all to capitalist private property. *Der heilige Max. Dokumente des Sozialismus* III, 363. Marx goes on to make a number of very fine observations about the effects of reification upon language. A philological study from the standpoint of historical materialism could profitably begin here. See Karl Marx and Friedrich Engels, *The German Ideology*, trans. C. P. Magill, *Collected Works* (London: Lawrence & Wishart, 1976), vol. 5, p. 230.

17 *Capital* III, pp. 384–5.

18 Ibid., p. 809.

19 Max Weber, *Gesammelte politische Schriften* (Munich, 1921), pp. 140–2. Weber's reference to the development of English law has no bearing on our problem. On the gradual ascendancy of the principle of economic calculation, see also A. Weber, *Über den Standort der Industrien* (Tübingen, 1909), especially p. 216.

20 Max Weber, *Wirtschaft und Gesellschaft* (Tübingen, 1922), p. 491.

21 Ibid., p. 129.

22 If we do not emphasise the class character of the state in *this* context, this is because our aim is to understand reification as a *general* phenomenon constitutive of the *whole* of bourgeois society. But for this the question of class would have to begin with the machine.

23 Cf. Max Weber, *Politische Schriften*, p. 154.

24 Cf. the essay by A. Fogarasi in *Kommunismus*, Jg. II, No. 25/26.

25 *Die Metaphysik der Sitten*, Pt. I, § 24.

26 Frederick Engels, *The Origin of the Family, Private Property and the State*, trans. Alec West, in Karl Marx, *Selected Works*, 2 vols. (London: Lawrence & Wishart, 1950), vol. II, p. 293.

27 *Capital* III, p. 239.

28 Ibid., p. 183.

29 *Capital* I, p. 356.

30 Letter to Conrad Schmidt in S.W. II, pp. 447–8.

31 *A Contribution to the Critique of Political Economy*, p. 276.

32 Ibid., p. 21.

33 Rudolf Hilferding, *Das Finanzkapital. Eine Studie Über die jüngste Entwicklung des Kapitalismus* (Vienna, 1910), 2nd edn, pp. 378–9.

34 *Capital* II, pp. 75–6.

35 *Die Akkumulation des Kapitals*, 1st edition (Leipzig, 1921), pp. 78–9. It would be a fascinating task to work out the links between this process and the development of the great rationalist systems.

36 Quoted by Carl Bergbohm, *Jurisprudenz und Rechtsphilosphie* (Leipzig, 1892), vol. I, p. 170.

37 Ibid., p. 375.

38 Preuss, *Zur Methode der juristischen Begriffsbildung*. In Schmollers Jahrbuch, 1900, p. 370.

39 *Lehrbuch des Naturrechts*, Berlin, 1799, § 141. Marx's polemic against Hugo (Nachlass I, pp. 268 et seq.) is still on Hegelian lines.

40 Hans Kelsen, *Hauptprobleme der Staatsrechtslehre* (Tübingen, 1923), p. 411 (my italics).

41 Feliz Somló, *Juristische Grundlehre* (Leipzig, 1917), p. 177.

2
Heidegger on Nietzsche

Considered by many to be the greatest philosopher of the twentieth century, Martin Heidegger (1889–1976) has also been reviled for his too intimate association with the Nazis. Heidegger studied under Edmund Husserl and, like Lukács, was influenced by Søren Kierkegaard and the attempt to move beyond neo-Kantianism. His most important work, *Being and Time* (1927), develops Husserl's approach to phenomenology to reveal Heidegger's distinctive investigation of ontology. For Heidegger, rigorous investigation into human being (*Dasein*) provides a way into what he calls fundamental ontology and the meaning of Being (*Sein*). According to Heidegger, Western thought and metaphysics have neglected or forgotten the importance of the 'ontological difference' between beings and Being. Heidegger is interested in the difference between what it means for a being to be a kind of being and what it means for a being to 'be'. The claim that a being 'is' human is thus two claims, a claim that it is a human kind of being and a claim that 'Being' as such exists. For something to be what it 'is' presupposes an answer to the question why there are beings at all and not nothing. Most forms of knowledge, especially scientific knowledge, forget the extent to which it is assumed that existence exists and is meaningful. Heidegger seeks to re-open or remember the question of what Being 'is' through problems of time and history. Human beings interpret what the world 'is' through their own kinds of temporality and historicity. Human beings 'exist' in time rather than as beings that can stand outside of time. For Heidegger, the hermeneutics of human existence go beyond textual or theological interpretation to question the meaning of existence and the limits of human transcendence. He reconfigures hermeneutics accordingly as the way human beings interpret Being from within the human horizons of death.

Only the first half of *Being and Time* (1927) was completed. Thereafter, Hedeigger's thought underwent what has become known as the 'turn' (*die Kehre*), often understood as the turn from the emphasis on human being to Being as such. This turn involves a renewed interest in language and the language of metaphysics. The essay by Gadamer included in this anthology provides an introduction to Heidegger's later philosophy. After *Being and Time*, Heidegger's thought seeks to overcome the history of Western metaphysics since the Greeks. This overcoming, or overturning, motivates Heidegger's interpretation of Nietzsche as the last metaphysician of Western thought. Heidegger's understanding of the way truth is concealed and disclosed in language often makes Heidegger's rhetoric deliberately opaque. In his lectures on Nietzsche the effort to provide an exposition reveals Heidegger at his most accessible. It remains an open question how far Heidegger provides a rigorous introduction to Nietzsche's thought and how far he appropriates Nietzsche's thought to provide an exposition of his own thinking.

'The Eternal Recurrence of the Same and the Will to Power' provides the text of two lectures written in 1939 but not delivered, and not published until 1961. These lectures were intended as the conclusion of a series of lecture courses Heidegger delivered from 1936 to 1940. These lectures are thus situated within Heidegger's turn towards the overcoming or destruction of metaphysics and come just after the most politically sensitive period of his involvement with the Nazi Party around 1933–4. Heidegger later claimed, controversially, that these lectures provided an implicit critique of Nazi ideology.

The political ambiguity of Heidegger's thought has proved intensely problematic, not least for those who share some of his hostility to the technocratic world of modern capitalism. Even those who have been most explicitly hostile to Heidegger, such as Adorno in *Negative Dialectics*, share important philosophical problems, notably the critique of scientific reason. Heidegger influenced Marcuse's critical theory, the Marxist existentialism of Sartre and the phenomenology of Levinas. These thinkers, along with Merleau-Ponty, Lacan, Foucault, Derrida and Deleuze, are critical of Heidegger but develop aspects of his thought. Heidegger's interpretation of Nietzsche, for example, provides a model for Derridean deconstruction and what became known, more generally, as post-structuralism. Derrida's understanding of 'différance' and 'deconstruction' translates Heidegger's conception of 'ontological difference' and the 'destruction' (*Destruktion*) of metaphysics. Some of Derrida's most important essays deconstruct the obscured question of sexual difference in Heidegger's thought. Heidegger's Nietzsche can be compared with Deleuze's interpretation of Nietzsche and Kant in this anthology, but implicit dialogues with Heidegger run throughout modern thought, though it remains difficult to understand Heidegger's thought as critique.

FURTHER READING

Primary works

Martin Heidegger, *Basic Writings*, ed. David Farrell Krell, revised edition (London: Routledge, 1993); *An Introduction to Metaphysics*, trans. Ralph Manheim (New Haven and London: Yale University Press, 1959); *Pathmarks*, ed. William

McNeill (Cambridge: Cambridge University Press, 1998); *The Question Concern-ing Technology and Other Essays*, trans. William Lovitt (New York: Harper and Row, 1977), including 'The Word of Nietzsche: "God is Dead" ', pp. 53–112.

Secondary works

Theodor Adorno, *Negative Dialectics*, trans. E. B. Ashton (London: Routledge and Kegan Paul, 1973).

David B. Allison, ed., *The New Nietzsche: Contemporary Styles of Interpretation* (Cambridge, MA: MIT, 1985).

Jacques Derrida, *Of Spirit: Heidegger and the Question*, trans. Geoffrey Bennington and Rachel Bowlby (Chicago: Chicago University Press, 1989); and *'Geschlecht*: Sexual Difference, Ontological Difference', trans. Ruben Bevezdivin, *A Derrida Reader: Be-tween the Blinds*, ed. Peggy Kamuf (Hemel Hempstead: Harvester Wheatsheaf, 1991), pp. 380–402.

H. L. Dreyfus and H. Hall, eds., *Heidegger: A Critical Reader* (Oxford: Blackwell, 1992).

Michel Foucault, 'Nietzsche, Freud, Marx', and 'Nietzsche, Genealogy, History', *Aesthet-ics, Method, and Epistemology: Essential Works of Foucault*, vol. 2, ed. James D. Faubion (London: Allen Lane/Penguin, 1998), pp. 269–78, 369–91.

Hans-Georg Gadamer, *Truth and Method* (London: Sheed and Ward, 1979).

Charles Guignon, ed., *The Cambridge Companion to Heidegger* (Cambridge: Cambridge University Press, 1993).

Jürgen Habermas, 'The Undermining of Western Rationalism through the Critique of Metaphysics: Martin Heidegger', *The Philosophical Discourse of Modernity*, trans. Fred-erick Lawrence (Cambridge: Polity, 1987), pp. 131–60.

Michael Inwood, ed., *A Heidegger Dictionary* (Oxford: Blackwell, 1999).

Karl Jaspers, *Nietzsche* (1935), trans. Charles F. Wallraff and Frederick J. Schmitz (Tucson: University of Arizona, 1965).

Pierre Klossowski, *Nietzsche and the Vicious Circle*, trans. Daniel W. Smith (London: Athlone, 1997).

Cristina Lafont, *Heidegger, Language and World-Disclosure*, trans. Graham Harman (Cam-bridge: Cambridge University Press, 2000).

Herman Philipse, *Heidegger's Philosophy of Being: A Critical Interpretation* (Princeton, NJ: Princeton University Press, 1998).

O. Pöggeler, *Martin Heidegger's Path of Thinking* (Atlantic Highlands, NJ: Humanities Press, 1987).

John Sallis, ed., *Reading Heidegger: Commemorations* (Bloomington and Indianapolis: Indiana University Press, 1993).

Richard Wolin, ed., *The Heidegger Controversy: A Critical Reader* (Cambridge, MA and London: MIT, 1993).

Martin Heidegger, 'The Eternal Recurrence of the Same and the Will to Power' (1939), trans. and ed. David Farrell Krell, *Nietzsche*, 4 vols., vol. III (San Francisco: Harper and Row, 1987), pp. 161–83.

At first there seems to be not a trace of truth in the claim that Nietzsche's philosophy is the *consummation* of Western metaphysics. For by abolishing the "suprasensuous world" that has served heretofore as the "true" world his philosophy appears rather to reject all metaphysics and to take steps toward its ultimate abnegation. To be sure, Nietzsche's fundamental thought, "the will to power," still refers in some way to an interpretation of the beingness of beings as a whole, namely, as will. Willing goes together with knowing. In the context of Schelling's and Hegel's projects, knowing and willing constitute the essence of reason. In the context of the Leibnizian projection of the substantiality of substance, knowing and willing are thought as *vis primitiva activa et passiva* [the originary active and passive force]. However, the thought of will to power, especially in its biologistic configuration, appears to abandon the realm of this project; rather than consummating the tradition of metaphysics, it seems to truncate that tradition by disfiguring and trivializing it.

What the word *consummation* means; what precisely may *not* be used as a standard for taking its measure; to what extent we can fasten onto a "doctrine" in it; in what way the consummation keeps to the guiding projection (beings' coming to light in Being) that articulates and grounds metaphysics as such; whether the consummation fulfills the guiding projection in its ultimate possibilities, thereby allowing it to stand outside all inquiry – none of these things can be discussed here.

The belief that Nietzsche's philosophy merely distorts, trivializes, and dogmatically abjures prior metaphysics is simply an illusion, albeit a very stubborn one, one that persists as long as we represent his fundamental thought superficially. The superficiality arises from our postponement of a historical meditation on Western metaphysics, as well as from our practice of reflecting on the various projections that evolved from particular fundamental positions solely within the limits of what is asserted in those projections. In doing the latter, we forget that these utterances inevitably speak out of a background, a background from which they emerge; such utterances do not explicitly interrogate that background but return to it unwittingly in their very speech. The various funda-mental positions understand the beingness of beings in a projection that was cast long before they themselves emerged, as far back as our Greek beginnings. These positions take the Being of beings as having been determined in the sense of permanence of presence. If we think these fundamental metaphysical positions within the scope of this guiding projection, we can preserve ourselves from the temptation to grasp Nietzsche's philosophy superficially and to pigeonhole it with the help of the usual historiological labels – as "Heraclitean," as a "metaphysics of the will," or as a "philosophy of life."

If we think in terms of the guiding projection of the beingness of beings, the projection that sustains the entire history of metaphysics even as it surpasses that history at its very commencement, then we will recognize what is metaphysically necessary and ultimate in the doctrine of the eternal recurrence of the same. When we define the interconnection of this doctrine with the fundamental thought of will to power, we bring Nietzsche's philosophy to the fore as the final distinctive position in the history of Western metaphysics. Given such an insight, Nietzsche's philosophy impels us toward the necessity of that confrontation in and for which Western metaphysics, as the totality of a history that has been accomplished, is consigned to what has been, that is to say, is consigned to an ultimate futurity. What has been liberates what apparently is merely past into its essence; specifically, it trans-lates the commencement, which apparently has foundered once and for all, into its character as a commencement. Because of this character, the commencement surpasses everything that follows it, and hence is futural. The past as *essentially unfolding*, that is, beingness projected in sundry ways as the veiled truth of Being, holds sway over everything that is taken to be current and actual, the latter by virtue of its actuating power.

In order to define the interconnection of eternal recurrence of the same and will to power, our reflections must execute the following six steps:

1   In terms of the history of metaphysics, the thought of eternal recurrence of the same anticipates in thought the fundamental thought of will to power; that is to say, it thinks that thought to the point of consummation.
2   In terms of metaphysics, in its modern phase and in the history of its end, both thoughts think the self-same.
3   In the essential unity of the two thoughts, the metaphysics that is approaching consummation utters its final word.
4   The fact that their essential unity remains unspoken founds the age of consummate meaninglessness.
5   This age fulfills the essence of modernity; now, for the first time, modernity comes into its own.
6   Viewed historically, such fulfillment − cloaked in concealment and running counter to bemused popular opinion − is the need characteristic of the transition that embraces all that has been and prepares what is to come. It is transition to guardianship over the truth of Being.

I

Will to power is the essence of power itself. It consists in power's overpowering, that is, its self-enhancement to the highest possible degree. Will does not hover beyond power; it is rather the empowering command within the essence of power to exercise power. The metaphysical determination of Being as will to power remains unthought in its decisive import, and falls prey to misinterpretation, as long as Being is posited solely as power or merely as will, and as long as will to power is explained in the sense of will as power or power as will. To think Being, the beingness of beings, as will to power means to conceive of Being as the unleashing of power to its essence; the unleashing transpires in such a way that unconditionally empowering power posits the exclusive preeminence of beings over Being. Whereas beings possess objective actuality, Being collapses into oblivion.

What this unleashing of power to its essence is, Nietzsche is unable to think. Nor can any metaphysics think it, inasmuch as metaphysics cannot put the matter into question.

On the contrary, Nietzsche thinks his interpretation of the Being of beings as will to power in an essential unity with that determination of Being which arose in the rubric "the eternal recurrence of the same."

Reckoned chronologically, Nietzsche pursued the thought of eternal return of the same before he conceived of will to power, even though intimations of the latter may be found every bit as early. Yet the thought of return is above all earlier *in terms of the matter;* that is to say, it is more forward-reaching, although Nietzsche himself was never able explicitly to think through its essential *unity* with will to power as such, nor to elevate it into a metaphysical conception. Just as little did Nietzsche recognize the truth of the thought of return in terms of the history of metaphysics. The reason for this is not that the thought remained in any way obscure to him, but that like all metaphysicians prior to him Nietzsche was unable to find his way back to the fundamental traits of the guiding metaphysical projection. For the general traits of the metaphysical projection of beings upon beingness, and thereby the representation of beings as such in the domain of presence and permanence, can be known only when we come to experience that projection as historically cast. An experience of this kind has nothing in common with the explanatory theories that metaphysics every now and again proposes concerning itself. Nietzsche too elaborates only these kinds of explanations – which, however, we dare not level off by calling them a "psychology of metaphysics."

"Recurrence" thinks the permanentizing of what becomes, thinks it to the point where the *becoming* of what becomes is secured in the *duration of its becoming.* The "eternal" thinks the permanentizing of such constancy in the direction of its circling back into itself and forward toward itself. Yet what becomes is not the unceasing otherness of an endlessly changing manifold. What becomes is the same itself, and that means the one and selfsame (the identical) that in each case is within the difference of the other. The presence of the one identical element, a presence that comes to be, is thought in the same. Nietzsche's thought thinks the constant permanentizing of the becoming of whatever becomes into the only kind of presence there is – the self-recapitulation of the identical.

This "selfsame" is separated as by an abyss from the singularity of the unrepeatable enjoining of all that coheres. Out of *that* enjoining alone does the difference commence.

The thought of return is not Heraclitean in the sense usually expounded by our historians of philosophy. But it thinks – in a way that has meanwhile become foreign to anything Greek – the formerly projected essence of beingness (permanence of presence), thinks it in its exitless and involuted consummation. Thus the beginning is brought to the fulfillment of its end. Thought concerning truth, in the sense of the essence of *alētheia*, whose essential advent sustains Being and allows it to be sheltered in its belonging to the commencement, is more remote than ever in this last projection of beingness. In Nietzsche's thinking, "truth" has petrified and become a hollow essence: it has the sense of a univocal accord with beings as a whole, in such a way that within this univocity the unstrained voice of Being can never be heard.

The history of the truth of Being ends when its primordial essence is utterly lost. That loss was prepared by the sudden collapse of ungrounded *alētheia*. Yet at the same time the historical illusion necessarily arises that the primordial unity of *physis* in its original configuration has been recovered once again. For in the very early period of metaphysics it was sundered into "Being" and "Becoming." What was sundered in this way was distributed between the two definitive realms, to wit, the true and the apparent worlds.

But, people say, what else can the cancellation of the distinction between the two, the crossing out of these two distinct worlds, mean than the fact that we are finding our way back to the commencement and thereby overcoming metaphysics? Nevertheless, Nietzsche's doctrine does not overcome metaphysics: it is the uttermost unseeing adoption of the very guiding projection of metaphysics. Yet precisely for that reason it is also something essentially other than a flaccid historiological reminiscence of ancient doctrines concerning the cyclical course of cosmic processes.

As long as we designate the thought of return as an unproven and unprovable eccentricity, and as long as we account it one of Nietzsche's poetic and religious caprices, we drag the thinker down to the flatlands of current opinion. If that were the end of the matter, then we might have to resign ourselves to this demotion as the result of those always inevitable misinterpretations by contemporary know-it-alls. Yet something else is at stake here. Inadequate interrogation of the meaning of Nietzsche's doctrine of return, when viewed in terms of the history of metaphysics, shunts aside the most intrinsic need that is exhibited in the course of the history of Western thought. It thus confirms, by assisting those machinations that are oblivious to Being, the utter abandonment of Being.

When that happens we forfeit the very first precondition that anyone would have to satisfy in order to grasp as Nietzsche's fundamental metaphysical thought the ostensibly more accessible thought of will to power. For if will to power constitutes the essential character of the beingness of beings, it must think whatever it is that the eternal recurrence of the same is thinking.

II

When in our meditations we bring the guiding projection of all metaphysics to closer inspection, we see that both thoughts think the same thing – will to power in terms of modernity, eternal recurrence of the same in terms of the history of the end. That guiding projection places beings as such in the open region of permanence and presence, representing them in their universal character with a view to their beingness. Which realm it is that yields our representations of permanence and presencing, indeed, the permanentizing of presence itself, never troubles the guiding projection of metaphysics. Metaphysics keeps strictly to the open region of its projection and interprets the permanentizing of presencing variously in accord with the fundamental experience of the already predetermined beingness of beings. Yet if a meditation stirs that gradually gets into its purview that which lightens, that which propriates all the openness of what is open, permanentizing and presencing will themselves be interrogated with a view to their essence. Both will show themselves as essentially bound up with time. Simultaneously, they will demand of us that we rid ourselves of whatever it is we usually designate in the word *time*.

Will to power may now be conceived of as the permanentizing of surpassment, that is, of Becoming; hence as a transformed determination of the guiding metaphysical projection. The eternal recurrence of the same unfurls and displays its essence, so to speak, as the most constant permanentizing of the becoming of what is constant. Yet, to be sure, all this emerges solely within the scope of that interrogation that has put beingness into question with a view to its projective realm and the grounding of that realm. For such interrogation, the guiding projection of metaphysics and thus metaphysics itself have already been thoroughly overcome; they are no longer admitted as constituting the primary and solely definitive realm.

And yet we may initially try to be guided toward the identity of "eternal recurrence of the same" and "will to power" within the perspectives of metaphysics and with the help of its distinctions. The lecture courses "*The Will to Power as Art*" and "*The Eternal Recurrence of the Same*" pursue a path by which we may see the *inner unity* of these two. From the outset, the eternal recurrence of the same and will to power are grasped as fundamental determinations of beings as such and as a whole – will to power as the peculiar coinage of "what-being" at the historic end, and eternal recurrence of the same as the coinage of "that-being." The *necessity* of grounding this distinction is surely recognized in an unpublished lecture course I taught during the year 1927; nevertheless, the essential origin of the distinction remains concealed there.

This distinction – and the prepotence of the elements thereby distinguished – rules unchallenged throughout the entire history of metaphysics and grows ever more self-evident. In what does it have its ground? What-being (*to ti estin*) and that-being (*to estin*) are coextensive in their differentiation with the distinction that everywhere sustains metaphysics, the distinction that is firmly established in the Platonic differentiation of *ontōs on* [being in its Being] and *mē on* [nonbeing]. Although first established in Platonism, established there once and for all, the distinction proves capable of transformation – to the point of unrecognizability. (See Aristotle, *Metaphysics* Z 4, 1030a 17.) The *ontōs on*, that which has the character of being – and that means "true" being, "true" in the sense of *alētheia* – is a "vision," a profile that comes to presence. In such presence there occurs essentially at one and the same time *what* a being is and *that* it – in the presentness of its profile – is. The "true world" is the world decided in advance with regard to its *that*. Yet insofar as it is true, and thus distinguished from the semblant; and insofar as the merely apparent world *manifests* what-being only in a hazy sort of way, hence "truly" "*is*" not, even if at the same time it is not merely nothing but a being; insofar as all this is the case, the "*that* it is" comes to obtrude precisely in the *mē on*. It comes to appear as a stripping away of the pure "visage" in which the "what" shows itself. The *to ti estin* and the *to estin* (the *ti* [what] and the *hoti* [that]) go their separate ways with and in the distinction of the *ontōs on* and the *mē on*. That-being becomes the distinguishing characteristic of each "this" (*tode ti*) and of the *hekaston* [each] as such; at the same time, these cause the relevant what-being (*eidos*) to appear, in this way alone determining a *that* for Being, and thus determining a being as a particular given. The *idea* now explicitly becomes an *eidos* in the sense of the *morphē* [form] of *hyle* [matter], in such a way that beingness is transposed to a *synolon* [gathered whole] that does not cancel the distinction. (With regard to the original Greek sense of *morphē*, which is quite different from the later distinction between *forma* and *materia*, see Aristotle, *Physics* B 1.) Under many guises, "form" assumes center stage in subsequent times, in particular because of the biblical notion of creation, as *existentia, essentia,* and the *principium individuationis*. What-being and that-being evanesce to vacuous "concepts of reflection" as the unquestioned acceptance of beingness waxes. They persevere with a power that becomes all the more tenacious as metaphysics is increasingly accepted as something self-evident.

Is it any wonder that the distinction between what-being and that-being once again comes to the fore most conspicuously at the consummation of Western metaphysics? Yet the *distinction as such* is forgotten, so that the two fundamental determinations of beings as a whole – will to power and eternal recurrence of the same – are uttered in such a way that although they are metaphysically homeless, as it were, they are posited unconditionally.

Will to power says *what* the being "is." The being is that which (as power) it empowers.

Eternal recurrence of the same designates the *how* in which the being that possesses such a "what" character is. It designates its "factualness" as a whole, its "that it is." Because Being as eternal recurrence of the same constitutes the permanentizing of presence, it is most permanent; it is the unconditioned *that*.

We must at the same time recall something else: the fulfillment of metaphysics tries on the very basis of that metaphysics to overcome the distinction between the "true" and the "merely apparent" worlds. At first it tries to do this simply by inverting those two worlds. Of course, the inversion is not merely a mechanical overturning, whereby the lower, the sensuous realm, assumes the place of the higher, the suprasensuous – an overturning in which these two realms and their locales would remain unchanged. The inversion transforms the lower, the sensuous realm, into "life" in the sense of will to power. In the essential articulation of will to power the suprasensuous is transformed into a securing of permanence.

In accordance with this overcoming of metaphysics, that is, this transformation of metaphysics into its final possible configuration, the very distinction between what-being and that-being is inevitably shunted aside. It thus *remains unthought*. What-being (will to power) is nothing "in itself" to which that-being, by some happy circumstance, is allotted. What-being, as essence, conditions the very animation of life (value). In such conditioning, what-being is at the same time the sole proper *that* of animate beings – and here that means beings as a whole.

On the basis of this cohesion of that-being and what-being (a cohesion that is now quite the opposite of the primordial encompassment of the *estin* by the *einai* of the *ontōs on* as idea), will to power and eternal recurrence of the same may no longer merely cohere as determinations of Being: they must say the *selfsame* thing. At the end of the history of metaphysics, the thought of eternal recurrence of the same expresses precisely what will to power, as the fundamental trait of the beingness of beings, says at the consummation of modernity. Will to power is self-surpassment into the possibilities of becoming that pertain to a commandeering which now begins to install itself. Such self-surpassment remains in its innermost core a permanentizing of Becoming as such. Self-surpassment stands opposed to all mere continuation into the endless, which is foreign and inimical to it.

As soon as we are in a position to think through the pure selfsameness of will to power and eternal recurrence of the same in every direction and in every one of its adopted guises, we shall find the basis for first measuring both of these fundamental thoughts in their particularity and in accord with their metaphysical scope. These thoughts provide an occasion for thinking back to the first commencement. For they constitute the fulfillment of that commencement, empowering unconditionally the nonessence that already emerges on the scene with the *idea*. From that fulfillment unfolds a meditation on the perennially undefined and ungrounded truth of Being. Thus begins the transition toward an interrogation of this truth.

III

The selfsame utterance in the essential unity of will to power and the eternal recurrence of the same is the final word of metaphysics. "Final," in the sense of exhaustive consummation, must also in a certain sense mean "first." The latter, *physis*, commences by rending itself straightaway into the ostensible opposition of Being and Becoming. Upsurgent presencing, unexamined, and not projected upon its character as "time," is always and everywhere apprehended with a view to one thing alone: coming to be and passing away, becoming and change, remaining and enduring. In this last-mentioned respect the Greeks view Being proper; indeed, for them every change is at first called *ouk on* [not-being], later *mē on* [nonbeing], but still defined as *on*. Being and Becoming are divided into two realms that are separated by a *khōrismos* [gap]. Thus they belong to a locale that is defined by these realms; here they take up their residence. To what extent does Aristotle overcome the *khōrismos* in the *ousia* of the *tode ti* [the "this"] and the *hekaston* [the "each"]? To the extent that Being becomes *ousia* solely as *entelekheia* [entelechy] and *energeia* [actuality].

Being ultimately steps into the arena with its opponent, Becoming, inasmuch as the latter claims Being's place. The opposition of the two unfolds on the plain of the "actual," a terrain that is never expressly perceived as such. Being's own actuality makes a claim on it, since it stands opposed to the nonactual, the null; yet such actuality also demands for itself the character of Becoming, since it does not wish to be a petrified, "life"-less thing at hand. Hegel executes the first step in the surpassment of this opposition on behalf of "Becoming," although he grasps the latter in terms of the suprasensuous and the absolute Idea, as its self-presentation. Nietzsche, inverting Platonism, transposes Becoming to the "vital" sphere, as the chaos that "bodies forth." That inversion, extinguishing as it does the opposition of Being and Becoming, constitutes the fulfillment proper. For now there is no way out, either in such rending or in a more appropriate fusion. This becomes manifest in the fact that "Becoming" claims to have usurped the prerogative of Being, whereas the prepotence of Becoming puts a final seal on the ultimate confirmation of Being's unshaken power. Being is the permanentizing (securing) of presencing, inasmuch as the interpretation of beings and their beingness as Becoming permanentizes Becoming as unconditioned presence. In order to shore up its prepotence, Becoming heeds the beck and call of permanentizing presencing. The primordial truth of Being holds sway in this particular permanentizing, albeit unrecognized and ungrounded, deviant in its utterly oblivious nonessence. Such empowering of Becoming to the status of Being deprives the former of its ultimate possibility for preeminence and restores to the latter its primordial essence (as bound up with *physis*); an essence, to be sure, that is consummate nonessence. Now beingness is all there is, and beingness sees to it all: alteration *and* permanence. It satisfies unconditionally the claims of being (as "life"). Providing such satisfaction, beingness appears to be beyond all question. It offers the most spacious quarters.

The essential sequence in this final phase of metaphysics, that is, the final phase of the projection of beingness upon permanentizing of presencing, is announced in the corresponding definition of the essence of "truth." Now the last reverberations of any intimation of *alētheia* fade. Truth becomes rightness, in the sense of a commanding absorption by the one who commands into the compulsion to self-surpassment. All correctness is merely a rehearsal of and an opportunity for such surpassing; every fixation merely a foothold for dissolving all things in Becoming, hence a purchase for willing the permanentizing of "chaos." Now the sole appeal is to the vitality of life. The primordial essence of truth is transformed in such a way that its metamorphosis amounts to a shunting aside (though not an annihilation) of essence. Verity dissolves in the presence of an empowering of power, a presence caught up at some point of its recurrence. Truth is once again the very same as Being, except that the latter has in the meantime been overtaken by the fulfillment of its nonessence. Yet when truth as correctness and as unconcealment has been leveled to "life-size"; when it is shunted aside in this way; then the *essence* of truth has surrendered its jurisdiction altogether. It no longer rises to the challenge of inquiry. It wanders without prospect in the region of "perspectives" and "horizons" that are bereft of every clearing. But what *then*? Then the bestowal of meaning gets under way as a "revaluation of all values." "Meaninglessness" is the only thing that makes "sense." Truth is "rightness," that is to say, supreme will to power. Only an unconditioned dominion over the earth by human beings will be right for such "rightness." Instituting planetary dominion, however, will itself be but the consequence of an unconditioned *anthropomorphism*.

IV

Precisely here the age of *consummate meaninglessness* begins. In such a designation the word *meaninglessness* is to be taken as a concept of thought that thinks the history of Being. Such thinking leaves metaphysics as a whole (with all its inversions and deviations in the direction of revaluations) behind. According to *Being and Time*, "meaning" designates the realm of projection, designates it in accord with its own proper intent (that is, in accord with its unique question concerning the "meaning of Being"), as the clearing of Being, the clearing that is opened and grounded in projection. Such projection is that in the thrown project which propriates as the essential unfolding of truth.

Meaninglessness is lack of the truth (clearing) of Being. Every possibility of such a projection founders because metaphysics has shunted aside the essence of truth. When the very question concerning the essence of the truth of *beings* and of our comportment toward beings is decided, meditation on the truth of Being, as the more original question concerning the essence of truth, can only remain in default. Advancing through a metamorphosis from *adaequatio* to certitude, truth has established itself as the *securing* of beings in their *perfectly accessible disposability*. That transformation ordains the prepotence of beingness, thus defined, as *malleability*. Beingness as malleability remains at the beck and call of that Being which has released itself into sheer accessibility through calculation, into the disposability of the beings appropriate to it by way of unconditioned planning and arranging.

The prepotence of Being in *this* essential configuration is called *machination*. It prevents any kind of grounding of the "projections" that are under its power and yet are themselves none the less powerful. For machination is the prepotence of all unquestioning self-assurance and certitude in securing. Machination alone can hold the stance it adopts toward itself under its unconditioned self-command. Machination makes itself permanent. When meaninglessness comes to power by dint of machination, the suppression of meaning and thus of all inquiry into the truth of Being must be replaced by machination's erection of "goals" (values). One quite reasonably expects new values to be propagated by "life," even though the latter has already been totally mobilized, as though total mobilization were something in itself and not the organization of unconditioned meaninglessness by and for will to power. Such positings and empowerings of power no longer conform to "standards of measure" and "ideals" that could be grounded in themselves; they are "in service" to sheer expansion of power and are valued purely according to their estimated use-value. The age of consummate meaninglessness is therefore the era in which "worldviews" are invented and promulgated with a view to their power. Such worldviews drive all calculability of representation and production to the extreme, originating as they do essentially in mankind's self-imposed instauration of self in the midst of beings – in the midst of mankind's unconditioned hegemony over all sources of power on the face of the earth, and indeed its dominion over the globe as such.

Whatever beings in their individual domains may be, whatever used to be defined as their *quiddity* in the sense of the "Ideas," now becomes something that the self-instauration can reckon with in advance, as with that which gauges the *value* of every productive and representative being as such (every work of art, technical contrivance, institution of government, the entire personal and collective order of human beings). Calculation on behalf of this self-instauration invents "values" (for our culture and for the nation). Value translates the essentiality of essence (that is, of beingness) into an object of calculation, something that can even be estimated in terms of quantity and spatial extension. Magnitude now attains to the very essence of grandeur – in the gigantic. The gigantic does *not* first of all *result from* the enhancement of the minuscule; it is not something that grows by accretion. It is the essential ground, the motor, and the goal of enhancement, which in turn consists in something other than quantitative relations.

The fulfillment of metaphysics, that is, the erection and entrenchment of consummate meaninglessness, thus remains nothing else than ultimate submission to the end of metaphysics – in the guise of "revaluation of all values." For Nietzsche's completion of metaphysics is *from the first* an inversion of Platonism (the sensuous becomes the true, the suprasensuous the semblant, world). But insofar as the Platonic "Idea" in its modern dress has become a "principle of reason" and hence a "value," the inversion of Platonism becomes a "revaluation of all values." Here inverted Platonism becomes blindly inflexible and superficial. *All that is left is the solitary superficies of a "life" that empowers itself to itself for its own sake.* If metaphysics begins as an explicit interpretation of beingness as *idea*, it achieves its uttermost end in the "revaluation of all values." The solitary superficies is what *remains after* the abolition of the "true" *and* the "semblant" worlds. It appears as the selfsame of eternal recurrence of the same and will to power.

As a revaluator of all values, Nietzsche testifies to the fact that he belongs ineluctably to metaphysics and thereby to its abyssal separation from *every possibility* of another commencement. Nietzsche himself does not know the distance that is measured out in this final step. And yet – did not Nietzsche succeed in positing a new "meaning" beyond all the teetering goals and ideals of earlier times, and thus beyond their annihilation? Did he not in his thinking anticipate "overman" as the "meaning" of the "earth"?

However, "meaning" is once again for him "goal" and "ideal." "Earth" is the name for the life that *bodies forth*, the rights of the sensuous. "Overman" is for him the consummation of what was the last man, making fast what was long *not yet* firmly defined, namely, that animal which still craved and lunged after ideals somewhere at hand and "true in themselves." Overman is extreme *rationalitas* in the empowering of *animalitas;* he is the *animal rationale* that is fulfilled in *brutalitas*. Meaninglessness now becomes the "meaning" of beings as a whole. The unquestionability of Being decides what beings are. Beingness is left to its own devices as liberated machination. Not only must humanity now "make do" without "a truth" but the *essence* of truth itself is dispatched to oblivion. For that reason, it is all a matter of "making do," and of some sort – any sort – of "values."

And yet the age of consummate meaninglessness possesses greater powers of invention, more forms of activity, more triumphs, and more avenues for getting all these things into the public eye than any age hitherto. It is therefore destined to fall prey to the presumption that it is the first age to discover "meaning," the first age to "bestow" meaning on everything that is "worth serving." Of course, the kind of wage it demands for its services has become exorbitant. The age of consummate meaninglessness insists on paving the way for its own essence, insists on it quite boisterously, and even violently. It seeks unthinking refuge in its own peculiar "superworld." It proceeds to the final confirmation of the prepotence of metaphysics in the form of Being's abandonment of beings. Thus the age of consummate meaninglessness does not stand on its own. It fulfills the essence of a concealed history – no matter how gratuitously and high-handedly our age seems to treat that subject on the highways and byways of its "histories."

V

The essence of modernity is fulfilled in the age of consummate meaninglessness. No matter how our histories may tabulate the concept and course of modernity, no matter which phenomena in the fields of politics, poetry, the natural sciences, and the social order they may appeal to in order to explain modernity, no historical meditation can afford to bypass two mutually related essential determinations within the history of modernity: first, that man installs and secures himself as *subiectum*, as the nodal point for beings as a whole; and secondly, that the beingness of beings as a whole is grasped as the representedness of whatever can be produced and explained. If it is Descartes and Leibniz who give essential shape to the first explicit metaphysical founding of modern history – Descartes by defining the *ens* as *verum* in the sense of *certum*, that is, as the *indubitatum* of *mathesis universalis*; Leibniz by interpreting the *substantialitas* of *substantia* as *vis primitiva* with the fundamental character of a "two-pronged" representing or *repraesentatio* – then the fact that in a history of Being we designate these names and give some thought to them suggests something quite different from the usual observations that have been made in the history of philosophy or in intellectual history concerning these figures.

Those fundamental metaphysical positions are not some supplementary, tangential, or even transcendent conceptual formulation of a history that has its origins elsewhere; nor are they pre-established doctrines that modern history somehow obeys or actualizes on its way to be. In either case the truth of metaphysics, a truth that grounds history, is being thought too extrinsically and too superficially in terms of its immediate impact. Whether we play down or exaggerate its value, we underestimate the matter in question by essentially misunderstanding it. For the determination of man as *subiectum* and of beings as a whole as "world picture" can only have sprung from the history of Being itself – here meaning the history of the transformation and the devastation of its ungrounded truth. (On the concept of "world picture," see the 1938 lecture "The Grounding of the Modern Picture of the World in Metaphysics," published in *Holzwege* [*Pathways*] in 1950 under the title "The Age of the World Picture.") Whatever the degree and the direction of any given scientific insight into the transformation of fundamental metaphysical positions; whatever the manner and the extent of any active reordering of beings in the light of this transformation of human beings and of beings as a whole; none of these things ever enters into the orbit of the history of Being itself. They always serve as mere foregrounds that, when understood in terms of the task of the meditation, always merely give themselves out to be the real thing.

The meaninglessness in which the metaphysical articulation of modernity is consummated becomes something we can know as the essential fulfillment of this age only when it is apprehended together with the transformation of man to *subiectum* and the determination of beings as the represented and produced character of the objective. Then it becomes clear that meaninglessness is the prefigured consequence of the finality of modern metaphysics in its very beginnings. Truth as certitude becomes the monotony that is injected into beings as a whole when they are served up for man's securing of permance, man now having been left to his own devices. This monotony is neither imitation nor empathy with regard to a being that would be true "in itself." Rather, it is a (mis)calculating overpowering of beings through the liberation of beingness into machination. Machination itself means the essence of beingness that is disposed toward the malleability in which everything is made out ahead of time to be "do-able" and altogether at our disposal. Corresponding to this process, representation is the (mis)calculating, securing pacing-off of the horizons that demarcate everything we can perceive along with its explicability and its use.

Beings are released to their possibilities to become; in these possibilities they are made permanent – in accord with machination. Truth as securing univocity grants machination exclusive pre-eminence. When certitude becomes the one and only, beings alone remain essential; never again beingness itself, to say nothing of its clearing. *When Being lacks the clearing, beings as a whole lack meaning.*

The subjectivity of the *subiectum*, which has nothing to do with an individuation that is bound up with the ego, is fulfilled in the calculability and manipulability of everything that lives, in the *rationalitas of animalitas*, in which the "overman" finds his essence. The extremity of subjectivity is reached when a particular illusion becomes entrenched – the illusion that all the "subjects" have disappeared for the sake of some transcendent cause that they now all serve. With the completion of modernity history capitulates to historiology, which is of the same essential stamp as technology. The unity of these powers of machination founds a position of power for man. That position is essentially violent. Only within a horizon of meaninglessness can it guarantee its subsistence and, ceaselessly on the hunt, devote itself entirely to one-upmanship.

VI

The essential, historic culmination of the final metaphysical interpretation of beingness as will to power is captured in the eternal recurrence of the same, captured in such a way that every possibility for the essence of truth to emerge as what is most worthy of question founders. Meaninglessness now attains power, defining in unconditional terms the horizon of modernity and enacting its fulfillment. The latter does not by any means become perspicuous to itself – that is, to the consciousness that essentially impels and secures historiologically and technologically – as a petrifaction and demise of something that was once achieved. It announces itself rather as an emancipation that step-by-step leaves its former self behind and enhances every thing in every way. The measureless has now disguised itself as self-overpowering power, as that which alone has permanence. Under such a cloak, the measureless can itself become the standard. When the standard of measure is shaped in such a way (as the measurelessness of one-upmanship), measuring rods and pegs can be cut to size, so that everyone now can measure up as painlessly as possible, demonstrating to everyone else all the impressive things he can do and proving to himself that he really must be all right. Such proofs are simultaneously taken to be a verification of goals, avenues, and realms of established efficacy. Everything we can do confirms all that we have already done, and all that we have done cries out for our doing it; every action and thought has committed itself totally to making out what it is that can be done. Everywhere and always machination, cloaking itself in the semblance of a measured ordering and controlling, confronts us with beings as the sole hierarchy and causes us to forget Being. What actually happens is that Being abandons beings: Being lets beings be on their own *and thereby refuses itself.*

Insofar as this *refusal* is experienced, a clearing of Being *has already occurred.* For such refusal is not nothing, is not even negative; it is not some lack, is not something truncated. It is the primordial and initial revelation of Being as worthy of question – of Being as Being.

Everything depends on our inhering in this clearing that is propriated by Being itself – never made or conjured by ourselves. We must overcome the compulsion to lay our hands on everything. We must learn that unusual and singular things will be demanded of those who are to come.

Truth announces the dominion of *its* essence: the clearing of self-concealing. History is the history of *Being.* Those who are struck by the clearing of refusal, those who do not know which way to turn in the face of it, are those who flee meditation: duped too long by beings, they are so alienated from Being that they cannot even come up with a reason to be suspicious of it. Still trapped in utter servitude to a metaphysics they think they have long since suppressed, they seek escape routes to some arcane realm, some world beyond the sensuous. They flee into mysticism (which is the mere counterimage of metaphysics) or, frozen in the posture of calculation, they appeal to "values." "Values," utterly transformed into calculable items, are the only ideals that still function for machination: culture and cultural values as grist for the mill of propaganda, art products as serviceable objects – at exhibitions of our achievements and as decorations for parade floats.

We neither know nor risk something other, something that in times to come will be the *one and only: the truth of Being*. For, however ungrounded it may be, it haunts the first commencement of our history. We neither know nor risk inherence in that truth from which alone world and earth strive to acquire their essence for man. Man experiences in such strife the response of his essence to the god of Being. Prior gods are the gods that have been.

The consummation of metaphysics as the essential fulfillment of modernity is an end only because its historical ground is itself a transition to the other commencement. The latter does not leap outside the history of the first, does not renounce what has been, but goes back into the grounds of the first commencement. With this return it takes on another sort of permanence. Such permanence is not defined in terms of the preservation of any given present thing. It bends to the task of preserving what is to come. What has been in the first commencement is thereby compelled to rest in the abyss of its heretofore ungrounded ground. It thus for the first time becomes history.

Such transition is not progress, nor is it a dreamy voyage from the prior to the new. The transition is seamless, inasmuch as it pertains to the decision of primordial commencement. The latter cannot be grasped by historical retrogressions or by historical maintenance of what has come down to us. Commencement only *is* in commencing. Commencement is the handing-over that is tradition. Preparation of such a commencement takes up that questioning by which the questioner is handed over to that which answers. Primordial questioning itself never replies. For primordial questioning, the sole kind of thinking is one that attunes man to hear the voice of Being. It is a thinking that enables man to bend to the task of guardianship over the truth of Being.

3

Adorno on Freud

Theodor Adorno (1903–69) was one of the leading figures of Frankfurt School Critical Theory, working alongside Max Horkheimer, Herbert Marcuse and others. Adorno wrote early dissertations on Husserl, Freud and Kierkegaard, and through the 1930s emerged as an unorthodox neo-Marxist thinker, influenced by Georg Lukács and Walter Benjamin. His two major critical works are *Dialectic of Enlightenment*, written with Max Horkheimer, and *Negative Dialectics*. Horkheimer's programme for the Institute for Social Research sought to renew the critical theory of the young Marx. The emancipatory potential of ideology-critique was to be guided by historical and empirical investigations. By the time Horkheimer and Adorno wrote *Dialectic of Enlightenment* in the 1940s, their analysis of the history of Western thought was bleaker, moving closer to Freud's account of civilization's discontents. Their conception of enlightenment develops the critique of enlightenment in Hegel and Nietzsche, but seeks to understand rationality's responsibility for the historical catastrophes of fascism and state capitalism. For Adorno, negative dialectic seeks to liberate thinking from the violence of instrumental rationality by developing new conceptions of experience, art and cognition. Although Adorno's thought set itself against systematic or foundational theories of knowledge, he pursues his historical critique of pure experience with remarkable persistence. He was critical of the phenomenological approaches developed by Husserl and Heidegger. For all his evident debts to Kant, Hegel and Marx, there is an intriguing philosophical ambivalence towards Nietzsche and Freud and their reconfiguration of experience. In Adorno's break with more conventional approaches to ideology-critique, there is also an intimate dialogue with Walter Benjamin's way of constellating history and experience.

As Gillian Rose suggested, Adorno is perhaps the only neo-Marxist to make Nietzsche's criticism of logic or identity into social criticism. Adorno's rhetoric has a Nietzschean style of argument developed through self-critical aphorisms. Sentences proceed by cancelling or negating what appears to have been asserted. In the essay that follows, for example, Adorno writes that: 'Objective truth itself is necessarily also untruth', or that: 'Rationalizations are the scars of reason in a state of unreason.' Such propositions can seem contradictory or nonsensical unless they are understood as critical resistances to identity-thinking. Where a Hegelian speculative proposition might claim that rationality is the truth of unreason, Adorno's propositions negate their own terms, as in the claim that rationality is not rational. His propositions remain suspended within critical aporia and performative contradiction. The determination to resist rationality's tendency to transcend its limitations is linked to the deter-mination to understand the social and historical nature of such limitations. Adorno's thought finds truth in the phenomenon analysed, but the propos-itional consequences are cast in negative forms.

Adorno's virtuoso negotiations of aporia and negativity have been criticized by subsequent critical theorists and more orthodox Marxists. He has been accused of overstating the value of art, of neglecting sociological and political specification, and of relying on a formulaic critique of capitalism. His approach to the history of modern rationality has also been characterized as unduly pessimistic and reductive, with a nostalgia for the highest qualities of bourgeois culture. Adorno's many eloquent expositors have shown how criticisms of Adorno often rest on misunderstandings of his thought and style, not least the way his most forceful statements undermine their own authority. Many of his most provocative assertions deliberately over-state propositions in part to dismantle thought's tendency to over-reach itself. The dismantling of thought from within through a process of immanent critique lends itself to superficial comparisons with Derridean deconstruction. While both Adorno and Derrida work to unbind the metaphysical assumptions of Western thought, Adorno is more concerned to show how philosophical questions are socially and histor-ically determined.

Along with Marcuse's more famous appropriation of Freud in *Eros and Civilization*, Frankfurt School Critical Theory reinterpreted Freud's thought critically. This reception of Freud's work resists the philosophical tendency to ignore or caricature Freud's work, while reading psychoanalysis against its claims. Within an inter-disciplinary framework, then, Adorno and others sought to integrate insights from Freud into a critical theory of society. As the following extract from Adorno's critique of psychoanalysis suggests, Adorno develops an immanent and critical analysis, while illuminating the relation between concepts and the historical conditions of thought. Adorno's assessment of Freud's unen-lightened enlightenment appears severe, but the critical reworking of psycho-analysis is developed throughout Adorno's work. The use of psychoanalysis to negotiate the tension between sociology and psychology informs Adorno's contributions to the critical and empirical research project published as *The Authoritarian Personality* and Adorno's essays on the culture industry, notably 'Freudian Theory and the Pattern of Fascist Propaganda'. As if to dramatize the problems involved in his critical reinterpretation of Freud, Adorno's *Minima Moralia* offers the aphorism that: 'In psycho-analysis nothing is true except the exaggerations.'

FURTHER READING

Primary works

Theodor Adorno and Max Horkheimer, *Dialectic of Enlightenment*, trans. John Cumming (London: Verso, 1979); Theodor Adorno and others, *The Authoritarian Personality* (New York: Harper and Row, 1950); Theodor Adorno, *Aesthetic Theory*, trans. Robert Hullot-Kentor (Minneapolis: University of Minnesota Press, 1997); *Negative Dialectics*, trans. E. B. Ashton (London: Routledge and Kegan Paul, 1973); *Metaphysics: Concept and Problems*, trans. Edmund Jephcott (Stanford, CA: Stanford University Press, 2001); *Kant's Critique of Pure Reason*, trans. Rodney Livingstone (Stanford, CA: Stanford University Press, 2001); *Minima Moralia*, trans. E. F. N. Jephcott (London: New Left Books, 1974).

Secondary works

Andrew Arato and Eike Gebhardt, eds., *The Essential Frankfurt School Reader* (Oxford: Blackwell, 1978), esp. Theodor Adorno, 'Freudian Theory and the Pattern of Fascist Propaganda', pp. 118–37.

Seyla Benhabib, Wolfgang Bonß and John McCole, eds., *On Max Horkheimer: New Perspectives* (Cambridge, MA: MIT, 1993).

J. M. Bernstein, *Adorno: Disenchantment and Ethics* (Cambridge: Cambridge University Press, 2001).

Susan Buck-Morss, *The Origin of Negative Dialectics: Theodor W. Adorno, Walter Benjamin and the Frankfurt Institute* (Hassocks: Harvester, 1977).

Paul Connerton, *The Tragedy of Enlightenment: An Essay on the Frankfurt School* (Cambridge: Cambridge University Press, 1980).

Jürgen Habermas, 'The Entwinement of Myth and Enlightenment: Max Horkheimer and Theodor Adorno', *The Philosophical Discourse of Modernity*, trans. Frederick Lawrence (Cambridge: Polity, 1987), pp. 106–30.

Axel Honneth, *The Fragmented World of the Social: Essays in Social and Political Philosophy*, ed. Charles W. Wright (Albany: SUNY, 1995).

Max Horkheimer, *Critical Theory: Selected Essays*, trans. Matthew J. O'Connell and others (New York: Continuum, 1982).

Fredric Jameson, *Late Marxism: Adorno, or, the Persistence of the Dialectic* (London: Verso, 1990).

Simon Jarvis, *Adorno: A Critical Introduction* (Cambridge: Polity, 1998).

Martin Jay, *The Dialectical Imagination: A History of the Frankfurt School and the Institute of Social Research, 1923–1950* (Boston: Little, Brown and Co., 1973).

Herbert Marcuse, *Eros and Civilization: A Philosophical Enquiry into Freud* (Boston: Beacon, 1966).

Brian O'Connor, ed., *The Adorno Reader* (Oxford: Blackwell, 2000).

Gillian Rose, *The Melancholy Science: An Introduction to the Thought of Theodor W. Adorno* (London: Macmillan, 1978).

Albrecht Wellmer, 'Reason, Utopia, and the *Dialectic of Enlightenment*', *Habermas and Modernity*, ed. Richard J. Bernstein (Cambridge: Polity, 1985), pp. 35–66.

Joel Whitebook, *Perversion and Utopia: A Study in Psychoanalysis and Critical Theory* (Cambridge, MA: MIT, 1995).

Theodor Adorno, 'Sociology and Psychology' (1955), trans. Irving N. Wohlfarth, *New Left Review*, 47 (1967), pp. 79–97.

Social developments thus affect even the most recent trends in psychology. Despite the ever-widening rift between society and psychology, society reaches repressively into all psychology in the form of censorship and superego. As part of the progressive integration of society, socially rational behaviour gets melted together with the psychological residues. But the revisionists who perceive this give an oversimplified account of the interaction of the mutually alienated institutions id and ego. They posit a direct connection between the instinctual sphere and social experience. The latter, however, takes place, according to Freudian topology, only at the outer layer of the ego which has been allotted the task of testing reality. But inside the instinctual dynamic, reality is 'translated' into the language of the id. If there is any truth in Freud's notion of the archaic and indeed possibly 'timeless' nature of the unconscious, then concrete social circumstances and motivations cannot enter it without being altered and 'reduced'.

The time-lag between consciousness and the unconscious is itself the stigma of the contradictory development of society. Everything that got left behind is sedimented in the unconscious and has to foot the bill for progress and enlightenment. Its backwardness becomes Freud's 'timelessness'. Today it harbours even the demand for happiness, which does indeed begin to look 'archaic' as soon as it aims not at fulfilment but at some purely somatic, fragmented, local gratification, which increasingly turns into 'having some fun' the more diligently consciousness aspires to the condition of adultness. Psychology insulates itself against society, like society against psychology, and regresses. Under the pressure of society the psychological sector responds in the end only to sameness and proves incapable of experiencing the specific. The traumatic is the abstract. The unconscious therein resembles the abstract society it knows nothing about, and can be used to weld it together.

Freud should not be reproached for having neglected the concrete social dimension, but for being all too untroubled by the social origin of this abstractness, the rigidity of the unconscious, which he registers with the undeviating objectivity of the natural scientist. The impoverishment that has resulted from an unending tradition of the negative is hypostatized into an ontological property. The historical dimension becomes changeless; the psychic, in return, is made into an historical event. In making the leap from psychological images to historical reality, he forgets what he himself discovered – that all reality undergoes modification upon entering the unconscious – and is thus misled into positing such factual events as the murder of the father by the primal horde. It is this short-circuit between reality and the unconscious which lends psychoanalysis its apocryphal features. Such ideas as the crudely literal conception of the Moses legend have served to buttress the resistances of the official sciences that have no trouble in disproving them.

Freud's Myths

What Kardiner has called Freud's 'myths – the translation of the intra-psychic into the dubiously factual – recurs wherever Freud too perpetrates ego-psychology, in his case an ego-psychology of the id, and treats the id as if it possessed the consummate rationality of the Viennese banker it at times really does resemble. In his all too refutable striving to gain a foothold in irrefutable facts, Freud unwittingly sanctions society's belief in the usual criteria of the very science that he challenged. For the sake of these criteria, the Freudian child is a little man and his world that of a man. Thus, no less than its sociologically well-versed counterpart, a psychology that turns in on itself is aped by the society it refuses to heed.

The psyche that has been extracted from the social dialectic and investigated as an abstract 'for itself' under the microscope has become an object of scientific inquiry all too consistent with a society that hires and fires people as so many units of abstract labour-power. Freud's critics have seized on his mechanistic bias. Both his determinism and also such implicit categories as the preservation of energy, the transformation of one form of energy into another and the subsumption of successive events under general laws, are reminiscent of scientific procedure. The concrete upshot of his 'naturalist' posture is the consistent exclusion of the new, the reduction of psychic life to a repetition of what happened in the past.

But all this has a highly progressive meaning. Freud was the first to register the full implications of the Kantian critique of an ontology of the soul, of 'rational psychology': the soul of Freudian psychology, as part of the already constituted world, falls within the province of the constitutive categories of empirical analysis. Freud put an end to the ideological transfiguration of the soul as a residual form of animism. It is no doubt the theory of childhood sexuality that most thoroughly undermines all metaphysical humbug about the soul. The psychoanalytic denunciation of man's unfreedom and degradation in an unfree society resembles the materialist critique of a society blindly dominated by its economy. But under its deadly medical gaze unfreedom becomes petrified into an anthropological constant, and the quasi-scientific conceptual apparatus thereby overlooks everything in its object that is not merely object – namely, its potential for spontaneity. The more strictly the psychological realm is conceived as an autonomous, self-enclosed play of forces, the more completely the subject is drained of his subjectivity. The objectless subject that is thrown back on himself freezes into an object. It cannot break out of its immanence and amounts to no more than equations of libidinal energy. The soul that is broken down into its own laws is a soul no longer: only the groping for what it itself is not would merit the name. This is no mere epistemological matter but extends even as far as the therapeutic outcome, those desperately realistic people who have literally transformed themselves into machines in order to get on all the more successfully within their limited sphere of interests, their 'subjectivism'.

The Concept of Rationalization

As soon as psychological concepts are as rigorously developed as Freud's, the neglected divergence of psychology and society takes its revenge. This can be demonstrated in the case of the concept of rationalization which was originally introduced by Jones[1] and then found its place in standard analytic theory. It designates all those statements which, quite apart from their truth content, fulfil certain functions within the psychic economy of the speaker, the commonest being defence against unconscious tendencies. Such utterances are invariably the object of a psychoanalytic critique analogous, as has often been noted, to the Marxist doctrine of ideology: their objective function is to conceal, and the analyst is out to establish both their falsehood and their necessity and to bring what was hidden to light. But there exists no pre-established harmony between the immanent psychological critique of rationalization and its real content. The same statement can be true or false, depending on whether it is judged according to reality or its psycho-dynamic context; indeed, this dual aspect is crucial to rationalizations, because the unconscious takes the line of least resistance and therefore latches on to whatever pretexts reality offers; and, what is more, the sounder their basis in reality, the more unassailably they can operate.

In its rationalizations, which involve both rationality and irrationality, the psychological subject ceases to be merely psychological. The analyst who takes pride in his realism thus becomes an out-and-out dogmatist the moment he disregards the real, objective aspects of rationalization in favour of its closed, immanently psychological context. But a sociology which, conversely, took rationalizations at face-value would be no less questionable. Private rationalization, the self-deception of the subject, is not identical with the objective untruth of public ideology. The individual's defence-mechanisms will, however, constantly seek support from their already well-established and widely endorsed counterparts in society at large. The phenomenon of rationalization, that is, the mechanism whereby objective truth can be made to enter the service of subjective untruth (a mechanism that can be amply documented in the social psychology of typical contemporary defence-mechanisms), betrays not merely neurosis but a false society. Objective truth itself is necessarily also untruth as long as it is not the whole truth of the subject, and serves both by its function and its indifference to its subjective genesis to camouflage merely particular interests. Rationalizations are the scars of reason in a state of unreason.

Ferenczi, perhaps the most unfaltering and liberated of the psychoanalysts, focused precisely on the rationalizations of the superego, the collective norms of individual behaviour that psychologically unsophisticated morality calls conscience. It is here more than anywhere else that the historical transformation in the function of psychoanalysis from a radical medium of enlightenment to practical adjustment to existing conditions is most strikingly apparent. Once it was the compulsive features of the superego that were stressed and analysis was required to do away with them. Such progressive intentions tolerate no unconscious controls even for the purpose of controlling the unconscious. Hardly any of this impetus still remains in today's psychoanalytic literature. Once his difficulties with the original conscious, preconscious and unconscious 'systems' had led Freud to reorganize the analytic topology under the categories id, ego and superego, it was all too easy to predicate the psychoanalytical picture of the good life on their mutual harmony. In particular, psychopaths – today a tabooed concept – are interpreted as lacking a well-developed superego, which, within reasonable limits, is thus held to be a necessity after all. But it is a mockery of the analytic principle to tolerate irrationalities merely because they stem from society and because an organized society is supposedly unthinkable without them.

Kant and Freedom

The distinction popular these days between a 'neurotic', that is, compulsive, and a 'healthy', that is, conscious superego betrays all the signs of the patchwork job. Along with its opaqueness a 'conscious' superego would lose precisely the authority for the sake of which its apologists cling to it. Kantian ethics, which centres round a quite unpsychologically conceived notion of conscience residing in the intelligible realm, is not to be confused with an updated psychoanalysis which arrests the process of enlightenment for fear that otherwise the conscience will be in trouble. Kant knew full well why he contrasted psychology and the idea of freedom: the play of forces with which psychoanalysis is concerned belongs in his system to the 'phenomenal' realm of causality. The crux of his doctrine of freedom is a conception incompatible with any empiricism – that moral objectivity, and the just social order it implies, cannot be measured by the way things and men happen at any given time to be. The psychologist's attitude of tactful permissiveness towards conscience destroys precisely that objectivity by utilizing it as a mere tool. The goal of the 'well-integrated personality' is objectionable because it expects the individual to establish an equilibrium between conflicting forces which does not obtain in existing society – nor should it, because those forces are not of equal moral merit. People are taught to forget the objective conflicts which necessarily repeat themselves in every individual, instead of being helped to grapple with them.

The well-balanced person who no longer sensed the inner conflict of psychological forces, the irreconcilable claims of id and ego, would not thereby have achieved an inner resolution of social conflicts. He would be confusing his psychic state – his personal good fortune – with objective reality. His integration would be a false reconciliation with an unreconciled world, and would presumably amount in the last analysis to an 'identification with the aggressor', a mere character-mask of subordination. The concept of integration which is today becoming increasingly dominant, especially in therapy, denies the genetic principle and immediately hypostatizes supposedly constitutional psychic forces such as consciousness and instinct, between which some balance is to be struck, instead of recognizing them as moments of a self-division which cannot be resolved within the confines of the psyche.

Freud's incisive polemic against the idea of psychosynthesis,[2] a fancy expression invented by hard-headed academics out to smear analysis as mechanistic, if not destructive, and to claim to be sole suppliers of the constructive approach, should be extended to include the ideal of integration, a threadbare version of the bad old notion of 'personality'. Whether the complete, all-round development of the whole man is, in fact, worth emulating may be questioned. A 'blond Siegfried' is the phrase with which Benjamin characterized the ideal of the genital character that was in vogue about 20 years ago among psychoanalysts; in the meantime they have come to prefer well-balanced people with a well-developed superego instead. The 'good' Freudian uninhibited by repressions would, in the existing acquisitive society, be almost indistinguishable from the hungry beast of prey and an eloquent embodiment of the abstract utopia of the subject, or, in today's jargon, the 'image of man', whose autonomous development was unimpeded by society. The psychologists' attack on their scapegoat, the herd animal, can be paid back with interest by a social critique of the superman whose freedom remains false, neurotically greedy, 'oral', as long as it presupposes unfreedom. Every 'image of man' is ideology except the negative one.

Conformity as an Ideal

If, for instance, the appeal goes out today for the all-round personality as opposed to the specialization inseparable from the division of labour, this merely sets a premium on the undifferentiated, the crude and the primitive, and ultimately exalts the extroversion of the go-getters, those who are atrocious enough to adapt to an atrocious life. Whatever qualities at present genuinely anticipate a more human existence are always simultaneously, in the eyes of the existing order, damaged rather than harmonious things. Mandeville's thesis that private vices are public virtues can be applied *mutatis mutandis* to the relation between psychology and society: what is characterologically dubious often represents what is objectively better: it is not the normal man but rather the unswerving specialist that is productive. Already at the beginning of the bourgeois era only the internalization of repression made possible that increase in human productivity which could here and now enable people to live in luxury; and, likewise, psychological defects signify something radically different in the context of the tangled whole than within the psychic household of the individual.

It would not be difficult for psychology to diagnose the behaviour of, say, the now obsolete figure of the collector as neurotic, and relate it to the anal syndrome; but without libidinal fixation on things, tradition and indeed humanity itself would scarcely be possible. A society that rids itself of that syndrome only to throw everything away like empty tins hardly deals any differently with human beings. We know too, to what an extent the libidinal cathexis of technology is today a regressive symptom, but without such regressions the technical inventions that may yet one day banish hunger and senseless suffering would hardly have been made. Psychologists can loftily belittle nonconformist politicians by showing how they have not solved their Oedipus complex, but without their spontaneity society would remain eternally doomed to reproduce that self-same Oedipus complex in every one of its members. Whatever rises above the existent is threatened with disintegration, and is thus mostly more than ever at the mercy of the existent.

'Character,' the opposite of the boundlessly elastic, subjectless subject, is, without doubt, archaic. In the end it proves to be not freedom but a superseded phase of unfreedom: when the Americans say 'He's quite a character', they mean he's a figure of fun, an oddity, a poor fellow. As late as in Nietzsche's time the psychological ideals were still the proper target for criticism, but today it is even more the psychological ideal as such, in all its various forms, that should come under attack. No longer is individual man the key to humanity. The kindly, established sages of today, moreover, are mere variants of führer propaganda.

Function of the Superego

The cultivation of the superego arbitrarily breaks off the process of psychoanalytic enlightenment. But to make a public profession of consciencelessness is to sanction atrocity. So heavily weighs the conflict of social and psychological insight. It was ineffectual comfort to claim, as already Kant implied, that what has hitherto been achieved at such unspeakable cost by an irrational conscience can be accomplished by conscious insight into social necessities without the havoc that Nietzsche's philosophy never ceases to denounce. The resolution of the antinomy of universal and particular remains mere ideology as long as the instinctual renunciation society expects of the individual neither can be objectively justified as true and necessary nor later provides him with the delayed gratification. This kind of irrationality is stifled by conscience. The goals of the psychic economy and the life-process of society simply cannot be reduced to a common formula. What society, for the sake of its survival, justly demands of each individual is at the same time also unjust for each individual and, ultimately, for society itself; what psychology takes to be mere rationalization is often socially necessary. In an antagonistic society each individual is non-identical with himself, both social and psychological character[3] at once, and, because of the split, maimed from the outset. It is no accident that the irreconcilability of an undiminished, unmutilated existence with bourgeois society has remained the fundamental theme of bourgeois realist art from *Don Quixote* via Fielding's *Tom Jones* up to Ibsen and the moderns. Right becomes wrong, foolishness or guilt.

What appears to the subject as his own essence, what over against the estranged social necessities he takes to be his very own, is a mere illusion when measured against those necessities. This invests all psychology with an element of futility. In disparaging the sphere we today call psychology as contingent and irrelevant beside the transcendental, objective sphere of spirit (Geist), the great idealist tradition, as represented by Kant and Hegel, sees more deeply into society than an empiricism that, while thinking itself sceptical, clings to the individualist facade. It could almost be said that the better one understands a person's psychology the further one removes oneself from an understanding of his social fate and of society itself and thereby – without the psychological insight being any the less valid – of the person as he really is. But it is another aspect of the 'totalitarian' nature of present society that, perhaps more completely than in the past, people as such reinforce with the energy of their ego the assimilation society imposes on them; and that they blindly pursue their self-alienation to the point of an illusory identity between what they are in themselves and what they are for themselves. Because, given objective possibilities, adjustment to society should no longer be a necessity, it takes more than simple adjustment to stick it out in existing society. Self-preservation succeeds only to the extent that, as a result of self-imposed regression, self-development fails.

As the co-ordinator of all psychic impulses and the principle which constitutes individual identity in the first place, the ego also falls within the province of psychology. But the 'reality-testing' ego not merely borders on the non-psychological, outer world to which it adjusts, but constitutes itself through objective moments beyond the immanence of the psyche, through the adequacy of its judgements to states of affairs. Although itself psychic in origin it is supposed to arrest the play of inner forces and check it against reality: this is one of the chief criteria for determining its 'health'. The concept of the ego is dialectical, both psychic and extrapsychic, a quantum of libido and the representative of outside reality.

Positive and Negative Ego-functions

Freud did not investigate this dialectic. As a result, his immanently psychological statements about the ego involuntarily contradict one another and disrupt the closed system he strives to establish. The most flagrant of the contradictions is that the ego, while encompassing the activities of consciousness, is itself conceived to be essentially unconscious. This is only very inadequately conveyed by Freud's external and oversimplified topology, in which consciousness is situated at the far rim of the ego, the area directly bordering on reality.[4] The upshot is that the ego is supposed to be both, *qua* consciousness, the opposite of repression, and, *qua* unconscious, the repressive agency itself. The introduction of the superego may be attributed to the intention of bringing some kind of order into this intricate state of affairs. In the Freudian system there is a total lack of any adequate criteria for distinguishing 'positive' from 'negative' ego-functions, above all, sublimation from repression. Instead, the concept of what is socially useful or productive is rather innocently dragged in. But in an irrational society the ego cannot perform at all adequately the function allotted to it by that society. The ego is necessarily burdened with psychic tasks that are irreconcilable with the psychoanalytic conception of the ego. To be able to assert itself in reality, the ego has to understand reality and operate consciously. But to enable the individual to effect the often senseless renunciations imposed on him, the ego has to set up unconscious prohibitions and to remain largely confined to the unconscious.

Freud did not fail to point out that the instinctual renunciation demanded of the individual is not rewarded by such compensations as would on conscious grounds alone justify it.[5] But since instinctual life does not obey the stoical philosophy of its learned analyst – no-one knew this better than Freud himself – the rational ego, judged by the principle of psychic economy Freud himself stipulated, is clearly unequal to its task. It has itself to become unconscious, part of the instinctual dynamic it is still, however, supposed to transcend. The ego's cognitive activity, performed in the interests of self-preservation, has to be constantly reversed, and self-awareness forgone, in the interests of self-preservation. The conceptual contradiction that Freud can be so elegantly shown to be guilty of is thus not the fault of loose thinking but of life and death.

Ego and Non-ego

But the ego, which, as reality-principle, is always also non-ego, is predisposed for its dual role by its own make-up. In so far as it has to see to the irreconcilable claims both of the libido and of actual self-preservation, it is constantly taxed beyond its powers. It by no means commands that firmness and sureness it flaunts in the direction of the id. Great psychologists of the ego such as Marcel Proust have, on the contrary, established the precariousness of all ego-identity. The reason for this is, to be sure, less the flow of time than the actual dynamic of the psyche. Where the ego fails to develop its intrinsic potential for self-differentiation, it will regress, especially towards what Freud called ego-libido,[6] to which it is most closely related, or will at least mingle its conscious functions with unconscious ones. What actually wanted to get beyond the unconscious then re-enters the service of the unconscious and may thus even strengthen its force. This is the psychodynamic scheme of 'rationalizations'.

Analytic ego-psychology has hitherto not devoted sufficient attention to the feed-back of ego into id because it simply took over from the Freudian taxonomy the concepts ego and id as fixed entities. The ego that withdraws back into the unconscious does not simply cancel itself out but retains several of the features it had acquired as a societal agent. But it subordinates them to the dictates of the unconscious. In this way an illusory harmony between reality-principle and pleasure-principle is brought about. With the transposition of the ego into the unconscious the quality of the drives is modified in turn; they are diverted towards characteristic ego-goals which contradict those of the primary libido. The kind of instinctual energy on which the ego draws in advancing towards its supreme sacrifice, that of consciousness, is of the anaclitic type Freud called narcissism. This is the irresistible conclusion to be drawn from the body of social-psychological findings about the currently prevalent forms of regression,[7] in which the ego is both negated and falsely, irrationally, rigidified. The socialized narcissism characteristic of the most recent mass movements and dispositions invariably combines the ruthlessly partial rationality of self-interest with a destructive, self-destructive, misshapen irrationality, in analysing which Freud carried on where Mac-Dougall and Le Bon had left off.

The Role of Narcissism

The introduction of the concept of narcissism counts among Freud's most magnificent discoveries, although psychoanalytic theory has still not proved quite equal to it. In narcissism the self-preserving function of the ego is, on the surface at least, retained, but, at the same time, split off from that of consciousness and thus lost to rationality. All defence-mechanisms bear the imprint of narcissism: the ego experiences its frailty in relation to the instincts as well as its powerlessness in the world as 'narcissistic injury'. The work of the defence-mechanisms, however, is not registered by consciousness, and is indeed hardly carried out by the ego itself but rather by a psychodynamic derivative, a hybrid, ego-oriented and yet unsublimated, undifferentiated form of libido. It is even questionable whether it is the ego that performs the function of repression, the chief of all the so-called defence-mechanisms. Perhaps the repressive agency itself should be regarded as ego-oriented, narcissistic libido which has ricocheted back from its real goals and then fused with moments specific to the ego. In which case, 'social psychology' would not be, as people today would like to think, essentially ego-psychology, but libido psychology.

Freud considered repression and sublimation to be equally precarious. He held the id's libido quantum to be so much larger than that of the ego that in case of conflict the id is always bound to regain the upper hand. Not merely is the spirit willing but the flesh weak, as theologians have always taught, but the mechanisms of ego-formation are themselves fragile. This is why it so readily allies itself with those very regressions inflicted on the instincts by their repression. Hence the partial legitimacy of the revisionists' complaint that Freud underestimated those social moments which are mediated through the ego but remain psychologically relevant. Karen Horney, for example, claims against Freud that it is illegitimate to derive the feeling of helplessness from early childhood and the oedipus situation; it stems, in her view, from real social helplessness, which may already have been experienced in childhood (for which Horney shows little interest). Now it would certainly be dogmatic if one wanted to separate the ubiquitous feeling of helplessness, of which precisely the revisionists have given very subtle descriptions,[8] from its present social causes. But experiences of real helplessness are anything but irrational – and they are actually hardly psychological. On their own they might be expected to prompt resistance to the social system rather than further assimilation to it. What people know about their helplessness in society belongs to their ego – understood not merely as the fully conscious faculty of judgement but as the whole web of its social relations. But as soon as the experience is turned into the 'feeling of helplessness' the specifically psychological element has entered in, the fact that individuals, precisely, *cannot* experience or confront their helplessness.

Internalization of Social Sanctions

This repression of their powerlessness points not merely to the disproportion between the individual and his powers within the whole but still more to injured narcissism and the fear of realizing that they themselves go to make up the false forces of domination before which they have every reason to cringe. They have to convert the experience of helplessness into a 'feeling' and let it settle psychologically in order not to think beyond it. It is the age-old pattern of the internalization of social sanctions. Id-psychology is mobilized by ego-psychology with the help of demagogy and mass culture. The latter merely process the raw material supplied to them by the psychodynamics of those they weld into masses. The ego hardly has any other choice than either to change reality or to withdraw back to the id. In interpreting this as a simple fact of ego-psychology, the revisionists mistake it for a mere epiphenomenon.

What in fact happens is that those infantile defence-mechanisms are selectively mobilized which, in a given historical situation, best dovetail into the pattern of the ego's social conflicts. It is this, and not that stand-by, wish-fulfilment, which explains the hold mass culture exerts over people. There is no 'neurotic personality of our time' – the name alone is a diversionary tactic – rather the objective situation does determine the course regressions will take. While conversion hysteria is today on the decrease, conflicts in the area of narcissism are more noticeable than 60 years ago, and manifest-ations of paranoid tendencies, too, are increasingly apparent. Whether there really exist more paranoiacs than previously can be left unanswered; there are no comparative figures even for the recent past. But a situation that threatens everyone, and in some of its achievements outdoes paranoid fantasies, particularly invites paranoia, perhaps, indeed, this can be said in general of dialectical nodal points in history. Against the superficial historicism of the revisionists Hartmann acknowledges that a given social structure selects but does not 'express', specific psychological tendencies.[9]

No doubt concrete historical components already enter early childhood experience, thereby disproving Freud's crude doctrine of the timeless quality of the unconscious. But the mimetic responses of small children on perceiving that their father does not guarantee them the protection they hanker after are not the work of the ego. It is precisely here that even Freud's psychology is all too ego-oriented. His magnificent discovery of infantile sexuality will cease to do violence only when we learn to understand the infinitely subtle and yet utterly sexual impulses of children. In their perceptive world, poles apart from that of the grown-ups, a fleeting smell or a gesture take on dimensions that the analyst, faithful to adult criteria, would like to attribute solely to their observation of their parents' coitus.

'Defence-mechanisms'

The difficulties with which the ego confronts psychology are nowhere more apparent than in Anna Freud's theory of the so-called defence-mechanisms. Her point of departure is what analysis initially terms resistance to the making conscious of the id. 'Since it is the aim of the analytic method to enable ideational representatives of the repressed instincts to enter consciousness, i.e. to encourage these inroads by the id, the ego's defensive operations against such representatives automatically assume the character of active resistance to analysis.'[10] The concept of defence already stressed by Freud in the 'Studies in Hysteria'[11] is now applied to the whole realm of ego-psychology and a list is assembled of nine defence-mechanisms familiar from psychoanalytic practice which all supposedly represent measures taken by the ego against the id: 'regression, repression, reaction-formation, isolation, undoing, projection, introjection, turning against the self, and reversal'.[12] To these 'we must add a tenth, which pertains rather to the study of the normal than to that of neurosis: sublimation, or displacement of instinctual aims'.[13]

   A closer consideration confirms the doubts raised by the enumerability of these nicely pigeon-holed mechanisms. Already Sigmund Freud had made out of the originally central concept of repression a mere 'special method of defence'.[14] But repression and regression, which he wisely never strictly differentiated from one another, unquestionably play their part in all the ego-activities listed by Anna Freud; whereas other activities such as 'undoing' or the 'identification with the aggressor'[15] which Anna Freud so convincingly describes, as special cases of the mechanisms of repression and regression, hardly belong on the same logical plane. In this juxtaposition of highly disparate mechanisms a certain faltering of rigorous theory in the face of the empirically observed material is to be detected. In subsuming both repression and sublimation under the rubric of defence, his daughter refuses still more categorically than Freud himself to make a clear distinction between the two. Such psychic activities as do not directly further instinctual gratification or self-preservation – in Freud they still pass for 'cultural achievements' – are, for her, and by no means for her alone, at bottom pathological. Similarly, contemporary psychoanalytic theory believes on the basis of clinical observation that in accounting for music as a defence against paranoia it has exhausted the topic; if it only pursued its thesis to its logical conclusion, it would have to ban all music.[16] From here it is no longer very far to those biographical psychoanalyses that think they are saying something important about Beethoven in pointing to his personal paranoia, and then wonder how such a man could have written music whose fame impresses them more than a truth their system prevents them from apprehending.

Authoritarianism and Anna Freud

Such filiations between the theory of defences and the reduction of psychoanalysis to a conformist interpretation of the reality-principle are not wholly lacking even in Anna Freud's book. She devotes a chapter to the relation of ego and id during puberty. Puberty is, in her eyes, essentially a conflict between the 'influx of libido'[17] into the psychic sphere and the ego's defence against the id. It is to this that 'intellectualization at puberty'[18] is attributed. 'There is a type of young person whose sudden spurt in intellectual development is no less noticeable and surprising than his rapid development in other directions ... When the pre-pubertal period begins, a tendency for the concrete interests of the latency-period to give place to abstractions becomes more and more marked. In particular, adolescents of the type whom Bernfeld describes as characterized by "prolonged puberty" have an insatiable desire to think about abstract subjects, to turn them over in their minds, and to talk about them. Many of the friendships of youth are based on and maintained by this desire to meditate upon and discuss such subjects together. The range of these abstract interests and of the problems which these young people try to solve is very wide. They will argue the case for free love or marriage and family life, a free-lance existence or the adoption of a profession, roving or settling down, or discuss philosophical problems such as religion or free thought, or different political theories, such as revolution *versus* submission to authority, or friendship itself in all its forms. If, as sometimes happens in analysis, we receive a faithful report of the conversations of young people or if – as has been done by many of those who make a study of puberty – we examine the diaries and jottings of adolescents, we are not only amazed at the wide and unfettered sweep of their thought but impressed by the degree of empathy and understanding manifested, by their apparent superiority to more mature thinkers and sometimes even by the wisdom which they display in the handling of the most difficult problems.'[19]

But this respect rapidly vanishes: 'We revise our opinion when we turn from the examination of the adolescent's intellectual processes themselves to consider how they fit into the general picture of his life. We are surprised to discover that this fine intellectual performance makes little or no difference to his actual behaviour. His empathy with the mental processes of other people does not prevent him from displaying the most outrageous lack of consideration towards those nearest to him. His lofty view of love and of the obligations of a lover does not mitigate the infidelity and callousness of which he is repeatedly guilty in his various love-affairs. The fact that his understanding of and interest in the structure of society often far exceeds those of later years does not assist him in the least to find his true place in social life, nor does the many-sidedness of his interests deter him from concentrating entirely upon a single point – his preoccupation with his own personality.'[20] With such judgements psycho-analysis, which once set out to break the power of the father image, firmly takes the side of the fathers, who either smile at the children's high-faluting ideas with a droop at the corner of their mouth or else rely on life to teach them what's what, and who consider it more important to earn money than get silly ideas into one's head. The attitude of mind that distances itself from the realm of immediate ends and means, and is given the chance to do so during the brief years in which it is its own master before being

absorbed and dulled by the necessity to earn a living, is slandered as mere narcissism. The powerlessness and fallibility of those who still believe in other possibilities is made out to be their own vain fault; what is blamed on their own inadequacies is much more the fault of a social order that constantly denies them the possible and breaks what potential people possess. The psychological theory of defence-mechanisms places itself   •
squarely in an old anti-intellectual bourgeois tradition.

From this arsenal, too, is fetched the stereotype argument that attacks not the conditions that stifle a powerless ideal but the ideal itself and those that cherish it. However much what Anna Freud calls 'these young people's, behaviour differs, for real no less than psychological reasons, from their state of mind, this very disparity holds more promise than the norm of unmediated identity between consciousness and reality whereby a person may think only what his existence can cash. As if adults lacked the inconsiderateness, infidelity and callousness that Anna Freud blames on 'young people' – the only difference between them being that the brutality later loses the ambivalence that still characterizes it at least while it is in conflict with an awareness of possible better things, and can even oppose what it later identifies with. 'We recognize', says Anna Freud, 'that we have here something quite different from intellectuality in the ordinary sense of the term.'[21] The psychologist holds up before imaginary adolescents intellectuality 'in the ordinary sense of the term', however ordinary it may be, without considering that even 'ordinary' derives from less ordinary intellectuality and that, as schoolboys or young students, few intellectuals are as mean as when they then barter their minds on the competitive market. The young person Anna Freud reproaches for 'evidently deriving gratification from the mere process of thinking, speculating or discussing'[22] has every reason to feel gratified: he will have to wean himself quickly enough to the privilege, instead of having to 'think out the right line of behaviour'[23] as the philistine does.

'Their ideals of friendship and undying loyalty are simply a reflection of the disquietude of the ego when it perceives the evanescence of all its new and passionate object-relations',[24] we read a little further on, and Margit Dubowitz of Budapest is thanked for the suggestion that 'the tendency of adolescents to brood on the meaning of life and death reflects the destructive activities in their own psyche'.[25] It is a moot point whether the spiritual breathing-space that bourgeois existence grants at least its better-placed members who serve as psychoanalytic material is, in fact, as futile and ineffectual as it appears in the patient free-associating on the couch; but there would certainly exist neither friendship and loyalty nor any significant thought without this breathing-space which, in the spirit and with the help of a well-integrated psychoanalysis, present society is preparing to reduce.

Genesis and Truth

The balance-sheet of the psychic economy necessarily registers as defence, illusion and neurosis anything the ego does to attack the conditions that drive it to defence, illusion and neurosis; in substituting the genesis of a thought for its truth, a thorough-going psychologism becomes the subversion of all truth and lends support to the status quo while simultaneously condemning its mirror-images in the subject. The bourgeoisie in its late phase is incapable of thinking genesis and validity in their simultaneous unity and difference. The wall of congealed labour, the objectified result, has come to seem impenetrable and timeless, and the dynamic, which, as human labour, is in fact an objective moment, is subtracted from that objective dimension and shifted into the isolated subject. Thereby, however, the part played by the subjective dynamic is reduced to mere illusoriness and simultaneously opposed to any insight into objective conditions: any such insight is suspected of being a futile self-reflection of the subject.

Husserl's campaign against psychologism – which coincides in time exactly with the early beginnings of psychoanalysis – the doctrine of logical absolutism which at all levels separates the validity of intellectual constructs from their genesis and fetishizes the former, is only the obverse side of an approach that sees nothing but the genesis, not its relation to objectivity, and ultimately abolishes the very notion of truth in favour of the reproduction of the existent. The two extreme opposites, both conceived, significantly, amidst the apologetics of an obsolutely semi-feudal Austria, ultimately converge. The status quo is either hypostatized as the content of 'intentions' or protected against all criticism by the further subordination of such criticism to psychology.

The ego-functions psychoanalysis takes such pains to separate from one another are inextricably intertwined. The difference is in reality that between the claims of society and those of the individual. For this reason the sheep cannot be separated from the goats in ego-psychology. The original cathartic method demands that the unconscious become conscious. But since Freudian theory also defined the ego, which must indeed cope with contradictory tasks, as the agent of repression, analysis should, pursued to its logical conclusion, simultaneously dismantle the ego – namely, its resistances, the work of the defence-mechanisms, without which, however, the ego could not conceivably retain its identity against the multiplicity of impulses pressing in on it. This leads to the absurd conclusion that in therapeutic practice the defence-mechanisms are to be sometimes broken through and sometimes strengthened – a view which Anna Freud explicitly supports.[26]

The Continuum between Neurosis and Psychosis

Psychotics' defences are thus supposed to be built up and neurotics' defences broken down. The psychotic's ego-defences are to prevent instinctual chaos and disintegration, and treatment is confined to 'supportive therapy'. In the case of neuroses the traditional cathartic technique is adhered to because here the ego can allegedly cope with the instincts. This nonsensically dualistic practice disregards the basic affinity that, according to psychoanalytic doctrine, exists between neurosis and psychosis. If a continuum is actually imagined to exist between compulsive neurosis and schizophrenia, there can be no justification for insisting on more consciousness for one patient while trying to keep another 'capable of functioning' and protecting him against the acute danger that is at the same time invoked as the first patient's salvation. Since ego-weakness has latterly been numbered among the most crucial neurotic structures,[27] any treatment that still further curtails the ego appears problematic.

The societal antagonism reappears in the goal of analysis, which no longer knows, and cannot know, where it wants to get the patient, to the happiness of freedom or to happiness in unfreedom. It dodges the issue by giving the well-to-do who can afford it protracted cathartic treatment and the poor patient, who has soon to be back at his job, mere therapeutic support – a division that makes neurotics of the rich and psychotics of the poor. This tallies with statistics that demonstrate correlations between schizophrenia and low social status.[28] It is an open question, however, whether depth-analysis is ultimately preferable to more superficial therapy, and whether those patients do not come off better who at least remain able to work and do not have to surrender themselves body and mind to the analyst with the vague prospect that the transference which is growing stronger with each passing year will one day dissolve.

Psychological therapy, too, is warped by the contradiction of sociology and psychology: whatever course it opts for is the wrong one. If analysis dissolves resistances, it weakens the ego, and fixation on the analyst is more than a mere transitory phase; it is, rather, the replacement for the ego the patient is being deprived of. If it strengthens the ego, then, according to orthodox theory, analysis to a large extent also strengthens the forces whereby it keeps the unconscious down, the defence-mechanisms that allow the unconscious to continue its destructive activities.

The Need for Differentiation

Psychology is no preserve of the particular, sheltered against exposure to the universal. With the intensification of social antagonisms, clearly, the thoroughly liberal and individualistic concept of psychology tends increasingly to forfeit its meaning. The pre-bourgeois order does not yet know psychology, the over-socialized society knows it no longer. Analytic revisionism is the counterpart of such a society. It is commensurate with the shifting relation between society and the individual. The social power-structure hardly needs the mediating agencies of ego and individuality any longer. An outward sign of this is, precisely, the spread of so-called ego-psychology, whereas in reality the individual psychological dynamic is replaced by the partly conscious and partly regressive adjustment of the individual to society. The remnants of irrationality function merely as so much oil to be squirted into the works. The truly contemporary types are those whose actions are motivated neither by an ego nor, strictly speaking, unconsciously, but mirror objective trends like an automaton. Together they enact a senseless ritual to the beat of a compulsively repetitive rhythm and become emotionally impoverished: with the destruction of the ego, narcissism, or its collectivistic derivatives, is heightened. A brutal, total, standardizing society arrests all differentiation, and to this end it exploits the primitive core of the unconscious. Both conspire to annihilate the mediating ego; the triumphant archaic impulses, the victory of id over ego, harmonize with the triumph of society over the individual.

Psychoanalysis in its most authentic and by now already obsolete form comes into its own as a report on the forces of destruction rampant in the individual amidst a destructive society. What remains untrue about psychoanalysis is its claim to totality, its own over-identification with the momentum of history; starting out with Freud's early assertions that analysis seeks merely to add something more to existing knowledge, it culminates in his late dictum that 'sociology too, dealing as it does with the behaviour of people in society, cannot be anything but applied psychology.'[29]

On what is, or used to be, its home ground, psychoanalysis carries specific conviction; the further it removes itself from that sphere, the more its theses are threatened alternately with shallowness or wild over-systematization. If someone makes a slip of the tongue and a sexually loaded word comes out, if someone suffers from agoraphobia or if a girl walks in her sleep, psychoanalysis not merely has its best chances of therapeutic success but also its proper province, the relatively autonomous, monadological individual as arena of the unconscious conflict between instinctual drive and prohibition. The further it departs from this area, the more tyrannically it has to proceed and the more it has to drag what belongs to the dimension of outer reality into the shades of psychic immanence. Its delusion in so doing is not dissimilar from that 'omnipotence of thought' which it itself criticized as infantile.

It is not that the ego constitutes an autonomous second source of psychic life in addition to the id, which psychoanalysis rightly concentrated on as long as it had its own specific province, but that, for better or for worse, the ego has separated off from the pure immediacy of the instinctual impulses – a process whereby the area of conflict that is the actual domain of psychoanalysis first came into being. The ego, as the result of a genetic process, is both so much instinct and something else. Psychoanalytic logic, being incapable of thinking this contradiction, has to reduce everything to the same first principle, to what the ego once was. In cancelling out the differentiation synonymous with the emergence of the ego, it becomes the ally of regression, its own worst enemy. For the essence is not abstract repetition but the differentiated universal. That large sensitivity to difference which is the hallmark of the truly humane develops out of the most powerful experience of difference, that of the sexes. In reducing everything it calls unconscious, and ultimately all individuality, to the same thing, psychoanalysis seems to be the victim of a familiar homosexual mechanism, the inability to perceive differences. Homosexuals exhibit a certain experiential colour-blindness, an incapacity to apprehend individuality; women are, in the double sense, 'all the same' to them.

This scheme, the inability to love – for love intends, inextricably, the universal in the particular – is the basis of that analytic coldness which has been much too superficially attacked by the revisionists; it combines with aggressive tendencies which serve to conceal the real instinctual drives. From the outset, psychoanalysis is, well before its commercialization, attuned to prevailing reification. When a famous analytic teacher lays down the principle that asocial and schizoid children should be assured how much one likes them, the demand that one should love a repulsively aggressive child makes a mockery of everything analysis stood for; it was precisely Freud who once rejected the commandment that one should without distinction love all mankind.[30] Such indiscriminate love goes along with contempt for mankind: this is why it befits professional counsellors of soul-guidance. Its inherent tendency is to check and arrest the spontaneous impulses it releases: the undifferentiated concept under which it subsumes deviations is invariably another instrument of domination. A technique intended to cure the instincts of their bourgeois distortions further subjects them to the distortions of emancipation. It trains those it encourages to champion their drives to become useful members of the destructive whole.

NOTES

1   cf. Ernest Jones, 'Rationalization in Every-Day Life', in *The Journal of Abnormal Psychology*, 1908.
2   'But I cannot think . . . that any new task is set us by this psychosynthesis. If I allowed myself to be frank and uncivil I should say it was nothing but an empty phrase. I will limit myself to remarking that it is merely pushing a comparison so far that it ceases to have any meaning, or . . . that it is an unjustifiable

exploitation of a name ... What is psychical is something so unique and peculiar to itself that no one comparison can reflect its nature ... The comparison with chemical analysis has its limitation: for in mental life we have to deal with trends that are under a compulsion towards unification and combination ... In actual fact, indeed, the neurotic patient presents us with a torn mind, divided by resistances. As we analyse it and remove the resistances, it grows together; the great unity which we call his ego fits into itself all the instinctual impulses which before had been split off and held apart from it. The psychosynthesis is thus achieved during analytic treatment without our intervention, automatically and inevitably ... It is not true that something in the patient has been divided into its components and is now quietly waiting for us to put it somehow together again.' (Sigmund Freud, *Complete Works*, Standard Edition (London, 1953–); Vol. 17, 'Lines of Advance in Psychoanalytic Therapy', p. 160–1.)

3   cf. Walter Benjamin, 'Standort der französischen Schriftsteller', in *Zeitschrift für Sozialforschung*, 3rd Vol., 1934, p. 66.

4   Freud, *Works*, Vol. 22, p. 58 and p. 75.

5   cf. Freud, *Works*, Vol. 9, '"Civilised" Sexual Morality and Modern Nervous Illness.'

6   cf. Freud, *Works*, Vol. 19, 'A Short Outline of Psycho-Analysis.'

7   cf. William Buchanan and Hadley Cantril, *How Nations See Each Other*, Urbana 1953, p. 57.

8   cf. Erich Fromm, 'Zum Gefühl der Ohnmacht', in *Zeitschrift für Sozialforschung*, Vol. 6, 1937, p. 95 et seq.

9   cf. Heinz Hartmann, 'The Application of Psychoanalytic Concepts in Social Science', in *The Psychoanalytic Quarterly*, Vol. XIX, no. 3, 1950, p. 388.

10   Anna Freud, *The Ego and the Mechanisms of Defence*, New York, 1946, p. 32.

11   cf. Sigmund Freud, *Works*, Vol. 2, p. 269.

12   Anna Freud. ibid., p. 47.

13   Ibid.

14   cf. Sigmund Freud, *Works*, Vol. 20, 'Inhibitions, Symptom and Anxiety', p. 164, and Anna Freud, ibid., p. 45.

15   Anna Freud, ibid., p. 117.

16   On the psychoanalytic controversy about music cf. especially Heinrich Racker, 'Contribution to Psychoanalysis of Music', in *American Imago*, Vol. VIII, No. 2, June 1951, p. 129 et seq., especially p. 157.

17   Anna Freud, ibid., p. 158.

18   Ibid., p. 172.

19   Ibid., p. 174–5.

20   Ibid., p. 175.

21   Ibid., p. 175.

22   Ibid., p. 176.

23   Ibid., p. 176 et seq.

24   Ibid., p. 177.

25   Ibid., p. 177, footnote.

26   'The only situation in which this promise [e.g. that once id-impulses are made conscious they are less dangerous and more amenable to control than when unconscious] may prove illusory is that in which the defence has been undertaken because the patient dreads the strength of his instincts. This most deadly struggle of the ego to prevent itself from being submerged by the id, as, for instance, when psychosis is taking one of its periodic turns for the worse, is essentially a matter of quantitative relations. All that the ego asks for in such a conflict is to be reinforced. In so far as analysis can strengthen it by bringing the unconscious id-contents into consciousness, it has a therapeutic effect here also. But, in so far as the bringing of the unconscious activities of the ego into consciousness has the effect of disclosing the defensive processes and rendering them inoperative, the result of analysis is to weaken the ego still further and to advance the pathological process.' (Anna Freud, ibid., p. 70 et seq.) But according to analytic theory this 'only situation', the fear of the strength of the instincts, would be the reason for all defence.

27   Herrmann Nunberg, 'Ichstärke und Ichschwäche', in *Internationale Zeitschrift für Psychoanalyse*, Vol. XXIV, 1939.

28   cf. August B. Hollingshead and Frederick C. Redlich, 'Social Stratification and Schizophrenia', in *American Sociological Review*, Vol. 19, No. 3, p. 302 et seq.

29   Sigmund Freud, *Works*, Vol. 22, 'New Introductory Lectures on Psychoanalysis', p. 179.

30 'A love that does not discriminate seems to me to forfeit a part of its own value, by doing an injustice to its object ... not all men are worthy of love.' (Freud, *Works*, Vol. 21, 'Civilization and its Discontents', p. 102.)

4

Merleau-Ponty on Lukács

Maurice Merleau-Ponty (1908–61) was, along with Jean-Paul Sartre, the major French philosopher of the period after 1945. Merleau-Ponty's work appropriated the phenomenological approaches of Husserl and Heidegger to develop a new phenomenology of perception. Merleau-Ponty's radical reinterpretation of Husserl continued Husserl's critique of psychology but put new emphasis on the body's role in perception. In a number of detailed analyses he showed how the body is 'our' general medium for being in the world and also a necessarily subjective medium. Reinterpreting mind–body relations, Merleau-Ponty offered a new account of freedom and action, an account that was also critical of Sartre's claims for human, individual freedom. The debate with Sartre extended into what became a major political breach and a quarrel that focused the intellectual concerns of the period.

Differences in their conceptions of existentialism are perhaps most acute around the ethics of freedom but this also took the form of significant disagreement about the ongoing validity of Marxism. Their divergence was made explicit in *Adventures of the Dialectic*, from which the essay ' "Western" Marxism' is taken. Merleau-Ponty stressed the contingency of historical significance against the claims of revolutionary parties to know history. This motivates a critique of the opportunist, indeed undialectical abuse of dialectical thought within Marxism. Merleau-Ponty explores such questions through reinterpretations of Max Weber, Lenin, Trotsky and Sartre. The chapter on 'Western Marxism' focuses on the work of Georg Lukács, providing a succinct introduction to *History and Class Consciousness*, and an ambivalent call to renew Lukács' philosophy of history.

The return to the Hegelian sources of Marxism has become a characteristic manoeuvre through which Western Marxists distance themselves from dogmatic and reductive forms of 'dialectical materialism'. The term 'Western' Marxism is taken by Merleau-Ponty from the account in Karl Korsch's *Marxism and Philosophy* of how Marxist-Leninists used this term pejoratively to describe figures such as Lukács and Korsch. 'Western' Marxism came to stand, more generally, for the diffuse traditions of Marxist and neo-Marxist thought critical of Eastern and Soviet Marxism. Perry Anderson's *Considerations on Western Marxism* (1976), for example, suggests that the key figures in Western Marxism are Lukács, Korsch and Gramsci; Adorno, Marcuse and Benjamin; Sartre and Althusser; and Della Volpe and Colletti; with a loosely geographical configuration around Germany, France and Italy. Merleau-Ponty stands in a critical relation to such groupings, and comes closer to a more fundamental break with Marxism as such. Merleau-Ponty's work nevertheless exemplifies Western Marxism's critical re-reading of Marxism in opposition to Communist Party orthodoxy. According to Merleau-Ponty, the 'realism' of communism gives lip service to the dialectic, while Lukács' dialectical approach to history attempts to wrap realism in the dialectic. He goes on to provide a sustained critique of Sartre's confusion of political expediency and philosophical Marxism. Merleau-Ponty's essay is self-critical, taking issue with the Marxist voluntarism exemplified in his own earlier book *Humanism and Terror*. In a provocative formulation from the epilogue to *Adventures of the Dialectic*, Merleau-Ponty suggests that the kinds of Marxism that remain true whatever happens provide not a philosophy of history, but 'Kant in disguise'. This motivates the widely felt need to bridge the gulf between existential ethics at the level of both the individual and the political reality of collectives.

Merleau-Ponty's subsequent thought breaks with Marxism, becoming almost an early form of post-Marxism. In a 1956 essay 'On De-Stalinization', for example, Merleau-Ponty called for 'a de-Stalinization which is unchecked, consequential, and extended beyond the frontiers of communism to the whole Left that communism has "frozen"'. The more lasting interest of Merleau-Ponty's later work is in his return to the phenomenology of perception, language and art, including the tantalizingly incomplete reflections published posthumously in *The Visible and the Invisible*. Sartre's later *Critique of Dialectical Reason* sought to answer the problems raised by Merleau-Ponty. Although Merleau-Ponty was also a friend of Jacques Lacan and an earlier proponent of the significance of Saussure and Lévi-Strauss, he became a key figure against which post-structuralism defined itself. Althusser's Marxism defended Marx against the existentialist, humanist and Hegelian Marxism associated with Merleau-Ponty and Sartre, while thinkers as diverse as Deleuze, Derrida, Foucault and Lyotard were critical of Merleau-Ponty's approach to phenomenology, politics and dialectic. Although often overshadowed by Heidegger and Husserl, Merleau-Ponty's philosophical contribution to phenomenology is more sensitive to the politics of philosophy.

FURTHER READING

Primary works

Maurice Merleau-Ponty, *Humanism and Terror*, trans. John O'Neill (Boston: Beacon, 1969); *Signs*, trans. Richard C. McCleary (Evanston, IL: Northwestern

University Press, 1964), which includes the essay 'On De-Stalinization'; *The Visible and the Invisible*, trans. Alphonso Lingis (Evanston, IL: Northwestern University Press, 1968); *Sense and Non-Sense*, trans. Hubert L. Dreyfus and Patricia Allen Dreyfus (Evanston, IL: Northwestern University Press, 1964); *The Prose of the World*, trans. John O'Neill (Evanston, IL: Northwestern University Press, 1973); *Phenomenology of Perception*, trans. Colin Smith (London: Routledge and Kegan Paul, 1962).

Secondary works

Perry Anderson, *Considerations on Western Marxism* (London: New Left Books, 1976).

Raymond Aron, *Marxism and the Existentialists* (New York and Evanston: Harper and Row, 1969), esp. 'The Adventures and Misadventures of Dialectics', pp. 45–80.

Judith Butler, 'Sexual Ideology and Phenomenological Description: A Feminist Critique of Merleau-Ponty's *Phenomenology of Perception*', *The Thinking Muse: Feminism and Modern French Philosophy*, eds. Jeffner Allen and Iris Marion Young (Bloomington: Indiana University Press, 1989), pp. 85–100.

Barry Cooper, *Merleau-Ponty and Marxism: From Terror to Reform* (Toronto: Toronto University Press, 1979).

Thomas R. Flynn, *Sartre and Marxist Existentialism* (Chicago: University of Chicago Press, 1984).

Axel Honneth, 'Embodied Reason: On the Rediscovery of Merleau-Ponty', *The Fragmented World of the Social*, ed. Charles W. Wright (Albany: SUNY, 1995), pp. 150–7.

Galen A. Johnson, ed., *The Merleau-Ponty Aesthetics Reader: Philosophy and Painting* (Evanston, IL: Northwestern University Press, 1993).

Galen A. Johnson and Michael B. Smith, eds., *Ontology and Alterity in Merleau-Ponty* (Evanston, IL: Northwestern University Press, 1990).

Emmanuel Levinas, 'On Intersubjectivity: Notes on Merleau-Ponty', *Outside the Subject*, trans. Michael B. Smith (London: Athlone, 1993), pp. 96–103.

George Lichtheim, *Marxism in Modern France* (New York: Columbia, 1966).

Jean-François Lyotard, *Phenomenology*, trans. Brian Beakley (Albany: SUNY, 1991).

Gary Brent Madison, *The Phenomenology of Merleau-Ponty* (Athens, OH: Ohio University Press, 1981).

Mark Poster, *Existential Marxism in Postwar France: From Sartre to Althusser* (Princeton: Princeton University Press, 1977).

Jean-Paul Sartre, *Critique of Dialectical Reason*, 2 vols. (London: Verso, 1976, 1991).

Hugh J. Silverman, ed., *Philosophy and Non-Philosophy Since Merleau-Ponty* (New York and London: Routledge, 1988), esp. Maurice Merleau-Ponty, *Philosophy and Non-Philosophy Since Hegel*, pp. 9–83.

Jon Stewart, ed., *The Debate Between Sartre and Merleau-Ponty* (Evanston, IL: Northwestern University Press, 1998).

Bernhard Waldenfels, Jan M. Broekman and Ante Pazanin, eds., *Phenomenology and Marxism*, trans. J. Claude Evans, Jr (London: Routledge and Kegan Paul, 1984).

Scott Warren, *The Emergence of Dialectical Theory* (Chicago: University of Chicago Press, 1984).

Maurice Merleau-Ponty, ' "Western" Marxism', *Adventures of the Dialectic* (1955), trans. Joseph Bien (Evanston, IL: Northwestern University Press, 1973), pp. 30–58.

At the beginning of the twentieth century, Marxists found themselves confronted by a problem which had been hidden from Marx by the remnants of Hegelian dogmatism: can one overcome relativism, not by ignoring it, but by truly going beyond it, by going further in the same direction? Weber had glimpsed the road to follow, namely, ideal types, significations that we introduce into our representation of the past that would cut us from it only if they were arbitrary. But they themselves are part of history: history as a science, with its methods and its idealizations, is an aspect of history as reality, of the capitalistic rationalization. Our ideas, our significations, precisely because they are relative to our time, have an intrinsic truth that they will teach to us if we succeed in placing them in their proper context, in understanding them rather than merely suffering them. We are able to speak of the metamorphosis of the past through knowledge only because we measure the distance there is between the past and this knowledge. History is not only an object in front of us, far from us, beyond our reach; it is also our awakening as subjects. Itself a historical fact, the true or false consciousness that we have of our history cannot be simple illusion. There is a mineral there to be refined, a truth to be extracted, if only we go to the limits of relativism and put it, in turn, back into history. We give a form to history according to our categories; but our categories, in contact with history, are themselves freed from their partiality. The old problem of the relations between subject and object is transformed, and relativism is surpassed as soon as one puts it in historical terms, since here the object is the vestige left by other subjects, and the subject – historical understanding – held in the fabric of history, is by this very fact capable of self-criticism. There is an oscillation from one to the other which, as much as we could hope for, reduces the distance between knowledge and history. It is along this road that Weber stops. He does not pursue the relativization of relativism to its limits. He always considers the circle of the present and the past, of our representation and real history, as a vicious circle. He remains dominated by the idea of a truth without condition and without point of view. By comparison with this absolute knowledge, with this pure theory, our progressive knowledge is degraded to the rank of opinion, of simple appearance. Would not a more radical criticism, the unrestricted recognition of history as the unique milieu of our errors and our verifications, lead us to recover an absolute in the relative?

This is the question that Georg Lukács asks of his teacher, Weber.[1] He does not reproach him for having been too relativistic but rather for not having been relativistic enough and for not having gone so far as to "relativize the notions of subject and object." For, by so doing, one regains a sort of totality. Certainly nothing can change the fact that our knowledge is partial in both senses of the word. It will never be confused with the historical in-itself (if this word has a meaning). We are never able to refer to completed totality, to universal history, as if we were not within it, as if it were spread out in front of us. The totality of which Lukács speaks is, in his own terms, "the totality of observed facts," not of all possible and actual beings but of our coherent arrangement of all the known facts. When the subject recognizes himself in history and history in himself, he does not dominate the whole, as the Hegelian philosopher does, but at least he is engaged in a work of totalization. He knows that no historical fact will ever have its whole meaning for us unless it has been linked to all the facts we are able to know, unless it has been referred to as a particular moment in a single enterprise which unites them, unless it has been placed in a vertical history which is the record of attempts which had a meaning, of their implications and of their conceivable continuations. If one takes on the responsibility of deciphering fundamental choices in history, there is no reason to limit oneself to partial and discontinuous intuitions. Lukács completely accepts the analysis sketched by Weber of the Calvinistic choice and of the capitalistic spirit; he only wishes to continue it. The Calvinistic choice needs to be confronted with all the others; and all choices must together form a single action if each of them is to be understood. The dialectic is this continued intuition, a consistent reading of actual history, the re-establishment of the tormented relations, of the interminable exchanges, between subject and object.[2] There is only one knowledge, which is the knowledge of our world in a state of becoming, and this becoming embraces knowledge itself. But it is knowledge that teaches us this. Thus, there is that moment in which knowledge looks back on its origins, recaptures its own genesis, equals as knowledge what it was as event, gathers itself together in order to totalize itself, and tends toward consciousness. The same whole is, in the first relationship, history; in the second, philosophy. History is philosophy realized, as philosophy is history formalized, reduced to its internal articulations, to its intelligible structure.

For Lukács, Marxism is, or should be, this integral philosophy without dogma. Weber understood materialism as an attempt to deduce all culture from economics. For Lukács, it is a way of saying that the relations among men are not the sum of personal acts or personal decisions, but pass through things, the anonymous roles, the common situations, and the institutions where men have projected so much of themselves that their fate is now played out outside them. "As . . . the personal interests become self-contained in class interests, the personal conduct of the individual re-objectifies itself (*sich versachlichen*), necessarily alienates itself (*entfremden*), and at the same time exists without him as an . . . independent force."[3] In the nineteenth century, especially through the development of production, "the material forces become saturated with spiritual life (*mit geistigem Leben ausgestattet werden*) and human existence is dulled (to the point that it becomes) a material force (*zu einer materiellen Kraft verdummt*)."[4] This exchange, by which things become persons and persons things, lays the foundation for the unity of history and philosophy. It makes all problems historical but also all history philosophical, since forces are human projects become institutions. Capital, says Marx in a famous passage, is "not a thing, but a social relationship between persons mediated by things (*nicht eine Sache, sondern ein durch Sachen vermitteltes gesellschaftliches Verhältnis zwischen Personen*)."[5] Historical materialism is not the reduction of history to one of its sectors. It states a kinship between the person and the exterior, between the subject and the object, which is at the bottom of the alienation of the subject in the object and, if the movement is reversed, will be the basis for the reintegration of the world with man.

Marx's innovation is that he takes this fact as fundamental, whereas, for Hegel, alienation is still an operation of the spirit on itself and thus is already overcome when it manifests itself. When Marx says that he has put the dialectic back on its feet or that his dialectic is the "contrary" of Hegel's, this cannot be simply a matter of exchanging the roles of the spirit and the "matter" of history, giving to the "matter" of history the very functions Hegel accorded to the spirit. As it becomes material, the dialectic must grow heavy. In Marx spirit becomes a thing, while things become saturated with spirit. History's course is a becoming of meanings transformed into forces or institutions. This is why there is an inertia of history in Marx and also an appeal to human invention in order to complete the dialectic. Marx cannot therefore transfer to, and lay to the account of, matter the *same* rationality which Hegel ascribed to spirit. The meaning of history appears in what he calls "human matter," an ambiguous setting where ideas and rationality do not find the *de jure* existence which in Hegel they owed to the dogma of totality as completed system and to the dogma of philosophy as the intellectual possession of this system. It is true that Marx often seems to claim the very authority of Hegel's absolute knowledge for his own antidogmatic criticism when, for example, he says that reason "has always existed though not always in a rational form."[6] But what is a reason which does not yet have the form of reason? Unless he claimed as his own the all-encompassing philosophical consciousness which he reproaches in Hegel, how could Marx affirm that reason pre-existed its manifestations and itself organized the coincidence of events from which its history benefited? Lukács thinks that Marxism cannot claim as its own this rationalistic dogma:

> But it must not be forgotten that "the ruse of reason" can only claim to be more than a myth if authentic reason can be discovered and demonstrated in a truly concrete manner. In that case it becomes a brilliant explanation for stages in history that have not yet become conscious. But these can only be understood and evaluated as stages from a standpoint already achieved by a reason that has discovered itself.[7]

In considering his past, man finds its meaning retrospectively in the coming-about of a rationality, the absence of which was not at first a simple privation but truly a state of nonreason, and which, at the moment this rationality appears, has the right to subordinate what precedes it only in the exact measure to which rationality comprehends this as its own preparation. Thus, Marxism disassociates the rationality of history from any idea of necessity. Rationality is necessary neither in the sense of physical causality, in which the antecedents determine the consequents, nor even in the sense of the necessity of a system, in which the whole precedes and brings to existence what happens. If human society does not become aware of the meaning of its history and of its contradictions, all one can say is that the contradictions will occur again, always more violently, by a sort of "dialectical mechanics."[8] In other words, the dialectic of things only makes the problems more urgent. It is the total dialectic, in which the subject interposes its authority, which can find a solution to the problems.[9] Marxism cannot hide the *Weltgeist* in matter. It must justify in another way the meaning of history, and it can do so only by conceiving a historical selection which eliminates the antinomistic realities from the course of history but does not have, in itself and without men's initiative, the power to create a coherent and homogeneous system.

Marxism understood in such a way had to be a revolutionary philosophy precisely because it refused to be a dogmatic philosophy of history. Two moments which succeed each other perpetually in it, but each time at a higher level, composed its spiral movement – a reading of history which allows its philosophical meaning to appear, and a return to the present which lets philosophy appear as history.

If the man of a capitalist society looks back to its origins, he gets the impression that he is witnessing the "realization of society (*Vergesellschaftung der Gesellschaft*)." A precapitalistic society, for example a caste society, divides itself into sectors which scarcely belong to the same social world. The canals and roads created by the process of production to join these sectors are at each moment blocked by relationships of prestige and by the brute facts of tradition. The economic function is never without its religious, legal, or moral components, which do not have exact equivalents in economic language. We must not merely say that these societies are unaware of their economic substructure, as if it were there and they only failed to see it – in Lukács' terms, as if falling bodies were there before Galileo. We must say that these societies are not economically based, as if what we call the imagination of history had established them in a fantastic order (where misery, of course, is very real). The economic analysis would miss criteria essential to the distribution of privileges; and if relationships between castes are religiously observed by the exploited as well as by the exploiter, it is because these relationships cannot be challenged as long as men do not think of themselves as partners in a common work of production. Lukács says that between the fragments of social life which admit of an economic interpretation are inserted "interworlds" which are dominated by relationships of blood, sex, or mythical kinship. This society, he continues, has not cut the "umbilical cord" which binds it to prehistory or nature. It has not yet defined itself as a relationship of man with man. Capitalist society, on the contrary, places all who live in it under the common denominator of work and in this sense is homogeneous. Even the wage system, that is to say, exploitation, places all those who participate in it within a single market. Here the phantasms and ideologies can in principle be recognized for what they are. There is in the system itself, whether it is made explicit or not, a distinction between appearance and reality, because there is truly, both within the boundaries of a single State and in the entire capitalistic world, a unity beneath local phenomena. Because there is a truly common ground, destinies can be compared. A balance sheet, or a calculation of the social whole, is conceivable because the system is deliberately rational, is designed to refund more than it costs, and translates everything it consumes and produces into the universal language of money. In saying that capitalism is a "socialization of society," one states, therefore, an observable property. It is not that all other societies are nothing but a sketch of this one: for themselves, as we have said, they are something completely different. The notion of precapitalism under which we are grouping them pell-mell is obviously egocentric. A true knowledge of "precapitalism" will demand that one rediscover it as it has been lived – as it was in its own eyes. What we have just said about it is rather the point of view of capitalism on what preceded it; and to get to the integral truth, one will have to go beyond the limits of the capitalistic present. But even if it is partial, this point of view about precapitalism is well founded. The comparison is not false, even if it is not exhaustive. The direction of development marked out in this way is not a fiction. The capitalistic structure has displaced the precapitalistic ones. One is witness to the historical work through which the currents of production break open new cleavages or dismantle and destroy the traditional partitions. The movement is accelerated by violence when established capitalism tries to take over and control backward societies. Nothing permits one to say that this transition is necessary, that capitalism is contained within precapitalism as its inevitable future, or that it contains to any great degree all that has preceded it, or, finally, that any society, to go beyond capitalism, must inevitably pass through a capitalistic phase. All these conceptions of development are mechanical. A dialectical conception demands only that, between capitalism, where it exists, and its antecedents, the relationship be one of an integrated society to a less integrated one. The formula *Vergesellschaftung der Gesellschaft* says nothing more.

This formula makes immediately evident a philosophical meaning of social development which, however, is not transcendent to it. To say that there is a "socialization of society" is to say that men begin to exist for one another, that the social whole retraces its dispersion in order to totalize itself, that it goes beyond various partitions and taboos, toward transparency, that it arranges itself as a center or an interior from which it is possible to think it, that it gathers itself around an anonymous project in relation to which various attempts, errors, progress, and a history would be possible, and, finally, that brute existence is transformed into its truth and tends toward meaning. The question is not, of course, to derive a collective consciousness from the social whole. Consciousness is presupposed in this description. Society would never become conscious of itself if it were not already made up of conscious subjects. What one wants to say is that the consciousness of principle which is at the outset granted to men finds a complicity in the structuration realized by history. This complicity allows consciousness to become knowledge of the social. Thus, in the eyes of consciousness, its "object," society, comes to meet consciousness and, so to speak, prepares itself to be known by establishing a decisive relationship with itself. There are different relationships of society with itself, and it is this that prevents us from placing them all at an equal distance from consciousness on the pretext that they are all its "objects." As a living body, given its behavior, is, so to speak, closer to consciousness than a stone, so certain social structures are the cradle of the knowledge of society. Pure consciousness finds its "origin" in them. Even if the notion of interiority, when applied to a society, should be understood in the figurative sense, we find, all the same, that this metaphor is possible with regard to capitalistic society but not so with regard to precapitalistic ones. This is enough for us to say that the history which produced capitalism symbolizes the emergence of a subjectivity. There are subjects, objects, there are men and things, but there is also a third order, that of relationships between men inscribed in tools or social symbols. These relationships have their development, their advances, and their regressions. Just as in the life of the individual, so in this generalized life there are tentative aims, failure or success, reaction of the result on the aim, repetition or variation, and this is what one calls history.

When one says that Marxism finds a meaning in history, it should not be understood by this that there is an irresistible orientation toward certain ends but rather that there is, immanent in history, a problem or a question in relation to which what happens at each moment can be classified, situated, understood as progress or regression, compared with what happens at other moments, can be expressed in the same language, understood as a contribution to the same endeavor, and can in principle furnish a lesson. In short it *accrues* with the other results of the past to form a single significant whole. The principle of the logic of history is not that all problems posed are solved in advance,[10] that the solution precedes the problem, or that there would be no question if the answer did not pre-exist somewhere, as if history were built on exact ideas. One should rather formulate it negatively: there is no event which does not bring further precision to the permanent problem of knowing what man and his society are, which does not make this problem a present concern, which does not bring back the paradox of a society of exploitation that is nonetheless based on the recognition of man by man. The "socialization of society" does not mean that the development of history is subordinated to an eternal essence of society. Rather, it means only that the moments of this development are interconnected, complement one another, step by step constitute a single event, and that the negative conditions of a solution are thus brought together. This sober principle requires neither that backward civilizations be completely surpassed by our own (it can, on the contrary, be, as Lukács says, that, in a time when the capitalistic apparatus with its constraints was not yet formed, culture attained expressions of the world which have an "eternal charm") nor that the progress achieved in later civilizations be regarded as absolute progress. First of all, it is only in the structure of the whole that there is progress. The balance sheet of history shows that, taken as a whole, there is a growing relationship of man to man. This does not alter the fact that, right now, the piece of furniture built by the craftsman speaks more eloquently of man than furniture made by the machine. But there is more to be said. Even in considering the whole of a civilization, its progress is secure only when followed by further progress. It cannot stand still. Historical accumulation or "sedimentation" is not a deposit or a residue. The very fact that an advance has occurred changes the situation; and to remain equal to itself, progress has to face the changes that it instigated. If, on the contrary, the progress that has been achieved becomes immobilized, it is already lost. All progress is then relative in the profound sense that the very historical movement which inscribes it in things brings to the fore the problem of decadence. Revolution become institution is already decadent if it believes itself to be accomplished. In other words, in a concrete conception of history, where ideas are nothing more than stages of the social dynamic, all progress is ambiguous because, acquired in a crisis situation, it creates a condition from which emerge problems that go beyond it.

The sense of history is then threatened at every step with going astray and constantly needs to be reinterpreted. The main current is never without countercurrents or whirlpools. It is never even given as a fact. It reveals itself only through asymmetries, vestiges, diversions, and regressions. It is comparable to the sense of perceived things, to those reliefs which take form only from a certain point of view and never absolutely exclude other modes of perception. There is less a sense of history than an elimination of non-sense. No sooner does the direction of becoming indicate itself than it is already compromised. It is always in retrospect that an advance can be affirmed: it was not implied in the past, and all that one can say is that, if it is real progress, it takes up problems immanent in the past. The bourgeoisie established itself as ruling class, but the very development of its power, by isolating in the midst of the new society another class which is not integrated into this society and by accentuating the conflict between the demands immanent in production and the forms to which the bourgeois society subjects its production, shows that it is not a universal class. "The limit of capitalism is capital itself" (Marx). While they may be termed "progressist" when compared with what preceded them, the capitalist forms are soon regressive or decadent when compared to the productive forces which capitalism itself has created. These forms were at first a projection of human freedom. With decadence, the product becomes detached from productive activity and even takes possession of it. Objectification becomes reification (*Verdinglichung*). In the period of transition, doubt is possible concerning the historical function of this or that form, and, moreover, the passage to decadence is not made in all sectors of history at the same moment. A difficult analysis will always be necessary to determine at a given moment what has kept, and what has lost, historical actuality. In a sense, everything is justified, everything is or has been true; in another sense, everything is false, unreal, and the world will begin when one has changed it. Revolution is the moment when these two perspectives are united, when a radical negation frees the truth of the entire past and allows the attempt to recover it. But when can one think that the moment of negation has passed, when must one begin the recovery? Within the revolution itself the scintillation of truth and falsity continues. The development which is outlined in things is so incomplete that it is left to consciousness to complete it. In rediscovering its birth certificate and its origins in history, consciousness perhaps thought it had found a guide to rely on, but now it is consciousness which must guide the guide. The two relationships – consciousness as a product of history, history as a product of consciousness – must be maintained together. Marx unites them in making consciousness, not the source of social being, not the reflection of an external social being, but a singular sphere where all is false and all is true, where the false is true as false and the true is false as true.

This is how Lukács sees the meaning of the theory of ideologies. This mixture of truth and falsity is already inextricable in the ideologies of science. The bourgeois conception of science taught us to think of the social as a second nature and inaugurated its objective study, just as capitalist production opened up a vast field of work. But, just as the capitalistic forms of production end by paralyzing the productive forces out of which they were born, the "natural laws of the social order," detached from the historical structure of which they are the expression and considered as the features of an eternal countenance of the universe, conceal the profound dynamic of the whole. A difficult critique is necessary if we are to go beyond scientism without sliding back to prescience, if we are to maintain the relative right of objective thought against object-ivism, if we are to articulate the universe of the dialectic with the universe of science. The difficulty is even greater when one turns to literature. One must insist on this, for with his theory of ideologies and of literature, not changed in thirty years, Lukács is trying to preserve – and his enemies are trying to attack – a Marxism which incorporates subjectivity into history without making it an epiphenomenon. He is trying to preserve the philosophical marrow of Marxism, its cultural value, and finally its revolutionary meaning, which, as we shall see, is an integral part of Marxism. Many Marxists are satisfied to say that consciousness is in principle mystified and therefore that literature is suspect. They do not see that, if consciousness were ever absolutely cut off from truth, they themselves would be reduced to silence, and no thought, not even Marxism, would ever be able to lay a claim to truth. There is no point in answering that Marxism is true, and alone true, as the ideology of the rising class, because, as Lenin says, Marxism and the theory of the social are initially brought to the working class from outside. This means that there can be truth outside the proletariat and that, inversely, not everything that comes from the proletariat is true, since the proletariat, in a society where it is powerless, is contaminated by its bourgeoisie. Thus Marxism needs a theory of consciousness which accounts for its mystification without denying it participation in truth. It is toward this theory that Lukács was leaning in his book of 1923. We cannot, he said, establish "an inflexible confrontation of true and false."[11] Hegel was able to integrate falsity into the logic of history only as partial truth, that is to say, only after having subtracted precisely what makes it false. Thus for him synthesis is transcendent with regard to the moments which prepare it. In Marx, on the contrary, since the dialectic is history itself, it is the whole experience of the past, without philosophical preparation, without transposition or suppression, which must pass into the present and into the future. " . . . in so far as the 'false' is an aspect of the 'true', it is both 'false' and 'non-false.' "[12] Even illusions have some sort of sense and call for deciphering because they always present themselves against the background of a lived relationship with the social whole and because they are thus not like something mental, opaque, and isolated; instead, like the expressions of faces or of speeches, they bring with them an underlying meaning that unmasks them, and they hide something only by exposing it. Lukács still holds today[13] that, because literature is the expression of the lived world, it never expresses the postulates of a single class but rather the class's meeting and eventual collision with other classes. Literature is then always the reflection of the whole, even if the class perspective distorts this reflection. Balzac's very prejudices helped him to see certain aspects of his time to which a more "advanced" mind, such as Stendhal, remained indifferent. As long as the writer still has a writer's integrity, that is to say, as long as he gives a picture of the world in which he lives, his work, through interpretation, always touches truth. Because the artist gives himself the strange task of objectifying a life, with all its ramifications in its surroundings, literature cannot simply be false. Consciousness, the relation of the self to itself, is "*subjectively* justified in the social and historical situation, as something which can and should be understood, i.e. as 'right.' At the same time, *objectively*, it bypasses the essence of the evolution of society as a 'false consciousness.' "[14] To say that it is "false consciousness" is not to state the thesis of an essential "falsity of consciousness." It is, on the contrary, to say that something within warns it that it is not altogether correct and invites it to rectify itself. This fundamental relationship with truth allows past literature to furnish models for the present. Literature is mystification only in decadence. This is when consciousness becomes ideology, mask, diversion, because it gives up domination of the social whole and can only be used for hiding it. In the rising period of capitalism, literature remained a sufficient expression of the human whole. It must perhaps even be said that the great bourgeois literature is the only model we have at our disposal. In the other camp, the society in which the proletariat tries its best to suppress itself as a class, writers, as Gorki said, necessarily lag behind the workers and can only be the unfaithful heirs of bourgeois culture. If, on the other hand, one considers a classless society, finally realized, it is not a "proletarian" culture which it produces but one which is beyond classes. One can therefore ask oneself whether for the moment a culture other than bourgeois culture is possible. In any case, we have no other example of ruling-class literature, where an energetic attempt to express the world has been made, than that of capitalism in its organic phase. This is why, after the war, Lukács still proposed Goethe, Balzac, and Stendhal as models for revolutionary writers. Now, as soon as one admits that man is open to truth through his lived relationship with totality, one defines an order of expression which does not conform to that of everyday action. The demands of discipline could not possibly be the same for militants, who act at the level of the immediate, and for the writer, who prepares instruments of knowledge, valid, in principle, at least for some time and perhaps forever. There would be a political action and a cultural action which are not always parallel. To transfer the rules of the first to those of the second would be to make culture a form of propaganda. That is why, a few years ago, Lukács was still defending the writers who were fellow travelers of the Party and were called "snipers." It is not that he ever excluded literature from history but rather that he distinguished between the "center" and the "periphery" of historical dialectic, between the rhythm of political action and that of culture. The two develop-ments are convergent, but truth does not march with the same step in both cases. This results from a double relationship that an integral philosophy admits of between individuals and historical totality. It acts on us; we are in it at a certain place and in a certain position; we respond to it. But we also live it, speak about it, and write about it. Our experience everywhere overflows our standpoint. We are in it, but it is completely in us. These two relationships are concretely united in every life. Yet they never merge. They could be brought back to unity only in a homogeneous society where the situation would no more restrain life than life imprisons our gaze. All Marxism which does not make an epiphenomenon of consciousness inevitably limps, sometimes on one side, sometimes on the other.

Such, according to Lukács, is the philosophical reading of history. As we see, it does not have an overview of events, it does not seek in them the justification of a pre-established schema. Rather, it questions events, truly deciphers them, and gives them only as much meaning as they demand. By an apparent paradox, it is precisely this rigor, this sobriety, for which he was reproached by Marxists. Lukács rehabilitated consciousness in principle beyond ideologies but at the same time refused it the *a priori* possession of the whole. He never claimed to exhaust the analysis of the precapitalistic past, and for him the rationality of history was only a postulation of its capitalistic development. Most Marxists do exactly the opposite. They contest the existence of consciousness in principle and, without saying so, grant themselves the intelligible structure of the whole, and then discover all the more easily the meaning and the logic of each phase in that they have dogmatically presupposed the intelligible structure of the whole. The exceptional merit of Lukács – which makes his book, even today, a philosophical one – is precisely that his philosophy was not by implication to be understood as dogma but was to be practiced, that it did not serve to "prepare" history, and that it was the very chain of history grasped in human experience. His philosophical reading of history brought to light, behind the prose of everyday existence, a recovery of the self by itself which is the definition of subjectivity. But this philosophical meaning remained tied to the articulations of history, undetachable from them; and finally the operation of philosophical focusing had its ballast, its counterpart, in a historical fact, the existence of the proletariat. We are not changing direction. We are simply deepening the analysis by now showing that philosophy is history, as, before, we showed that history is philosophy.

The philosophical reading of history is not a simple application of concepts of consciousness, of truth and totality, badly disguised under historical rags, for this focusing, this placing in perspective, is accomplished in history itself by the proletariat. In creating an expropriated class – men who are commodities – capitalism forces them to judge commodities according to human relationships. Capitalism makes evident *a contrario* the "relations between persons" which are its reality but which it is very careful to hide, even from itself. It is not the philosopher who looks for the criteria of a judgement of capitalism in a conception of the "reign of freedom." It is capitalism which gives rise to a class of men who cannot stay alive without repudiating the status of commodity imposed upon them. The proletariat is commodity seeing itself as commodity, at the same time distinguishing itself from this, challenging the "eternal" laws of political economy, and discovering, under the supposed "things," the "process" which they hide – that is to say, the dynamic of production, the social whole as "production and reproduction of itself."[15] The proletariat is an "intention of totality" or the "totality in intention,"[16] "the correct view of the over–all economic situation."[17] The realization of society that capitalism has sketched, left in suspense, and finally thwarted is taken up by the proletariat, because, being the very failure of the capitalistic intention, it is, by position, "at the focal point of the socialising process."[18] The "socialising" function of capitalism passes to the proletariat. At the same time, the proletariat *is* this philosophical meaning of history that one might have thought was the work of the philosopher, because it is the "self-consciousness of the object (*das Selbstbewusstsein des Gegenstandes*)."[19] It furnishes this identity of subject and object that philosophical knowledge perceives abstractly as the condition of truth and the Archimedes' point of a philosophy of history. "For this class the knowledge of self signifies at the same time a correct knowledge of the entire society. . . . Consequently . . . this class is at one and the same time the subject and the object of knowledge."[20]

> In the period of the "pre-history of human society" and of the struggles between classes the only possible function of truth is to establish the various possible attitudes to an essentially uncomprehended world in accordance with man's needs in the struggle to master his environment. Truth could only achieve an 'objectivity' relative to the standpoint of the individual classes and the objective realities corresponding to it. But as soon as mankind has clearly understood and hence *restructured* the foundations of its existence, truth acquires a wholly novel aspect.[21]

The "historical mission of the proletariat," which is the absolute negation of class, the institution of a classless society, is at the same time a philosophical mission of the advent of truth. "For the proletariat the truth is a weapon that brings victory; and the more ruthless, the greater the victory."[22] It is not, first of all, as it is for Weber, in the existence of the man of culture or the historian but rather in the "object," in the proletarian, that rationalization and truth are elaborated. History provides its own interpretation by producing, along with the proletariat, its own consciousness.

But what do we mean when we say that the proletariat is the truth of the historical whole? We have already encountered the question and the following false dilemma. Either one truly places oneself in history, and then each reality is fully what it is, each part is an incomparable whole; none can be reduced to being a sketch of what is to follow, none can claim to be in truth what the past sketched. Or one wants a logic of history and wants it to be a manifestation of truth; but there is no logic except for a consciousness, and it is necessary to say either that the proletarians know the totality of history or that the proletariat is in itself (that is to say, in our eyes, not for itself) a force which leads to the realization of the true society. The first conception is absurd. Marx and Lukács cannot think of putting the total knowledge of history into the proletariat and into history, under the form of distinct thought and will, in the mode of psychic existence. In Lukács' terms, the proletariat is totality only in "intention." As for Marx, we have only to cite again the famous sentence: "The question is not what goal is *envisaged* for the time being by this or that member of the proletariat, or even by the proletariat as a whole. The question is *what is the proletariat* and what course of action will it be forced historically to take in conformity with its own *nature*."[23] But then, even if Marxism and its philosophy of history are nothing else than the "secret of the proletariat's existence," it is not a secret that the proletariat itself possesses but one that the theoretician deciphers. Is this not to admit that, by means of a third party, it is still the theoretician who gives his meaning to history in giving his meaning to the existence of the proletariat? Since the proletariat is not the subject of history, since the workers are not "gods," and since they receive a historical mission only in becoming the opposite, namely, "objects" or "commodities," is it not necessary that, as with Hegel, the theoretician or the philosopher remains the only authentic subject of history, and is not subjectivity the last word of this philosophy? Just because the historical mission of the proletariat is enormous, and because it should, as "universal class" or "final class," end what was the unvarying regime of history before it, it is necessary that it be fashioned by an unlimited negation which it contains in itself as class. "*The proletariat only perfects itself by annihilating and transcending itself, by creating the classless society through the successful conclusion of its own class struggle.*"[24] Does this not mean that its function prevents it from existing as a compact and solid class? In a society of classes it does not yet completely exist; afterwards, it no longer exists as a distinct class. To the extent that it is, it is a power of continuous suppression, and even its own suppression. Is this not to recognize that it is historically nearly unreal, that it chiefly exists negatively, which is to say, as idea in the thought of the philosopher? Does this not amount to admitting that one has missed the realization of philosophy in history that Lukács, after Marx, wanted to obtain?

On the contrary, for Lukács it is here that the essential and most innovative notion of Marxism appears. The difficulty exists only if the proletariat must become either subject or object for the theoretician. This is precisely the alternative that Marx puts aside by introducing a new mode of historical existence and of meaning: *praxis*. Everything that we have mentioned concerning the relationships between subject and object in Marxism was only an approximation of praxis. Class consciousness in the proletariat is not a state of mind, nor is it knowledge. It is not, however, a theoretician's conception because it is a praxis; that is to say, it is less than a subject and more than an object; it is a polarized existence, a possibility which appears in the proletarian's situation at the juncture of things and his life. In short – Lukács here uses Weber's term – it is an "objective possibility."

Precisely because this difficult notion was new, it was poorly understood. Yet this is what makes Marxism another philosophy and not simply a materialistic transposition of Hegel. Engels says in passing: "Practice, namely experiment and industry (*Die Praxis, nämlich das Experiment und die Industrie*),"[25] which defines it by contact with the sentient or the technique and carries the opposition between *theōria* and *praxis* back to the vulgar distinction between the abstract and the concrete. If praxis were nothing more, it would be impossible to see how Marx could make it rival contemplation as a fundamental mode of our relationship with the world. Experiment and industry put in the place of theoretical thought would result in a form of pragmatism or empiricism; in other words, the whole of *theōria* would be reduced to one of its parts, for experimentation is a modality of knowledge, and industry also rests on a theoretical knowledge of nature. Experiment and industry do not cover this "critico-practical revolutionary activity," which is the definition of praxis in the first of the *Theses on Feuerbach*. Engels does not see what Marx calls "the vulgar and Judaic phenomenal form of praxis." Lukács says that one should reach the "philosophical-dialectical" meaning of it,[26] which can be stated more or less as follows: it is the inner principle of activity, the global project which sustains and animates the productions and actions of a class, which delineates for it both a picture of the world and its tasks in that world, and which, keeping in mind exterior conditions, assigns it a history.[27] This project is not the project of *someone* – of some proletarians, of all proletarians, or of a theoretician who arrogates to himself the right of reconstructing their profound will. It is not, like the meaning of our thoughts, a closed, definitive unity. It is the cluster of relations of an ideology, a technique, and a movement of productive forces, each involving the others and receiving support from them, each, in its time, playing a directive role which is never exclusive, and all, together, producing a qualified phase of social development. As the milieu of these exchanges, praxis goes far beyond the thought and feeling of the proletarians, and yet, says Lukács, it is not a "mere fiction,"[28] a disguise invented by the theoretician for his own ideas of history. It is the proletarians' common situation, the system of what they do on all levels of action, a supple and malleable system which allows for all sorts of individual mistakes and even collective errors but which always ends by making its weight felt. Thus, it is a vector, an attraction, a possible state, a principle of historical selection, and a diagram of existence.

It will be objected that the proletarians do not share a common situation, that their conduct has no logic, that the particulars of their lives do not converge, and finally that the proletariat has unity only in the eyes of an external spectator who dominates history, since by hypothesis the proletarians themselves can be mistaken. This brings back the alternative: either they are subjects of history, and then they are "gods"; or it is the theoretician who supposes a historical mission for them, and then they are only objects of history. Marx's answer would be that there is no *theoretical* way of going beyond the dilemma. In the face of contemplating consciousness, the theoretician must either command or obey, be subject or object, and, correlatively, the proletariat must obey or command, be object or subject. For theoretical consciousness there is no middle ground between democratic consultation of the proletarians, which reduces proletarian praxis to their thought and their feelings of the moment and relies on the "spontaneity of the masses," and bureaucratic cynicism, which substitutes, for the existing proletariat, the idea made of it by the theoretician. But in practice the dilemma is transcended because praxis is not subjugated to the postulate of theoretical consciousness, to the rivalry of consciousnesses. For a philosophy of praxis, knowledge itself is not the intellectual possession of a signification, of a mental object; and the proletarians are able to carry the meaning of history, even though this meaning is not in the form of an

"I think." This philosophy does not take as its theme consciousnesses enclosed in their native immanence but rather men who explain themselves to one another. One man brings his life into contact with the apparatuses of oppression, another brings information from another source on this same life and a view of the total struggle, that is to say, a view of its political forms. By this confrontation, theory affirms itself as the rigorous expression of what is lived by the proletarians, and, simultaneously, the proletarians' life is transposed onto the level of political struggle. Marxism avoids the alternative because it takes into consideration, not idle, silent, and sovereign consciousnesses, but the exchange between workers, who are also speaking men – capable, therefore, of making their own the theoretical views proposed to them – and theoreticians, who are also living men – capable, therefore, of collecting in their theses what other men are in the process of living.

When one founds Marxist theory on proletarian praxis, one is not therefore led to the "spontaneous" or "primitive" myth of the "revolutionary instinct of the masses." The profound philosophical meaning of the notion of praxis is to place us in an order which is not that of knowledge but rather that of communication, exchange, and association. There is a proletarian praxis which makes the class exist before it is known. It is not closed in on itself, it is not self-sufficient. It admits and even calls for a critical elaboration and for rectification. These controls are procured by a praxis of a superior degree, which is, this time, the life of the proletariat in the Party. This higher praxis is not a reflection of the initial praxis; it is not contained in it in miniature; it carries the working class beyond its immediate reality; it expresses it, and here, as everywhere else, the expression is creative. But it is not arbitrary. The Party must establish itself as the expression of the working class by making itself accepted by the working class. The Party's operation must prove that beyond capitalistic history there is another history, wherein one does not have to choose between the role of subject and object. The proletariat's acknowledgment of the Party is not an oath of allegiance to persons. Its counterpart is the acknowledgment of the proletariat by the Party. This is certainly not to say that there is a submission of the Party to the proletarians' opinions just as they are; rather, there is the statutory aim of making them attain political life. This exchange, in which no one commands and no one obeys, is symbolized by the old custom which dictates that, in a meeting, speakers join in when the audience applauds. What they applaud is the fact that they do not intervene as persons, that in their relationship with those who listen to them a truth appears which does not come from them and which the speakers can and must applaud. In the communist sense, the Party is this communication; and such a conception of the Party is not a corollary of Marxism – it is its very center. Unless one makes another dogmatism of it (and how is one to do so, since one cannot start from the self-certainty of a universal subject), Marxism does not have a total view of universal history at its disposal; and its entire philosophy of history is nothing more than the development of partial views that a man situated in history, who tries to understand himself, has of his past and of his present. This conception remains hypothetical until it finds a unique guarantee in the existing proletariat and in its assent, which allows it to be valid as the law of being. The Party is then like a mystery of reason. It is the place in history where the *meaning which is* understands itself, where the concept becomes life; and, avoiding the test which authenticates Marxism, any deviation which would assimilate the relationships of Party and class to the relationships of chief and troops would make an "ideology" of it. Then history as science and history as reality would remain disjointed, and the Party would no longer be the laboratory of history and the beginning of a true society. The great Marxists realized so well that problems of organization command the value of truth in Marxism that they went so far as to admit that theses, however well-founded, must not be imposed on the proletarians against their will, because their rejection signifies that subjectively the proletariat is not ripe for them and, thus, that these theses are premature and, finally, false. Nothing remains to their defenders but to explain them anew, once the teachings of events will have made them convincing. Class consciousness is not an absolute knowledge of which the proletarians are miraculously the trustees. It has to be formed and straightened out, but the only valid politics is the one which makes itself accepted by the workers. It is not a question of entrusting to the proletariat the task of deciphering the situation and elaborating theses and the political line. It is not even a question of continually translating into clear language for the proletarians the full revolutionary implication of their actions. This would sometimes make them feel that the weight of the resistance to be overcome is too heavy – a resistance which they will overcome without being aware that they are doing so; and, in any case, this would amount to warning the enemy. The theoretician therefore is in front of the proletariat, but, as Lenin said, only a step in front of it. In other words, the masses are never the simple means of a great politics which is worked out behind their backs. Led, but not maneuvered, the masses bring the seal of truth to the politics of the Party.

In what sense are we employing the word truth? It is not the truth of realism, the correspondence between the idea and the external thing, since the classless society is to be made, not already made, since the revolutionary politics is to be invented, not being already there, implicit in the existing proletariat, and since, finally, the proletariat is to be convinced and not merely consulted. Revolutionary politics cannot bypass this moment when it dares to step into the unknown. It is even its specific character to go into the unknown, since it wishes to put the proletariat in power as negation of capitalism and as sublation of itself. Thus, the truth of Marxism is not the truth one attributes to the natural sciences, the similarity of an idea and its external *ideatum*;[29] it is rather *nonfalsity*, the maximum guarantee against error that men may demand and get. The theoretician and the proletarians have to make a history in which they are included. They are therefore, at the same time, subjects and objects of their undertaking, and this creates for them a simultaneous possibility of understanding history, of finding a truth in it, and of being mistaken as to its developing meaning. We can say, then, that there is truth when there is *no disagreement* between the theoreticians and the proletarians, when the political idea is not challenged by known facts, although one can never be sure that it will not be challenged at some future date. Truth itself is then conceived as a process of indefinite verification, and Marxism is, at one and the same time, a philosophy of violence and a philosophy without dogmatism. Violence is necessary only because there is no final truth in the contemplated world; violence cannot therefore pride itself on having an absolute truth. Certainly, in action, in revolutionary periods, violence has the aspect of dogma. But there remains a difference, which can be seen in the long run, between a new dogmatism and a politics which puts generalized self-criticism into power. The *Stimmung* of Lukács, and, we believe, of Marxism, is thus the conviction of being, not in the truth, but on the threshold of truth, which is, at the same time, very near, indicated by all the past and all the present, and at an infinite distance in a future which is to be made.

We have seen history trace a philosophical itinerary which is realized only through us and through our decision; we have seen the subject find its certitude in adhering to a historical force in which the subject recognizes itself because this force is the power of a principle of negativity and self-criticism. For Lukács the essential feature of Marxism as dialectical philosophy is this meeting of event and meaning. Josef Revai, one of his companions in this struggle, who hailed his book as an event[30] and who today has become one of his principal critics, went so far as to propose a sort of Marxist irrationalism. Lukács himself carries out Marx's program, which is to destroy speculative philosophy but to do so by realizing it. The problem of the thing-in-itself, says Revai, reappears in the philosophy of history under the form of a divergence between actual history and the image we ourselves make of it; to Lukács he objects that

> The identical subject-object of the capitalistic society is not identifiable with the unique subject of all history, which is postulated only as correlative and cannot be embodied concretely. ...The modern proletariat which fights for communism is not at all the subject of ancient or feudal society. It understands these epochs as its own past and as stages which lead to itself. Thus it is not their subject.[31]

The proletariat "projects" a subject into the past which totalizes the experience of the past and undoubtedly projects into the empty future a subject which concentrates the meaning of the future. This is a well-founded "conceptual mythology," but a mythology, since the proletariat is not truly able to enter into a precapitalistic past or a postcapitalistic future. The proletariat does not realize the identification of subject and history. It is nothing but the "carrier"[32] of a myth which presents this identification as desirable. This extension offered by Revai reduces Lukács' philosophical effort to nothing because, if the proletariat is only the carrier of a myth, the philosopher, even if he judges this myth to be well founded, decides this in his profound wisdom or unlimited audacity, which becomes a court of last appeal. In such a situation the historical movement which puts the proletariat in power no longer has philosophical substance. It no longer has this privilege, which is also a duty, of being the realization of the true society and of the truth. Lukács' effort was precisely to show that the empirical proletariat, surpassed by the richness of a history which it cannot represent to itself either as it was or as it will be, retains, nevertheless, an implicit totality and is in itself the universal subject which, because it is self-critical and sublates itself, can become for itself only through the indefinite development of the classless society. The essential feature of Lukács' thought was no longer to put the total meaning of history in a mythical "world spirit" but on a level with the proletarians' condition in a provable and verifiable process without an occult background. Revai stated that Marx "introduced the future into the domain of the revolutionary dialectic, not as positing a goal or an end, or as the necessary advent of a natural law, but as an active reality which dwells in the present and determines it."[33] This hold on the future – and, moreover, on the past, which remains to be unveiled in its true light – was, for Lukács, guaranteed to the proletariat because the proletariat is the work of negativity. If the proletariat is nothing but a carrier of myths, the whole meaning of the revolutionary enterprise is in danger.

This meaning, according to Lukács, is not entirely defined by any particular objective, not even those which revolutionary politics proposes for itself day by day, not even by the ideology diffused by this politics. The meaning of the revolution is to be revolution, that is to say, universal criticism, and, in particular, criticism of itself. The characteristic of historical materialism, he said, is to apply itself to itself, that is to say, to hold each of its formulations as provisional and relative to a phase of development and, by constantly refining itself, to proceed toward a truth which is always to come. Take, for example, the ideology of historical materialism. When the foundations of capitalistic society are destroyed and the proletariat takes power, said Lukács, the doctrine "changes function." Its purpose before was to discredit bourgeois ideologies (even if they contained some truth) by unmasking the interests they defended. It was then one of the weapons of the proletarian struggle. When the proletariat directs its struggle from above, when the management of the economy begins to obey its demands and to follow human norms, true knowledge and a regression of ideologies, including those used at first by the proletariat, inevitably accompany the development of production. The solidarity of "matter" and spirit, which in the capitalistic phase of history meant the decadence of a knowledge which no longer expressed the social totality and served only to mask it, now means a liberation of both knowledge and production. It is, then, the task of historical materialism to recognize what was purely polemical in the representations of history with which it had satisfied itself, and to develop into true knowledge as society develops into classless society. And Lukács invited his country's sociologists to rediscover the richness of the precapitalistic past beyond Engels' explanatory diagrams.[34]

The coming-to-be of truth, the core of history, gives to Marxism the validity of a strict philosophy and distinguishes it from any kind of psychologism and historicism. In this regard, Lukács thinks that the vague slogan of humanism should be reconsidered. The very concept of man must be rendered dialectical; and if by "man" one understood a positive nature or attributes, Lukács would no more accept this idol than any other. We have seen that, if one goes deeply enough into relativism, one finds there a transcendence of relativism, and one would miss this transcendence if one were to absolutize the relative. Man is not the measure of all things if man is a species or even a psychic phenomenon equipped with a certain set of principles or an unconditional will. "The measure," says Lukács, "should itself be measured,"[35] and it can be measured only by truth. Under the myth of Platonic recollection[36] there is this always valid view that truth is of another species than the positivity of being, that it is elsewhere, that it is to be made. "The criterion for correctness of thought is without doubt reality. But reality does not exist; it becomes; and it does not become without the collaboration of thought (*nicht ohne Zutun des Denkens*)."[37]

> ...the criterion of truth is provided by relevance to reality. This reality is by no means identical with empirical existence. This reality is not, it becomes. ...But when the truth of becoming is the future that is to be created but has not yet been born, when it is the new that resides in the tendencies that (with our conscious aid) will be realized, then the question whether thought is a reflection appears quite senseless.[38]

What worries Lukács in humanism is that it offers us a given being to admire. To put man in the place of God is to displace, defer, and "abstractly negate"[39] the absolute.

Our task, rather, is to make the abstract fluid, diffuse it in history, "understand" it as process.

Nothing is further from Marxism than positivistic prose: dialectical thought is always in the process of extracting from each phenomenon a truth which goes beyond it, waking at each moment our astonishment at the world and at history. This "philosophy of history" does not so much give us the keys of history as it restores history to us as permanent interrogation. It is not so much a certain truth hidden behind empirical history that it gives us; rather it presents empirical history as the genealogy of truth. It is quite superficial to say that Marxism unveils the meaning of history to us: it binds us to our time and its partialities; it does not describe the future for us; it does not stop our questioning – on the contrary, it intensifies it. It shows us the present worked on by a self-criticism, a power of negation and of sublation, a power which has historically been delegated to the proletariat. Max Weber ended by seeing in our historical participation an initiation into the universe of culture and, through that, into all times. For Lukács, it is not only the thought of the historian or the theoretician but a class which thus transforms the particular into the universal. But for him, as for Weber, knowledge is rooted in existence, where it also finds its limits. The dialectic is the very life of this contradiction. It is the series of progressions which it accomplishes. It is a history which makes itself and which nevertheless is to be made, a meaning which is never invalid but is always to be rectified, to be taken up again, to be maintained in the face of danger, a knowledge limited by no positive irrationality but a knowledge which does not actually contain the totality of accomplished and still to be accomplished reality and whose ability to be exhaustive is yet to be factually proved. It is a history-reality which is judge or criterion of all our thoughts but which itself is nothing else than the advent of consciousness, so that we do not have to obey it passively but must think it in accordance with our own strength. These reversible relationships prove that, when Marxism focuses everything through the perspective of the proletariat, it focuses on a principle of universal strife and intensifies human questioning instead of ending it.

If we have undertaken to recall Lukács' attempt (very freely, and emphasizing certain points that in his work were only indicated), it is not because something of it remains in today's Marxism or even because it is one of those truths which only by chance miss the historical record. We shall see, on the contrary, that there was something justified in the opposition it encountered. But it was necessary to recall this lively and vigorous attempt, in which the youth of revolution and Marxism lives again, in order to measure today's communism, to realize what it has renounced and to what it has resigned itself. By thus remaining in the superstructures, by trying to find out how communism theoretically conceives the relationships between subject and history, one undoubtedly skims over political history, but a certain sense of its evolution appears with an incomparable distinctness. The intellectual history of communism is not indifferent – even, and especially, for a Marxist; it is one of the detectors of communist reality. Perhaps, in the end, the "detour" via philosophy is much less conjectural than a political, social, or economic analysis which, in the absence of sufficient information, is often only a construct in disguise. Let us try, then, to ask the communist question once again by confronting Lukács' attempt with the orthodox philosophy that was preferred to it.

NOTES

1 We are especially thinking of his 1923 book, *Geschichte und Klassenbewusstsein* (History and Class Consciousness).

2 Thus, despite Engels, Lukács refuses to admit the prime importance of the dialectic of nature – nature is unaware of the subject. But the passage of the subject into the object and of the object into the subject is the driving force of dialectic. Only in a secondary or derivative sense is there a dialectic of nature. The nature that *we* observe offers data of reciprocal action and quantitative leaps, but, as in the case of movement in Zeno, this dialectic fails. It is a destruction of opposites. They are resolved only in history and man.

3 Karl Marx and Friedrich Engels, *The German Ideology*, ed. S. Ryazanskaya (Moscow, 1964).

4 Karl Marx, *The Class Struggles in France, 1848 to 1850* (Moscow, 1952).

5 In German the complete sentence reads, "Er entdeckte, dass das Kapital nicht eine Sache ist, sondern ein durch Sachen vermitteltes gesellschaftliches Verhältniss zwischen Personen" (Karl Marx, *Das Kapital* [Hamburg, 1890], I, 731; *Capital*, trans. Samuel Moore and Edward Aveling [New York, 1906], p. 839).

6 "... nur nicht immer in der vernünftigen Form," "Nachlass," I, 381, cited by Lukács in *Geschichte und Klassenbewusstsein* (Berlin, 1923), p. 32. English translation by Rodney Livingstone, *History and Class Consciousness* (Cambridge, Mass.: M.I.T. Press, 1971), p. 18. [In subsequent notes the German edition will be cited as *GK*, the translation as ET.]

7 *GK*, p. 162; ET, p. 146.

8 *GK*, p. 216; ET, p. 198.

9 Lukács sketches here a Marxist criticism of the idea of progress which would be full of lessons for contemporary Marxists who are so far removed from the dialectic that they often confuse it with the bourgeois optimism of progress. He says that the ideology of progress is an expedient which consists in placing a contradiction which has already been reduced to a minimum against the backdrop of an unlimited time and in supposing that it will there resolve itself. Progress dissolves the beginning and the end, in the historical sense, into a limitless natural process and hides from man his own role.

10 Marx did say that humanity does not ask questions which it cannot resolve. But this possibility is certainly not, in his eyes, a pre-existence of the solution in the problem since elsewhere he has admitted that history can fail. The solution is possible in the sense that no destiny opposes it or since, as Max Weber has said, there is no irrational reality. But indeterminate adversity without intention or law can cause it to miscarry.

11 *GK*, p. 61; ET, p. 50.

12 *GK*, p. 12; ET, p. xlvii.

13 Georg Lukács, *Karl Marx und Friedrich Engels als Literaturhistoriker* (Berlin, 1947); see, e.g., pp. 141, 150.

14 *GK*, p. 62; ET, p. 50.

15 *GK*, pp. 27–28; ET, p. 14.

16 *GK*, p. 190; ET, p. 174.

17 *GK*, p. 88; ET, p. 75.

18 *GK*, p. 193; ET, p. 176.

19 *GK*, p. 195; ET, p. 178.

20 *GK*, p. 14; ET, p. 2.

21 *GK*, pp. 206–7; ET, p. 189.

22 *GK*, p. 80; ET, p. 68.

23 Karl Marx, *The Holy Family*, cited by Lukács, *GK*, p. 57; ET, p. 46.

24 *GK*, p. 93; ET, p. 80.

25 Cited by Lukács, *GK*, p. 145; ET, p. 131.

26 *GK*, p. 146; ET, p. 132.

27 In a review of Bukharin's *Theory of Historical Materialism* (*Archiv für die Geschichte des Sozialismus und der Arbeiterbewegung*, XI [1925], 216–24), Lukács shows that, far from exhausting the historical activity of society, the technical derives from it. From the classical through the mediaeval economies, it is not technical changes which explain changes in modes of labor; on the contrary, these changes are understandable only through social history. More precisely, it is necessary to distinguish the results of

a technique (the results of classical techniques are sometimes superior to those of the Middle Ages) from its principle (that of mediaeval economy, regardless of its results, represents progress because the rationalization extends to modes of labor and the Middle Ages renounces servile labor). It is this new principle of free labor, the disappearance of the unlimited resources of servile labor, which demands the technical transformations of the Middle Ages, just as, in antiquity, it is the existence of servile manpower which blocks the development of corporations and professions and, finally, that of cities. In speaking of the change from the Middle Ages to capitalism, the decisive factor is not the coming of manufacturing, a completely quantitative change, but rather the division of labor, the relations of forces in the enterprise, the coming of mass consumption. Technical transformation happens when the "narrow technical base" of manufacturing comes into contradiction with the needs of production that it has engendered (*Das Kapital*, I, 333; ET, p. 404, cited by Lukács in the same review, p. 221). Techniques realized apart from man would be a "fetishistic transcendental principle in the face of man" (ibid., p. 219), but Marxism, on the contrary, wants "to reduce all economic and 'sociological' phenomena to a social relation of man with man" (ibid., p. 218).

28   *Ibid.*, p. 88; ET, p. 75.

29   In the already cited review of Bukharin's book, Lukács reproaches the author for having suggested that the date of events and the speed of the historical process are not predictable because we have "not as yet" the knowledge of their quantitative laws. For Lukács, the difference between history and nature is not this alone, which would be totally subjective: it is objective and qualitative. In social situations there are only "tendencies"; and this is so, not because we do not have sufficient knowledge of them, but because this mode of existence is essential to the social event. As he again writes in *History and Class Consciousness*, history is not "exact." The only exact sciences are those whose object is made up of constant elements. This is not the case with history if it is to be able to be transformed by a revolutionary praxis (*GK*, p. 18; ET, pp. 5–6).

30   Revai said that Lukács' book is "the first attempt to make conscious what is Hegelian in Marx, the dialectical 'it is'; by its depth, its richness of content, its art of testing apparently purely philosophical general propositions against concrete and particular problems, it is far superior to the works which until now have been dealing with the philosophical basis of Marxism as a special problem. Besides this, it is the first attempt to deal with the history of philosophy in terms of historical materialism, and, from a purely philosophical point of view, it is the first time we have indeed gone beyond a philosophy which hardens itself into a theory of knowledge" (Josef Revai, review of Lukács' *History and Class Consciousness, Archiv für die Geschichte des Sozialismus und der Arbeiterbewegung*, XI [1925], 227–36).

31   *Ibid.*, p. 235.

32   *Ibid.*

33   *Ibid.*, p. 233.

34   See "The Changing Function of Historical Materialism" in *GK*, pp. 229–60; ET, pp. 223–55.

35   *GK*, p. 204; ET, p. 187.

36   *GK*, p. 220; ET, pp. 201–2.

37   *GK*, p. 223; ET, p. 204 (modified).

38   *GK*, pp. 222–23; ET, pp. 203–4.

39   *GK*, p. 208; ET, p. 190.

5

Marcuse on Sartre

Herbert Marcuse (1898–1979) was one of the major representatives of Frankfurt School Critical Theory and in the 1960s became the most prominent figure of the American New Left. He studied with both Heidegger and Husserl, and his early work attempts to negotiate the relation between phenomenology and historical materialism. Throughout Marcuse's work there is an emphasis on negation, resistance and rebellion which suggests an almost romantic approach to radical freedom, an interest which might also be characterized as utopian. This existentialist orientation to freedom and action is juxtaposed, in Marcuse's work, with a recognition of the need to develop a critical theory of society. Marcuse's critical sociology combines insights from Hegel, Marx, Weber and Freud. Although he identified his work with Marxism, he was critical of state socialism and Communist Party orthodoxy, a critique substantiated in his book *Soviet Marxism: A Critical Analysis*. Marcuse's eclectic relation to Marxism owes more to the radicalism of the young Marx than to the more scientific critique of Marx's *Capital*.

Heidegger's *Being and Time* influenced Marcuse's early book *Hegel's Ontology and the Theory of Historicity* (1932). Marcuse subsequently re-evaluated his thought in the light of reading Marx's *Economic and Philosophical Manuscripts*. His approach emphasized the existential dynamics of the young Marx and a radical re-reading of Hegel. In the 1930s he wrote a number of key essays in the development of the Institute for Social Research and what became Frankfurt School Critical Theory, notably 'The Concept of Essence' and 'Philosophy and Critical Theory', essays subsequently collected in *Negations*. Marcuse developed his attempt to think through the difference between philosophy and social theory in *Reason and Revolution: Hegel and the Rise of Social Theory* (1941). As a way of reading Marxist existentialism back into Hegel, this work bears comparison with Alexandre Kojève's *Introduction to the Reading of Hegel*, which was influential on the French reception of Hegel. Marcuse's subsequent work, notably *Eros and Civilization* (1955), attempted to synthesize problems around labour and alienation through an amalgam of Marx and Freud. Highly influential on the emerging radicalism of sexual politics, Marcuse's thought became a target both for psychoanalytic critics and for those who rejected any synthesis of psychoanalysis with Marxism. Marcuse prefigures a range of arguments within post-structuralism and feminism while also galvanizing sceptical accounts of the history of sexuality, such as those of Michel Foucault. In *One Dimensional Man* (1964) Marcuse's account of capitalism as a totally administered society popularized themes in Adorno and Horkheimer's *Dialectic of Enlightenment*, although Marcuse remained more optimistic about the radical potential within contemporary society. His account of scientific 'reason' and the domination of nature more explicitly engages Max Weber's sociological accounts of rationalization and the 'spirit' of capitalism.

Marcuse's work has been overshadowed recently by the work of Adorno, Habermas and Foucault. This may be a reaction, as with Sartre, to Marcuse's public notoriety, or because his thought provides an accessible sketch of key themes with less difficulty, rigour or style. His work is nevertheless central to Frankfurt School Critical Theory and to a range of radical reinterpretations of Marxism, with intriguing resonances in the work of Slavoj Žižek. Marcuse's trajectory took him from the attempt to synthesize Heideggerian phenomenology and historical materialism into a new kind of Hegelian Marxism informed by Freud. This trajectory prefigured many of the key dialogues between French existentialism and Marxism, and provides the context for Marcuse's critical essay 'Sartre's Existentialism'. Marcuse provides a critical sketch both of Sartre's thought and of the tensions in own thought. In a later epilogue to this essay, Marcuse recognized that Sartre's subsequent thought developed a more sustained relation to Marxism and to this extent their respective careers responded to shared recognitions of the problems outlined in Marcuse's essay.

FURTHER READING

Primary works

Herbert Marcuse, *Counter-Revolution and Revolt* (Boston: Beacon Press, 1972); *Hegel's Ontology and the Theory of Historicity*, trans. Seyla Benhabib (Cambridge, MA: MIT, 1987); *Eros and Civilization: A Philosophical Inquiry into Freud* (Boston: Beacon Press, 1956); *From Luther to Popper*, trans. Joris De Bres (London: Verso, 1983), previously published as *Studies in Critical Philosophy* (1972); *One Dimensional Man: Studies in the Ideology of Advanced Industrial Society* (London: Routledge and Kegan Paul, 1964); *Reason and Revolution: Hegel and the Rise of Social Theory*, 2nd edition with Supplementary Chapter (London: Routledge & Kegan Paul, 1955; 1st edition 1941); *Negations: Essays in Critical Theory*, trans. Jeremy J. Shapiro (Harmondsworth: Penguin, 1968); *Soviet Marxism: A Critical Analysis* (London: Routledge and Kegan Paul, 1958); *Technology, War and Fascism: Collected Papers, Volume One*, ed. Douglas Kellner (London: Routledge, 1998); *Towards a Critical Theory of Society: Collected Papers, Volume Two*, ed. Douglas Kellner (London: Routledge, 2001).

Secondary works

C. Fred Alford, *Science and the Revenge of Nature: Marcuse and Habermas* (Gainesville: University of Florida Press, 1985).

Raymond Aron, *Marxism and the Existentialists* (New York: Harper and Row, 1969).

Ronald Aronson, *Jean-Paul Sartre – Philosophy in the World* (London: Verso, 1980).

John Bokina and Timothy J. Lukes, eds., *Marcuse: From the New Left to the Next Left* (Kansas: University Press of Kansas, 1994).

Peter Caws, *Sartre* (London: Routledge and Kegan Paul, 1979).

Wilfrid Desan, *The Marxism of Jean-Paul Sartre* (Garden City, NY: Doubleday, 1965).

Helmut Dubiel, *Theory and Politics: Studies in the Development of Critical Theory*, trans. Benjamin Gregg (Cambridge, MA: MIT, 1985).

Thomas R. Flynn, *Sartre and Marxist Existentialism* (Chicago: University of Chicago Press, 1984).

Vincent Geoghegan, *Reason and Eros: The Social Theory of Herbert Marcuse* (London: Pluto, 1981).

André Gorz, 'Sartre and Marx', *Western Marxism: A Critical Reader*, ed. New Left Review (London: Verso, 1977), pp. 176–200.

Jürgen Habermas, 'Psychic Thermidor and the Rebirth of Rebellious Subjectivity', *Habermas and Modernity*, ed. Richard J. Bernstein (Cambridge: Polity, 1985), pp. 67–77.

Christina Howells, ed., *The Cambridge Companion to Sartre* (Cambridge: Cambridge University Press, 1992).

Martin Jay, *The Dialectical Imagination: A History of the Frankfurt School and the Institute of Social Research, 1923–50* (London: Heinemann, 1973).

Barry Katz, *Herbert Marcuse and the Art of Liberation: An Intellectual Biography* (London: Verso, 1982).

Douglas Kellner, *Herbert Marcuse and the Crisis of Marxism* (London: Macmillan, 1984).

Alexandre Kojève, *Introduction to the Reading of Hegel*, trans. James H. Nichols, Jr. (Ithaca and London: Cornell University Press, 1980).

Timothy J. Lukes, *The Flight into Inwardness: An Exposition and Critique of Herbert Marcuse's Theory of Liberative Aesthetics* (London and Toronto: Associated University Presses, 1986).

Alasdair MacIntyre, *Marcuse* (London: Fontana / Collins, 1970).

William McBride, *Sartre's Political Theory* (Bloomington: Indiana University Press, 1991).

Alain Martineau, *Herbert Marcuse's Utopia* (Montreal: Harvest Press, 1986).

Drew Milne, 'Between Philosophy and Critical Theory: Marcuse', *Edinburgh Encyclopedia of Continental Philosophy*, ed. Simon Glendinning (Edinburgh: Edinburgh University Press, 1999), pp. 461–70.

Robert Pippin, Andrew Feenberg and Charles P. Webel, eds., *Marcuse: Critical Theory and the Promise of Utopia* (London: Macmillan, 1988).

Morton Schoolman, *The Imaginary Witness: The Critical Theory of Herbert Marcuse* (New York: Free Press, 1980).

Bernhard Waldenfels, Jan M. Broekman and Ante Pazanin, eds., *Phenomenology and Marxism*, trans. J. Claude Evans, Jr (London: Routledge and Kegan Paul, 1984).

Joel Whitebook, *Perversion and Utopia: A Study in Psychoanalysis and Critical Theory* (Cambridge, MA: MIT, 1995).

Herbert Marcuse, 'Sartre's Existentialism' (1948), *Studies in Critical Philosophy*, trans. Joris De Bres (London: New Left Books, 1972), pp. 159–189 (paperback edition retitled *From Luther to Popper*; London: Verso, 1983).

Introduction

'The following pages deal with the sentiment of absurdity which prevails in our world.' This opening sentence of Albert Camus's *Le Mythe de Sisyphe* conveys the climate in which Existentialism originates. Camus does not belong to the existentialist school, but the basic experience which permeates his thought is also at the root of Existentialism. The time is that of the totalitarian terror: the Nazi regime is at the height of its power; France is occupied by the German armies. The values and standards of western civilization are co-ordinated and superseded by the reality of the fascist system. Once again, thought is thrown back upon itself by a reality which contradicts all promises and ideas, which refutes rationalism as well as religion, idealism as well as materialism. Once again, thought finds itself in the Cartesian situation and asks for the one certain and evident truth which may make it still possible to live. The question does not aim at any abstract idea but at the individual's concrete existence: what is the certain and evident experience which can provide the foundation for his life here and now, in this world?

Like Descartes, this philosophy finds its foundation in the self-certainty of the Cogito, in the consciousness of the Ego. But whereas for Descartes the self-certainty of the Cogito revealed a rational universe, governed by meaningful laws and mechanisms, the Cogito now is thrown into an 'absurd' world in which the brute fact of death and the irretrievable process of Time deny all meaning. The Cartesian subject, conscious of its power, faced an objective world which rewarded calculation, conquest, and domination; now the subject itself has become absurd and its world void of purpose and hope. The Cartesian *res cogitans* was opposed by a *res extensa* which responded to the former's knowledge and action; now the subject exists in an iron circle of frustration and failure. The Cartesian world, although held together by its own rationality, made allowance for a God who cannot deceive; now the world is godless in its very essence and leaves no room for any transcendental refuge.

The reconstruction of thought on the ground of absurdity does not lead to irrationalism. This philosophy is no revolt against reason; it does not teach abnegation or the *credo quia absurdum*. In the universal destruction and disillusion, one thing maintains itself: the relentless clarity and lucidity of the mind which refuses all shortcuts and escapes, the constant awareness that life has to be lived 'without appeal' and without protection. Man accepts the challenge and seeks his freedom and happiness in a world where there is no hope, sense, progress and morrow. This life is nothing but 'consciousness and revolt', and defiance is its only truth. Camus's *Mythe de Sisyphe* recaptures the climate of Nietzsche's philosophy:

> Absurd man envisages a burning and icy universe, transparent and limited, where nothing is possible but everything is given, beyond which is extinction and the void.[1]

Thought moves in the night, but it is the night

> of desperation which remains lucid, polar night, eve of the mind out of which will perhaps rise that white and integral clarity which designs every object in the light of the intellect.[2]

The experience of the 'absurd world' gives rise to a new and extreme rationalism which separates this mode of thought from all fascist ideology. But the new rationalism defies systematization. Thought is held in abeyance between the 'sentiment of absurdity' and its comprehension, between art and philosophy. Here, the ways part. Camus rejects existential philosophy: the latter must of necessity 'explain' the inexplicable, rationalize the absurdity and thus falsify its reality. To him, the only adequate expression is living the absurd life, and the artistic creation, which refuses to rationalize ('raisonner le concret') and which 'covers with images that which makes no sense' ('ce qui n'a pas de raison'). Sartre, on the other hand, attempts to develop the new experience into a philosophy of the concrete human existence: to elaborate the structure of 'being in an absurd world' and the ethics of 'living without appeal'.

The development of Sartre's Existentialism spans the period of the war, the Liberation, and reconstruction. Neither the triumph nor the collapse of fascism produces any fundamental change in the existentialist conception. In the change of the political systems, in war and peace, before and after the totalitarian terror – the structure of the 'réalité humaine' remains the same. 'Plus ça change, plus c'est la même chose.' The historical absurdity which consists in the fact that after the defeat of fascism the world did not collapse, but relapsed into its previous forms, that it did not leap into the realm of freedom but restored with honour the old management – this absurdity lives in the existentialist conception. But it lives in the existentialist conception as a metaphysical, not as a historical fact. The experience of the absurdity of the world, of man's failure and frustration, appears as the experience of his ontological condition. As such, it transcends his historical condition. Sartre defines Existentialism as a doctrine according to which 'existence precedes and perpetually creates the essence'.[3] But in his philosophy, the existence of man, in creating his essence, is itself determined by the perpetually identical ontological structure of man, and the various concrete forms of man's existence serve only as examples of this structure. Sartre's existential analysis is a strictly philosophical one in the sense that it abstracts from the historical factors which constitute the empirical concreteness: the latter merely illustrates Sartre's metaphysical and meta-historical conceptions. In so far as Existentialism is a philosophical doctrine, it remains an idealistic doctrine: it hypostatizes specific historical conditions of human existence into ontological and metaphysical characteristics. Existentialism thus becomes part of the very ideology which it attacks, and its radicalism is illusory. Sartre's *L'Être et le Néant*, the philosophical foundation of Existentialism, is an ontological-phenomenological treatise on human freedom and could as such come out under the German occupation (1943). The essential freedom of man, as Sartre sees it, remains the same before, during, and after the totalitarian enslavement of man. For freedom is the very structure of human being and cannot be annihilated even by the most adverse conditions: man is free even in the hands of the executioner. Is this not Luther's comforting message of Christian liberty?

Sartre's book draws heavily on the philosophy of German idealism, in which Luther's Protestantism has found its transcendental stabilization. At the outset, Sartre's concept of the free subject is a reinterpretation of Descartes's Cogito, but its development follows the tradition of German rather than French rationalism. Moreover Sartre's book is in large parts a restatement of Hegel's *Phenomenology of Mind* and Heidegger's *Sein und Zeit*. French Existentialism revives many of the intellectual tendencies which were prevalent in the Germany of the twenties and which came to naught in the Nazi system.

But while these aspects seem to commit Existentialism to the innermost tendencies of bourgeois culture, others seem to point in a different direction. Sartre himself has protested against the interpretation of human freedom in terms of an essentially 'internal' liberty – an interpretation which his own analysis so strongly suggests – and he has explicitly linked up his philosophy with the theory of the proletarian revolution.[4]

Existentialism thus offers two apparently contradictory aspects: one the modern reformulation of the perennial ideology, the transcendental stabilization of human freedom in the face of its actual enslavement; the other the revolutionary theory which implies the negation of this entire ideology. The two conflicting aspects reflect the inner movement of existentialist thought[5] which reaches its object, the concrete human existence, only where it ceases to analyse it in terms of the 'free subject' and describes it in terms of what it has actually become: a 'thing' in a reified world. At the end of the road, the original position is reversed: the realization of human freedom appears, not in the *res cogitans*, the 'Pour-soi', but in the *res extensa*, in the body as thing. Here, Existentialism reaches the point where philosophical ideology would turn into revolutionary theory. But at the same point, Existentialism arrests this movement and leads it back into the ideological ontology.

The elucidation of this hidden movement requires a critical restatement of some of the basic conceptions of *L'Être et le Néant*.

I

L'Être et le Néant starts with the distinction of two types of being – Being-for-itself (Pour-soi; consciousness, cogito) and Being-in-itself (En-soi). The latter (roughly identical with the world of things, objectivity) is characterized by having no relation to itself, being what it is, plainly and simply, beyond all becoming, change, and temporality (which emerge only with the Pour-soi), in the mode of utter contingency. In contrast, the Being-for-itself, identical with the human being, is the free subject which continually 'creates' its own existence; Sartre's whole book is devoted to its analysis. The analysis proceeds from the question as to the 'relationship' (*rapport*) between these two types of being. Following Heidegger, subjectivity and objectivity are understood, not as two separate entities between which a relationship must only be established, but as essential 'togetherness', and the question aims at the full and concrete structure of this togetherness.

> The concrete can be only the synthetic totality of which consciousness as well as phenomenon (Being-in-itself) constitute but moments. The concrete – that is man in the world. . . .[6]

The question thus aims at the full and concrete structure of the human being as being-in-the-world (*la réalité humaine*).

In order to elucidate this structure, the analysis orients itself on certain typical 'human attitudes' (*conduites exemplaires*). The first of these is the attitude of questioning (*l'attitude interrogative*), the specific human attitude of interrogating, reflecting on himself and his situation at any given moment. The interrogation implies a threefold (potential) negativity: the not-knowing, the permanent possibility of a negative answer, and the limitation expressed in the affirmative answer: 'It is thus and not otherwise.' The interrogative attitude thus brings to the fore the fact that man is surrounded by and permeated with negativity:

> It is the permanent possibility of not-being, outside of us and in us, which conditions our questions about being (EN, p. 40).

However, the negativity implied in the interrogative attitude serves only as an example and indication of the fundamental fact that negativity surrounds and permeates man's entire existence and all his attitudes:

> The necessary condition which makes it possible to say 'no' is that the not-being is perpetually present, in us and outside of us, is that the void haunts being (EN, p. 47).

Negativity originates with and constantly accompanies the human being, manifesting itself in a whole series of negations (*néantisations*) with which the human being experiences, comprehends, and acts upon himself and the world. The totality of these negations constitutes the very being of the subject: man exists 'as perpetually detaching himself from what is' (EN, p. 73); he transcends himself as well as his objects toward his and their possibilities, he is always 'beyond' his situation, 'wanting' his full reality. By the same token, man does not simply exist like a thing (*en soi*) but makes himself and his world exist, 'creates' himself and his world at any moment and in any situation.

This characterization of the 'réalité humaine' (which is hardly more than a restatement of the idealistic conception of the Cogito or Selfconsciousness, especially in the form in which the *Phenomenology of Mind* develops this conception) furnishes the fundamental terms of Sartre's Existentialism – the terms which guide the subsequent development of his philosophy. There is first of all the identification of the human being with liberty. The series of negations by which man constitutes himself and his world at the same time constitutes his essential freedom:

> [Liberty] arises with the negation of the appeals of the world, it appears from the moment when I detach myself from the world where I had engaged myself so that I perceive myself as consciousness (EN, p. 77).

Human freedom thus conceived is not one quality of man among others, nor something which man possesses or lacks according to his historical situation, but is the human being itself and as such:

> That which we call liberty is therefore indistinguishable from the being of the 'human reality'. Man does not first exist in order to be free subsequently, but there is no difference between his being and his free-being [being-free] (EN, p. 61).

Secondly, from the identification of the human being with freedom follows the full and unqualified responsibility of man for his being. In order to concretize his idea of freedom and responsibility, Sartre adapts Heidegger's emphasis on the *Geworfenheit* of man into a pre-given 'situation'. Man always finds himself and his world in a situation which appears as an essentially external one (the situation of his family, class, nation, race, etc.). Likewise, the objects of his environment are not his own: they were manufactured as commodities; their form and their use are pre-given and standardized. However, this essential 'contingency' of man's situation is the very condition of life of his freedom and responsibility. His contingent situation becomes 'his' in so far as he 'engages' himself in it, accepts or rejects it. No power in heaven or on earth can force him to abdicate his freedom: he himself, and he alone is to decide and choose what he is.

Thirdly, man is by definition (that is to say, by virtue of the fact that he is, as 'être-pour-soi', the permanent realization of his possibilities) nothing but self-creation. His Being is identical with his activity (action), or rather with his (free) acts. 'L'homme est ce qu'il fait', and, vice versa, everything that is is a 'human enterprise'.

> Man engages in his life, designs its shape, and outside this shape, there is nothing. ... Man is nothing else but a series of enterprises (undertakings), he is the sum total, the organization, the ensemble of the relationships which constitute these enterprises (EN, pp. 57ff.).

Human existence is at any moment a 'project' that is being realized, freely designed and freely executed by man himself, or, man's existence is nothing but his own fundamental project. This dynamics is based on the fact that man's actual situation never coincides with his possibilities, that his Being is essentially being-in-want-of (*manque*). However, the want is not want of something, so that the want would disappear with its satisfaction; it is the manifestation of the basic negativity of the human being:

> Human reality is not something which first exists in order to want for this or that later; it exists as want and in close synthetic union with what it wants. ... In its coming into being, (human) reality is cognizant of itself as an incomplete being. ... Human reality is a perpetual reaching for a coincidence which is never accomplished (EN, pp. 132ff.).

The existentialist dynamics is thus not an aimless and senseless one: the 'projet fondamental' which is man's existence aims at the ever lacking coincidence with himself, at his own completeness and totality. In other words, the *Pour-soi* constantly strives to become *En-soi*, to become the stable and lasting foundation of his own being. But this project, which would make the *Pour-soi* an *En-soi* and vice versa, is eternally condemned to frustration, and this ontological frustration shapes and permeates the entire Being of man:

> Human reality suffers in its being because it emerges into existence as though perpetually haunted by a totality which it is without being able to be it, since in effect it cannot attain Being-in-itself without losing Being-for-itself. It is therefore essentially unhappy consciousness (EN, p. 134).

Sartre's ontological analysis has herewith reached its centre: the determination of the human being as frustration, *Scheitern*, 'échec'. All fundamental human relationships, the entire 'human enterprise' are haunted by this frustration. However, precisely because frustration is permanent and inevitable (since it is the ontological characteristic of the human being), it is also the very foundation and condition of human freedom. The latter is what it is only in so far as it 'engages' man within his contingent situation, which in turn, since it is a pre-given situation, prevents him once and for all from ever becoming the founder of his own Being-for-himself. The circle of ontological identifications is thus closed: it combines Being and Nothing, freedom and frustration, self-responsible choice and contingent determination. The *coincidentia oppositorum* is accomplished, not through a dialectical process, but through their simple establishment as ontological characteristics. As such, they are transtemporally simultaneous and structurally identical.

The ontological analysis of the *l'être-pour-soi* furnishes the framework for the interpretation of the *l'existence d'autrui*, of the Other. This transition presents a decisive methodological problem. Sartre has followed so closely the idealistic conception of Self-Consciousness (*Cogito*) as the transcendental origin and 'creator' of all Being that he constantly faces the danger of transcendental solipsism. He takes up the challenge in an excellent critique of Husserl and Heidegger (and Hegel), in which he shows that their attempts to establish the Being of the Other as an independent ontological fact fail, that in all of them the existence of the Other is more or less absorbed into the existence of the Ego (EN, pp. 288ff.). Sartre himself renounces all efforts to derive ontologically the existence of the Other:

> The existence of the Other has the nature of a contingent and irreducible fact. The Other is encountered; he is not constituted (by the Ego) (EN, p. 307).

However, he continues, the Cogito provides the only point of departure for the understanding of the existence of the Other because all 'fait contingent', all 'nécessit de fait' is such only for and by virtue of the Cogito:

> The *Cogito* (examined once again) must cast me outside of itself onto the Other. ... We must ask the Being-for-itself to give us the Being-for-another; absolute immanence must cast us back into absolute transcendence (EN, pp. 308ff.).

The experience of the Cogito which establishes the independent existence of the Other is that of 'being-looked-at by another [man]'. The relation of being-seen by another (man) constitutes, for the Cogito, 'l'existence d'autrui':

> My perception of the Other in the world as probably being (a) man relates to my permanent possibility of being-seen-by-him. ... On principle, the Other is he who looks at me (EN, p. 315).

'Le regard d'autrui' becomes constitutive of the fundamental interhuman relationships. Sartre illustrates this by the example of a jealous lover who peeps through a keyhole. In this situation, he suddenly feels himself seen by another man. With this glance, he becomes somebody whom another (man) knows in his innermost being, who *is* that which the other sees. His own possibilities are taken away from him (he cannot hide where he intended to hide, he cannot know what he desired to know, etc.); his entire world at once has a new, different focus, structure, and meaning: it emerges as the other's world and as a world-for-the-other. His being thus emerges, in a strict sense, as being 'at the liberty' of the other: from now on,

> it is a question of my being as it is inscribed in and through the liberty of the Other. Everything occurs as though I possessed a dimension of being from which I was separated by a profound void, and this void is the liberty of the Other (EN, p. 320).

The other's glance turns me into an object, turns my existence into 'nature', alienates my possibilities, 'steals' my world.

> By the very emergence of his existence, I have an appearance, a nature; the existence of the Other is my original sin (EN, p. 321).

The appearance of the Other thus transforms the world of the Ego into a world of conflict, competition, alienation, 'reification'. The Other, that is 'la mort cachée de mes possibilités'; the Other, that is he who usurps my world, who makes me an 'object of appreciation and appraisal', who gives me my 'value'.

> Thus, being seen constitutes me as being without any defence against a liberty which is not my liberty. In this sense we may consider ourselves as 'slaves' in so far as we appear to the Other. But this bondage is not the historical and surmountable result of the life of an abstract consciousness (EN, pp. 391ff.).

This conception of the Other as the irreconcilable antagonist of the Ego now serves as the basis for Sartre's interpretation of the interhuman relationships. They are primarily corporal relationships (as already indicated by the constitutive role attributed to the '*regard*'). However, the body enters these relationships not merely as a physical-biological 'thing' but as the manifestation of the individuality and contingency of the Ego in his 'rapport transcendant' with the world (EN, pp. 391ff.). The original experience of the Other as the source of alienation and reification calls for two fundamental reactions which constitute the two fundamental types of interhuman relationships: (1) the attempt, on the part of the Ego, to deny the liberty and mastery of the Other and to make him into an objective thing, totally dependent on the Ego; or, (2) to assimilate his liberty, to accept it as the foundation of the Ego's own liberty and thereby to regain the free Ego (EN, p. 430). The first attitude leads to Sadism, the second to Masochism. But the essential frustration which marks all existential 'projects' of the Ego also characterizes these attempts: the complete enslavement of the Other transforms him into a thing, annihilates him *as* the (independent) Other and thus annihilates the very goal which the Ego desired to attain. Similarly, the complete assimilation to the Other transforms the Ego into a thing, annihilates it as a (free) subject and thus annihilates the very freedom which the Ego desired to regain. The frustration suffered in the sadistic attitude leads to the adoption of the masochistic attitude, and vice versa:

> Each of them implies the death of the other, that is, the failure of the one motivates the adoption of the other. Therefore, my relations with the Other are not dialectical but circular, although each attempt is enriched by the failure of the other (EN, p. 230).

The two fundamental human relationships produce and destroy themselves 'en cercle' (EN, p. 431).

The only remaining possible attitude toward the Other is that which aims directly at his utter destruction, namely, hate. However, this attitude too fails to achieve the desired result: the liberation of the Ego. For even after the death of the Other (or the Others), he (or they) remain as 'having been' and thus continue to haunt the Ego's conscience.

The conclusion: since

> all the complex attitudes of men toward each other are only variations of these two attitudes (and of hate) (EN, 477)

there is no breaking out of the circle of frustration. On the other hand, man *must* 'engage' in one of these attitudes because his very reality consists in nothing but such 'engagement'. Thus, after the failure of each attempt,

> there is no alternative left for the Being-for-itself but to return into the circle and to be tossed about indefinitely from one to the other of these two fundamental attitudes (EN, p. 484).

Here, the image of Sisyphus and his absurd task appears most naturally as the very symbol of man's existence. Here, too, Sartre deems it appropriate to add in a footnote that 'these considerations do not exclude the possibility of a morality of liberation and salvation'; however, such a morality requires a 'radical conversion, which we cannot discuss in this place'.

II

The main ontological argument is concluded by this analysis of the fundamental interhuman relationships; the remaining part of the book is taken up by a synopsis of the 'réalité humaine' as it has emerged in the preceding interpretation. The synopsis is guided by the concept of freedom. The ontological analysis had started with the identification of Ego (Cogito) and freedom. The subsequent development of the existential characteristics of the Ego had shown how his freedom is inextricably tied up within the contingency of his 'situation', and how all attempts to make himself the free foundation of his existence are eternally condemned to frustration. The last part of Sartre's book resumes the discussion at this point in order to justify finally, in the face of these apparent contradictions, the ontological identification of human being and freedom.

For Sartre, the justification cannot be that which is traditionally featured in idealistic philosophy, namely, the distinction between transcendental and empirical freedom. This solution cannot suffice for him because his analysis of the Ego does not remain within the transcendental-ontological dimension. Ever since his Ego, in the Third Part of his book, had to acknowledge the existence of the Other as a plain 'nécessité de fait', his philosophy had left the realm of pure ontology and moved within the ontic-empirical world.

Sartre thus cannot claim that his philosophy of freedom is a transcendental-ontological one and therefore neither committed nor equipped to go into the (empirical) actuality of human freedom. Quite in contrast to Heidegger (whose existential analysis claims to remain within the limits of pure ontology), Sartre's philosophy professes to be an '-ism', Existentialism, that is to say, a *Weltanschauung* which involves a definite attitude toward life, a definite morality, 'une doctrine d'action' (EH, p. 95). Sartre must therefore show the actuality of the entire 'existentialist' conception of man. The last part of *L'Être et le Néant* is chiefly dedicated to this task.

Sartre attempts to demonstrate that the ontological definition actually defines the 'réalité humaine', that man is in *reality* the free being-for-himself which the existential ontology posits.

We have seen that, according to Sartre, man, as a Being-for-itself that does not simply exist but exists only in so far as it 'realizes' itself, is essentially act, action, activity.

> Man is free because he is not merely himself but present to himself. The being which (merely) is what it is cannot be free. Freedom is, actually, the void which is in man's heart and which forces the human reality to *create itself* rather than to *be* (EN, p. 516).

This 'se faire' applies to every single moment in man's life: whatever he does or does not do, whatever he is or is not − he himself has 'chosen' it, and his choice was absolutely and perfectly free:

> Our existence is actually our original choice (EN, p. 539).

As against this proclamation of the absolute freedom of man, the objection arises immediately that man is in reality determined by his specific socio-historical situation, which in turn determines the scope and content of his liberty and the range of his 'choice'.

'La réalité humaine', that is, for example, a French worker under the German occupation, or a sales clerk in New York. His liberty is limited, and his choice is prescribed to such an extent that their interpretation in the existentialist terms appear like mere mockery. Sartre accepts the challenge and sets out to prove that even in a situation of extreme determinateness, man is and remains absolutely free. True, he says, the worker may live in a state of actual enslavement, oppression, and exploitation, but he has freely 'chosen' this state, and he is free to change it at any moment. He has freely chosen it because 'enslavement', 'oppression', 'exploitation' have meaning only for and by the 'Pour-soi' which has posited and accepted these 'values' and suffers them. And he is free to change his condition at any moment because these values will cease to exist for him as soon as he ceases to posit, accept, and suffer them. Sartre understands this freedom as a strictly individual liberty, the decision to change the situation as a strictly individual project, and the act of changing as a strictly individual enterprise.

The fact that for the individual worker such individual action would mean loss of his job and probably lead to starvation, imprisonment, and even death, does not invalidate his absolute freedom, for it is again a matter of free choice to value life and security higher than starvation, imprisonment, and death. The existentialist proposition thus leads inevitably to the reaffirmation of the old idealistic conception that man is free even in chains, or, as Sartre formulates it: 'but the executioner's tools cannot dispense us from being free' (EN, p. 587).

However, Sartre does not want to have this proposition interpreted in the sense of a merely 'internal' freedom. The slave is literally and actually free to break his chains, for the very meaning ('sens') of his chains reveals itself only in the light of the goal which he chooses: to remain a slave or to risk the worst in order to liberate himself from enslavement.

> If, for example, he chooses to revolt, slavery, far from being first an obstacle to this revolt, takes its meaning and its coefficient of adversity only from this revolt (EN, p. 635).

All adversities, obstacles, limitations to our liberty, are thus posited by and emerge ('surgir') with ourselves; they are parts of the free 'project' which is our existence (EN, pp. 562, 569).

> The coefficient of adversity of things...cannot be an argument against our freedom because it is *through us*, that is, through the preliminary setting of a goal that this coefficient of adversity emerges. The very rock which displays profound resistance if I wish to change its position, will, on the other hand, be a precious help to me if I wish to climb it in order to contemplate the countryside (EN, p. 562).

Sartre does not hesitate to push this conception to its last consequences. Being a Frenchman, a Southerner, a worker, a Jew – is the result of the 'Pour-soi's' own 'making'. By the same token, all the restrictions, obstacles, prohibitions which society places upon the Jew 'exist' only because and in so far as the Jew 'chooses' and accepts them:

> 'No Jews allowed here', 'Jewish restaurant, Aryans forbidden to enter', etc., can only have meaning on and through the foundation of my free choice (EN, p. 607).

> It is only by recognizing the liberty...of the anti-Semites and by assuming this being-Jewish which I represent to them, that being-Jewish will appear as the external objective limit of my situation. If, on the other hand, it pleases me to consider them simply as objects, my being-Jewish disappears immediately to give way to the simple consciousness of being a free transcendence (EN, p. 610).

The treatise on human freedom has here reached the point of self-abdication. The persecution of the Jews, and 'les tenailles du bourreau' are the terror which is the world today, they are the brute reality of unfreedom. To the existentialist philosopher, however, they appear as examples of the existence of human freedom. The fact that Sartre's demonstration is ontologically correct and a time-honoured and successful feature of idealism only proves the remoteness of this demonstration from the 'réalité humaine'. If philosophy, by virtue of its existential-ontological concepts of man or freedom, is capable of demonstrating that the persecuted Jew and the victim of the executioner are and remain absolutely free and masters of a self-responsible choice, then these philosophical concepts have declined to the level of a mere ideology, an ideology which offers itself as a most handy justification for the persecutors and executioners – them-selves an important part of the 'réalité humaine'. It is true that the 'Pour-soi', *qua* 'Pour-soi', is and remains free in the hands of the numerous executioners who provide the numerous opportunities for exercising existential freedom, but this freedom has shrunk to a point where it is wholly irrelevant and thus cancels itself. The free choice between death and enslavement is neither freedom nor choice, because both alternatives destroy the 'réalité humaine' which is supposed to be freedom. Established as the locus of freedom in the midst of a world of totalitarian oppression, the 'Pour-soi', the Cartesian Cogito, is no longer the jumping-off point for the conquest of the intellectual and material world, but the last refuge of the individual in an 'absurd world' of prostration and failure. In Sartre's philosophy, this refuge is still equipped with all the paraphernalia which characterized the heydays of individualistic society. The 'Pour-soi' appears with the attributes of absolute autonomy, perpetual ownership, and perpetual appropriation (just as the Other appears as the one who usurps, appropriates, and appraises my world, as the 'thief' of my possibilities). Behind the nihilistic language of Existentialism lurks the ideology of free competition, free initiative, and equal opportunity. Everybody can 'transcend' his situation, carry out his own project: everybody has his absolutely free choice. However adverse the conditions, man must 'take it' and make compulsion his self-realization. Everybody is master of his destiny. But in the face of an 'absurd world' without meaning and reward, the attributes of the heroic period of bourgeois society assume naturally an absurd and illusory character. Sartre's 'Pour-soi' is closer to Stirner's *Einziger und sein Eigentum* than to Descartes's *Cogito*. In spite of Sartre's insistence on the Ego's *Geworfenheit* (being thrown into a pre-given contingent situation), the latter seems to be wholly absorbed by the Ego's ever-transcending power which posits, as its own free project, all the obstacles encountered on its way. True, man is thrown into a 'situation' which he himself has not created, and this situation may be such that it 'alienates' his freedom, degrades him into a thing. The process of 'reification' appears in manifold forms in Sartre's philosophy: as the subordination of the 'Pour-soi' to the standardized technics of everyday life (EN, pp. 495ff., 594), and as the interchangeability of the individual (EN, p. 496). But to Sartre reification as well as its negation are only obstacles on which man's freedom thrives and feeds itself: they become parts of the Cogito's existential project, and the whole process once again serves to illustrate the perpetual liberty of the 'Pour-soi' which finds only itself in the most alienated situation.

The Self-consciousness that finds itself in its Being-for-Others: Sartre's Existentialism thus revives Hegel's formula for the free and rational condition of man. To Hegel, however, the realization of this condition is only the goal and end of the entire historical process. Sartre takes the ontological shortcut and transforms the process into the metaphysical condition of the 'Pour-soi'. Sartre accomplishes this transformation by a trick: the term 'Pour-soi' covers the We as well as the I; it is the collective as well as the individual self-consciousness.

le Pour-soi 'fait qu'il soit daté par ses techniques'. .... (EN, p. 604).

... se fait Français, meridional, ouvrier (EN, p. 606).

Thus, the 'Pour-soi' creates nation, class, class distinctions, etc., makes them parts of his own free 'project', and, consequently, is 'responsible' for them. This is the fallacious identification of the ontological and historical subject. While it is a truism to say that the *ideas* 'nation', 'class', etc., arise with and 'exist' only for the 'Pour-soi', 'nation', 'class', etc., are not created by the 'Pour-soi', but by the action and reaction of specific social groups under specific historical conditions. To be sure, these groups are composed of individuals who may be ontologically characterized as 'Pour-soi', but such character-ization is totally irrelevant to the understanding of their concreteness. The ontological concept of the 'Pour-soi', which defines equally the wage earner and the entrepreneur, the sales clerk and the intellectual, the serf and the landlord, prejudices the analysis of their concrete existence: in so far as the different existential situations are interpreted in terms of the realization of the 'Pour-soi', they are reduced to the abstract denominator of a universal essence. In subsuming the various historical subjects under the ontological idea of the 'Pour-soi', and making the latter the guiding principle of the existential philosophy, Sartre relegates the specific differences which constitute the very concrete-ness of human existence to mere manifestations of the universal essence of man – thus offending against his own thesis that 'existence creates the essence'. Reduced to the role of examples, the concrete situations cannot bridge the gap between the terms of ontology and those of existence. The ontological foundation of Existentialism frustrates its effort to develop a philosophy of the concrete human existence.

The gap between the terms of ontology and those of existence is concealed by the equivocal use of the term 'is'. Sartre's 'is' functions indiscriminately and without medi-ation as the copula in the definition of the essence of man, and as the predication of his actual condition. In this twofold sense, the 'is' occurs in propositions like 'Man is free', 'is his own project', etc. The fact that, in the empirical reality, man is not free, not his own project, is obliterated by the inclusion of the negation into the definition of 'free', 'project', etc. But Sartre's concepts are, in spite of his dialectical style and the pervasive role of the negation, decidedly undialectical. In his philosophy, the negation is no force of its own but is *a priori* absorbed into the affirmation. True, in Sartre's analysis, the develop-ment of the subject through its negation into the self-conscious realization of its project appears as a process, but the process-character is illusory: the subject moves in a circle.

Existentialist freedom is safe from the tribulations to which man is subjected in the empirical reality. However, in one respect, the empirical reality does not affect Sartre's concept of human liberty. Although the freedom which is operative as the very being of the 'Pour-soi' accompanies man in all situations, the scope and degree of his freedom varies in his different situations: it is smallest and dimmest where man is most thoroughly 'reified', where he is least 'Pour-soi'. For example, in situations where he is reduced to the state of a thing, an instrument, where he exists almost exclusively as body, his 'Pour-soi' has all but disappeared. But precisely here, where the ontological idea of freedom seems to evaporate together with the 'Pour-soi', where it falls almost entirely into the sphere of things – at this point a new image of human freedom and fulfilment arises. We shall now discuss the brief appearance of this image in Sartre's philosophy.

III

In illustrating the permanent transcendence of the 'Pour-soi' beyond every one of its contingent situations (a transcendence which, however free, remains afflicted with the very contingency it transcends), Sartre uses the term 'jouer à être'. He introduces the term in describing the behaviour of a 'garçon de café'. The waiter's behaviour exemplifies the manner in which man has to 'make himself what he is' (EN, p. 98): every single one of the waiter's motions, attitudes, and gestures shows that he is constantly aware of the obligation to be a waiter and to behave as a waiter, and that he is trying to discharge this obligation. He 'is' not a waiter, he rather 'makes' himself a waiter. Now 'being a waiter' consists of a set of standardized and mechanized motions, attitudes, and gestures which almost amount to being an automaton. Such a set of behaviour patterns is expected from a waiter, and he tries to live up to this expectation: he 'plays' the waiter, he 'plays' his own being. The obligation to be what he is thus becomes a play, a performance, and the freedom of the 'Pour-soi' to transcend his contingent condition (being-a-waiter) shows forth as the freedom to play, to perform.

Can the example be generalized so that the transcendence of the *Cogito*, the realization of its freedom, shows forth as a permanent and ubiquitous play, a 'jouer à être'? Sartre strongly suggests such generalization, although he does not make the concept of 'jouer à être' the guiding idea of his analysis. But at least at one decisive place, he does link it with the general condition of man. The essential contingency of human existence coagulates in the fact that man is and remains his past, and that this past prevents him once and for all from freely creating his being.

> [The past is] the fact which cannot determine the content of my motivations but which passes through them with its contingence because they can neither suppress nor change it. The past is rather that which the motivations necessarily carry with them and modify. . . . This is what causes me, at each instant, *not to be* a diplomat or a sailor, but rather a professor, although I can only play this being without ever being able to rejoin it (EN, pp. 162ff.).

But if man can only play his being, then the freedom of the 'Pour-soi' is in reality nothing but his ability to act a prescribed role in a play in which neither his part nor its interpretation is of his own free choosing. The *Cogito*'s transcendence, instead of showing forth as the very root of man's power over himself and his world, would appear as the very token of his being for others. Moreover, and most important, his liberty would lie, not in the 'free' transcendence of the *Cogito* but rather in its negation: in the cancellation of that performance in which he has to play permanently the 'Pour-soi' while actually being-for-others. But the negation of the 'Pour-soi' is the 'En-soi', the negation of the *Cogito* is the state of being a thing, nature. The analysis is thus driven into the sphere of reification: this sphere seems to contain the possibility of a freedom and satisfaction which are quite different from that of the *Cogito* and its activity.

The state of reification as the lever for the liberation of man appears in Sartre's philosophy on two different levels: (1) on the level of the individual existence as the 'attitude of (sexual) desire', (2) on the socio-historical level as the revolutionary attitude of the proletariat. Sartre does not establish the link between these two levels: whereas the first is intrinsically connected with the main philosophical argument, the second remains extraneous to it and is developed only outside *L'Être et le Néant*, in the article 'Matérialisme et Révolution'.

According to Sartre, 'le désir' is essentially 'le désir sexuel'. To him, sexuality is not 'un accident contingent lié à notre nature physiologique', but a fundamental structure of the 'Pour-soi' in its being-for-others (EN, pp. 452ff.). He had previously described the two chief types of human relations in terms of sexual relations (sadism and masochism); now sexuality becomes the force which cancels the entire apparatus of existentialist freedom, activity, and morality.

'Le désir' becomes this force first by virtue of the fact that it is the negation of all activity, all 'performance': 'Le désir n'est pas désir de *faire*' (EN, p. 454).

Whatever activity the desire may engender, all 'technique amoureuse', accrues to it from outside. The desire itself is 'purement et simplement désir d'un object transcendant', namely, 'désir d'un corps'. And this object is desired purely and simply as what it is and appears, in its brute 'facticité'.

In describing the 'désir sexuel' and its object, Sartre emphasizes the characteristics which make this relation the very opposite of the 'Pour-soi' and its activity:

> ...in sexual desire consciousness is as though dulled; one appears to let oneself be pervaded by the mere facticity (of one's existence as body), to cease fleeing from it, and to glide into a passive ascent to desire (EN, p. 457).

This is the coming-to-rest of the transcending *Cogito*, the paralysis of its freedom, 'projects' and performances. And the same force which cancels the incessant performance of the 'Pour-soi' also cancels its alienation. The 'désir sexuel' reveals its object as stripped of all the attitudes, gestures, and affiliations which make it a standardized instrument, reveals the 'corps comme chair' and thereby 'comme révélation fascinante de la facticité' (EN, p. 458). Enslavement and repression are cancelled, not in the sphere of purposeful, 'projective' activity, but in the sphere of the 'corps vécu comme chair', in the 'trame d'inertie' (EN, p. 458). By the same token, the image of fulfilment and satisfaction is, not in the ever transcending 'Pour-soi', but in its own negation, in its pure 'être-là', in the fascination of its being an object (for itself and for others). Reification itself thus turns into liberation.

The 'désir sexuel' accomplishes this negation of the negation not as a mere relapse into animal nature, but as a free and liberating human relation. In other words, the 'désir sexuel' is what it is only as activity of the 'Pour-soi', an activity, however, which is rather the negation of all activity and which aims at the liberation of the pure presence to its object. This activity is 'la caresse'.

Desire expresses itself through caress as thought does through language (EN, p. 459). The breaking of the reified world, the revelation of the 'Chair . . . comme contingence pure de la présence' is only brought about by the 'caresse':

> Caress causes the Other to be born as flesh for me and for himself. . . . Caress reveals the flesh by divesting the body of its action, by isolating it from the possibilities which surround it . . . (EN, p. 459).

It is thus in complete isolation from its possibilities, oblivious of its freedom and responsibility, divested of all its performances and achievements, in being a pure 'object' ('corps vécu comme chair') that the *Ego* finds itself in the Other. The relationships among men have become relationships among things, but this fact is no longer concealed and distorted by societal fetishes and ideologies. Reification no longer serves to perpetuate exploitation and toil but is in its entirety determined by the 'pleasure principle'.

Moreover, the fundamental change in the existential structure caused by the 'désir sexuel' affects not only the individuals concerned but also their (objective) world. The 'désir sexuel' has, according to Sartre, a genuinely cognitive function: it reveals the (objective) world in a new form.

> If my body ... is no longer felt to be the instrument which can be used by any other instrument, that is, as the synthetic organization of my acts in the world, if it is lived as flesh, it is then, as reverberation of my flesh, that I seize the objects in the world. This means that I make myself passive in relationship to them. ... A contact as caress means that my perception is not utilization of an object and not the transcending of the present with a view to a goal. To perceive an object, in the attitude of desire, is to caress myself with it (EN, p. 461).

The 'attitude désirante' thus releases the objective world as well as the *Ego* from domination and manipulation, cancels their 'instrumentality', and, in doing so, reveals their own pure presence, their 'chair'.

We have seen that the fixation on the property relation permeates Sartre's entire book: not only the relation between the 'Pour-soi' and 'En-soi', but also the fundamental relationships between the 'Pour-soi' and 'l'autrui', the interhuman relationships are eventually interpreted in terms of 'appropriation'. Finally, the 'désir sexuel' is the attempt to appropriate freely the liberty of the Other. That all these appropriations turn out to be futile and self-defeating only renews and perpetuates the attempt to appropriate. And the one point, the one moment which appears as fulfilment, possession, is where and when man becomes a thing: body, flesh; and his free activity becomes complete inertia: caressing the body as thing. The *Ego*, thus far separated from the 'things' and therefore dominating and exploiting them, now has become a 'thing' itself – but the thing, in turn, has been freed to its own pure existence. The Cartesian gap between the two substances is bridged in that both have changed their substantiality. The *Ego* has lost its character of being 'Pour-soi', set off from and against everything other-than-the *Ego*, and its objects have assumed a subjectivity of their own. The 'attitude désirante' thus reveals (the possibility of) a world in which the individual is in complete harmony with the whole, a world which is at the same time the very negation of that which gave the *Ego* freedom only to enforce its free submission to necessity. With the indication of this form of the 'réalité humaine', Existentialism cancels its own fundamental conception.

In the sphere of the individual existence, the cancellation is only a temporary one: the free satisfaction afforded in the 'attitude désirante' is bound to end in new frustration. Confined within the circle of sadistic and masochistic relationships, man is driven back into the transcending activity of the 'Pour-soi'. But the image which has guided Sartre's analysis to seek the reality of freedom in the sphere of reification and alienation also leads him into the socio-historical sphere. He tests his conception in a critical discussion of Historical Materialism.

IV

In Sartre's interpretation of the socio-historical sphere, the reification of the subject (which, in the private sphere, appeared as the 'corps vécu comme chair') manifests itself in the existence of the industrial worker. The modern entrepreneur tends to reduce the worker to the state of a thing by assimilating his behaviour to [that of] properties (тм, 10, p. 15).

In view of the brute mechanization of the worker and his work, in view of his complete subjugation to the capitalistic machine process, it would be ridiculous to preach him the 'internal' liberty which the philosophers have preached throughout the centuries:

> The revolutionary himself... distrusts freedom. And rightly so. There has never been lack of prophets to proclaim to him that he was free, and each time in order to cheat him (тм, 10, p. 14).

Sartre mentions in this connection the Stoic concept of freedom, Christian liberty, and Bergson's idea of freedom:

> They all come back to a certain internal liberty which man can preserve in any situation whatsoever. This internal liberty is nothing but an idealistic mystification ... (тм, 10, p. 14).

It would seem that Sartre's own ontological concept of freedom would well be covered by this verdict of 'idealistic mystification', and *L'Être et le Néant* provides little ground for evading it. Now he recognizes the fact that, in the empirical reality, man's existence is organized in such a way that his freedom is totally 'alienated', and that nothing short of a revolutionary change in the social structure can restore the development of his liberty (тм, 9, pp. 15–16). If this is true, if, by the organization of society, human freedom can be alienated to such an extent that it all but ceases to exist, then the content of human freedom is determined, not by the structure of the 'Pour-soi', but by the specific historical forces which shape the human society. However, Sartre tries to rescue his idea of freedom from Historical Materialism. He accepts the revolution as the only way to the liberation of mankind, but he insists that the revolutionary solution presupposes man's freedom to *seize* this solution, in other words, that man must be free '*prior*' to his liberation. Sartre maintains that this presupposition destroys the basis of materialism, according to which man is wholly determined by the material world. But according to Historical Materialism, the revolution remains an act of freedom – in spite of all material determination. Historical Materialism has recognized this freedom in the important role of the maturity of the revolutionary consciousness. Marx's constant emphasis on the material determination of the consciousness in all its manifestations points up the relationships between the subject and his world as they actually prevail in the capitalist society, where freedom has shrunk to the possibility of recognizing and seizing the necessity for liberation.

In the concrete historical reality, the freedom of the 'Pour-soi', to whose glorification Sartre devotes his entire book, is thus nothing but one of the preconditions for the possibility of freedom – it is not freedom itself. Moreover, isolated from the specific historical context in which alone the 'transcendence' of the subject may become a precondition of freedom, and hypostatized into the ontological form of the subject as such, this transcendental liberty becomes the very token of enslavement. The anti-fascist who is tortured to death may retain his moral and intellectual freedom to 'transcend' this situation: he is still tortured to death. Human freedom is the very negation of that transcendental liberty in which Sartre sees its realization. In *L'Être et le Néant* this negation appeared only in the 'attitude désirante': it was the loss of the 'Pour-soi', its reification in the 'corps vécu comme chair' which suggested a new idea of freedom and happiness.

Similarly, in Sartre's interpretation of the socio-historical sphere, it is the existence, not of the free but of the reified subject which points the way toward real liberation. The wage labourer, whose existence is that of a thing, and whose activity is essentially action on things, conceives of his liberation naturally as a change in the relationship between man and things. Sartre interprets the process between capital and wage labour in terms of the Hegelian process between master and servant. The labourer, who works in the service of the entrepreneur on the means of production, transforms, through his labour, these means into the instruments for his liberation. True, his labour is imposed upon him, and he is deprived of its products, but 'within these limitations', his labour confers upon him 'la mâitrise sur les choses':

> The worker sees himself as the possibility of modifying endlessly the form of material objects by acting on them in accordance with certain universal rules. In other words, it is the determinateness of matter which offers him the first view of his freedom. ... He transcends his state of slavery through his action on things, and things give back to him, by the very rigidity of their bondage, the image of a tangible freedom which consists of modifying them. And since the outline of tangible freedom appears to him shackled to determinism, it is not surprising that he visualizes the relationship of man to man, which appears to him as that of tyrannic liberty to humbled obedience, replaced by a relationship of man to thing, and finally, since, from another point of view, the man who controls things is in turn a thing himself, by the relationship of thing to thing (TM, 10, pp. 15–16).

Sartre maintains that the materialistic conception of freedom is itself the victim of reification in so far as it conceives the liberated world in terms of a new relationship among things, a new organization of things. As the liberation originates in the process of labour, it remains defined by this process, and the liberated society appears only as 'une entreprise harmonieuse d'exploitation du monde' (TM, 10, p. 17). The result would simply be 'a more rational organization of society' (TM, 10, p. 21) – not the realization of human freedom and happiness.

This critique is still under the influence of 'idealistic mystifications'. The 'more rational organization of society', which Sartre belittles as 'simplement', is the very precondition of freedom. It means the abolition of exploitation and repression in all their forms. And since exploitation and repression are rooted in the material structure of society, their abolition requires a change in this structure: a more rational organization of the relationships of production. In Historical Materialism, this organization of the liberated society is so little 'defined by labour' ('définie par le travail') that Marx once formulated the Communist goal as the 'abolition of labour', and the shortening of the working day as the precondition for the establishment of the 'realm of freedom'. The formula conveys the image of the unfettered satisfaction of the human faculties and desires, thus suggesting the essential identity of freedom and happiness which is at the core of materialism.

Sartre notes that throughout history, materialism was linked with a revolutionary attitude:

> No matter how far back I go, I find it [materialistic faith] linked with the revolutionary attitude (TM, 9, pp. 15–16).

Indeed, the materialist faith was revolutionary in so far as it was materialistic, that is to say, as it shifted the definition of human freedom from the sphere of consciousness to that of material satisfaction, from toil to enjoyment, from the moral to the pleasure principle. The idealistic philosophy has made freedom into something frightening and tyrannic, bound up with repression, resignation, scarcity, and frustration. Behind the idealistic concept of freedom lurked the demand for an incessant moral and practical performance, an enterprise the profits of which were to be invested ever again in the same activity – an activity which was really rewarding only for a very small part of the population. The materialistic conception of freedom implies the discontinuation of this activity and performance: it makes the reality of freedom a pleasure. Prior to the achievement of this 'utopian' goal, materialism teaches man the necessities which determine his life in order to break them by his liberation. And his liberation is nothing less than the abolition of repression.

Sartre hits upon the revolutionary function of the materialistic principle in his inter-pretation of the 'attitude désirante': there, and only there, is his concept of freedom identical with the abolition of repression. But the tendencies which make for the destruc-tion of his idealistic conception remain confined within the framework of philosophy and do not lead to the destruction of the ideology itself. Consequently, in Sartre's work, they manifest themselves only as a disintegration of the traditional philosophical 'style'. This disintegration is expressed in his rejection of the 'esprit de sérieux' (seriousness).

V

According to Sartre, the 'esprit de sérieux' must be banned from philosophy because, by taking the 'réalité humaine' as a totality of objective relationships, to be understood and evaluated in terms of objective standards, the 'esprit de sérieux' offends against the free play of subjective forces which is the very essence of the 'réalité humaine'. By its very 'style' philosophy thus fails to gain the adequate approach to its subject. In contrast, the existentialist style is designed to assert, already through the mode of presentation, the absolutely free movement of the *Cogito*, the 'Pour-soi', the creative subject. Its 'jouer à être' is to be reproduced by the philosophical style. Existentialism plays with every affirmation until it shows forth as negation, qualifies every statement until it turns into its opposite, extends every position to absurdity, makes liberty into compulsion and compulsion into liberty, choice into necessity and necessity into choice, passes from philosophy to *belles lettres* and vice versa, mixes ontology and sexology, etc. The heavy seriousness of Hegel and Heidegger is translated into artistic play. The ontological analysis includes a series of 'scènes amoureuses', and the existentialist novel sets forth philosophical theses in italics.

This disintegration of the philosophical style reflects the inner contradictions of all existential philosophy: the concrete human existence cannot be understood in terms of philosophy. The contradiction derives from the historical conditions under which Western philosophy has developed and to which it remained committed throughout its development. The separation of the intellectual from the material production, of leisure and the leisure class from the underlying population, of theory from practice caused a fundamental gap between the terms of philosophy and the terms of existence. When

Aristotle insisted that philosophy presupposed the establishment of the arts directed to the necessities of life, he defined not only the situation of the philosopher but of philosophy itself. The content of the basic philosophical concepts implies a degree of freedom from the necessities of life which is enjoyed only by a small number of men. The general concepts which aim at the structures and forms of being transcend the realm of necessity and the life of those who are confined to this realm. Their existence is not on the philosophical level. Conversely philosophy does not possess the conceptual instruments for comprehending their existence, which is the concreteness of the 'réalité humaine'. The concepts which do adequately describe this concreteness are not the exemplifications and particularizations of any philosophical concept. The existence of a slave or of a factory worker or of a sales clerk is not an 'example' of the concept of being or freedom or life or man. The latter concepts may well be 'applicable' to such forms of existence and 'cover' them by their scope, but this coverage refers only to an irrelevant part or aspect of the reality. The philosophical concepts abstract necessarily from the concrete existence, and they abstract from its very content and essence; their generality transcends the existence *qualitatively*, into a different *genus*. Man as such, as 'kind', is the genuine theme of philosophy; his *hic et nunc* is the ὕλη (matter, stuff) which remains outside the realm of philosophy. Aristotle's dictum that man is an ultimate indivisible kind (ἔσχατον ἄτομον; ἄτομον εἶδος; ἄτομον τῷ γένει), which defies further concretization pronounces the inner impossibility of all existential philosophy.

Against its intentions and efforts, Existentialism demonstrates the truth of Aristotle's statement. We have seen how, in Sartre's philosophy, the concept of the 'Pour-soi' vacillates between that of the individual subject and that of the universal *Ego* or consciousness. Most of the essential qualities which he attributes to the 'Pour-soi' are qualities of man as a *genus*. As such, they are *not* the essential qualities of man's concrete existence. Sartre makes reference to Marx's early writings, but not to Marx's statement that man, in his concrete historical existence, is not (yet) the realization of the *genus* man. This proposition states the fact that the historical forms of society have crippled the development of the general human faculties, of the *humanitas*. The concept of the *genus* man is thus at the same time the concept of the abstract-universal and of the *ideal* man – but is *not* the concept of the 'réalité humaine'.

But if the 'réalité humaine' is not the concretization of the *genus* man, it is equally indescribable in terms of the individual. For the same historical conditions which crippled the realization of the *genus* man also crippled the realization of his individuality. The activities, attitudes, and efforts which circumscribe his concrete existence are, in the last analysis, not his but those of his class, profession, position, society. In this sense is the life of the individual indeed the life of the universal, but this universal is a configuration of specific historical forces, made up by the various groups, interests, institutions, etc., which form the social reality. The concepts which actually reach the concrete existence must therefore derive from a theory of society. Hegel's philosophy comes so close to the structure of the concrete existence because he interprets it in terms of the historical universal, but because he sees in this universal only the manifestation of the Idea he remains within the realm of philosophical abstraction. One step more toward concretization would have meant a transgression beyond philosophy itself.

Such transgression occurred in the opposition to Hegel's philosophy. Kierkegaard and Marx are frequently claimed as the origins of existential philosophy. But neither

Kierkegaard nor Marx wrote existential philosophy. When they came to grips with the concrete existence, they abandoned and repudiated philosophy. Kierkegaard comes to the conclusion that the situation of man can be comprehended and 'solved' only by theology and religion. For Marx, the conception of the 'réalité humaine' is the critique of political economy and the theory of the socialist revolution. The opposition against Hegel pronounces the essential inadequacy of philosophy in the face of the concrete human existence.

Since then, the gap between the terms of philosophy and those of existence has widened. The experience of the totalitarian organization of the human existence forbids to conceive freedom in any other form than that of a free society.

NOTES

1   A. Camus, *Le Mythe de Sisyphe*, Paris, 1946, pp. 83ff.
2   Ibid., pp. 89ff.
3   In *Les Lettres françaises*, 24 November, 1945. Cf. also Sartre, *L'Existentialisme est un humanisme*, Paris, 1946, p. 17 (henceforth referenced in text thus: EH).
4   'Matérialisme et Révolution' in *Les Temps modernes*, I, 9 and 10, Paris, June and July 1946 (henceforth referenced in text thus: TM, 9, 10).
5   Unless otherwise stated, 'existentialist' and 'Existentialism' refer only to Sartre's philosophy.
6   *L'Être et le Néant*, Paris, 1943, p. 38 (henceforth referenced in text thus: EN).

6

Levinas on Husserl

Emmanuel Levinas (1906–95) was one of the first to introduce Husserl's thought to France in the 1930s with his book *The Theory of Intuition in Husserl's Phenomenology* (1930). Expositions of Husserl dominate Levinas's early work and it is not until the publication of *Totality and Infinity* (1961) that Levinas's distinctive approach matures. Levinas was, then, a contemporary of Sartre and Merleau-Ponty but it was not until the 1980s that a renewed interest in ethics and subjectivity became focused on the reception of his work. As with Heidegger, the language of Levinas's later work becomes increasingly distinctive and idiosyncratic in ways that are not simply rhetorical but integral to his philosophical approach. A series of terms become associated with the problems Levinas seeks to address, most notably with his conception of the 'Other'. The concern of *Totality and Infinity* develops Husserlian phenomenology into ethical investigation of face-to-face encounters with the 'Other'. Ethical obligations to the 'Other' involve Levinas in a critique of the reduction of the other to 'the same'. The 'same' marks the force of understanding the Other within some totality or whole.

Levinas shares aspects of Adorno's critique of 'identity'-thinking, but seeks a more profound break with dialectical thinking. His later thought also breaks with Husserl and Heidegger, arguing against the way Husserl's transcendental ego and Heidegger's *Dasein* function as totalizing centres in their thought. Against the abstractions of ontology, then, Levinas analyses the ethics of the 'Other' through the encounter with the face and speech of another person. Our responsibility to others, for Levinas, is not reciprocal or based on recognition, but an asymmetrical and unlimited respect for an other's otherness. The experience of radical alterity destabilizes the conventional orientations of philosophical thought. Levinas shares some of Kierkegaard's resistance to the power of dialectical thought exemplified by Hegel, and, like Kierkegaard, suggests how an ethics of the other returns philosophy to religious questions. The problem posed for readers by the relation between Levinas's many religious writings and his more explicitly philosophical texts is as awkward as it is for readers of Kierkegaard. Jacques Derrida's critical essay 'Violence and Metaphysics: An Essay on the Thought of Emmanuel Levinas' argues that Levinas remains complicit with Western metaphysics. But as Derrida himself suggests, many of the most distinctive features of Levinas's thought renew a dialogue between Judaism and Western philosophy.

Levinas's essay 'Reflections on Phenomenological "Technique"' (1959) comes just before the breakthrough announced by *Totality and Infinity*. The essay here needs to be read as prefiguring his more distinctive contribution, providing both a suggestive exploration of Husserl's work and an introduction to Levinas's emerging difference. His exegesis of the outlines of Husserlian thought combines with an original appropriation that opens up new paths. His consideration of the shared thinking of Husserlian phenomenology offers a synthetic overview that points beyond phenomenology. Intimations regarding 'lyric phrasing' and the idea of God resonate with the way he compares Husserl with Kant, Hegel and Bergson to suggest a critical reckoning. Levinas is more concerned to draw out the spirit rather than the method of Husserlian phenomenology. Part of the interest, then, is the way Levinas condenses different moments in the development of Husserl's thought. Some of the more technical features of Husserl's vocabulary are presented schematically without developing a phenomenological exposition. The exegesis takes the form of essayistic reflections against the grain of Husserlian analysis.

Husserlian thought has fewer affinities with the hermeneutic 'readings' of philosophical traditions offered by other philosophers. Merleau-Ponty's *Phenomenology of Perception*, for example, works within a Husserlian approach that often cites Husserl but rarely offers explicit 'readings' of Husserl that might clarify similarities and differences. Adorno's *Against Epistemology*, by contrast, offers an immanent critique of Husserl whose results are negative rather than sympathetic. Levinas's essay is unusual in providing an introduction to Husserl that is immanent, sympathetic and critical. Levinas's critical reading remains within the traditions suggested by Husserl, but the abrupt quality of the synoptic perspective implies different concerns. In his response to questions put to his essay, Levinas talks of going beyond the Husserlian conception of the subject and intentionality. Through a phenomenology of the other person, he suggests, it might be possible to see that another person's alterity consists in being 'more' than the 'I' or 'me' of the subject. He also points out that such a phenomenology would break with Husserl. To the extent that this essay is faithful to Husserlian phenomenology it remains on the cusp of that break. Levinas's move 'beyond' Husserl is sketched in subsequent essays from the 1970s which are included in *Discovering Existence with Husserl*.

FURTHER READING

Primary works

Emmanuel Levinas, *The Theory of Intuition in Husserl's Phenomenology*, trans. Andre Orianne (Evanston, IL: Northwestern University Press, 1973; with new preface by Richard A. Cohen, 1995); *God, Death, and Time*, trans. Bettina Bergo (Stanford, CA: Stanford University Press, 2000); *Totality and Infinity*, trans. Alphonso Lingis (Pittsburgh: Duquesne University Press, 1969); *Basic Philosophical Writings*, eds. Adriaan T. Peperzak, Simon Critchley and Robert Bernasconi (Bloomington and Indianapolis: Indiana University Press, 1996); *Discovering Existence with Husserl*, trans. Richard A. Cohen and Michael B. Smith (Evanston, IL: Northwestern University Press, 1998); *Collected Philosophical Papers*, trans. Alphonso Lingis (Dordrecht, Boston and London: Kluwer, 1993).

Secondary works

Theodor Adorno, *Against Epistemology: A Metacritique, Studies in Husserl and the Phenomenological Antinomies*, trans. Willis Domingo (Oxford: Blackwell, 1982).

R. Bernasconi and S. Critchley, eds. *Re-Reading Levinas* (Bloomington: Indiana University Press, 1991).

R. Bernasconi and D. Wood, eds., *The Provocation of Levinas: Rethinking the Other* (London and New York: Routledge, 1988).

Richard Cohen, ed., *Face to Face with Levinas* (New York: State University of New York Press, 1986).

Simon Critchley, *The Ethics of Deconstruction: Derrida and Levinas* (Oxford: Blackwell, 1992).

Simon Critchley and Robert Bernasconi, *The Cambridge Companion to Levinas* (Cambridge: Cambridge University Press, 2002).

Jacques Derrida, 'Violence and Metaphysics: An Essay on the Thought of Emmanuel Levinas', trans. A. Bass, *Writing and Difference* (London: Routledge, 1978), pp. 79–153.

Jacques Derrida, *Speech and Phenomena*, trans. David B. Allison (Evanston, IL: Northwestern University Press, 1973).

Frederick Ellison and Peter McCormack, eds., *Husserl: Expositions and Appraisals* (Notre Dame and London: University of Notre Dame Press, 1977).

Frederick Ellison and Peter McCormack, eds., *Husserl: Shorter Works* (Brighton, Sussex: Harvester, 1981).

Sean Hand, ed., *The Levinas Reader* (Oxford: Blackwell, 1989).

Edmund Husserl, *Ideas: General Introduction to Pure Phenomenology*, trans. W. R. Boyce Gibson (London: George Allen and Unwin, 1931).

Edmund Husserl, *Cartesian Meditations: An Introduction to Phenomenology*, trans. Dorion Cairns (The Hague: Martinus Nijhoff, 1977).

Edmund Husserl, *Phenomenology and the Crisis of Philosophy*, trans. Quentin Lauer (New York: Harper and Row, 1965).

John Llewelyn, *Emmanuel Levinas: The Genealogy of Ethics* (London: Routledge, 1995).

Maurice Merleau-Ponty, *Phenomenology of Perception*, trans. Colin Smith (London: Routledge, 1962).

Adriaan T. Peperzak, *Beyond: The Philosophy of Emmanuel Levinas* (Evanston, IL: Northwestern University Press, 1997).

Adriaan T. Peperzak, ed., *Ethics as First Philosophy: The Significance of Emmanuel Levinas for Philosophy, Literature and Religion* (New York: Routledge, 1995).

Emmanuel Levinas, 'Reflections on Phenomenological "Technique"' (1959), *Discovering Existence with Husserl*, trans. Richard A. Cohen and Michael B. Smith (Evanston, IL: Northwestern University Press, 1998), pp. 91–102.

Philosophy has not become a rigorous science, pursued by a team of investigators, arriving at definitive results. It is very likely that philosophy resists this mode of spiritual life. But some Husserlian hopes have been realized. *Phenomenology unites philosophers*, although not in the way in which Kantianism united Kantians or Spinozism Spinozans. Phenomenologists are not bound to the theses formulated by Husserl; they do not devote themselves exclusively to the exegesis or the history of his writings. It is a way of proceeding that they have in common. They agree on approaching questions in a certain way, rather than on adhering to a certain number of fixed propositions.

To present Husserlian phenomenology as a method would be to insist on the obvious. Such is not exactly our purpose. We simply want to point out some procedures, techniques almost, used quasispontaneously by those who have been shaped even partially by the Husserlian work. Phenomenology is a method in an eminent sense, for it is essentially open. It can be practiced in the most diverse domains, rather like the method of mathematical physics after Galileo and Descartes, dialectics after Hegel and especially Marx, or psychoanalysis after Freud. One can carry out a phenomenology of the sciences, of Kantianism, of socialism, as well as a phenomenology of phenomenology itself. But the way it has been practiced since the *Logical Investigations*, in which it was "tested in action," the style it has taken on, the refutations and confirmations to which it has subjected thought, do not always coincide with what Husserl understands strictly by method. On this point, his work does not seem to have exerted influence through the methodological considerations in which it abounds. Besides, most of the time those methodological considerations already express positions, responses to problems, rather than rules for the art of dealing with them.

I do not mean to say that these theses are not essential to the practice of the method. But the theories concerning intuition, ideas, reduction, and constituted and constituting intersubjectivity – without which, Husserl declares, phenomenological analysis would not rise to philosophical dignity – are in reality elements of a system, rather than a route leading to the discovery of a system. They count as method in the sense that all knowledge of being counts as method. If one takes them as rules of method they appear too formal.

The phenomenological reduction claims to open up, behind the naive vision of things, the field of a radical experience, allowing reality to appear in its ultimate structure. It would suffice, then, to receive it as it is given. Philosophers have never sought and promised anything but the vision of the truly real behind common and abstract experience. This field of transcendental facts that the seeing of essences or the phenomenological reduction claims to open up requires a way of being treated that constitutes the "lyric phrasing," as it were, of phenomenological research. Of this *way*, Husserl's work furnishes the prototype rather than the technology.

Despite the wealth of analyses and the profundity of views that so many remarkable works of phenomenology have produced in France, Germany, and elsewhere since the war, I would like, in all modesty, to mention some of those elementary movements of thought that have come from the Husserlian manner. Thus we are not concerned with judging systems by showing how they are put together, and even less with judging the Husserlian system – as it appears in the works published during his lifetime, and in its evolution through the posthumous works – by its technique. This historian's game of who is the cleverest, the historian or the author he is examining, is vain and unworthy. I would like simply to highlight a series of gestures that determine, for the outside observer, the physiognomy of one thinker, and lend a family resemblance to several others.

Our reflections, developed without systematizing intent, concern the notions of description, intentionality, sensibility, and subjectivity. I apologize for the disparate character of these reflections.

1. In phenomenology one no longer deduces, in the mathematical or logical sense of the word. Moreover, the facts which the phenomenological reduction opens up are not there to suggest or to confirm hypotheses. There is neither deduction nor induction. The facts of consciousness do not lead to any principle that explains them. The "becauses" which appear in the texts merely establish the primacy of one fact over another; they never rise above the phenomena. "Because" the synthesis of sensible perception is never completed, the existence of the exterior world is relative and uncertain. But the relativity and uncertainty of the exterior world signify nothing other than the incomplete character of the synthesis or perception of the sensible. The abstract notions which the terms "relativity" and "uncertainty" express cannot be *separated* from the phenomena or from their unfolding which these terms summarize. Without these phenomena, these terms become abstract and equivocal.

The ideal of absolute existence, by contrast with which the existence of the world is posited as relative, is, in turn, taken from the description of the "fulfillment" of a "signitive" intention by an intuition. The conclusion does not (as in scholastic or Cartesian proofs) result in a truth superior to the facts that suggest it. Nor does it result in an intuition in Bergson's sense, which goes beyond description toward a truth expressed by the formula "everything happens as if."

The experience of the facts of consciousness is the origin of all the notions that can be legitimately employed. Description – and this is the exceptional claim in which it asserts its philosophical dignity – has recourse to no previously *separated* notion that would allegedly be necessary to description. Thus, in Descartes, the description of the *cogito* – in the imperfection of its doubt – eventually acknowledges its reference to the idea of the infinite and perfect: the idea of the perfect, given in advance, makes the description of finitude possible. Phenomenological description seeks the significance of the finite within the finite itself: hence the particular style of the description. Whenever a philosopher of the classical type insists on the imperfection of a phenomenon of knowledge, phenomenology, not content with the negation included in this imperfection, posits instead this negation as constitutive of the phenomenon. If feeling is an obscure fact of psychological life, phenomenological description will take this obscurity as a positive characteristic of feeling, and not conceive of it as a clarity simply diminished. If a remembering is always modified by the present wherein it returns, phenomenology will not speak of a falsified remembrance, but will make of this alteration the essential nature of remembering. A memory exact in itself and independent of the present that modifies it is an *abstraction*, a source of equivocation. The legitimate notion of remembering must be taken from the concrete situation of lived memory. Even for God, remembering has this structure which emerges from description. "Even for God" – the formula is remarkable. We do not need the idea of God – of the infinite and perfect – to become aware of the finitude of phenomena; the essence of the phenomenon such as it is manifested at the finite level is its essence in itself. Even for God – all the being of the object is in its truth, as we would say today.

This reversal into "positivity" and "essential structure" of what remained a setback, a lack, or an empirical contingency for a philosophy that measured the given from the height of the ideal (but which Kant had already denounced as transcendental illusion), gives a decidedly dialectical character to these descriptions. What seemed at first a setback – the incompletion of a series of the thing's aspects – is a thing's mode of completion; what deforms memory is just what constitutes the sui generis reliability of the memory. Soon the doubts that traversed and shattered Kierkegaardian faith will be taken to authenticate this faith; the god who is hidden will be precisely, in his dissimulation, the god who is revealed. The contradictory ambiguity of notions (to be distinguished from the equivocation of words) will constitute their essence. Philosophies – very beautiful ones – of ambiguity will become possible. The immediate link between concepts will be symptomatic of oversights and abstractions, of the unauthentic. One will tread with extreme caution. A halting gait, and happily so! It will bring closest to its goal a way of thinking that wants above all to grasp itself without surpassing itself; for all surpassing, from the point of view of this way of thinking, proceeds most often from nonreflection, presumption, and opinion, from nonphilosophy.

There is in this independence of the finite with regard to the infinite the hallmark of a post-Kantian philosophy. All pre-Kantian idealism contained an essential role for reason, that of making it possible to survey and judge experience; or, if you will, it was still an idealism with the idea of infinity. Phenomenology is the paradox of an idealism without reason. Reason, for Husserl, does not signify a way to rise above the data directly; it is equivalent to experience, to its privileged moment of "*leibhaft*," presence of the object, presence of the object "in flesh and blood" so to speak.

2. Phenomenology is a destruction of representation and the theoretical object. It denounces contemplation of the object (which nevertheless it seems to have promoted) as an abstraction, a partial vision of being, a *forgetting* (as we might say in modern terms), *of its truth. To intend the object, to represent it to oneself, is already to forget the being of its truth.*

To do phenomenology is to denounce the direct vision of the object as naive. Husserl's phenomenology, which finds the leading thread of intentional analysis (which has often been denounced as logicism or objectivism) in the regions of the eidetic sciences, takes the object as its point of departure, but upstream from the current that constitutes it. It starts at the extreme limit of the abstraction that in naive realism (naive for just this reason) is taken for being itself.

This position is clear very early, as far back as in the second volume of the *Logical Investigations*. It is said, to be sure, in a language very different, and with much less pathos. But our language only amplifies the expansion of Husserl's phenomenology, which in its entirety proceeds from the *Logical Investigations*.

Going back to the things themselves signifies first of all not limiting oneself to words, which intend only an absent reality. Husserl recognizes this imperfection of the *signitive* aim in the equivocation that ineluctably slips into verbal thought. Equivocation, an apparently minor fault, which could be dispelled, or so it would appear, with a bit of clarity of thought, is now posited as inevitable, or as essential to a thought that limits itself to words. Equivocation is the child of the void or the rarified atmosphere of abstraction. But the recourse to intuitive thought, to *Erfüllung* [fulfillment] as opposed to *signitive* thought, does not put an end to equivocations, which threaten *every vision fixed on an object*. The return to the acts in which the intuitive presence of objects is unveiled is necessary in order to put an end to equivocation, that is, to abstraction and the partialness of the relationship with the object. *The true return to things is the return to the acts in which the intuitive presence of things is unveiled.* This is certainly the great shock given by the *Logical Investigations* – particularly since the first volume of this work, the *Prolegomena*, and all that is said in the second and third Investigations in favor of the object and its essence, blocked giving a psychologistic interpretation to this recourse to acts of consciousness. Thus, as early as in the *Logical Investigations* we find the affirmation of what appears to us to dominate the phenomenologists' way of proceeding: *access to the object is part of the object's being.*

It matters little that acts in which the object will appear in the guise of a simple transcendent pole continue to be described by Husserl as theoretical acts. What is distinctive to all these analyses is the regressive movement from the object to the concrete fulfillment of its constitution, in which sensibility will play the primary role.

It is evident that it was Kant who first worked in this way, when he deformalized the abstract idea of simultaneity (linking it to the idea of reciprocal action) and the idea of succession (subordinating it to physical causality). One idea calls forth another, which it does not contain analytically. But despite what some have said about Husserl's constitution, it will not play the role that it plays in Kant, as the common use of the term would suggest. For phenomenologists, the constitution of the object does not have as its goal the *justification of the use of concepts or categories*, or, as Kant calls it, their deduction. The Husserlian constitution is a reconstitution of the object's concrete being, a return to everything that has been forgotten in the attitude fixed on an object; the latter being not a thought but a technique. And this distinction between thought and technique, which reappears in the *Crisis*, was drawn very early by Husserl. Already according to the *Prolegomena*[1] the scientist is not required to comprehend entirely what he does; he *acts* on his object. Theoretical thought is, in this sense, technique. In discovering the object, it ignores the paths that led to it, and that constitute the ontological locus of that object, the being of which it is but an abstraction. The phenomenological way consists in recovering these access routes, in recovering all the self-evidences traversed and forgotten. They make up the ontological weight of the object that seems to transcend them.

The being of an entity is the drama that – through remembrance and forgetfulness, constructions and ruins, falls and ascents – led to the abstraction, to the entity that claims to be outside this drama. In the next, post-Husserlian, stage of phenomenology, events charged with yet more pathos, and nothing less than the whole of European history, will be brought into this drama. The object of our theoretical life is but a fragment of a world that it dissimulates. The drama must be recovered by phenomenologists, for it determines the meaning of that abstract object, and because it is its truth.

Here the procedures of Husserlian phenomenology recall certain distinctions in Hegelian phenomenology: abstract thought – understanding – is that which aims at the in-itself. It must be made to relate to the absolute and to the concrete, to reason. Or was it, quite to the contrary, the Kantian distinction between the concept of the understanding and the idea of reason (the latter being separated from the sensible, but aiming for this very reason at a necessary illusion) that prepared the phenomenological notion of a thought that remains abstract despite its certitudes?

3. The laying bare, in the abstract object, of its ways of appearing, implies on the one hand that there is an essential correspondence between objects and the subjective acts necessary for their appearing. We shall speak of this now. On the other hand, phenomenology is characterized by the considerable and original role that sensibility plays for it in the work of truth; we will come back to this.

The notions examined by phenomenologists are no longer entities to which there are in principle a multiplicity of paths. The way a notion or an entity is accessible, the movements of the mind that conceive it, are not just (in the name of some arbitrary but coherent legislation) fixed for each notion. These movements performed to permit the manifestation of the notion to a mind – *are as it were the fundamental ontological event of that very notion*. The role that a given historical situation plays in Hegel, outside of which such and such idea or other is not even *thinkable*, is played in Husserl by the configuration of subjective procedures that for him is equally necessary and irreplaceable. The beloved, the implement, or the work of art exist and are "substances," each in its own way. And the way cannot be separated from the "intentions" that sketch it out.

As early as in the *Logical Investigations* the revelation of beings, in the form of logical entities, constitutes the very being of these entities. The being of beings lies in their truth: *the essence of beings is in the truth or the revelation of their essence.*

Thus, phenomenology as a revelation of beings is a *method of the revelation of their revelation.* Phenomenology is not just the fact of letting phenomena appear as they appear; this appearing, this phenomenology, is the essential event of being.

The being of objects being in their revelation, the very nature of the problems phenomenology deals with changes. It will no longer be a question of proofs of existence. *We are straightaway within being; we are ourselves part of its play*; we are partners in the revelation. It remains for us only to describe these modes of revelation which are modes of existence. Already ontology in the Heideggerian sense replaces metaphysics, for revelation is the principal event of being. Truth, as we would say today, is the very essence of being. Problems concerning reality consist in describing the way in which reality receives a meaning that clarifies or reveals it, or the way in which that meaning is given to it.

The fact that being is revelation, that the essence of being is its truth, is expressed in the notion of intentionality. Intentionality does not consist in affirming the correlation between subject and object. To affirm intentionality as a central theme of phenomenology is not even to conceive of the correlation between subject and object as a *kind* of intentionality. The representation of the object by a spectator whose gaze is fixed on it is realized at the price of manifold neglect and forgetting. Such a representation is abstract in the Hegelian sense. Because being consists in revealing itself, it is enacted as intentionality. The object, by contrast, is a way in which, par excellence, the being that reveals itself lets the history of its self-evidence be forgotten. The object, a correlate of theoretical consideration, produces the illusion that it signifies by itself. This is why, in Husserl, phenomenology begins with the object and Nature, the quintessence of objectivity, and then moves back toward their intentional implications.

4. It is characteristic of phenomenology's procedure to accord a primary place in constitution to sensibility. Even when Husserl affirms the ideality of concepts and of syntactic relations, he makes them rest on the sensible. There is the well-known text: "The idea of a pure intellect, interpreted as a faculty of pure thought (of categorial action), entirely cut off from a faculty of sensibility, could only have been conceived before the elementary analysis of knowledge."[2]

Sensibility is not considered as simple matter, crudely given, to which a spontaneous act of thought is applied, whether to give it form or to bring out relations from it by abstraction. It does not designate the element of receptivity in an objectifying spontaneity. It does not appear as a stammering thought that errs and falls into illusion, nor as the springboard for rational knowledge. The sensible is not an *Aufgabe* [task] in the neo-Kantian sense, nor an obscure thought in the Leibnizian sense. The new way of treating sensibility consists in conferring upon it, in its very obtuseness, and in its thickness, a signification and a wisdom of its own and a kind of intentionality. The senses make sense.

Every intellectual construction will receive from the sensible experience it claims to transcend the very style and dimension of its architecture. Sensibility does not simply record facts; it unfolds a world from which the highest works of spirit stem and from which they will not be able to escape. From the threads intertwined with the "content" of sensations are woven "forms" that – like space and time in Kant – mark every object that will subsequently be presented to thought.

A weave of intentionalities can be perceived in the hyletic data themselves. These intentionalities are not a simple repetition of the intentionality leading toward the non-ego, in which the localization, the weight of the ego, its *now*, are already forgotten. The relations that *Experience and Judgement* show us in the prepredicative sphere are not simple prefigurations. Sensibility marks the subjective character of the subject, the very movement back toward the point of departure of all receiving (in this sense, the principle), the movement back to the *here* and *now* from which everything happens for the first time. The *Urimpression* [primal impression] is the individuation of the subject. "The *Urimpression* is the absolute beginning, the primal source, that from which all the rest is engendered. It itself is not engendered, it does not arise through generation, but *genesi spontanea*, it is primal generation [*Urzeugung*] . . . it is primal creation [*Urschöpfung*]."[3]

Sensibility is thus intimately tied to time-consciousness: it is the present around which being is oriented. Time is not conceived as a form of the world, nor even as a form of psychological life, but as the articulation of subjectivity. Time is not a scansion of the interior life, but as it were the pattern of the primary and fundamental relations that tie the subject to being and cause it to arise out of the *now*. There is a dialectic of engagement and disengagement, through the execution of the *now*, in which Husserl discerns at once the passivity of the impression and the activity of the subject. But there, contrary to Hegel, a tearing away of the subject from any system and totality occurs, a retrogressive transcendence setting out from the immanence of the conscious state, a retro-cendence.

Time, the essential mark of sensibility in philosophy since Plato, becomes, as the existence of the subject, the source of all meaning. All the relations that structure consciousness as subjectivity are since Husserl described in terms of time as much as in terms of intentionality. The temporal structure – the mode of temporalization – of a notion replaces its definition.

Sensibility is thus not simply an amorphous content, a fact in the sense employed in empiricist psychology. It is "intentional" in that it *situates* all content, and is situated not in relation to objects but in relation *to itself*. It is the *zero* point of situation, the origin of the fact of being situated itself. Prepredicative or lived relations are established as initial attitudes taken from this zero point. The sensible is a modification of the *Urimpression*, which is the *here* and *now* par excellence. It is difficult not to see in this description of sensibility the sensible lived at the level of *one's own body* [*corps propre*] whose fundamental event lies in the feat of *self-adherence* [*se tenir*] – that is, of adhering to itself like the body that stands *itself* on its legs. This feat *coincides* with that of *orienting* oneself, that is, taking an attitude with regard to. . . . There is, here, a new characteristic of the subjective; the subjective does not retain the arbitrary meaning of the passive and the nonuniversal. It inaugurates the origin, the beginning, and, in a sense very different from cause or premise, the principle. This notion of sensibility is certainly caught sight of by Kant (perhaps it already presides over the transcendental aesthetic) when, in the famous article "Was heißt sich im Denken orientieren" ["What Is Orientation in Thinking?"], he attributes the possibility of orienting oneself in geometrical space to the distinction between the right hand and the left. He relates this distinction to *Gefühl* – sensibility – which implies an incarnate geometrician and not a simple reflection of that object-space that by convention is called the subject.

From the *Logical Investigations* and *The Phenomenology of Internal Time-Consciousness* to *Experience and Judgement*, Husserl's phenomenology inaugurates this new notion of sensibility and subjectivity. Historians are struck by the fact that the description of this sensible and passive consciousness is immediately overturned when it is put into relation with the activity of the subject of which it is supposed to be the fulfillment. In reality one may wonder whether this ambiguity is not essential to sensibility, whether the reference to the subject's activity does not confer upon sensibility precisely this role of subjectivity-origin. Indeed, it anticipates contemporary phenomenology's speculations on the role of the body in subjectivity. The ambiguity of passivity and activity in the description of sensibility captures in reality this new type of consciousness that will be called one's own body, the body-subject. The subject as body and not as a simple parallel to the represented object.

It is to the degree that the concept of the subject is linked to sensibility, or that individuation coincides with the ambiguity of the *Urimpression*, in which activity and passivity meet, in which the *now* is prior to the historical manifold that it will constitute, that phenomenology preserves the person. The latter does not dissolve into the work constituted or conceived by it, but always remains transcendent, on the hither side. And in this sense I think that phenomenology is situated at the antipodes of the position maintained by Spinoza or Hegel, where thought absorbs the thinker, where the thinker is dissolved in the eternity of discourse. Because of sensibility, the "eternity" of ideas refers to a *head* that thinks, a subject that is temporally present. This is where the connection between being and time is effectuated in Husserl. Herein lies the profound kinship between phenomenology and Bergsonism.

The ego as *now* is not defined by anything other than itself; that is, it is not defined, it borders nothing, it remains outside of the system. This is why the entire analysis of prepredicative passivity is affirmed, in the last instance, as the activity of a subject. The latter is always a transcendence within immanence; it does not coincide with the heritage of its existence. The ego even precedes its sensible work. It is nowise a quality. Or, it is in a certain sense indeed a quality – but it is the possibility of apprehending itself once more in this quality. The dialectic of the sensible upon which Hegel's phenomenology of spirit opens does not apply to Husserl's sensible, which is absolutely subject. Universality is constituted from a subject that is not absorbed in it. To be sure this in no way indicates that the universal is a mode of existence wherein humanity is simply led astray. But it does indicate that when the universal is separated from the ego that constitutes it and that it does not exhaust, it is an abstract mode of existence.

In the final analysis, the phenomenological ego does not appear in the history it constitutes, but in consciousness. And thus it is torn from the totality. It can break with the past and is not, in this rupture with the past, in spite of itself, the continuator of that past, which a sociology or psychoanalysis will retrieve. It can break away, and consequently can speak.

5. Ancient metaphysics distinguished the appearance of phenomena from their signification. A notion was not measured by the meaning it had for consciousness; its relationship with consciousness was only one of the vicissitudes of its being. As if from the outside, one embraced both the notion and consciousness with a look respectful of the old logical norms derived from contemplative thought. Thus, for example, in Plato's *Parmenides*, the *relation* between the absolute and the consciousness that thinks it compromises this very absolute, for an absolute in a relation is a self-contradictory notion. *In phenomenology the being of an entity is determined by its truth* – by its phosphorescence, by the meaning of the intentions that have access to it, and by the "intentional" history it concludes.

Henceforth one speaks of structures of being without referring right away to logical norms. Paradoxical notions are welcome, such as the much-discussed circle of understanding, in which the whole presupposes the parts but the parts refer to the whole; or the notion of the *Zeug* [gear] in which the structure of *in order to* is not bolstered by any category of substance; or the reference to nothingness in connection with anxiety, in violation of all the Eleatic principles; or, in Husserl himself, the essential incompleteness of the objective sphere, inexact concepts, and the ideality of essences.

Situations, the intention of which is not reducible to knowledge, can be posited as conditions of knowledge, without this positing taking on the appearance of an irrational decision. A fully phenomenological way of proceeding is to discover, for relations of knowledge, foundations that properly speaking lack the structure of knowledge, not because these foundations impose themselves without certainty, but because as anterior and conditioning they are more certain than certainty, more rational than reason.

To be sure, in Husserl's work itself, intentions that intend the object never rest on a nonobjectifying basis. But sensibility and passivity – the "hyletic data" jealously maintained at the basis of a consciousness whose movement toward the outside Husserl, better than anyone else, has shown – relieve his concept of subjectivity of the role of being the object's simple replica, and lead us to what lies on the hither side of the subject–object correlation and its privilege.

Similarly, the reduction to primordial egological knowledge, through which, in Husserl's fifth Cartesian Meditation, the constitution of intersubjectivity begins, does not end in self-evidence structured as objective knowledge (because of its monadological character). Yet this egological knowledge is a situation whose function it is to found objectivity.

Phenomenologists move with ease in these relations between the subject and being, which are not reducible to knowledge but which, nevertheless, as revelation of being, contain truth. The mode of being thus revealed is articulated in terms of the subjective intentions to which it reveals itself. Nothing is more characteristic of phenomenological reflection than the idea of intentional relations maintained with correlates that are not representations and do not exist as substances.

Here, too, Kant is among the precursors in his theory of the postulates of practical reason that makes use of "original *a priori* principles . . . that resist every possible intuition of theoretical reason."[4] There is truth without there being representation: "*Dieses Fürwahrhalten . . . dem Grade nach keinem Wissen nachsteht, ob es gleich der Art nach davon völlig verschieden ist.*" ["This assent . . . is in no degree inferior to cognition, even though it is wholly different in kind."][5]

6. The phenomenological reduction was a radical way of suspending the natural approach, which posits the world as an object, a radical struggle against the abstraction that the object epitomizes.

But it did not succeed in putting the whole of the universe between parentheses on the side of the noemata. In much of contemporary phenomenological work, the reduction has become a laying out of realities, which for the natural attitude had been objects, in a perspective wherein they appear as *modes of apprehension*. The reduction becomes a *subjectivization* of being, an apperception of hitherto objects as *subjective* conditions of objects, origins of and principles for objects. We are now witnessing not merely an extraordinary subjectivization of the body and its physical organs; we discover the earth, the sky, the bridge, and the temple, as ways of access to being and as moments of subjectivity. As early as in the *Ideas*, sensory perception not only supplies a point of departure for scientific construction; it establishes the locus the constructed intelligible object will never leave. The object of science will have to be brought back to this locus in order for it to be grasped in its concrete being. It may be said that phenomenology lays claim to the irrevocable privilege of the world perceived by the concrete man who lives his life. It is surely this thesis from the *Ideas* that Heidegger takes up again, when he affirms that the place delineated by *building* contains geometrical space, which itself can contain nothing.

The subjectivization of what not so long ago were empirical realities does not consist in transforming them into *contents* of consciousness or into givens, but in discovering them as *containers* and *givers*. There are no definitively given qualities; every quality is a relation. Its intelligibility no longer depends on the reducibility of a notion to a principle or an end, or to the system in which it would have its place, but to its function in the transcendence of intentionality. Every given, even the earth, the body, and things, are moments of the work of *Sinngebung* [bestowal of meaning]. Whence a deformalization of objective, scientific reality. It is caught up in relations of the *object to its condition*. These relations are neither analytic, synthetic, nor dialectic, but intentional.

This new connection between givens and other givens that serve as their "subjective" condition gives the spectator who remains outside a new way of opening up concepts.

NOTES

The abbreviations used in the notes are as follows:

LU   = Edmund Husserl, *Logische Untersuchungen*, 2nd edn., 2 vols. (Halle: Niemeyer, 1912, 1921). The second part of vol. II, published in 1921, is referred to by Levinas as vol. III; thus references to this work are abbreviated as *LU* I, II and III.

LI   = *Logical Investigations*, trans. J. N. Findlay, 2 vols. with consecutive pagination (New York: Humanities Press, 1970).

ZB   = *Husserls Vorlesungen zur Phaenomenologie des inneren Zeitbewußtseins*, ed. M. Heidegger, in *Jahrbuch für Philosophie und phaenomenologische Forschung* 9 (Halle, 1928).

PITC = Edmund Husserl, *The Phenomenology of Internal Time-Consciousness*, ed. M. Heidegger, trans. J. S. Churchill (Bloomington: Indiana University Press, 1964).

1   LU I, 9–10; LI, 58–59.
2   LU III, 183; LI, 818.
3   *ZB*, 451; PITC, 131.
4   Immanuel Kant, *Critique of Pure Reason*.
5   *Was heißt sich im Denken orientieren* ["What Is Orientation in Thinking?"], ed. E. Cassirer (Berlin), 360.

7

Gadamer on Heidegger

Hans-Georg Gadamer (1900–2002) was a contemporary of Martin Heidegger and studied with him in the 1920s. Gadamer's work shares much with Heidegger, but is perhaps most distinctive in its special emphasis on hermeneutic problems in philosophy. His unusual distinction is to have suggested new ways of thinking that do not so much break with Heidegger as offer different ways of articulating shared concerns. This means that Gadamer's claims for originality are somewhat overshadowed by the importance of Heidegger, though Gadamer's insistence on hermeneutics involves greater emphasis on interpretative traditions and conversations developed through readings of earlier texts. This emphasis on textual interpretation provides its most sustained exposition in Gadamer's principal work *Truth and Method* (1965), which, like Levinas's *Totality and Infinity* (1961), came relatively late in the consolidation of Gadamer's position as a major thinker.

Whereas Heidegger's later writings are often obscure and only with difficulty understood as readings of other texts, Gadamer's work is developed through more conventional modes of exposition. The status of 'reading' is for Gadamer a question that emerges within traditions of hermeneutic thought rather than through the history of philosophy as a self-contained tradition. The traditions of hermeneutic thought in biblical interpretation and what became literary criticism are often resistant to philosophy. Although Gadamer appropriates hermeneutics for philosophical thought, there is a reciprocity with texts and traditions of textual transmission that goes against the grain of 'pure' philosophy. Indeed, Gadamer is critical of many of the ways in which the models of philosophy have been based on mathematics or science rather than on the way problems are given from within historical traditions of interpretation. The problem of understanding a philosophical or theological text is less a problem of scientific method, then, than of a rigorous understanding of the historicity and spirit of a text. Developing out of Schleiermacher's conception of hermeneutics as an 'art' rather than a science of understanding, Gadamer seeks to show the philosophical implications of more restricted 'methods' of understanding. Against the tendency of biblical or literary interpretation to restrict itself to the authority of the text interpreted, Gadamer shows how understanding is itself one of the ways in which human beings exist in the world. This existence, moreover, is thrown in the world such that it seeks to go beyond the limits of human understanding to encounter truth. The hermeneutic circle opens up a series of relations between the horizons with which understanding is already familiar, and that which is unfamiliar, unintelligible or historically distanced. The limits of our present horizons of understanding are enabling conditions of understanding and no mode of self-critical awareness can fully transcend the historically mediated prejudices of these horizons. Critical awareness has to reckon with the effective history which gives us these horizons, and the limits of prejudice (*Vorurteil*) or prejudgement are inevitably controversial. The central insight of *Truth and Method* is that philosophical hermeneutics is not a question of method or formal analysis, but an ontological rethinking of the encounter with truth.

Gadamer's essay 'Heidegger's Later Philosophy' first appeared as an introduction to a German edition of Martin Heidegger's essay 'The Origin of the Work of Art', and is sympathetic and collaborative rather than critical. Gadamer seeks to outline Heidegger's turn (*die Kehre*) from *Being and Time* towards new ways of approaching the truth of art. The question of how truth is revealed or disclosed by art also suggests how art conceals and hides truth. The approach to art is suggestive for any hermeneutic approach to texts. Heidegger and Gadamer also sketch a poetics of Being that radically reorients philosophy away from consciousness towards language and historicity. Gadamer's conception of hermeneutics attempts to disclose unspoken suggestions in the way tradition speaks to us. This is both a universal task and a task confined within the limits of human temporality. Part of the strength of Gadamer's thought is its willingness to enter into dialogue with texts which are both close and distant in spirit, for example, with the thought of Plato, Hegel and Wittgenstein. Some of Gadamer's critics have questioned this claim for universality within philosophical hermeneutics by attempting to delimit questions that are properly those of science and social science. An important early response to Gadamer is provided by Jürgen Habermas in *On the Logic of the Social Sciences*, which generated a reply from Gadamer and further response from Habermas. Habermas argues that reflection can break with the authority of tradition in a critique of the limits of hermeneutics. Habermas also pays tribute to the way Gadamer builds bridges. In Habermas's rather sharp and suggestive metaphor, he suggests that Gadamer urbanizes the Heideggerian province. Curiously, Gadamer's dialogues with the appropriation of Heidegger in the work of French thinkers such as Jacques Derrida have been less productive.

FURTHER READING

Primary works

Hans-Georg Gadamer, *Truth and Method*, trans. William Glen-Doepel, eds. John Cumming and Garrett Barden, 2nd edition (London: Sheed and Ward, 1979);

Heidegger's Ways, trans. John W. Stanley (Albany: SUNY, 1994); *Hegel's Dialectic: Five Hermeneutical Studies*, trans. P. Christopher Smith (New Haven and London: Yale University Press, 1976); *Philosophical Hermeneutics*, trans. David E. Linge (Berkeley: University of California Press, 1976); *Reason in the Age of Science*, trans. Frederick G. Lawrence (Cambridge, MA: MIT, 1981).

Secondary works

Robert J. Dostal, ed., *The Cambridge Companion to Gadamer* (Cambridge: Cambridge University Press, 2002).

Jürgen Habermas, *On the Logic of the Social Sciences* (1967), trans. Shierry Weber Nicholsen and Jerry A. Stark (Cambridge: Polity, 1988).

Jürgen Habermas, 'Hans-Georg Gadamer: Urbanizing the Heideggerian Province' (1979), in *Philosophical-Political Profiles*, trans. Frederick G. Lawrence (Cambridge, MA: MIT, 1983), pp. 189–197.

Lewis E. Hahn, ed., *The Philosophy of Hans-Georg Gadamer* (LaSalle, IL: Open Court, 1997).

Martin Heidegger, *Basic Writings*, ed. David Farrell Krell, revised edition (London: Routledge, 1993).

Martin Heidegger, *Pathmarks*, ed. William McNeill (Cambridge: Cambridge University Press, 1998).

Alan How, *The Habermas–Gadamer Debate and the Nature of the Social* (Aldershot: Avebury, 1995).

Cristina Lafont, *The Linguistic Turn in Hermeneutic Philosophy*, trans. José Medina (Cambridge, MA: MIT, 1999).

Cristina Lafont, *Heidegger, Language and World-Disclosure*, trans. Graham Harman (Cambridge: Cambridge University Press, 2000).

Jeff Malpas, Ulrich Arnswald and Jens Kertscher, eds., *Gadamer's Century: Essays in Honor of Hans-Georg Gadamer* (Cambridge, MA: MIT, 2002).

Diane P. Michelfelder and Richard E. Palmer, eds., *Dialogue and Deconstruction: The Gadamer–Derrida encounter* (Albany: SUNY, 1989).

Kurt Mueller-Vollmer, ed., *The Hermeneutics Reader* (Oxford: Blackwell, 1986) (includes Hans-Georg Gadamer, 'Rhetoric, Hermeneutics, and the Critique of Ideology: Metacritical Comments on *Truth and Method*', pp. 274–92, and Jürgen Habermas, 'On Hermeneutics' Claim to Universality', pp. 294–319).

Richard E. Palmer, *Hermeneutics: Interpretation Theory in Schleiermacher, Dilthey, Heidegger, and Gadamer* (Evanston, IL: Northwestern University Press, 1969).

Paul Ricoeur, *Hermeneutics & the Human Sciences*, ed. and trans. John B. Thompson (Cambridge: Cambridge University Press, 1981).

Hugh J. Silverman, ed., *Gadamer and Hermeneutics* (New York: Routledge, 1991).

B. Wachterhauser, ed., *Hermeneutics and Modern Philosophy* (Albany: SUNY, 1986).

Joel C. Weinsheimer, *Gadamer's Hermeneutics: A Reading of* Truth and Method (New Haven: Yale University Press, 1985).

Kathleen Wright, ed., *Festivals of Interpretation: Essays on Hans-Georg Gadamer's Work* (Albany: SUNY, 1990).

Hans-Georg Gadamer, 'Heidegger's Later Philosophy' (1960), *Philosophical Hermeneutics*, trans. David E. Linge (Berkeley and Los Angeles: University of California Press, 1976), pp. 213–28.

When we look back today on the time between the two world wars, we can see that this pause within the turbulent events of our century represents a period of extraordinary creativity. Omens of what was to come could be seen even before the catastrophe of World War I, particularly in painting and architecture. But for the most part, the general awareness of the time was transformed only by the terrible shock that the slaughters of World War I brought to the cultural consciousness and to the faith in progress of the liberal era. In the philosophy of the day, this transformation of general sensibilities was marked by the fact that with one blow the dominant philosophy that had grown up in the second half of the nineteenth century in renewal of Kant's critical idealism was rendered untenable. "The collapse of German idealism," as Paul Ernst called it in a popular book of the time,[1] was placed in a world-historical context by Oswald Spengler's *The Decline of the West*. The forces that carried out the critique of this dominant Neo-Kantian philosophy had two powerful precursors: Friedrich Nietzsche's critique of Platonism and Christendom, and Søren Kierkegaard's brilliant attack on the *Reflexionsphilosophie* of speculative idealism. Two new philosophical catchwords confronted the Neo-Kantian preoccupation with methodology. One was the *irrationality of life*, and of historical life in particular. In connection with this notion, one could refer to Nietzsche and Bergson, but also to the great historian of philosophy Wilhelm Dilthey. The other catchword was *Existenz*, a term that rang forth from the works of Søren Kierkegaard, the Danish philosopher of the first part of the nineteenth century, whose influence was only beginning to be felt in Germany as a result of the Diedrichs translation. Just as Kierkegaard had criticized Hegel as the philosopher of reflection who had forgotten existence, so now the complacent system-building of Neo-Kantian methodologism, which had placed philosophy entirely in the service of establishing scientific cognition, came under critical attack. And just as Kierkegaard – a Christian thinker – had stepped forward to oppose the philosophy of idealism, so now the radical self-criticism of the so-called dialectical theology opened the new epoch.

Among the forces that gave philosophical expression to the general critique of liberal culture-piety and the prevailing academic philosophy was the revolutionary genius of the young Heidegger. Heidegger's appearance as a young teacher at Freiburg University in the years just after World War I created a profound sensation. The extraordinarily forceful and profound language that resounded from the rostrum in Freiburg already betrayed the emergence of an original philosophical power. Heidegger's *magnum opus, Being and Time*, grew out of his fruitful and intense encounter with contemporary Protestant theology during his appointment at Marburg in 1923. Published in 1927, this book effectively communicated to a wide public something of the new spirit that had engulfed philosophy as a result of the convulsions of World War I. The common theme that captured the imagination of the time was called existential philosophy. The contemporary reader of

Heidegger's first systematic work was seized by the vehemence of its passionate protest against the secured cultural world of the older generation and the leveling of all individual forms of life by industrial society, with its ever stronger uniformities and its techniques of communication and public relations that manipulated everything. Heidegger contrasted the concept of the authenticity of Dasein, which is aware of its finitude and resolutely accepts it, with the "They," "idle chatter" and "curiosity," as fallen and inauthentic forms of Dasein. The existential seriousness with which he brought the age-old riddle of death to the center of philosophical concern, and the force with which his challenge to the real "choice" of existence smashed the illusory world of education and culture, disrupted well-preserved academic tranquility. And yet his was not the voice of a reckless stranger to the academic world – not the voice of a bold and lonely thinker in the style of Kierkegaard or Nietzsche – but of a pupil of the most distinguished and conscientious philosophical school that existed in the German universities of the time. Heidegger was a pupil of Edmund Husserl, who pursued tenaciously the goal of establishing philosophy as a rigorous science. Heidegger's new philosophical effort also joined in the battle cry of phenomenology, "To the things themselves." The thing he aimed at, however, was the most concealed question of philosophy, one that for the most part had been forgotten: What is being? In order to learn how to ask this question, Heidegger proceeded to define the being of human Dasein in an ontologically positive way, instead of understanding it as "merely finite," that is, in terms of an infinite and always existing Being, as previous metaphysics had done. The ontological priority that the being of human Dasein acquired for Heidegger defined his philosophy as "fundamental ontology." Heidegger called the ontological determinations of finite human Dasein determinations of existence "existentials." With methodical precision, he contrasted these basic concepts with the categories of the present-at-hand that had dominated previous metaphysics. When Heidegger raised once again the ancient question of the meaning of being, he did not want to lose sight of the fact that human Dasein does not have its real being in determinable presence-at-hand, but rather in the dynamic of the care with which it is concerned about its own future and its own being. Human Dasein is distinguished by the fact that it understands itself in terms of its being. In order not to lose sight of the finitude and temporality of human Dasein, which cannot ignore the question of the meaning of its being, Heidegger defined the question of the meaning of being within the horizon of time. The present-at-hand, which science knows through its observations and calculations, and the eternal, which is beyond everything human, must both be understood in terms of the central ontological certainty of human temporality. This was Heidegger's new approach, but his goal of thinking being as time remained so veiled that *Being and Time* was promptly designated as "hermeneutical phenomenology," primarily because self-understanding still represented the real foundation of the inquiry. Seen in terms of this foundation, the understanding of being that held sway in traditional metaphysics turns out to be a corrupted form of the primordial understanding of being that is manifested in human Dasein. Being is not simply pure presence or actual presence-at-hand. It is finite, historical Dasein that "is" in the real sense. Then the ready-to-hand has its place within Dasein's projection of a world, and only subsequently does the merely present-at-hand receive its place.

But various forms of being that are neither historical nor simply present-at-hand have no proper place within the framework provided by the hermeneutical phenomenon of self-understanding: the timelessness of mathematical facts, which are not simply observable entities present-at-hand; the timelessness of nature, whose ever-repeating patterns hold sway even in us and determine us in the form of the unconscious; and finally the timelessness of the rainbow of art, which spans all historical distances. All of these seem to designate the limits of the possibility of hermeneutical interpretation that Heidegger's new approach opened up. The unconscious, the number, the dream, the sway of nature, the miracle of art – all these seemed to exist only on the periphery of Dasein, which knows itself historically and understands itself in terms of itself. They seem to be comprehensible only as limiting concepts.

It was a surprise, therefore, in 1936, when Heidegger dealt with the origin of the work of art in several addresses. This work had begun to have a profound influence long before it was first published in 1950, when it became accessible to the general public as the first essay in *Holzwege*.[2] For it had long been the case that Heidegger's lectures and addresses had everywhere aroused intense interest. Copies and reports of them were widely disseminated, and they quickly made him the focus of the very "idle chatter" that he had characterized so acrimoniously in *Being and Time*. In fact, his addresses on the origin of the work of art caused a philosophical sensation.

It was not merely that Heidegger now brought art into the basic hermeneutical approach of the self-understanding of man in his historicity, nor even that these addresses understood art to be the act that founds whole historical worlds (as it is understood in the poetic faith of Hölderlin and George). Rather, the real sensation caused by Heidegger's new experiment had to do with the startling new conceptuality that boldly emerged in connection with this topic. "World" and "earth" were key terms in Heidegger's discussion. From the very beginning, the concept of the world had been one of Heidegger's major hermeneutical concepts. As the referential totality of Dasein's projection, "world" constituted the horizon that was preliminary to all projections of Dasein's concern. Heidegger had himself sketched the history of this concept of the world, and in particular, had called attention to and historically legitimated the differ-ence between the anthropological meaning of this concept in the New Testament (which was the meaning he used himself) and the concept of the totality of the present-at-hand. The new and startling thing was that this concept of the world now found a counterconcept in the "earth." As a whole in which human self-interpretation takes place, the concept of the world could be raised to intuitive clarity out of the self-interpretation of human Dasein, but the concept of the earth sounded a mythical and gnostic note that at best might have its true home in the world of poetry. At that time Heidegger had devoted himself to Hölderlin's poetry with passionate intensity, and it is clearly from this source that he brought the concept of the earth into his own philoso-phy. But with what justification? How could Dasein, being-in-the-world, which understands itself out of its own being, be related ontologically to a concept like the "earth" – this new and radical starting point for all transcendental inquiry? In order to answer this question we must return briefly to Heidegger's earlier work.

Heidegger's new approach in *Being and Time* was certainly not simply a repetition of the spiritualistic metaphysics of German idealism. Human Dasein's understanding of itself out of its own being is not the self-knowledge of Hegel's absolute spirit. It is not a self-projection. Rather, it knows that it is not master of itself and its own Dasein, but comes upon itself in the midst of beings and has to take itself over as it finds itself. It is a "thrown-projection." In one of the most brilliant phenomenological analyses of *Being and Time,* Heidegger analyzed this limiting experience of Dasein, which comes upon itself in the midst of beings, as "disposition" [*Befindlichkeit*], and he attributed to disposition or mood [*Stimmung*] the real disclosure of being-in-the-world. What is come upon in disposition represents the extreme limit beyond which the historical self-understanding of human Dasein could not advance. There was no way to get from this hermeneutical limiting concept of disposition or moodfulness to a concept such as the earth. What justification is there for this concept? What warrant does it have? The important insight that Heidegger's "The Origin of the Work of Art" opened up is that "earth" is a necessary determination of the being of the work of art.

If we are to see the fundamental significance of the question of the nature of the work of art and how this question is connected with the basic problems of philosophy, we must gain some insight into the prejudices that are present in the concept of a philosophical aesthetics. In the last analysis, we need to overcome the concept of aesthetics itself. It is well known that aesthetics is the youngest of the philosophical disciplines. Only with the explicit restriction of Enlightenment rationalism in the eighteenth century was the autonomous right of sensuous knowledge asserted and with it the relative independence of the judgment of taste from the understanding and its concepts. Like the name of the discipline itself, the systematic autonomy of aesthetics dates from the aesthetics of Alexander Baumgarten. Then in his third Critique – the *Critique of Aesthetic Judgment* – Kant established the problem of aesthetics in its systematic significance. In the subjective universality of the aesthetic judgment of taste, he discovered the powerful and legitimate claim to independence that aesthetic judgment can make over against the claims of the understanding and morality. The taste of the observer can no more be comprehended as the application of concepts, norms, or rules than the genius of the artist can. What sets the beautiful apart cannot be exhibited as a determinate, knowable property of an object, but manifests itself in a subjective factor: the intensification of the *Lebensgefühl* (life-feeling) through the harmonious correspondence of imagination and understanding. What we experience in beauty – in nature as well as in art – is the total animation and free interplay of all our spiritual powers. The judgment of taste is not knowledge, yet it is not arbitrary. It involves a claim to universality that can establish the autonomy of the aesthetic realm. We must acknowledge that this justification of the autonomy of art was a great achievement in the age of the Enlightenment, with its insistence on the sanctity of rules and moral orthodoxy. This is particularly the case at just that point in German history when the classical period of German literature, with its center in Weimar, was seeking to establish itself as an aesthetic state. These efforts found their conceptual justification in Kant's philosophy.

Basing aesthetics on the subjectivity of the mind's powers was, however, the beginning of a dangerous process of subjectification. For Kant himself, to be sure, the determining factor was still the mysterious congruity that obtained between the beauty of nature and the subjectivity of the subject. In the same way, he understood the creative genius who transcends all rules in creating the miracle of the work of art to be a favorite of nature. But this position presupposes the self-evident validity of the natural order that has its ultimate foundation in the theological idea of the creation. With the disappearance of this context, the grounding of aesthetics led inevitably to a radical subjectification in further development of the doctrine of the freedom of the genius from rules. No longer derived from the comprehensive whole of the order of being, art comes to be contrasted with actuality and with the raw prose of life. The illuminating power of poesy succeeds in reconciling idea and actuality only within its own aesthetic realm. This is the idealistic aesthetics to which Schiller first gave expression and that culminated in Hegel's remarkable aesthetics. Even in Hegel, however, the theory of the work of art still stood within a universal ontological horizon. To the extent that the work of art succeeds at all in adjusting and reconciling the finite and the infinite, it is the tangible indication of an ultimate truth that philosophy must finally grasp in conceptual form. Just as nature, for idealism, is not merely the object of the calculating science of the modern age, but rather the reign of a great, creative world power that raises itself to its perfection in self-conscious spirit, so the work of art too, in the view of these speculative thinkers, is an objectification of spirit. Art is not the perfected concept of spirit, but rather its manifestation on the level of the sense intuition of the world. In the literal sense of the word, art is an intuition of the world [*Welt-Anschauung*].

If we wish to determine the point of departure for Heidegger's meditation on the nature of the work of art, we must keep clearly in mind that the idealistic aesthetics that had ascribed a special significance to the work of art as the organon of a nonconceptual understanding of absolute truth had long since been eclipsed by Neo-Kantian philosophy. This dominant philosophical movement had renewed the Kantian foundation of scientific cognition without regaining the metaphysical horizon that lay at the basis of Kant's own description of aesthetic judgment, namely, a teleological order of being. Consequently, the Neo-Kantian conception of aesthetic problems was burdened with peculiar prejudices. The exposition of the theme in Heidegger's essay clearly reflects this state of affairs. It begins with the question of how the work of art is differentiated from the thing. The work of art is also a thing, and only by way of its being as a thing does it have the capacity to refer to something else, for instance, to function symbolically, or to give us an allegorical understanding. But this is to describe the mode of being of the work of art from the point of view of an ontological model that assumes the systematic *priority of scientific cognition*. What really "is" is thing-like in character; it is a fact, something given to the senses and developed by the natural sciences in the direction of objective cognition. The significance and value of the thing, however, are secondary forms of comprehension that have a mere subjective validity and belong neither to the original givenness itself nor to the objective truth acquired from it. The Neo-Kantians assumed that the thing alone is objective and able to support such values. For aesthetics, this assumption would have to mean that even the work of art possesses a thing-like character as its most prominent feature. This thing-like character functions as a substructure upon which the real aesthetic form rises as a superstructure. Nicolai Hartmann still describes the structure of the aesthetic object in this fashion.

Heidegger refers to this ontological prejudice when he inquires into the thing-character of the thing. He distinguishes three ways of comprehending the thing that have been developed in the tradition: it is the bearer of properties; it is the unity of a manifold of perceptions; and it is matter to which form has been imparted. The third of these forms of comprehension, in particular – the thing as form and matter – seems to be the most directly obvious, for it follows the model of production by which a thing is manufactured to serve our purposes. Heidegger calls such things "implements." Viewed theologically, from the standpoint of this model, things in their entirety appear as manufactured items, that is, as creations of God. From man's perspective, they appear as implements that have lost their implement-character. Things are *mere* things, that is, they are present without reference to serving a purpose. Now Heidegger shows that this concept of being-present-at-hand, which corresponds to the observing and calculating procedures of modern science, permits us to think neither the thing-like character of the thing nor the implement-character of the implement. In order to focus attention on the implement-character of the implement, therefore, he refers to an artistic representation – a painting by Van Gogh depicting a peasant's shoes. The implement itself is perceived in this work of art – not an entity that can be made to serve some purpose or other, but something whose very being consists in having served and in still serving the person to whom it belongs. What emerges from the painter's work and is vividly depicted in it is not an incidental pair of peasant's shoes. The emergence of truth that occurs in the work of art can be conceived from the work alone, and not at all in terms of its substructure as a thing.

These observations raise the question of what a work is that truth can emerge from it in this way. In contrast to the customary procedure of starting with the thing-character and object-character of the work of art, Heidegger contends that a work of art is characterized precisely by the fact that it is *not* an object, but rather stands in itself. By standing in itself it not only belongs to its world; its world is present in it. The work of art opens up its own world. Something is an object only when it no longer fits into the fabric of its world because the world it belongs to has disintegrated. Hence a work of art is an object when it becomes an item of commercial transaction, for then it is worldless and homeless.

The characterization of the work of art as standing-in-itself and opening up a world with which Heidegger begins his study consciously avoids going back to the concept of genius that is found in classical aesthetics. In his effort to understand the ontological structure of the work independently of the subjectivity of the creator or beholder, Heidegger now uses "earth" as a counterconcept alongside the concept of the "world" to which the work belongs and which it erects and opens up. "Earth" is a counterconcept to world insofar as it exemplifies self-concealment and concealing as opposed to self-opening. Clearly, both self-opening and self-concealing are present in the work of art. A work of art does not "mean" something or function as a sign that refers to a meaning; rather, it presents itself in its own being, so that the beholder must tarry by it. It is so very much present itself that the ingredients out of which it is composed – stone, color, tone, word – only come into a real existence of their own within the work of art itself. As long as something is mere stuff awaiting its rendering, it is not really present, that is, it has not come forth into a genuine presence. It only comes forth when it is used, when it is bound into the work. The tones that constitute a musical masterwork are tones in a more real sense than all other sounds or tones. The colors of a painting are colors in a more genuine sense than even nature's wealth of colors. The temple column manifests the stone-like character of its being more genuinely in rising upward and supporting the temple roof than it did as an unhewn block of stone. But what comes forth in this way in the work is precisely its concealedness and self-concealing – what Heidegger calls the being of the earth. The earth, in truth, is not stuff, but that out of which everything comes forth and into which everything disappears.

At this point, form and matter, as reflective concepts, prove to be inadequate. If we can say that a world "arises" in a great work of art, then the arising of this world is at the same time its entrance into a reposing form. When the form stands there it has found its earthly existence. From this the work of art acquires its own peculiar repose. It does not first have its real being in an experiencing ego, which asserts, means, or exhibits something and whose assertions, opinions, or demonstrations would be its "meaning." Its being does not consist in its becoming an experience. Rather, by virtue of its own existence it is an event, a thrust that overthrows everything previously considered to be conventional, a thrust in which a world never there before opens itself up. But this thrust takes place in the work of art itself in such a fashion that at the same time it is sustained in an abiding [ins Bleiben geborgen]. That which arises and sustains itself in this way constitutes the structure of the work in its tension. It is this tension that Heidegger designates as the conflict between the world and the earth. In all of this, Heidegger not only gives a description of the mode of being of the work of art that avoids the prejudices of traditional aesthetics and the modern conception of subjectivity, he also avoids simply renewing the speculative aesthetics that defined the work of art as the sensuous manifestation of the Idea. To be sure, the Hegelian definition of beauty shares with Heidegger's own effort the fundamental transcendence of the antithesis between subject and object, I and object, and does not describe the being of the work of art in terms of the subjectivity of the subject. Nevertheless, Hegel's description of the being of the work of art moves in this direction, for it is the sensuous manifestation of the Idea, conceived by self-conscious thought, that constitutes the work of art. In thinking the Idea, therefore, the entire truth of the sensuous appearance would be cancelled. It acquires its real form in the concept. When Heidegger speaks of the conflict between world and earth and describes the work of art as the thrust through which a truth occurs, this truth is not taken up and perfected in the truth of the philosophical concept. A unique manifestation of truth occurs in the work of art. The reference to the work of art in which truth comes forth should indicate clearly that for Heidegger it is meaningful to speak of an *event* of truth. Hence Heidegger's essay does not restrict itself to giving a more suitable description of the being of the work of art. Rather, his analysis supports his central philosophical concern to conceive being itself as an event of truth.

The objection is often made that the basic concepts of Heidegger's later work cannot be verified. What Heidegger intends, for example, when he speaks of being in the verbal sense of the word, of the event of being, the clearing of being, the revealment of being, and the forgetfulness of being, cannot be fulfilled by an intentional act of our subjectivity. The concepts that dominate Heidegger's later philosophical works are clearly closed to subjective demonstration, just as Hegel's dialectical process is closed to what Hegel called representational thinking. Heidegger's concepts are the object of a criticism similar to Marx's criticism of Hegel's dialectic in the sense that they too are called "mythological."

The fundamental significance of the essay on the work of art, it seems to me, is that it provides us with an indication of the later Heidegger's real concern. No one can ignore the fact that in the work of art, in which a world arises, not only is something meaningful given to experience that was not known before, but also something new comes into existence with the work of art itself. It is not simply the manifestation of a truth, it is itself an event. This offers us an opportunity to pursue one step further

Heidegger's critique of Western metaphysics and its culmination in the subjectivism of the modern age. It is well known that Heidegger renders *aletheia*, the Greek word for truth, as *unhiddenness*. But this strong emphasis on the privative sense of *aletheia* does not mean simply that knowledge of the truth tears truth out of the realm of the unknown or hiddenness in error by an act of robbery (*privatio* means "robbery"). It is not the only reason why truth is not open and obvious and accessible as a matter of course, though it is certainly true and the Greeks obviously wanted to express it when they designated beings as they are as unhidden. They knew that every piece of knowledge is threatened by error and falsehood, that it is a question of avoiding error and gaining the right representation of beings as they are. If knowledge depends on our leaving error behind us, truth is the pure unhiddenness of beings. This is what Greek thought had in view, and in this way it was already treading the path that modern science would eventually follow to the end, namely, to bring about the correctness of knowledge by which beings are preserved in their unhiddenness.

In opposition to all this, Heidegger holds that unhiddenness is not simply the character of beings insofar as they are correctly known. In a more primordial sense, unhiddenness "occurs," and this occurrence is what first makes it possible for beings to be unhidden and correctly known. The hiddenness that corresponds to such primordial unhiddenness is not error, but rather belongs originally to being itself. Nature, which loves to hide itself (Heraclitus), is thus characterized not only with respect to its possibility of being known, but rather with respect to its being. It is not only the emergence into the light but just as much the hiding of itself in the dark. It is not only the unfolding of the blossom in the sun, but just as much its rooting of itself in the depths of the earth. Heidegger speaks of the "clearing of being," which first represents the realm in which beings are known as disclosed in their unhiddenness. This coming forth of beings into the "there" of their Dasein obviously presupposes a realm of openness in which such a "there" can occur. And yet it is just as obvious that this realm does not exist without beings manifesting themselves in it, that is, without there being a place of openness that openness occupies. This relation is unquestionably peculiar. And yet even more remarkable is the fact that only in the "there" of this self-manifestation of beings does the hiddenness of being first present itself. To be sure, correct knowledge is made possible by the openness of the there. The beings that come forth out of unhiddenness present themselves for that which preserves them. Nevertheless, it is not an arbitrary act of revealing, an act of robbery, by which something is torn out of hiddenness. Rather, this is all made possible only by the fact that revealment and hiddenness are an event of being itself. To understand this fact helps us in our understanding of the nature of the work of art. There is clearly a tension between the emergence and the hiddenness that constitute the being of the work itself. It is the power of this tension that constitutes the form-niveau of a work of art and produces the brilliance by which it outshines everything else. Its truth is not its simple manifestation of meaning, but rather the unfathomableness and depth of its meaning. Thus by its very nature the work of art is a conflict between world and earth, emergence and hiddenness.

But precisely what is exhibited in the work of art ought to be the essence of being itself. The conflict between revealment and concealment is not the truth of the work of art alone, but the truth of every being, for as unhiddenness, truth is always such an *opposition of revealment and concealment*. The two belong necessarily together. This obviously means that truth is not simply the mere presence of a being, so that it stands, as it were, over against its correct representation. Such a concept of being unhidden would presuppose the subjectivity of the Dasein that represents beings. But beings are not correctly defined in their being if they are defined merely as objects of possible representation. Rather, it belongs just as much to their being that they withhold themselves. As unhidden, truth has in itself an inner tension and ambiguity. Being contains something like a hostility to its own presentations, as Heidegger says. What Heidegger means can be confirmed by everyone: the existing thing does not simply offer us a recognizable and familiar surface contour; it also has an inner depth of self-sufficiency that Heidegger calls its "standing-in-itself." The complete unhiddenness of all beings, their total objectification (by means of a representation that conceives things in their perfect state) would negate this standing-in-itself of beings and lead to a total leveling of them. A complete objectification of this kind would no longer represent beings that stand in their own being. Rather, it would represent nothing more than our opportunity for using beings, and what would be manifest would be the will that seizes upon and dominates things. In the work of art, we experience an absolute opposition to this will-to-control, not in the sense of a rigid resistance to the presumption of our will, which is bent on utilizing things, but in the sense of the superior and intrusive power of a being reposing in itself. Hence the closedness and concealment of the work of art is the guarantee of the universal thesis of Heidegger's philosophy, namely, that beings hold themselves back by coming forward into the openness of presence. The standing-in-itself of the work betokens at the same time the standing-in-itself of beings in general.

This analysis of the work of art opens up perspectives that point us further along the path of Heidegger's thought. Only by way of the work of art were the implement-character of the implement and, in the last analysis, the thingness of the thing able to manifest themselves. All-calculating modern science brings about the loss of things, dissolving their character of standing-in themselves, which "can be forced to do nothing," into the calculated elements of its projects and alterations, but the work of art represents an instance that guards against the universal loss of things. As Rilke poetically illuminates the innocence of the thing in the midst of the general disappearance of thingness by showing it to the angel,[3] so the thinker contemplates the same loss of thingness while recognizing at the same time that this very thingness is preserved in the work of art. Preservation, however, presupposes that what is preserved still truly exists. Hence the very truth of the thing is implied if this truth is still capable of coming forth in the work of art. Heidegger's essay, "What Is a Thing?" thus represents a necessary advance on the path of his thought.[4] The thing, which formerly did not even achieve the implement-status of being-present-to-hand, but was merely present-at-hand for observation and investigation, is now recognized in its "whole" being [in seinem "heilen" Sein] as precisely what cannot be put to use.

From this vantage point, we can recognize yet a further step on this path. Heidegger asserts that the essence of art is the process of poeticizing. What he means is that the nature of art does not consist in transforming something that is already formed or in copying something that is already in being. Rather, art is the project by which something new comes forth as true. The essence of the event of truth that is present in the work of art is that "it opens up an open place." In the ordinary and more restricted sense of the word, however, poetry is distinguished by the intrinsically linguistic character that differentiates it from all other modes of art. If the real project and the genuine artistic element in every art – even in architecture and in the plastic arts – can be called "poetry," then the project that occurs in an actual poem is bound to a course that is already marked out and cannot be projected anew simply from out of itself, the course already prepared by language. The poet is so dependent upon the language he inherits and uses that the language of his poetic work of art can only reach those who command the same language. In a certain sense, then, the "poetry" that Heidegger takes to symbolize the projective character of all artistic creation is less the project of building and shaping out of stone or color or tones than it is their secondary forms. In fact, the process of poeticizing is divided into two phases: into the project that has already occurred where a language holds sway, and another project that allows the new poetic creation to come forth from the first project. But the primacy of language is not simply a unique trait of the poetic work of art; rather, it seems to be characteristic of the very thing-being of things themselves. The work of language is the most primordial poetry of being. The thinking that conceives all art as poetry and that discloses that the work of art is language is itself still on the way to language.

NOTES

1 Cf. Paul Ernst, *Der Zusammenbruch des deutschen Idealismus* (Munich: G. Müller, 1918).
2 Cf. Martin Heidegger, "Über den Ursprung des Kunstwerkes," in *Holzwege* (Frankfurt: Klostermann, 1950), pp. 7–68.
3 [Gadamer is referring to the angel motif in Rilke's *Duino Elegies*. – Trans.]
4 Cf. Heidegger, *Die Frage nach dem Ding: Zu Kants Lehre von den transzendentalen Grundsätzen* (Tubingen: Max Niemeyer, 1962). English translation: *What Is a Thing?*, trans. Barton and Deutsch (Chicago: Henry Regnery, 1967).

8

Deleuze on Nietzsche and Kant

Gilles Deleuze (1925–95) was among the pioneers of what became known as post-structuralism and deconstruction, a role announced by his seminal work *Difference and Repetition* (1968). Deleuze's conception of difference reworks Heidegger's 'ontological difference'. Where Levinas poses the problem of the 'same' and the 'other', Deleuze suggests how repetition cannot be explained by forms of identity in concepts or representations. He seeks instead to understand repetition as a mode of difference that goes beyond the identity of concepts. Although often compared with Jacques Derrida, Deleuze's work also has a distinctive experimental dimension developed in collaboration with Félix Guattari. The most notable works to emerge from this collaboration were the two-volume study of capitalism, schizophrenia and the genealogy of desire entitled *Anti-Oedipus* and *A Thousand Plateaus*. The rhetorical irreverence of these texts approaches the limits of sense. The presiding spirit is Nietzsche. As with Nietzsche's genealogy of morals, their poetics of desire challenges conventional forms of argument and overturns the pieties of philosophy and psychoanalysis. With Michel Foucault, Deleuze and Guattari shared a radical conception of the body and power that opened up new configurations of philosophical thought. Foucault's preface described *Anti-Oedipus* as a book of ethics, a guide to non-fascist arts of living. The friendship between Deleuze and Foucault went through various phases of reciprocal influence and disagreement through to Deleuze's book *Foucault* (1986).

Deleuze also wrote a number of more conventional studies in the history of philosophy. These studies work through immanent exegeses of thinkers such as Liebniz, Spinoza, Hume, Kant and Bergson, stretching the text under interpretation to breaking point. A number of problems recur in Deleuze's critique of Western philosophy, not least his resistance to Hegel and dialectical thought, and an interest in new conceptions of events, bodies and images. Deleuze seeks a new thinking, beyond the existing logics of sense and representation, a search that also motivates his writings on literature, painting and cinema. In *Kant's*

Critical Philosophy (1963), for example, Deleuze's preface offers 'four poetic formulas' from *Hamlet*, Rimbaud, and Kafka to suggest a deeply romantic Kant so as to stage the difference between Kant's work and its contemporary relevance. This gesture points to the constitutive difference in Deleuze's work between his relatively austere philosophical readings and the more rhetorical excesses of a radical literary aesthetic. The juxtaposition of stringent critical reconstructions and more subversively anarchic texts suggests the need to read these conflicting dimensions of Deleuze's work back into each other, and with a developed scepticism as to the rhetorical concerns involved. The dynamics of his work involve an ongoing renegotiation of philosophical and literary boundaries.

Deleuze's radical experiments and his critical reconstruction of the history of philosophy take a decisive early form in *Nietzsche and Philosophy* (1962), from which the following extract is taken. *Nietzsche and Philosophy* is widely seen as a decisive moment in the French reception of Nietzsche, but it also differentiates Deleuze's approach to Kant. As with Heidegger's interpretations of Kant and Nietzsche, Deleuze's interpretation is partial and strategic, seeking to provide synthetic perspectives that sketch new directions for thought. Deleuze has a distinctive style of philosophical paraphrase. His confident reconstruction of Nietzsche's thought as a dynamic whole bears comparison with Heidegger's interpretation of Nietzsche. Deleuze's exposition of Nietzschean 'critique', for example, goes against the tenor of Nietzsche's own accounts of his thinking to juxtapose Nietzsche with Kant. The resulting unstable combination of Nietzsche and Kant remains a powerful current in contemporary thought, not least in resistances to dialectics. Deleuze intimates his polemic against Hegel and Marx to suggest his own conception of critique. In the conclusion to *Nietzsche and Philosophy*, Deleuze suggests there is no possible compromise between Hegel and Nietzsche. The radicalism of Nietzsche, for Deleuze, extends to the demystification of dialectics in what Deleuze calls Nietzsche's anti-dialectic discoveries. The more contemporary polemic against dialectic marks the limits of Deleuze's reinvention of Nietzsche.

FURTHER READING

Primary works

Gilles Deleuze, *Difference and Repetition* (1968), trans. Paul Patton (New York: Columbia University Press, 1994); *The Logic of Sense* (1969), trans. Mark Lester (New York: Columbia University Press, 1990); *Kant's Critical Philosophy* (1963), trans. Hugh Tomlinson and Barbara Habberjam (London: Athlone, 1984); *Foucault* (1986), trans. Sean Hand (Minneapolis: University of Minnesota Press, 1988); *Negotiations, 1972–1990*, trans. Martin Joughin (New York: Columbia University Press, 1995); *Pure Immanence*, trans. Anne Boyman (Cambridge, MA: MIT, 2001).

Gilles Deleuze and Félix Guattari, *Anti-Oedipus: Capitalism and Schizophrenia*, trans. Robert Hurley, Mark Seem and Helen R. Lane (London: Athlone, 1984); *A*

Thousand Plateaus, trans. Brian Massumi (Minneapolis: University of Minnesota Press, 1987); *Kafka: Toward a Minor Literature*, trans. Dana Polan (Minneapolis: University of Minnesota Press, 1986); *What is Philosophy?*, trans. Hugh Tomlinson and Graham Burchell (New York: Columbia University Press, 1994).

Secondary works

David B. Allison, ed., *The New Nietzsche: Contemporary Styles of Interpretation* (Cambridge, MA: MIT, 1985).

Alain Badiou, *Deleuze: The Clamor of Being*, trans. Louise Burchill (Minneapolis: University of Minnesota Press, 2000).

Ronald Bogue, *Deleuze and Guattari* (London: Routledge, 1989).

Constantin V. Boundas, *The Deleuze Reader* (Oxford: Blackwell, 1993).

Constantin V. Boundas and Dorothea Olkowski, eds., *Gilles Deleuze and the Theater of Philosophy* (London: Routledge, 1994).

Ian Buchanan, *Deleuzism: A Metacommentary* (Durham, NC and Edinburgh: Duke University Press and Edinburgh University Press, 2000).

Ian Buchanan, ed., *A Deleuzian Century?* (Durham, NC: Duke University Press, 1999).

Ian Buchanan and Claire Colebrook, eds., *Deleuze and Feminist Theory* (Edinburgh: Edinburgh University Press, 2000).

Michel Foucault, 'Theatrum Philosophicum', *Aesthetics, Method, and Epistemology: Essential Works of Foucault*, vol. 2, ed. James D. Faubion (London: Allen Lane / Penguin, 1998), pp. 343–68 (also in *Language, Counter-Memory, Practice*, trans. Donald F. Bouchard and Sherry Simon (Ithaca: Cornell University Press, 1977), pp. 165–96).

Gary Genosko, ed., *Deleuze and Guattari: Critical Assessments*, 3 vols. (London: Routledge, 2000).

Philip Goodchild, *Deleuze and Guattari: An Introduction to the Politics of Desire* (London: Sage, 1996).

Michael Hardt, *Gilles Deleuze: An Apprenticeship in Philosophy* (London: UCL, 1993).

Eleanor Kaufman and Kevin Jon Heller, *Deleuze and Guattari: New Mappings in Politics, Philosophy, and Culture* (Minneapolis: University of Minnesota Press, 1998).

John Marks, *Gilles Deleuze: Vitalism and Multiplicity* (London: Pluto, 1998).

Dorothea Olkowski, *Gilles Deleuze and the Ruin of Representation* (Berkeley and Los Angeles: University of California Press, 1999).

Paul Patton, ed., *Deleuze: A Critical Reader* (Oxford: Blackwell, 1996).

Gilles Deleuze, 'Critique', *Nietzsche and Philosophy* (1962), trans. Hugh Tomlinson (London: Athlone, 1984), pp. 73–94.

1   Transformation of the Sciences of Man

In Nietzsche's view the balance sheet of the sciences is a depressing one: *passive, reactive* and *negative* concepts predominate everywhere. They always try to interpret phenomena in terms of reactive forces. We have already seen this in the case of physics and biology. But when we look seriously at the sciences of man we see the development of the reactive and negative interpretation of phenomena: "utility", "adaptation", "regulation" and even "forgetting" serve as explanatory concepts (GM 12) [see Abbreviations]. Ignorance of origins and of the genealogy of forces is obvious everywhere – in the sciences of man and even in those of nature. It could be said that the scientist sets up the triumph of reactive forces as his model and wants to chain thought to it. He makes much of his respect for facts and his love of truth. But the "fact" is an interpretation: what type of interpretation? Truth expresses a will: who wills truth? And what does he who says "I am seeking the truth" will? Science today is taking the exploration of nature and man further than ever in a particular direction, but it is also taking submission to the ideal and the established order further than ever. Scholars, even democratic and socialist ones, do not lack piety, they have merely invented a theology which no longer depends on the heart.[1] "Observe the ages in the history of peoples when the scholar steps into the foreground: they are ages of exhaustion, often of evening and decline" (GM III 25 p. 154).

The misrecognition of action, of all that is active, is obvious in the sciences of man: for example, action is judged in terms of its *utility*. It would be precipitate to say that utilitarianism is today an outdated doctrine. In the first place, if this is so it is partly thanks to Nietzsche. Furthermore, a doctrine only lets itself become outdated when it has spread its principles and hidden its postulates in the doctrines which succeed it. Nietzsche asks; what does the concept of utility refer to? That is: to whom is an action useful or harmful? *Who* considers action from the standpoint of its utility or harmfulness, its motives and consequences? Not the one who acts: he does not "consider" action. It is rather the third party, the sufferer or the spectator. He is the person who considers the action that he does not perform – precisely because he does not perform it – as something to evaluate from the standpoint of the advantage which he draws or can draw from it. The person who does not act considers that he possesses a natural light over action, that he deserves to derive advantage or profit from it (GM 12 and 10, BGE 260). We can guess the source of "utility": it is the source of all passive concepts in general, *ressentiment*, nothing but the requirements of *ressentiment*. Utility serves us as an example here. But, in any case, the taste for replacing real relations between forces by an abstract relation which is supposed to express them all, as a measure, seems to be an integral part of science and also of philosophy. In this respect Hegel's objective spirit is no more valid than the no less "objective" concept of utility. Now, in this abstract relation, whatever it is, we always end up replacing real activities (creating, speaking, loving etc.) by the third party's perspective on these activities: the essence of the activity is confused with the gains of a third party, which he claims that he ought to profit from, whose benefits he claims the right to reap (whether he is God, objective spirit, humanity, culture or even the proletariat . . .).

Take another example, that of linguistics. Language is usually judged from the standpoint of the hearer. Nietzsche dreams of another philology, an active philology. The secret of the word is no more on the side of the one who hears than the secret of the will is on the side of the one who obeys or the secret of force on the side of the one who reacts. Nietzsche's active philology has only one principle: a word only means[2] something insofar as the speaker *wills* something by saying it; and one rule: treating speech as a real activity, placing oneself at the point of view of the speaker. "The lordly right of giving names extends so far that one should allow oneself to conceive the origin of language itself as an expression of power on the part of rulers: they say 'this *is* this and this', they seal every thing and event with a sound and, as it were, take possession of it" (GM I2 p. 26). Active linguistics looks to discover who it is that speaks and names. "Who uses a particular word, what does he apply it to first of all; himself, someone else who listens, something else, and with what intention? What does he will by uttering a particular word?" The transformation of the sense of a word means that someone else (another force and another will) has taken possession of it and is applying it to another thing because he wants something else. The whole Nietzschean conception of etymology and philology, which is often misunderstood, depends on this principle and this rule. – Nietzsche applies it brilliantly in the *Genealogy of Morals* where he considers the word "good", its etymology, its sense and the transformation of this sense: he shows how the word "good" was originally created by the masters who applied it to themselves, then taken from their mouths by the slaves, who were then able to call the masters "the evil ones" (GM I 4, 5, 10, 11).

What would a truly active science be like, one permeated by active concepts like this new philology? Only an active science is capable of discovering active forces and also of recognising reactive forces for what they are – forces. Only an active science is capable of interpreting real activities and real relations between forces. It therefore appears in three forms. A *symptomatology*, since it interprets phenomena, treating them as symptoms whose sense must be sought in the forces that produce them. A *typology*, since it interprets forces from the standpoint of their quality, be it active or reactive. A *genealogy*, since it evaluates the origin of forces from the point of view of their nobility or baseness, since it discovers their ancestry in the will to power and the quality of this will. All the sciences, including the sciences of nature, are brought together in such a conception, as are science and philosophy (GM I Final Note). When science stops using passive concepts it stops being a positivism and philosophy ceases to be a utopia, a reverie on activity which makes up for this positivism. The philosopher as such is a symptomatologist, a typologist and a genealogist. We can recognise the Nietzschean trinity of the "philosopher of the future": the *philosopher-physician* (the physician interprets symptoms), the *philosopher-artist* (the artist moulds types), the *philosopher-legislator* (the legislator determines rank, genealogy) (cf. PTG, VP IV).

2   The Form of the Question in Nietzsche

Metaphysics formulated the question of essence in the form: "what is . . . ?" We have perhaps picked up the habit of considering that this question is obvious; in fact we owe it to Socrates and Plato. We must go back to Plato to see just how far the question "what is . . . ?" presupposes a particular way of thinking. Plato asks: "what is beauty? what is justice?" etc. He wants to oppose this form of the question to all other forms. He sometimes sets Socrates against very young men, sometimes against stubborn old men, sometimes against famous sophists. They all seem to produce the same form of reply, citing *the one that* is just, *the one that* is beautiful: a young virgin, a mare, a cooking pot . . . [3] Socrates triumphs: one does not reply to the question "what is beauty?" by citing *the one that* is beautiful. So we get the distinction, dear to Plato, between beautiful things – which are only beautiful, for example, accidentally and according to becoming – and Beauty – which is nothing but beautiful, necessarily beautiful, *the one that is beautiful* in its being and essence. This is why, in Plato, the opposition of essence and appearance, of being and becoming, depends primarily on a mode of questioning, a form of question. Nevertheless, we should ask ourselves whether Socrates' triumph is deserved. For this Socratic method does not seem to be fruitful: it dominates the so-called "aporetic" dialogues, where nihilism is king. It is undoubtedly a blunder to cite something beautiful when you are asked "what is beauty?" But it is less certain that the question: "what is beauty?" is not itself a blunder. It is by no means certain that it is legitimate and well put, even and above all as a way of discovering essence. Sometimes a brief flash of light in the dialogues gives us a momentary indication of what the sophist idea was. Mixing the sophists up with old men and youngsters is a procedure of amalgamation. The sophist Hippias was not a child who was content to answer the question "which one?" when asked the question "what is?" He thought that the question "which one?" was the best kind of question, the most suitable one for determining essence. For it does not refer, as Socrates believed, to discrete examples, but to the continuity of concrete objects taken in their becoming, to the becoming-beautiful of all the objects citable or cited as examples. Asking which one is beautiful, which one is just and not what beauty is, what justice is, was therefore the result of a worked-out method, implying an original conception of essence and a whole sophistic art which was opposed to the dialectic. An empirical and pluralist art.

"What is it? I cried out with curiosity – *which one is it?* you ought to ask! Thus spoke Dionysus, then kept quiet in his own special way, that is to say, in an enticing way."[4] According to Nietzsche the question "which one?" (*qui*) means this: what are the forces which take hold of a given thing, what is the will that possesses it? Which one is expressed, manifested and even hidden in it? We are led to essence only by the question: which one? For *essence is merely the sense and value of the thing*; essence is determined by the forces with affinity for the thing and by the will with affinity for these forces. Moreover, when we ask the question "what is it?" (*qu'est-ce que*) we not only fall into the worst metaphysics but in fact we merely ask the question "which one?" in a blind, unconscious and confused way. The question "what is it?" is a way of establishing a sense seen from another point of view. Essence, being, is a perspectival reality and presupposes a plurality. Fundamentally it is always the question "What is it *for me*?" (for us, for everyone that sees etc.) (VP I 204). When we ask what beauty is we ask from what standpoint things appear beautiful: and something which does not appear beautiful to us, from what standpoint would it become so? And for a particular thing, what are the forces which make or would make it beautiful by appropriating it, what are the other factors which yield to these or, on the contrary, resist them. The pluralist art does not deny essence: it makes it depend, in each case, on an affinity of phenomena and forces, on a coordination of force and will. The essence of a thing is discovered in the force which possesses it and which is expressed in it, it is developed in the forces with affinity for this first one, endangered or destroyed by the forces which are opposed to it and which can take hold of it. Essence is always sense and value. And so the question "which one?" reverberates in and for all things: which forces, which will? This is the *tragic* question. At the deepest level the whole of it is held out to Dionysus. For

Dionysus is the god who hides and reveals himself, Dionysus is will, Dionysus is the one that . . . The question "which one?" finds its supreme instance[5] in Dionysus or in the will to power; Dionysus, the will to power, is the one that answers it each time it is put. We should not ask "which one wills?", "which one interprets?", "which one evaluates?" for everywhere and always the will to power is *the one that* (VP I 204). Dionysus is the god of transformations, the unity of multiplicity, the unity that affirms multiplicity and is affirmed of it. "Which one is it?" – it is always him. This is why Dionysus keeps tantalisingly quiet: to gain time to hide himself, to take another form and to change forces. In Nietzsche's work the admirable poem "Ariadne's Complaint" expresses this fundamental relation between a way of questioning and the divinity hidden behind every question – between the pluralist question and Dionysian or tragic affirmation (DD "Ariadne's Complaint").

3   Nietzsche's Method

From this form of question there derives a method. Any given concept, feeling or belief will be treated as symptoms of a will that wills something. What does *the one that* says this, that thinks or feels that, will? It is a matter of showing that he could not say, think or feel this particular thing if he did not have a particular will, particular forces, a particular way of being. What does he will the one who speaks, loves or creates? And conversely what does the one who profits from an action that he does not do, the one who appeals to "disinterestedness", what does he will? And what about the ascetic, and the utilitarians with their concept of utility? And Schopenhauer when he creates the strange concept of a *negation of the will*? Was this true? But what do they ultimately want, the truth-seekers, those who say: I'm looking for the truth.[6] – Willing is not an act like any other. Willing is the critical and genetic instance of all our actions, feelings and thoughts. The method is as follows: relating a concept to the will to power in order to make it the symptom of a will without which it could not even be thought (nor the feeling experienced, nor the action undertaken). This method corresponds to the tragic question. It is itself the *tragic method*. Or, more precisely, if we remove from the word "drama" all the Christian and dialectical pathos which taints it, it is the method of *dramatisation*. "What do you will?" Ariadne asks Dionysus. What a will wants – this is the latent content of the corresponding thing.

We must not be deceived by the expression: *what* the will wants. What a will wants is not an object, an objective or an end. Ends and objects, even motives, are still symptoms. What a will wants, depending on its quality, is to affirm its difference or to deny what differs. Only qualities are ever willed: the heavy, the light . . . What a will wants is always its own quality and the quality of the corresponding forces. As Nietzsche says of the noble, affirmative and light soul, it has "some fundamental certainty . . . in regard to itself, something which may not be sought or found and perhaps may not be lost either" (BGE 287 p. 196). Thus, when we ask: "what does the one who thinks this want?" we do not abandon the fundamental question "which one?" we merely give it a rule and a methodical development. We are demanding that the question be answered not by *examples* but by the determination of a *type*. And, a type is in fact constituted by the quality of the will to power, the nuance of this quality and the corresponding relation of forces: everything else is symptom. What a will wants is not an object but a type, the type of the one that speaks, of the one that thinks, that acts, that does not act, that reacts etc. A type can only be defined by determining what the will wants in the exemplars of this type. What does the one that seeks truth want? This is the only way of knowing which one seeks truth. The method of dramatisation is thus presented as the only method adequate to Nietzsche's project and to the form of the questions that he puts: a differential, typological and genealogical method.

There is, however, a second objection to such a method: its anthropological character. But all we need to consider is the *type* of man himself. If it is true that the triumph of reactive forces constitutes man, then the whole method of dramatisation aims to discover other types expressing other relations of forces, to discover another quality of the will to power capable of transmuting its too-human nuances. According to Nietzsche the inhuman and the superhuman – a thing, an animal or a god – are no less capable of dramatisation than a man or his determinations. They too are transformations of Dionysus, symptoms of a will which wants something. They too express a type, a type of forces unknown to man. The method of dramatisation surpasses man on every side. A will of the Earth, what would a will capable of affirming the Earth be like? What does it want, this will without which the Earth itself remains meaningless? What is its quality, a quality which also becomes the quality of the Earth? Nietzsche replies: "The weightless..."[7]

4   Against His Predecessors

What does "will to power" mean? Not, primarily, that the will wants power, that it desires or seeks out power as an end, nor that power is the motive of the will. The expression "desiring power" is no less absurd than "willing to live". He who shot the doctrine of "will to life" at truth certainly did not hit the truth: this will does not exist! "For what does not exist cannot will; but that which is alive, how could it still will to live?" (Z II "Of Self-Overcoming" p. 138 and Z III "Of Three Evil Things"). This is why, in spite of appearances, Nietzsche is of the opinion that the will to power is an entirely new concept that he has created himself and introduced into philosophy. He says, with appropriate modesty; "To conceive psychology as I have done, as morphology and the development-theory of the will to power – has never yet so much entered the mind of anyone else: insofar as it is permissible to see in what has hitherto been written a symptom of what has hitherto been kept silent" (BGE 23 p. 38). But more than one writer before Nietzsche had spoken of a will to power or something analogous; more than one after Nietzsche spoke of it again. But the latter were no more disciples of Nietzsche than the former were his masters. They always spoke of it in the sense expressly condemned by Nietzsche: as if power were the ultimate aim of the will and also its essential motive. *As if power were what the will wanted.* But, such a conception implies at least three misunderstandings which threaten the whole philosophy of the will:

(1) Power is interpreted as the object of a *representation*. In the expression "the will wants power or desires domination", the relation of representation and power is so close that all power is represented and every representation is of power. The aim of the will is also the object of representation and vice versa. In Hobbes, man in the state of nature

wants to see his superiority represented and recognised by others. In Hegel, consciousness wants to be recognised by another and represented as self-consciousness. Even in Adler it is still a matter of the representation of a superiority which, when necessary, compensates for the existence of an organic inferiority. In all these cases power is always the object of a representation, of a *recognition* which materially presupposes a comparison of consciousnesses. It is therefore necessary for the will to power to have a corresponding motive which would also serve as the motor of comparison: vanity, pride, self-love, display or even a feeling of inferiority. Nietzsche asks: *who* conceives of the will to power as a will to get oneself recognised? Who conceives of power itself as the object of a recognition? Who essentially wants to be represented as superior and even wants his inferiority to be represented as superiority? It is the sick who want "to represent superiority under any form whatsoever" (GM III 14). "It is the slave who seeks to persuade us to have a good opinion of him; it is also the slave who then bends his knee before these opinions as if it wasn't him who produced them. And I repeat: vanity is an atavism."[8] What we present to ourselves as power itself is merely the representation of power formed by the slave. What we present to ourselves as the master is the idea of him formed by the slave, the idea formed by the slave when he imagines himself in the master's place, it is the slave as he is when he actually triumphs, "this need *for* the noble is fundamentally different from the needs of the noble soul itself, and in fact an eloquent and dangerous sign of its lack" (BGE 287 p. 196). Why have philosophers accepted this false image of the master which resembles only the triumphant slave? Everything is ready for an eminently dialectical sleight of hand: having put the slave into the master, they realise that the truth of the master is in the slave. In fact everything has happened between slaves, conquering or conquered. The mania for representing, for being represented, for getting oneself represented; for having representatives and representeds: this is the mania that is common to all slaves, the only relation between themselves they can conceive of, the relation that they impose with their triumph. The notion of representation poisons philosophy: it is the direct product of the slave and of the relations between slaves, it constitutes the worst, most mediocre and most base interpretation of power (VP III 254).

(2) What is the nature of this first error of the philosophy of the will? When we make power an object of representation we necessarily make it dependent upon the factor according to which a thing is represented or not, recognised or not. Now, only values which are already current, only accepted values, give criteria of recognition in this way. The will to power, understood as the will to get oneself recognised, is necessarily the will to have the values current in a given society attributed to oneself (power, money, honours, reputation).[9] But here again, who conceives of power as the acquisition of assignable values? "The common man never had any value but that which was attributed to him; in no way accustomed to positing values himself, he attributed to himself no other value than that which was recognised in him" (BGE 261), or even that which he got them to recognise. Rousseau reproached Hobbes for having produced a portrait of man in the state of nature which presupposed society. In a very different spirit an analogous reproach is found in Nietzsche: the whole conception of the will to power, from Hobbes to Hegel, presupposes the existence of established values that wills seek only to have attributed to themselves. What seems symptomatic in this philosophy of the will is conformism, absolute misrecognition of the will to power as *creation* of new values.

(3) We must still ask: how are established values attributed? It is always as the result of a combat, a struggle, whatever form this takes – whether secret or open, honest or underhand. From Hobbes to Hegel the will to power is engaged in combat, precisely because the combat determines those who will profit from current values. It is characteristic of established values to be brought into play in a struggle, but it is characteristic of the struggle to be always referred to established values: whether it is struggle for power, struggle for recognition or struggle for life – the schema is always the same. One cannot over emphasise *the extent to which the notions of struggle, war, rivalry or even comparison are foreign to Nietzsche and to his conception of the will to power*. It is not that he denies the existence of struggle: but he does not see it as in any way creative of values. At least, the only values that it creates are those of the triumphant slave. Struggle is not the principle or the motor of hierarchy but the means by which the slave reverses hierarchy. Struggle is never the active expression of forces, nor the manifestation of a will to power that affirms – any more than its result expresses the triumph of the master or the strong. Struggle, on the contrary, is the means by which the weak prevail over the strong, because they are the greatest number. This is why Nietzsche is opposed to Darwin: Darwin confused struggle and selection. He failed to see that the result of struggle was the opposite of what he thought; that it does select, but it selects only the weak and assures their triumph (VP I 395, TI). Nietzsche says of himself that he is much too well bred to struggle.[10] He also says of the will to power: "Abstraction being made from struggle" (VP II 72).

5   Against Pessimism and Against Schopenhauer

These three misunderstandings would be unimportant if they did not introduce an extremely unfortunate "tone" or emotional tonality into the philosophy of the will. The essence of the will is always discovered with grief and dejection. All those who discover the essence of the will in a will to power or something analogous never stop complaining about their discovery, as if they ought to draw from it the strange resolve to flee from it or to ward off its effects. It is as if the essence of the will puts us into an unlivable, untenable and deceptive situation. And this is easily explained: making the will a will to power in the sense of a "desire to dominate", philosophers see this desire as infinite; making power an object of representation they see the unreal character of a thing represented in this way; engaging the will to power in combat they see the contradiction in the will itself. According to Hobbes the will to power is as if in a dream from which only the fear of death will rescue it. Hegel insists on the unreality of the situation of the master, for the master depends on the slave for recognition. Everyone puts contradiction into the will and also the will into contradiction. Represented power is only appearance; the essence of the will does not establish itself in what is willed without losing itself in appearance. Thus philosophers promise the will a *limitation*, a rational or contractual limitation which is the only thing which will be able to make it livable and resolve contradiction. Schopenhauer does not inaugurate a new philosophy of the will in any of these respects. On the contrary, his genius consists in drawing out the extreme consequences of the old philosophy, in pushing the old philosophy as far as it can go. Schopenhauer is not content with an essence of the will, he makes the will the essence of things, "the world seen from the inside". The will has become essence in general and in itself. But, on this basis, what it wants (its objectification) has become representation, appearance in general. Its contradiction become the basic contradiction: as essence it wills the appearance in which it is reflected. "The fate which awaits the will in the world in which it is reflected" is just the suffering of this contradiction. This is the formula of the will to live; the world as will *and* representation. We recognise here the development of a mystification which began with Kant. By making will the essence of things or the world seen from the inside, the distinction between two worlds is denied in principle: the same world is both sensible and super-sensible. But while denying this distinction between worlds one merely replaces it with the distinction between interior and exterior – which is just like that between essence and appearance, that is to say like the two worlds themselves. By making will the essence of the world Schopenhauer continues to understand the world as an illusion, an appearance, a representation (BGE 36, VP I 216 and III 325). – Limiting the will is therefore not going to be enough for Schopenhauer. The will must be denied, it must deny itself. The Schopenhauerian choice: "We are stupid beings or, at best, beings who suppress themselves" (VP III 40). Schopenhauer teaches us that a rational or contractual limitation of the will is not enough, that we must go all the way to mystical suppression. This was the aspect of Schopenhauer that was influential, that influenced Wagner, for example: not his critique of metaphysics, not his "cruel sense of reality", not his anti-Christianity, nor his profound analysis of human mediocrity, not the way in which he showed that phenomena are symptoms of a will, but the complete opposite, the way in which he made the will less and less bearable, less and less livable, at the same time as he was christening it will to live . . . (GS 99).

6 Principles for the Philosophy of the Will

According to Nietzsche the philosophy of the will must replace the old metaphysics: it destroys and supersedes it. Nietzsche thinks that he produced the first philosophy of the will, that all the others were the final avatars of metaphysics. The philosophy of the will as he conceives it has two principles which together form the glad tidings: "willing = creating" and "will = joy", "my *willing* always comes to me as my liberator and bringer of joy. Willing liberates: that is the true doctrine of will and freedom – thus Zarathustra teaches you" (Z II "On the Blissful Isles" p. 111). "Will – that is what the liberator and bringer of joy is called: thus I have taught you my friends! But now learn this as well; The will itself is still a prisoner. Willing liberates . . . " (Z II "Of Redemption" p. 161). "That willing becomes not-willing – how you, my brothers, know this fable-song of madness! I have led you away from these fable-songs when I taught you: 'The will is a creator'" (ibid. p. 162). "It is the intrinsic *right of masters* to create values" (BGE 261 p. 179). Why does Nietzsche present these two principles, creation and joy, as the main point of Zarathustra's teaching, as the two ends of a hammer head which must drive in and pull out? Although these principles may appear vague or undetermined they take on an extremely precise meaning if one understands their critical aspect, that is to say, the way in which they are opposed to previous conceptions of the will. Nietzsche says: the will to power has been conceived as if the will wanted power, as if the power were what the will wanted. Consequently power has turned into something represented, an idea of power of the slave and the impotent was formed, power was judged according to the attribution of ready-made established values; the will to power was not conceived of independently of a combat in which the prize was these established values; consequently the will to power was identified with contradiction and the suffering of contradiction. Against this *fettering* of the will Nietzsche announces that willing *liberates*; against the *suffering* of the will Nietzsche announces that the will is *joyful*. Against the image of a will which dreams of having *established* values attributed to it Nietzsche announces that to will is *to create* new values.

Will to power does not mean that the will wants power. Will to power does not imply any anthropomorphism in its origin, signification or essence. Will to power must be interpreted in a completely different way: power is *the one that* wills in the will. Power is the genetic and differential element in the will. This is why the will is essentially creative. This is also why power is never measured against representation: it is never represented, it is not even interpreted or evaluated, it is "the one that" interprets, "the one that" evaluates, "the one that" wills. But what does it will? It wills precisely that which derives from the genetic element. The genetic element (power) determines the relation of force with force and qualifies related forces. As plastic element it simultaneously determines and is determined, simultaneously qualifies and is qualified. What the will to power wills is a particular relation of forces, a particular quality of forces. And also a particular quality of power: affirming or denying. This complex, which varies in every case, forms a type to which given phenomena corres- pond. All phenomena express relations of forces, qualities of forces and of power, nuances of these qualities, in short, a type of force and will. In Nietzsche's terms, we must say that every phenomenon not only reflects a type which constitutes its sense and value, but also the will to power as the element from which the signification of its sense and the value of its value derive. *In this way the will to power is essentially creative and giving*: it does not aspire, it does not seek, it does not desire, above all it does not desire power. It *gives*: power is something inexpressible in the will (something mobile, variable, plastic); power is in the will as "the bestowing virtue", through power the will itself bestows sense and value.[11] We should not ask whether, in the final analysis, the will to power is unitary or multiple – this would show a general misunderstanding of Nietzsche's philosophy. The will to power is plastic, inseparable from each case in which it is determined; just as the eternal return is being, but being which is affirmed of becoming, the will to power is unitary, but unity which is affirmed of multiplicity. The monism of the will to power is inseparable from a pluralist typology.

The element which creates sense and values must also be defined as the *critical* element. A type of forces not only signifies a quality of forces but a relation between qualified forces. The active type not only designates active forces but a hierarchical whole in which active forces prevail over the reactive forces and where reactive forces are acted; conversely the reactive type designates a whole in which reactive forces triumph and separate active forces from what they can do. It is in this sense that the type implies the quality of power by which certain forces prevail over others. *High* and *noble* designate, for Nietzsche, the superiority of active forces, their affinity with affirmation, their tendency to ascend, their lightness. *Low* and *base* designate the triumph of reactive forces, their affinity with the negative, their heaviness or clumsiness. Many phenomena can only be interpreted as expressing this heavy triumph of reactive forces. Is the whole human phenomenon not an example of this? There are things which are only able to exist through reactive forces and their victory. There are things which can only be said, thought or felt, values which can only be believed, if one is animated by reactive forces. Nietzsche makes this more specific; if one has a heavy and base soul. There is a certain baseness of the soul which is more than error, more than stupidity itself.[12] Thus the typology of forces and the doctrine of the will to power are inseparable, in turn, from a critique which can be used to determine the genealogy of values, their nobility and baseness. – Of course one may ask in what sense and why noble is "worth more" than base or high "worth more" than low. By what right? There is no possible reply to this question if as we consider the will to power in itself or abstractly, as merely endowed with two opposite qualities, affirmation and negation. Why should affirmation be better than negation?[13] We will see that the solution can only be given by the test of the eternal return: what is better and better absolutely is that which returns, that which can bear returning, that which wills its return. The test of the eternal return will not let reactive forces subsist, any more than it will let the power of denying subsist. The eternal return transmutes the negative: it turns the heavy into something light, it makes the negative cross over to affirmation, it makes negation a power of affirming. But negation in this new form has become critique: destruction becomes active, aggression profoundly linked to affirmation. Critique is destruction as joy, the aggression of the creator. The creator of values cannot be distinguished from a destroyer, from a criminal or from a critic: a critic of established values, reactive values and baseness.[14]

7 Plan of *The Genealogy of Morals*

The Genealogy of Morals is Nietzsche's most systematic book. Its interest is twofold: in the first place it is presented neither as a collection of aphorisms nor as a poem, but as a key for the interpretation of aphorisms and the evaluation of poems (GM Preface 8). In the second place it gives a detailed analysis of the reactive type, of the mode and principle of the triumph of reactive forces. The first essay deals with *ressentiment*, the second with bad conscience and the third with the ascetic ideal: *ressentiment*, bad conscience and the ascetic ideal are the figures of the triumph of reactive forces and also the forms of nihilism. – This double aspect of *The Genealogy of Morals* – its presentation as key for interpretation in general and as analysis of the reactive type in particular – is not accidental. Indeed, is it not the pressure of reactive forces themselves that puts obstacles in the way of the arts of interpretation and evaluation, that perverts genealogy and reverses hierarchy? The two aspects of *The Genealogy of Morals* thus form a *critique*. But what critique is and in what sense philosophy is a critique – all this remains to be analysed.

We know that reactive forces triumph by relying on a fiction. Their victory always rests on the negative as something imaginary: they separate active force from what it can do. Active force thus becomes reactive in reality, but as a result of a mystification.

(1) From the first essay Nietzsche presents *ressentiment* as "an imaginary revenge", "an essentially spiritual vindication" (GM 17 and 10). Moreover, the constitution of *ressentiment* implies a *paralogism* that Nietzsche analyses in detail: the paralogism of force separated from what it can do (GM I 13).

(2) The second essay underlines the fact that bad conscience is inseparable from "spiritual and imaginary events" (GM II 18). Bad conscience is by nature *antinomic*, expressing a force which is turned against itself.[15] In this sense it is the basis of what Nietzsche calls "the inverted world" (GM III 14 p. 124). We may note, in general, how much Nietzsche enjoys underlining the insufficiency of the Kantian conception of antinomy: Kant did not understand their source or their true extention.[16]

(3) Finally, the ascetic ideal refers to the deepest mystification – that of the *Ideal*, which includes all the others, all the fictions of morality and knowledge. *Elegantia syllogismi*, Nietzsche says. Here we are dealing with a will that wants nothingness, "but it is at least, and always remains, a will" (GM III 28).

We are merely trying to bring out the formal structure of the *Genealogy of Morals*. If we stop thinking that the organisation of the three essays is fortuitous we must conclude that Nietzsche, in the *Genealogy of Morals*, wanted to rewrite the *Critique of Pure Reason*. Paralogism of the soul, antinomy of the world, mystification of the ideal: Nietzsche thinks that the idea of critique is identical to that of philosophy but that this is precisely the idea that Kant has missed, that he has compromised and spoilt, not only in its application but in principle. Chestov takes pleasure in finding the true *Critique of Pure Reason* in Dostoyevsky, in the *Notes From the Underground*. It is, in fact, primarily a Nietzschean idea to say that Kant's critique failed. But Nietzsche does not rely on anyone but himself to conceive and accomplish the true critique. This project is of great importance for the history of philosophy; for it runs counter not only to Kantianism, with which it competes, but to the whole Kantian inheritance, to which it is violently opposed. What became of critique after Kant, from Hegel to Feuerbach via the famous "critical critique"? – It became an art by which mind, self-consciousness, the critic himself, adapted themselves to things and ideas; or an art by which man reappropriated determinations which he claimed to have been deprived of: in short, the dialectic. But this dialectic, this new critique, carefully avoids asking the preliminary question: "*Who must undertake critique, who is fit to undertake it?*" They talk of reason, spirit, self-consciousness and man; but *to whom* do all these concepts refer? They do not tell us who man or spirit is. Spirit seems to hide forces which are ready to be reconciled with any kind of power, with Church or State. When the little man reappropriates little things, when the reactive man reappropriates reactive determinations, is it thought that critique has made great progress, that it has thereby proved its activity? If man is a reactive being what right has he to undertake a critique? Does the recuperation of religion stop us being religious? By turning theology into anthropology, by putting man in God's place, do we abolish the essential, that is to say, the place? All these ambiguities begin with the Kantian critique.[17] In Kant, critique was not able to discover the truly active instance which would have been capable of carrying it through. It is exhausted by compromise: it never makes us overcome the reactive forces which are expressed in man, self-consciousness, reason, morality and religion. It even has the opposite effect – it turns these forces into something a little more "our own". Finally, Nietzsche's relation to Kant is like Marx's to Hegel: Nietzsche stands critique on its feet, just as Marx does with the dialectic. But this analogy, far from reconciling Marx and Nietzsche, separates them still further. For the dialectic comes from the original Kantian form of critique. There would have been no need to put the dialectic back on its feet, nor "to do" any form of dialectics if critique itself had not been standing on its head from the start.

8 Nietzsche and Kant from the Point of View of Principles

Kant is the first philosopher who understood critique as having to be total and positive *as* critique. Total because "nothing must escape it"; positive, affirmative, because it can not restrict the power of knowing without releasing other previously neglected powers. But what are the results of such a vast project? Can the reader seriously believe that, in the *Critique of Pure Reason*, "Kant's *victory* over the dogmatic concepts of theology ('God', 'soul', 'freedom', 'immorality') damaged that ideal" (GM III 25 p. 156) and can we really believe that Kant "ever had any intention of doing such a thing"? As for the *Critique of Practical Reason* does not Kant admit, from its opening pages, that it is not really a critique at all? He seems to have confused the positivity of critique with a humble recognition of the rights of the criticised. There has never been a more conciliatory or respectful total critique. This opposition between project and results (moreover between the general project and the particular intentions) is easily explained. Kant merely pushed a very old conception of critique to the limit, a conception which saw critique as a force which should be brought to bear on all claims to knowledge and truth, but not on knowledge and truth themselves; a force which should be brought to bear on all claims to morality, but not on morality itself. Thus total critique turns into the politics of compromise: even before the battle the spheres of influence have already been shared out. Three ideals are distinguished: what can I know? what should I do? what can I hope for? Limits are drawn to each one, misuses and trespasses are denounced, but the uncritical character of each ideal remains at the heart of Kantianism like the worm in the fruit: true knowledge, true morality and true religion. What Kant still calls – in his own terms – a fact: the fact of morality, the fact of knowledge . . . The Kantian taste for the demarcation of domains was finally freed, allowed to play its own game, in the *Critique of Judgement*; we learn here what we had known from the start, that the only object of Kant's critique is justification, it begins by believing in what it criticises.

Is this the announcement of the great politics? Nietzsche notes that there has not yet been a "great politics". Critique is nothing and says nothing insofar as it is content to say that true morality makes fun of morality. Critique has done nothing insofar as it has not been brought to bear on truth itself, on true knowledge, on true morality, on true religion.[18] Every time that Nietzsche denounces virtue he is not denouncing false virtues, nor those which make use of virtue as a mask. It is virtue itself in itself, that is to say the pettiness of true virtue, the unbelievable mediocrity of true morality, the baseness of its authentic values that he attacks. "Zarathustra leaves no doubt at this point: he says that it was insight precisely into the good, the 'best', that made him shudder at man in general; that it was from this aversion that he grew wings" (EH IV pp. 330–31). However much we criticise false morality or false religion we remain poor critics, "her majesty's opposition", sad apologists. It is a "justice of the peace's" critique. We may criticise pretenders, we may condemn those who trespass on domains, but we regard the domains themselves as sacred. Similarly for knowledge: a critique worthy of the name must not bear on the pseudo-knowledge of the unknowable, but primarily on the true knowledge of what can be known (VP I 189). This is why Nietzsche, in this domain as in others, thinks that he has found the only possible principle of a total critique in what he calls his "perspectivism": there are no moral facts or phenomena, but only a moral interpretation of phenomena (VP II 550); there are no illusions of knowledge, but knowledge itself is an illusion; knowledge is an error, or worse, a falsification.[19] (Nietzsche owes this final proposition to Schopenhauer. This was the way in which Schopenhauer interpreted Kantianism, radically transforming it in an opposite direction to the dialecticians. Schopenhauer was thus able to prepare the principle of critique: he had stumbled across its weak point, morality.)

9   Realisation of Critique

Kant's genius, in the *Critique of Pure Reason*, was to conceive of an immanent critique. Critique must not be a critique of reason by feeling, by experiencing or by any kind of external instance. And what is criticised is no longer external to reason: we should not seek, in reason, errors which have come from elsewhere – from body, senses or passions – but illusions coming from reason as such. Now, caught between these two demands, Kant concludes that critique must be a critique *of* reason *by* reason itself. Is this not the Kantian contradiction, making reason both the tribunal and the accused; constituting it as judge and plaintiff, judging and judged? (VP I 185). – Kant lacked a method which permitted reason to be judged from the inside without giving it the task of being its own judge. And, in fact, Kant does not realise his project of immanent critique. Transcendental philosophy discovers conditions which still remain external to the conditioned. Transcendental principles are principles of conditioning and not of internal genesis. We require a genesis of reason itself, and also a genesis of the understanding and its categories: what are the forces of reason and of the understanding? What is the will which hides and expresses itself in reason? What stands behind reason, in reason itself? In the will to power and the method which derives from it Nietzsche has at his disposal a principle of internal genesis. When we compared the will to power with a transcendental principle, when we compared nihilism in the will to power with an *a priori* structure, our main aim was to indicate how they differed from psychological determinations. Nevertheless, in Nietzsche, principles are never transcendental; it is these very principles which are replaced by genealogy. Only the will to power as genetic and genealogical principle, as legislative principle, is capable of realising internal critique. Only the will to power makes a transmutation possible.

In Nietzsche the *philosopher-legislator* appears as the philosopher of the future; to legislate means to create values. "*Actual philosophers . . . are commanders and law givers*" (BGE 211 p. 123). This is the Nietzschean inspiration behind Chestov's fine writings: "For us all truths derive from the *parere* – even metaphysical ones. And nevertheless, the only source of metaphysical truths is the *jubere*, insofar as men will not participate in the *jubere*, it will seem to them that metaphysics is impossible." "The Greeks felt that submission, the obedient acceptance of all that presents itself, hides true being from man. In order to reach true reality one must consider oneself as the master of the world, one must learn to command and create . . . Here, where sufficient reason is lacking and where, according to us, all possibility of thinking ceases, they saw the beginning of metaphysical truth."[20] It is not that the philosopher must add the activity of the legislator to his other activities because he is in the best position to do this – as if his own subjection to wisdom qualified him to discover the best possible laws to which men in their turn ought to be subjected. The point is a completely different one: that the philosopher, as philosopher, *is not* a sage, that the philosopher, as philosopher, ceases to obey, that he replaces the old wisdom by command, that he destroys the old values and creates new ones, that the whole of his science is legislative in this sense. "Their 'knowing' is creating, their *creating* is a law-giving, their will to truth is – *will to power*" (BGE 211 p. 123). While it is true that this idea of the philosopher has presocratic roots it seems that its reappearance in the modern world is Kantian and critical. *Jubere* instead of *parere*: is this not the essence of the Copernican revolution and the way in which critique is opposed to the old wisdom, to dogmatic or theological subjection? The idea that *philosophy legislates* as *philosophy* makes the idea that critique *as* critique is internal complete: together they form Kantianism's principal achievement, its liberating achievement.

But in what way did Kant understand his idea of philosophy-legislation? Why does Nietzsche, at the very moment when he seems to revive and develop the Kantian idea, rank Kant among the "philosophical labourers", those who are content to make inventories of current values, the opposite of the philosophers of the future? (BGE 211 p. 123). For Kant, what legislates (in a domain) is always one of our faculties: understanding, reason. We are legislators ourselves only insofar as we make proper use of this faculty and allot our other faculties tasks which conform to it. We are legislators only insofar as we submit to one of our faculties, as it were the whole of ourselves. But to what do we submit in such a faculty, to what forces? Understanding and reason have a long history: they are instances which still make us obey when we no longer want to obey anyone. When we stop obeying God, the State, our parents, reason appears and persuades us to continue being docile because it says to us: it is you who are giving the orders. Reason represents our slavery and our subjection as something superior which make us reasonable beings. Under the name of practical reason, "Kant invented a reason expressly for those cases in which one has no need to bother about reason: namely, when the needs of the heart, when morality, when 'duty' speaks".[21] And, finally, what is concealed in the famous Kantian unity of legislator and subject? Nothing but a renovated theology, theology with a protestant flavour: we are burdened with the double task of priest and believer, legislator and subject. Kant's dream was not to abolish the distinction between two worlds (sensible and super-sensible) but to secure *the unity of the personal* in the two worlds. The same person as legislator and subject, as subject and object, as noumenon and phenomenon, as priest and believer. This arrangement succeeds as theology: "Kant's success is only a theologian's success" (AC 10). Can we really believe that by installing the priest and the legislator *in us* we stop being primarily believers and subjects? The legislators and the priest practise the ministry, the legislation and the representation of established values; all they do is internalise current values. Kant's "proper usage of the faculties" mysteriously coincides with these established values: true knowledge, true morality, true religion...

10   Nietzsche and Kant from the Point of View of Consequences

The Nietzschean and the Kantian conceptions of critique are opposed on five main points.

(1) Genetic and plastic principles that give an account of the sense and value of beliefs, interpretations and evaluations rather than transcendental principles which are simple conditions for so-called facts.

(2) A thought which thinks *against* reason rather than a thought that believes itself to be legislative because it is subject to reason alone – "That which will always be impossible, a reasonable being" (Z). It is a serious mistake to think that irrationalism opposes anything but thought to reason – whether it be the rights of the given, of the heart, of feeling, caprice or passion. In irrationalism we are concerned only with thought, only with thinking. What is opposed to reason is thought itself; what is opposed to the reasonable being is the thinker himself.[22] Because it is reason which receives and expresses the rights of that which dominates thought, thought reconquers its rights and becomes a legislator against reason: *the dicethrow*, this was the sense of the dicethrow.

(3) The genealogist rather than the Kantian legislator. Kant's legislator is an arbitrator, a justice of the peace who supervises the distribution of domains and the allocation of established values. The genealogical inspiration is the opposite of the judicial inspiration. The genealogist is the true legislator. The genealogist is something of a fortune-teller, the philosopher of the future. He does not foretell a critical peace but wars such as we have never known (EH IV 1). He also sees thinking as judging, but judging is evaluating and interpreting, it is creating values. The problem of judgement becomes that of justice and hierarchy.

(4) The reactive man serving himself rather than the reasonable being, functionary of current values, both priest and believer, legislator and subject, conquering and conquered slave. But, in that case, which one undertakes critique? What is the critical standpoint? The critical instance is not the realised man, nor any sublimated form of man, spirit, reason or self-consciousness. It is neither God nor man – for there is still not enough difference between man and God, they can replace each other too easily. The critical instance is the will to power, the critical perspective is that of the will to power. But in what form? Not that of the Overman who is the positive product of critique itself. But there is a "relatively superhuman type" (EH IV 5): the critical type, man *insofar as he wants to be gone beyond, overcome* ... "But you could transform yourselves into forefathers and ancestors of the Overman: and let this be your finest creation!" (Z II "On the Blissful Isles" p. 110).

(5) The aim of critique is not the ends of man or of reason but in the end the Overman, the overcome, overtaken man. The point of critique is not justification but a different way of feeling: another sensibility. [. . .]

ABBREVIATIONS OF NIETZSCHE'S WORKS

BT   *The Birth of Tragedy* (1871) Trans. W. Kaufmann, Random House, 1967
UM   *Untimely Meditations* (1873–76)
HH   *Human, all-too Human* (1878)
WS   *The Wanderer and His Shadow* (1879)
D   *Daybreak* (1880) Trans. R. J. Hollingdale, CUP, 1982
GS   *The Gay Science* (1882) Trans. W. Kaufmann, Random House, 1974

Z   *Thus Spoke Zarathustra* (1883–85) Trans. R. J. Hollingdale, Penguin Books, 1961

BGE   *Beyond Good and Evil* (1886) Trans. R. J. Hollingdale, Penguin Books, 1973

GM   *On the Genealogy of Morals* (1887) Trans. Kaufmann and Hollingdale, Random House, 1967

TI   *The Twilight of the Idols* (1881) Trans. R. J. Hollingdale, Penguin Books, 1968

NW   *Nietzsche contra Wagner* (1888) Trans. W. Kaufmann, The Viking Press, 1954

AC   *The Antichrist* (1888) Trans. R. J. Hollingdale, Penguin, 1968

DD   *Dionysian Dithyrambs* (1888)

EH   *Ecce Homo* (1888) Trans. W. Kaufmann, Random House, 1967

PTG   *Philosophy in the Tragic Age of the Greeks* Trans. M. Cowan, Gateway

VP   *La Volonté de Puissance* Trans. G. Bianquis (from the edition of F. Würzbach), NRF, 1935 and 1937

WP   *The Will to Power* Trans. Kaufmann and Hollingdale, Random House, 1968

NOTES

1   GM III 23–25. On the psychology of the scholar, BGE 206–207.

2   [*Translator's note*:] The expression translated here as "means" is *veut dire*, literally "wants or wills to say". The French sentence reads "un mot ne veut dire quelque chose que dans la mesure où celui qui le dit veut quelque chose en le distant", relating "willing to say" to "willing something" in a way which cannot be simply translated into English. Throughout this translation I have used both "wills" and "wants" for *vouloir* and its derivatives.

3   [*Translator's note*:] Deleuze's exposition of Nietzsche's change in the "form of the question" is central to his interpretation. The change hinges on the difference, in French, between the questions *qu'est-ce que?* and *qui?* This would usually be translated as the difference between the questions "what?" and "who?" But the word *qui?* has a wider sense than the English "who?", picking out particulars of all kinds not just persons. Deleuze suggested translating *qui?* as "which (one)?" since "it is never a person" that is being asked for. He discusses "the form of the question" in the Conclusion and also in the Preface to the English translation.

4   WS Sketch for a Preface, 10 (French translation, Henri Albert, p. 226).

5   [*Translator's note*:] The French word *instance* has a range of senses rather different from the English word – including both "insistence" and "authority" and excluding the sense of "example" which the word has in English. The different senses have been played on by a number of recent French philosophical writers in ways which are very difficult to translate and it has become common practice to retain the word in English.

6   This is always Nietzsche's method, in all his books. It is presented in an especially systematic manner in GM.

7   Z Prologue 3 p. 42: "The Overman is the meaning of the earth. Let your will say: The Overman *shall be* the meaning of the Earth!" Z III "Of the Spirit of Gravity" p. 210: "He who will one day teach men to fly will have moved all boundary stones; all boundary stones will themselves fly into the air to him, he will baptise the earth anew – as 'the weightless'."

8   BGE 261. On the "aspiration to distinction" cf. D 113: "He who aspires to distinction has his eye ceaselessly on his neighbour and wants to know what his feelings are; but the sympathy and abandon which this penchant needs to satisfy itself are far from being inspired by innocence, compassion or benevolence. On the contrary, one wants to perceive or guess in what way the neighbour *is suffering*, internally or externally to our sight, how he is losing power over himself and giving way to the impression that our hand or sight make on him."

9   VP IV 522: "How impossible is it for a demagogue to clearly represent a *higher nature* to himself. As if the essential trait and the true value of higher men consisted in their aptitude to stir up the masses, in short, in the effect that they produce. But the higher nature of the great man resides in the incommunicable thing that differentiates him from others of a different rank." (Effect that they produce = demagogic representation that they make of themselves = established values that are attributed to them.)

10 EH II 9 p. 255: "No trace of *struggle* can be demonstrated in my life: I am the opposite of a heroic nature. 'Willing' something, 'striving' for something, envisaging a 'purpose', a 'wish' – I know none of this from experience."

11 Z III "Of the Three Evil Things" p. 97: "Desire for power: but who shall call it *desire* . . . Oh who shall find the rightful baptismal and virtuous name for such a longing! 'Bestowing virtue' – that is the name Zarathustra once gave the unnameable."

12 cf. Nietzsche's judgements on Flaubert: he discovered stupidity but not the baseness of the soul which it presupposes (BGE 218).

13 There can be no preestablished values here to decide which is *better than*; cf. VP II 530. "I distinguish an ascendent type of life and a type of decadence, decomposition, weakness. Is it thought that the question of precedence between these two types is still in balance?"

14 Z Prologue 9: "the destroyer, the criminal – but he is the creator"; Z I 15 "whoever creates must always destroy".

15 GM II 18: "contradictory concepts such as *selflessness, self-denial, self-sacrifice* . . . their delight is tied to cruelty", p. 88.

16 The source of antinomy is the bad conscience (GM II). Antinomy is expressed as the opposition of morality and life (VP I 304, PTG II, GM III).

17 AC 10 p. 121: "Among Germans one will understand immediately when I say that philosophy has been corrupted by theologian blood. The Protestant pastor is the grandfather of German philosophy, Protestantism itself is its original sin . . . Kant's success is merely a theologian's success."

18 GS 345 p. 285: "the more refined . . . uncover and criticise the perhaps foolish opinions of a people about their morality, or of humanity about all human morality – opinions about its origin, religious sanction, the superstition of free will and things of that sort – and then suppose that they have criticised the morality itself".

19 VP I and II (cf. knowledge defined as "error which becomes organic and organised").

20 Chestov, "La Seconde Dimension de la Pensée", *NRF*, Sept. 1932.

21 VP I 78/WP 414 – analogous passage, AC 12.

22 UM I "David Strauss" 1; III "Schopenhauer Educator" 1: the opposition of private and public thinker (the public thinker is a "cultivated philistine", representing reason). An analogous theme is found in Kierkegaard, Feuerbach and Chestov.

9

Althusser on Marx

Louis Althusser (1918–90) was probably the most influential thinker after 1945 to identify with Marxist-Leninism and the traditions of classical Marxism. Althusser nevertheless conflated a series of otherwise conflictual approaches to generate an idiosyncratic return to Marx. Although loosely identified with structuralist Marxism, Althusser's work became influential as one among a number of post-structuralist attempts to overturn the authority of existential Marxism and phenomenology. Althusserian Marxism came to represent a new compound of ideology critique, involving a triple alliance between psychoanalysis, linguistics and discourse theory, and a new emphasis on scientificity and the analysis of the state. Althusser's attempts to rethink the role of ideology were particularly influential on cultural studies and the way 'subjects' are interpellated by the seemingly intractable forces of capitalism and patriarchy. The Althusserian combination of ideology critique and psychoanalysis suggested ways in which feminists might, for example, understand the deep psychic structures at work in modern society, analysing what Frederic Jameson later called 'the political unconscious'.

Althusser's work was resisted by many Marxists, notably for the way he overstates certain theoretical claims in his reading of Marx. In particular, Althusser's unusual conception of the status of science and the relation between theory and practice differs from more classical Marxist conceptions of praxis. His rethinking of Marxism generated what might be called the 'theory effect', a generalized theoretical resistance to more humanist and empirical approaches to historical study. In *The Poverty of Theory*, for example, E. P. Thompson defended the scientificity of historical materialism and accused Althusser of theoretical formalism, a charge reflected in the way Thompson's title reworks the attack on Proudhon in Marx's book *The Poverty of Philosophy*. Althusser's critics have continued to contest the radical status of 'theory' claimed by Althusser. This resistance to theory echoed more general resistances to theory in the many conflations of critical and literary theory, in which 'theory' itself became associated with radical challenges to conventional approaches and disciplines. The shift from Terry Eagleton's Althusserian book *Criticism and Ideology* to the more iconoclastic and Brechtian strategies of Eagleton's *Literary Theory: An Introduction*, is symptomatic. Many of those who passed through an Althusserian phase subsequently became interested in the work of Derrida and Foucault without revisiting the problems raised by Althusser's contradictory relation to Marxist thought, as though Althusser were the last word in any attempt to make Marxism viable for critical theory.

Althusser's early work, featured in *The Spectre of Hegel*, included a dissertation on Hegel but his later work assimilated ideas from Claude Lévi-Strauss's approach to structural anthropology and from Jacques Lacan's return to Freud through structural linguistics. Emerging through conflict with the humanist strains of Western Marxism exemplified by Lukács and Sartre, Althusser sought to develop a more scientific and anti-humanist account of Marx and Marxism. Concerned to identify Marx's break from Hegelian thought, Althusser developed his approach through strategic readings of Marx, readings focused on the 'scientific' achievement of Marx's *Capital*. In *Reading Capital*, Althusser acknowledges that his reformulation of symptomatic reading was influenced by Lacan's reading of Freud, and also by the approaches to the re-reading of intellectual history and the history of science suggested by Gaston Bachelard, Jean Cavaillès, Georges Canguilhem and Michel Foucault. Thus while Althusser's work challenges the philosophical aporia of classical Marxism and Western Marxist thought, his work also needs to be situated within the conflicts of French philosophy and above all in the claims of scientific reason.

One important feature of Althusser's approach is to pose the difficulty of a Marxist reading of Marx, not least in the light of the vicissitudes of twentieth-century Marxism. Althusser suggests a conception of reading which is rigorously formal, seeking a philosophically self-critical and scientific approach almost to the extent of rejecting conventional Marxist conceptions of history. This new approach has implications for the status of philosophical and critical reading beyond the specific problems posed by Marx and Marxist discourse, opening out questions which become characteristic of post-structuralist approaches to critical reading and the theory of literary production developed by Pierre Macherey. Althusser's collaborators, notably Etienne Balibar, Jacques Rancière and Pierre Macherey, have continued to explore and develop aspects of Althusser's work but working at some distance from Althusser's more polemical formulations. While Althusser's influence has waned, his thinking remains an important point of reference for Marxist cultural critics, such as Frederic Jameson, and for non-Marxist approaches to philosophy and discourse, most notably as an implicit influence on the work of Michel Foucault. Althusser also remains a target for readings of Marx and Marxism that take issue with Althusser in the work of Michel Henry, Jacques Derrida and Slavoj Žižek.

FURTHER READING

Primary works

Louis Althusser and Etienne Balibar, *Reading Capital*, trans. Ben Brewster (London: New Left Books / Verso, 1970).

Louis Althusser, *The Spectre of Hegel: Early Writings*, trans. G. M. Goshgarian (London: Verso, 1997); *Essays on Ideology*, trans. Ben Brewster and Graham Lock (London: Verso, 1984); *Lenin and Philosophy and Other Essays*, trans. Ben Brewster (London: New Left Books, 1971); *For Marx*, trans. Ben Brewster (London: New Left Books, 1977).

Secondary works

Perry Anderson, *Arguments within English Marxism* (London: Verso, 1980).

Etienne Balibar, *The Philosophy of Marx*, trans. Chris Turner (London: Verso, 1995).

Ted Benton, *The Rise and Fall of Structural Marxism: Althusser and His Influence* (London: Macmillan, 1984).

Alex Callinicos, *Althusser's Marxism* (London: Pluto, 1976).

Terry Eagleton, *Criticism and Ideology: A Study in Marxist Literary Theory* (London: Verso, 1978).

Terry Eagleton, *Literary Theory: An Introduction*, 2nd edition (Oxford: Blackwell, 1996).

Gregory Elliott, ed., *Althusser: A Critical Reader* (Oxford: Blackwell, 1994).

Gregory Elliott, *Althusser: The Detour of Theory* (London: Verso, 1987).

André Glucksmann, 'A Ventriloquist Structuralism', *Western Marxism: A Critical Reader*, ed. New Left Review (London: Verso, 1977), pp. 282–314.

Frederic Jameson, *The Political Unconscious: Narrative as a Socially Symbolic Act* (London: Methuen, 1981).

E. Ann Kaplan and Michael Sprinker, eds., *The Althusserian Legacy* (London: Verso, 1993).

Jacques Lezra, ed., *Depositions: Althusser, Balibar, Macherey and the Labor of Reading, Yale French Studies* no. 88 (New Haven: Yale University Press, 1996).

Pierre Macherey, *A Theory of Literary Production*, trans. Geoffrey Wall (London: Routledge and Kegan Paul, 1978).

Juliet Mitchell, *Women: The Longest Revolution* (London: Virago, 1984).

Mark Poster, *Existential Marxism in Postwar France: From Sartre to Althusser* (Princeton: Princeton University Press, 1977).

Ali Rattansi, ed., *Ideology, Method and Marx* (London: Routledge, 1989), especially Jacques Rancière, 'The Concept of "Critique" and the "Critique of Political Economy"', trans. Ben Brewster, pp. 74–180.

Robert Paul Resch, *Althusser and the Renewal of Marxist Social Theory* (Berkeley and Los Angeles: University of California Press, 1992).

Steven B. Smith, *Reading Althusser: An Essay on Structural Marxism* (Ithaca: Cornell University Press, 1984).

Michael Sprinker, *Imaginary Relations: Aesthetics and Ideology in the Theory of Historical Materialism* (London: Verso, 1987).

E. P. Thompson, *The Poverty of Theory and Other Essays* (London: Merlin, 1978).

Louis Althusser, 'From *Capital* to Marx's Philosophy' (1965; first published 1968), *Reading Capital*, trans. Ben Brewster (London: Verso, 1970), pp. 13–34.

1

Of course, we have all read, and all do read *Capital*. For almost a century, we have been able to read it every day, transparently, in the dramas and dreams of our history, in its disputes and conflicts, in the defeats and victories of the workers' movement which is our only hope and our destiny. Since we 'came into the world', we have read *Capital* constantly in the writings and speeches of those who have read it for us, well or ill, both the dead and the living, Engels, Kautsky, Plekhanov, Lenin, Rosa Luxemburg, Trotsky, Stalin, Gramsci, the leaders of the workers' organizations, their supporters and opponents: philosophers, economists, politicians. We have read bits of it, the 'fragments' which the conjuncture had 'selected' for us. We have even all, more or less, read Volume One, from 'commodities' to the 'expropriation of the expropriators'.

But some day it is essential to read *Capital* to the letter. To read the text itself, complete, all four volumes, line by line, to return ten times to the first chapters, or to the schemes of simple reproduction and reproduction on an enlarged scale, before coming down from the arid table-lands and plateaus of Volume Two into the promised land of profit, interest and rent. And it is essential to read *Capital* not only in its French translation (even Volume One in Roy's translation, which Marx revised, or rather, rewrote), but also in the German original, at least for the fundamental theoretical chapters and all the passages where Marx's key concepts come to the surface.

That is how we decided to read *Capital*. The studies that emerged from this project are no more than the various individual protocols of this reading: each having cut the peculiar oblique path that suited him through the immense forest of this Book. And we present them in their immediate form without making any alterations so that all the risks and advantages of this adventure are reproduced; so that the reader will be able to find in them new-born the experience of a reading; and so that he in turn will be dragged in the wake of this first reading into a second one which will take us still further.

2

But as there is no such thing as an innocent reading, we must say what reading we are guilty of.

We were all philosophers. We did not read *Capital* as economists, as historians or as philologists. We did not pose *Capital* the question of its economic or historical content, nor of its mere internal 'logic'. We read *Capital* as philosophers, and therefore posed it a different question. To go straight to the point, let us admit: we posed it the question of its *relation to its object*, hence both the question of the specificity of its *object*, and the question of the specificity of its *relation* to that object, i.e., the question of the nature of the type of discourse set to work to handle this object, the question of scientific discourse. And since there can never be a definition without a difference, we posed *Capital* the question of the specific difference both of its object and of its discourse — asking ourselves at each step in our reading, what distinguishes the object of *Capital* not only from the object of classical (and even modern) political economy, but also from the object of Marx's Early Works, in particular from the object of the *1844 Manuscripts*; and hence what distinguishes the discourse of *Capital* not only from the discourse of classical economics, but also from the philosophical (ideological) discourse of the Young Marx.

To have read *Capital* as economists would have meant reading it while posing the question of the economic content and value of its analyses and schemes, hence comparing its discourse with an object already defined outside it, without questioning that object itself. To have read *Capital* as historians would have meant reading it while posing the question of the relation between its historical analyses and a historical object already defined outside it, without questioning that object itself. To have read *Capital* as logicians would have meant posing it the question of its methods of exposition and proof, but in the abstract, once again without questioning the object to which the methods of this discourse relate.

To read *Capital* as philosophers is precisely to question the specific object of a specific discourse, and the specific relationship between this discourse and its object; it is therefore to put to the *discourse-object* unity the question of the epistemological status which distinguishes this particular unity from other forms of discourse-object unity. Only this reading can determine the answer to a question that concerns the place *Capital* occupies in the history of knowledge. This question can be crystallized as follows: is *Capital* merely one ideological product among others, classical economics given a Hegelian form, the imposition of anthropological categories defined in the philosophical Early Works on the domain of economic reality; the 'realization' of the idealist aspirations of the *Jewish Question* and the *1844 Manuscripts*? Is *Capital* merely a continuation or even culmination of classical political economy, from which Marx inherited both object and concepts? And is *Capital* distinguished from classical economics not by its object, but only by its *method*, the dialectic he borrowed from Hegel? Or, on the contrary, does *Capital* constitute a real epistemological mutation of its object, theory and method? Does *Capital* represent the founding moment of a new discipline, the founding moment of a science — and hence a real event, a theoretical revolution, simultaneously rejecting the classical political economy and the Hegelian and Feuerbachian ideologies of its prehistory — the absolute beginning of the history of a science? And if this new science is the theory of *history* will it not make possible in return a knowledge of its own *prehistory* — and hence a clear view of both classical economics and the philosophical works of Marx's Youth? Such are the implications of the epistemological question posed to *Capital* by a philosophical reading of it.

Hence a philosophical reading of *Capital* is quite the opposite of an innocent reading. It is a guilty reading, but not one that absolves its crime on confessing it. On the contrary, it takes the responsibility for its crime as a 'justified crime' and defends it by proving its necessity. It is therefore a special reading which exculpates itself as a reading by posing every guilty reading the very question that unmasks its innocence, the mere question of its innocence: *what is it to read?*

3

However paradoxical it may seem, I venture to suggest that our age threatens one day to appear in the history of human culture as marked by the most dramatic and difficult trial of all, the discovery of and training in the meaning of the 'simplest' acts of existence: seeing, listening, speaking, reading – the acts which relate men to their works, and to those works thrown in their faces, their 'absences of works'. And contrary to all today's reigning appearances, we do not owe these staggering knowledges to psychology, which is built on the absence of a concept of them, but to a few men: Marx, Nietzsche and Freud. Only since Freud have we begun to suspect what listening, and hence what speaking (and keeping silent), *means* (*veut dire*); that this '*meaning*' (*vouloir dire*) of speaking and listening reveals beneath the innocence of speech and hearing the culpable depth of a second, *quite different* discourse, the discourse of the unconscious.[1] I dare maintain that only since Marx have we had to begin to suspect what, in theory at least, *reading* and hence writing *means* (*veut dire*). It is certainly no accident that we have been able to reduce all the ideological pretensions which reigned on high over the *1844 Manuscripts*, and still craftily haunt the temptations to historicist backsliding in *Capital*, to the explicit innocence of a *reading*. For the Young Marx, to know the essence of things, the essence of the historical human world, of its economic, political, aesthetic and religious productions, was simply to *read* (*lesen, herauslesen*) in black and white the presence of the 'abstract' essence in the transparency of its 'concrete' existence. This immediate reading of essence in existence expresses the religious model of Hegel's Absolute Knowledge, that End of History in which the concept at last becomes fully visible, present among us in person, tangible in its sensory existence – in which *this* bread, *this* body, *this* face and *this* man are the Spirit itself. This sets us on the road to understanding that the yearning for a reading *at sight*, for Galileo's '*Great Book of the World*' itself, is older than all science, that it is still silently pondering the religious fantasies of epiphany and parousia, and the fascinating myth of the Scriptures, in which the body of truth, dressed in its words, is the Book: the Bible. This makes us suspect that to treat nature or reality as a Book, in which, according to Galileo, is spoken the silent discourse of a language whose 'characters are triangles, circles and other geometrical figures', it was necessary to have a certain idea of *reading* which makes a written discourse the immediate transparency of the true, and the real the discourse of a voice.

   The first man ever to have posed the problem of *reading*, and in consequence, of *writing*, was Spinoza, and he was also the first man in the world to have proposed both a theory of history and a philosophy of the opacity of the immediate. With him, for the first time ever, a man linked together in this way the essence of reading and the essence of history in a theory of the difference between the imaginary and the true. This explains to us why Marx could not possibly have become Marx except by founding a theory of history and a philosophy of the historical distinction between ideology and science, and why in the last analysis this foundation was consummated in the dissipation of the religious myth of *reading*. The Young Marx of the *1844 Manuscripts* read the human essence at sight, immediately, in the transparency of its alienation. *Capital*, on the contrary, exactly measures a distance and an internal dislocation (*décalage*) in the real, inscribed in its *structure*, a distance and a dislocation such as to make their own effects themselves illegible, and the illusion of an immediate reading of them the ultimate apex of their effects: *fetishism*. It was essential to turn to history to track down this myth of reading to its lair, for it was from the history in which they offered it the cult of their religions and philosophies that men had projected it onto nature, so as not to perish in the daring project of knowing it. Only from history in thought, the theory of history, was it possible to account for the historical religion of reading: by discovering that the truth of history cannot be read in its manifest discourse, because the text of history is not a text in which a voice (the Logos) speaks, but the inaudible and illegible notation of the effects of a structure of structures. A reading of some of our expositions will show that, far from making metaphorical suggestions, I take the terms I am using literally. To break with the religious myth of reading: with Marx this theoretical necessity took precisely the form of a rupture with the Hegelian conception of the whole as a 'spiritual' totality, to be precise, as an *expressive* totality. It is no accident that when we turn the thin sheet of the theory of reading, we discover beneath it a theory of *expression*, and that we discover this theory of the expressive totality (in which each part is *pars totalis*, immediately expressing the whole that it inhabits in person) to be the theory which, in Hegel, for the last time and on the terrain of history itself, assembled all the complementary religious myths of the voice (the Logos) speaking in the sequences of a discourse; of the Truth that inhabits its Scripture; – and of the ear that hears or the eye that reads this discourse, in order to discover in it (if they are pure) the speech of the Truth which inhabits each of its Words in person. Need I add that once we have broken with the religious complicity between Logos and Being; between the Great Book that was, in its very being, the World, and the discourse of the knowledge of the world; between the essence of things and its reading; – once we have broken those tacit pacts in which the men of a still fragile age secured themselves with magical alliances against the precariousness of history and the trembling of their own daring – need I add that, once we have broken these ties, a new conception of *discourse* at last becomes possible?

4

Returning to Marx, we note that not only in what he says but in what he does we can grasp the transition from an earlier idea and practice of reading to a new practice of reading, and to a theory of history capable of providing us with a new theory of *reading*.

When we read Marx, we immediately find a *reader* who *reads* to us, and out loud. The fact that Marx was a prodigious reader is much less important for us than the fact that Marx felt the need to fill out his text by reading out loud, not only for the pleasure of quotation, or through scrupulousness in his references (his accuracy in this was fanatical, as his opponents learnt to their cost), not only because of the intellectual honesty which made him always and generously recognize his debts (alas, *he* knew what a debt was), but for reasons deeply rooted in the theoretical conditions of his work of discovery. So Marx reads out loud to us, not only in the *Theories of Surplus Value*[2] (a book which remains essentially in note form), but also in *Capital*: he reads Quesnay, he reads Smith, he reads Ricardo, etc. He reads them in what seems a perfectly lucid way: in order to support himself with what is correct in what they say, and in order to criticize what is false in what they say – in sum, to *situate* himself with respect to the acknowledged masters of Political Economy. However, the reading Marx makes of Smith and Ricardo is only lucid for a certain reading of this reading: for an immediate reading that does not question what it reads, but takes the obvious in the text read for hard cash. In reality, Marx's reading of Smith-Ricardo (they will be my example here) is, on *looking* at it closely, a rather special one. It is a double reading – or rather a reading which involves two radically different reading principles.

In the *first reading*, Marx reads his predecessor's discourse (Smith's for instance) through his own discourse. The result of this reading through a grid, in which Smith's text is seen through Marx's, projected onto it as a measure of it, is merely a summary of concordances and discordances, the balance of what Smith discovered and what he missed, of his merits and failings, of his presences and absences. In fact, this reading is a retrospective theoretical reading, in which what Smith could not see or understand appears only as a radical omission. Certain of these omissions do refer to others, and the latter to a primary omission – but even this reduction restricts us to the observation of presences and absences. As for the omissions themselves, this reading does not provide reasons for them, since the observation of them destroys them: the continuity of Marx's discourse shows the lacunae in Smith's discourse which are invisible (to Smith) beneath the apparent continuity of his discourse. Marx very often explains these omissions by Smith's distractions, or in the strict sense, his *absences*: he did not *see* what was, however, staring him in the face, he did not grasp what was, however, in his hands. '*Oversights*' (*bévues*) all more or less related to the '*enormous oversight*', the confusion of constant capital and variable capital which dominates all classical economics with its 'incredible' aberration. This reduces every weakness in the system of concepts that makes up knowledge to a psychological weakness of 'vision'. And if it is absences of *vision* that explain these *oversights*, in the same way and by the same necessity, it is the presence and acuteness of 'vision' that will explain these '*sightings*' (*vues*): all the knowledges recognized.

This single logic of sighting and oversight thus reveals itself to us as what it is: the logic of a conception of knowledge in which all the work of knowledge is reduced in principle to the recognition of the mere relation of *vision*; in which the whole nature of its object is reduced to the mere condition of a *given*. What Smith did not see, through a weakness of vision, Marx sees: what Smith did not see was perfectly visible, and it was because it was visible that Smith could fail to see it while Marx could see it. We are in a circle – we have relapsed into the mirror myth of knowledge as the vision of a given object or the reading of an established text, neither of which is ever anything but transparency itself – the sin of blindness belonging by right to vision as much as the virtue of clear-sightedness – to the eye of man. But as one is always treated as one treats others, this reduces Marx to Smith minus the myopia – it reduces to nothing the whole gigantic effort by which Marx *tore* himself from Smith's supposed myopia; it reduces to a mere difference of *vision* this day in which all cats are no longer grey; it reduces to nothing the historical distance and theoretical dislocation (*décalage*) in which Marx thinks the theoretical difference that nevertheless separates him from Smith for ever. And finally, we too are condemned to the same fate of vision – condemned to see in Marx only what he *saw*.

5

But there is in Marx a *second quite different reading*, with nothing in common with the first. The latter, which is only sustained by the dual and conjoint observation of presences and absences, of sights and oversights, can itself be blamed for a remarkable oversight: it does not *see* that the combined existence of sightings and oversights in an author poses a problem, the problem of their *combination*. It does not see this problem, precisely because this problem is only visible insofar as it is invisible, because this problem concerns something quite different from given objects that can be seen so long as one's eyes are clear: a necessary invisible connexion between the field of the visible and the field of the invisible, a connexion which defines the necessity of the obscure field of the invisible, as a necessary effect of the structure of the visible field.

But in order to make what I mean by this more comprehensible, I shall leave this abrupt posing of the question in suspense for the moment, and make a detour back to it through an analysis of the *second kind of reading* we find in Marx. I only need one example: the admirable Chapter XIX of *Capital*, on wages (T.II, pp. 206ff.; Vol. I, pp. 535ff.),[3] secretly reflected backstage in Engels's extraordinary theoretical remarks in his Preface to Volume Two (pp. 14–19).

I therefore quote Marx, *reader* of the classical economists:

> Classical political economy naïvely borrowed from everyday life the category 'price of labour' without any prior verification, and then asked the question, how is this price determined? It soon recognized that the relations of demand and supply explained, in regard to the price of labour, as of all other commodities, nothing but the oscillations of the market-price above or below a certain figure. If demand and supply balance, the variation in prices they produce ceases, but then the effect of demand and supply ceases, too. At the moment when demand and supply are in equilibrium, the price of labour no longer depends on their action and must be determined as if they did not exist. This price, the centre of gravity of the market prices, thus emerged as the true object of scientific analysis.
>
> The same result was obtained by taking a period of several years and calculating the averages to which the alternative rising and falling movements could be reduced by continuous compensations. This left an average price, a relatively constant magnitude, which predominates over the oscillations in the market prices and regulates them internally. This average price, the Physiocrats' 'necessary price' – Adam Smith's 'natural price' – can, with labour, as with all other commodities, be nothing else than its *value* expressed in money. 'The commodity,' says Smith, 'is then sold for precisely *what it is worth*.'
>
> In this way, classical political economy believed it had ascended from the accidental prices of labour to the real value of labour. It then determined this value by the value of the subsistence goods necessary for the maintenance and reproduction of the labourer. *It thus unwittingly changed terrain* by substituting for the value of labour, up to this point, *the apparent object of its investigations*, the value of labour power, a power which only exists in the personality of the labourer, and is as different from its function, labour, as a machine is from its performance. Hence the course of the analysis had led them forcibly not only from the market prices of labour to its necessary price and its value, but had led to their resolution of the so-called value of labour into the value of labour power, so that from then on the former should have been treated merely as a phenomenal form of the latter.

The result the analysis led to, therefore, was *not a resolution of the problem as it emerged at the beginning, but a complete change in the terms of that problem.*

Classical economy never arrived at an awareness of this substitution, exclusively pre-occupied as it was with the difference between the current prices of labour and its value, with the relation of this value to the values of commodities, to the rate of profit, etc. The deeper it went into the analysis of value in general, the more the so-called value of labour led it into inextricable contradictions... (T.II, pp. 208–9; Vol. I, pp. 537–8)

I take this astonishing text for what it is: a protocol of Marx's *reading* of classical economics. Here again it is tempting to believe that we are destined to a conception of reading which adds up the balance of sightings and oversights. Classical political economy certainly saw that... but it did not see that... it 'never arrived at' a sight of... Here again, it seems as if this balance of sights and oversights is found beneath a grid, the classical absences revealed by the Marxist presences. But there is one small, one very small difference, which, I warn the reader straight away, we have no intention of *not seeing*! It is this: what classical political economy does not see, is not what it does not see, it is *what it sees*; it is not what it lacks, on the contrary, it is *what it does not lack*; it is not what it misses, on the contrary, it is *what it does not miss*. The oversight, then, is not to see what one sees, the oversight no longer concerns the object, but *the sight* itself. The oversight is an oversight that concerns *vision*: non-vision is therefore inside vision, it is a form of vision and hence has a necessary relationship with vision.

We have reached our real problem, the problem that exists *in* and is posed *by* the actual identity of this organic confusion of non-vision in vision. Or rather, in this observation of non-vision, or of oversight, we are no longer dealing with a reading of classical economics through the grid of Marx's theory alone, with a comparison between classical theory and Marxist theory, the latter providing the standard – for we never compare classical theory with anything *except itself*, its non-vision with its vision. We are therefore dealing with our problem in its pure state, defined in a single domain, without any regression to infinity. To understand this necessary and paradoxical identity of non-vision and vision within vision itself is very exactly to pose our problem (the problem of the necessary connexion which unites the visible and the invisible), and to pose it properly is to give ourselves a chance of solving it.

6

How, therefore, is this identity of non-vision and vision in vision possible? Let us reread our text carefully. In the course of the questions classical economics asked about the 'value of labour' something very special has happened. Classical political economy has '*produced*' (just as Engels will say, in the Preface to Volume Two, that phlogistic chemistry 'produced' oxygen and classical economics 'produced' surplus value) a correct answer: the value of 'labour' is equal to the value of the subsistence goods necessary for the reproduction of 'labour'. A correct answer is a correct answer. Any reader in the 'first manner' will give Smith and Ricardo a good mark and pass on to other observations. Not Marx. For what we shall call his eye has been attracted by a remarkable property of this answer; *it is the correct answer to a question that has just one failing: it was never posed.*

The original question as the classical economic text formulated it was: what is the value of labour? Reduced to the content that can be rigorously defended in the text where classical economics produced it, the answer should be written as follows: '*The value of* labour ( ) *is equal to the value of the subsistence goods necessary for the maintenance and reproduction of labour ( ).*' There are two *blanks*, two absences in the text of the answer. Thus Marx makes us *see* blanks in the text of classical economics' answer; but that is merely to make us see what the classical text itself says while not saying it, does not say while saying it. Hence it is not Marx who says what the classical text does not say, it is not Marx who intervenes to impose from without on the classical text a discourse which reveals its silence – *it is the classical text itself which tells us that it is silent*: its silence is *its own words*. In fact, if we suppress our 'slots', our blanks, we still have the same discourse, the same apparently 'full' sentence: '*the value of labour is equal to the value of the subsistence goods necessary for the maintenance and reproduction of labour.*' But this sentence means nothing: what is the maintenance of 'labour'? what is the reproduction of 'labour'? The substitution of one word for another at the end of the answer: 'labourer' for 'labour', might seem to settle the question. '*The value of labour is equal to the value of the subsistence goods necessary for the maintenance and reproduction of the labourer.*' But as the labourer is not the labour the term at the end of the sentence now clashes with the term at the beginning: they do not have the same content and the equation cannot be made, for it is not the labourer who is bought for the wages, but his 'labour'. And how are we to situate the first labour in the second term: 'labourer'? In even uttering this sentence, therefore, precisely at the level of the term '*labour*', at the beginning and end of the answer, there is something lacking, and this lack is strictly designated by the function of the terms themselves in the whole sentence. If we suppress our slots – our blanks – we are merely reconstituting a sentence which, if it is taken literally, itself designates in itself these *points of emptiness*, restores these slots as the marks of an omission produced by the 'fullness' of the utterances itself.

This omission, located *by the answer* in the answer itself immediately next to the word '*labour*', is no more than the presence in the answer of the absence of its question, the omission *of its question*. For the question posed does not seem to contain anything by which to *locate* in it this omission. '*What is the value of labour?*' is a sentence identical to a concept, it is a concept-sentence which is content to *utter* the concept 'value of labour', an utterance-sentence which does not designate any omission in itself, unless it is itself as a whole, as a concept, a question *manqué*, a concept *manqué*, the omission (*manque*) of a concept. It is the answer that answers us about the question, since the question's only space is this very concept of 'labour' which is designated by the answer as *the site of the omission*. It is the answer that tells us that the question is *its own omission*, and nothing else.

If the answer, including its omissions, is correct, and if *its* question is merely the omission of its concept, it is because the answer is the answer to *a different question*, which is peculiar in one respect, it has not been uttered in the classical economic text, but is uttered as slots in its answer, precisely *in the slots in its answer*. That is why Marx can write:

> *The result the analysis led to, therefore, was not a resolution of the problem as it emerged at the beginning, but a complete change in the terms of the problem.*

That is why Marx can pose the unuttered *question*, simply by uttering the concept present in an unuttered form in the emptinesses in the *answer*, sufficiently present in this answer to produce and reveal these emptinesses as the emptinesses of a presence. Marx re-establishes the continuity of the utterance by introducing/re-establishing in the utterance the concept of *labour power*, present in the emptinesses in the utterance of classical political economy's answer – and at the same time as establishing/re-establishing the continuity of the answer, by the utterance of the concept of labour power, he produces the as yet unposed question, which the as yet un-asked-for answer answered.

The answer then becomes: '*The value of labour-power is equal to the value of the subsistence goods necessary for the maintenance and reproduction of labour power*' – and *its* question is produced as follows: '*what is the value of labour power?*'

This restoration of an utterance containing emptinesses and this production of *its* question out of the answer enable us to bring to light the reasons why classical economics was blind to what it nevertheless saw, and thus to explain the non-vision inside its vision. Moreover, it is clear that the mechanism whereby Marx is able to see what classical economics did not see while seeing it, is identical with the mechanism whereby Marx saw what classical economics did not see at all – and also, at least in principle, identical with the mechanism whereby we are at this moment reflecting this operation of the sighting of a non-sight of the seen, by *reading* a text by Marx which is itself a *reading* of a text of classical economics.

7

We have now reached the point we had to reach in order to discover from it the reason for this *oversight* where a *sighting* is concerned: we must completely reorganize the idea we have of knowledge, we must abandon the mirror myths of immediate vision and reading, and conceive knowledge as a production.

What made the mistake of political economy possible does indeed affect the *transformation of the object* of its oversight. What political economy does not see is not a pre-existing object which it could have seen but did not see – but an object which it produced itself in its operation of knowledge and which did not pre-exist it: precisely the production itself, which is identical with the object. What political economy does not see is what it *does*: its production of a new answer without a question, and simultaneously the production of a new latent question contained by default in this new answer. Through the lacunary terms of its new answer political economy produced a new question, but '*unwittingly*'. It made '*a complete change in the terms of the*' original '*problem*', and thereby produced a new problem, but without knowing it. Far from knowing it, it remained convinced that it was still on the terrain of the old problem, whereas it has '*unwittingly changed terrain*'. Its blindness and its 'oversight' lie in this misunderstanding, between what it produces and what it sees, in this '*substitution*', which Marx elsewhere calls a '*play on words*' (*Wortspiel*) that is necessarily impenetrable for its author.

Why is political economy necessarily blind to what it produces and to its work of production? Because its eyes are still fixed on *the old question*, and it continues to relate its new answer to its old question; because it is still concentrating on the old '*horizon*' (*Capital*, T.II, p. 210) within which the new problem '*is not visible*' (ibid.). Thus the metaphors in which Marx thinks this necessary 'substitution' suggest the image of a change of terrain and a corresponding change of horizon. They raise a crucial point which enables us to escape from the psychological reduction of the 'oversight' or 'unwittingness'. In fact, what is at stake in the production of this new problem contained *unwittingly* in the new answer is not a particular new object which has emerged among other, already identified objects, like an unexpected guest at a family reunion; on the contrary, what has happened involves a transformation of the *entire* terrain and its *entire* horizon, which are the background against which the new problem is produced. The emergence of this new critical problem is merely a particular index of a possible critical transformation and of a possible latent mutation which affect the reality of this terrain throughout its extent, including the extreme limits of its 'horizon'. Putting this fact in a language I have already used,[4] the production of a new problem endowed with this *critical* character (critical in the sense of a critical situation) is the unstable index of the possible production of a new theoretical *problematic*, of which this problem is only one symptomatic mode. Engels says this luminously in his Preface to Volume Two of *Capital*: the mere 'production' of oxygen by phlogistic chemistry, or of surplus value by classical economics, contains the wherewithal not only to modify the old theory *at one point*, but also to 'revolutionize *all* economics' or *all* chemistry (Vol. II, p. 15). Hence what is in balance in this unstable and apparently local event is the possibility of a revolution in the old theory and hence in the old problematic *as a totality*. This introduces us to a fact peculiar to the very existence of science: it can only pose problems on the terrain and within the horizon of a definite theoretical structure, its problematic, which constitutes its absolute and definite condition of possibility, and hence the absolute determination of *the forms in which all problems must be posed*, at any given moment in the science.[5]

This opens the way to an understanding of the determination of the *visible* as visible, and conjointly, of the invisible as invisible, and of the organic link binding the invisible to the visible. Any object or problem situated on the terrain and within the horizon, i.e., in the definite structured field of the theoretical problematic of a given theoretical discipline, is visible. We must take these words literally. The sighting is thus no longer the act of an individual subject, endowed with the faculty of 'vision' which he exercises either attentively or distractedly; the sighting is the act of its structural conditions, it is the relation of immanent reflection[6] between the field of the problematic and *its* objects and *its* problems. Vision then loses the religious privileges of divine reading: it is no more than a reflection of the immanent necessity that ties an object or problem to its conditions of existence, which lie in the conditions of its production. It is literally no longer the eye (the mind's eye) of a subject which *sees* what exists in the field defined by a theoretical problematic: it is this field itself which *sees itself* in the objects or problems it defines – sighting being merely the necessary reflection of the field on its objects. (This no doubt explains a 'substitution' in the classical philosophies of vision, which are very embarrassed by *having* to say *both* that the light of vision comes from the eye, *and* that it comes from the object.)

The same connexion that defines the visible also defines the invisible as its shadowy obverse. It is the field of the problematic that defines and structures the invisible as the defined excluded, *excluded* from the field of visibility and *defined* as excluded by the existence and peculiar structure of the field of the problematic; as what forbids and represses the reflection of the field on its object, i.e., the necessary and immanent inter-relationship of the problematic and one of its objects. This is the case with oxygen in the phlogistic theory of chemistry, or with surplus value and the definition of the 'value of labour' in classical economics. These new objects and problems are necessarily *invisible* in the field of the existing theory, because they are not objects of this theory, because they are *forbidden* by it – they are objects and problems necessarily without any necessary relations with the field of the visible as defined by this problematic. They are invisible because they are rejected in principle, repressed from the field of the visible: and that is why their fleeting presence in the field when it does occur (in very peculiar and symptomatic circumstances) *goes unperceived*, and becomes literally an undivulgeable absence – since the whole function of the field is not to see them, to forbid any sighting of them. Here again, the invisible is no more a function of *a subject's sighting* than is the visible: the invisible is the theoretical problematic's non-vision of its non-objects, the invisible is the darkness, the blinded eye of the theoretical problematic's self-reflection when it scans its non-objects, its non-problems without seeing them, *in order not to look at them*.

And since, to use terms adopted from some very remarkable passages in the preface to Michel Foucault's *Histoire de la Folie*,[7] we have evoked the conditions of possibility of the visible and the invisible, of the inside and the outside of the theoretical field that defines the visible – perhaps we can go one step further and show that *a certain relation of necessity* may exist between the visible and the invisible thus defined. In the development of a theory, the invisible of a visible field is not generally *anything whatever* outside and foreign to the visible defined by that field. The invisible is defined by the visible as *its* invisible, *its* forbidden vision: the invisible is not therefore simply what is outside the visible (to return to the spatial metaphor), the outer darkness of exclusion – but the *inner darkness of exclusion*, inside the visible itself because defined by its structure. In other words, the seductive metaphors of the terrain, the horizon and hence the limits of a visible field defined by a given problematic threaten to induce a false idea of the nature of this field, if we think this field literally according to the spatial metaphor[8] as a space limited by *another space outside it*. This other space is also in the first space which contains it as its own denegation; this other space is the first space in person, which is only defined by the denegation of what it excludes from its own limits. In other words, all its limits are *internal*, it carried its outside inside it. Hence, if we wish to preserve the spatial metaphor, the paradox of the theoretical field is that it is an *infinite* because *definite* space, i.e., it has no limits, no external frontiers separating it from nothing, precisely because it is *defined* and limited within itself, carrying in itself the finitude of its definition, which, by excluding what it is not, makes it what it is. Its *definition* (a scientific operation *par excellence*), then, is what makes it both *infinite in its kind*, and marked inside itself, in all its determinations, by what is excluded from it *in it* by its very definition. And when it happens that, in certain very special critical circumstances, the development of the questions produced by the problematic (in the present case, the development of the questions of political economy investigating the 'value of labour') leads to the *production* of the *fleeting presence of an aspect* of its invisible within the visible field of the existing problematic – this product can then only be *invisible*, since the light of the field scans it blindly without reflecting on it. This invisible thus disappears as a theoretical lapse, absence, lack of symptom. It manifests itself exactly as it is: invisible to theory – and that is why Smith made his 'oversight'.

To see this invisible, to see these 'oversights', to identify the lacunae in the fullness of this discourse, the blanks in the crowded text, we need something quite different from an acute or attentive gaze; we need an *informed* gaze, a new gaze, itself produced by a reflection of the 'change of terrain' on the exercise of vision, in which Marx pictures the transformation of the problematic. Here I take this transformation for a fact, without any claim to analyse the mechanism that unleashed it and completed it. The fact that this *'change of terrain'* which produces as its effect this metamorphosis in the gaze, was itself only produced in very specific, complex and often dramatic conditions; that it is absolutely irreducible to the idealist myth of a mental decision to change 'view-points'; that it brings into play a whole process that the subject's sighting, far from producing, merely reflects in its own place; that in this process of real transformation of the means of production of knowledge, the claims of a 'constitutive subject' are as vain as are the claims of the subject of vision in the production of the visible; that the whole process takes place in the dialectical crisis of the mutation of a theoretical structure in which the 'subject' plays, not the part it believes it is playing, but the part which is assigned to it by the mechanism of the process – all these are questions that cannot be studied here. It is enough to remember that the subject must have occupied its new place in the new terrain,[9] in other words that the subject must already, even partly unwittingly, have been installed in this new terrain, for it to be possible to apply to the old invisible the informed gaze that will make that invisible visible. Marx can see what escaped Smith's gaze because he has already occupied this new terrain which, in what new answers it had produced, had nevertheless been produced though unwittingly, by the old problematic.

8

Such is Marx's second reading: a reading which might well be called *'symptomatic'* (*symptomale*), insofar as it divulges the undivulged event in the text it reads, and in the same movement relates it to *a different text*, present as a necessary absence in the first. Like his first reading, Marx's second reading presupposes the existence of *two texts*, and the measurement of the first against the second. But what distinguishes this new reading from the old one is the fact that in the new one the *second text* is articulated with the lapses in the first text. Here again, at least in the way peculiar to theoretical texts (the only ones whose analysis is at issue here), we find the necessity and possibility of one reading on two bearings simultaneously.

In the papers you are about to *read*, and which do not escape the law I have pronounced – assuming that they have some claim to be treated, for the time being at least, as discourses with a theoretical meaning – we have simply tried to apply to Marx's reading the *'symptomatic'* reading with which Marx managed to read the illegible in Smith, by measuring the problematic initially visible in his writings against the invisible problematic contained in the paradox of *an answer which does not correspond to any question posed.* You will also find that the infinite distance which separates Marx from Smith and in consequence our relation to Marx from Marx's relation to Smith, is the following radical difference: whereas in his text Smith produces an answer which not only does not answer any of the immediately preceding questions, but does not even answer *any* other question he ever posed anywhere in his work; with Marx, on the contrary, when he does happen to formulate *an answer without a question*, with a little patience and perspicacity we can find *the question* itself *elsewhere*, twenty or one hundred pages further on, with respect to some other object, enveloped in some other matter, or, on occasion, in Engels's immediate comments on Marx, for Engels has flashes of profound inspiration.[10] And if, as I have dared suggest, there is undoubtedly in Marx an important *answer* to a *question that is nowhere posed*, an answer which Marx only succeeds in formulating on condition of multiplying the images required to render it, the answer of the '*Darstellung*' and its avatars, it is surely because the age Marx lived in did not provide him, and he could not acquire in his lifetime, an adequate concept with which to think what he produced: *the concept of the effectivity of a structure on its elements*. It will no doubt be said that this is merely a word, and that only the word is missing, since the *object* of the word is there complete. Certainly, but this word is a *concept*, and the repercussions of the structural lack of this concept can be found in certain precise theoretical effects on certain assignable *forms* of Marx's discourse, and in certain of his identifiable *formulations* which are not without their consequences. Which may help to illuminate, but this time *from within*, i.e., not as a relic of a past, a survival, a raffish 'flirtation' (the famous '*kokettieren*'), or a trap for fools (the advantage of my dialectic is that I say things little by little – and when they think I have finished, and rush to refute me, they merely make an untimely manifestation of their asininity! – Letter to Engels, 27 June 1867), the *real presence* of certain Hegelian forms and references in the discourse of *Capital*. *From within*, as the exact measurement of a disconcerting but inevitable absence, the absence of the concept (and of all the sub-concepts) *of the effectivity of a structure on its elements* which is the visible/invisible, absent/present keystone of his whole work. Perhaps therefore it is not impermissible to think that if Marx does 'play' so much with Hegelian formulae in certain passages, the game is not just raffishness or sarcasm, but *the action of a real drama*, in which old concepts desperately play the part of something absent *which is nameless*, in order to call it onto the stage in person – whereas they only 'produce' its presence in their failures, in the dislocation between the characters and their roles.

If it is true that the identification and location of this omission, which is a *philosophical* omission, can also lead us to the threshold of Marx's philosophy, we can hope for other gains from it in the theory of history itself. A conceptual omission that has not been divulged, but on the contrary, consecrated as a non-omission, and proclaimed as a fullness, may, in certain circumstances, seriously hinder the development of a science or of certain of its branches. To be convinced of this we need only note that a science only progresses, i.e., *lives*, by the extreme attention it pays to the points where it is theoretically fragile. By these standards, it depends less for its life on what it knows than on what it *does not know*: its absolute precondition is to focus on this unknown, and to pose it in the rigour of a problem. But the unknown of a science is not what empiricist ideology thinks: its 'residue', what it leaves out, what it cannot conceive or resolve; but *par excellence* what it contains that is fragile despite its apparently unquestionable 'obviousness', certain silences in its discourse, certain conceptual omissions and lapses in its rigour, in brief, everything in it that 'sounds hollow' to an attentive ear, despite its fullness.[11] If it is true that a science progresses and lives by knowing how to hear what 'sounds hollow' in it, some part of the life of the Marxist theory of history perhaps depends on this precise point where Marx shows us in a thousand ways the presence of a concept essential to his thought, but absent from his discourse.

9

This then is the guilt of our philosophical reading of *Capital*: it reads Marx according to the rules of a reading in which he gave us a brilliant lesson in his own reading of classical political economy. Our admission of this crime is deliberate, we shall fetter ourselves to it, anchor ourselves in it, cling fiercely to it as the point which must be hung on to at all costs if we hope to establish ourselves on it one day, recognizing the infinite extent contained within its minute space: the extent of Marx's *philosophy*.

We are all seeking this philosophy. The protocols of *The German Ideology*'s philosophical rupture do not give us it in person. Nor do the earlier *Theses on Feuerbach*, those few lightning flashes which break the night of philosophical anthropology with the fleeting snap of a new world glimpsed through the retinal image of the old. Nor, finally, at least insofar as their immediate form is concerned, however genial their clinical judgement, do the criticisms in *Anti-Dühring*, where Engels had to '*follow Herr Dühring into that vast territory in which he dealt with all things under the sun and some others as well*' (Moscow and London, 1959, p. 10), the territory of philosophical ideology, or of a world outlook inscribed in the form of a 'system' (p. 10). For to think that all Marx's philosophy can be found in the few quivering sentences of the *Theses on Feuerbach*, i.e., in the Works of the Break,[12] is to deceive oneself remarkably as to the conditions indispensable to the growth of a radically new theory, which needs time to mature, define itself and grow. 'After its first presentation to the world in Marx's *The Poverty of Philosophy* and in *The Communist Manifesto*,' writes Engels, '*this mode of outlook of ours . . . passed through an incubation period of fully twenty years before the publication of Capital*' (p. 14). Similarly, to believe that we can get all Marx's philosophy directly from the polemical formulations of a work that joins battle on the enemy's terrain, i.e., in the terrain of philosophical *ideology*, as *Anti-Dühring* very often does (and *Materialism and Empirio-Criticism* does later), is to deceive ourselves as to the laws of ideological struggle, as to the nature of the *ideology* which is the stage on which this indispensable struggle is fought, and as to the necessary distinction between the philosophical ideology in which this ideological struggle is fought, and the Theory or Marxist philosophy which appears on this stage to give battle there. To concentrate exclusively on the Works of the Break or on the arguments of the later ideological struggle is in practice to fall into the '*oversight*' of not seeing that the place we are given in which to *read* Marx's philosophy in person is *par excellence* his masterpiece, *Capital*. But we have known this for a long time; since Engels, who told us so in black and white, particularly in the extraordinary Preface to Volume Two of *Capital*, which will be a school text some day; and since Lenin, who repeated that Marx's philosophy was entirely to be found in the '*Logic of Capital*', the Logic Marx '*did not have time*' to write.

Let no one argue against this that we are living in a different century, that much water has flowed under the bridge and that our problems are no longer the same. We are discussing living water which has not yet flowed away. We are familiar with enough historical examples, beginning with that of Spinoza, where men have worked ferociously to wall up for ever and bury deep in the earth sources which were made to quench their thirsts, but which their fear will not tolerate. For nearly a century academic philosophy has buried Marx in the earth of silence, the earth of the cemetery. In the same period, Marx's comrades and successors had to contend with the most dramatic and urgent struggles, and Marx's philosophy passed completely into their historical enterprises, their economic, political and ideological action, and into the indispensable works that guided and instructed that action. In this long period of struggles, the *idea* of Marx's *philosophy*, the *consciousness* of its specific existence and function, which are indispensable to the purity and rigour of the knowledges that underlay all the action, were safeguarded and defended against all temptations and hostility. I need no other proof of this than that cry of scientific conscience, *Materialism and Empirio-Criticism*, and all of Lenin's work, that permanent revolutionary manifesto for *knowledge*, for scientific theory – and for '*partisanship in philosophy*', the principle that dominates everything, and is nothing but the most acute consciousness of scientificity in its lucid and intransigent rigour. That is what we have been given, and what defines our task today: a number of *works*, some produced by the theoretical practice of a science (with *Capital* at the top of the list), the others produced by economic and political practice (all the transformations that the history of the workers' movement has imposed on the world) or by reflection on this practice (the economic, political and ideological texts of the great Marxists). These works carry with them not only the Marxist theory of history, contained in the theory of the capitalist mode of production and in all the fruits of revolutionary action; but also Marx's *philosophical* theory, in which they are thoroughly steeped, though sometimes unwittingly, even in the inevitable approximations of its *practical* expression.

When once before[13] I claimed that it was necessary to give to this *practical* existence of Marxist philosophy, which exists in person in the practical state in that scientific practice of the analysis of the capitalist mode of production, *Capital*, and in the economic and political practice of the history of the worker's movement, the *form of theoretical existence indispensable* to its needs and our needs, I merely proposed a labour of investigation and critical elucidation, which would analyse one with another, according to the nature of their peculiar modalities, the different *degrees* of this existence, i.e., the different *works* which are the raw material of our reflection. I merely proposed a '*symptomatic*' *reading* of the works of Marx and of Marxism, one with another, i.e., the progressive and systematic production of a reflection of the problematic on its objects such as to make them *visible*, and the disinterment, the production of the deepest-lying problematic which will allow us to *see* what could otherwise only have existed allusively or practically. As a function of this demand, I can claim to have *read* the specific theoretical form of the Marxist dialectic in its directly political existence (and actively political: the policies of a revolutionary leader – Lenin – immersed in the revolution); as a function of this principle, I can claim to have treated Mao Tse-tung's 1937 text on contradiction as a description of the structures of the Marxist dialectic reflected in political practice. But this *reading* was not, nor could have been, a direct reading or the merely '*generalizing*' reading which Marxist philosophy is too often reduced to, but which, beneath the word *abstraction* with which it is covered, is no more than the confirmation of the religious or empiricist myth of reading, for the summation of individual readings that it resumed does not for one moment deliver us from this myth. This reading was in principle a *dual* reading, the result of a different, 'symptomatic' reading, which introduced into a *question* an answer given to its absent question.

To speak plainly, it was only possible to pose to the practical political analyses Lenin gives us of the conditions for the revolutionary explosion of 1917 the question of the *specificity* of the Marxist dialectic on the basis of an *answer* which lacked the proximity of its *question*, an answer situated *at another place* in the Marxist works at our disposal, precisely the *answer* in which Marx declared that he had '*inverted*' the Hegelian dialectic. This answer by 'inversion' was Marx's answer to the following (absent) question: what is the specific difference distinguishing the Marxist dialectic from the Hegelian dialectic? But this answer by 'inversion', like classical political economy's answer by 'the value of labour', is noteworthy in that it contains inside it an internal lack: an interrogation of the inversion metaphor shows that it cannot itself think itself, and hence that it both points to a real but absent problem, a real but absent question outside itself, and to the conceptual emptiness or ambiguity corresponding to this absence, the *absence of a concept behind a word*. Treating this absence of the concept beneath the presence of a word as a symptom put me on to the track of the formulation of the question implied and defined by its absence. However imperfect and provisional it may have been, my 'reading' of Lenin's texts was only possible on condition that it posed these texts the theoretical question whose active answer they represented, although their level of existence was far from purely theoretical (since these texts describe, for practical purposes, the structure of the conjuncture in which the Soviet Revolution exploded). This 'reading' enabled me to sharpen the question, and then to pose the question thus transformed to other, equally symptomatic texts existing at a different level, to Mao Tse-tung's text, and also to a methodological text like Marx's *1857 Introduction*. The question forged out of the first answer emerged transformed anew, and suitable for a reading of other works: today, *Capital*. But here again, to read *Capital*, we have resorted to a series of dual, i.e., 'symptomatic' readings: we have read *Capital* in order to make visible whatever invisible survivals there are in it, but in the present state of our forces, the backward step necessary for this 'reading' has taken all the space we could obtain for it from a second reading performed simultaneously of Marx's Early Works, in particular of the *1844 Manuscripts*, and therefore of the problematic which constitutes the background to his works, Feuerbach's anthropological problematic and Hegel's problematic of absolute idealism.

If the question of Marx's philosophy, i.e. of his differential specificity, emerges even only slightly altered and sharpened from this first reading of *Capital*, it should make other 'readings' possible, first other readings of *Capital*, which will give rise to new differential sharpenings, and then readings of other Marxist works: for example, an informed reading of Marxist texts which are philosophical (but trapped in the inevitable forms of ideological struggle) such as Engels's *Anti-Dühring* and *Dialectics of Nature*, and Lenin's *Materialism and Empirio-Criticism* (and the *Philosophical Notebooks*); or again a 'reading' of those other practical works of Marxism which are so abundant today and exist in the historical reality of socialism and of the newly liberated countries advancing towards socialism. I have left these classical philosophical texts so late deliberately for the simple reason that, before the definition of the essential principles of Marxist philosophy, i.e., before managing to establish the indispensable minimum for the consistent existence of Marxist philosophy in its difference from all philosophical ideology, it was not possible to *read* these classical texts, which are not scholarly but militant texts, other than to the enigmatic letter of their *ideological* expression, without being able to show why this expression had necessarily to take the *form* of ideological expression, i.e., without being able to isolate this form in its real essence. The same is true of the 'reading' of the still theoretically opaque works of the history of the workers' movement, such as the 'cult of personality' or the very serious conflict which is our present drama: perhaps this 'reading' will one day be possible on condition that we have correctly identified in the rational works of Marxism the resources for the production of the concepts indispensable to an understanding of the reasons for this unreason.[14]

May I sum up all this in one sentence? This sentence describes a circle: a philosophical reading of *Capital* is only possible as the application of that which is the very object of our investigation, Marxist philosophy. This circle is only epistemologically possible because of the existence of Marx's philosophy in the works of Marxism. It is therefore a question of producing, in the precise sense of the word, which seems to signify making manifest what is latent, but which really means transforming (in order to give a pre-existing raw material the form of an object adapted to an end), something which in a sense *already exists*. This production, in the double sense which gives the production operation the necessary form of a circle, is the *production of a knowledge*. To conceive Marx's philosophy in its specificity is therefore to conceive the essence of the very movement with which the knowledge of it is produced, or to conceive knowledge as *production*. [. . .]

NOTES

1   We owe this result, which has revolutionized our *reading* of Freud to Jacques Lacan's intransigent and lucid – and for many years isolated – theoretical effort. At a time when the radical novelty of what Jacques Lacan has given us is beginning to pass into the public domain, where everyone can make use of it and profit by it in his own way, I feel bound to acknowledge my debt to an exemplary reading lesson which, as we shall see, goes beyond its object of origin in some of its effects. I feel bound to acknowledge this *publicly*, so that 'the tailor's labour (does not) disappear . . . into the coat' (Marx), even into my coat. Just as I feel bound to acknowledge the obvious or concealed debts which bind us to our masters in reading learned works, once Gaston Bachelard and Jean Cavaillès and now Georges Canguilhem and Michel Foucault.

2   Two volumes out of three translated into English and published by Lawrence and Wishart.

3   References to *Capital* Volume One are given first to Roy's French translation in the three volumes of the Éditions Sociales version (T.I, T.II, T.III) and then to the English translation of Moore and Aveling in one volume published by Lawrence and Wishart (Vol. I). References to Volumes Two and Three are given to the English translation only (Vol. II, Vol. III).

4   *For Marx*, Allen Lane The Penguin Press, London 1969, pp. 46, 66–70, etc.

5   Auguste Comte often came very close to this idea.

6   'Relation of immanent reflection': this 'reflection' itself poses a theoretical problem which I cannot deal with here.

7   Plon, Paris 1961; abridged translation, *Madness and Civilization*, Tavistock Press, London 1967.

8   The recourse made in this text to spatial metaphors (field, terrain, space, site, situation, position, etc.) poses a theoretical problem: the problem of the validity of its *claim* to existence in a discourse with scientific pretensions. The problem may be formulated as follows: *why* does a certain form of scientific discourse necessarily need the use of metaphors borrowed from non-scientific disciplines?

9   I retain the spatial metaphor. But the change of terrain takes place *on the spot*: in all strictness, we should speak of the mutation of the *mode* of theoretical production and of the change of function of the subject induced by this change of mode.

10   If I may invoke my personal experience, I should like to give two precise examples of this presence *elsewhere* in Marx or in Engels of the question absent from its answer. At the cost of a decidedly laborious investigation, the text of which (*For Marx*, pp. 89ff) bears the mark of these difficulties, I succeeded in identifying a pertinent absence in the idea of the 'inversion' of the Hegelian dialectic by Marx: the absence of its concept, and therefore of its question. I managed to reconstruct this *question* laboriously, by showing that the 'inversion' Marx mentions had as its effective content a revolution in the problematic. But later, reading Engels's Preface to Volume Two of *Capital*, I was stupefied to find that the question I had had such trouble in formulating was there in black and white! Engels expressly identifies the 'inversion', the 'setting right side up again' of the chemistry and political economy which had been standing on their heads, with a change in their 'theory', and therefore in their problematic. Or again: in one of my first essays, I had suggested that Marx's theoretical revolution lay not in his change of the answers, but in his change of the questions, and that therefore Marx's revolution in the theory of history consisted of a '*change of elements*' by which he moved from the terrain of ideology to the terrain of science (*For Marx*, p. 47). But recently, reading the chapter of *Capital* on wages, I was stupefied to see that Marx used the very expression '*change of terrain*' to express this change of theoretical problematic. Here again, the question (or its concept) which I had laboriously reconstituted out of its *absence* in one precise point of Marx's, Marx himself gave in black and white *somewhere else* in his work.

11   Pierre Macherey: 'A propos de la rupture', *La Nouvelle Critique*, Paris, May 1965, p. 139.

12   *For Marx*, pp. 34–5.

13   *For Marx*, pp. 164ff.

14   The same applies to the 'reading' of those new works of Marxism which, sometimes in surprising forms, contain in them something essential to the future of socialism: what Marxism is producing in the vanguard countries of the 'third world' which is struggling for its freedom, from the guerillas of Vietnam to Cuba. It is vital that we be able to 'read' these works before it is too late.

10

Derrida on Lévi-Strauss

Jacques Derrida (1930–) is one of the most influential and prolific among recent philosophers, producing avowedly *written* texts which have influenced literary studies, as well as offering provocative readings of philosophy from Plato to the present. Derrida came to prominence in the late 1960s as a major figure in the reassessment of phenomenology and structuralism which became known as post-structuralism. In 1967 Derrida published his first three books, *Speech and Phenomena, Of Grammatology* and *Writing and Difference*, which mark out his characteristic concerns and mode of writing. *Speech and Phenomena* offers a critical reading of the importance ascribed to speech by Husserl. *Of Grammatology* and *Writing and Difference* trace a range of related philosophical problems through interwoven essays which establish the reading strategies and critical questions associated with the project of deconstruction. 'Structure, Sign and Play in the Discourse of the Human Sciences' was published in *Writing and Difference* and intervenes in the context of a new emphasis on linguistics and the human sciences, an emphasis exemplified by the structuralist anthropologist Claude Lévi-Strauss (1908–). Derrida questions the concept of structure in Lévi-Strauss's work, situating structuralism within Western philosophy and reasserting philosophical aporia otherwise ignored by social scientists. Derrida's essay was first delivered in 1966 at a conference in Johns Hopkins University, Baltimore. The conference proceedings, published as *The Languages of Criticism and the Sciences of Man: The Structuralist Controversy*, provide a record of responses to Derrida's lecture and suggest the range of participants in dialogue. This book and Derrida's essay in particular are often taken as the seminal moment through which post-structuralism and Derridean deconstruction were introduced into the USA.

Derrida has often pointed out that deconstruction is not to be understood as critique, a method, or a theory. These negative remarks make a positive characterization difficult, but Derrida's work could be described as a mode of philosophical writing which questions the limits of philosophy and of writing.

Derrida's immanent readings are reworked as writings to show how the claims of writing are obscured in philosophy. Idealizations of speech, consciousness and presence mystify the importance of writing otherwise necessary for philosophy's own articulation. Out of an analysis of the way such seemingly binary oppositions as speech/writing have structured philosophical texts, Derrida seeks first to reverse the hierarchy implicit within these oppositions, and then to radicalize this reversal so as to disseminate a new sense of the way texts and concepts are complicit with the assumptions of Western metaphysics. Deconstruction, then, combines close reading and analysis with questions and strategies of rewriting. As writing, the rhetoric exceeds any attempt to determine critical consequences in the form of rules, laws or propositions.

Derrida inherits much from Heidegger's readings of Kant and Nietzsche. His work reconfigures the limits of metaphysics broached in Heidegger. Heidegger's interpretation of Nietzsche, for example, provides a model for Derridean deconstruction. Derrida's understanding of 'différance' and 'deconstruction' can be read as translations of Heidegger's conception of 'ontological difference' and the 'destruction' (Destruktion) of metaphysics. Deconstruction differs in its emphasis on writing. Derrida's approach to critical reading can also be compared with the techniques of symptomatic reading developed by Freud, Lacan and Althusser. Although Derrida's work often offers itself as a strategic intervention with political purpose, perhaps most notably in Specters of Marx, much of the reception of Derrida's work has been too quick to understand deconstruction as a form of ideology critique or an implicitly materialist attack on the idealism of Western metaphysics. Derrida's work, moreover, has not restricted itself to avowedly philosophical texts, but has engaged writers such as Saussure and Freud, whose work might appear marginal to philosophy. Thus, although Derrida's work continually returns to the founding questions of philosophy, his essays also question the boundaries between philosophy and other kinds of writing, not least literature.

Insofar as Derrida's readings reveal the conditions of possibility informing texts, literary oeuvres or philosophical projects, deconstruction can be said to offer critiques, readings which show how quasi-transcendental claims are immanent within texts but in ways that remain constitutively uncertain or aporetic. Insofar as Derrida's readings are themselves constituted as writings, the critical reflexivity of Derrida's work seeks to stage the limits of philosophy through rhetorics which come closer to a philosophical poetics than to philosophical critique. In Glas, for example, Derrida arranges his text in parallel columns which interweave discussions of Hegel's philosophy with Jean Genet's fiction such that the authority of Derrida's deconstruction of both is as much literary as it is philosophical. Indeed, Jürgen Habermas, among others, has accused Derrida of levelling the generic boundaries between philosophy and literature, and of giving undue primacy to the importance of philosophical rhetoric. Derrida's work has nevertheless been salutary in revealing a series of productive blindspots and problems, not least the differences between philosophical critique, critical reading and literary criticism.

FURTHER READING

Primary works

Jacques Derrida, *Speech and Phenomena*, trans. David B. Allison (Evanston, IL: Northwestern University Press, 1973); *Of Grammatology*, trans. Gayatri Chakravorty Spivak (Baltimore and London: Johns Hopkins University Press, 1976); *Writing and Difference*, trans. Alan Bass (London: Routledge and Kegan Paul, 1978); *Dissemination*, trans. Barbara Johnson (Chicago: University of Chicago Press, 1981); *Margins of Philosophy*, trans. Alan Bass (Chicago: University of Chicago Press, 1982); *Glas*, trans. John P. Leavey and Richard Rand (Lincoln and London: University of Nebraska Press, 1986); *Specters of Marx*, trans. Peggy Kamuf (New York and London: Routledge, 1994); *Positions: Interviews, 1974–1994*, ed. Elisabeth Weber, trans. Peggy Kamuf and others (Stanford, CA: Stanford University Press, 1995); *Limited Inc* (Evanston, IL: Northwestern University Press, 1988).

Secondary works

Geoff Bennington and Jacques Derrida, *Jacques Derrida* (revised edition, 1999).

Geoffrey Bennington, *Interrupting Derrida* (London: Routledge, 2000).

Peter Dews, 'Jacques Derrida: The Transcendental and Difference', *Logics of Disintegration: Post-Structuralist Thought and the Claims of Critical Theory* (London: Verso, 1987), pp. 1–43.

Rodolphe Gasché, *The Tain of the Mirror: Derrida and the Philosophy of Reflection* (Cambridge, MA and London: Harvard University Press, 1986).

Rodolphe Gasché, *Inventions of Difference: On Jacques Derrida* (Cambridge, MA and London: Harvard University Press, 1994).

Jürgen Habermas, *The Philosophical Discourse of Modernity*, trans. Frederick G. Lawrence (Cambridge: Polity, 1987).

Irene E. Harvey, *Derrida and the Economy of Différance* (Bloomington: Indiana University Press, 1985).

Marcel Hénaff, *Claude Lévi-Strauss and the Making of Structural Anthropology*, trans. Mary Baker (Minneapolis: University of Minnesota, 1998).

Marian Hobson, *Jacques Derrida: Opening Lines* (London and New York: Routledge, 1998).

Nancy J. Holland, ed., *Feminist Interpretations of Jacques Derrida* (University Park, PA: University of Pennsylvania Press, 1997).

Christina Howells, *Derrida: Deconstruction from Phenomenology to Ethics* (Cambridge: Polity, 1998).

Richard Macksey and Eugenio Donato, eds., *The Languages of Criticism and the Sciences of Man: The Structuralist Controversy* (Baltimore: Johns Hopkins University Press, 1970).

Gary B. Madison, ed., *Working through Derrida* (Evanston, IL: Northwestern University Press, 1993).

John P. Muller and William J. Richards, eds., *The Purloined Poe: Lacan, Derrida, and Psychoanalytic Reading* (Baltimore and London: Johns Hopkins University Press, 1988).

David Pace, *Claude Lévi-Strauss: The Bearer of Ashes* (London: Routledge, 1983).

David Wood and Robert Bernasconi, eds., *Derrida and Différance* (Evanston, IL: Northwestern University Press, 1988).

David Wood, ed., *Derrida: A Critical Reader* (Oxford: Blackwell, 1992).

Jacques Derrida, 'Structure, Sign and Play in the Discourse of the Human Sciences' (1966), *Writing and Difference*, trans. Alan Bass (London: Routledge and Kegan Paul, 1978), pp. 278–93.

> *We need to interpret interpretations more than to interpret things.*
> Montaigne

Perhaps something has occurred in the history of the concept of structure that could be called an "event," if this loaded word did not entail a meaning which it is precisely the function of structural – or structuralist – thought to reduce or to suspect. Let us speak of an "event," nevertheless, and let us use quotation marks to serve as a precaution. What would this event be then? Its exterior form would be that of a *rupture* and a *redoubling*.

It would be easy enough to show that the concept of structure and even the word "structure" itself are as old as the *epistēmē* – that is to say, as old as Western science and Western philosophy – and that their roots thrust deep into the soil of ordinary language, into whose deepest recesses the *epistēmē* plunges in order to gather them up and to make them part of itself in a metaphorical displacement. Nevertheless, up to the event which I wish to mark out and define, structure – or rather the structurality of structure – although it has always been at work, has always been neutralized or reduced, and this by a process of giving it a center or of referring it to a point of presence, a fixed origin. The function of this center was not only to orient, balance, and organize the structure – one cannot in fact conceive of an unorganized structure – but above all to make sure that the organizing principle of the structure would limit what we might call the *play* of the structure. By orienting and organizing the coherence of the system, the center of a structure permits the play of its elements inside the total form. And even today the notion of a structure lacking any center represents the unthinkable itself.

Nevertheless, the center also closes off the play which it opens up and makes possible. As center, it is the point at which the substitution of contents, elements, or terms is no longer possible. At the center, the permutation or the transformation of elements (which may of course be structures enclosed within a structure) is forbidden. At least this permutation has always remained *interdicted* (and I am using this word deliberately). Thus it has always been thought that the center, which is by definition unique, constituted that very thing within a structure which while governing the structure, escapes structurality. This is why classical thought concerning structure could say that the center is, paradoxically, *within* the structure and *outside it*. The center is at the center of the totality, and yet, since the center does not belong to the totality (is not part of the totality), the totality *has its center elsewhere*. The center is not the center. The concept of centered structure – although it represents coherence itself, the condition of the *epistēmē* as philosophy or science – is contradictorily coherent. And as always, coherence in contradiction expresses the force of a desire. The concept of centered structure is in fact the concept of a play based on a fundamental ground, a play constituted on the basis of a fundamental immobility and a reassuring certitude, which itself is beyond the reach of play. And on the basis of this certitude anxiety can be mastered, for anxiety is invariably the result of a certain mode of being implicated in the game, of being caught by the game, of being as it were at stake in the game from the outset. And again on the basis of what we call the center (and which, because it can be either inside or outside, can also indifferently be called the origin or end, *archē* or *telos*), repetitions, substitutions, transformations, and permutations are always *taken* from a history of meaning [*sens*] – that is, in a word, a history – whose origin may always be reawakened or whose end may always be anticipated in the form of presence. This is why one perhaps could say that the movement of any archaeology, like that of any eschatology, is an accomplice of this reduction of the structurality of structure and always attempts to conceive of structure on the basis of a full presence which is beyond play.

If this is so, the entire history of the concept of structure, before the rupture of which we are speaking, must be thought of as a series of substitutions of center for center, as a linked chain of determinations of the center. Successively, and in a regulated fashion, the center receives different forms or names. The history of metaphysics, like the history of the West, is the history of these metaphors and metonymies. Its matrix – if you will pardon me for demonstrating so little and for being so elliptical in order to come more quickly to my principal theme – is the determination of Being as *presence* in all senses of this word. It could be shown that all the names related to fundamentals, to principles, or to the center have always designated an invariable presence – *eidos, archē, telos, energeia, ousia* (essence, existence, substance, subject) *alētheia*, transcendentality, consciousness, God, man, and so forth.

The event I called a rupture, the disruption I alluded to at the beginning of this paper, presumably would have come about when the structurality of structure had to begin to be thought, that is to say, repeated, and this is why I said that this disruption was repetition in every sense of the word. Henceforth, it became necessary to think both the law which somehow governed the desire for a center in the constitution of structure, and the process of signification which orders the displacements and substitutions for this law of central presence – but a central presence which has never been itself, has always already been exiled from itself into its own substitute. The substitute does not substitute itself for anything which has somehow existed before it. Henceforth, it was necessary to begin thinking that there was no center, that the center could not be thought in the form of a present-being, that the center had no natural site, that it was not a fixed locus but a function, a sort of nonlocus in which an infinite number of sign-substitutions came into play. This was the moment when language invaded the universal problematic, the moment when, in the absence of a center or origin, everything became discourse – provided we can agree on this word – that is to say, a system in which the central signified, the original or transcendental signified, is never absolutely present outside a system of differences. The absence of the transcendental signified extends the domain and the play of signification infinitely.

Where and how does this decentering, this thinking the structurality of structure, occur? It would be somewhat naïve to refer to an event, a doctrine, or an author in order to designate this occurrence. It is no doubt part of the totality of an era, our own, but still it has always already begun to proclaim itself and begun to *work*. Nevertheless, if we wished to choose several "names," as indications only, and to recall those authors in whose discourse this occurrence has kept most closely to its most radical formulation, we doubtless would have to cite the Nietzschean critique of metaphysics, the critique of the concepts of Being and truth, for which were substituted the concepts of play, interpretation, and sign (sign without present truth); the Freudian critique of self-presence, that is, the critique of consciousness, of the subject, of self-identity and of self-proximity or self-possession; and, more radically, the Heideggerean destruction of metaphysics, of onto-theology, of the determination of Being as presence. But all these destructive discourses and all their analogues are trapped in a kind of circle. This circle is unique. It describes the form of the relation between the history of metaphysics and the destruction of the history of metaphysics. There is no sense in doing without the concepts of metaphysics in order to shake metaphysics. We have no language – no syntax and no lexicon – which is foreign to this history; we can pronounce not a single destructive proposition which has not already had to slip into the form, the logic, and the implicit postulations of precisely what it seeks to contest. To take one example from many: the metaphysics of presence is shaken with the help of the concept of *sign*. But, as I suggested a moment ago, as soon as one seeks to demonstrate in this way that there is no transcendental or privileged signified and that the domain or play of signification henceforth has no limit, one must reject even the concept and word "sign" itself – which is precisely what cannot be done. For the signification "sign" has always been understood and determined, in its meaning, as sign-of, a signifier referring to a signified, a signifier different from its signified. If one erases the radical difference between signifier and signified, it is the word "signifier" itself which must be abandoned as a metaphysical concept. When Lévi-Strauss says in the preface to *The Raw and the Cooked* that he has "sought to transcend the opposition between the sensible and the intelligible by operating from the outset at the level of signs,"[1] the necessity, force, and legitimacy of his act cannot make us forget that the concept of the sign cannot in itself surpass this opposition between the sensible and the intelligible. The concept of the sign, in each of its aspects, has been determined by this opposition throughout the totality of its history. It has lived only on this opposition and its system. But we cannot do without the concept of the sign, for we cannot give up this metaphysical complicity without also giving up the critique we are directing against this complicity, or without the risk of erasing difference in the self-identity of a signified reducing its signifier into itself or, amounting to the same thing, simply expelling its signifier outside itself. For there are two heterogenous ways of erasing the difference between the signifier and the signified: one, the classic way, consists in reducing or deriving the signifier, that is to say, ultimately in *submitting* the sign to thought; the other, the one we are using here against the first one, consists in putting into question the system in which the preceding reduction functioned: first and foremost, the opposition between the sensible and the intelligible. For the *paradox* is that the metaphysical reduction of the sign needed the opposition it was reducing. The opposition is systematic with the reduction. And what we are saying here about the sign can be extended to all the concepts and all the sentences of metaphysics, in particular to the discourse on "structure." But there are several ways of being caught in this circle. They are all more or less naïve, more or less empirical, more or less systematic, more or less close to the formulation – that is, to the formalization – of this circle. It is these differences which explain the multiplicity of destructive discourses and the disagreement between those who elaborate them.

Nietzsche, Freud, and Heidegger, for example, worked within the inherited concepts of metaphysics. Since these concepts are not elements or atoms, and since they are taken from a syntax and a system, every particular borrowing brings along with it the whole of metaphysics. This is what allows these destroyers to destroy each other reciprocally – for example, Heidegger regarding Nietzsche, with as much lucidity and rigor as bad faith and misconstruction, as the last metaphysician, the last "Platonist." One could do the same for Heidegger himself, for Freud, or for a number of others. And today no exercise is more widespread.

What is the relevance of this formal schema when we turn to what are called the "human sciences"? One of them perhaps occupies a privileged place – ethnology. In fact one can assume that ethnology could have been born as a science only at the moment when a decentering had come about: at the moment when European culture – and, in conse-quence, the history of metaphysics and of its concepts – had been *dislocated*, driven from its locus, and forced to stop considering itself as the culture of reference. This moment is not first and foremost a moment of philosophical or scientific discourse. It is also a moment which is political, economic, technical, and so forth. One can say with total security that there is nothing fortuitous about the fact that the critique of ethnocentrism – the very condition for ethnology – should be systematically and historically contempor-aneous with the destruction of the history of metaphysics. Both belong to one and the same era. Now, ethnology – like any science – comes about within the element of discourse. And it is primarily a European science employing traditional concepts, how-ever much it may struggle against them. Consequently, whether he wants to or not – and this does not depend on a decision on his part – the ethnologist accepts into his discourse the premises of ethnocentrism at the very moment when he denounces them. This necessity is irreducible; it is not a historical contingency. We ought to consider all its implications very carefully. But if no one can escape this necessity, and if no one is therefore responsible for giving in to it, however little he may do so, this does not mean that all the ways of giving in to it are of equal pertinence. The quality and fecundity of a discourse are perhaps measured by the critical rigor with which this relation to the history of metaphysics and to inherited concepts is thought. Here it is a question both of a critical relation to the language of the social sciences and a critical responsibility of the discourse itself. It is a question of explicitly and systematically posing the problem of the status of a discourse which borrows from a heritage the resources necessary for the deconstruction of that heritage itself. A problem of *economy* and *strategy*.

If we consider, as an example, the texts of Claude Lévi-Strauss, it is not only because of the privilege accorded to ethnology among the social sciences, nor even because the thought of Lévi-Strauss weighs heavily on the contemporary theoretical situation. It is above all because a certain choice has been declared in the work of Lévi-Strauss and because a certain doctrine has been elaborated there, and precisely, in a *more or less explicit manner*, as concerns both this critique of language and this critical language in the social sciences.

In order to follow this movement in the text of Lévi-Strauss, let us choose as one guiding thread among others the opposition between nature and culture. Despite all its rejuvenations and disguises, this opposition is congenital to philosophy. It is even older than Plato. It is at least as old as the Sophists. Since the statement of the opposition *physis/nomos, physis/technē*, it has been relayed to us by means of a whole historical chain which opposes "nature" to law, to education, to art, to technics – but also to liberty, to the arbitrary, to history, to society, to the mind, and so on. Now, from the outset of his researches, and from his first book (*The Elementary Structures of Kinship*) on, Lévi-Strauss simultaneously has experienced the necessity of utilizing this opposition and the impossibility of accepting it. In the *Elementary Structures*, he begins from this axiom or definition: that which is *universal* and spontaneous, and not dependent on any particular culture or on any determinate norm, belongs to nature. Inversely, that which depends upon a system of *norms* regulating society and therefore is capable of *varying* from one social structure to another, belongs to culture. These two definitions are of the traditional type. But in the very first pages of the *Elementary Structures* Lévi-Strauss, who has begun by giving credence to these concepts, encounters what he calls a *scandal*, that is to say, something which no longer tolerates the nature/culture opposition he has accepted, something which *simultaneously* seems to require the predicates of nature and of culture. This scandal is the *incest prohibition*. The incest prohibition is universal; in this sense one could call it natural. But it is also a prohibition, a system of norms and interdicts; in this sense one could call it cultural:

> Let us suppose then that everything universal in man relates to the natural order, and is characterized by spontaneity, and that everything subject to a norm is cultural and is both relative and particular. We are then confronted with a fact, or rather, a group of facts, which, in the light of previous definitions, are not far removed from a scandal: we refer to that complex group of beliefs, customs, conditions and institutions described succinctly as the prohibition of incest, which presents, without the slightest ambiguity, and inseparably combines, the two characteristics in which we recognize the conflicting features of two mutually exclusive orders. It constitutes a rule, but a rule which, alone among all the social rules, possesses at the same time a universal character.[2]

Obviously there is no scandal except within a system of concepts which accredits the difference between nature and culture. By commencing his work with the *factum* of the incest prohibition, Lévi-Strauss thus places himself at the point at which this difference, which has always been assumed to be self-evident, finds itself erased or questioned. For from the moment when the incest prohibition can no longer be conceived within the nature/culture opposition, it can no longer be said to be a scandalous fact, a nucleus of opacity within a network of transparent significations. The incest prohibition is no longer a scandal one meets with or comes up against in the domain of traditional concepts; it is something which escapes these concepts and certainly precedes them – probably as the condition of their possibility. It could perhaps be said that the whole of philosophical conceptualization, which is systematic with the nature/culture opposition, is designed to leave in the domain of the unthinkable the very thing that makes this conceptualization possible: the origin of the prohibition of incest.

This example, too cursorily examined, is only one among many others, but nevertheless it already shows that language bears within itself the necessity of its own critique. Now this critique may be undertaken along two paths, in two "manners." Once the limit of the nature/culture opposition makes itself felt, one might want to question systematically and rigorously the history of these concepts. This is a first action. Such a systematic and historic questioning would be neither a philological nor a philosophical action in the classic sense of these words. To concern oneself with the founding concepts of the entire history of philosophy, to deconstitute them, is not to undertake the work of the philologist or of the classic historian of philosophy. Despite appearances, it is probably the most daring way of making the beginnings of a step outside of philosophy. The step "outside philosophy" is much more difficult to conceive than is generally imagined by those who think they made it long ago with cavalier ease, and who in general are swallowed up in metaphysics in the entire body of discourse which they claim to have disengaged from it.

The other choice (which I believe corresponds more closely to Lévi-Strauss's manner), in order to avoid the possibly sterilizing effects of the first one, consists in conserving all these old concepts within the domain of empirical discovery while here and there denouncing their limits, treating them as tools which can still be used. No longer is any truth value attributed to them; there is a readiness to abandon them, if necessary, should other instruments appear more useful. In the meantime, their relative efficacy is exploited, and they are employed to destroy the old machinery to which they belong and of which they themselves are pieces. This is how the language of the social sciences criticizes *itself*. Lévi-Strauss thinks that in this way he can separate *method* from *truth*, the instruments of the method and the objective significations envisaged by it. One could almost say that this is the primary affirmation of Lévi-Strauss; in any event, the first words of the *Elementary Structures* are: "Above all, it is beginning to emerge that this distinction between nature and society ('nature' and 'culture' seem preferable to us today), while of no acceptable historical significance, does contain a logic, fully justifying its use by modern sociology as a methodological tool."[3]

Lévi-Strauss will always remain faithful to this double intention: to preserve as an instrument something whose truth value he criticizes.

On the one hand, he will continue, in effect, to contest the value of the nature/culture opposition. More than thirteen years after the *Elementary Structures, The Savage Mind* faithfully echoes the text I have just quoted: "The opposition between nature and culture to which I attached much importance at one time ... now seems to be of primarily methodological importance." And this methodological value is not affected by its "ontological" nonvalue (as might be said, if this notion were not suspect here): "However, it would not be enough to reabsorb particular humanities into a general one. This first enterprise opens the way for others which ... are incumbent on the exact natural sciences: the reintegration of culture in nature and finally of life within the whole of its physico-chemical conditions."[4]

On the other hand, still in *The Savage Mind*, he presents as what he calls *bricolage* what might be called the discourse of this method. The *bricoleur*, says Lévi-Strauss, is someone who uses "the means at hand," that is, the instruments he finds at his disposition around him, those which are already there, which had not been especially conceived with an eye to the operation for which they are to be used and to which one tries by trial and error to adapt them, not hesitating to change them whenever it appears necessary, or to try several of them at once, even if their form and their origin are heterogenous – and so forth. There is therefore a critique of language in the form of *bricolage*, and it has even been said that *bricolage* is critical language itself. I am thinking in particular of the article of G. Genette, "Structuralisme et critique littéraire," published in homage to Lévi-Strauss in a special issue of *L'Arc* (no. 26, 1965), where it is stated that the analysis of *bricolage* could "be applied almost word for word" to criticism, and especially to "literary criticism."

If one calls *bricolage* the necessity of borrowing one's concepts from the text of a heritage which is more or less coherent or ruined, it must be said that every discourse is *bricoleur*. The engineer, whom Lévi-Strauss opposes to the *bricoleur*, should be the one to construct the totality of his language, syntax, and lexicon. In this sense the engineer is a myth. A subject who supposedly would be the absolute origin of his own discourse and supposedly would construct it "out of nothing," "out of whole cloth," would be the creator of the verb, the verb itself. The notion of the engineer who supposedly breaks with all forms of *bricolage* is therefore a theological idea; and since Lévi-Strauss tells us elsewhere that *bricolage* is mythopoetic, the odds are that the engineer is a myth produced by the *bricoleur*. As soon as we cease to believe in such an engineer and in a discourse which breaks with the received historical discourse, and as soon as we admit that every finite discourse is bound by a certain *bricolage* and that the engineer and the scientist are also species of *bricoleurs*, then the very idea of *bricolage* is menaced and the difference in which it took on its meaning breaks down.

This brings us to the second thread which might guide us in what is being contrived here.

Lévi-Strauss describes *bricolage* not only as an intellectual activity but also as a mythopoetical activity. One reads in *The Savage Mind*, "Like *bricolage* on the technical plane, mythical reflection can reach brilliant unforeseen results on the intellectual plane. Conversely, attention has often been drawn to the mythopoetical nature of *bricolage*."[5]

But Lévi-Strauss's remarkable endeavor does not simply consist in proposing, notably in his most recent investigations, a structural science of myths and of mythological activity. His endeavor also appears – I would say almost from the outset – to have the status which he accords to his own discourse on myths, to what he calls his "mythologicals." It is here that his discourse on the myth reflects on itself and criticizes itself. And this moment, this critical period, is evidently of concern to all the languages which share the field of the human sciences. What does Lévi-Strauss say of his "mythologicals"? It is here that we rediscover the mythopoetical virtue of *bricolage*. In effect, what appears most fascinating in this critical search for a new status of discourse is the stated abandonment of all reference to a *center*, to a *subject*, to a privileged *reference*, to an origin, or to an absolute *archia*. The theme of this decentering could be followed throughout the "Overture" to his last book, *The Raw and the Cooked*. I shall simply remark on a few key points.

1. From the very start, Lévi-Strauss recognizes that the Bororo myth which he employs in the book as the "reference myth" does not merit this name and this treatment. The name is specious and the use of the myth improper. This myth deserves no more than any other its referential privilege: "In fact, the Bororo myth, which I shall refer to from now on as the key myth, is, as I shall try to show, simply a transformation, to a greater or lesser extent, of other myths originating either in the same society or in neighboring or remote societies. I could, therefore, have legitimately taken as my starting point any one representative myth of the group. From this point of view, the key myth is interesting not because it is typical, but rather because of its irregular position within the group."[6]

2. There is no unity or absolute source of the myth. The focus or the source of the myth are always shadows and virtualities which are elusive, unactualizable, and

nonexistent in the first place. Everything begins with structure, configuration, or relationship. The discourse on the acentric structure that myth itself is, cannot itself have an absolute subject or an absolute center. It must avoid the violence that consists in centering a language which describes an acentric structure if it is not to shortchange the form and movement of myth. Therefore it is necessary to forego scientific or philosophical discourse, to renounce the *epistēmē* which absolutely requires, which is the absolute requirement that we go back to the source, to the center, to the founding basis, to the principle, and so on. In opposition to *epistemic* discourse, structural discourse on myths – *mythological* discourse – must itself be *mythomorphic*. It must have the form of that of which it speaks. This is what Lévi-Strauss says in *The Raw and the Cooked*, from which I would now like to quote a long and remarkable passage:

> The study of myths raises a methodological problem, in that it cannot be carried out according to the Cartesian principle of breaking down the difficulty into as many parts as may be necessary for finding the solution. There is no real end to methodological analysis, no hidden unity to be grasped once the breaking-down process has been completed. Themes can be split up *ad infinitum*. Just when you think you have disentangled and separated them, you realize that they are knitting together again in response to the operation of unexpected affinities. Consequently the unity of the myth is never more than tendential and projective and cannot reflect a state or a particular moment of the myth. It is a phenomenon of the imagination, resulting from the attempt at interpretation; and its function is to endow the myth with synthetic form and to prevent its disintegration into a confusion of opposites. The science of myths might therefore be termed "anaclastic," if we take this old term in the broader etymological sense which includes the study of both reflected rays and broken rays. But unlike philosophical reflection, which aims to go back to its own source, the reflections we are dealing with here concern rays whose only source is hypothetical . . . And in seeking to imitate the spontaneous movement of mythological thought, this essay, which is also both too brief and too long, has had to conform to the requirements of that thought and to respect its rhythm. It follows that this book on myths is itself a kind of myth.[7]

This statement is repeated a little farther on: "As the myths themselves are based on secondary codes (the primary codes being those that provide the substance of language), the present work is put forward as a tentative draft of a tertiary code, which is intended to ensure the reciprocal translatability of several myths. This is why it would not be wrong to consider this book itself as a myth: it is, as it were, the myth of mythology."[8] The absence of a center is here the absence of a subject and the absence of an author: "Thus the myth and the musical work are like conductors of an orchestra, whose audience becomes the silent performers. If it is now asked where the real center of the work is to be found, the answer is that this is impossible to determine. Music and mythology bring man face to face with potential objects of which only the shadows are actualized . . . Myths are anonymous."[9] The musical model chosen by Lévi-Strauss for the composition of his book is apparently justified by this absence of any real and fixed center of the mythical or mythological discourse.

Thus it is at this point that ethnographic *bricolage* deliberately assumes its mythopoetic function. But by the same token, this function makes the philosophical or epistemological requirement of a center appear as mythological, that is to say, as a historical illusion.

Nevertheless, even if one yields to the necessity of what Lévi-Strauss has done, one cannot ignore its risks. If the mythological is mythomorphic, are all discourses on myths equivalent? Shall we have to abandon any epistemological requirement which permits us to distinguish between several qualities of discourse on the myth? A classic, but inevitable question. It cannot be answered – and I believe that Lévi-Strauss does not answer it – for as long as the problem of the relations between the philosopheme or the theorem, on the one hand, and the mytheme or the mythopoem, on the other, has not been posed explicitly, which is no small problem. For lack of explicitly posing this problem, we condemn ourselves to transforming the alleged transgression of philosophy into an unnoticed fault within the philosophical realm. Empiricism would be the genus of which these faults would always be the species. Transphilosophical concepts would be transformed into philosophical naïvetés. Many examples could be given to demonstrate this risk: the concepts of sign, history, truth, and so forth. What I want to emphasize is simply that the passage beyond philosophy does not consist in turning the page of philosophy (which usually amounts to philosophizing badly), but in continuing to read philosophers *in a certain way*. The risk I am speaking of is always assumed by Lévi-Strauss, and it is the very price of this endeavor. I have said that empiricism is the matrix of all faults menacing a discourse which continues, as with Lévi-Strauss in particular, to consider itself scientific. If we wanted to pose the problem of empiricism and *bricolage* in depth, we would probably end up very quickly with a number of absolutely contradictory propositions concerning the status of discourse in structural ethnology. On the one hand, structuralism justifiably claims to be the critique of empiricism. But at the same time there is not a single book or study by Lévi-Strauss which is not proposed as an empirical essay which can always be completed or invalidated by new information. The structural schemata are always proposed as hypotheses resulting from a finite quantity of information and which are subjected to the proof of experience. Numerous texts could be used to demonstrate this double postulation. Let us turn once again to the "Overture" of *The Raw and the Cooked*, where it seems clear that if this postulation is double, it is because it is a question here of a language on language:

> If critics reproach me with not having carried out an exhaustive inventory of South American myths before analyzing them, they are making a grave mistake about the nature and function of these documents. The total body of myth belonging to a given community is comparable to its speech. Unless the population dies out physically or morally, this totality is never complete. You might as well criticize a linguist for compiling the grammar of a language without having complete records of the words pronounced since the language came into being, and without knowing what will be said in it during the future part of its existence. Experience proves that a linguist can work out the grammar of a given language from a remarkably small number of sentences ... And even a partial grammar or an outline grammar is a precious acquisition when we are dealing with unknown languages. Syntax does not become evident only after a (theoretically limitless) series of events has been recorded and examined, because it is itself the body of rules governing their production. What I have tried to give is an outline of the syntax of South American mythology. Should fresh data come to hand, they will be used to check or modify the

formulation of certain grammatical laws, so that some are abandoned and replaced by new
ones. But in no instance would I feel constrained to accept the arbitrary demand for a total
mythological pattern, since, as has been shown, such á requirement has no meaning.[10]

Totalization, therefore, is sometimes defined as *useless*, and sometimes as *impossible*. This is
no doubt due to the fact that there are two ways of conceiving the limit of totalization.
And I assert once more that these two determinations coexist implicitly in Lévi-Strauss's
discourse. Totalization can be judged impossible in the classical style: one then refers to
the empirical endeavor of either a subject or a finite richness which it can never master.
There is too much, more than one can say. But nontotalization can also be determined in
another way: no longer from the standpoint of a concept of finitude as relegation to the
empirical, but from the standpoint of the concept of *play*. If totalization no longer has any
meaning, it is not because the infiniteness of a field cannot be covered by a finite glance or
a finite discourse, but because the nature of the field – that is, language and a finite
language – excludes totalization. This field is in effect that of *play*, that is to say, a field of
infinite substitutions only because it is finite, that is to say, because instead of being an
inexhaustible field, as in the classical hypothesis, instead of being too large, there is
something missing from it: a center which arrests and grounds the play of substitutions.
One could say – rigorously using that word whose scandalous signification is always
obliterated in French – that this movement of play, permitted by the lack or absence of a
center or origin, is the movement of *supplementarity*. One cannot determine the center
and exhaust totalization because the sign which replaces the center, which supplements it,
taking the center's place in its absence – this sign is added, occurs as a surplus, as a
supplement. The movement of signification adds something, which results in the fact that
there is always more, but this addition is a floating one because it comes to perform a
vicarious function, to supplement a lack on the part of the signified. Although Lévi-
Strauss in his use of the word "supplementary" never emphasizes, as I do here, the two
directions of meaning which are so strangely compounded within it, it is not by chance
that he uses this word twice in his "Introduction to the Work of Marcel Mauss," at one
point where he is speaking of the "overabundance of signifier, in relation to the signifieds
to which this overabundance can refer":

> In his endeavor to understand the world, man therefore always has at his disposal a surplus
> of signification (which he shares out amongst things according to the laws of symbolic
> thought – which is the task of ethnologists and linguists to study). This distribution of a
> *supplementary* allowance [*ration supplémentaire*] – if it is permissible to put it that way – is
> absolutely necessary in order that on the whole the available signifier and the signified it
> aims at may remain in the relationship of complementarity which is the very condition of
> the use of symbolic thought.[11]

(It could no doubt be demonstrated that this *ration supplémentaire* of signification
is the origin of the *ratio* itself.) The word reappears a little further on, after Lévi-Strauss
has mentioned "this floating signifier, which is the servitude of all finite thought":

> In other words – and taking as our guide Mauss's precept that all social phenomena can be
> assimilated to language – we see in *mana, Wakau, oranda* and other notions of the same
> type, the conscious expression of a semantic function, whose role it is to permit symbolic

thought to operate in spite of the contradiction which is proper to it. In this way are explained the apparently insoluble antinomies attached to this notion . . . At one and the same time force and action, quality and state, noun and verb; abstract and concrete, omnipresent and localized – *mana* is in effect all these things. But is it not precisely because it is none of these things that *mana* is a simple form, or more exactly, a symbol in the pure state, and therefore capable of becoming charged with any sort of symbolic content whatever? In the system of symbols constituted by all cosmologies, *mana* would simply be a zero symbolic value, that is to say, a sign marking the necessity of a symbolic content *supplementary* [my italics] to that with which the signified is already loaded, but which can take on any value required, provided only that this value still remains part of the available reserve and is not, as phonologists put it, a group-term.

Lévi-Strauss adds the note:
"Linguists have already been led to formulate hypotheses of this type. For example: 'A zero phoneme is opposed to all the other phonemes in French in that it entails no differential characters and no constant phonetic value. On the contrary, the proper function of the zero phoneme is to be opposed to phoneme absence.' (R. Jakobson and J. Lutz, "Notes on the French Phonemic Pattern," *Word* 5, no. 2 [August 1949]: 155.) Similarly, if we schematize the conception I am proposing here, it could almost be said that the function of notions like *mana* is to be opposed to the absence of signification, without entailing by itself any particular signification."[12]

The *overabundance* of the signifier, its *supplementary* character, is thus the result of a finitude, that is to say, the result of a lack which must be *supplemented*.

It can now be understood why the concept of play is important in Lévi-Strauss. His references to all sorts of games, notably to roulette, are very frequent, especially in his *Conversations*,[13] in *Race and History*,[14] and in *The Savage Mind*. Further, the reference to play is always caught up in tension.

Tension with history, first of all. This is a classical problem, objections to which are now well worn. I shall simply indicate what seems to me the formality of the problem: by reducing history, Lévi-Strauss has treated as it deserves a concept which has always been in complicity with a teleological and eschatological metaphysics, in other words, paradoxically, in complicity with that philosophy of presence to which it was believed history could be opposed. The thematic of historicity, although it seems to be a somewhat late arrival in philosophy, has always been required by the determination of Being as presence. With or without etymology, and despite the classic antagonism which opposes these significations throughout all of classical thought, it could be shown that the concept of *epistēmē* has always called forth that of *historia*, if history is always the unity of a becoming, as the tradition of truth or the development of science or knowledge oriented toward the appropriation of truth in presence and self-presence, toward knowledge in consciousness-of-self. History has always been conceived as the movement of a resumption of history, as a detour between two presences. But if it is legitimate to suspect this concept of history, there is a risk, if it is reduced without an explicit statement of the problem I am indicating here, of falling back into an ahistoricism of a classical type, that is to say, into a determined moment of the history of metaphysics. Such is the algebraic formality of the problem as I see it. More concretely, in the work of Lévi-Strauss it must be recognized that the respect for structurality, for the internal originality of the structure, compels a neutralization of time and history. For

example, the appearance of a new structure, of an original system, always comes about –
and this is the very condition of its structural specificity – by a rupture with its past, its
origin, and its cause. Therefore one can describe what is peculiar to the structural
organization only by not taking into account, in the very moment of this description, its
past conditions: by omitting to posit the problem of the transition from one structure to
another, by putting history between brackets. In this "structuralist" moment, the
concepts of chance and discontinuity are indispensable. And Lévi-Strauss does in fact
often appeal to them, for example, as concerns that structure of structures, language, of
which he says in the "Introduction to the Work of Marcel Mauss" that it "could only
have been born in one fell swoop":

> Whatever may have been the moment and the circumstances of its appearance on the scale
> of animal life, language could only have been born in one fell swoop. Things could not
> have set about acquiring signification progressively. Following a transformation the study
> of which is not the concern of the social sciences, but rather of biology and psychology, a
> transition came about from a stage where nothing had a meaning to another where
> everything possessed it.[15]

This standpoint does not prevent Lévi-Strauss from recognizing the slowness, the
process of maturing, the continuous toil of factual transformations, history (for example,
Race and History). But, in accordance with a gesture which was also Rousseau's and
Husserl's, he must "set aside all the facts" at the moment when he wishes to recapture
the specificity of a structure. Like Rousseau, he must always conceive of the origin of a
new structure on the model of catastrophe – an overturning of nature in nature, a
natural interruption of the natural sequence, a setting aside *of* nature.

Besides the tension between play and history, there is also the tension between play
and presence. Play is the disruption of presence. The presence of an element is always a
signifying and substitutive reference inscribed in a system of differences and the
movement of a chain. Play is always play of absence and presence, but if it is to be
thought radically, play must be conceived of before the alternative of presence and
absence. Being must be conceived as presence or absence on the basis of the possibility
of play and not the other way around. If Lévi-Strauss, better than any other, has brought
to light the play of repetition and the repetition of play, one no less perceives in his
work a sort of ethic of presence, an ethic of nostalgia for origins, an ethic of archaic and
natural innocence, of a purity of presence and self-presence in speech – an ethic,
nostalgia, and even remorse, which he often presents as the motivation of the ethno-
logical project when he moves toward the archaic societies which are exemplary
societies in his eyes. These texts are well known.

Turned towards the lost or impossible presence of the absent origin, this structuralist
thematic of broken immediacy is therefore the saddened, *negative*, nostalgic, guilty,
Rousseauistic side of the thinking of play whose other side would be the Nietzschean
affirmation, that is the joyous affirmation of the play of the world and of the innocence of
becoming, the affirmation of a world of signs without fault, without truth, and without
origin which is offered to an active interpretation. *This affirmation then determines the
noncenter otherwise than as loss of the center.* And it plays without security. For there is a *sure*
play: that which is limited to the *substitution* of *given* and *existing, present,* pieces. In

absolute chance, affirmation also surrenders itself to *genetic* indetermination, to the *seminal* adventure of the trace.

There are thus two interpretations of interpretation, of structure, of sign, of play. The one seeks to decipher, dreams of deciphering a truth or an origin which escapes play and the order of the sign, and which lives the necessity of interpretation as an exile. The other, which is no longer turned toward the origin, affirms play and tries to pass beyond man and humanism, the name of man being the name of that being who, throughout the history of metaphysics or of ontotheology – in other words, throughout his entire history – has dreamed of full presence, the reassuring foundation, the origin and the end of play. The second interpretation of interpretation, to which Nietzsche pointed the way, does not seek in ethnography, as Lévi-Strauss does, the "inspiration of a new humanism" (again citing the "Introduction to the Work of Marcel Mauss").

There are more than enough indications today to suggest we might perceive that these two interpretations of interpretation – which are absolutely irreconcilable even if we live them simultaneously and reconcile them in an obscure economy – together share the field which we call, in such a problematic fashion, the social sciences.

For my part, although these two interpretations must acknowledge and accentuate their difference and define their irreducibility, I do not believe that today there is any question of *choosing* – in the first place because here we are in a region (let us say, provisionally, a region of historicity) where the category of choice seems particularly trivial; and in the second, because we must first try to conceive of the common ground, and the *différance* of this irreducible difference. Here there is a kind of question, let us still call it historical, whose *conception, formation, gestation,* and *labor* we are only catching a glimpse of today. I employ these words, I admit, with a glance toward the operations of childbearing – but also with a glance toward those who, in a society from which I do not exclude myself, turn their eyes away when faced by the as yet unnamable which is proclaiming itself and which can do so, as is necessary whenever a birth is in the offing, only under the species of the nonspecies, in the formless, mute, infant, and terrifying form of monstrosity.

NOTES

1 *The Raw and the Cooked*, trans. John and Doreen Wightman (New York: Harper and Row, 1969), p. 14. [Translation somewhat modified.]

2 *The Elementary Structures of Kinship*, trans. James Bell, John von Sturmer, and Rodney Needham (Boston: Beacon Press, 1969), p. 8.

3 Ibid., p. 3.

4 *The Savage Mind* (London: George Weidenfeld and Nicolson; Chicago: The University of Chicago Press, 1966), p. 247.

5 Ibid., p. 17.

6 *The Raw and the Cooked*, p. 2.

7 Ibid., pp. 5–6.

8 Ibid., p. 12.

9 Ibid., pp. 17–18.

10 Ibid., pp. 7–8.

11 "Introduction à l'oeuvre de Marcel Mauss," in Marcel Mauss, *Sociologie et anthropologie* (Paris: P.U.F., 1950), p. xlix.

12 Ibid., pp. xlix–l.

13 George Charbonnier, *Entretiens avec Claude Lévi-Strauss* (Paris: Plon, 1961).

14 *Race and History* (Paris: Unesco Publications, 1958).

15 "Introduction à l'oeuvre de Marcel Mauss," p. xlvi.

11

Foucault on Derrida

The work of Michel Foucault (1926–84) exemplifies a more general shift from philosophical critique into the critical examination of intellectual disciplines, histories and practices. Associated with 'post-structuralism', Foucault's work emerges less as a series of readings of precursors than as a combination of intellectual history and the critique of power. A number of his key works take particular institutions, practices or areas of social discipline and seek to provide alternative conceptions of the power relations involved. *Madness and Civilization* (1961) and *The Birth of the Clinic* (1963) provide strategic critiques of the treatment of insanity and the institutions of medicine, while *Discipline and Punish: The Birth of the Prison* (1975) offers a comparable critique of the institution of the prison. Two of his most overtly theoretical books, *The Order of Things* (1966) and *The Archaeology of Knowledge* (1969), provide a methodological account of Foucault's critical relation to structuralism. His 'archaeology' of the way different 'epistemes' work as shifting structural paradigms developed in the 1970s towards a more overtly Nietzschean approach to the genealogy of thought, focusing on questions of power, knowledge and ethics. This shift is evidenced by his three-volume work *The History of Sexuality* (1976–84) which offers an alternative genealogy of practices and pleasure read back into Greek thought.

Although influenced by his teacher Louis Althusser and by his reading of Heidegger, Foucault's engagement with their work remains implicit rather than being spelt out in critical essays. The more explicit object of analysis in Foucault's work is the network of intellectual disciplines and institutions often thought of as marginal to philosophical texts. The impression that Foucault's work is intellectual history is somewhat misleading, however, since he is less concerned with empirical history or historiographical research than with a strategic critique of the genealogy of ideas. There is, then, a loose affinity with Max Weber, working at the boundaries between philosophy, sociology and anthropology, though Foucault is markedly indifferent to traditional conceptions of politics and economics. Critical of the operations of power in thought and in society, Foucault's approach owes more to Nietzsche than to Marx or Freud. He offers genealogies of particular problems and social myths, rather than working within more general accounts of capitalism or psychology. Although not directly influenced, his critique of enlightenment and of social and intellectual administration has affinities with the Frankfurt School. This affinity has been recognized in the importance ascribed to Foucault's work by second-generation Frankfurt School theorists, though the German reception of Foucault often underplays his radicalization of intellectual presentation and style. The work of another French Nietzschean, Gilles Deleuze, comes closer to the critical spirit of Foucault's work. The more diffuse reception of Foucault's work can be traced as an animating influence on disciplinary paradigms such as new historicism, cultural materialism and queer theory. He has influenced a number of intellectuals working against the grain of theory or philosophy who offer situated modes of intellectual history and critical intervention.

Foucault's essay 'My Body, This Paper, This Fire' first appeared as an appendix to the 1972 revised edition of Histoire de la folie, translated as Madness and Civilization. Foucault's response to Derrida's critique of his work suggests local rivalries and disagreements, as well as a contrast between their approaches. Both Foucault and Derrida offer innovative interpretations of texts which nevertheless rest much of their authority on their ability to work as detailed readings. Foucault is concerned, then, to contest both the detail and the implicit methodology of Derridean deconstruction so as to highlight the qualitative legitimacy of his own approach to discursive analysis. At one level the difference can be understood as a disagreement about the status of texts as opposed to discourses. For Foucault, discourses are implicated in social actions and institutions that go beyond what can be explicated from the logic of particular texts. At another level, the disagreement concerns the limits of philosophy and the extent to which it is possible to conceive of discourses, such as the discourse of madness, beyond the authority of philosophy. Foucault defends his work against the accusation that his account of madness remains complicit with the categories of Western metaphysics. This motivates Foucault's concluding remarks, which suggest that Derrida's approach to close reading can be understood not as a radical exploration of the limits of metaphysics, but as a continuation of the authoritative pedagogy of academic philosophy. This accusation also echoes one of Foucault's most famous essays, 'What Is an Author?', which seeks to shift interpretation beyond the immanent textuality of close reading towards the way the authority of the 'author' works as a discursive practice.

FURTHER READING

Primary works

Michel Foucault, Madness and Civilization: A History of Insanity in the Age of Reason, trans. Richard Howard (London: Tavistock, 1967); The Birth of the Clinic: An Archaeology of Medical Perception, trans. A. M. Sheridan (London: Tavistock, 1973); Discipline and Punish: The Birth of the Prison, trans. A. M. Sheridan (London:

Allen Lane, 1977); *The Order of Things: An Archaeology of the Human Sciences* (London: Tavistock, 1970); *The Archaeology of Knowledge*, trans. A. M. Sheridan Smith (London: Tavistock, 1972); *The History of Sexuality*, 3 vols., trans. Robert Hurley (London: Allen Lane, 1979–86); *Remarks on Marx*, trans. R. James Goldstein and James Cascaito (New York: Semiotext(e), 1991); 'What Is Critique?', *The Politics of Truth: Michel Foucault*, eds. Sylvère Lotringer and Lysa Hochroth (New York: Semiotext(e), 1997); James D. Faubion, ed., *Essential Works of Foucault, 1954–1984*, 3 vols., trans. Robert Hurley and others (London: Allen Lane, 1997–9).

Secondary works

Judith Butler, *Gender Trouble* (London: Routledge, 1990).

Arnold I. Davidson, ed., *Foucault and His Interlocutors* (Chicago: University of Chicago Press, 1997), esp. Jacques Derrida, '"To Do Justice to Freud": The History of Madness in the Age of Psychoanalysis', trans. Pascale-Anne Brault and Michael Naas.

Gilles Deleuze, *Foucault*, trans. Sean Hand (London: Athlone, 1988).

Jacques Derrida, 'Cogito and the History of Madness', *Writing and Difference*, trans. Alan Bass (London: Routledge and Kegan Paul, 1978), pp. 31–63.

Hubert L. Dreyfus and Paul Rabinow, *Michel Foucault: Beyond Structuralism and Hermeneutics*, 2nd edition (Chicago: University of Chicago Press, 1983).

François Ewald, ed., *Michel Foucault, Philosopher*, trans. Timothy J. Armstrong (New York: Harvester Wheatsheaf, 1992).

Thomas R. Flynn, *Sartre, Foucault, and Historical Reason* (Chicago: University of Chicago Press, 1997).

Jan Goldstein, ed., *Foucault and the Writing of History* (Oxford: Blackwell, 1994).

Gary Gutting, *The Cambridge Companion to Foucault* (Cambridge: Cambridge University Press, 1994).

Susan J. Hekman, ed., *Feminist Interpretations of Michel Foucault* (University Park, PA: Pennsylvania State University Press, 1996).

David Couzens Hoy, *Foucault: A Critical Reader* (Oxford: Blackwell, 1986).

Michael Kelly, ed., *Critique and Power: Recasting the Foucault–Habermas Debate* (Cambridge, MA: MIT, 1994).

Hans Herbert Kögler, *The Power of Dialogue: Critical Hermeneutics after Gadamer and Foucault*, trans. Paul Hendrickson (Cambridge, MA: MIT, 1996).

Lois McNay, *Foucault: A Critical Introduction* (New York: Continuum, 1994).

Richard Marsden, *The Nature of Capital: Marx after Foucault* (London: Routledge, 1999).

Mark Poster, *Foucault, Marxism and History* (Cambridge: Polity, 1984).

Paul Rabinow, ed., *The Foucault Reader* (Harmondsworth: Penguin, 1986).

Jana Sawicki, *Disciplining Foucault: Feminism, Power, and the Body* (London: Routledge, 1991).

Barry Smart, *Foucault, Marxism and Critique* (London: Routledge, 1983).

Barry Smart, ed., *Michel Foucault: Critical Assessments*, 3 vols. (London: Routledge, 1994).

Rudi Visker, *Michel Foucault: Genealogy as Critique*, trans. Chris Turner (London: Verso, 1995).

Michel Foucault, 'My Body, This Paper, This Fire' (1966), trans. Geoff Bennington, *Aesthetics, Method, and Epistemology: Essential Works of Foucault*, vol. 2, ed. James D. Faubion (London: Allen Lane / Penguin, 1998), pp. 393–417.

On pages 56–59 of *Histoire de la folie* [*Madness and Civilization*][a] I said that dreams and madness have neither the same status nor the same role in the development of Cartesian doubt: dreams allow me to doubt this place where I am, this sheet of paper I see, this hand I hold out; but madness is not an instrument or stage of doubt; for "*I* who am thinking cannot be mad." Madness is therefore excluded, contrary to the skeptical tradition, which made it one of the reasons for doubting.

To sum up Derrida's objection to this thesis, it is no doubt best to quote the passage where he gives most energetically his reading of Descartes [*Meditations on First Philosophy*, first meditation].

> Descartes has just said that all knowledge of sensory origin could deceive him. He pretends to put to himself the astonished objection of the imaginary nonphilosopher who is frightened by such audacity and says: no, not all sensory knowledge, for then you would be mad and it would be unreasonable to follow the example of madmen, to put forward a madman's discourse. Descartes *echoes* this objection: since I am here, writing, and you understand me, I am not mad, nor are you, and we are all sane here. The example of madness is therefore not indicative of the fragility of the sensory idea. So be it. Descartes acquiesces to this natural point of view, or rather he pretends to be sitting back in this natural comfort the better, the more radically and the more definitively to spring out of it and unsettle his interlocutor. So be it, he says, you think that I would be extravagant to doubt that I am sitting near the fire, etc., that I would be extravagant to follow the example of madmen. I will therefore propose a hypothesis which will seem much more natural to you, will not disorient you, because it concerns a more common, and more universal experience than that of madness: the experience of sleep and dreams. Descartes then elaborates the hypothesis that will ruin *all* the *sensory* foundations of knowledge and will lay bare only the *intellectual* foundations of certainty. This hypothesis above all will not run from the possibility of extravagances – epistemological ones – much more serious than madness.
>
> The reference to dreams does not, therefore, fall short of a madness potentially respected or even excluded by Descartes: quite the contrary. It constitutes, in the methodical order which here is ours, the hyperbolical exasperation of the hypothesis of madness. This latter affected only certain areas of sensory perception, and in a contingent and partial way. Moreover, Descartes is concerned here not with determining the concept of madness but with utilizing the popular notion of extravagance for juridical and methodological ends, in order to ask questions of principle regarding only the *truth* of ideas. ([Derrida's footnote] *Madness, theme or index*: what is significant is that Descartes, at bottom, never speaks of madness itself in this text. Madness is not his theme. He treats it as the index of a question of principle, and epistemological value. It will be said, perhaps, that this is the sign of a profound exclusion. But this silence on madness itself simultaneously signifies the opposite

of an exclusion, since it is not a question of madness in this text, not even to exclude it. It is not in the *Meditations* that Descartes speaks of madness itself.) What must be grasped here is that *from this point of view* the sleeper, or the dreamer, is madder than the madman. Or, at least, the dreamer, insofar as concerns the problem of knowledge which interests Descartes here, is further from true perception than the madman. It is in the case of sleep, and not in that of extravagance, that the *absolute totality* of ideas of sensory origin becomes suspect, is stripped of "objective value" as M. Guéroult puts it. The hypothesis of extravagance is therefore not a good example, a revelatory example, a good instrument of doubt – and for at least two reasons. (a) It does not cover the *totality* of the field of sensory perception. The madman is not always wrong about everything; he is not wrong often enough, is never mad enough. (b) It is not a useful or happy example pedagogically, because it meets the resistance of the non-philosopher who does not have the audacity to follow the philosopher when the latter agrees that he might indeed be mad at the very moment when he speaks.

Derrida's augmentation is remarkable for its depth and perhaps even more so for its frankness. The stakes of the debate are clearly indicated: Could there be anything anterior or exterior to philosophical discourse? Can its condition reside in an exclusion, a refusal, a risk avoided, and, why not, a fear? Derrida rejects this suspicion passionately. "*Pudenda origo*," as Nietzsche said, about the religious and their religion.

Let us confront Derrida's analyses and Descartes's texts.

1 The Privileges of Dreams Over Madness

Derrida: "Dreaming is a more common, and more universal experience than that of madness." "The madman is not always wrong about everything." "Madness affects only certain areas of sensory perception, and in a contingent and partial way."

Now, Descartes does not say that dreaming is "more common and more universal than madness." Nor does he say that madmen are only mad from time to time and on particular points. Let us listen instead to his evocation of people who "insist constantly that they are kings." Is the madness of these men who think they are kings, or have a body made of glass, more intermittent than dreams?

Yet it is a fact that in the progression of his doubt, Descartes privileges dreaming over madness. Let us leave undecided for the moment the problem of whether madness is excluded, merely neglected, or taken up in a broader and more radical testing.

Scarcely has Descartes cited the example of madness only to abandon it, than he evokes the case of dreams: "However, I must here take into account the fact that I am a man, and consequently have the habit of sleeping, and imagining in my dreams the same or sometimes more unlikely things than these deranged people do when awake."

So dreams have a double advantage. On the one hand, they are capable of giving rise to extravagances that equal or sometimes exceed those of madness. On the other hand, they have the property of happening habitually. The first advantage is of a logical and demonstrative order: everything that madness (the example I have just left to one side) could make me doubt can also be rendered uncertain by dreams. In their power to make uncertain, dreams are not outdone by madness; and none of the demonstrative force of madness is lost by dreams when I need to convince myself of all that I must call into doubt. The other advantage of dreams is of a quite different order: they are frequent, they happen often; my memories of them are recent, it is not difficult to have access to these vivid memories which they leave. In short, this is a practical advantage when it is no longer a question of demonstrating, but of performing an exercise, and calling up a memory, a thought, a state, in the very movement of meditation.

The extravagance of dreams guarantees their *demonstrative* character as an *example*: their frequency ensures their *accessibility* as an *exercise*. And it is indeed this quality of accessibility which preoccupies Descartes here, certainly more so than the demonstrative quality, which he mentions once and for all, as if to make sure that the hypothesis of madness can be abandoned without regret. On the other hand, the theme that dreams happen very often returns several times. "I am a man, and consequently I am in the habit of sleeping," "how many times has it happened that I have dreamed at night," "what happens in sleep," "thinking about it carefully I remember having often been mistaken while asleep."

I am afraid that Derrida has confused these two aspects of dreaming. It is as if he had covered them both with one word that joins them together by force: "universal." If they could be described as "universal," dreams would happen to everyone and about everything. Dreams would indicate that everything could be doubted by everyone. But this forces the words; it goes far beyond what Descartes's text says; or, rather, it falls far short of the peculiarities of that text; it effaces the clear distinction between the extravagance of dreams and their frequency; it erases the specific role of these two characteristics (demonstration and exercise) in Descartes's discourse; it omits the greater importance accorded to habit than to extravagance.

But why is it important that dreams should be familiar and accessible?

2   My Experience of Dreams

Derrida: "The reference to dreams constitutes, in the methodical order which here is ours, the hyperbolical exasperation of the hypothesis of madness."

Before re-reading the paragraph on dreams,[1] let us keep in mind what has just been said: "But just a moment – these are madmen, and I should be no less extravagant if I were to follow their examples."

The discourse then runs as follows: a resolution on the part of the meditating subject to take into consideration that he is a man, that he does sometimes sleep and dream; the appearance of a memory, or rather of a multitude of memories, of dreams that coincide exactly, point by point, with today's perception (sitting here, fully dressed, beside the fire); and yet, a feeling that there is a difference between this perception and that memory, a difference not only noted but brought about by the subject in the very movement of his meditation (I look at this paper; I shake my head, I reach out my hand to make the difference between waking and sleeping stand out sharply); but then come further memories, at a second level (the sharpness of this impression has often formed part of my dreams); with these memories, the vivid feeling that I am awake disappears; it is replaced by the clear vision that there is no certain index that can separate sleep and waking; an observation that provokes in the meditating subject an astonishment such that the lack of differentiation between waking and sleeping provokes the near certainty of being asleep.

It is clear that making sleep and waking into a theme for reflection is not the only consequence of the resolution to think about dreaming. In the very movement that proposes it and makes it vary, this theme *takes effect* in the meditating subject in the form of memories, sharp impressions, voluntary gestures, felt differences, more memories, clear vision, astonishment, and a lack of differentiation very close to the feeling of being asleep. To think of dreams is not to think of something external, whose causes and effects I could know, nor is it to evoke no more than a strange phantasmagoria, or the movements of the brain which can provoke it; thinking about dreams, when one applies oneself to it, is such that its effect is that of blurring the perceived limits of sleeping and waking for the meditating subject at the very heart of his meditation. The subject who thinks of dreaming *is thereby disturbed*. Applying one's mind to dreams is not an indifferent task: perhaps it is indeed in the first place a self-suggested theme; but it quickly turns out to be a risk to which one is exposed. A risk, for the subject, of being modified; a risk of no longer being at all sure of being awake; a risk of *stupor*, as the Latin text says.

And it is here that the example of dreaming shows another of its privileges: dreams may well modify the meditating subject to this extent, but they do not prevent him, in the very heart of this *stupor*, from continuing to meditate, to meditate validly, to see clearly a certain number of things or principles, in spite of the lack of distinction, however deep, between waking and sleeping. Even though I am no longer sure of being awake, I remain sure of what my meditation allows me to see: this is just what is shown by the following passage, which begins, precisely, with a sort of hyperbolic resolution, "let us suppose, then, that we are asleep," or as the Latin text says more forcefully, "*Age somniemus*." Thinking about dreams had led me to uncertainty; uncertainty, through the astonishment it provoked, led me to the near-certainty of being asleep; this near-certainty is now made by my resolutions into a systematic pretense. The meditating subject is put to sleep by way of artifice: "*Age somniemus*," and on this basis the meditation will be able to develop anew.

We can now see all the possibilities furnished by the dream's property of being, not universal, certainly, but modestly habitual.

1. It is a possible, immediately accessible experience, the model for which is put forward by countless memories.

2. This possible experience is not only a theme for meditation: it is really and actually produced in meditation, according to the following series: thinking of the dream, remembering the dream, trying to separate the dream from waking, no longer knowing whether one is dreaming or not, acting voluntarily as though one were dreaming.

3. By means of this meditative exercise, thinking about dreaming takes effect in the subject himself: it modifies the subject by striking him with *stupor*.

4. But in modifying him, in making of him a subject uncertain of being awake, thinking about dreams does not disqualify him as meditating subject: even though transformed into a "subject supposedly asleep," the meditating subject can safely pursue the progression of his doubt.

But we must go back and compare this experience of dreams with the example of madness which immediately precedes it.

3   The "Good" and the "Bad" Example

Derrida: "What must be grasped here is that from this point of view the sleeper, or the dreamer, is madder than the madman."

For Derrida, madness is not excluded by Descartes: it is simply neglected. Neglected in favor of a better and more radical example. The example of dreams extends, completes and generalizes what the example of madness indicated so inadequately. To pass from madness to dreams is to pass from a "bad" to a "good" instrument of doubt.

Now I believe that the opposition between dreams and madness is of a quite different type. We must compare Descartes's two paragraphs step by step, and follow the system of their opposition in detail.

1. The *nature* of the meditative exercise. This appears clearly in the *vocabulary* used. In the madness paragraph, a vocabulary of comparison. If I wish to deny that "these hands and this body are mine," I must "compare myself to certain deranged people" (*comparare*) but I would be extravagant indeed "if I followed their examples" (*si quod ab iis exemplum ad me transferrem*: if I applied to myself some example coming from them). The madman: an external term to which I compare myself.

In the dream-paragraph, a vocabulary of memory. "I am in the habit of imagining in my dreams"; "how many times has it happened that I . . . "; "thinking carefully about it, I remember." The dreamer: that which I remember having been; from the depths of my memory rises the dreamer that I was myself, that I will be again.

2. The *themes* of the meditative exercise. They appear in the examples that the meditating subject proposed by himself.

Examples of madness: thinking one is a king when one is poor; imagining one's body is made of glass or that one is a jug. Madness is the entirely other; it deforms and transports; it gives rise to another scene.

Examples of dreams: being seated (as I am at this moment); feeling the heat of the fire (as I feel it today); reaching out my hand (as I decide, at this moment, to do). The dream does not shift the scene; it doubles the demonstratives that point to the scene where I am (this hand? Perhaps a different hand, in image. This fire? Perhaps a different fire, a dream). Dream-imagination pins itself onto present perception at every point.

3. The *central test* of the exercise. This consists in the search for difference; can I take these proposed themes into account in my meditation? Can I seriously wonder whether my body is made of glass, or whether I am naked in my bed? If I can, then I am obliged to doubt even my own body. On the other hand, my body is saved if my meditation remains quite distinct from madness and dreams.

Distinct from dreams? I put it to the test: I remember dreaming that I was nodding my head. I will therefore nod my head again, here and now. Is there a difference? Yes – a certain clarity, a certain distinctness. But, and this is the second stage of the test, can this clarity and distinctness be found in the dream? Yes, I have a clear memory that it was so. Therefore what I supposed was the criterion of difference (clarity and distinctness) belongs indifferently to both dreams and waking perception; so it cannot make the difference between them.

Distinct from madness? The test is immediately carried out. Or, rather, looking more closely, the test does not take place as it does in the case of dreams. There is, in fact, no question of trying to take myself to be a madman who takes himself to be a king; nor is there any question of wondering if I am a king (or a captain from Tours) who takes himself to be a philosopher shut up in a room to meditate. What is different with madness does not have to be tested, it is established. Scarcely are the themes of extravagance evoked than the distinction bursts out like a shout: "*sed amentes sunt isti.*"

4. *The effect of the exercise.* This appears in the sentences, or rather in the decision-sentences, which end both passages.

Madness-paragraph: "But just a moment – these are madmen" (third person plural, they, the others, *isti*); "I should be no less extravagant if I followed their example": it would be madness (note the conditional) even to try the test, to wish to imitate all these delights, and to play the fool with fools, as fools do. Imitating madmen will not persuade me that I am mad (as thinking of dreams will in a moment convince me that I am perhaps asleep); it is the very project of imitating them that is extravagant. The extravagance applies to the very idea of putting it to the test, and that is why the test fails to take place and is replaced by a mere registering of difference.

Dream-paragraph: the sentence "*these* are madmen" corresponds to "*I* am quite astonished" (*obstupescere*: the stupor of indistinctness responds to the shout of difference); and the sentence "I should be no less extravagant if . . . " is answered by "my astonishment (*stupor*) is such that it is almost capable of convincing me that I am asleep." The test that has been effectively tried has "taken" so well that here I am (note the present indicative) in uncertainty as to whether I am awake. And it is in this uncertainty that I decide to continue my meditation.

It would be mad to want to act the madman (and I abandon the idea); but to think about dreaming is already to have the impression of being asleep (and that is what I shall meditate on).

It is extraordinarily difficult to remain deaf to the way these two paragraphs echo one another. Difficult not to be struck by the complex system of oppositions which underlies them. Difficult not to recognize in them two parallel but different exercises: that of the *demens*, and that of the *dormiens*. Difficult not to hear the words and sentences confront each other on both sides of the "however," the importance of which Derrida so deeply underlined, though I think he was wrong not to analyze its function in the play of the discourse. Difficult indeed, to say simply that among the reasons for doubt, madness is an insufficient and pedagogi-cally clumsy example, because the dreamer is in any case much madder than the madman.

The whole discursive analysis shows that the establishment of nonmadness (and the rejection of the test) is not continuous with the test of sleep (and the observation that one is perhaps asleep).

But why this rejection of the test of the *demens*? From the fact that it does not take place, can one draw the conclusion that it is excluded? After all, Descartes speaks so little, and so briefly, about madness . . .

4   The Disqualification of the Subject

Derrida: "What is significant is that Descartes, at bottom, never speaks of madness in this text . . . it is not a question of madness in this text, not even to exclude it."

On several occasions Derrida wisely points out that in order to understand Descartes's text properly it is necessary to refer to the original Latin version. He recalls – and he is quite right – the words used by Descartes in the famous sentence: "But just a moment: these are madmen (*sed amentes sunt isti*), and I should be no less extravagant (*demens*) if I were to follow their examples." Unfortunately, he takes the analysis no further than this simple reminder of the words.

Let us return to the passage itself: "How could I deny that these hands and this body are mine, except by comparing myself to certain deranged people . . . ?" (The term used here is *insani*). Now what are these *insani* who take themselves to be kings or jugs? They are *amentes*; and I should be no less *demens* if I were to apply their examples to myself. Why these three terms, or rather why use firstly the term *insanus*, then the couple *amens-demens*? When it is a matter of characterizing them by the implausibility of their imagination, the madmen are called *insani*: a word that belongs as much to current vocabulary as to medical terminology. As far as the signs of it are concerned, to be *insanus* is to take oneself to be what one is not, to believe in fancies, to be the victim of illusions. As for its causes, it comes from having the brain gorged with vapor. But when Descartes wants no longer to characterize madness but to affirm that I ought not to follow the example of madmen, he uses the terms *demens* and *amens*: terms that are in the first place juridical, before being medical, which designate a whole category of people incapable of certain religious, civil, and judicial acts. The *dementes* do not have total possession of their rights when it comes to speaking, promising, pledging, signing, starting a legal action, etc. *Insanus* is a characterizing term; *amens* and *demens* are disqualifying ones. In the former, it is a question of signs; in the others, of capacity.

The two sentences: In order to doubt my body, I must "compare myself to certain deranged people," and "but just a moment – these are madmen," are not the proof of an impatient and annoyed tautology. It is in no way a matter of saying, "one must be mad or act like madmen," but, "these are madmen and I am not mad." It would be a singular flattening of the text to sum it up as Derrida does: "since I am here . . . I am not mad, nor are you, we are all sane here." The development of the text is quite different: to doubt one's body is to be like those with deranged minds, the sick, the *insani*. Can I follow their example and at least feign madness for my own part, and make me uncertain in my own mind whether I am mad or not? I cannot and must not. For these *insani* are *amentes*; and I would be just as *demens* as they, and juridically disqualified if I followed . . .

Derrida has obscurely sensed this juridical connotation of the word. He returns to it several times, insistently and hesitantly. Descartes, he says, "treats madness as an index of a question of principle and epistemological value." Or again: "Descartes is concerned here not with determining the concept of madness but with utilizing the popular notion of extravagance for juridical and methodological ends, in order to ask questions of principle regarding only the truth of ideas." Yes, Derrida is right to emphasize that it is a question of right at this point. Yes, he is right again to say that Descartes did not want to "determine the concept of madness" (and who ever made out that he did?). But he is wrong not to have seen that Descartes's text plays on the gap between two types of determinations of madness (medical on the one hand and juridical on the other). Above all, he is wrong to say hastily that the question of right posed here concerns "the truth of ideas," when in fact, as is clearly stated, it concerns the qualification of the subject.

The problem can, then, be posed thus. Can I doubt my own body, can I doubt my actuality? The example of madmen, of the *insani* invites me to do so. But comparing myself to them and acting like them implies that I, too, will become demented, incapable and disqualified in my enterprise of meditation: I should be no less *demens* if I followed their examples. But if, on the other hand, I take the example of dreaming, if I pretend to dream, then *dormiens* though I am, I will be able to continue meditating, reasoning, seeing clearly. *Demens* I shall be unable to continue: at the hypothesis alone I am obliged to stop, envisage something else, see if another example allows me to doubt my body. *Dormiens*, I can continue with my meditation; I remain qualified to think, and I therefore make my resolution: "*Age somniemus,*" which leads to a new stage of meditation.

It would have to be a very distant reading which could assert that "it's not a question of madness in this text."

Alright, you say. Let us admit, in spite of Derrida, that it is necessary to pay such great attention to the text, and to all its little differences. For all that, have you demonstrated that madness is well and truly excluded from the progress of doubt? Does not Descartes refer to it again with reference to the imagination? Will it not be a question of madness when he discovers the extravagance of painters, and all the fantastic illusions they invent?

5   The Extravagance of Painters

Derrida: "What [Descartes] seemed previously to exclude...as extravagance, he here admits as a possibility in dreams...Now, within these representations, these images, these ideas in the Cartesian sense, everything may be fictitious and false, as in the representations of those painters whose imaginations, as Descartes expressly says, 'are extravagant enough to invent something so new that its like has never been seen before.'"

It will indeed be a question of madness several more times in the rest of Descartes's work. And its disqualifying role for the meditating subject will in no way prevent meditation from bearing on it, for it is not for the content of these extravagances that madness is put out of play; that only happens for the subject who wants "to play the fool" and meditate at the same time, when in fact it is a matter of knowing if the subject can take madness in hand, imitate it, feign it, and risk no longer being sure whether or not he is rational. I think I have made this point: madness is excluded by the subject who doubts as a means of qualifying himself as doubting subject. But it is not excluded as an object of reflection and knowledge. Is it not characteristic that the madness talked of by Descartes in the paragraph studied above is defined in medical terms, as the result of a "brain deranged or gorged with the black vapors of bile"?

But Derrida could insist and stress the fact that madness is found again in the movement of doubt, mixed up with the imagination of painters. It is manifestly present as is indicated by the word "extravagant" used to describe the imagination of painters: "If it is possible that their imagination is extravagant enough to invent something so new that we have never seen anything like it...certainly at the very least the paints [*couleurs*] with which they compose it must be real." Derrida has realized perfectly what is odd about the expression: "their imagination is extravagant enough." So well has he realized it that he underlines it in his quotation as the peg on which to hang his whole demonstration. And I subscribe wholly to the necessity of isolating these words and keeping them well to one side.

But for a different reason – simply because they *do not appear* in Descartes's text. They are an addition by the translator. The Latin text says only: "*si forte aliquid excogitent ad eo novum ut nihil*...*"*; "if perhaps they invent something so new." It is curious that in support of his thesis Derrida should have spontaneously chosen, retained and underlined what precisely is *only* found in the French translation of the *Meditations*; curious, too, that he should insist, and assert that the word "extravagant" has been "expressly" used by Descartes.

It does not appear, then, that the example of dreaming is for Descartes only a generalization or radicalization of the case of madness. It is not as a feeble, inferior, "unrevealing," "ineffectual" example that madness is distinguished from dreaming; and it is not for its lesser value that, once evoked, it is as if left to one side. The example of madness stands against that of dreaming; they are confronted the one with the other and opposed according to a whole system of differences which are clearly articulated in Descartes's discourse.

And I am afraid that Derrida's analysis neglects many of these differences. Literal differences between words (*comparare/reminiscere; exemplum transferre*/to persuade; conditional/indicative). Thematic differences between images (being beside the fire, holding out one's hand and opening one's eyes/taking oneself to be a king, being covered in gold, having a body made of glass); textual differences in the disposition and opposition of paragraphs (the first plays on the distinction between *insanus* and *demens*, and on the *juridical implication* of *demens* by *insanus*; the second plays on the distinction "remembering being asleep/being persuaded that one is asleep," and on the *real passage* from the one to the other in a mind that applies itself to such a memory). But, above all, differences at the level of what happens in the meditation, at the level of the *events* that follow one another; *acts* carried out by the meditating subject (comparison/reminiscence); *effects* produced in the meditating subject (sudden and immediate perception of a difference/astonishment– stupor–experience of a lack of distinction); the qualification of the meditating subject (invalidated if he were *demens*; validated even if he were *dormiens*).

It is clear that this last set of differences controls all the others; it refers less to the signifying organization of the text than to the series of events (acts, effects, qualifications) which the discursive practice of meditation carries with it: it is a question of the modifications of the subject by the very exercise of discourse. And I have the feeling that if a reader as remarkably assiduous as Derrida has missed so many literary, thematic or textual differences, then this is through having misunderstood those differences which are the principle of these others; namely, the "discursive differences."

We must keep in mind the very title of "meditations." Any discourse, whatever it be, is constituted by a set of utterances which are produced each in its place and time, as so many discursive events. If it is a question of a pure demonstration, these utterances can be read as a series of events linked one to another according to a certain number of formal rules; as for the subject of the discourse, he is not implicated in the demonstration – he remains, in relation to it, fixed, invariable and as if neutralized. On the other hand, a "meditation" produces, as so many discursive events, new utterances that carry with them a series of modifications of the enunciating subject: through what is said in meditation, the subject passes from darkness to light, from impurity to purity, from the constraint of passions to detachment, from uncertainty and disordered movements to the serenity of wisdom, and so on. In meditation, the subject is ceaselessly altered by his own movement; his discourse provokes effects within which he is caught; it exposes him to risks, makes him pass through trials or temptations, produces states in him, and confers on him a status or qualification he did not hold at the initial moment. In short, meditation implies a mobile subject modifiable through the effect of the discursive events that take place. From this one, one can see what a demonstrative meditation would be: a set of discursive events which constitute at once groups of utterances linked one to another by formal rules of deduction, and series of modifications of the enunciating subject which follow continuously one from another. More precisely, in a demonstrative meditation the utterances, which are formally linked, modify the subject as they develop, liberating him from his convictions or on the contrary inducing systematic doubts, provoking illuminations or resolutions, freeing him from his attachments or immediate certainties, including new states. But, inversely, the decisions, fluctuations, displacements, primary or acquired qualifications of the subject make sets of new utterances possible, which are in their turn deduced regularly one from another.

The *Meditations* require this double reading: a set of propositions forming a *system*, which each reader must follow through if he wishes to feel their truth, and a set of modifications forming an *exercise*, which each reader must effect, by which each reader must be affected, if he in turn wants to be the subject enunciating this truth on his own behalf. And if there are indeed certain passages of the *Meditations* which can be deciphered exhaustively as a systematic stringing together of propositions – moments of pure deduction – there exist on the other hand sorts of "chiasmas," where the two forms of discourse intersect, and where the exercise modifying the subject orders the succession of propositions, or controls the junction of distinct demonstrative groups. It seems that the passage on madness and dreaming is indeed of this order.

Let us take it up again now as a whole and as an intersection of the demonstrative and ascetic schemas.

1. The immediately preceding passage presents itself as a practical syllogism.

> I ought to be wary of something that has deceived me once
> My senses, through which I have received the truest and surest things I possess, have
>   deceived me, and more than once
> I ought therefore no longer to trust them.

Clearly, it is here a question of a deductive fragment whose import is completely general: *all* that I have taken to be the most *true* falls under the sway of doubt, along with the senses which furnished it. A fortiori, there can therefore remain nothing that does not become at least as doubtful. Need I generalize any further? Derrida's hypothesis, that the (ineffectual) example of madness, and the (effectual) example of dreaming are summoned to operate this generalization, and to carry the syllogism of doubt farther forward, can thus not be retained. But then by what are they summoned?

2. They are summoned less by an objection or restriction than by a resistance: there are perceptible things that "one cannot rationally doubt." It is the word "*plane*" that the translator renders by "rationally." What then is this "impossibility," given that we have just established a completely binding syllogism? What, then, is this obstacle that opposes our doubting "entirely," "wholly," "completely" (rationally?) given that we've just performed a rationally unassailable piece of reasoning? It is the impossibility of this subject's really effecting such a generalized doubt in the exercise which modifies him; it is the impossibility of constituting oneself as universally doubting subject. What is still a problem, after a syllogism of such general import, is the taking-up of the advice of prudence into effective doubt, the transformation of the subject "knowing he must doubt everything" into a subject "applying his resolution-to-doubt to everything." We see why the translator has rendered "*plane*" as "rationally": by wanting to carry through this qualification "rational" that I brought into play at the very beginning of the meditations (and in at least three forms: having a sufficiently mature mind, being free of cares and passions, being assured of a peaceful retreat). If I am to resolve myself to doubt everything thoroughly, must I first disqualify myself as rational? If I want to maintain my qualification as rational, must I give up carrying out this doubt, or at least carrying it out in general terms?

The importance of the words "being able to doubt completely" consists in the fact that they mark the point of intersection of the two discursive forms – that of the system and that of the exercise: at the level of ascetic discursivity, one cannot yet doubt rationally. It is thus this level that will control the following development, and what is involved in it is not the extent of doubtful things but the status of the doubting subject, the qualificative elaboration that allows him to be at once "all-doubting" yet rational.

But what, then, is the obstacle, the resistance point of the exercise of doubt?

3. My body, and the immediate perception I have of it? More exactly an area defined as "the vivid and the near" (in opposition to all those "distant" and "weak" things which I can *place* in doubt without difficulty): I am here, wearing a dressing gown, sitting beside the fire – in short, the whole system of actuality which characterizes this moment of my meditation. It is of the first importance that Descartes here involves not the certainty that one may have in general of one's own body but, rather, everything that, at this precise *instant* of meditation, resists *in fact* the carrying-out of doubt by the subject who is *currently* meditating. Clearly, it is not certain things that in themselves (by their nature, their universality, their intelligibility) resist doubt but, rather, that which characterizes the actuality of the meditating subject (the place of his meditation, the gesture he is in the process of making, the sensations that strike him). If he really doubted all this system of actuality, would he still be rational? Would he not precisely be renouncing all these guarantees of rational meditation which he gave himself in choosing, as has just been said, the moment of the undertaking (quite late in life, but not too late: the moment that must not be allowed to slip past has come), its conditions (peace and quiet, with no cares to form distractions), its place (a peaceful retreat). If I

must begin doubting the place where I am, the attention I am paying to this piece of paper, and this heat from the fire which marks my present moment, how could I remain convinced of the rational character of my undertaking? In placing this actuality in doubt, am I not at the same time going to render impossible all rational meditation and remove all value from my resolution to discover the truth at last?

It is in order to reply to this question that two examples are called on, side by side, both of which force one to call into doubt the subject's system of actuality.

4. First example: madness. Madmen indeed are completely deluded as to what constitutes their actuality: they believe they are dressed when they are naked, kings when they are poor. But can I take up this example on my own account? Is it through this that I shall be able to transform into an effective resolution the proposition that we must doubt everything which comes to us from dreams? Impossible: "isti sunt dementes," that is, they are juridically disqualified as rational subjects, and to qualify myself among them, following them ("transfer their example to me") would disqualify me in my turn, and I should not be able to be a rational subject of meditation ("I should be no less extravagant"...). If one uses the example of madness to move from systems to askēsis, from the proposition to the resolution, it is quite possible to constitute oneself as a subject having to call everything into doubt, but it is impossible to remain qualified as a subject conducting rationally his meditation through doubt to an eventual truth. The resistance of actuality to the exercise of doubt is reduced by too strong an example: it carries away with it the possibility of meditating validly; the two qualifications "doubting subject" and "meditating subject" are not in this case simultaneously possible.

That madness is posited as disqualificatory in any search for truth, that it is not "rational" to call it up to carry out necessary doubt, that one cannot feign it even for a moment, that this impossibility is immediately obvious in the assignation of the term *demens*: this is indeed the decisive point at which Descartes parts company with all those for whom madness can be in one way or another the bringer or revealer of truth.

5. Second test: dreaming. Madness has therefore been excluded, not as an insufficient example but as an excessive and impossible test. Dreaming is now invoked: because it renders the actuality of the subject no less doubtful than does madness (one thinks one is sitting at table and one is naked in one's bed); and because it offers a certain number of differences with respect to madness – it forms part of the virtualities of the subject (I am a man), of his frequently actualized virtualities (I often sleep and dream), of his memories (I clearly remember having dreamed), and of his memories, which can return as the most vivid of impressions (to the point where I can compare my present impression validly with my memory of my dream). From these properties of dreaming, it is possible for the subject to conduct the exercise of a calling into doubt of his own actuality. First stage (which defines the test): I remember having dreamed what I now perceive as my actuality. Second stage (which for a moment appears to invalidate the test): the gesture I make in the very instant of my meditation to find out if I am asleep indeed appears to have the clarity and distinction of waking perception. Third stage (which validates the test): I remember not only the images of my dream, but also their clarity, as great as that of my current impressions. Fourth stage (which concludes the test): at one and the same time *I see manifestly* that there is no certain mark for distinguishing dream from reality; *and* I am so *surprised* that I am no longer sure whether

at this precise moment I am asleep or not. These two sides of the successful test (uncertain stupor and manifest vision) indeed constitute the subject as *effectively doubting* his own actuality, and as *validly continuing a meditation* that puts to one side everything that is not manifest truth. The two qualifications (doubting everything that arrives through the senses and meditating validly) are really effected. The syllogism had required that they be simultaneously in play; the subject's consciousness of his actuality had formed an obstacle to the accomplishment of this requirement. The attempt to use the example of madmen as a base had confirmed this incompatibility; the effort made to actualize the vividness of dreams showed, on the one hand, that this incompatibility is not insurmountable. And the meditating subject becomes doubting subject at the end of opposing tests: one that has constituted the subject as rational (as opposed to the disqualified madman), and one that also constituted the subject as doubting (in the lack of distinction between dreaming and waking).

Once this qualification of the subject has finally been achieved ("*Age somniemus*"), systematic discursivity will once again be able to intersect with the discourse of the exercise, take the upper hand, place intelligible truths under examination, until a new ascetic stage constitutes the meditating subject as threatened with universal error by the "great trickster." But even at that stage of the meditation, the qualification as "nonmad" (like the qualification as "potential dreamer") will remain valid.

It seems to me that Derrida has vividly and deeply sensed that this passage on madness has a singular place in the development of the *Meditations*. And he transcribes his feeling into his text, at the very moment at which he attempts to master it.

1. In order to explain that the question of madness should appear at this precise point of the *Meditations*, Derrida invents an alternation of voices that would displace, reject, and drive out of the text itself the difficult exclamation: "but just a moment – these are madmen."

Derrida did indeed find himself faced with a knotty problem. If, as he supposes, it is true that this whole movement of the first meditation operates a generalization of doubt, why does it pause, if only for a moment, over madness or even over dreaming? Why take pains to demonstrate that vivid and recent sensations are no less doubtful than the palest and most distant ones, once it has been established, *in general terms*, that what comes via the senses must not be trusted? Why make this swerve toward the particular point of my body, this paper, this fire? Why make a detour toward the singular trickeries of madness and dreaming?

Derrida gives to this deviation the status of a break. He imagines a foreign intervention, the scruple or reticence of a straggler worried by the movement overtaking him and fighting a last-minute rearguard action. Descartes has scarcely said that we must not trust the senses when a voice would be raised, the voice of a peasant foreign to all philosophical urbanity; he would, in his simple way, try to broach, or at least to limit the thinker's resolution: "I'm quite happy for you to doubt certain of your perceptions, but . . . that you are sitting here, by the fire, saying these things, holding that paper in your hands and other things of the same nature."[2] You'd have to be mad to doubt them, or rather, only madmen can make mistakes about such certain things. And I'm certainly not mad. It is at this point that Descartes would take over again and say to this obstinate yokel: I'm quite prepared to admit that you're not mad, since you're unwilling to be so;

but remember that you dream every night, and that your nightly dreams are no less mad than this madness you refuse. And the naive reticence of the objector who cannot doubt his body because he does not want to be mad would be conquered by the example of dreaming, so much "more natural," "more common," "more universal."

Derrida's hypothesis is a seductive one. It resolves with the utmost nicety his problem, which is to show that the philosopher goes directly to the calling into question of the "totality of beingness" [*la totalité de l'étantité*], that this is precisely the form and philosophical mark of his procedure; if he happens to stop for a moment at a "being-ness" as singular as madness, this can only be if some innocent tugs at his sleeves and questions him; by himself he would never have lingered among these stories of jugs and naked kings. In this way the rejection of madness, the abrupt exclamation "but just a moment − these are madmen" is itself rejected by Derrida and three times enclosed *outside* philosophical discourse: first, since it is another subject speaking (not the philosopher of the *Meditations* but the objector raising his scarcely refined voice); second, because he speaks from a place which is that of nonphilosophical naïveté; and, finally, because the philosopher takes over again and by quoting the "stronger," more "telling" example of dreaming disarms the objection and makes the very man who refuses madness accept something far worse.

But it is now clear what price Derrida has to pay for his skillful hypothesis. The omission of a certain number of *literal* elements (which appear as soon as one takes the trouble to compare the Latin text with the French translation); the elision of *textual* differences (the whole play of semantic and grammatical opposition between the dream paragraph and that on madness): finally, and above all, the erasure of the essential *discursive* determination (the double web of exercise and demonstration). Curiously, by imagining that other naive objecting voice behind Descartes's writing, Derrida has fudged all the text's differences; or, rather, in erasing all these differences, in bringing the test of madness and that of dreaming as close together as possible, in making the one the first faint failed draft of the other, in absorbing the insufficiency of the one in the universality of the other, Derrida is continuing the Cartesian exclusion. For Descartes, the meditating subject had to exclude madness by qualifying himself as not mad. And this exclusion is, in its turn, no doubt too dangerous for Derrida: no longer for the disqualification with which it threatens the philosophizing subject but for the qualification with which it would mark philosophical discourse; it would indeed determine it as "other" than the discourse of madness; it would establish between them a relationship of exteriority; it would send philosophical discourse across to the "other side," into the pure presumption of not being mad. Separation, exteriority, a determination from which the philosopher's discourse must indeed be saved if it is to be a "project for exceeding every finite and determinate totality." This Cartesian exclusion must then be excluded because it is determining. And Derrida is obliged to proceed to three operations to do this, as we can see: first, he affirms, against all the visible economy of the text, that the power of doubt specific to madness is a fortiori included in dreaming; second, he imagines (to account for the fact that there is any question of madness in spite of everything) that it is someone else who excludes madness, on his own account and following the oblique line of an objection; finally, he removes all philosophical status from this exclusion by denouncing its naive rusticity. Reverse the Cartesian exclusion and make it an inclusion; exclude the excluder by giving his discourse the status of an objection; exclude the exclusion by rejecting it into prephilosophical naïveté: Derrida has needed to do no less than this to get through Descartes's text and reduce the question of madness to nothing. We can see the result: the elision of the text's differences and the compensatory invention of a difference of voices lead Descartes's exclusion to a second level; philosophical discourse is finally excluded from excluding madness.

2. But madness does not allow itself to be reduced in this way. Even supposing that Descartes was "not speaking" of madness, at the point in his text where it is a question of *insani* and *dementes*, supposing that he gave way for a moment to a yokel in order to raise such a crude question, could it not be said that he proceeds, albeit in an insidious and silent manner, to exclude madness?

Could it not be said that Descartes has *de facto* and constantly avoided the question of madness?

Derrida replies to this objection in advance: Yes indeed, Descartes fully faces up to the risk of madness; not as you pretend in a prefatorial and almost marginal way with reference to some business about jugs and naked kings, but at the very heart of his philosophical enterprise, at the precise moment where his discourse, separating itself from all natural considerations on the errors of the senses or the engorgements of the brain, takes on its radical dimension in hyperbolic doubt and the hypothesis of the evil genius. *That* is where madness is called into question and faced up to; with the evil genius I indeed suppose that I am even more radically mistaken than those who think they have a body made of glass – even go so far as persuading myself that two and three do not perhaps add up to five; then with the *cogito* I reach that extreme point, that excess with respect to any determination which allows me to say, whether mistaken or not, whether mad or not, I am. The evil genius would indeed be the point at which philosophy itself, in the excess proper to it, risks madness; and the *cogito* would be the moment at which madness is erased (not because of an exclusion but because its determination when faced with reason would stop being pertinent). According to Derrida, then, we should not attach too much importance to this little farce of the peasant who interrupts at the beginning of the text with his village idiots: in spite of all their motley, they do not manage to pose the question of madness. On the other hand, all the threats of Unreason would be at play beneath the far more disturbing and gloomy figure of the evil genius. Similarly, the taking up by dreams of the worst extravagances of madmen at the beginning of the text would be an easy victory; on the other hand, after the great panic of the evil genius, we should need no less than the point of the *cogito* (and its excess with respect to the "totality of beingness") to make the determinations of madness and dreams appear to be nonradical. The great solemn theater of the universal trickster and of the "I think" would repeat the still natural fable of the madman and the sleeper, but this time in philosophical radicality.

To hold such an interpretation, Derrida had to deny that it was a question of madness at the point where madness was named (and in specific, carefully differentiated terms); now he has to demonstrate that there is a question of madness at the point where it is not named. Derrida puts this demonstration into operation through two series of semantic derivations. It is enough to quote them:

Evil genius: "total madness," "total panic," "disorder of the body" and "subversion of pure thought," "extravagance," "panic that I cannot master."

Cogito: "mad audacity," "mad project," "project which recognizes madness as its freedom," "disorder and inordinate nature of hyperbole," "unheard-of and singular excess," "excess tending toward Zero and Infinity," "hyperbolic point which ought to be, like all pure madness in general, silent."

All these derivations around Descartes's text are necessary for the evil genius and the *cogito* to become, as Derrida wishes, the true scene of confrontation with madness. But more is needed: he has to erase from Descartes's texts themselves everything showing that the episode of the evil genius is a voluntary, controled exercise, mastered and carried out from start to finish by a meditating subject who never lets himself be surprised. If it is true that the hypothesis of the malign genius carries the suspicion of error far beyond those illusions of the senses exemplified by certain madmen, then he who forms this fiction (and by the very fact that he forms it voluntarily and as an exercise) escapes the risk of "receiving them into his belief," as is the case and misfortune of madmen. He is tricked, but not convinced. Perhaps everything is illusion, but no credulity attaches to it. No doubt the evil genius tricks far more than does an engorged brain; he can give rise to all the illusory decors of madness, but he is something quite different from madness. It could even be said that he is the contrary of madness: since in madness *I believe* that an illusory purple covers my nudity and my poverty, while the hypothesis of the evil genius permits *me not to believe* that my body and hands exist. As to the extent of the trap, it is true that the evil genius is not outdone by madness; but, in the position of the subject with respect to the trap, there is a rigorous opposition between evil genius and madness. If the evil genius takes on the powers of *madness*, this is only after the exercise of meditation has excluded the risk of *being mad.*

Let us reread Descartes's text. "I shall think that the sky, the air, the earth, colors, figures, sounds, and all other external things are nothing but illusions and daydreams" (whereas the madman thinks that his illusions and daydreams are really the sky, the air and all external things). "I shall consider myself as having no hands, no eyes ... but believing falsely that I have all these things" (whereas the madman believes falsely that his body is made of glass, but does *not* consider himself as believing it falsely). "I shall take great care not to receive any falsity into my belief" (whereas the madman receives all falsities).

It is clear: faced with the cunning trickster, the meditating subject behaves not like a madman in a panic at universal error but as a no less cunning adversary, always alert, constantly rational, and remaining in the position of master with respect to his fiction: I shall prepare my mind so well for all the ruses of this great trickster that however powerful and cunning he may be, he will be unable to catch me out. How far we are from Derrida's pretty variations on themes: "total madness, total panic which *I am unable to master,* since it is *inflicted* by hypothesis and *I am no longer responsible for it.*" How is it possible to imagine that the meditating subject should no longer be responsible for what he himself calls "this painful and laborious design"?

Perhaps we should ask how it is that an author as meticulous as Derrida, and as attentive to texts, could have been guilty of so many omissions but could also operate so many displacements, transpositions, and substitutions? But perhaps we should ask this to the extent that in his reading Derrida is doing no more than revive an old tradition. He is, moreover, aware of this; and this conformity seems, justifiably, to comfort him. He shies in any case from thinking that the classical interpreters have missed through lack of attention the singularity of the passage on madness and dreaming.

On one fact at least I am in agreement: it is not as an effect of their lack of attention that, before Derrida and in like manner, the classical interpreters erased this passage from Descartes. It is by system. A system of which Derrida is the most decisive modern representative, in its final glory: the reduction of discursive practices to textual traces; the elision of the events produced therein and the retention only of marks for a reading; the invention of voices behind texts to avoid having to analyze the modes of implication of the subject in discourses; the assigning of the originary as said and unsaid in the text to avoid placing discursive practices in the field of transformations where they are carried out.

I will not say that it is a metaphysics, metaphysics itself or its closure which is hiding in this "textualization" of discursive practices. I'll go much farther than that: I shall say that what can be seen here so visibly is a historically well determined little pedagogy. A pedagogy that teaches the pupil there is nothing outside the text, but that in it, in its gaps, its blanks and its silences, there reigns the reserve of the origin; that it is therefore unnecessary to search elsewhere, but that here, not in the words, certainly, but in the words under erasure, in their *grid*, the "sense of being" is said. A pedagogy that gives conversely to the master's voice the limitless sovereignty that allows it to restate the text indefinitely.

Father Bourdin supposed that, according to Descartes, it was impossible to doubt things that were certain, even if one were asleep or mad. With respect to a well-founded certainty, the fact of dreaming or of raving would not be pertinent. Descartes replies very explicitly to this interpretation: "I do not remember having said anything of the sort, nor even having dreamed it while asleep." Indeed – nothing can be clearly or distinctly conceived of which is not true (and at this level, the problem of knowing whether or not the conceiver is dreaming or raving does not need to be asked). But, Descartes adds immediately, who then can *distinguish* "what is clearly conceived and what only seems and appears to be so"? Who, then, as thinking and meditating subject, can know whether he knows clearly or not? Who, then, is capable of not deluding himself as to his own certainty and of not being caught out by it? Except precisely those who are not mad? Those who are "wise." And Descartes retorts, with Father Bourdin in his sights: "But as only the wise can distinguish what is clearly conceived from what only seems and appears to be so, I am not surprised that this fellow can't tell the difference between them."

NOTES

a   [This essay appears as an appendix in the 1972 edition of *Histoire de la folie* (Paris: Plon) but is not included in the English translation (*Madness and Civilization*). It is a response to Jacques Derrida's critique of the *Histoire* in "Cogito and the History of Madness." This translation, by Geoff Bennington, has been slightly amended. Translations of the passages quoted from Derrida are taken, with some modifications, from the version by Alan Bass in *Writing and Difference* (London: Routledge, 1978). The translation of the French words "extravagance" and "extravagant" poses some problems: Bass habitually, but not exclusively, uses "insanity" and "insane," and it is true that the French words carry an overtone of madness absent from most uses of the English cognate forms. However, in the discussion of the "extravagance" of painters, the translation "insanity" is clearly excessive, and Bass resorts to the English "extravagance." I have preferred to use this form throughout in the interests of consistency and clarity and have modified Bass's version of Derrida accordingly. – Transl. Ed.]

1   I use this term paragraph out of amusement, convenience, and fidelity to Derrida. Derrida says in a picturesque and jocular manner: "Descartes starts a new paragraph" [*va à la ligne*]. We know this is quite mistaken.

2   I am quoting Derrida. In Descartes's text, these things it is so difficult to doubt are characterized not by their "nature," but by their proximity and their vividness – by their relation to the meditating subject.

12

Habermas on Benjamin

Jürgen Habermas (1929–) is the major figure among the second generation of Frankfurt School critical theorists who came to prominence in the 1960s. He was a pupil of Adorno, but his early work *The Structural Transformation of the Public Sphere* can be read as a more historically determinate account of enlightenment than that provided by Adorno and Horkheimer in *Dialectic of Enlightenment*. Subsequent works, through to the substantial volumes *The Theory of Communicative Action* (2 vols., 1984–7) and *Between Facts and Norms* (1996), move away from the work of earlier Frankfurt School theorists. Habermas is less sceptical about the value of reason, science and knowledge in modern society, and more concerned to offer a positive and sociologically flexible account of modern society, while recognizing the distortions and irrationality of bureaucracy, technology and industrialization. Habermas's early works, such as *Knowledge and Human Interests* (1968), attempt to rethink Hegel, Marx, Weber, Freud and Lukács within a neo-Marxist paradigm. His subsequent work has abandoned any vestigial relation to Marxism and the critique of political economy. Whereas Adorno, Horkheimer and Marcuse suggest how modern rationality has ideological affinities with fascism, Stalinism, state capitalism and administered rationality, Habermas's work is informed by the less revolutionary and more social-democratic spirit of post-war reconstruction. In the process, critical characterizations of capitalism have given way to the defence of modernity within a loosely neo-Kantian differentiation of the legitimacy of science, morality and art.

The project of modernity, understood by Habermas as processes of rationalization, emancipation and social modernization, remains unfinished. In defending the legitimacy of modernity, Habermas is critical of the Nietzschean and anti-enlightenment strains of Frankfurt School critical theory. This has brought him into conflict with post-structuralism and postmodernism. Although Habermas is sympathetic to traditions of thought underlying post-structuralism, notably Kant and Heidegger, there are nevertheless marked differences. In *The Philosophical Discourse of Modernity* he characterizes post-structuralists, such as Lyotard,

Derrida and Foucault, as neo-conservative opponents of modernity. This rather sweeping critique of post-structuralism has come to play an important role in debates about postmodernism. The critique of power offered by Habermas nevertheless has affinities with the work of Foucault and there are ongoing attempts to synthesize aspects of Foucault's work within Frankfurt School critical theory. One key difference with Foucault is Habermas's attempt to provide normative grounds for a critique of modern society. The difficulty is to find ways of grounding a critique of the abuse of power which can somehow transcend the distorted conditions of modern thought. This has involved Habermas in attempting to ground different regulative principles or norms. The difference in this emphasis on normative critique comes out sharply in debates with Gadamer. His subsequent work sketches neo-Kantian claims for the normative value of universal pragmatics, ideal speech situations and inter-subjective rationality. In this vein, Habermas has influenced the general shift away from subject–object conceptions of thought and epistemology towards hermeneutics and the philosophy of language. This renewed interest has been most productive in illuminating struggles for recognition associated with civil society, democracy and the inter-subjective, legal and institutional conditions of discourse and understanding.

Despite his affinities with social science, the characteristic form through which Habermas has presented his thought is the critical essay. Rather than providing analytic arguments or empirical evidence, his critiques seek to show the aporia and limitations of earlier philosophical works. This strategy is most successful where the object or figure under analysis can be reconstrued with sufficient sympathy to convince proponents of the position being criticized that Habermas has correctly identified key problems. Where the critique offered is less immanent and more a question of externally imposed positions and schemes, the argument has a correspondingly diminished force. This accords with Habermas's account of the inter-subjective exchanges characteristic of modern rationality and context-specific conditions of agreement and disagreement. Habermas's essay on Walter Benjamin (1892–1940) is a fascinating example of this mode of intellectual exchange, not least because Habermas seeks to isolate the defensible rationality at the core of Benjamin's notoriously elusive thought, while also identifying key aporia and weaknesses. Also of interest is the way Habermas distinguishes Benjamin's philosophy of language and situates Benjamin's conception of critique. Habermas's essay provides a succinct critical introduction to Benjamin and a strategic intervention in the confusingly eclectic reception of Benjamin. Read back into Habermas's work, this essay exemplifies the way Habermas settles his accounts with earlier critical theorists.

FURTHER READING

Primary works

Jürgen Habermas, *The Philosophical Discourse of Modernity*, trans. Frederick Lawrence (Cambridge: Polity, 1987); *The Structural Transformation of the Public*

Sphere, trans. Thomas Burger (Cambridge: Polity, 1991); *Knowledge and Human Interests*, trans. Jeremy J. Shapiro (London: Heinemann, 1971); *The Theory of Communicative Action*, 2 vols., trans. Thomas McCarthy (Cambridge: Polity, 1984–7); *Between Facts and Norms: Contributions to a Discourse Theory of Law and Democracy*, trans. William Rehg (Cambridge: Polity, 1996); *On the Logic of the Social Sciences*, trans. Shierry Weber Nicholsen and Jerry A. Stark (Cambridge: Polity, 1988).

Secondary works

Theodor W. Adorno and others, *The Positivist Dispute in German Sociology*, trans. Glyn Adey and David Frisby (London: Heinemann, 1976).

Theodor Adorno, 'Introduction to Benjamin's *Schriften*', *Notes to Literature*, vol. 2, trans. Shierry Weber Nicholsen (New York: Columbia University Press, 1992), pp. 220–32.

Walter Benjamin, *Selected Writings*, vol. 1, *1913–1926* and vol. 2, *1927–1934*, eds. Michael W. Jennings, Howard Eiland and Gary Smith (Cambridge, MA: Harvard University Press, 1996, 1999); *The Arcades Project*, trans. Howard Eiland and Kevin McLaughlin (Cambridge, MA: Harvard University Press, 1999).

Jay Bernstein, *Recovering Ethical Life: Jürgen Habermas and the Future of Critical Theory* (London: Routledge, 1995).

Richard J. Bernstein, ed., *Habermas and Modernity* (Cambridge: Polity, 1985).

Craig Calhoun, ed., *Habermas and the Public Sphere* (Cambridge, MA: MIT, 1992).

Maeve Cooke, *Language and Reason: A Study of Habermas's Pragmatics* (Cambridge, MA: MIT, 1994).

Peter Dews, *Logics of Disintegration* (London: Verso, 1987).

Peter Dews, ed., *Autonomy and Solidarity: Interviews with Jürgen Habermas* (London: Verso, 1986).

Peter Dews, ed., *Habermas: A Critical Reader* (Oxford: Blackwell, 1998).

David Couzens Hoy and Thomas A. McCarthy, *Critical Theory* (Oxford: Blackwell, 1994).

David Ingram, *Habermas and the Dialectic of Reason* (New Haven: Yale University Press, 1987).

Michael Kelly, ed., *Critique and Power: Recasting the Habermas–Foucault Debate* (Cambridge: Polity, 1994).

Garbis Kortian, *Metacritique: The Philosophical Argument of Jürgen Habermas*, trans. John Raffan (Cambridge: Cambridge University Press, 1980).

Thomas A. McCarthy, *The Critical Theory of Jürgen Habermas*, revised edition (Cambridge: Polity, 1984).

William Outhwaite, ed., *The Habermas Reader* (Cambridge: Polity, 1996).

David Rasmussen, *Reading Habermas* (Oxford: Blackwell, 1990).

David Rasmussen and James Swindal, eds., *Jürgen Habermas* (London: Sage, 2002).

Gary Smith, ed., *Benjamin: Philosophy, History, Aesthetics* (Chicago and London: 1989).

Gary Smith, ed., *On Walter Benjamin: Critical Essays and Recollections* (Cambridge, MA and London: MIT, 1988).

John B. Thompson and David Held, eds., *Habermas: Critical Debates* (London: Macmillan, 1982).

Stephen K. White, *The Recent Work of Jürgen Habermas* (Cambridge: Cambridge University Press, 1988).

Jürgen Habermas, 'Walter Benjamin: Consciousness-Raising or Rescuing Critique' (1972), trans. Frederick Lawrence, Philosophical-Political Profiles (Cambridge, MA: MIT, 1983), pp. 129–63.

Benjamin is relevant even in the trivial sense: In relation to him there is a division of opinion. The battle lines drawn during the short, almost eruptive period of the influence of Benjamin's *Schriften*[1] in Germany were presaged in Benjamin's biography. The constellation of Scholem, Adorno, and Brecht, a youthful dependence on the school reformer Gustav Wyneken, and later closer relations with the surrealists were decisive for Benjamin's life history. Scholem, his most intimate friend and mentor, is today represented by Scholem the unpolemical, sovereign, and totally inflexible advocate of the dimension in Benjamin that was captivated with the traditions of Jewish mysticism.[2] Adorno, Benjamin's heir, partner, and forerunner all in one person, not only introduced the first wave of the posthumous reception of Benjamin but also put his lasting imprint on it.[3] After the death of Peter Szondi[4] (who doubtless would have stood here today in my place), Adorno's place was taken mainly by Benjamin's editors, Tiedemann and Schweppenhäuser.[5] Brecht, who must have served as a kind of reality principle for Benjamin, brought Benjamin around to breaking with his esotericism of style and thought. In Brecht's wake, the Marxist theoreticians of art H. Brenner, H. Lethen, and M. Scharang[6] put Benjamin's late work into the perspective of the class struggle. Wyneken, whom Benjamin (who was active in the Free School Community) repudiated as a model while still a student,[7] signalizes ties and impulses that continue on; the youthful conservative in Benjamin has found an intelligent and valiant apologist in Hannah Arendt,[8] who would protect the suggestible, vulnerable aesthete, collector, and private scholar against the ideological claims of his Marxist and Zionist friends. Finally, Benjamin's proximity to surrealism has again been brought to our attention with the second wave of the Benjamin reception that took its impetus from the student revolt; the works by Bohrer and Bürger, among others, document this.[9]

Between these fronts there is emerging a Benjamin philology that relates to its subject in a scholarly fashion and respectably gives notice to the incautious that this is no longer an unexplored terrain.[10] In relation to the factional disputes that have nearly splintered the image of Benjamin, this academic treatment furnishes a corrective, if anything, but surely not an alternative. Moreover, the competing interpretations have not been simply tacked on. It was not mere mysterymongering that led Benjamin, as Adorno reports, to keep his friends apart from one another. Only as a surrealistic scene could one imagine, say, Scholem, Adorno, and Brecht sitting around a table for a peaceful symposium, with Breton and Aragon crouching nearby, while Wyneken stands by the door, all gathered for a debate on Bloch's *Spirit of Utopia* or even Klages's *Mind as Adversary of the Soul*. Benjamin's intellectual existence had so much of the surreal about it that one should not confront it with facile demands for consistency. Benjamin brought together motifs that ordinarily run at cross purposes, but he did not actually unite them, and had he united them he would have done so in as many unities as there are moments in which the interested gaze of succeeding interpreters breaks through the crust and penetrates to where the stones still have life in them. Benjamin belongs to those authors on whom it is not possible to gain a purchase, whose work is destined for disparate effective histories; we encounter these authors only in the sudden flash of relevance with which a thought achieves dominance for brief seconds of history. Benjamin was accustomed to explaining the nature of relevance in terms of a Talmudic legend according to which "the angels – new each moment in countless hosts – (were) created so that, after they had sung their hymn before God, they ceased to exist and passed away into nothingness." (*GS* II p. 246)

I would like to start from a statement Benjamin once turned against the procedure of cultural history: "It [cultural history] increases the burden of treasures that is piled on the back of humanity. But it does not bestow upon us the power to shake it off, so as to put it at our disposal." (F, p. 36) Benjamin sees the task of criticism precisely in this. He deals with the documents of culture (which are at the same time those of barbarism) not from the historicist viewpoint of stored-up cultural goods but from the critical viewpoint (as he so obstinately expresses it) of the decline of culture into "goods that can become an object of possession for humanity." (F, p. 35) Benjamin says nothing, of course, about the "overcoming of culture" [*Aufhebung der Kultur*].

1

Herbert Marcuse speaks of the overcoming of culture in a 1937 essay, "The Affirmative Character of Culture."[11] As regards classical bourgeois art, he criticizes the two-sidedness of a world of beautiful illusion that has been established autonomously, beyond the struggle of bourgeois competition and social labor. This autonomy is illusory because art permits the claims to happiness by individuals to hold good only in the realm of fiction and casts a veil over the unhappiness of day-to-day reality. At the same time there is something true about the autonomy of art because the ideal of the beautiful also brings to expression the longing for a happier life, for the humanity, friendliness, and solidarity withheld from the everyday, and hence it transcends the status quo: "Affirmative culture was the historical form in which were preserved those human wants which surpassed the material reproduction of existence. To that extent, what is true of the form of social reality to which it belonged holds for it as well: Right is on its side. Certainly, it exonerated 'external relationships' from responsibility for the 'vocation of humanity,' thus stabilizing their injustice. But it also held up to them the image of a better order as a task." (*Negations*, p. 120) In relation to this art, Marcuse makes good the claim of ideology critique to take at its word the truth that is articulated in bourgeois ideals but has been reserved to the sphere of the beautiful illusion – that is, to overcome art as a sphere split off from reality.

If the beautiful illusion is the medium in which bourgeois society actually expresses its own ideals but at the same time hides the fact that they are held in suspense, then the practice of ideology critique on art leads to the demands that autonomous art be overcome and that culture in general be reintegrated into the material processes of life. The revolutionizing of bourgeois conditions of life amounts to the overcoming of culture: "To the extent that culture has transmuted fulfillable, but factually unfulfilled, longings and instincts, it will lose its object. ...Beauty will find a new embodiment when it no longer is represented as real illusion but, instead, expresses reality and joy in reality." (*Negations*, pp. 130 ff.)

In the face of the mass art of fascism, Marcuse could not have been deceived about the possibility of a false overcoming of culture. Against it he held up another kind of politicization of art, which thirty years later seemed to assume concrete shape for a moment in the flower-garlanded barricades of the Paris students. In his *Essay on Liberation*[12] Marcuse interpreted the surrealist praxis of the youth revolt as the overcoming of art with which art passes over into life.

A year before Marcuse's essay on the affirmative character of culture, Benjamin's treatise *The Work of Art in the Age of its Technological Reproducibility* (I, pp. 219–251) had appeared in the same journal, *Zeitschrift für Sozialforschung*. It seems as if Marcuse only recast Benjamin's more subtle observations in terms of the critique of ideology. The theme is once again the overcoming of autonomous art. The profane cult of beauty first developed in the Renaissance and remained valid for 300 years. (I, p. 224) In the measure that art becomes dissociated from its cultic basis, the illusion of its autonomy disappears. (I, p. 230) Benjamin grounds his thesis that "art has escaped from the realm of 'beautiful illusion'" by pointing to the altered status of the work of art and to its altered mode of reception.

With the destruction of the aura, the innermost symbolic structure of the work of art is shifted in such a way that the sphere removed from the material processes of life and counterbalancing them falls apart. The work of art withdraws its ambivalent claim to superior authenticity and inviolability. It sacrifices both historical witness and cultic trappings to the art spectator. Already in 1927 Benjamin noted that "what we used to call art only starts 2 meters away from the body." (*GS* II, p. 622) The trivialized work of art gains its value for exhibition at the cost of its cultural value.[13]

To the altered structure of the work of art corresponds a changed organization of the perception and reception of art. As autonomous, art is set up for individual enjoyment; after the loss of its aura it is geared to reception by the masses. Benjamin contrasts the contemplation of the isolated, art-viewing individual with the diffusion of art within a collective, stimulated by its appeal. "In the degeneration of the bourgeoisie, meditation became a school for asocial behavior; it was countered by diversion as a variety of social behavior." (I, p. 238) Moreover, in this collective reception Benjamin sees an enjoyment of art that is at once instructive and critical.

I believe I can distill from these not completely consistent utterances the notion of a mode of reception that Benjamin acquired from the reactions of a relaxed, and yet mentally alert, film-viewing public:

> Let us compare the screen on which a film unfolds with the canvas of a painting. The painting invites the viewer to contemplation; before it the viewer can abandon himself to his own flow of associations. Before the movie frame, he cannot do so. ...In fact, when a person views these constantly changing (film) images, his stream of associations is immediately disrupted. This constitutes the shock effect of the film, which like all shock effects needs to be parried by a heightened presence of mind. Because of its technical structure, the film has liberated the physical shock effect from the moral cushioning in which Dadaism had, as it were, held it. (I, p. 238)

In a succession of discrete shocks, the art work deprived of its aura releases experiences that used to be enclosed within an esoteric style. In the mentally alert elaboration of this shock Benjamin notices the exoteric dissolution of a cultic spell that bourgeois culture inflicts on the solitary spectator in virtue of its affirmative character.

Benjamin conceives the functional transformation of art, which takes place the moment the work of art is freed "from its parasitic dependence on ritual," as the politicizing of art. "Instead of being based on ritual, it begins to be based on another practice – politics." (*I*, p. 224) In the claim of fascist mass art to be political, Benjamin, like Marcuse, sees the risk in the overcoming of autonomous art. Nazi propaganda art carries out the liquidation of art as pertaining to an autonomous realm, but behind the veil of politicization it really serves the aestheticizing of naked political violence. It replaces the degraded cult value of bourgeois art with a manipulatively produced one. The cultic spell is broken only to be revived synthetically; mass reception becomes mass suggestion.[14]

Benjamin's theory of art appears to develop a notion of culture proper to the critique of ideology, which Marcuse will take up a year later; however, the parallels alone are deceptive. I note four essential differences:

● Marcuse deals with the exemplary forms of bourgeois art in accord with ideology critique, inasmuch as he fastens on the contradiction between the ideal and the real. From this critique results an overcoming of autonomous art only as the consequence of an idea. In contrast, Benjamin does not raise critical demands against a culture still unshaken in its substance. Instead, he describes the factual process of the disintegration of the aura, upon which bourgeois art grounds the illusion of its autonomy. He proceeds descriptively. He observes a functional change in art, which Marcuse only anticipates for the moment in which the conditions of life are revolutionized.

● It is thus striking that Marcuse, like most other proponents of idealist aesthetics, limits himself to the periods acknowledged within bourgeois consciousness as classical. He is oriented toward a notion of artistic beauty taken from the symbolic forms within which essence comes to appearance. The classic works of art (in literature this means especially the novel and the bourgeois tragic drama) are suitable objects for a critique of ideology precisely because of their affirmative character, just as in the realm of political philosophy rational natural right is suitable on account of its affirmative character. Benjamin's interest, however, is in the nonaffirmative forms of art. In his investigation of the baroque tragic drama he found in the allegorical a concept that contrasted with the individual totality of the transfigurative work of art.[15] Allegory, which expresses the experience of the passionate, the oppressed, the unreconciled, and the failed (that is, the negative), runs counter to a symbolic art that prefigures and aims for positive happiness, freedom, reconciliation, and fulfillment. Whereas the latter needs ideology critique for decodifying and overcoming, the former is itself suggestive of critique: "What has survived is the extraordinary detail of the allegorical references: an object of knowledge whose haunt lies amid the consciously constructed ruins. Criticism is the mortification of the works. This is cultivated by the essence of such production more readily than by any other." (*O*, p. 182)

In this connection, it is furthermore remarkable that Marcuse spares the transformation of bourgeois art by the avant-garde from the direct grasp of ideology critique,
whereas Benjamin shows the process of the elimination of autonomous art within
the history of modernity. Benjamin, who regards the emergence of the metropolitan
masses as a "matrix from which all traditional behavior toward works of art emerges
rejuvenated" (I, p. 239), uncovers a point of contact with this phenomenon precisely
in the works that seem to be hermetically closed off from it: "The masses are so
interiorized by Baudelaire that one searches in vain for clarification of them by him."
("On Some Motifs in Baudelaire," I, pp. 155–200) [For this reason Benjamin
opposes the superficial understanding of *l'art pour l'art*: "This is the moment to
embark on a work that would illuminate as no other the crisis of the arts that we
are witnessing: a history of esoteric poetry. . . . On its last page one would have to
find the x-ray image of surrealism." (R, p. 184)] Benjamin pursues the traces of
modernity because they lead to the point where "the realm of poetry is exploded
from within." (R, p. 178) The insight into the necessity for overcoming autonomous
art arises from the reconstruction of what avant-garde art exposes about bourgeois art
in transforming it.

• Finally, the decisive difference with Marcuse lies in Benjamin's conceiving the
dissolution of autonomous art as the result of an upheaval in techniques of reproduction. In a comparison of the functions of painting and photography, Benjamin
demonstrates in exemplary fashion the consequences of new techniques moving to
the fore in the nineteenth century. In contrast with the traditional printing methods
of pouring, casting, woodcarving, engraving, and lithography, these techniques
represent a new developmental stage that may be comparable to the invention of
the printing press. In his own day Benjamin could observe a development in
phonograph records, films, and radio, which was accelerated by electronic media.
The techniques of reproduction impinge on the internal structure of works of art.
The work sacrifices its spatio-temporal individuality, on the one hand, but on the
other hand it purchases more documentary authenticity. The temporal structure of
ephemerality and repeatability, which replaces the uniqueness and duration typical of
the temporal structure of the autonomous work of art, destroys the aura, "the unique
appearance of a distance," and sharpens a "sense for sameness in the world." (I, pp.
222 ff.) Things stripped of their aura move nearer the masses, as well, because the
technical medium intervening between the selective organs of sense and the object
copies the object more exactly and realistically. The authenticity of the subject
matter, of course, requires the constructive use of means for realistic replication
(that is, montage and captioning of photographs).[16]

2

As these differences make clear, Benjamin does not let himself be guided by the concept
of art based on ideology critique. With the dissolution of autonomous art, he has
something else in mind than does Marcuse with his demand for the overcoming of
culture. Whereas Marcuse confronts ideal and reality and highlights the unconscious

content of bourgeois art that legitimates bourgeois reality while unintentionally de-nouncing it, Benjamin's analysis forsakes the form of self-reflection. Whereas Marcuse (by analytically disintegrating an objective illusion) would like to prepare the way for a transformation of the thus unmasked material relationships of life and to initiate an overcoming of the culture within which these relationships of life are stabilized, Benjamin cannot see his task to be an attack on an art that is already caught up in a process of dissolution. His art criticism behaves conservatively toward its objects, whether he is dealing with baroque tragic drama, with Goethe's *Elective Affinities*, with Baudelaire's *Fleurs du Mal*, or with the Soviet films of the early 1920s. It aims, to be sure, at the "mortification of the works" (O, p. 182), but the criticism practices this mortification of the art work only to transpose what is worth knowing from the medium of the beautiful into that of the true and thereby to rescue it.

Benjamin's peculiar conception of history explains the impulse toward rescuing:[17] There reigns in history a mystical causality of the sort that "a secret agreement (comes about) between past generations and ours." "Like every generation that preceded us, we have been endowed with a *weak* messianic power, a power on which the past has a claim." ("Theses on the Philosophy of History," I, p. 254) This claim can only be redeemed by an ever-renewed critical exertion of historical vision toward a past in need of redemption; this effort is conservative in an eminent sense, for "every image of the past that is not recognized by the present as one of its own concerns threatens to disappear irretrievably." (I, p. 255) If this claim is not met, then danger threatens "both for the continuance of the tradition and for its recipients."[18]

For Benjamin the continuum of history consists in the permanence of the unbearable and progress is the eternal return of catastrophe: "The concept of progress is to be founded within the idea of catastrophe." Benjamin notes in a draft of his work on Baudelaire that "the fact that 'everything just keeps on going' is the catastrophe." This is why "rescuing" has to cling "to the little crack within the catastrophe." (GS, I, p. 513) The concept of a present in which time stops and comes to rest belongs to Benjamin's oldest insights. In the "Theses on the Philosophy of History," written shortly before his death, the following statement is central: "History is the object of a construction whose site forms not homogeneous and empty time but time filled by the 'presence of the now' (*Jetztzeit; nunc stans*). Thus, to Robespierre ancient Rome was a past charged with the time of the now, which he blasted out of the continuun of history." (I, p. 261) One of Benjamin's earliest essays, "The Life of Students," starts off in a similar sense:

> There is an apprehension of history that, trusting in the endlessness of time, discriminates only the different tempos of humans and epochs, which roll rapidly or slowly along the highway of progress. ... The following treatment, on the contrary, is concerned with a distinct condition in which history rests as if gathered into one burning point, as has always been the case with the utopian images of thinkers. The elements of the final condition do not lie evident as shapeless, progressive tendencies, but are embedded in *any* present time as the most imperiled, scorned, and derided creations and ideas. (GS, II, p. 75)

To be sure, the interpretation of the rescuing intervention into the past has shifted since the doctrine of ideas presented in Benjamin's book on baroque tragic drama. The retrospective gaze was then supposed to gather the phenomenon rescued, inasmuch as it escaped processes of becoming and passing away, into the fold of the world of ideas; with its entry into the sphere of the eternal, the primordial event was supposed to shed its pre- and post-history (now become virtual) like a curtain of natural history. (O, pp. 45–47) This constellation of natural history and eternity later gives way to the constellation of history and the time of the now; the messianic cessation of the event takes over the place of the origin.[19] But the enemy that threatens the dead as much as the living when rescuing criticism is missing and forgetting takes its place remained one and the same: the dominance of mythic fate. Myth is the mark of a human race hopelessly deprived of its vocation to a good and just life and exiled into the cycle of sheer reproduction and survival.[20] The mythic fate can be brought to a standstill only for a transitory moment. The fragments of experience that have been wrung at such moments from fate (from the continuum of empty time) for the relevance of the time of the now shape the duration of the endangered tradition. The history of art belongs to this tradition. Tiedemann quotes from the Paris Arcades project the following passage: "In every true work of art there is a place where a cool breeze like that of the approaching dawn breathes on whoever puts himself there. It follows from this that art, which was often enough regarded as refractory toward any relationship with progress, can serve its *authentic* distinctiveness. Progress is at home not in the continuity of the flow of time, but in its interferences: wherever something genuinely new makes itself felt for the first time with the sobriety of dawn." (Tiedemann, *Studien*, pp. 103 ff.)

Benjamin's partially carried out plan for a primal history of modernity also belongs in this context. Baudelaire became central for Benjamin because his poetry brings to light "the new within the always-the-same, and the always-the-same within the new." (GS, I, p. 673)

Within the headlong processes of antiquation, which understands and misunderstands itself as progress, Benjamin's criticism uncovers the coincidence of time immemorial. It identifies within the modernization of forms of life propelled by the forces of production a compulsion toward repetition which is just as pervasive under capitalism – the always-the-same within the new. However, in doing this, Benjamin's criticism aims – and in this it is distinguished from critique of ideology – at rescuing a past charged with the *Jetztzeit*. It ascertains the moments in which the artistic sensibility puts a stop to fate draped as progress and enciphers the utopian experience in a dialectical image – the new within the always-the-same. The reversal of modernity into primal history has an ambiguous meaning for Benjamin. Myth belongs to primordial history, as does the content of the images. These alone can be broken away from myth. They have to be revived in another, as it were, awaited present and brought to "readability" for the sake of being preserved as tradition for authentic progress.[21] Benjamin's antievolutionary conception of history, in accord with which the *Jetztzeit* runs perpendicular to the continuum of natural history, is not rendered utterly blind toward steps forward in the emancipation of the human race. However, it judges with a profound pessimism the chances that the punctual breakthroughs that undermine the always-the-same will combine into a tradition and not be forgotten.

Benjamin is acquainted with a continuity that, in its linear progress, breaks through the cycle of natural history and thereby menaces the lastingness of tradition. This is the continuity of demystification, whose final stage Benjamin diagnoses as the loss of aura: "In prehistoric times, because of the absolute emphasis on its cult value, the work of art was an instrument of magic. Only later did it come to be recognized as a work of art. In the same way today, because of the absolute emphasis on its exhibition value, the work of art becomes a structure with entirely new functions, among which the one we are conscious of, the artistic function, later may be recognized as incidental." (*I*, p. 225) Benjamin does not explain this deritualization of art, yet it has to be understood as part of the world-historical process of rationalization that the developmental surge of the forces of production causes in social forms of life through revolutionizing the mode of production. Max Weber uses the term *disenchantment* too. Autonomous art became established only to the degree that, with the rise of civil society, the economic and political system was uncoupled from the cultural system and traditionalistic world views were undermined by the basic ideology of fair exchange, thus freeing the arts from the context of ritual.[22] In the first place, art owes to its commodity character its liberation for the private enjoyment of the bourgeois reading, theater-going, exhibition-going, and concert-going public that was coming into being in the seventeenth and eighteenth centuries.[23] The advance of the process to which art owes its autonomy leads to its liquidation as well. In the nineteenth century the public made up of bourgeois private persons gave way to the laboring populace of large urban collectives. Thus, Benjamin concentrates on Paris as the large city *par excellence*. He also concentrates on mass art, since "photography and the film provide the most suitable means" to recognize the "deritualization of art." (*I*, p. 225)

3

On no point did Adorno contradict Benjamin as vigorously as on this one. He regarded the mass art emerging with the new techniques of reproduction as a degeneration of art. The market that first made possible the autonomy of bourgeois art permitted the rise of a culture industry that penetrates the pores of the work of art itself and, along with art's commodity character, imposes on the spectator the attitudes of a consumer. Adorno first developed this critique in 1938, using jazz as an example, in his essay "The Fetish Character in Music and the Regression of Listening."[24] He summarized and generalized the criticism – since carried out with regard to a number of different objects – in his volume on aesthetic theory (*GS*) under the title "Art Deprived of Its Artistic Character":

> Of the autonomy of works of art – which stirs the customers of culture to indignation that one should consider it as something better – there is nothing left except the fetish character of the commodity. ... The work of art is disqualified as the *tabula rasa* for subjective projections. The poles of its deprivation are that it becomes both just one thing among others and the vehicle for the psychology of the beholder. What reified works of art no longer say, the beholder replaces with the standardized echo of himself, which he receives from them. The culture industry sets this mechanism in motion and exploits it. ... (p. 33)

The ingredient of historical experience in this critique of the culture industry is disappointment, not so much about the history of the decline of art, religion, and philosophy as about the history of the parodies of their overcoming. The constellation of bourgeois culture in the age of its classical development was, to put it rather roughly, characterized by the dissolution of traditional images of the world, first by the retreat of religion into the sphere of privatized faith, then by the alliance of empiricist and relationalist philosophy with the new physics, and finally by an art which, having become autonomous, took up the complementary positions on behalf of the victims of bourgeois rationalization. Art was the preserve for a satisfaction, be it only virtual, of those needs that became, so to speak, illegal within the material processes of life in bourgeois society: the need for a mimetic relation with external nature and the nature of one's own body, the need for life together in solidarity, and, in general, the need for the happiness of a communicative experience removed from the imperatives of purposive rationality and leaving room for fantasy and spontaneous behavior. This constellation of bourgeois culture was by no means stable; it lasted, as did liberalism itself, only a moment; then it fell prey to the dialectic of the enlightenment (or, rather, to capitalism as its irresistible vehicle).

Hegel announced the loss of aura in his *Lectures on Aesthetics*.[25] In conceiving art and religion as restricted forms of absolute knowledge which philosophy as the free thinking of the absolute spirit penetrates, he set in motion the dialectic of a "sublation" [*Aufhebung*], which immediately transcended the limits of the Hegelian logic. Hegel's disciples achieved secular critiques of religion and then philosophy in order finally to allow the sublation of philosophy and its realization to come to term in the overcoming of political violence; this was the hour when Marxist ideology critique was born. What in the Hegelian construction was still veiled now came into the foreground: the special status assumed by art among the figures of the absolute spirit to the extent that it did not (like religion once it became subjectivized and philosophy once it became scientific) take over tasks in the economic and political system, but gathered residual needs that could not be satisfied in the "system of needs." Consequently, the sphere of art was spared from ideology critique right down to our century. When it finally fell subject to ideology critique, the ironic overcoming of religion and philosophy already stood in full view.

Today not even religion is a private matter, but with the atheism of the masses the utopian contents of the tradition have gone under as well. Philosophy has been stripped of its metaphysical claim, but within the dominant scientism even the constructions before which a wretched reality was supposed to justify itself have disintegrated. In the meantime, even a "sublation" of science is at hand. This destroys the illusion of autonomy, but less for the sake of discursively guiding the scientific system than for the sake of functionalizing it for unreflected interests.[26] Adorno's critique of a false elimination of art should also be seen in this context; it does destroy the aura, but along with the dominative organization of the work of art it liquidates its truth at the same time.

Disappointment with false overcoming, whether of religion, philosophy, or art, can evoke a reaction of restraint, if not of hesitancy, of the sort that one would rather be mistrustful of absolute spirit's becoming practical than consent to its liquidation. Connected with this is an option for the esoteric rescue of moments of truth. This distinguishes Adorno from Benjamin, who insists that the true moments of the tradition will be rescued for the messianic future either exoterically or not at all. In opposition to the false overcoming of religion, Adorno – like Benjamin an atheist, if not in the same way – proposes bringing in utopian contents as the ferment for an uncompromisingly critical thought, but precisely not in the form of a universalized secular illumination. In opposition to the false overcoming of philosophy, Adorno – an antipositivist, like Benjamin – proposes bringing a transcendent impetus into a critique that is in a certain way self-sufficient, but does not penetrate into the positive sciences in order to become universal in the form of a self-reflection of the sciences. In opposition to the false overcoming of autonomous art, Adorno presents Kafka and Schoenberg, the hermetic dimension of modernity, but precisely not the mass art that makes the auratically encapsulated experience public. After reading the manuscript of Benjamin's essay on the work of art, Adorno (in a letter dated March 18, 1936) objects to Benjamin that "the center of the autonomous work of art does not itself belong on the side of myth." He continues: " . . . Dialectical though your work may be, it is not so in the case of the autonomous work of art itself; it disregards the elementary experience which becomes more evident to me every day in my own musical experience – that precisely the utmost consistency in the technological law of autonomous art changes this art and, instead of rendering it into a taboo or a fetish, approximates it to the state of freedom, of something that can consciously be produced and made."[27] After the destruction of the aura, only the formalist work of art, inaccessible to the masses, resists the pressures toward assimilation to the needs and attitudes of the consumer as determined by the market.

Adorno follows a strategy of hibernation, the obvious weakness of which lies in its defensive character. Interestingly, Adorno's thesis can be documented with examples from literature and music only insofar as these remain dependent on techniques of reproduction that prescribe isolated reading and contemplative listening (the royal road of bourgeois individuation). In contrast, for arts received collectively – architecture, theater, painting – just as for popular literature and music, which have become dependent on electronic media, there are indications of a development that points beyond mere culture industry and does not *a fortiori* invalidate Benjamin's hope for a generalized secular illumination.

Of course, the deritualization of art has an ambiguous meaning for Benjamin too. It is as if Benjamin were afraid of myth's being eradicated without any intervening liberation – as if myth would have to be given up as beaten, but its content could be preserved for transposition into tradition, in order to triumph even in defeat. Now that myth is wearing the robes of progress, the images that tradition can find only within the innermost recesses of myth are in danger of toppling over and being forever lost to rescuing criticism. The myth nesting within modernity, which is expressed in positivism's faith in progress, is the enemy against which Benjamin sets the entire pathos of rescuing. Far from being a guarantee of liberation, deritualization menaces us with a specific loss of experience.

4

Benjamin was always ambivalent about the loss of aura.[28] In the aura of a work of art is enclosed the historical experience of a past *Jetztzeit* in need of revitalization; the undialectical destruction of aura would be a loss of that experience. When Benjamin, as a student, still trusted himself to sketch "The Program of Coming Philosophy" (*GS,*

II, p. 159), the notion of an unmutilated experience already stood at the center of his reflections. At that time, Benjamin polemicized against "experience reduced to point zero, the minimum of significance," against the experience of physical objects with respect to which Kant had paradigmatically oriented his attempt at an analysis of the conditions of possible experience. Against this, Benjamin defended the more complex modes of experience of people living close to nature, madmen, seers, and artists. At that time he still had hopes of restoring a systematic continuum of experience through metaphysics. Later he assigned this task to art criticism, supposing that *it* would transpose the beautiful into the medium of the true, by which transposition "truth is not an unveiling, which annihilates the mystery, but a revelation and a manifestation that does it justice." (*O*, p. 31) The concept of aura ultimately takes the place of the beautiful illusion as the necessary outer covering, which, as it disintegrates, reveals the mystery of complex experience: "Experience of aura thus rests on the transposition of a response common in human relationships to the relationship between the inanimate or natural object and human beings. The person whom we look at, or who feels he is being looked at, looks at us in turn. To perceive the aura of an object means to invest it with the capacity to look at us in turn." (*I*, p. 298)

The auratic appearance can occur only in the intersubjective relationship of the I with its counterpart, the alter ego. Wherever nature gets so "invested" that it opens its eyes to look at us in return, the object is transformed into a counterpart. Universal animation of nature is the sign of magical world views in which the split between the sphere of the objectified, over which we have manipulative disposal, and the realm of the intersubjective, in which we encounter one another communicatively, has not yet been achieved. Instead, the world is organized according to analogies and correspondences for which totemistic classifications supply an example. A subjectivistic remainder of the perception of such correspondences are the synaesthetic associations.[29]

In the light of the appearance of aura, Benjamin develops the emphatic notion of an experience that needs to be critically conserved and appropriated if the messianic promise of happiness is ever to be redeemed. On the other hand, he also treats the loss of aura in a positive way. This ambiguity is also expressed in Benjamin's emphasis on just those achievements in autonomous art that are also distinctive of the deritualized work of art. Art fully stripped of the cultic element – and surrealist art, whose proponents have once again taken up Baudelaire's notion of *correspondances*, is exemplary in this regard – has the same aim as autonomous art, namely to experience objects within the network of rediscovered correspondences as a counterpart that makes one happy: "The *correspondances* constitute the court of judgement before which the object of art is found to be one that forms a faithfully reproduced image – which, to be sure, makes it entirely problematic. If one attempted to reproduce even this aporia in the material of language, one would define beauty as the object of experience in the state of resemblance." (*I*, p. 99, n. 13) The ambiguity can be resolved only if we separate the cultic moment in the notion of the auratic appearance from the universal moments. With the overcoming of autonomous art and the collapse of aura, the esoteric access to the work of art and its cultic distance from the viewer disappear. Hence, the contemplation characteristic of the solitary enjoyment of art disappears too. However, the experience released by the shattered shell of aura, namely the transformation of the object into a counterpart, was already contained in the experience of aura as well. A field of surprising correspondences between animate and inanimate nature is thereby opened up wherein things, too, encounter us in the structure of vulnerable intersubjectivity. In such structures, the essence that appears escapes the grasp after immediacy without any distance at all; the proximity of the other refracted in the distance is the signature of a possible fulfillment and a mutual happiness.[30] Benjamin's intention aims at a condition in which the esoteric experiences of happiness have become public and universal, for only in a context of communication into which nature is integrated in a brotherly fashion, as if it were set upright once again, can human subjects open up their eyes to look in return.

The deritualization of art conceals the risk that the work of art also sacrifices the experiential content along with its aura and becomes trivial. On the other hand, the collapse of aura opens up the chance of universalizing and stabilizing the experience of happiness. The absence of a protective shell around a happiness that has become exoteric and has dispensed with auratic refraction grounds an affinity with the experience of the mystic, who in the experience of rapture is more interested in the actuality of the nearness and sensible presence of God than in God himself. Only the mystic closes his eyes and is solitary; his experience as well as its transmission is esoteric. Exactly this moment separates the experience of happiness that Benjamin's rescuing criticism validates from religious experience. Benjamin therefore calls *secular* the illumination he elucidates in terms of the effect of surrealistic works that are no longer art in the sense of autonomous works but manifestation, slogan, document, bluff, and counterfeit. Such works bring us to the awareness that "we penetrate the mystery only to the degree that we recognize in it the everyday world, by virtue of a dialectical optic that knows the everyday as impenetrable, the impenetrable as everyday." (R, p. 190) This experience is secular because it is exoteric.[31]

No interpretation – however insistent in wrestling for the soul of a friend, as is Scholem's contribution to the volume *Zur Aktualität Walter Benjamins*[32] – can dismiss Benjamin's break with esotericism. In the face of the rise of fascism, political insight forced Benjamin to break with that esotericism of the true for which the young Benjamin had reserved the dogmatic concept of doctrine.[33] Benjamin once wrote to Adorno that "speculation sets out upon its necessarily bold flight with some prospect of success only if, instead of donning the waxen wings of esotericism, it sees its source of power in construction alone." (*NLR*, p. 76) Benjamin turned against the esotericism of fulfillment and happiness just as decisively. His intention – and this sounds like a repudiation of Scholem – is "the true, creative *overcoming* of religious illumination . . . a *secular* illumination, a materialist, anthropological inspiration" (R, p. 179), for which solitary ecstasy could at most serve as a primer.

If we look back at Benjamin's thesis about the overcoming of autonomous art from this point, we see why it cannot be a thesis of ideology critique: Benjamin's theory of art is a theory of experience (but not of the experience of reflection).[34] In the forms of secular illumination, the experience of aura has burst the protective auratic shell and become exoteric. It does not derive from an analysis that sheds light on what has been suppressed and sets free what has been repressed. It is gained in a manner other than reflection would be capable of, namely by taking up again a semantics that is pried piece by piece from the interior of myth and released messianically (that is, for purposes of emancipation) into works of great art at the same time as it is preserved. What is unexplainable in this conception is the peculiar undertow that must be stemmed by rescuing criticism: Without its permanent exertion, it seems, the transmitted testimony of punctual liberations from myth and the semantic contents wrung from it would have to fall into a void; the contents of tradition would fall victim to forgetfulness without leaving a trace. Why? Benjamin was obviously of the opinion that meaning was not a good capable of being increased, and that experiences of an unimpaired interchange with nature, with other people, and with one's self cannot be engendered at will. Benjamin thought instead that the semantic potential on which human beings draw in order to invest the world with meaning and make it accessible to experience was first deposited in myth and needs to be released from it, and that this potential cannot be expanded but only transformed. Benjamin was afraid that semantic energies might escape during this transformation and be lost to humanity. His linguistic philosophy affords a foothold for this perspective of decline and fall; the theory of experience is founded in it.[35]

5

Throughout his life, Benjamin adhered to a mimetic theory of language. Even in the later works he comes back to the onomatopoetic character of single words and even of language as a whole. It is unimaginable to him that words are related to reality accidentally. Benjamin conceives words as names. In giving names to things, however, we can either hit their essence or miss the mark; naming is a kind of translation of the nameless into names, a translation from the incomplete language of nature into the language of humans. Benjamin did not consider the special property of language to lie in its syntactical organization (in which he had no interest) or in its representational function (which he regarded as subordinate to its expressive function[36]). It is not the specifically human properties of language that interest Benjamin but the function that links it with animal languages. Expressive speech, he thinks, is only one form of the animal instinct that is manifested in expressive movements. Benjamin brings this together with the mimetic capacity to perceive and reproduce similarities. An example is dance, in which expression and mimesis are fused. He cites a statement by Mallarmé: "The dancer is not a woman but a metaphor that can bring to expression an aspect of the elementary forms of our existence: a sword, a drinking cup, a flower, or anything else." (GS, p. 478) The primordial mimesis is the representation of correspondences in images: "As is known, the sphere of life that formerly seemed to be governed by the law of similarity was comprehensive; it ruled both microcosm and macrocosm. But these natural correspondences acquire their real importance only if we recognize that they serve without exception to stimulate and awaken the mimetic capacity in the human being that responds to them." (R, p. 333) Whatever is expressed in linguistic physiognomy or in expressive gestures generally is not a mere subjective state but, by way of this, the as-yet-uninterrupted connection of the human organism with surrounding nature; expressive movements are systematically linked with the qualities of the environment that evoke them. As adventurous as this mimetic theory of language sounds, Benjamin is correct in supposing that the oldest semantic stratum is that of expression. The expressive richness of the language of primates is well researched, and, according to Ploog, "to the extent that language is entoned emotional expression, there is no

basic difference from the vocal expressive capacity of the nonhuman family of primates."[37]

One might speculate that a semantic basis from the subhuman forms of communication entered into human language and represents a potential in meanings that is
incapable of being increased and with which humans interpret the world in light of
their needs and thereby engender a network of correspondences. Be that as it may,
Benjamin counts on such a mimetic capacity with which the species on the verge of
becoming human was equipped before it entered upon the process of reproducing itself.
It is one of Benjamin's fundamental (non-Marxist) convictions that meaning is not
produced by labor, as value is, but can at most be transformed in dependence upon the
process of production.[38] The historically changing interpretation of needs feeds from a
potential with which the species has to economize, because although we can indeed
transform it we cannot enrich it:

> It must be borne in mind that neither mimetic powers nor mimetic objects or referents
> (which, one could add, have stored away in them something of the releasing qualities of
> whatever is compelling and pregnant) remain the same in the course of thousands of years.
> Rather, we must suppose that the gift of producing similarities (for example, in dances,
> whose oldest function was this), and therefore also the gift of recognizing them, have
> changed with historical development. The direction of this change seems definable as the
> increasing decay of the mimetic faculty. (R, pp. 333–334)

This process has an ambiguous significance.

In the mimetic capacity, Benjamin sees not only the source of the wealth of meaning
that human needs, released in the socio-cultural form of life, pour out in language over a
world that is thereby humanized. He also sees in the gift of perceiving similarities the
rudimentary form of the once-violent compulsion to become similar, to be forced into
adaptation – the animal legacy. To this extent, the mimetic capacity is also the signature
of a primordial dependence on the violent forces of nature; it is expressed in magical
practices, lives on in the primal anxiety of animistic world views, and is preserved in
myth. The vocation of the human species, then, is to liquidate that dependence without
sealing off the powers of mimesis and the streams of semantic energies, for that would be
to lose the poetic capacity to interpret the world in the light of human needs. This is the
secular content of the messianic promise. Benjamin has conceived the history of art,
from the cultic to the postauratic, as the history of the attempts to represent in images
these insensible similarities or correspondences but at the same time to loose the spell
that once rested on this mimesis. Benjamin called these attempts divine, because they
break myth while preserving and setting free its richness.

If we follow Benjamin this far, the question arises what is the source of those divine
forces that at once preserve and liberate. Even the criticism whose conservative-
revolutionary power Benjamin counts on has to be directed retrospectively toward
past *Jetztzeiten*; it lights on structures in which contents recovered from the myth (that
is, documents of past deeds of liberation) have been deposited. Who produces these
documents? Who are their authors? Benjamin obviously did not want to rely, in an
idealist way, on an underivable illumination of great authors, and thus on an utterly
nonsecular source. Indeed he was close enough to the idealist answer to the question,

for a theory of experience grounded in a mimetic theory of language permits no other response. Benjamin's political insights stood opposed to this, however. Benjamin, who uncovered the prehistoric world by way of Bachofen, knew Schuler, studied and appreciated Klages, and corresponded with Carl Schmitt – this Benjamin, as a Jewish intellectual in the Berlin of the 1920s could still not ignore where his (and our) enemies stood. This awareness compelled him to a materialist response.

This is the background to Benjamin's reception of historical materialism, which he naturally had to unite with the messianic conception of history developed on the model of rescuing criticism. This domesticated historical materialism was supposed to supply an answer to the open question about the subject of the history of art and culture, an answer at once materialist and yet compatible with Benjamin's own theory of experience. To have thought he had achieved this was Benjamin's mistake and the wish of his Marxist friends.

Ideology critique's concept of culture has the advantage of introducing the cultural tradition methodologically as a part of social evolution and making it accessible to a materialist explanation. Benjamin went behind this concept, because the kind of criticism that appropriates the history of art under the aspects of rescuing the messianic moments and preserving an endangered semantic potential has to comprehend itself not as reflection on a process of self-formation but as identification and *re-trieval* of emphatic experiences and utopian contents. Benjamin also conceived the philosophy of history as a theory of experience.[39] Within this framework, however, a materialist explanation of the history of art – which Benjamin, for political reasons, does not want to give up – is not possible in any direct way. That is why he tries to integrate this doctrine with basic assumptions of historical materialism. He announces his intention in the first of his "Theses on the Philosophy of History": The hunchbacked dwarf theology is supposed to take the puppet historical materialism into its service. This attempt must fail, because the materialist theory of social development cannot simply be fitted into the anarchical conception of the *Jetztzeiten* that intermittently break through fate as if from above. Historical materialism, which reckons on progressive steps not only in the dimension of productive forces but in that of domination as well, cannot be covered over with an antievolutionary conception of history as with a monk's cowl. My thesis is that Benjamin did not succeed in his intention of uniting enlightenment and mysticism because the theologian in him could not bring himself to make the messianic theory of experience serviceable for historical materialism. That much, I believe, has to be conceded in Scholem's favor.

I would like now to take up two difficulties: the odd adaptation of Marxian critique of ideology and the idea of a politicized art.

6

In 1935, at the behest of the Institute for Social Research, Benjamin prepared an exposé in which he presented for the first time some motifs of the Paris Arcades Project (*Paris, Capital of the Nineteenth Century*). Looking back on the lengthy history of its preparation, Benjamin writes in a letter to Adorno about a process of recasting that "has brought the entire mass of thought, which was metaphysically motivated at the start, to a state in which the universe of dialectical images has been secured against the objections provoked by metaphysics." (B, 2, p. 664) By this he is referring to "the new and incisive sociological perspectives that provide a secure framework for the span of interpretation." (B, 2, p. 665) Adorno's response to this exposé and his critique of the first study on Baudelaire that Benjamin offered the *Zeitschrift für Sozialforschung* three years later reflect very exactly the way Benjamin makes original use of Marxist categories – and in terms of both what Adorno understands and what he misunderstands.[40] Adorno's impression is that Benjamin does violence to himself in the Arcades Project in order to pay tribute to Marxism, and that this turns out for the good of neither. He warns against a procedure that "gives to conspicuous individual features from the realm of the superstructure a 'materialist' turn by relating them, without mediation and perhaps even causally, to corresponding features of the base." (NLR, p. 71) He refers particularly to the merely metaphorical use of the category of commodity fetishism, concerning which Benjamin had announced in a letter to Scholem that it stood at the center of the new work in the same way the concept of the tragic drama stood at the center of his book about the Baroque. Adorno lances the superficially materialist tendency to relate "the contents of Baudelaire's work immediately to adjacent features in the social history of his time, and, as much as possible, to those of an economic kind." (NLR, p. 70) In doing so, Benjamin gives Adorno the impression of a swimmer "who, covered with great goose pimples, plunges into cold water." (Ibid.) This sharp-sighted judgement, which loses none of its trenchancy even when Adorno's rivalry with Brecht is taken into account, still contrasts oddly with the unintelligent insistence that his friend might wish to make good the "omitted theory" and the "lacking interpretation" so that the dialectical mediation between cultural properties and the overall social process would become visible. Adorno never noticeably hesitated to attribute to Benjamin the precise intention of ideology critique that he followed in his own work, and in this he was wrong. This error is shown in exemplary fashion by the objections that were supposed to have moved Benjamin to revise the notion of dialectical image that was central to his theory of experience so that "a purification of the theory itself might be achieved." (NLR, p. 54) Adorno does not see how legitimate it is to want to carry out the project for a primal history of modernity – which aims at decodifying a semantics that has been buried and is threatened with forgetfulness – by hermeneutical means, through the interpretation of dialectical images. For Benjamin, imaginal fantasies of the primal past are set loose under the impulse of the new, in which the continuity of the always the same is carried on; they "mingle with the new to give birth to utopias." (R, p. 148)

Benjamin's exposé speaks of the collective unconscious as the store-house of experiences. Adorno is rightly put off by this use of language; however, he is quite incorrect in thinking that disenchantment of the dialectical image has to lead back to an unbroken mythic thinking, for the archaic dimension of modernity – in which Adorno would see Hell instead of the golden age – contains just the potentialities for experience that point the way to the utopian condition of a liberated society. The model is the French Revolution's recourse to Roman antiquity. Here Benjamin uses a comparison with the realization of dream elements upon waking, which was developed into a technique in surrealism and which Benjamin misleadingly calls a classic instance of dialectical thinking. Adorno takes Benjamin too literally here. Transposing the dialectical image into consciousness as a dream seems to him to be naked subjectivism. The fetish character of commodities, he contends against Benjamin, is no mere fact of consciousness but is dialectical in the eminent sense that it produces consciousness – archaic images – within alienated bourgeois individuals. However, Benjamin has no need to take up this claim of ideology critique; he does not want to reach behind the formations of consciousness to the objectivity of an evaluation process by means of which the commodity as fetish gains power over the consciousness of individuals. Benjamin wants and needs to investigate only "the mode of apprehension of the fetish character in the collective consciousness," because dialectical images are phenomena of consciousness and not (as Adorno thought) transposed into consciousness.

Of course, Benjamin also deceived himself about the difference between his manner of proceeding and the Marxist critique of ideology. In the manuscripts for the Arcades Project he once puts it as follows: "If the base determines the superstructure to a certain extent in regard to the material for thought and experience, and if this determination is, however, not that of a simple mirroring, how then is it to be characterized, quite apart from the cause behind emergence (!)? As its expression. The superstructure is the expression of the base. The economic conditions under which the society exists come to expression in the superstructure." (cited after Tiedemann, *Studien*, p. 106) Expression is a category of Benjamin's theory of experience; it is related to those insensible correspondences between animate and inanimate nature upon which the physiognomical gaze of the child and of the artist rests. Expression, for Benjamin, is a separate category that is more akin to what Kassner or even Klages intended than to the base-superstructure theorem. The same misunderstanding is shown in relation to the critique of ideology as practiced by Adorno, when Benjamin remarks about chapters of his later book on Wagner that "*one* tendency of this work interested (me) in particular: situating the physiognomical immediately, almost without psychological mediation, within the social realm." (*B*, 2, p. 741) In fact Benjamin did not have psychology in mind, but neither was he concerned with a critique of necessarily false consciousness. His criticism was concerned with doing justice to the collective fantasy images deposited in the expressive qualities of daily life as well as in literature and art. These images arise from the secret communication between the oldest semantic potentials of human needs and the conditions of life generated by capitalism.

In their correspondence concerning the Arcades Project, Adorno appeals to the goal "for the sake of which you sacrifice theology." (*NLR*, p. 54) Benjamin had surely made this sacrifice, inasmuch as he now accepted mystical illumination only as secular (i.e., universalizable) exoteric experience. However, Adorno, who in comparison with Benjamin was certainly the better Marxist, did not see that his friend was never prepared to give up the theological heritage, inasmuch as he always kept his mimetic theory of language, his messianic theory of history, and his conservative-revolutionary understanding of criticism immune against objections from historical materialism (to the degree that this puppet could not simply be brought under his direction). This can also be seen in Benjamin's assent to the instrumental politicization of art, where he confessed to being an engaged Communist. I understand this assent, which becomes clearest in the lecture "The Author as Producer" (*R*, pp. 220–238), as a perplexity resulting from the fact that an immanent relation to political praxis is by no means to be gained from rescuing critique, as it is from consciousness-raising critique.

When it uncovers within apparently universal interests the particular interest of the ruling class, ideology critique is a political force. Insofar as it shakes the normative structures that hold the consciousness of the oppressed captive and comes to term in political action, ideology critique aims to dismantle the structural violence invested in institutions. It is oriented toward the participatory eradication of the violence thus set loose. Structural violence can also be released preventatively or reactively from above; then it has the form of a fascist partial mobilization of the masses, who do not eradicate the violence unleashed but "act it out" in a diffuse manner.

I have shown that there is no room in this relational frame of reference of ideology critique for the type of criticism developed by Benjamin. A criticism that sets out to rescue semantic potential with a leap into past *Jetztzeiten* has a highly mediated position relative to political praxis. On this, Benjamin did not manage to achieve sufficient clarity.

In the early essay "Toward a Critique of Violence," Benjamin differentiates law-making violence from law-keeping violence. The latter is the legitimate violence exercised by the organs of the state; the former is the structural violence set loose in war and civil strife, which is present latently in all institutions.[41] Law-making violence, unlike law-keeping violence, does not have an instrumental character; instead it "manifests itself." And, to be sure, the structural violence embodied in interpretations and institutions is manifested in the sphere that Benjamin, like Hegel, reserves for destiny or fate (the fates of wars and families). Of course, changes in the sphere of natural history change nothing: "A gaze directed only at what is close at hand can perceive at most a dialectical rising and falling in the law-making and law-preserving formations of violence. ... This lasts until either new forces or those suppressed earlier triumph over the hitherto law-making violence and thus found a new law, which is destined in turn to decay." (R, p. 300) Here again we meet Benjamin's conception of fate, which affirms a natural historical continuum of the always the same and excludes cumulative changes in the structures of domination.

This is where the figure of rescuing criticism sets in. Benjamin then shapes the concept of revolutionary violence in accord with this figure; he invests with all the insights of praxis the act of interpretation that extracts from the past work of art the punctual breakthrough from the continuum of natural history and makes it relevant for the present. This is then the "pure" or "divine" violence that aims at "breaking the cycle under the spell of mythical forms of law." (Ibid.) Benjamin conceptualizes the "pure" violence in the framework of his theory of experience; hence, he has to divest it of the attributes of purposive rational action: Revolutionary violence, like mythical violence, manifests itself – it is the "highest manifestation of unalloyed violence in humans." (Ibid.) In a consistent way, Benjamin refers to Sorel's myth of the general strike and to an anarchistic praxis characterized by the way it bans the instrumental character of action from the realm of political praxis and negates purposive rationality in favor of a "politics of pure means": "The violence (of such a praxis) may be assessed no more from its effects than from its goals, but only from the law of its means." (R, p. 292)

That was in 1920. Nine years later Benjamin wrote his famous essay on the surrealist movement, in which Baudelaire's idea of an intimate connection between dream and deed had in the meantime gained ascendancy. What Benjamin had conceived as pure violence had, in the surrealist provocation, surprisingly taken shape: In the nonsensical acts of the surrealist, art was translated into expressive activity; the separation between poetic and political action had been overcome. Thus, Benjamin could see in surrealism the confirmation of his theory of art. Nonetheless, the illustrations of pure violence offered by surrealism found in Benjamin an ambivalent spectator. Politics as show, or even poeticizing politics – when Benjamin saw these realizations, he did not want after all to close his mind to the difference in principle between political action and manifestation: "This would mean the complete subordination of the methodical and disciplinary preparation for revolution to a praxis oscillating between training for it and celebrating its imminent onset." (R, p. 199) Encouraged by his contact with Brecht, Benjamin thus parted with his earlier anarchist inclinations; he then regarded the relationship of art and political praxis primarily from the viewpoint of the organizational and propagandistic utility of art for the class struggle. The resolute politicizing of art was a concept that he found ready at hand. He may have had good reasons for taking up this notion, but it did not have a systematic relation to his own theory of art and history. Inasmuch as Benjamin accepted it without any bother, he mutely admitted that an immanent relation to praxis cannot be gained from his theory of experience: The experience of shock is not an action, and secular illumination is not a revolutionary deed.[42]

Benjamin's intention was to "enlist the services" of historical materialism for the theory of experience, but that intention had to lead to an identification of ecstasy and politics that Benjamin could not have wanted. The liberation from cultural tradition of semantic potentials that must not be lost to the messianic condition is not the same as the liberation of political domination from structural violence. Benjamin's relevance does not lie in a theology of revolution.[43] His relevance can be seen if we attempt now, conversely, to "enlist the services" of Benjamin's theory of experience for historical materialism.

7

A dialectical theory of progress, which historical materialism claims to be, is on its guard; what presents itself as progress can quickly show itself to be the perpetuation of what was supposedly overcome. More and more theorems of counter-enlightenment have therefore been incorporated into the dialectic of the enlightenment, and more and more elements of a critique of progress have been incorporated into the theory of progress – all for the sake of an idea of progress that is subtle and relentless enough not to let itself be blinded by the mere illusion of emancipation. Of course, this dialectical theory of progress has to contradict the thesis that emancipation itself mystifies.[44]

In the concept of exploitation that was determinative for Marx's critique, poverty and domination were still one. The development of capitalism has taught us in the meantime to differentiate between hunger and oppression. The deprivations that can be provided against by an increase in the standard of living are different from those that can be helped, not by the growth of social wealth, but by that of freedom. In *Natural Right and Human Dignity* Bloch introduced into the concept of progress distinctions that were made necessary by the success of the forces of production developed under capitalism.[45] The more the possibility grows in developed societies of uniting repression with

prosperity (that is, satisfying demands directed to the economic system without necessarily having to redeem the genuinely political exigencies), the more the accent shifts
from the elimination of hunger to emancipation.

In the tradition that reaches back to Marx, Benjamin was one of the first to emphasize
a further moment in the concepts of exploitation and progress: besides hunger and
repression, failure; besides prosperity and liberty, happiness. Benjamin regarded the
experience of happiness he named secular illumination as bound up with the rescuing
of tradition. The claim to happiness can be made good only if the sources of that
semantic potential we need for interpreting the world in the light of our needs are not
exhausted. Cultural goods are spoils that the ruling elite carries in its triumphal parade,
and so the process of tradition has to be disentangled from myth. The liberation of
culture is certainly not possible without the overcoming of the repression anchored in
institutions. Yet, for a moment the suspicion cannot help but arise that an emancipation
without happiness and lacking in fulfillment might not be just as possible as relative
prosperity without the elimination of repression. This question is not without risks;
however, on the verge of *posthistoire*, where symbolic structures are exhausted, worn
thin, and stripped of their imperative functions, neither is it entirely idle.

Benjamin would not have posed this question. He insisted on a happiness at once
most spiritual and most sensual as an experience for the masses. Indeed, he was almost
terrified by the prospect of the possibility of the definitive loss of this experience,
because, with his gaze fixed on the messianic condition, he observed how progress
was successively cheated for the sake of its fulfillment by progress itself. The critique of
the Kautskian way of viewing progress is therefore the political context of the "Theses
on the Philosophy of History." Even if one does not argue with respect to each of the
three dimensions discussed above that progress in the increase of prosperity, the expansion of liberty, and the promotion of happiness does not represent real progress as long
as prosperity, liberty, and happiness have not become universal, it still can plausibly be
argued with respect to the hierarchy of the three components that prosperity without
liberty is not prosperity and that liberty without happiness is not liberty. Benjamin was
profoundly imbued by this: We cannot be sure about even partial progress before the
Last Judgement. Naturally, Benjamin wove this emphatic insight into his conception of
fate, according to which historical changes effect no change unless they are reflected in
the orders of happiness: "The order of the secular should be erected upon the idea of
happiness." (*R*, p. 312) In this totalizing perspective, the cumulative development of the
productive forces and the directional change of the structures of interaction are wound
down into an undifferentiated reproduction of the always-the-same. Before Benjamin's
Manichean gaze, progress can be perceived only at the solar prominences of happiness;
history spreads out like the orbiting of a dead planet upon which, now and then,
lightning flashes down. This forces us to construe the economic and political systems in
concepts that would really only be adequate to cultural processes: Within the ubiquity
of the context of guilt, revolutions are submerged beyond recognition – revolutions
that, for all their questionable partiality, take place not only in the dimensions of the
forces of production and of social wealth but even in the dimension in which distinctions are infinitely difficult to make in the face of the weight of repression. (I mean
progress, which is certainly precarious and permanently threatened by reversal, in the
products of legality if not in the formal structures of morality.) In the melancholy of

remembering what has been missed and in conjuring up moments of happiness that are in the process of being extinguished, the historical sense for secular progress is in danger of atrophy. No doubt these advances generate their regressions, but this is where political action starts.

Benjamin's critique of empty progress is directed against a joyless reformism whose sensorium has long since been stunted as regards the difference between an improved reproduction of life and a fulfilled life (or, better, a life that is not a failure). But this criticism becomes sharp only when it succeeds in making this difference visible in connection with the uncontemptible improvements of life. These improvements create no new memories, but they dissolve old and dangerous ones. The step-by-step negations of poverty and even repression are, it has to be conceded, oddly without traces; they make things easier, but they do not fulfill, for only alleviation that was remembered would be a preparatory stage for fulfillment. In the face of this situation, there are in the meantime two overworked positions. The counter-enlightenment based on a pessimistic anthropology would have us realize that utopian images of fulfillment are the life-serving fictions of a finite creature that will never be able to transcend its mere life to reach the good life. On the other side, the dialectical theory of progress is quite sure of its prognosis that successful emancipation also means fulfillment. Benjamin's theory of experience could – if it were not the monk's cowl but the core of historical materialism – oppose to the one position a grounded hope and to the other a prophylactic doubt.

Here we are talking only about the doubt that Benjamin's semantic materialism suggests: Can we preclude the possibility of a meaningless emancipation? In complex societies, emancipation means the participatory transformation of administrative decision structures. Is it possible that one day an emancipated human race could encounter itself within an expanded space of discursive formation of will and yet be robbed of the light in which it is capable of interpreting its life as something good? The revenge of a culture exploited over millennia for the legitimation of domination would then take this form: Right at the moment of overcoming age-old repressions, it would harbor no violence but it would have no content either. Without the influx of those semantic energies with which Benjamin's rescuing criticism was concerned, the structures of practical discourse – finally well established – would necessarily become desolate.

Benjamin comes close to wresting the reproach of empty reflection from the counter-enlightenment and appropriating it for a theory of progress. Whoever looks for Benjamin's relevance in this direction is of course open to the objection that emancipatory efforts, in the face of an unshaken political reality, should not be encumbered so light-heartedly with further mortgages, however sublime they might be – first things first. I of course think that a differentiated concept of progress opens a perspective that does not simply obstruct courage but can make political action more sure of hitting its mark, for under historical circumstances that prohibit the thought of revolution and give one reason to expect revolutionary processes of long duration, the idea of the revolution as the process of forming a new subjectivity must also be transformed. Benjamin's conservative-revolutionary hermeneutics, which deciphers the history of culture with a view to rescuing it for the upheaval, may point out one path to take.

A theory of linguistic communication that wanted to bring Benjamin's insights back into a materialist theory of social evolution would need to conceive two of Benjamin's theses together. I am thinking of the assertion that "there is a sphere of human agreement that is nonviolent to the extent that it is wholly inaccessible to violence: the proper sphere of 'mutual understanding,' language." (*R*, p. 289) And I am thinking of the warning that belongs with this: " . . . pessimism all along the line. Absolutely . . . , but above all mistrust, mistrust, and again mistrust in all reciprocal understanding between classes, between nations, between individuals. And unconditional trust only in I. G. Farben and the peaceful perfection of the Luftwaffe." (*R*, p. 191)

NOTES

1 W. Benjamin, *Schriften*, 2 vols., T. W. and Gretel Adorno, eds. (Frankfurt am Main, 1955). Citations and references in the text use available English translations where possible. Abbreviations to the editions used are as follows:

Briefe (*B*), Gershom Scholem and T. W. Adorno, eds. (Frankfurt, 1966).
"Correspondence with Benjamin" (*NLR*), *New Left Review* 81 (1972): 55–80.
"Edward Fuchs, Collector and Historian" (F), *New German Critique* 5 (1975): 27–58.
Gesammelte Schriften I–V (*GS*), Rolf Tiedemann and Hermann Schweppenhäuser, eds. (Frankfurt am Main, 1972–).
Illuminations (*I*), Hannah Arendt, ed. (New York, 1969).
The Origins of German Tragic Drama (*O*) (London, 1977).
Reflections (*R*), Peter Demetz, ed. (New York, 1978).

2 G. Scholem, "Walter Benjamin," in *Über Walter Benjamin* (Frankfurt, 1968) [English translation in Scholem, *Jews and Judaism in Crisis* (New York, 1976)]. See also "Walter Benjamin and His Angel" and "Two Letters to Walter Benjamin," ibid., and Scholem, "Nachwort," in W. Benjamin, *Berliner Chronik* (Frankfurt, 1970).
3 T. W. Adorno, *Über Walter Benjamin* (Frankfurt, 1970). In English, see "A Portrait of Walter Benjamin," in Adorno, *Prisms* (Cambridge, Mass., 1982).
4 P. Szondi, "Nachwort," in W. Benjamin, *Städtbilder* (Frankfurt, 1963).
5 R. Tiedemann, *Studien zur Philosophie W. Benjamins* (Frankfurt, 1965); Tiedemann, "Nachwort," in Benjamin, *Charles Baudelaire* (Frankfurt, 1969); Tiedemann, "Nachwort," in Benjamin, *Versuche über Brecht* (Frankfurt, 1966); H. Schweppenhäuser, "Einleitung," in Benjamin, *Über Haschish* (Frankfurt, 1972).
6 H. Brenner, "Die Lesbarkeit der Bilder. Skizzen zur Passagenentwurf," *alternativ* 59/60 (1968): 48ff.; H. Lethen, "Zur materialistischen Kunsttheorie Benjamins," ibid. 65/67 (1967): 225–232; M. Scharang, *Zur Emanzipation der Kunst* (Neuweid, 1971).
7 W. Benjamin, *Briefe*, vol. I, pp. 120ff.
8 H. Arendt, *Benjamin, Brecht. Zwei Essays* (Munich, 1971); "Introduction: Walter Benjamin 1892–1940," in *I.*
9 P. Bürger, *Der Französische Surrealismus* (Frankfurt, 1971); K. H. Bohrer, *Die gefährdete Phantasie oder Surrealismus und Terror* (Munich, 1970); E. Lenk, *Der springende Narziss* (Munich, 1971). Adorno's critique of surrealism may be found in *Noten zur Literatur* I (Frankfurt, 1958), pp. 153–160. Following him is H. M. Enzensberger, "Die Aporien der Avantgarde," in *Einzelheiten* (Frankfurt, 1962). On the status of the secondary literature see W. S. Rubin, "The D-S Expedition," *New York Review of Books* 18 (1972): 9–10.
10 See *Text und Kritik* 31/32 (1971), the issue dedicated to Benjamin, which has essays by B. Lindner, L. Wiesenthat, and P. Krumme and an annotated bibliography (pp. 85ff.) with references to uncompleted dissertations on Benjamin.
11 H. Marcuse, *Kultur und Gesellschaft* I (Frankfurt, 1965), pp. 56–101 [English translation: *Negations* (Boston, 1968), pp. 88–133].
12 H. Marcuse, *An Essay on Liberation* (Boston, 1969), especially chapter II. Marcuse has developed and also partially modified this perspective in "Art and Revolution," in *Counterrevolution and Revolt* (Boston, 1972). Cf. G. Rohrmoser, *Herrschaft und Versöhnung. Aesthetik und die Kulturrevolution des Westens* (Freiburg, 1972).

13 "Certain Madonnas remain covered nearly all year round; certain sculptures on medieval cathedrals are invisible to the spectator on ground level. With the emancipation of various art practices from ritual go increasing opportunities for the exhibition of their products." (*I*, p. 225)

14 "Fascist art is executed not only for the masses but also by the masses . . . [It] casts the ones performing as well as the recipients under a spell. Under this spell they must appear monumental to themselves, i.e., incapable of well-considered and independent actions. . . . Only in the attitude imposed on them by the spell, so Fascism teaches us, do the masses find their expression." (*GS* III, p. 488)

15 "Whereas in the symbol destruction is idealized and the transfigured face of nature is fleetingly revealed in the light of redemption, in allegory the observer is confronted with the *facies hippocratica* of history as a petrified, primordial landscape. . . . This is the heart of the allegorical way of seeing, of the baroque, secular explanation of history as the Passion of the world. Its importance resides solely in the stations of its declines." (*O*, p. 166)

16 Here, too, Benjamin sees Dadaism as a precursor of the technical arts by other means: "The revolutionary strength of Dadaism lay in testing art for its authenticity. One made still-lifes out of tickets, spools of cotton, cigarette butts, and mixed them with pictorial elements. One put a frame around the whole thing. And in this way one showed the public: Look, your picture frame explodes time; the smallest authentic fragment of everyday life says more than a painting. Just as a murderer's bloody fingerprint on a page says more than the book's text. Much of this revolutionary content has been rescued and redeemed by passing into photomontage." (*R*, p. 229)

17 Tiedemann, *Studien*, pp. 103ff.; H. D. Kittsteiner, "Die Geschichtsphilosophischen Thesen," *alternativ* 55/56 (1966): 243–251.

18 The rescuing power of a retrospective criticism is, of course, not to be confused with the empathy and reexperiencing that historicism took over from Romanticism: "With Romanticism begins the hunt for false wealth, for the assimilation of any past, not by a progressive emancipation of the human race in virtue of which it takes its own history into view with even more heightened awareness and constantly gets new angles on it, but by imitation, which ferrets out all the works from all the nations and world epochs that have ever lived." (*GS* II, p. 581) On the one hand, this is not a recommendation to apprehend history hermeneutically as a continuum of effective history or to reconstruct it as the self-formative process of the human species. Over against this stands the most profoundly antievolutionary conception of history.

19 B. Lindner, "Natur-Geschichte – eine Geschichtsphilosophie und Welterfahrung in Benjamins Schriften," *Text und Kritik* 31/32 (1971), at 56.

20 In this sense, enlightened sciences such as systems theory and behaviorist psychology conceive human beings as "mythic" natures.

21 "[I]ndeed this attainment of readability is a distinctive critical point interior to them (i.e., the dialectical images). Each present is determined by those specific images which are synchronic with it: Each now is the now of a distinctive recognizability. In the now the truth is changed with time to the explosion-point." (Cited in Tiedemann, *Studien*, p. 310)

22 "Autonomy" here designates the independence of the works of art in relation to the intentions of employing them, which are extrinsic to art. The autonomy of the *production* of art could already develop earlier, namely in the forms of support connected with patronage.

23 A. Hauser, *Sozialgeschichte der Kunst*, 2 vols. (Munich, 1953); J. Habermas, *Strukturwandel der Öffentlichkeit*, fifth edition (Neuweid, 1971), pp. 46ff.

24 T. W. Adorno, in *Dissonanzen* (Göttingen, 1969).

25 "Art in its beginnings still leaves something mysterious, a secret foreboding and a longing. . . . But if the perfect content has been perfectly revealed in artistic shapes, then the more farseeing spirit rejects this objective manifestation and turns back into its inner self. This is the case in our time. We may hope that art will always rise higher and grow to perfection, but the form of art has ceased to be the supreme need of the spirit. No matter how excellent we find the statues of the Greek gods, no matter how we see God the Father, Christ, Mary so estimably and perfectly portrayed, it is no help; we bow the knee no longer." (G. W. F. Hegel, *Aesthetics, Lectures on Fine Art I* (Oxford, 1975), p. 103)

26 J. Behrmann, G. Böhme, and W. van den Daele put forward this thesis in the manuscript Alternativen in der Wissenschaft.

27 T. W. Adorno, "Correspondence with Benjamin," *New Left Review* 81 (Sept.–Oct. 1972): 55–80, at 65.

28   "For the last time the aura emanates from the early photographs in the fleeting expression of a human face. This is what constitutes their melancholy and incomparable beauty." (*I*, p. 226)

29   "The important thing is that the *correspondances* record a concept of experience that includes ritual elements. Only by appropriating these elements was Baudelaire able to fathom the full meaning of the breakdown that he, a modern man, was witnessing. Only in this way was he able to recognize in it the challenge meant for him alone, a challenge he incorporated into the *Fleurs de Mal*." (*I*, p. 181) "Baudelaire describes eyes of which one is inclined to say that they have lost their ability to look." (*I*, p. 189)

30   On Adorno's speculations about reconciliation with nature, especially those presented in *Minima Moralia*, see my essay "Theodor W. Adorno, Ein philosophierende Intellektueller (1963)," in *Philoso-phisch-politische Profile* (Frankfurt, 1971).

31   This is why Benjamin does not accept private ecstasy or hashish as a model for this experience: "The reader, the thinker, the loiterer, the flâneur, are types of illuminati just as much as the opium eater, the dreamer, the ecstatic. And more profane." (*R*, p. 190)

32   *Zur Aktualität Walter Benjamins. Aus Anlass des 80. Geburtstages von Walter Benjamin*, S. Unseld, ed. (Frankfurt, 1972). See also "Walter Benjamin and His Angel," listed in note 2 above.

33   "[T]hus the demands on future philosophy can finally be put into words: to fashion a notion of knowledge on the basis of the Kantian system that corresponds to the concept of experience for which the knowledge is doctrine" (*GS* II, p. 168)

34   "It would be worth demonstrating that the theory of experience represents the by no means secret center of all Benjamin's conceptions." P. Krumme, "Zur Konzeption der dialektischen Bilder," *Text und Kritik* 31/32 (1971), p. 80, n. 5.

35   Already in the "Program of Coming Philosophy" there is the following suggestion: "A notion of [philosophy] gained through reflection on the linguistic nature of knowledge will create a correspond-ing notion of experience, which will also comprise areas whose true systematic ordering Kant did not achieve." (*GS* II, p. 168) Hamann had already attempted this during Kant's lifetime.

36   "The word must communicate *something* (other than itself). That is really the Fall of the spirit of language. The word as something externally communicating, as it were a parody of the expressly mediate word ..." (*R*, p. 327)

37   D. Ploog, "Kommunikation in Affengesellschaften und deren Bedeutung für die Verständesweisen des Menschen," in *Neue Anthropologie*, vol. 2, H.-G. Gadamer and P. Vogler, eds. On Benjamin's philoso-phy of language, which has been relatively neglected in the discussion until now, see H. H. Holz, "Prismatisches Denken," in *Über Walter Benjamin*.

38   The thesis "that meaning, significance, etc. – in a Marxist fashion – gets engendered only by the world-historical labor processes of the human species – in which it produces itself – Benjamin never made his own." (Lindner, "Natur-Geschichte," at 55)

39   Among other things, the fourteenth thesis on the philosophy of history proves this. Benjamin is interested in the experiential content of the French Revolution rather than the objective changes to which it led: "The French Revolution understood itself as Rome returned. It cited Rome precisely the way fashion cites a costume of the past." (*I*, p. 261)

40   I am referring to two letters from Adorno to Benjamin, dated August 2, 1935, and November 10, 1938 (*B* 1, pp. 671ff. and 782ff.; *NLR*, pp. 55–80). For Benjamin's answer, see *B* 1, pp. 790ff. On this whole complicated matter see Jacob Taubes, "Kultur und Ideologie," in *Spätkapitalismus oder Industrie-gesellschaft?* (Stuttgart, 1969).

41   In this context, Benjamin put forth a critique of parliamentarianism that drew Carl Schmitt's admir-ation: "They [the parliaments] offer the familiar, woeful spectacle because they have not remained conscious of the revolutionary forces to which they owe their existence. Accordingly, in Germany in particular, the last manifestation of such forces bore no fruit for parliaments. They lack the sense that a lawmaking violence is ... a supposedly nonviolent manner of dealing with political affairs." (*R*, p. 288)

42   On this see Bohrer, *Die gefährdete Phantasie*, especially pp. 53ff., and B. Lypp, *Ästhetischer Absolutismus und politische Vernunft* (Frankfurt, 1972).

43   See H. Salzinger, "W. Benjamin – Theologe der Revolution," *Kürbiskern* (1969): 629–647.

44   From this perspective, critical theory is viewed as "modern sophistry." See, for example, R. Bubner, "Was ist kritische Theorie?," in *Hermeneutik und Ideologiekritik* (Frankfurt, 1971).

45 "Social utopia aimed at human happiness, natural right, and human dignity. Social utopia portrayed relationships in which the miserable and heavy-laden were no longer to be found; natural right constructed relationships in which the downtrodden and the degraded disappear." (E. Bloch, *Naturrecht und menschliche Würde* (Frankfurt am Main, 1961), p. 13)

13
Rose on Lacan

Jacqueline Rose's work exemplifies the feminist rethinking of psychoanalysis which emerged in the 1970s and 1980s. Many feminists have been hostile to Freud, seeing his work as an ideological representation of patriarchal thought rather than as a critical resource. As Juliet Mitchell argues in *Psychoanalysis and Feminism* (1974), however, Freud's work can be understood not as a recommendation for a patriarchal society, but an analysis of one. Feminist appropriations of psychoanalysis are comparable to the no less strained relations between Marxism and psychoanalysis. The principal interest has been in ways in which psychoanalysis might illuminate ideological resistances to political change, but the attempt to politicize psychoanalysis has invariably proved difficult. Jacqueline Rose's work has engaged in strategies of critical and politicized reading informed by psychoanalysis and feminism. Her readings are developed in sympathy with psychoanalysis, but working outside the institutions and practices of psychoanalysis. The centrality of critical reading to her work also reflects the cross-fertilization of critical theory and literary criticism. This combination of theory and textual analysis also owes something to semiotics, literary theory and film theory, areas of thought important in the early transmission of Lacanian theory within the English-speaking world.

Along with Althusser, Foucault and Derrida, the work of Jacques Lacan (1901–81) was central to what became known as post-structuralism. A practising psychoanalyst rather than a professional philosopher, Lacan built his work around a series of controversial reinterpretations of Freud. Although staged as a return to Freud, Lacan's work challenged the authority of Freud's concepts and practices as well as challenging the institutions of psychoanalysis. Lacan sought to radicalize the implications of Freud's work, seeking to change psychoanalytic practices and to develop new ways of thinking. A friend of Merleau-Ponty, Lacan drew on Husserl, Heidegger and Kojève's reading of Hegel, but he rarely makes explicit reference to their work. Contemporary with the shift towards structuralism, he also drew on Claude Lévi-Strauss's structural anthropology and the structuralist theories of language associated with Ferdinand de Saussure. Lacan's writings make idiosyncratic and often cryptic uses of literary texts and surrealism. The resulting rhetoric is notoriously dense and difficult to decipher, generating a discourse whose difficulty resists any attempt to construe a Lacanian orthodoxy. This strategy is informed by an understanding of the dangers of orthodoxy and theoretical authority for psychoanalytic practice and for the institutions of psychoanalysis. Lacan's work seeks, accordingly, to develop a critical discourse of and for psychoanalysis. Among the most influential features of Lacan's thought are the ways in which he conceptualizes the structure of the unconscious by analogy with structuralist accounts of language, an analogy encapsulated in the claim that the unconscious is structured as, or like, a language. The emphasis on the role of speech and language not only generated new readings of Freud, but also suggested new modes of clinical practice and philosophy. As well as influencing Althusser, Lacan's work vied with Derrida's for critical ascendancy within Parisian thought, a rivalry evident in Derrida's deconstruction of Lacan's seminar on Edgar Allen Poe's story *The Purloined Letter*. Lacan's reformulation of psychoanalysis and language has also been controversial within various strands of Marxism and critical theory. Lacan's most recent and most extravagant proponent is Slavoj Žižek, but although Žižek offers confident expositions and illustrations of Lacanian theory, Žižek's Lacan is no less controversial than Lacan's Freud, not least in the way Žižek politicizes the significance of Lacan's work.

Rose's essay intervenes in the reception of Lacan by offering one of the most lucid presentations and expositions of key currents in Lacan's thinking. The considerable resistance of Lacan's work to such an exposition undermines the claims of immanent critique. Rose nevertheless offers a critical reconstruction which marks the limits of Lacan's understanding of femininity and sexual difference. Her essay was written to introduce a collection of translations of Lacan's articles and seminar discourses entitled *Feminine Sexuality*. The interest of this book is in posing what might be involved in a critical translation of Lacan's work which is relevant to feminism. More recently, Rose has performed a similar act of critical translation for Moustapha Safouan's *Jacques Lacan and the Question of Psychoanalytic Training* (2000). In her introduction she suggests that Safouan shows how Lacan's work and institutional trajectory can be read as a history of psychoanalysis and of its constitutive inability to match its institutions to its theory. Her introduction suggests, retrospectively, that it would have been impossible for her, as a woman, to have been involved in Lacan's project had she been in Paris. Indeed she explains the need to disentangle her enthusiasm for much of Lacan's thought from discomfort with Lacan's charismatic authority. This difficulty disables many of the attempts to appropriate Lacan's work, just as Lacan's texts disable authoritative readings. Insofar as Lacan's work has nevertheless been suggestive for different forms of critique, Rose's essay provides one of the most helpful critical translations.

FURTHER READING

Primary works

Jacqueline Rose, *Sexuality in the Field of Vision* (London: Verso, 1986); *States of Fantasy* (Oxford: Clarendon, 1996); *The Case of Peter Pan or the Impossibility of Children's Fiction*, revised edition (London: Macmillan, 1994); *The Haunting of Sylvia Plath* (London: Virago, 1991); *Why War? – Psychoanalysis, Politics, and the Return to Melanie Klein* (Oxford: Blackwell, 1993), with interview and bibliography of her work; Juliet Mitchell and Jacqueline Rose, eds., *Feminine Sexuality: Jacques Lacan and the École Freudienne*, trans. Jacqueline Rose (London: Macmillan, 1982).

Jacques Lacan, *Écrits: A Selection*, trans. Alan Sheridan (London: Tavistock, 1977); *The Four Fundamental Concepts of Psycho-analysis*, trans. Alan Sheridan (Harmondsworth: Penguin, 1979); *The Ethics of Psychoanalysis, 1959–1960*, trans. Dennis Porter (London: Tavistock / Routledge, 1992); *On Feminine Sexuality: The Limits of Love and Knowledge, 1972–3*, trans. Bruce Fink (London and New York: W. W. Norton, 1999).

Secondary works

Willy Apollon and Richard Feldstein, eds., *Lacan, Politics, Aesthetics* (Albany, NY: SUNY, 1996).

Jessica Benjamin, *The Bonds of Love: Psychoanalysis, Feminism, and the Problems of Domination* (London: Virago, 1988); *Like Subjects, Love Objects: Essays on Recognition and Sexual Difference* (New Haven: Yale University Press, 1995).

Richard Boothby, *Death and Desire: Psychoanalytic Theory in Lacan's Return to Freud* (New York: Routledge, 1991).

Peter Dews, 'Jacques Lacan: A Philosophical Rethinking of Freud' and 'Lacan and Derrida: Individuality and Symbolic Order', *Logics of Disintegration: Post-structuralist Thought and the Claims of Critical Theory* (London: Verso, 1987), pp. 45–86, 87–108.

Elizabeth Grosz, *Jacques Lacan: A Feminist Introduction* (London: Routledge, 1990).

Anika Lemaire, *Jacques Lacan* (London: Routledge, 1979).

Juliet Flower McCannell, *Figuring Lacan: Criticism and the Cultural Unconscious* (London: Croom Helm, 1986).

Juliet Mitchell, *Women: The Longest Revolution* (London: Virago, 1984).

Juliet Mitchell, *Psychoanalysis and Feminism* (London: Allen Lane, 1974).

John P. Muller and William J. Richards, eds., *The Purloined Poe: Lacan, Derrida, and Psychoanalytic Reading* (Baltimore and London: Johns Hopkins University Press, 1988).

Dany Nobus, ed., *Key Concepts in Lacanian Psychoanalysis* (London: Rebus, 1998).

Ellie Ragland-Sullivan and Mark Bracher, eds., *Lacan and the Subject of Language* (London: Routledge, 1991).

William J. Richardson, 'Lacan and Non-Philosophy', *Philosophy and Non-Philosophy Since Merleau-Ponty*, ed. Hugh J. Silverman (London: Routledge, 1988), pp. 120–35.

Elisabeth Roudinesco, *Jacques Lacan & Co: A History of Psychoanalysis in France, 1925–1985*, trans. Jeffrey Mehlman (London: Free Association Books, 1990).

Elisabeth Roudinesco, *Jacques Lacan*, trans. Barbara Bray (Cambridge: Polity, 1997).

Moustapha Safouan, *Jacques Lacan and the Question of Psychoanalytic Training*, trans. and
    introduced by Jacqueline Rose (Basingstoke: Macmillan, 2000).
Slavoj Žižek, *The Sublime Object of Ideology* (London: Verso, 1989).
Slavoj Žižek, *For They Know not What They Do: Enjoyment as a Political Factor* (London:
    Verso, 1991).

Jacqueline Rose, 'Feminine Sexuality: Jacques Lacan and the *École Freudienne*', *Sexuality in the Field of Vision* (London: Verso, 1986), pp. 49–81.

> *Freud argues that the only libido is masculine. Meaning what? other than that a whole field,*
> *which is hardly negligible, is thereby ignored. This is the field of all those beings who take on*
> *the status of the woman – if, indeed, this being takes on anything whatsoever of her fate.*
> Lacan, *Le séminaire XX: Encore* (1972–3), Paris 1975, p. 75
> (tr. *Feminine Sexuality*, p. 151)

The works of Jacques Lacan and the *école freudienne* on female sexuality return to and
extend the psychoanalytic debate of the 1920s and 1930s over femininity and sexual
difference in Freud.[1] They return to it by insisting that its implications for psychoanalysis have still not been understood; they extend it in so far as the issue itself – the question
of feminine sexuality – goes beyond psychoanalysis to feminism, as part of its questioning of how that sexuality comes to be defined.

In this sense, the writing examined in this essay bears all the signs of a repetition, a
resurfacing of an area of disagreement or disturbance, but one in which the issue at stake
has been thrown into starker relief. It is as if the more or less peaceful co-existence
which closed the debate of the 1920s and 1930s ('left, in a tacit understanding, to the
goodwill of individual interpretation'),[2] and the lull which it produced ('the lull experienced after the breakdown of the debate'),[3] concealed a trouble which was bound to
emerge again with renewed urgency. Today, that urgency can be seen explicitly as
political, so much so that in the controversy over Lacan's dissolution of his school in
1980, the French newspaper *Le Monde* could point to the debate about femininity as the
clearest statement of the political repercussions of psychoanalysis itself (*Le Monde*, 1 June
1980, p. xvi). Psychoanalysis is now recognised as crucial in the discussion of femininity
– how it comes into being and what it might mean. Lacan addressed this issue increasingly during the course of his work, and has been at the centre of the controversies
produced by that recognition.

In this context, the idea of a 'return to Freud' most commonly associated with Lacan
has a very specific meaning. It is not so much a return to the letter of Freud's text as the re-
opening of a case, a case which has already been fought and one which, if anything, in
relation to feminism, Freud could be said to have lost. In fact the relationship between
psychoanalysis and feminism might seem to start at the point where Freud's account of
sexual difference was rejected by analysts specifically arguing *for* women ('men analysts
have been led to adopt an unduly phallocentric view').[4] Most analysts have since agreed
on the limitations and difficulties of Freud's account. Those difficulties were fully

recognised by Lacan, but he considered that attempts to resolve them within psychoanalysis had systematically fallen into a trap. For they failed to see that the concept of the
phallus in Freud's account of human sexuality was part of his awareness of the problematic, if not impossible, nature of sexual identity itself. They answered it, therefore, by
reference to a pre-given sexual difference aimed at securing that identity for both sexes.
In doing so, they lost sight of Freud's sense that sexual difference is constructed at a price
and that it involves subjection to a law which exceeds any natural or biological division.
The concept of the phallus stands for that subjection, and for the way in which women
are very precisely implicated in its process.

The history of psychoanalysis can in many ways be seen entirely in terms of its
engagement with this question of feminine sexuality. Freud himself started with the analysis of the hysterical patient[5] (whom, it should be noted, he insisted could also be male[6]).
It was then his failure to analyse one such patient – 'Dora' – in terms of a normative concept of what a woman should be, or want, that led him to recognise the fragmented and
aberrant nature of sexuality itself. Normal sexuality is, therefore, strictly an *ordering*, one
which the hysteric refuses (falls ill). The rest of Freud's work can then be read as a description of how that ordering takes place, which led him back, necessarily, to the question
of femininity, because its persistence as a difficulty revealed the cost of that order.

Moreover, Freud returned to this question at the moment when he was reformu-
lating his theory of human subjectivity. Lacan took Freud's concept of the unconscious,
as extended and developed by the later texts[7] as the basis of his own account of
femininity (the frequent criticism of Lacan that he disregarded the later works is totally
unfounded here). He argued that failure to recognise the interdependency of these two
concerns in Freud's work – the theory of subjectivity and femininity together – has led
psychoanalysts into an ideologically loaded mistake, that is, an attempt to resolve the
difficulties of Freud's account of femininity by aiming to resolve the difficulty of
femininity itself. For by restoring the woman to her place and identity (which, they
argue, Freud out of 'prejudice' failed to see), they have missed Freud's corresponding
stress on the division and precariousness of human subjectivity itself, which was, for
Lacan, central to psychoanalysis' most radical insights. Attempts by and for women to
answer Freud have tended to relinquish those insights, discarding either the concept of
the unconscious (the sign of that division) or that of bisexuality (the sign of that
precariousness). And this has been true of positions as diverse as that of Jones (and
Horney) in the 1920s and 1930s and that of Nancy Chodorow[8] speaking from
psychoanalysis for feminism today.

Re-opening the debate on feminine sexuality must start, therefore, with the link
between sexuality and the unconscious. No account of Lacan's work which attempts to
separate the two can make sense. For Lacan, the unconscious undermines the subject
from any position of certainty, from any relation of knowledge to his or her psychic
processes and history, and *simultaneously* reveals the fictional nature of the sexual
category to which every human subject is none the less assigned. In Lacan's account,
sexual identity operates as a law – it is something enjoined on the subject. For him, the
fact that individuals must line up according to an opposition (having or not having the
phallus) makes that clear. But it is the constant difficulty, or even impossibility, of that
process which Lacan emphasised. Exposure of that difficulty within psychoanalysis and
for feminism is, therefore, part of one and the same project.

I

The link between sexuality and the unconscious is one that was constantly stressed by Lacan: 'we should not overlook the fact that sexuality is crucially underlined by Freud as being strictly consubstantial to the dimension of the unconscious'.[9] Other accounts, such as that of Ernest Jones, described the acquisition of sexual identity in terms of ego development and/or the maturation of the drives. Lacan considered that each of these concepts rests on the myth of a subjective cohesion which the concept of the unconscious properly subverts. For Lacan, the description of sexuality in developmental terms invariably loses sight of Freud's most fundamental discovery – that the unconscious never ceases to challenge our apparent identity as subjects.

Lacan's account of subjectivity was always developed with reference to the idea of a fiction. Thus, in the 1930s he introduced the concept of the 'mirror stage',[10] which took the child's mirror image as the model and basis for its future identifications. This image is a fiction because it conceals, or freezes, the infant's lack of motor co-ordination and the fragmentation of its drives. But it is salutary for the child, since it gives it the first sense of a coherent identity in which it can recognise itself. For Lacan, however, this is already a fantasy – the very image which places the child divides its identity into two. Furthermore, that moment only has meaning in relation to the presence and the look of the mother who guarantees its reality for the child. The mother does not (as in D. W. Winnicott's account)[11] mirror the child to itself; she grants an image *to* the child, which her presence instantly deflects. Holding the child is, therefore, to be understood not only as a containing, but as process of referring, which fractures the unity it seems to offer. The mirror image is central to Lacan's account of subjectivity, because its apparent smoothness and totality is a myth. The image in which we first recognise ourselves is a *misrecognition*. Lacan is careful to stress, however, that his point is not restricted to the field of the visible alone: 'the idea of the mirror should be understood as an object which reflects – not just the visible, but also what is heard, touched and willed by the child'.[12]

Lacan then takes the mirror image as the model of the ego function itself, the category which enables the subject to operate as 'I'. He supports his argument from linguistics, which designates the pronoun as a 'shifter'.[13] The 'I' with which we speak stands for our identity as subjects in language, but it is the least stable entity in language, since its meaning is purely a function of the moment of utterance. The 'I' can shift, and change places, because it only ever refers to whoever happens to be using it at the time.

For Lacan the subject is constituted through language – the mirror image represents the moment when the subject is located in an order outside itself to which it will henceforth refer. The subject is the subject *of* speech (Lacan's '*parle-être*'), and subject *to* that order. But if there is division in the image, and instability in the pronoun, there is equally loss, and difficulty, in the word. Language can only operate by designating an object in its absence. Lacan takes this further, and states that symbolisation turns on the object *as* absence. He gives as his reference Freud's early account of the child's hallucinatory cathexis of the object for which it cries, and his later description in *Beyond the Pleasure Principle* of the child's symbolisation of the absent mother in play.[14] In the first example, the child hallucinates the object it desires; in the second, it throws a cotton reel out of its cot in order to symbolise the absence and the presence of the mother. Symbolisation starts, therefore, when the child gets its first sense that something could be missing; words stand for objects, because they only have to be spoken at the moment when the first object is lost. For Lacan, the subject can only operate within language by constantly repeating that moment of fundamental and irreducible division. The subject is therefore constituted in language *as* this division or splitting (Freud's *Ichspaltung*, or splitting of the ego).

Lacan termed the order of language the symbolic, that of the ego and its identifications the imaginary (the stress, therefore, is quite deliberately on symbol and image, the idea of something which 'stands in'). The real was then his term for the moment of impossibility onto which both are grafted, the point of that moment's endless return.[15]

Lacan's account of childhood then follows his basic premise that identity is constructed in language, but only at a cost. Identity shifts, and language speaks the loss which lay behind that first moment of symbolisation. When the child asks something of its mother, that loss will persist over and above anything which she can possibly give, or say, in reply. Demand always 'bears on something other than the satisfaction which it calls for',[16] and each time the demand of the child is answered by the satisfaction of its needs, so this 'something other' is relegated to the place of its original impossibility. Lacan terms this 'desire'. It can be defined as the 'remainder' of the subject, something which is always left over, but which has no content as such. Desire functions much as the zero unit in the numerical chain – its place is both constitutive *and* empty.

The concept of desire is crucial to Lacan's account of sexuality. He considered that the failure to grasp its implications leads inevitably to a reduction of sexuality back into the order of a need (something, therefore, which could be satisfied). Against this, he quoted Freud's statement: 'we must reckon with the possibility that something in the nature of the sexual instinct itself is unfavourable to the realisation of complete satisfaction'.[17]

At the same time 'identity' and 'wholeness' remain precisely at the level of fantasy. Subjects in language persist in their belief that somewhere there is a point of certainty, of knowledge and of truth. When the subject addresses its demand outside itself to another, this other becomes the fantasied place of just such a knowledge or certainty. Lacan calls this the Other – the site of language to which the speaking subject necessarily refers. The Other appears to hold the 'truth' of the subject and the power to make good its loss. But this is the ultimate fantasy. Language is the place where meaning circulates – the meaning of each linguistic unit can only be established by reference to another, and it is arbitrarily fixed. Lacan, therefore, draws from Saussure's concept of the arbitrary nature of the linguistic sign – introduced in his *Course in General Linguistics* – the implication that there can be no final guarantee or securing of language. There is, Lacan writes, 'no Other of the Other', and anyone who claims to take up this place is an imposter (the Master and/or psychotic).

Sexuality belongs in this area of instability played out in the register of demand and desire, each sex coming to stand, mythically and exclusively, for that which could satisfy and complete the other. It is when the categories 'male' and 'female' are seen to represent an absolute and complementary division that they fall prey to a mystification in which the difficulty of sexuality instantly disappears: 'to disguise this gap by relying on the virtue of the "genital" to resolve it through the maturation of tenderness . . . , however piously intended, is nonetheless a fraud'.[18] Lacan therefore argued that psychoanalysis should not try to produce 'male' and 'female' as complementary entities, sure of each other and of their own identity, but should expose the fantasy on which this notion rests.

There is a tendency, when arguing for the pre-given nature of sexual difference, for the specificity of male and female drives, to lose sight of the more radical aspects of Freud's work on sexuality – his insistence on the disjunction between the sexual object and the sexual aim, his difficult challenge to the concept of perversion, and his demand that heterosexual object-choice be explained and not assumed.[19] For Lacan, the 'vicissitudes' of the instinct ('instinct' was the original English translation for the German word *trieb*) cannot be understood as a deviation, accident or defence on the path to a normal heterosexuality which would ideally be secured. Rather the term 'vicissitude' indicates a fundamental difficulty inherent in human sexuality, which can be seen in the very concept of the drive.

The concept of the drive is crucial to the discussion of sexuality because of the relative ease with which it can be used to collapse psychoanalysis into biology, the dimension from which, for Lacan, it most urgently needed to be retrieved. He rejected the idea of a gradual 'maturation' of the drive, with its associated emphasis on genital identity (the 'virtue' of the genital) because of the way it implies a quasi-biological sequence of sexual life. Instead he stressed the resistance of the drive to any biological definition.

The drive is not the instinct precisely because it cannot be reduced to the order of need (Freud defined it as an internal stimulus only to distinguish it immediately from hunger and thirst). The drive is divisible into pressure, source, object and aim; and it challenges any straightforward concept of satisfaction – the drive can be sublimated and Freud described its object as 'indifferent'. What matters, therefore, is not what the drive *achieves*, but its *process*. For Lacan, that process reveals all the difficulty which characterises the subject's relationship to the Other. In his account, the drive is something in the nature of an appeal, or searching out, which always goes beyond the actual relationships on which it turns. Although Freud did at times describe the drive in terms of an economy of pleasure (the idea that tension is resolved when the drive achieves its aim), Lacan points to an opposite stress in Freud's work. In *Beyond the Pleasure Principle*, when Freud described the child's game with the cotton reel, what he identified in that game was a process of pure repetition which revolved around the object as lost. Freud termed this the death drive. Analysts since Freud (specifically Melanie Klein) have taken this to refer to a primordial instinct of aggression. For Freud there could be no such instinct, in that all instincts are characterised by their aggression, their tenacity or insistence (exactly their *drive*). It is this very insistence which places the drive outside any register of need, and beyond an economy of pleasure. The drive touches on an area of excess (it is 'too much'). Lacan calls this *jouissance* (literally 'orgasm', but used by Lacan to refer to something more than pleasure which can easily tip into its opposite).

In Lacan's description of the transformation of the drive (its stages), the emphasis is always on the loss of the object around which it revolves, and hence on the drive itself as a representation. Lacan therefore took one step further Freud's own assertion that the drive can only be understood in terms of the representation to which it is attached, by arguing that the structure of representation is present in the very process of the drive. For Lacan, there is always distance in the drive and always a reference to the Other (he added to the oral and anal drives the scopic and invocatory drives whose objects are the look and the voice). But because of its relation to the question of sexual difference, he made a special case for the genital drive in order to retrieve it from the residual biologism to which it is so easily assimilated: 'There is no genital drive. It can go and get f... [...] on the side of the Other.'[20] In one of his final statements, Lacan again insisted that Freud had seen this, despite his equation of the genital and the reproductive at certain moments of his work.[21]

When Lacan himself did refer to biology, it was in order to remind us of the paradox inherent in reproduction itself, which, as Freud pointed out, represents a victory of the species over the individual. The 'fact' of sexed reproduction marks the subject as '*subject to*' death.[22] There is a parallel here with the subject's submission to language, just as there is an analogy between the endless circulation of the drive and the structure of meaning itself ('a topological unity of the gaps in play').[23] At moments, therefore, it looks as if Lacan too is grounding his theory of representation in the biological facts of life. But the significant stress was away from this, to an understanding of how representation determines the limits within which we experience our sexual life. If there is no straightforward biological sequence, and no satisfaction of the drive, then the idea of a complete and assured sexual identity belongs in the realm of fantasy.

The structure of the drive and what Lacan calls the 'nodal point' of desire are the two concepts in his work as a whole which undermine a normative account of human sexuality, and they have repercussions right across the analytic setting. Lacan considered that an emphasis on genital maturation tends to produce a dualism of the analytic relationship which can only reinforce the imaginary identifications of the subject. The case of Dora illustrates only too well that the question of feminine sexuality brings with it that of psychoanalytic technique.[24] Thus by insisting to Dora that she was in love with Herr K., Freud was not only defining her in terms of a normative concept of genital heterosexuality, he also failed to see his own place within the analytic relationship, and reduced it to a dual dimension operating on the axes of identification and demand. By asking Dora to realise her 'identity' through Herr K., Freud was simultaneously asking her to meet, or reflect, his own demand. On both counts, he was binding her to a dual relationship in which the problem of desire has no place. For Lacan, there was always this risk that psychoanalysis will strengthen for the patient the idea of self-completion through another, which was the fantasy behind the earliest mother–child relationship. If the analyst indicates to the patient that she or he 'desires this or that object',[25] this can only block the emergence of desire itself.

Lacan therefore defined the objective of analysis as the breaking of any imaginary relationship between patient and analyst through the intervention of a third term which throws them both onto the axis of the symbolic. The intervention of a third term is the precondition of language (the use of the three basic pronouns 'I'/'you'/'he-she-it'), and it can be seen in the structure of the Oedipus complex itself. What matters here, however, is that the symbolic sets a limit to the 'imaginary' of the analytic situation. Both analyst and patient must come to see how they are constituted by an order which goes beyond their interaction as such: 'The imaginary economy only has a meaning and we only have a relation to it in so far as it is inscribed in a symbolic order which imposes a ternary relation.'[26]

By focusing on what he calls the symbolic order, Lacan was doing no more than taking to its logical conclusion Freud's preoccupation with an 'historic event' in the determination of human subjectivity (the myth of the primal horde). But for Lacan this is not some mythical moment of our past; it is the present order in which every individual subject must take up her or his place. His concern to break the duality of the analytic situation was part of his desire to bring this dimension back into the centre of our understanding of psychic life. The subject and the analytic process must break out of the imaginary dyad which blinds them to what is happening outside. As was the case with Freud, the concept of castration came into Lacan's account of sexuality as the direct effect of this emphasis. For Lacan, the increasing stress on the mother–child relationship in analytic theory, and the rejection of the concept of castration had to be seen as related developments, because the latter only makes sense with reference to the wider symbolic order in which that relationship is played out:

> Taking the experience of psychoanalysis in its development over sixty years, it comes as no surprise to note that whereas the first outcome of its origins was a conception of the castration complex based on paternal repression, it has progressively directed its interests towards the frustrations coming from the mother, not that such a distortion has shed any light on the complex.[27]

This was at the heart of Lacan's polemic. He considered that it was the failure to grasp the concept of the symbolic which has led psychoanalysis to concentrate increasingly on the adequacies and inadequacies of the mother–child relationship, an emphasis which tends to be complicit with the idea of a maternal role (the concept of mothering).[28] The concept of castration was central to Lacan because of the reference which it always contains to paternal law.

Addressing Melanie Klein, Lacan makes it clear that the argument for a reintroduction of the concept of desire into the definition of human sexuality is a return to, and a reformulation of, the law and the place of the father as it was originally defined by Freud ('a dimension . . . increasingly evaded since Freud'[29]):

> Melanie Klein describes the relationship to the mother as a mirrored relationship: the maternal body becomes the receptacle of the drives which the child projects onto it, drives motivated by aggression born of a fundamental disappointment. This is to neglect the fact that the outside is given for the subject as the place where the desire of the Other is situated, and where he or she will encounter the third term, the father.[30]

Lacan argued, therefore, for a return to the concept of the father, but this concept is now defined in relation to that of desire. What matters is that the relationship of the child to the mother is not simply based on 'frustration and satisfaction' ('the notion of frustration (which was never employed by Freud)'),[31] but on the recognition of her desire. The mother is refused to the child in so far as a prohibition falls on the child's desire to be what the mother desires (not the same, note, as a desire to possess or enjoy the mother in the sense normally understood):

What we meet as an accident in the child's development is linked to the fact that the child does not find himself or herself alone in front of the mother, and that the phallus forbids the child the satisfaction of his or her own desire, which is the desire to be the exclusive desire of the mother.[32]

The duality of the relation between mother and child must be broken, just as the analytic relation must be thrown onto the axis of desire. In Lacan's account, the phallus stands for that moment of rupture. It refers mother and child to the dimension of the symbolic which is figured by the father's place. The mother is taken to desire the phallus not because she contains it (Klein), but precisely because she does not. The phallus therefore belongs somewhere else; it breaks the two-term relation and initiates the order of exchange. For Lacan, it takes on this value as a function of the androcentric nature of the symbolic order itself (cf. section II below). But its status is in itself false, and must be recognised by the child as such. Castration means first of all this – that the child's desire for the mother does not refer *to* her but *beyond* her, to an object, the phallus, whose status is first imaginary (the object presumed to satisfy her desire) and then symbolic (recognition that desire cannot be satisfied).

The place of the phallus in the account, therefore, follows from Lacan's return to the position and law of the father, but this concept has been reformulated in relation to that of desire. Lacan uses the term 'paternal metaphor', metaphor having a very specific meaning here. First, as a reference to the act of substitution (substitution is the very law of metaphoric operation), whereby the prohibition of the father takes up the place originally figured by the absence of the mother. Secondly, as a reference to the status of paternity itself which can only ever logically be *inferred*. And thirdly, as part of an insistence that the father stands for a place and a function which is not reducible to the presence or absence of the real father as such:

> To speak of the Name of the Father is by no means the same thing as invoking paternal deficiency (which is often done). We know today that an Oedipus complex can be constituted perfectly well even if the father is not there, while originally it was the excessive presence of the father which was held responsible for all dramas. But it is not in an environmental perspective that the answer to these questions can be found. So as to make the link between the Name of the Father, in so far as he can at times be missing, and the father whose effective presence is not always necessary for him not to be missing, I will introduce the expression *paternal metaphor*.[33]

Finally, the concept is used to separate the father's function from the idealised or imaginary father with which it is so easily confused and which is exactly the figure to be got round, or past: 'Any discourse on the Oedipus complex which fails to bring out this figure will be inscribed within the very effects of the complex.'[34]

Thus when Lacan calls for a return to the place of the father he is crucially distinguishing himself from any sociological conception of role. The father is a function and refers to a law, the place outside the imaginary dyad and against which it breaks. To make of him a referent is to fall into an ideological trap: the 'prejudice which falsifies the conception of the Oedipus complex from the start, by making it define as natural, rather than normative, the predominance of the paternal figure'.[35]

There is, therefore, no assumption about the ways in which the places come to be fulfilled (it is this very assumption which is questioned). This is why, in talking of the genetic link between the mother and child, Lacan could refer to the 'vast social connivance' which *makes* of her the 'privileged site of prohibitions'.[36] And why Safouan, in an article on the function of the real father, recognises that it is the intervention of the third term which counts, and that nothing of itself requires that this should be embodied by the father as such.[37] Lacan's position should be read against two alternative emphases – on the actual behaviour of the mother alone (adequacy and inadequacy), and on a literally present or absent father (his idealisation and/or deficiency).

The concept of the phallus and the castration complex can only be understood in terms of this reference to prohibition and the law, just as rejection of these concepts tends to lose sight of this reference. The phallus needs to be placed on the axis of desire before it can be understood, or questioned, as the differential mark of sexual identification (boy or girl, having or not having the phallus). By breaking the imaginary dyad, the phallus represents a moment of division (Lacan calls this the subject's 'lack-in-being') which re-enacts the fundamental splitting of subjectivity itself. And by jarring against any naturalist account of sexuality ('phallocentrism . . . strictly impossible to deduce from any pre-established harmony of the said psyche to the nature it expresses'),[38] the phallus relegates sexuality to a strictly other dimension – the order of the symbolic outside of which, for Lacan, sexuality cannot be understood. The importance of the phallus is that its status in the development of human sexuality is something which nature *cannot* account for.

When Lacan is reproached with phallocentrism at the level of his theory, what is most often missed is that the subject's entry into the symbolic order is equally an exposure of the value of the phallus itself. The subject has to recognise that there is desire, or lack in the place of the Other, that there is no ultimate certainty or truth, and that the status of the phallus is a fraud (this is, for Lacan, the meaning of castration). The phallus can only take up its place by indicating the precariousness of any identity assumed by the subject on the basis of its token. Thus the phallus stands for that moment when prohibition must function, in the sense of whom may be assigned to whom in the triangle made up of mother, father and child, but at that same moment it signals to the subject that 'having' only functions at the price of a loss and 'being' as an effect of division. Only if this is dropped from the account can the phallus be taken to represent an unproblematic assertion of male privilege, or else lead to reformulations intended to guarantee the continuity of sexual development for both sexes (Jones).

It is that very continuity which is challenged in Lacan's account. The concept of the phallus and the castration complex testify above all to the problematic nature of the subject's insertion into his or her sexual identity, to an impossibility writ large over that insertion at the point where it might be taken to coincide with the genital drive. Looking back at Jones's answer to Freud, it is clear that his opposition to Freud's concept of the phallic phase involves a rejection of the dimension of desire, of the loss of the object, of the difficulty inherent in subjectivity itself. Just as it was Freud's failure to apply the concept of castration literally to the girl child which brought him up against the concept of desire.[39]

The subject then takes up his or her identity with reference to the phallus, but that identity is thereby designated symbolic (it is something enjoined on the subject). Lacan inverts Saussure's formula for the linguistic sign (the opposition between signifier and signified), giving primacy to the signifier over that which it signifies (or rather creates in that act of signification). For it is essential to his argument that sexual difference is a legislative divide which creates and reproduces its categories. Thus Lacan replaces Saussure's model for the arbitrary nature of the linguistic sign:

TREE

(which is indeed open to the objection that it seems to reflect a theory of language based on a correspondence between words and things), with this model:[40]

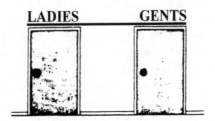

'Any speaking being whatever' must line up on one or other side of the divide.[41]

Sexual difference is then assigned according to whether individual subjects do or do not possess the phallus, which means not that anatomical difference *is* sexual difference (the one as strictly deducible from the other), but that anatomical difference comes to *figure* sexual difference, that is, it becomes the sole representative of what that difference is allowed to be. It thus covers over the complexity of the child's early sexual life with a crude opposition in which that very complexity is refused or repressed. The phallus thus indicates the reduction of difference to an instance of visible perception, a *seeming* value.

Freud gave the moment when the boy and girl child saw that they were different the status of a trauma in which the girl is seen to be lacking (the objections often start here). But something can only be *seen* to be missing according to a pre-existing hierarchy of values ('there is nothing missing in the real').[42] What counts is not the perception but its already assigned meaning – the moment therefore belongs in the symbolic. And if Lacan states that the symbolic usage of the phallus stems from its visibility (something for which he was often criticised), it is only in so far as the order of the visible, the apparent, the seeming is the object of his attack. In fact he constantly refused any crude identification of the phallus with the order of the visible or real ('one might say that this signifier is chosen as what stands out as most easily seized upon in the real of sexual copulation'),[43] and he referred it instead to that function of 'veiling' in which he locates the fundamental duplicity of the linguistic sign: 'All these propositions merely veil over the fact that the phallus can only play its role as veiled, that is, as in itself the sign of the latency with which everything signifiable is struck as soon as it is raised to the function of signifier'.[44]

Meaning is only ever erected, it is set up and fixed. The phallus symbolises the effects of the signifier in that having no value in itself, it can represent that to which value *accrues*.

Lacan's statements on language need to be taken in two directions – towards the fixing of meaning itself (that which is enjoined on the subject), and away from that very fixing to the point of its constant slippage, the risk or vanishing-point which it always contains (the unconscious). Sexuality is placed on both these dimensions at once. The difficulty is to hold these two emphases together – sexuality in the symbolic (an ordering), sexuality as that which constantly fails. Once the relationship between these two aspects of psychoanalysis can be seen, then the terms in which feminine sexuality can be described undergo a radical shift. The concept of the symbolic states that the woman's sexuality is inseparable from the representations through which it is produced ('images and symbols *for* the woman cannot be isolated from images and symbols *of* the woman . . . it is the representation of sexuality which conditions how it comes into play'),[45] but those very representations will reveal the splitting through which they are constituted as such. The question of what a woman is in this account always stalls on the crucial acknowledgement that there is absolutely no guarantee that she *is* at all (cf. section II below). But if she takes up her place according to the process described, then her sexuality will betray, necessarily, the impasses of its history.

Sexuality belongs for Lacan in the realm of masquerade. The term comes from Joan Rivière for whom it indicated a failed femininity.[46] For Lacan, masquerade is the very definition of 'femininity' precisely because it is constructed with reference to a male sign. The question of frigidity (on which, Lacan recognised, psychoanalysis 'gave up')[47] also belongs here, and it is described in 'The Meaning of the Phallus' as the effect of the status of the phallic term. But this does not imply that there is a physiology to which women could somehow be returned, or into which they could be freed. Rather the term 'frigidity' stands, on the side of the woman, for the difficulty inherent in sexuality itself, the disjunction laid over the body by desire, at the point where it is inscribed into the genital relation. Psychoanalysis now recognises that any simple criterion of femininity in terms of a shift of pleasure from clitoris to vagina is a travesty, but what matters is the fantasies implicated in either (or both). For both sexes, sexuality will necessarily touch on the duplicity which underpins its fundamental divide. As for 'normal' vaginal femininity, which might be taken as the recognition of the value of the male sign (a 'coming to' that recognition), it will always evoke the splitting on which its value is erected ('why not acknowledge that if there is no virility which castration does not consecrate, then for the woman it is a castrated lover or a dead man . . . who hides behind the veil where he calls on her adoration').[48]

The description of feminine sexuality is, therefore, an exposure of the terms of its definition, the very opposite of a demand as to what that sexuality should be. Where such a definition is given – 'identification with her mother as desiring and a recognition of the phallus in the real father',[49] it involves precisely a collapse of the phallus into the real and of desire into recognition – giving the lie, we could say, to the whole problem outlined.[50]

II

Three points emerge from what has been described so far:

1   anatomy is what figures in the account: 'for me "anatomy is not destiny", but that does not mean that anatomy does not figure',[51] but it *only figures* (it is a sham);
2   the phallus stands at its own expense and any male privilege erected upon it is an imposture: 'what might be called a man, the male speaking being, strictly disappears as an effect of discourse, ... by being inscribed within it solely as castration';[52]
3   woman is not inferior, she is *subjected:*

> That the woman should be inscribed in an order of exchange of which she is the object, is what makes for the fundamentally conflictual, and, I would say, insoluble, character of her position: the symbolic order literally submits her, it transcends her ... There is for her something insurmountable, something unacceptable, in the fact of being placed as an object in a symbolic order to which, at the same time, she is subjected just as much as the man.[53]

It is the strength of the concept of the symbolic that it systematically repudiates any account of sexuality which assumes the pre-given nature of sexual difference – the polemic within psychoanalysis and the challenge to any such 'nature' by feminism appear at their closest here. But a problem remains. Lacan's use of the symbolic at this stage relied heavily on Lévi-Strauss's notion of kinship in which women are defined as objects of exchange. As such it is open to the same objections as Lévi-Strauss's account in that it presupposes the subordination which it is intended to explain.[54] Thus while at first glance these remarks by Lacan seem most critical of the order described, they are in another sense complicit with that order and any argument constructed on their basis is likely to be circular.[55]

I think it is crucial that at the point where Lacan made these remarks he had a concept of full speech, of access to the symbolic order whose subjective equivalent is a successful linguistic exchange.[56] But his work underwent a shift, which totally undercut any such conception of language as mediation, in favour of an increasing stress on its fundamental division, and the effects of that division on the level of sexuality itself.

'There is no sexual relation' – this became the emphasis of his account. 'There is no sexual relation' because the unconscious divides subjects to and from each other, and because it is the myth of that relation which acts as a barrier against the division, setting up a unity through which this division is persistently disavowed. Hence the related and opposite formula 'There is something of One' (the two formulas should be taken together) which refers to that fantasied unity of relation ('*We are as one*. Of course everyone knows that it has never happened for two to make one, but still *we are as one*. That's what the idea of love starts out from... the problem then being how on earth there could be love for another'),[57] refers also to its suppression of division and difference ('Love your neighbour as yourself... the commandment lays down the abolition of sexual difference'),[58] to the very ideology of oneness and completion which, for Lacan, closes off the gap of human desire.

In the earlier texts, the unity was assigned to the imaginary, the symbolic was at least potentially its break. In the later texts, Lacan located the fantasy of 'sameness' within language and the sexual relation at one and the same time. 'There is no sexual relation' because subjects relate through what makes sense in *lalangue*.[59] This 'making sense' is a supplement, a making good of the lack of subjectivity and language, of the subject *in* language, against which lack it is set. Psychoanalysis states meaning to be sexual but it has left behind any notion of a repressed sexuality which it would somehow allow to speak. Meaning can only be described as sexual by taking the limits of meaning into account, for meaning in itself operates *at* the limit, the limits of its own failing: 'Meaning indicates the direction in which it fails.'[60] The stress, therefore, is on the constant failing within language and sexuality, which meaning attempts to supplement or conceal: 'Everything implied by the analytic engagement with human behaviour indicates not that meaning reflects the sexual but that it makes up for it.'[61] Sexuality is the vanishing-point of meaning. Love, on the other hand, belongs to the *Lust-Ich* or pleasure-ego which disguises that failing in the reflection of like to like (love as the ultimate form of self-recognition).

We could say that Lacan has taken the relationship between the unconscious and sexuality and has pushed it to its furthest extreme, producing an account of sexuality solely in terms of its divisions – the division *of* the subject, division *between* subjects (as opposed to relation). Hence the increasing focus on enunciation,[62] on language's internal division, and also the deliberate formalisation of the account – sexual difference as a divide, something to be laid out (exactly a formality, a question of form (the graph of *Encore*)).[63] The challenge to the unity of the subject, its seeming coherence, is then addressed to the discourse of sexuality itself: 'instead of one signifier we need to interrogate, we should interrogate the signifier One'.[64] Thus there is no longer imaginary 'unity' and then symbolic difference or exchange, but rather an indictment of the symbolic for the imaginary unity which its most persistent myths continue to promote.

Within this process, woman is constructed as an absolute category (excluded and elevated at one and the same time), a category which serves to guarantee that unity on the side of the man. The man places the woman at the basis of his fantasy, or constitutes fantasy through the woman. Lacan moved away, therefore, from the idea of a problematic but socially assured process of exchange (women as objects) to the construction of woman as a category within language (woman as *the* object, the fantasy of her definition). What is now exposed in the account is 'a carrying over onto the woman of the difficulty inherent in sexuality' itself.[65]

Lacan's later work on femininity, especially the seminar *Encore*, belong to this development. It goes further than, and can be seen as an attempt to take up the problems raised by, the work that precedes it. For whereas in the earlier texts the emphasis was on the circulation of the phallus in the process of sexual exchange, it is now effectively stated that if it is the phallus that circulates then there is no exchange (or relation). The question then becomes not so much the 'difficulty' of feminine sexuality consequent on phallic division, as what it means, given that division, to speak of the 'woman' at all. It is in many ways a more fundamental or 'radical' enquiry:

> whatever can be stated about the constitution of the feminine position in the Oedipus complex or in the sexual 'relation' concerns only a second stage, one in which the rules governing a certain type of exchange based on a common value have already been established. It is at a more radical stage, constitutive of those very rules themselves, that Freud points to one last question by indicating that it is the woman who comes to act as their support.[66]

In the later texts, the central term is the *object small a* [*objet a*], Lacan's formula for the lost object which underpins symbolisation, cause of and 'stand in' for desire. What the man relates to is this object and the 'whole of his realisation in the sexual relation comes down to fantasy'.[67] As the place onto which lack is projected, and through which it is simultaneously disavowed, woman is a 'symptom' for the man.

Defined as such, reduced to being nothing other than this fantasmatic place, the woman does not exist. Lacan's statement 'T̶h̶e̶ woman does not exist' is, therefore, the corollary of his accusation, or charge, against sexual fantasy. It means, not that women do not exist, but that her status as an absolute category and guarantor of fantasy (exactly *The* woman) is false (T̶h̶e̶). Lacan sees courtly love as the elevation of the woman into the place where her absence or inaccessibility stands in for male lack ('For the man, whose lady was entirely, in the most servile sense of the term, his female subject, courtly love is the only way of coming off elegantly from the absence of sexual relation'),[68] just as he sees her denigration as the precondition for man's belief in his own soul ('For the soul to come into being, she, the woman, is differentiated from it . . . called woman and defamed').[69] In relation to the man, woman comes to stand for both difference and loss: 'On the one hand, the woman becomes, or is produced, precisely as what he is not, that is, sexual difference, and on the other, as what he has to renounce, that is, *jouissance*.'[70]

Within the phallic definition, the woman is constituted as 'not all', in so far as the phallic function rests on an exception (the 'not') which is assigned to her. Woman is excluded *by* the nature of words, meaning that the definition poses her as exclusion. Note that this is not the same thing as saying that woman is excluded *from* the nature of words, a misreading which leads to the recasting of the whole problem in terms of woman's place outside language, the idea that women might have of themselves an entirely different speech.

For Lacan, men and women are only ever in language ('Men and women are signifiers bound to the common usage of language').[71] All speaking beings must line themselves up on one side or the other of this division, but anyone can cross over and inscribe themselves on the opposite side from that to which they are anatomically destined.[72] It is, we could say, an either/or situation, but one whose fantasmatic nature was endlessly reiterated by Lacan: 'these are not positions able to satify us, so much so that we can state the unconscious to be defined by the fact that it has a much clearer idea of what is going on than the truth that man is not woman'.[73]

The woman, therefore, is *not*, because she is defined purely against the man (she is the negative of that definition – 'man is *not* woman'), and because this very definition is designated fantasy, a set which may well be empty. If woman is 'not all', writes Lacan, then 'she' can hardly refer to all women.

As negative to the man, woman becomes a total object of fantasy (or an object of total fantasy), elevated into the place of the Other and made to stand for its truth. Since the place of the Other is also the place of God, this is the ultimate form of mystification ('the more man may ascribe to the woman in confusion with God . . . the less he is'). In so far as God 'has not made his exit',[74] so the woman becomes the support of his symbolic place. In his later work Lacan defined the objective of psychoanalysis as breaking the confusion behind this mystification, a rupture between the *object a* and the Other, whose conflation he saw as the elevation of fantasy into the order of truth. The *object a*, cause of desire and support of male fantasy, gets transposed onto the image of the woman as Other who then acts as its guarantee. The absolute 'Otherness' of the woman, therefore, serves to secure for the man his own self-knowledge and truth. Remember that for Lacan there can be no such guarantee – there is no 'Other of the Other'. His rejection of the category 'Woman', therefore, belonged to his assault on any unqualified belief in the Other as such: 'This ~~The~~ [of the woman] crossed through . . . relates to the signifier O when it is crossed through (Ø)'.[75]

Increasingly this led Lacan to challenge the notions of 'knowledge' and 'belief', and the myths on which they necessarily rely. All Lacan's statements against belief in the woman, against her status as knowing, problematic as they are, can only be understood as part of this constant undercutting of the terms on which they rest. In the later writing, Lacan continually returns to the 'subject supposed to know', the claim of a subject to know (the claim to know oneself as subject), and the different forms of discourse which can be organised around this position.[76] 'Knowing' is only ever such a claim, just as 'belief' rests entirely on the supposition of what is false. To believe in The Woman is simply a way of closing off the division or uncertainty which also underpins conviction as such. And when Lacan says that women do not know, while at one level he relegates women outside, and against the very mastery of his own statement, he was also recognising the binding, or restricting, of the parameters of knowledge itself ('masculine knowledge irredeemably an erring').[77]

The Other crossed through (Ø) stands against this knowledge as the place of division where meaning falters, where it slips and shifts. It is the place of *signifiance*, Lacan's term for this very movement in language against, or away from, the positions of coherence which language simultaneously constructs. The Other therefore stands against the phallus – its pretence to meaning and false consistency. It is from the Other that the phallus seeks authority and is refused.

The woman belongs on the side of the Other in this second sense, for in so far as *jouissance* is defined as phallic so she might be said to belong somewhere else. The woman is implicated, of necessity, in phallic sexuality, but at the same time it is 'elsewhere that she upholds the question of her own *jouissance*',[78] that is, the question of her status as desiring subject. Lacan designates this *jouissance* supplementary so as to avoid any notion of complement, of woman as a complement to man's phallic nature (which is precisely the fantasy). But it is also a recognition of the 'something more', the 'more than *jouissance*',[79] which Lacan locates in the Freudian concept of repetition –

what escapes or is left over from the phallic function, and exceeds it. Woman is, therefore, placed *beyond* (beyond the phallus). That 'beyond' refers at once to her total mystification as absolute Other (and hence nothing other than other), and to a *question*, the question of her own *jouissance*, of her greater or lesser access to the residue of the dialectic to which she is constantly subjected. The problem is that once the notion of 'woman' has been so relentlessly exposed as a fantasy, then any such question becomes an almost impossible one to pose.

Lacan's reference to woman as Other needs, therefore, to be seen as an attempt to hold apart two moments which are in constant danger of collapsing into each other – that which assigns woman to the negative place of its own (phallic) system, and that which asks the question as to whether women might, as a very effect of that assignation, break against and beyond that system itself. For Lacan, that break is always within language, it is the break of the subject *in* language. The concept of *jouissance* (what escapes in sexuality) and the concept of *signifiance* (what shifts within language) are inseparable.

Only when this is seen can we properly locate the tension which runs right through *Encore* between his critique of the forms of mystification latent to the category Woman, and the repeated question as to what her 'otherness' might be. A tension which can be recognised in the very query 'What does a woman want?' on which Freud stalled and to which Lacan returned. That tension is clearest in Lacan's appeal to St Theresa, whose statue by Bernini in Rome[80] he took as the model for an-other *jouissance* – the woman therefore as 'mystical' but, he insisted, this is not 'not political',[81] in so far as mysticism is · one of the available forms of expression where such 'otherness' in sexuality utters its most forceful complaint. And if we cut across for a moment from Lacan's appeal to her image as executed by the man, to St Theresa's own writings, to her commentary on 'The Song of Songs', we find its sexuality in the form of a disturbance which, crucially, she locates not on the level of the sexual content of the song, but on the level of its enunciation, in the instability of its pronouns – a precariousness in language which reveals that neither the subject nor God can be placed ('speaking with one person, asking for peace from another, and then speaking to the person in whose presence she is').[82] Sexuality belongs, therefore, on the level of its, and the subject's, *shifting*.

Towards the end of his work, Lacan talked of woman's 'anti-phallic' nature as leaving her open to that 'which of the unconscious cannot be spoken' (a reference to women analysts in which we can recognise, ironically, the echo of Freud's conviction that they would have access to a different strata of psychic life).[83] In relation to the earlier texts we could say that woman no longer masquerades, she *defaults:* 'the *jouissance* of the woman does not go without saying, that is, without the saying of truth', whereas for the man 'his *jouissance* suffices which is precisely why he understands nothing'.[84] There is a risk, here, of giving back to the woman a status as truth (the very mythology denounced). But for Lacan, this 'truth' of the unconscious is only ever that moment of fundamental division through which the subject entered into language and sexuality, and the constant failing of position within both.

This is the force of Lacan's account – his insistence that femininity can only be understood in terms of its construction, an insistence which produced in reply the same reinstatment of women, the same argument for *her* sexual nature as was seen in the 1920s and 1930s in response to Freud. This time the question of symbolisation, which was latent in the earlier debate, has been at the centre of that response. This is all the more clear in that the specificity of feminine sexuality in the more recent discussion[85] has explicitly become the issue of women's relationship to language. In so far as it is the order of language which structures sexuality around the male term, or the privileging of that term which shows sexuality to be constructed within language, so this raises the issue of women's relationship to that language and that sexuality simultaneously. The question of the body of the girl child (what she may or may not know of that body) as posed in the earlier debate, becomes the question of the woman's body as language (what, of that body, can achieve symbolisation). The objective is to retrieve the woman from the dominance of the phallic term and from language at one and the same time. What this means is that femininity is assigned to a point of origin prior to the mark of symbolic difference and the law. The privileged relationship of women to that origin gives them access to an archaic form of expressivity outside the circuit of linguistic exchange.

This point of origin is the maternal body, an undifferentiated space, and yet one in which the girl child recognises herself. The girl then has to suppress or devalue that fullness of recognition in order to line up within the order of the phallic term. In the argument for a primordial femininity, it is clear that the relation between the mother and child is conceived of as dyadic and simply reflective (one to one – the girl child fully *knows* herself in the mother) which once again precludes the concept of desire. Feminine specificity is, therefore, predicated directly onto the concept of an unmediated and unproblematic relation to origin.

The positions taken up have not been identical, but they have a shared stress on the specificity of the feminine drives, a stress which was at the basis of the earlier response to Freud. They take a number of their concepts directly from that debate (the concept of concentric feminine drives in Montrelay comes directly from Jones and Klein). But the effects of the position are different. Thus whereas for Jones, for example, those drives ideally anticipated and ensured the heterosexual identity of the girl child, now those same drives put at risk her access to any object at all (Montrelay)[86] or else they secure the woman to herself and, through that, to other women (Irigaray). Women are *returned*, therefore, in the account and to each other – against the phallic term but also against the loss of origin which Lacan's account is seen to imply. It is therefore a refusal of division which gives the woman access to a different strata of language, where words and things are not differentiated, and the real of the maternal body threatens or holds off woman's access to prohibition and the law.

There is a strength in this account, which has been recognised by feminism. At its most forceful it expresses a protest engendered by the very cogency of what Freud and then Lacan describe (it is the *effect* of that description).[87] And something of its position was certainly present in Lacan's earlier texts ('feminine sexuality . . . as the effort of a *jouissance* wrapped in its own contiguity').[88] But Lacan came back to this response in the later texts, which can therefore be seen as a sort of reply, much as Freud's 1931 and 1933 papers on femininity addressed some of the criticisms which he had received.

For Lacan, as we have seen, there is no pre-discursive reality ('How return, other than by means of a special discourse, to a pre-discursive reality?'),[89] no place prior to the law which is available and can be retrieved. And there is no feminine outside language. First, because the unconscious severs the subject from any unmediated relation to the body as such ('there is nothing in the unconscious which accords with the body'),[90] and secondly because the 'feminine' is constituted as a division in language, a division which produces the feminine as its negative term. If woman is defined as other it is because the definition produces her as other, and not because she has another essence. Lacan does not refuse difference ('if there was no difference how could I say there was no sexual relation'),[91] but for him what is to be questioned is the seeming 'consistency' of that difference – of the body or anything else – the division it enjoins, the definitions of the woman it produces.

For Lacan, to say that difference is 'phallic' difference is to expose the symbolic and arbitrary nature of its division as such. It is crucial – and it is something which can be seen even more clearly in the response to the later texts on femininity – that refusal of the phallic term brings with it an attempt to reconstitute a form of subjectivity free of division, and hence a refusal of the notion of symbolisation itself. If the status of the phallus is to be challenged, it cannot, therefore, be directly from the feminine body but must be by means of a different symbolic term (in which case the relation to the body is immediately thrown into crisis), or else by an entirely different logic altogether (in which case one is no longer in the order of symbolisation at all).

The demands against Lacan therefore collapse two different levels of objection – that the body should be mediated by language and that the privileged term of that mediation be male. The fact that refusal of the phallus turns out once again to be a refusal of the symbolic does not close, but leaves open as still unanswered, the question as to why that necessary symbolisation and the privileged status of the phallus appear as interdependent in the structuring and securing (never secure) of human subjectivity.

There is, therefore, no question of denying here that Lacan was implicated in the phallocentrism he described, just as his own utterance constantly rejoins the mastery which he sought to undermine. The question of the unconscious and of sexuality, the movement towards and against them, operated at exactly this level of his own speech. But for Lacan they function as the question of that speech, and cannot be referred back to a body outside language, a place to which the 'feminine', and through that, women, might escape. In the response to Lacan, therefore, the 'feminine' has returned as it did in the 1920s and 1930s in reply to Freud, but this time with the added meaning of a resistance to a phallic organisation of sexuality which is recognised as such. The 'feminine' stands for a refusal of that organisation, its ordering, its identity. For Lacan, on the other hand, interrogating that same organisation undermines any absolute definition of the 'feminine' at all.

Psychoanalysis does not produce that definition. It gives an account of how that definition is produced. While the objection to its dominant term must be recognised, it cannot be answered by an account which returns to a concept of the feminine as pre-given, nor by a mandatory appeal to an androcentrism in the symbolic which the phallus would simply reflect. The former relegates women outside language and history, the latter simply subordinates them to both.

Lacan's writing gives an account of how the status of the phallus in human sexuality enjoins on the woman a definition in which she is simultaneously symptom and myth. As long as we continue to feel the effects of that definition we cannot afford to ignore this description of the fundamental imposture which sustains it.

NOTES

1 This essay was originally published as the second part of the Introduction to *Feminine Sexuality – Jacques Lacan and the école freudienne*, edited by Juliet Mitchell and Jacqueline Rose, London 1982, New York 1983, a collection of articles relating to the question of feminine sexuality by the French psychoanalyst Jacques Lacan and members of his school of psychoanalysis, the *école freudienne*, founded in 1964 and dissolved by Lacan in 1980. The articles were put together and edited by Juliet Mitchell and myself with separate, but complementary, introductions tracing the terms of the psychoanalytic debate about femininity instigated in the 1920s and continued in the work of Lacan and in the responses to his writing. In the first part, Juliet Mitchell gave an extensive account of the dispute which took place in the 1920s and 30s over Freud's theories of femininity and the castration complex. For details of this dispute, readers are referred to Juliet Mitchell's Introduction, *Feminine Sexuality*, reprinted in Juliet Mitchell, *Women: The Longest Revolution*, London and New York 1984.

2 Lacan, 'Propos directifs pour un congrès sur la sexualité féminine' (1958), *Ecrits*, Paris 1966 (tr. 'Guiding Remarks for a Congress on Feminine Sexuality', *Feminine Sexuality*, pp. 88–89).

3 Ibid., p. 89.

4 Ernest Jones, 'The Early Development of Female Sexuality', *International Journal of Psychoanalysis* 8, 1927, p. 459.

5 Josef Breuer and Sigmund Freud, *Studies on Hysteria* (1893–5), *The Standard Edition of the Complete Psychological Works of Sigmund Freud* [SE], vol. 2 (1955); Penguin Freud Library [PF], vol. 3.

6 Freud, 'Observation of a Severe Case of Hemi-Anaesthesia in a Hysterical Male' (1886), SE 1.

7 Freud, *Beyond the Pleasure Principle* (1920), SE 18, PF 11; 'Splitting of the Ego in the Process of Defence' (1938), SE 23, PF 11.

8 Nancy Chodorow, *The Reproduction of Mothering, Psychoanalysis and the Sociology of Gender*, Berkeley and Los Angeles 1978, London 1979; see note 28 below.

9 Lacan, *The Four Fundamental Concepts of Psychoanalysis*, trans. Alan Sheridan, Harmondsworth 1977, p. 146.

10 Lacan, 'Le stade du miroir comme formateur de la fonction du Je' (1936), *Ecrits* (tr. 'The Mirror Stage as Formative of the Function of the I', *Ecrits: A Selection*, trans. Alan Sheridan, London 1977).

11 D. W. Winnicott, 'Mirror-Role of Mother and Family in Child Development' (1967), *Playing and Reality*, London 1971.

12 Lacan, 'Cure psychanalytique à l'aide de la poupée fleur', *Revue française de la psychanalyse* 4, October–December 1949, p. 567.

13 Emile Benveniste, 'La nature des pronoms', *Problèmes de linguistique générale*, 2 vols, Paris 1966, 1974 (tr. 'The Nature of Pronouns', *Problems in General Linguistics*, trans. Mary E. Meek, Florida 1971).

14 Freud, *Project for a Scientific Psychology* (1895), SE 1, p. 319; *Beyond the Pleasure Principle*, pp. 14–17; pp. 283–287.

15 This can be compared with, for example, Melanie Klein's account of symbol-formation (Melanie Klein, 'The Importance of Symbol Formation in the Development of the Ego', *IJPA* 11, 1930) and also with Hannah Segal's ('Notes on Symbol Formation', *IJPA* 38, 1957), where symbolisation is an effect of anxiety and a means of transcending it on the path to reality, a path which is increasingly assured by the strengthening of the ego itself. Cf. also Lacan's specific critique of Ernest Jones's famous article on symbolism (Ernest Jones, 'The Theory of Symbolism', *British Journal of Psychoanalysis* 11:2, 1916 and Jacques Lacan, 'A la mémoire d'Ernest Jones: sur sa théorie de symbolisme' (1959), *Ecrit*) which he criticised for its definition of language in terms of an increasing mastery or appropriation of reality, and for failing to see, therefore, the structure of metaphor (or substitution) which lies at the root of, and is endlessly repeated within, subjectivity in its relation to the unconscious. It is in this sense also that Lacan's emphasis on language should be differentiated from what he defined as 'culturalism', that is, from any conception of language as a social phenomenon which does not take into account its fundamental instability (language as constantly placing, and *displacing*, the subject).

16 Lacan, 'La signification du phallus' (1958), *Ecrits* (tr. 'The Meaning of the Phallus', *Feminine Sexuality*, p. 80).

17   Freud, 'On the Universal Tendency to Debasement in the Sphere of Love' (1912), SE 11, pp. 188–189; PF 7, p. 258.

18   'The Meaning of the Phallus', p. 81.

19   Freud, *Three Essays on the Theory of Sexuality* (1905), SE 7, pp. 144–146n; PF 7, p. 57n.

20   *The Four Fundamental Concepts*, p. 189.

21   *Ornicar?* 20–21, Summer 1980, p. 16. *Ornicar?* is the periodical of the department of psychoanalysis, under Lacan's direction up to 1981, at the University of Paris VIII (Vincennes).

22   *The Four Fundamental Concepts*, p. 205.

23   Ibid., p. 181.

24   See Lacan, 'Intervention on Transference'; also 'Dora – Fragment of an Analysis' in Rose, *Sexuality in the Field of Vision*.

25   Lacan, *Le séminaire II: Le moi dans la théorie de Freud et dans la technique de la psychanalyse* (1954–55), Paris 1978, p. 267 (tr. Sylvana Tomaselli, *The Ego in Freud's Theory and in the Technique of Psychoanalysis*, Cambridge 1987).

26   Ibid., p. 296.

27   'Guiding Remarks', p. 87.

28   Nancy Chodorow's reading of psychoanalysis for feminism (*The Reproduction of Mothering*) paradoxically also belongs here, and it touches on all the problems raised so far. The book attempts to use psychoanalysis to account for the acquisition and reproduction of mothering, but it can only do so by displacing the concepts of the unconscious and bisexuality in favour of a notion of gender imprinting ('the establishment of an unambiguous and unquestioned gender identity', p. 158 – the concept comes from Robert Stoller, 'A Contribution to the Study of Gender Identity', *IJPA* 45, 1965) which is compatible with a sociological conception of role. Thus the problem needing to be addressed – the acquisition of sexual identity and its difficulty – is sidestepped in the account. The book sets itself to question sexual *roles*, but only within the limits of an assumed sexual *identity*.

29   'La phase phallique et la portée subjective du complexe de castration', *Scilicet* 1, 1968; tr. 'The Phallic Phase and the Subjective Import of the Castration Complex', *Feminine Sexuality*, p. 117. *Scilicet* was the review published in Lacan's series, *Le champ freudien*, at Editions du Seuil in Paris; apart from those by Lacan, the articles in the first issues were unsigned.

30   Lacan, 'Les formations de l'inconscient', *Bulletin de Psychologie* 2, 1957–58, p. 13.

31   'The Meaning of the Phallus', p. 80.

32   'Les formations de l'inconscient', p. 14.

33   Ibid., p. 8

34   Moustapha Safouan, 'Is the Oedipus Complex Universal?' (tr. Ben Brewster from chapter 7 of *Etudes sur l'oedipe*, Paris 1974), *m/f* 5–6, 1981, p. 9.

35   'Intervention on Transference', p. 69.

36   Lacan, *Le séminaire XVII: L'envers de la psychanalyse* (1969–70), 6, p. 10 (unpublished seminar, references to week and page of the typescript).

37   Safouan, p. 127.

38   Lacan, 'D'une question préliminaire à tout traitement possible de la psychose' (1955–56), Ecrits (tr. 'On a Question Preliminary to any Possible Treatment of Psychosis', *Ecrits: A Selection*, p. 198).

39   For a fuller discussion of both of these points see 'The Phallic Phase', and 'Feminine Sexuality in Psychoanalytic Doctrine', in *Feminine Sexuality*.

40   Lacan, 'L'instance de la lettre dans l'inconscient ou la raison depuis Freud' (1957), Ecrits (tr. 'The Agency of the Letter in the Unconscious or Reason since Freud', *Ecrits: A Selection*, p. 151).

41   Lacan, 'Une lettre d'âmour', *Le séminaire XX: Encore* (1972–73), Paris 1975 (tr. 'A Love Letter', *Feminine Sexuality*, p. 150).

42   'The Phallic Phase', p. 113.

43   'The Meaning of the Phallus', p. 82.

44   Ibid., p. 82.

45   'Guiding Remarks', p. 90.

46   Joan Rivière, 'Womanliness as Masquerade', *IJPA* 10, 1929; reprinted in *Formations of Fantasy*, London 1986.

47   'Guiding Remarks', p. 89.

48 Ibid., p. 95.

49 Moustapha Safouan, *La sexualité féminine dans la doctrine freudienne*, Paris 1976, p. 110.

50 The difficulty of these terms is recognised by Safouan, but the problem remains; cf. also Eugénie Lemoine-Luccioni, *Partage des femmes* (Paris 1976) where there is the same collapse between the Other to be recognised by the woman in her advent to desire, and the real man whom, ideally, she comes to accept ('the Other, the man', p. 83; 'the Other, the man as subject', p. 87). There seems to be a constant tendency to literalise the terms of Lacan's account and it is when this happens that the definitions most easily recognised as reactionary tend to appear. We can see this in such apparently different areas as Maud Mannoni's translation of the name of the father into a therapeutic practice which seeks to establish the paternal genealogy of the psychotic child (Maud Mannoni, *L'enfant, sa 'maladie' et les autres*, Paris 1967; tr. *The Child, its 'Illness' and the Others*, London 1970) and in Lemoine-Luccioni's account of the real Other who ensures castration to the woman otherwise condemned to pure narcissism. Lemoine-Luccioni's account is in many ways reminiscent of that of Helene Deutsch ('The Significance of Masochism in the Mental Life of Women', *IJPA* 11, 1930) who described the transition to femininity in terms of a desire for castration which is produced across the woman's body by the man.

51 Safouan, *La sexualité féminine*, p. 131.

52 *L'envers de la psychanalyse*, 12, p. 4.

53 *Le moi dans la théorie de Freud*, pp. 304–305.

54 See Elizabeth Cowie, 'Woman as Sign', *m/f* 1, 1978.

55 Cf., for example, Gayle Rubin, 'The Traffic in Women', in Rayna M. Reiter, *Towards an Anthropology of Women* (New York 1975), which describes psychoanalysis as a 'theory about the reproduction of Kinship', losing sight, again, of the concept of the unconscious and the whole problem of sexual identity, reducing the relations described to a quite literal set of acts of exchange.

56 'The Function and Field of Speech and Language', in *Ecrits*.

57 *Encore*, p. 46.

58 Lacan, *Le séminaire XXI: Les non-dupes errent* (1973–74), unpublished typescript, 4, p. 3.

59 Lacan's term for Saussure's *langue* (language) from the latter's distinction between *langue* (the formal organisation of language) and *parole* (speech), the individual utterance. Lacan's term displaces this opposition in so far as, for him, the organisation of language can only be understood in terms of the subject's relationship to it. *Lalangue* indicates that part of language which reflects the laws of unconscious processes, but whose effects go beyond that reflection, and escape the grasp of the subject. (See *Encore*, pp. 126–127.)

60 'A Love Letter', p. 150.

61 *Les non-dupes errent*, 15, p. 9.

62 The term comes from Benveniste, his distinction between *énoncé* and *énonciation*, between the subject of the statement and the subject of the utterance itself. (See note 25 to 'Dora – Fragment of an Analysis' above.) Lacan sites the unconscious at the radical division of these instances, seen at its most transparent in the statement 'I am lying' where there are clearly two subjects, the one who is lying and the one who is not.

63 'A Love Letter', p. 149.

64 *Encore*, p. 23.

65 'The Phallic Phase', p. 118.

66 Ibid., pp. 118–119.

67 'A Love Letter, p. 157.

68 Lacan, 'Dieu et la jouissance de La femme', *Encore* (tr. 'God and the Jouissance of The Woman', *Feminine Sexuality*, p. 141).

69 'A Love Letter', p. 156.

70 Lacan, *Le séminaire XVIII: D'un discours qui ne sera pas semblant* (1970–71), 6, pp. 9–10; see also Otto Fenichel, in a paper to which Lacan often referred, on the refusal of difference which underpins the girl = phallus equation frequently located as a male fantasy: 'the differentness of woman is denied in both cases; in the one case, in the attempt to repress women altogether, in the other, in denying their individuality'. (Otto Fenichel, 'The Symbolic Equation: Girl = Phallus', *Psychoanalytic Quarterly* 18:3, 1949, p. 13.)

71 *Encore*, p. 36.

72 Note how this simultaneously shifts the concept of bisexuality – not an undifferentiated sexual nature prior to symbolic difference (Freud's earlier sense), but the availability to all subjects of both positions in relation to that difference itself.

73 *Les non-dupes errent*, 6, p. 9.

74 'A Love Letter', pp. 160, 154.

75 Ibid., p. 151.

76 Much of the difficulty of Lacan's work stemmed from his attempt to subvert that position from within his own utterance, to rejoin the place of 'non-knowledge' which he designated the unconscious, by the constant slippage or escape of his speech, and thereby to undercut the very mastery which his own position as speaker (master and analyst) necessarily constructs. In fact one can carry out the same operation on the statement 'I do not know' as Lacan performed on the utterance 'I am lying' (cf. note 62 above) – for, if I do not know, then how come I know enough to know that I do not know and if I do know that I do not know, then it is not true that I do not know. Lacan was undoubtedly trapped in this paradox of his own utterance.

77 *Les non-dupes errent*, 6, p. 11.

78 'The Phallic Phase', p. 121.

79 At times *jouissance* is opposed to the idea of pleasure as the site of this excess, but where *jouissance* is defined as phallic, Lacan introduces the concept of the supplement ('more than') with which to oppose it.

80 'What is her *jouissance*, her *coming* from?' ('God and the Jouissance of ~~The~~ Woman', p. 147) – a question made apparently redundant by the angel with arrow poised above her (the 'piercing' of Saint Theresa), and one whose problematic nature is best illustrated by the cardinals and doges in the gallery on either side of the 'proscenium' – *witnesses* to the staging of an act which, because of the perspective lines, they cannot actually *see* (Bernini, 'The Ecstasy of Saint Theresa', Santa Maria della Vittoria, Rome).

81 'God and the Jouissance of ~~The~~ Woman', p. 146.

82 Saint Theresa, *The Complete Works*, ed. Silverio de Santa Teresa P., English edition, Peers, London 1946, p. 359. Commentary on the line from the 'Song of Songs' – 'Let the Lord kiss me with the kiss of his mouth, for thy breasts are sweeter than wine'.

83 *Ornicar?*, 20–21, Summer 1980, p. 12. At the time of writing Lacan had just dissolved his school in Paris, rejoining in the utterance through which he represented that act – 'Je père-sévère' ('I persevere' – the pun is on 'per' and 'père' (father)) – the whole problem of mastery and paternity which has cut across the institutional history of his work. From the early stand against a context which he (and others) considered authoritarian, and the cancellation, as its effect, of his seminar on the Name of the Father in 1953, to the question of mastery and transference which lay behind the further break in 1964, and which so clearly surfaces in the dissolution here. It has been the endless paradox of Lacan's position that he has provided the most systematic critique of forms of identification and transference which, by dint of this very fact, he has come most totally to represent. That a number of women analysts (cf. note 85) have found their position in relation to this to be an impossible one, only confirms the close relation between the question of feminine sexuality and the institutional divisions and difficulties of psychoanalysis itself.

84 *Les non-dupes errent*, 7, p. 16.

85 In this last section I will be referring predominantly to the work of Michèle Montrelay and Luce Irigaray, the former a member of Lacan's school prior to its dissolution in January 1980 when she dissociated herself from him, the latter working within his school up to 1974 when she was dismissed from the newly reorganised department of psychoanalysis at the University of Paris VIII (Vincennes) on publication of her book, *Speculum de l'autre femme*. Both are practising psychoanalysts. Montrelay takes up the Freud-Jones controversy specifically in terms of women's access to language in her article 'Recherches sur la fémininité' (*Critique* 26, 1970; tr. Parveen Adams, 'Inquiry into Femininity'). Irigaray's book *Speculum* contained a critique of Freud's papers on femininity; her later *Ce sexe qui n'en est pas un* (Paris 1977; tr. Catherine Porter, *This Sex Which Is Not One*, Ithaca 1985) contains a chapter ('Cosi fan tutti') directly addressed to Lacan's *Encore*.

86 Montrelay attempts to resolve the 'Freud-Jones' controversy by making the two different accounts of femininity equal to *stages* in the girl's psychosexual development, femininity being defined as the passage from a concentric psychic economy to one in which symbolic castration has come into play.

Access to symbolisation depends on the transition, and it is where it fails that the woman remains bound to a primordial cathexis of language as the undifferentiated maternal body. Montrelay should, therefore, be crucially distinguished from Irigaray at this point, since for her such a failure is precipitant of anxiety and is in no sense a concept of femininity which she is intending to promote.

87 Note too the easy slippage from Irigaray's title *Ce sexe qui n'en est pas un*, 'This sex which isn't one', to Lacan's formula: 'This sex which isn't *one*'.
88 'Guiding Remarks', p. 97.
89 *Encore*, p. 33.
90 'Seminar of 21 January, 1975', p. 165.
91 *Les non-dupes errent*, 4, p. 18.

14

Bhabha on Fanon

Homi Bhabha (1949–) is a prominent and controversial figure in what has become known as postcolonial theory. The genesis of his characteristically restless and reflexive style can be traced back to what might be called the moment of 'theory' in literary studies in the 1970s and 1980s. This moment saw a pervasive radicalization and revision in the range of critical approaches deployed in the study of literary texts, developing unstable compounds of literary and critical theory. Literary theorists sought to appropriate insights from a range of disciplines, including linguistics, structuralism, Marxism, psychoanalysis and post-structuralism. An initial phase in literary theoretical work gave prominence to approaches developed out of the structuralist anthropology of Claude Lévi-Strauss whose work was itself influenced by the linguistics of Ferdinand de Saussure. Roland Barthes acted as a key mediating figure, especially for literary and cultural studies, in the subsequent shift from structuralism to post-structuralism. A number of those whose work is featured in this anthology were engaged in this shift, notably Althusser, Lacan, Foucault and Kristeva, though Derrida came to play the leading role in the theorization of literary studies in the English-speaking world. Much of the conceptual revision translated French philosophical thought into English-speaking contexts, with 'theory' acting as a crossroads between literary criticism, philosophy and a range of other disciplines.

The context of 'theory' in literary studies is important for understanding Bhabha's work because it helps to explain the array of theoretical positions and vocabularies he brings together. In one sense his essays extend a post-structuralist paradigm through an eclectic appropriation of selected aspects of French thought. In another sense, his work is part of a revision of post-structuralist motifs in the light of emerging inter-disciplinary contexts and the impact of globalization on the study of 'English' literature. Post-colonial theory emerged at the intersection between literary theory, cultural studies and the theorization of multicultural politics. Much of the impact of postcolonial theory lies in the questions posed for the 'universal', or indeed specifically 'Western', 'imperial' or 'colonial' dynamics in Western philosophy and theory. Edward Said's influential book *Orientalism* (1978), for example, questioned the Western construction of 'Oriental' culture and exposed the imperialist dynamics in Orientalist studies. As Bhabha puts it in his essay 'The Commitment to Theory' in *The Location of Culture*: 'Are the interests of "Western" theory necessarily collusive with the hegemonic role of the West as a power bloc? Is the language of theory merely another power ploy of the culturally privileged Western elite to produce a discourse of the Other that reinforces its own power–knowledge equation?' Another key feature of postcolonial theory is its focus on deconstructing essentialist conceptions of identity, origin and subjectivity. Analogous in this respect with queer theory, postcolonial theory has sought to unpick the essentialist categories at work in colonial, national and race ideology, suggesting an alternative, politicized and post-structuralist conception of identity as difference. The key term for this emphasis on identity as a fluid and indeterminate play of difference is 'hybridity', used variously to suggest spaces of mixed and ambivalently conflictual experience, or what Wilson Harris has called a certain void or misgiving which attends every assimilation of contraries.

Bhabha's work is at the centre of these developments in postcolonial theory, not least in his attempts to theorize hybridity. Within the project of politicizing the tendency for academic disciplines to insist on national or essentialist categories, such as 'Indian' literature or 'African-American' identity, Bhabha has insisted on the importance of theory in opening up the possibility of a third space of cultural negotiation. The challenge is to develop a critique of the legacies of imperialist and colonial identity formation without becoming imprisoned in anti-imperial or anti-colonial strategies of opposition. In order to develop such a critique Bhabha has drawn above all on a politicized reading of Derrida, Foucault's conception of power and knowledge, Fanon's psychoanalytic model of colonialism and Lacan's conceptions of the subject.

Frantz Fanon (1925–61) is a key figure in postcolonial debates and an important theorist of anti-colonial and anti-racist struggles. He combined psychoanalytic models of identity through a critical dialogue with Marxism and the politicized existentialism of Jean-Paul Sartre. Bhabha reads Fanon against the grain of Fanon's own theoretical and political contexts, so as to develop a new theoretical model, but Bhabha has been criticized by many, notably Cedric Robinson and Aijaz Ahmad, for misappropriating Fanon. Insofar as Bhabha's reading articulates a strategic intervention *through* Fanon rather than offering a faithful exposition, Bhabha's essay serves as an excellent introduction to the difficult status of critique in postcolonial theory and to the critical issues at play in the reception of Fanon's work.

FURTHER READING

Primary works

Homi Bhabha, *The Location of Culture* (London: Routledge, 1994); 'Difference, Discrimination, and the Discourse of Colonialism', *Politics of Theory*, ed. Francis

Barker and others (Colchester: University of Essex, 1983), pp. 194–211; Homi
Bhahba, ed., *Nation and Narration* (London: Routledge, 1990).

Frantz Fanon, *Black Skin, White Masks* (1952), trans. Charles Lam Markman
(London: Pluto, 1996); *Towards the African Revolution*, trans. Haakon Chevalier
(London: Writers and Readers, 1980); *Studies in a Dying Colonialism*, trans.
Haakon Chevalier (London: Earthscan, 1989); *The Wretched of the Earth*,
trans. Constance Farrington with preface by Jean-Paul Sartre (Harmondsworth:
Penguin, 1967).

Secondary works

Aijaz Ahmad, 'The Politics of Literary Postcoloniality', *Race and Class* 36(3) (1995).

Aijaz Ahmad, *In Theory: Classes, Nations, Literatures* (London: Verso, 1992).

Hussein Abadilahi Bulhan, *Frantz Fanon and the Psychology of Oppression* (New York:
Plenum, 1985).

Anthony Easthope, 'Bhabha, Hybridity, and Identity', *Textual Practice* 12(2) (1998).

Ragnar Farr, ed., *Mirage: Engimas of Race, Difference and Desire* (London: ICA, 1995).

Monika Fludernik, ed., *Hybridity and Postcolonialism: Twentieth-Century Indian Literature*
(Tübingen: Stauffenberg, 1998).

Henry Louis Gates, 'Critical Fanonism', *Critical Inquiry* 17 (Spring 1991): 457–70.

Lewis R. Gordon, *Fanon and the Crisis of European Man* (New York and London:
Routledge, 1995).

Lewis R. Gordon, T. Denean Sharpley-Whiting and Renée T. White, eds., *Fanon: A Critical
Reader* (Oxford: Blackwell, 1996).

Bart Moore-Gilbert, *Postcolonial Theory: Contexts, Practices, Politics* (London: Verso, 1997).

Wilson Harris, *Tradition, the Writer and Society* (London: New Beacon, 1973).

Ania Loomba, *Colonialism / Postcolonialism* (London: Routledge, 1998).

Richard C. Onwuanibe, *A Critique of Revolutionary Humanism: Frantz Fanon* (St Louis:
Warren H. Green, 1983).

Benita Parry, 'Problems in Current Theories of Colonial Discourse', *Oxford Literary
Review* 9 (1–2): 27–58 (also in *The Post-Colonial Studies Reader*, eds. Bill Ashcroft,
Gareth Griffiths and Helen Tiffin (London: Routledge, 1995)).

Benita Parry, 'Signs of Our Times: Discussion of Homi Bhabha's *The Location of Culture*',
Third Text 28/29 (Autumn / Winter, 1994): 5–24 (also in *The Third Text Reader on Art,
Culture and Theory*, eds. Rasheed Araaen, Sean Cubitt and Ziauddin Sarda (New York:
Continuum, 2002), pp. 243–55).

Cedric Robinson, 'The Appropriation of Frantz Fanon', *Race and Class* 35(1) (1993):
79–9.

Cedric Robinson, *Black Marxism: The Making of the Black Radical Tradition* (London: Zed
Press, 1983).

Edward Said, *Orientalism* (London: Routledge & Kegan Paul, 1978).

Ato Sekyi-Oto, *Fanon's Dialectic of Experience* (Cambridge, MA: Harvard University
Press, 1996).

Gayatri Chakravorty Spivak, *A Critique of Postcolonial Reason* (Cambridge, MA: Harvard
University Press, 1999).

Patrick Williams and Laura Chrisman, eds., *Colonial Discourse and Post-Colonial Theory*
(Hemel Hempstead: Harvester Wheatsheaf, 1993).

Robert J. Young, *White Mythologies: Writing History and Writing the West* (London:
Routledge, 1990), esp. 'The Ambivalence of Bhabha', pp. 141–56.

Homi Bhabha, 'Interrogating Identity: Frantz Fanon and the Postcolonial Prerogative' (1990), *The Location of Culture* (London: Routledge, 1994), pp. 40–65.

I

To read Fanon is to experience the sense of division that prefigures – and fissures – the emergence of a truly radical thought that never dawns without casting an uncertain dark. Fanon is the purveyor of the transgressive and transitional truth. He may yearn for the total transformation of Man and Society, but he speaks most effectively from the uncertain interstices of historical change: from the area of ambivalence between race and sexuality; out of an unresolved contradiction between culture and class; from deep within the struggle of psychic representation and social reality. His voice is most clearly heard in the subversive turn of a familiar term, in the silence of sudden rupture: '*The Negro is not. Any more than the white man.*'[1] The awkward division that breaks his line of thought keeps alive the dramatic and enigmatic sense of change. That familiar alignment of colonial subjects – Black/White, Self/Other – is disturbed with one brief pause and the traditional grounds of racial identity are dispersed, whenever they are found to rest in the narcissistic myths of negritude or white cultural supremacy. It is this palpable pressure of division and displacement that pushes Fanon's writing to the edge of things – the cutting edge that reveals no ultimate radiance but, in his words, 'exposed an utterly naked declivity where an authentic upheaval can be born'.[2]

The psychiatric hospital at Blida-Joinville is one such place where, in the divided world of French Algeria, Fanon discovered the impossibility of his mission as a colonial psychiatrist:

> If psychiatry is the medical technique that aims to enable man no longer to be a stranger to his environment, I owe it to myself to affirm that the Arab, permanently an alien in his own country, lives in a state of absolute depersonalization. . . . The social structure existing in Algeria was hostile to any attempt to put the individual back where he belonged.[3]

The extremity of this colonial alienation of the person – this end of the 'idea' of the individual – produces a restless urgency in Fanon's search for a conceptual form appropriate to the social antagonism of the colonial relation. The body of his work splits between a Hegelian–Marxist dialectic, a phenomenological affirmation of Self and Other and the psychoanalytic ambivalence of the Unconscious. In his desperate, doomed search for a dialectic of deliverance Fanon explores the edge of these modes of thought: his Hegelianism restores hope to history; his existentialist evocation of the 'I' restores the presence of the marginalized; his psychoanalytic framework illumin-ates the madness of racism, the pleasure of pain, the agonistic fantasy of political power.

As Fanon attempts such audacious, often impossible, transformations of truth and value, the jagged testimony of colonial dislocation, its displacement of time and person, its defilement of culture and territory, refuses the ambition of any total theory of colonial oppression. The Antillean *évolué* cut to the quick by the glancing look of a frightened, confused, white child; the stereotype of the native fixed at the shifting boundaries between barbarism and civility; the insatiable fear and desire for the Negro: 'Our women are at the mercy of Negroes... God knows how they make love';[4] the deep cultural fear of the black figured in the psychic trembling of Western sexuality – it is these signs and symptoms of the colonial condition that drive Fanon from one conceptual scheme to another, while the colonial relation takes shape in the gaps between them, articulated to the intrepid engagements of his style. As Fanon's texts unfold, the scientific fact comes to be aggressed by the experience of the street; sociological observations are intercut with literary artefacts, and the poetry of liberation is brought up short against the leaden, deadening prose of the colonized world.

What is the distinctive *force* of Fanon's vision? It comes, I believe, from the tradition of the oppressed, the language of a revolutionary awareness that, as Walter Benjamin suggests, 'the state of emergency in which we live is not the exception but the rule. We must attain to a concept of history that is in keeping with this insight.'[5] And the state of emergency is also always a state of *emergence*. The struggle against colonial oppression not only changes the direction of Western history, but challenges its historicist idea of time as a progressive, ordered whole. The analysis of colonial depersonalization not only alienates the Enlightenment idea of 'Man', but challenges the transparency of social reality, as a pre-given image of human knowledge. If the order of Western historicism is disturbed in the colonial state of emergency, even more deeply disturbed is the social and psychic representation of the human subject. For the very nature of humanity becomes estranged in the colonial condition and from that 'naked declivity' it emerges, not as an assertion of will nor as an evocation of freedom, but as an enigmatic questioning. With a question that echoes Freud's '*What does woman want?*', Fanon turns to confront the colonized world. 'What does a man want?' he asks, in the introduction to *Black Skin, White Masks*; 'What does the black man want?'

To this loaded question where cultural alienation bears down on the ambivalence of psychic identification, Fanon responds with an agonizing performance of self-images:

> I had to meet the white man's eyes. An unfamiliar weight burdened me. In the white world the man of color encounters difficulties in the development of his bodily schema.... I was battered down by tom-toms, cannibalism, intellectual deficiency, fetishism, racial defects. ... I took myself far off from my own presence. ... What else could it be for me but an amputation, an excision, a haemorrhage that spattered my whole body with black blood?[6]

From within the metaphor of vision complicit with a Western metaphysic of Man emerges the displacement of the colonial relation. The black presence runs the representative narrative of Western personhood: its past tethered to treacherous stereotypes of primitivism and degeneracy will not produce a history of civil progress, a space for the *Socius*; its present, dismembered and dislocated, will not contain the image of identity that is questioned in the dialectic of mind/body and resolved in the epistemology of appearance and reality. The white man's eyes break up the black man's body and in that act of epistemic violence its own frame of reference is transgressed, its field of vision disturbed.

'What does the black man *want?*' Fanon insists, and in privileging the psychic dimension he not only changes what we understand by a *political* demand but transforms the very means by which we recognize and identify its *human agency*. Fanon is not principally posing the question of political oppression as the violation of a human essence, although he lapses into such a lament in his more existential moments. He is not raising the question of colonial man in the universalist terms of the liberal–humanist (How does colonialism deny the Rights of Man?); nor is he posing an ontological question about Man's being (*Who* is the alienated colonial man?). Fanon's question is addressed not to such a unified notion of history nor to such a unitary concept of man. It is one of the original and disturbing qualities of *Black Skin, White Masks* that it rarely historicizes the colonial experience. There is no master narrative or realist perspective that provides a background of social and historical facts against which emerge the problems of the individual or collective psyche. Such a traditional sociological align-ment of Self and Society or History and Psyche is rendered questionable in Fanon's identification of the colonial subject who is historicized in the heterogeneous assem-blage of the texts of history, literature, science, myth. The colonial subject is always 'overdetermined from without', Fanon writes.[7] It is through image and fantasy – those orders that figure transgressively on the borders of history and the unconscious – that Fanon most profoundly evokes the colonial condition.

In articulating the problem of colonial cultural alienation in the psychoanalytic language of demand and desire, Fanon radically questions the formation of both individual and social authority as they come to be developed in the discourse of social sovereignty. The social virtues of historical rationality, cultural cohesion, the autonomy of individual consciousness assume an immediate, Utopian identity with the subjects on whom they confer a civil status. The civil state is the ultimate expression of the innate ethical and rational bent of the human mind; the social instinct is the progressive destiny of human nature, the necessary transition from Nature to Culture. The direct access from individual interests to social authority is objectified in the representative structure of a General Will – Law or Culture – where Psyche and Society mirror each other, transparently translating their difference, without loss, into a historical totality. Forms of social and psychic alienation and aggression – madness, self-hate, treason, violence – can never be acknowledged as determinate and constitutive conditions of civil authority, or as the ambivalent effects of the social instinct itself. They are always explained away as alien presences, occlusions of historical progress, the ultimate misrecognition of Man.

For Fanon such a myth of Man and Society is fundamentally undermined in the colonial situation. Everyday life exhibits a 'constellation of delirium' that mediates the normal social relations of its subjects: 'The Negro enslaved by his inferiority, the white man enslaved by his superiority alike behave in accordance with a neurotic orienta-tion.'[8] Fanon's demand for a psychoanalytic explanation emerges from the perverse reflections of civil virtue in the alienating acts of colonial governance: the visibility of cultural mummification in the colonizer's avowed ambition to civilize or modernize the native that results in 'archaic inert institutions [that function] under the oppressor's supervision like a caricature of formerly fertile institutions';[9] or the validity of violence in the very definition of the colonial social space; or the viability of the febrile, phantasmic images of racial hatred that come to be absorbed and acted out in the wisdom of the West. These interpositions, indeed collaborations of political and psychic violence *within* civic virtue, alienation within identity, drive Fanon to describe the splitting of the colonial space of consciousness and society as marked by a 'Manichaean delirium'.

The representative figure of such a perversion, I want to suggest, is the image of post-Enlightenment man tethered to, *not* confronted by, his dark reflection, the shadow of colonized man, that splits his presence, distorts his outline, breaches his boundaries, repeats his action at a distance, disturbs and divides the very time of his being. The ambivalent identification of the racist world – moving on two planes without being in the least embarrassed by it, as Sartre says of the anti-Semitic consciousness – turns on the idea of man as his alienated image; not Self and Other but the otherness of the Self inscribed in the perverse palimpsest of colonial identity. And it is that bizarre figure of desire, which splits along the axis on which it turns, that compels Fanon to put the psychoanalytic question of the desire of the subject to the historic condition of colonial man.

'What is often called the black soul is a white man's artefact,' Fanon writes.[10] This transference speaks otherwise. It reveals the deep psychic uncertainty of the colonial relation itself: its split representations stage the division of body and soul that enacts the artifice of identity, a division that cuts across the fragile skin – black and white – of individual and social authority. Three conditions that underlie an understanding of the *process of identification* in the analytic of desire emerge.

First: to exist is to be called into being in relation to an otherness, its look or locus. It is a demand that reaches outward to an external object and as Jacqueline Rose writes, 'It is the relation of this demand to the place of the object it claims that becomes the basis for identification.'[11] This process is visible in the exchange of looks between native and settler that structures their psychic relation in the paranoid fantasy of boundless possession and its familiar language of reversal: 'When their glances meet he [the settler] ascertains bitterly, always on the defensive, "They want to take our place." It is true for there is no native who does not dream at least once a day of setting himself up in the settler's place.'[12] It is always in relation to the place of the Other that colonial desire is articulated: the phantasmic space of possession that no one subject can singly or fixedly occupy, and therefore permits the dream of the inversion of roles.

Second: the very place of identification, caught in the tension of demand and desire, is a space of splitting. The fantasy of the native is precisely to occupy the master's place while keeping his place in the slave's *avenging* anger. 'Black skin, white masks' is not a neat division; it is a doubling, dissembling image of being in at least two places at once that makes it impossible for the devalued, insatiable *évolué* (an abandonment neurotic, Fanon claims) to accept the colonizer's invitation to identity: 'You're a doctor, a writer, a student, you're *different*, you're one of *us*.' It is precisely in that ambivalent use of 'different' – to be different from those that are different makes you the same – that the Unconscious speaks of the form of otherness, the tethered shadow of deferral and displacement. It is not the colonialist Self or the colonized Other, but the disturbing distance in-between that constitutes the figure of colonial otherness – the white man's artifice inscribed on the black man's body. It is in relation to this impossible object that the liminal problem of colonial identity and its vicissitudes emerges.

Finally, the question of identification is never the affirmation of a pre-given identity, never a *self*-fulfilling prophecy – it is always the production of an image of identity and the transformation of the subject in assuming that image. The demand of identification

– that is, to be *for* an Other – entails the representation of the subject in the differentiating order of otherness. Identification, as we inferred from the preceding illustrations, is
always the return of an image of identity that bears the mark of splitting in the Other
place from which it comes. For Fanon, like Lacan, the primary moments of such a
repetition of the self lie in the desire of the look and the limits of language. The
'atmosphere of certain uncertainty' that surrounds the body certifies its existence and
threatens its dismemberment.

II

Listen to my friend, the Bombay poet Adil Jussawalla, writing of the 'missing person'
that haunts the identity óf the postcolonial bourgeoisie:

> No Satan
> warmed in the electric coils of his creatures
> or Gunga Din
> will make him come before you.
> To see an invisible man or a missing person,
> trust no Eng. Lit. That
> puffs him up, narrows his eyes,
> scratches his fangs. Caliban
> is still not IT.
> But faintly pencilled
> behind a shirt . . .
> . . .
> savage of no sensational paint,
> fangs cancelled.[13]

As that voice falters listen to its echo in the verse of a black woman, descendant of
slaves, writing of the diaspora:

> We arrived in the Northern Hemisphere
> when summer was set in its way
> running from the flames that lit the sky
> over the Plantation.
> We were a straggle bunch of immigrants
> in a lily white landscape.
> . . .
> One day I learnt
> a secret art,
> Invisible-Ness, it was called.
> I think it worked
> as even now you look
> but never see me . . .
> Only my eyes will remain to watch and to haunt,
> and to turn your dreams
> to chaos.[14]

As these images fade, and the empty eyes endlessly hold their menacing gaze, listen finally to Edward Said's attempt to historicize their chaos of identity:

> One aspect of the electronic, postmodern world is that there has been a reinforcement of the stereotypes by which the Orient is viewed. . . . If the world has become immediately accessible to a Western citizen living in the electronic age, the Orient too has drawn nearer to him, and is now less a myth perhaps than a place criss-crossed by Western, especially American interests.[15]

I use these postcolonial portraits because they seize on the vanishing point of two familiar traditions in the discourse of identity: the philosophical tradition of identity as the process of self-reflection in the mirror of (human) nature; and the anthropological view of the difference of human identity as located in the division of Nature/Culture. In the postcolonial text the problem of identity returns as a persistent questioning of the frame, the space of representation, where the image – missing person, invisible eye, Oriental stereotype – is confronted with its difference, its Other. This is neither the glassy essence of Nature, to use Richard Rorty's image, nor the leaden voice of 'ideological interpellation', as Louis Althusser suggests.

What is so graphically enacted in the moment of colonial identification is the splitting of the subject in its historical place of utterance: '*No* Satan . . . /or Gunga Din/will make him come before you/*To see* an invisible man or a missing person,/trust *no* Eng. Lit.' (my emphases). What these repeated negations of identity dramatize, in their elision of the seeing eye that must contemplate what is missing or invisible, is the impossibility of claiming an origin for the Self (or Other) within a tradition of representation that conceives of identity as the satisfaction of a totalizing, plenitudinous object of vision. By disrupting the stability of the ego, expressed in the equivalence between image and identity, the secret art of invisibleness of which the migrant poet speaks changes the very terms of our recognition of the person.

This change is precipitated by the peculiar temporality whereby the subject cannot be apprehended without the absence or invisibility that constitutes it – 'as even now you look/but never see me' – so that the subject speaks, and is seen, from where it is *not*; and the migrant woman can subvert the perverse satisfaction of the racist, masculinist gaze that disavowed her presence, by presenting it with an anxious absence, a counter-gaze that turns the discriminatory look, which denies her cultural and sexual difference, back on itself.

The familiar space of the Other (in the process of identification) develops a graphic historical and cultural specificity in the splitting of the postcolonial or migrant subject. In place of that 'I' – institutionalized in the visionary, authorial ideologies of *Eng. Lit.* or the notion of 'experience' in the empiricist accounts of slave history – there emerges the challenge to see what is invisible, the look that cannot 'see me', a certain problem of the object of the gaze that constitutes a problematic referent for the language of the Self. The elision of the eye, represented in a narrative of negation and repetition – *no* . . . *no* . . . *never* – insists that the phrase of identity cannot be spoken, except by putting the eye/I in the impossible position of enunciation. *To see* a missing person, or *to look* at Invisibleness, is to emphasize the subject's *transitive* demand for a *direct* object of self-reflection, a point of presence that would maintain its privileged enunciatory position *qua subject.* To see a *missing person* is to *transgress* that demand; the 'I' in the position of mastery is, at *that same time*, the place of its absence, its *re*-presentation. We witness the alienation of the eye through the sound of the signifier as the scopic desire (to look/to be looked at) emerges and is erased in the *feint of writing*:

> But faintly pencilled
> behind a shirt,
> a trendy jacket or tie
> *if* he catches your eye,
> he'll come screaming at you like a jet –
> savage of no sensational paint,
> fangs cancelled.

Why does the faintly pencilled person fail to catch your eye? What is the secret of Invisibleness that enables the woman migrant to look without being seen?

What is interrogated is not simply the image of the person, but the discursive and disciplinary place from which questions of identity are strategically and institutionally posed. Through the progress of this poem 'you' are continually positioned in the space between a range of contradictory places that coexist. So that you find yourself at the point at which the Orientalist stereotype is evoked and erased *at the same time*, in the place where Eng. Lit. is *entstellt* in the ironic mimicry of its Indo-Anglican repetition. And this space of reinscription must be thought outside of those metaphysical philosophies of self-doubt, where the otherness of identity is the anguished *presence* within the Self of an existentialist agony that emerges when you look perilously through a glass darkly.

What is profoundly unresolved, even erased, in the discourses of poststructuralism is that *perspective of depth* through which the authenticity of identity comes to be reflected in the glassy metaphorics of the mirror and its mimetic or realist narratives. Shifting the frame of identity from the field of vision to the space of writing interrogates the third dimension that gives profundity to the representation of Self and Other – that depth of perspective that cineastes call the fourth wall; literary theorists describe it as the transparency of realist metanarratives. Barthes brilliantly diagnoses this as *l'effet du réel*, the 'profound, geological dimension'[16] of signification, achieved by arresting the linguistic sign in its *symbolic* function. The bilateral space of the symbolic consciousness, Barthes writes, massively privileges *resemblance*, constructs an *analogical* relation between signifier and signified that ignores the question of form, and creates a vertical dimension within the sign. In this scheme the signifier is always predetermined by the signified – that conceptual or real space that is placed prior to, and outside of, the act of signification.

From our point of view, this verticality is significant for the light it sheds on that *dimension of depth* that provides the language of Identity with its sense of reality – a measure of the 'me', which emerges from an acknowledgement of my inwardness, the depth of my character, the profundity of my person, to mention only a few of those qualities through which we commonly articulate our self-consciousness. My argument about the importance of *depth* in the representation of a unified image of the self is borne out by the most decisive and influential formulation on personal identity in the English empiricist tradition.

John Locke's famous criteria for the continuity of consciousness could quite legitimately be read in the symbolic register of resemblance and analogy. For the sameness of a rational being requires a consciousness of the past which is crucial to the argument – 'as far as this consciousness can be extended *backwards* to any past action or thought, so far reaches the identity of that person' – and is precisely the unifying third dimension. The agency of *depth* brings together in an analogical relation (dismissive of the differences that construct temporality and signification) 'that same consciousness uniting those distant actions into the same person, *whatever substances contributed to their production*' (my emphasis).[17]

Barthes's description of the sign-as-symbol is conveniently analogous to the language we use to designate identity. At the same time, it sheds light on the concrete linguistic concepts with which we can grasp how the language of personhood comes to be invested with a visuality or visibility of depth. This makes the moment of self-consciousness at once refracted and transparent; the question of identity always poised uncertainly, tenebrously, between shadow and substance. The symbolic consciousness gives the sign (of the Self) a sense of autonomy or solitariness 'as if it stands by itself in the world' privileging an individuality and a unitariness whose integrity is expressed in a certain richness of agony and anomie. Barthes calls it a mythic prestige, almost totemic in 'its form [which is] constantly exceeded by the power and movement of its content; . . . much less a codified form of communication than an (affective) instrument of participation.'[18]

This image of human identity and, indeed, human identity as *image* – both familiar frames or mirrors of selfhood that speak from deep within Western culture – are inscribed in the sign of resemblance. The analogical relation unifies the experience of self-consciousness by finding, within the mirror of nature, the symbolic certitude of the sign of culture based 'on an analogy with the compulsion to believe when staring at an object'.[19] This, as Rorty writes, is part of the West's obsession that our primary relation to objects and ourselves is analogous to visual perception. Pre-eminent among these representations has been the reflection of the self that develops in the symbolic consciousness of the sign. It marks out the discursive space from which *The real Me* emerges (initially as an assertion of the authenticity of the person) and then lingers on to reverberate – *The real Me?* – as a questioning of identity.

My purpose here is to define the space of the inscription or writing of identity – beyond the visual depths of Barthes's symbolic sign. The experience of the disseminating self-image goes beyond representation as the analogical consciousness of resemblance. This is not a form of dialectical contradiction, the antagonistic consciousness of master and slave, that can be sublated and transcended. The impasse or aporia of consciousness that seems to be the representative postmodernist experience is a peculiar strategy of doubling.

Each time the encounter with identity occurs at the point at which something exceeds the frame of the image, it eludes the eye, evacuates the self as site of identity and autonomy and – most important – leaves a resistant trace, a stain of the subject, a sign of resistance. We are no longer confronted with an ontological problem of being but with the discursive strategy of the moment of interrogation, a moment in which the demand for identification becomes, primarily, a response to other questions of signification and desire, culture and politics.

In place of the symbolic consciousness that gives the sign of identity its integrity and unity, its *depth*, we are faced with a dimension of doubling; a spatialization of the subject, that is occluded in the illusory perspective of what I have called the 'third dimension' of the mimetic frame or visual image of identity. The figure of the double – to which I now turn – cannot be contained within the analogical sign of resemblance; as Barthes said, this developed its totemic, vertical dimension only because 'what interests it in the sign is the signified: the signifier is always a determined element.'[20] For poststructuralist discourse, the priority (and play) of the signifier reveals the space of doubling (not depth) that is the very articulatory principle of discourse. It is through that space of enunciation that problems of meaning and being enter the discourses of poststructuralism, as the problematic of subjection and identification.

What emerges in the preceding poems, as the line drawing of trendy jacket and tie, or the eerie, avengeful disembodied eye, must not be read as a revelation of some suppressed truth of the postcolonial psyche/subject. In the world of double inscriptions that we have now entered, in this space of *writing*, there can be no such immediacy of a visualist perspective, no such face-to-face epiphanies in the mirror of nature. On one level, what confronts you, the reader, in the incomplete portrait of the postcolonial bourgeois – who looks uncannily like the metropolitan intellectual – is the ambivalence of your desire for the Other: '*You! hypocrite lecteur! – mon semblable, – mon frère!*'

That disturbance of your voyeuristic look enacts the complexity and contradictions of your desire to see, to fix cultural difference in a containable, *visible* object. The desire for the Other is doubled by the desire in language, which *splits the difference* between Self and Other so that both positions are partial; neither is sufficient unto itself. As I have just shown in the portrait of the missing person, the very question of identification only emerges *in-between* disavowal and designation. It is performed in the agonistic struggle between the epistemological, visual demand for a knowledge of the Other, and its representation in the act of articulation and enunciation.

> Look, a Negro ... Mama, see the Negro! I'm frightened ... I could no longer laugh, because I already know where there were legends, stories, history, and above all *historicity.* ... Then, assailed at various points, the corporeal schema crumbled, its place taken by a racial epidermal schema. ... It was no longer a question of being aware of my body in the third person but in a triple person. ... I was responsible for my body, for my race, for my ancestors.[21]

Fanon's *Black Skin, White Masks* reveals the doubling of identity: the difference between personal identity as an intimation of reality, or an intuition of being, and the psychoanalytic problem of identification that always begs the question of the subject: 'What does a man want?' The emergence of the human subject as socially and psychically authenticated depends on the *negation* of an originary narrative of fulfilment, or of an imaginary coincidence between individual interest or instinct and the General Will. Such binary, two-part, identities function in a kind of narcissistic reflection of the One in the Other, confronted in the language of desire by the psychoanalytic process of identification. For identification, identity is never an a priori, nor a finished product; it is only ever the problematic process of access to an image of totality. The discursive

conditions of this psychic image of identification will be clarified if we think of the
perilous perspective of the concept of the image itself. For the image – as point of
identification – marks the site of an ambivalence. Its representation is always spatially
split – it makes *present* something that is *absent* – and temporally deferred: it is the
representation of a time that is always elsewhere, a repetition.

The image is only ever an *appurtenance* to authority and identity; it must never be read
mimetically as the appearance of a reality. The access to the image of identity is only
ever possible in the *negation* of any sense of originality or plenitude; the process of
displacement and differentiation (absence/presence, representation/repetition) renders
it a liminal reality. The image is at once a metaphoric substitution, an illusion of
presence, and by that same token a metonym, a sign of its absence and loss. It is
precisely from this edge of meaning and being, from this shifting boundary of otherness
within identity, that Fanon asks: 'What does a *black* man want?'

> When it encounters resistance from the other, self-consciousness undergoes the experience
> of desire. . . . As soon as I desire I ask to be considered. I am not merely here and now,
> sealed into thingness. I am for somewhere else and for something else. I demand that
> notice be taken of my negating activity in so far as I pursue something other than life. . . .
> I occupied space. I moved towards the other . . . and the evanescent other, hostile, but
> not opaque, transparent, not there, disappeared. Nausea.[22]

From that overwhelming emptiness of nausea Fanon makes his answer: the black man
wants the objectifying confrontation with otherness; in the colonial psyche there is an
unconscious disavowal of the negating, splitting moment of desire. The place of the
Other must not be imaged, as Fanon sometimes suggests, as a fixed phenomenological
point opposed to the self, that represents a culturally alien consciousness. The Other
must be seen as the necessary negation of a primordial identity – cultural or psychic –
that introduces the system of differentiation which enables the cultural to be signified as
a linguistic, symbolic, historic reality. If, as I have suggested, the subject of desire is
never simply a Myself, then the Other is never simply an *It-self*, a front of identity, truth
or misrecognition.

As a principle of identification, the Other bestows a degree of objectivity, but its
representation – be it the social process of the Law or the psychic process of the Oedipus
– is always ambivalent, disclosing a lack. For instance, the common, conversational
distinction between the letter and spirit of the Law displays the otherness of Law itself;
the ambiguous grey area between Justice and judicial procedure is, quite literally, a
conflict of judgement. In the language of psychoanalysis, the Law of the Father or the
paternal metaphor cannot be taken at its word. It is a process of substitution and
exchange that inscribes a normative, normalizing place for the subject; but that metaphoric access to identity is exactly the place of prohibition and repression, a conflict
of authority. Identification, as it is spoken in the *desire of the Other*, is always a question of
interpretation, for it is the elusive assignation of myself with a one-self, the elision of
person and place.

If the differentiating force of the Other is the process of the subject's signification in
language and society's objectification in Law, then how can the Other disappear? Can
desire, the moving spirit of the subject, ever evanesce?

III

Lacan's excellent, if cryptic, suggestion that 'the Other is a dual entry matrix'[23] should be understood as the partial erasure of the *depth perspective* of the symbolic sign; through the circulation of the signifier in its doubling and displacing, the signifier permits the sign no reciprocal, binary division of form/content, superstructure/infrastructure, self/ other. It is only by understanding the ambivalence and the antagonism of the desire of the Other that we can avoid the increasingly facile adoption of the notion of a homogenized Other, for a celebratory, oppositional politics of the margins or minorities.

The performance of the doubleness or splitting of the subject is enacted in the *writing* of the poems I have quoted; it is evident in the play on the metonymic figures of 'missing' and 'invisibleness' around which their questioning of identity turns. It is articulated in those iterative instances that simultaneously mark the possibility and impossibility of identity, presence through absence. 'Only my eyes will remain to watch and to haunt,' warns Meiling Jin as that threatening part object, the disembodied eye – the evil eye – becomes the subject of a violent discourse of *ressentiment*. Here, phantasmic and (pre)figurative rage erases the naturalistic identities of I and We that narrate a more conventional, even realist history of colonial exploitation and metropolitan racism, within the poem.

The moment of seeing that is arrested in the evil eye inscribes a timelessness, or a freezing of time – 'remain/to watch and to haunt' – that can only be represented in the destruction of the *depth* associated with the sign of symbolic consciousness. It is a depth that comes from what Barthes describes as the *analogical* relation between superficial form and massive *Abgrund*: the 'relation of form and content [as] ceaselessly renewed by time (history); the superstructure overwhelmed by the infrastructure, without our ever being able to grasp the structure itself.'[24]

The eyes that remain – the eyes as a kind of *remainder*, producing an iterative process – cannot be part of this plenitudinous and progressive renewal of time or history. They are the signs of a structure of *writing* history, a *history* of the poetics of postcolonial diaspora, that the symbolic consciousness could never grasp. Most significantly, these partial eyes bear witness to a woman's writing of the postcolonial condition. Their circulation and repetition frustrate both the voyeuristic desire for the fixity of sexual difference and the fetishistic desire for racist stereotypes. The gaze of the evil eye alienates *both* the narratorial I of the slave and the surveillant eye of the master. It unsettles any simplistic polarities or binarisms in identifying the exercise of power – Self/Other – and erases the analogical dimension in the articulation of sexual difference. It is empty of that depth of verticality that creates a totemic resemblance of form and content (*Abgrund*) ceaselessly renewed and replenished by the groundspring of history. The evil eye – like the missing person – is nothing in itself; and it is this *structure of difference* that produces the hybridity of race and sexuality in the postcolonial discourse.

The elision of identity in these tropes of the 'secret art of Invisibleness' from which these writers speak is not an ontology of lack that, on its other side, becomes a nostalgic demand for a liberatory, non-repressed identity. It is the uncanny space and time *between* those two moments of being, their incommensurable differences – if such a place can be imagined – signified in the process of repetition, that give the evil eye or the missing person their meaning. Meaningless in/as themselves, these figures initiate the rhetorical excess of social reality and the psychic reality of social fantasy. Their poetic and political force develops through a certain strategy of duplicity or doubling (not resemblance, in Barthes's sense), which Lacan has elaborated as 'the process of gap' within which the relation of subject to Other is produced.[25] The primary duplicity of the missing person pencilled in before your eyes, or the woman's eyes that watch and haunt, is this: although these images emerge with a certain fixity and finality in the *present*, as if they are the last word on the subject, they cannot identify or interpellate identity as *presence*. This is because they are created in the ambivalence of a double time of iteration that, in Derrida's felicitous phrase, 'baffles the process of appearing by dislocating any orderly time at the center of the present'.[26] The effect of such baffling, in both poems, is to initiate a principle of undecidability in the signification of part and whole, past and present, self and Other, such that there can be no negation or transcendence of difference.

The naming of the missing person as 'Savage of no sensational paint' is a case in point. The phrase, spoken at the end of Adil Jussawalla's poem, neither simply returns us to the Orientalist discourse of stereotypes and exotica – Gunga Din – enshrined in the history of Eng. Lit., nor allows us to rest with the line drawing of the missing person. The reader is positioned – together with the enunciation of the question of identity – in an undecidable space between 'desire and fulfillment, between perpetration and its recollection. ... Neither future nor present, but between the two.'[27] The repetition of the Orientalia and their imperialist past are re-presented, made present semantically, within the same time and utterance as that in which their representations are negated syntactically – '*no* sensational paint/*Fangs cancelled*.' From that erasure, in the repetition of that 'no', without being articulated at all in the phrase itself, emerges the faintly pencilled presence of the missing person who, *in absentia*, is both present in, and constitutive of, the savagery. Can you tell the postcolonial bourgeois and the Western intellectual elite apart? How does the repetition of a part of speech – no! – turn the image of civility into the double of savagery? What part does the feint of writing play in evoking these faint figures of identity? And, finally, where do *we* stand in that uncanny echo between what may be described as the attenuation of identity and its simulacra?

These questions demand a double answer. In each of them I have posed a theoretical problem in terms of its political and social effects. It is the boundary between them that I have tried to explore in my vacillations between the texture of poetry and a certain textuality of identity. One answer to my questions would be to say that we now stand at the point in the poststructuralist argument where we can see the doubleness of its own grounds: the uncanny sameness-in-difference, or the alterity of Identity of which these theories speak, and from which, in forked tongues, they communicate with each other to constitute those discourses that we name postmodernist. The rhetoric of repetition or doubling that I have traced displays the art of *becoming* through a certain metonymic logic disclosed in the 'evil eye' or the 'missing person'. Metonymy, a figure of contiguity that substitutes a part for a whole (an eye for an I), must not be read as a form of simple substitution or equivalence. Its circulation of part and whole, identity and difference, must be understood as a *double movement* that follows what Derrida calls the logic or play of the 'supplement':

If it represents and makes an image, it is by the anterior default of a presence. Compensatory and vicarious, the supplement [evil eye] is an adjunct, a subaltern instance which *takes – the – place*. As substitute ... [missing person] ... it produces no relief, its place is assigned in the structure by the mark of an emptiness. Somewhere something can be filled up of itself ... only by allowing itself to be filled through sign and proxy.[28]

Having illustrated, through my reading of the poems above, the supplementary nature of the subject, I want to focus on the subaltern instance of metonymy, which is the *proxy* of both presence and the present: time (*takes place on*) and space (*takes place of* ...) at once. To conceptualize this complex doubling of time and space, as the site of enunciation, and the temporal conditionality of social discourse, is both the thrill and the threat of the poststructuralist and postmodernist discourses. How different is this representation of the sign from the symbolic consciousness where, as Barthes said, the relation of form and content is ceaselessly renewed by Time (as the *Abgrund* of the historical)? The evil eye, which seeks to outstare linear, continuist history and turn its progressive dream into nightmarish chaos, is exemplary once more. What Meiling Jin calls 'the secret art of Invisible-Ness' creates a crisis in the representation of personhood and, at the critical moment, initiates the possibility of political subversion. Invisibility erases the self-presence of that 'I' in terms of which traditional concepts of political agency and narrative mastery function. What *takes (the) place*, in Derrida's supplementary sense, is the disembodied evil eye, the subaltern instance, that wreaks its revenge by circulating, *without being seen*. It cuts across the boundaries of master and slave; it opens up a space *in-between* the poem's two locations, the Southern Hemisphere of slavery and the Northern Hemisphere of diaspora and migration, which then become uncannily doubled in the phantasmic scenario of the political unconscious. This doubling resists the traditional causal link that explains contemporary metropolitan racism as a result of the historical prejudices of imperialist nations. What it does suggest is the possibility of a new understanding of both forms of racism, based on their shared symbolic and spatial structures – Fanon's Manichaean structure – articulated within different temporal, cultural and power relations.

The *anti-dialectical* movement of the subaltern instance subverts any binary or sublatory ordering of power and sign; it defers the object of the look – 'as even now you look/but never see me' – and endows it with a strategic motion, which we may here, analogously, name the movement of the death drive. The evil eye, which is nothing in itself, exists in its lethal traces or effects as a form of iteration that arrests time – death/chaos – and initiates a space of *intercutting* that articulates politics/psyche, sexuality/race. It does this in a relation that is differential and strategic rather than originary, ambivalent rather than accumulative, doubling rather than dialectical. The play of the evil eye is camouflaged, invisible in the common, on-going activity of looking – making present, while it is implicated in the petrifying, unblinking gaze that falls Medusa-like on its victims – dealing death, extinguishing both presence and the present. There is a specifically feminist re-presentation of political subversion in this strategy of the evil eye. The disavowal of the position of the migrant woman – her social and political *invisibility* – is used by her in her secret art of revenge, *mimicry*. In that overlap of signification – in that fold of identification as cultural and sexual difference – the 'I' is the initial, initiatory signature of the subject; and the 'eye' (in its metonymic repetition) is the sign that initiates the terminal, arrest, death:

as even now you look
but never see me ...
Only my eyes will remain to haunt,
and to turn your dreams
to chaos.

It is in this overlapping space between the fading of identity and its faint inscription that I take my stand on the subject, amidst a celebrated gathering of poststructuralist thinkers. Although there are significant differences between them, I want to focus here on their attention to the place from which the subject speaks or is spoken.

For Lacan – who has used the arrest of the evil eye in his analysis of the gaze – this is the moment of 'temporal pulsation': '[The signifier in the field of the Other] petrif[ies] the subject in the same movement in which it calls the subject to speak as subject.'[29]

Foucault repeats something of the same uncanny movement of doubling when he elaborates on the 'quasi-invisibility of the statement':

> Perhaps it is like the over-familiar that constantly eludes one; those familiar transparencies, which although they conceal nothing in their density, are nevertheless not entirely clear. The enunciative level emerges in its very proximity. . . . It has this quasi-invisibility of the 'there is,' which is effaced in the very thing of which one can say: 'there is this or that thing. . . .' Language always seems to be inhabited by the other, the elsewhere, the distant; it is hollowed out by distance.[30]

Lyotard holds on to the pulsating beat of the time of utterance when he discusses the narrative of Tradition:

> Tradition is that which concerns time, not content. Whereas what the West wants from autonomy, invention, novelty, self-determination, is the opposite – to forget time and to preserve, and accumulate contents. To turn them into what we call history and to think that it progresses because it accumulates. On the contrary, in the case of popular traditions . . . nothing gets accumulated, that is the narratives must be repeated all the time because they are forgotten all the time. But what does not get forgotten is the temporal beat that does not stop sending the narratives to oblivion.
>
> . . .
>
> This is a situation of continuous embedding, which makes it impossible to find a first utterer.[31]

IV

I may be accused of a form of linguistic or theoretical formalism, of establishing a rule of metonymy or the supplement and laying down the oppressive, even universalist, law of difference or doubling. How does the poststructuralist attention to *écriture* and textuality influence my experience of myself? Not directly, I would answer, but then, have our fables of identity ever been unmediated by another; have they ever been more (or less) than a detour through the word of God, or the writ of Law, or the Name of the Father; the totem, the fetish, the telephone, the superego, the voice of the analyst, the closed ritual of the weekly confessional or the ever open ear of the monthly *coiffeuse*?

I am reminded of the problem of self-portraiture in Holbein's *The Ambassadors*, of which Lacan produces a startling reading. The two still figures stand at the centre of their world, surrounded by the accountrements of *vanitas* – a globe, a lute, books and compasses, unfolding wealth. They also stand in the moment of temporal instantaneity where the Cartesian subject emerges as the subjectifying relation of geometrical perspective, described above as the *depth* of the image of identity. But off-centre, in the foreground (violating the meaningful depths of the *Abgrund*), there is a flat spherical object, obliquely angled. As you walk away from the portrait and turn to leave, you see that the disc is a skull, the reminder (and remainder) of death, that makes visible nothing more than the alienation of the subject, the anamorphic ghost.[32]

Doesn't the logic of the supplement – in its repetition and doubling – produce a historylessness; a 'culture' of theory that makes it impossible to give meaning to historical specificity? This is a large question that I can only answer here by proxy, by citing a text remarkable for its postcolonial specificity and for its questioning of what we might mean *by* cultural specificity:

> A–'s a giggle now
> but on it Osiris, Ra.
> An अ an er . . . a cough,
> once spoking your valleys with light.
> But the a's here to stay.
> On it St Pancras station,
> the Indian and African railways.
> That's why you learn it today.
>   . . .
> 'Get back to your language,' they say.

These lines come from an early section of Adil Jussawalla's poem 'Missing Person'. They provide an insight into the fold between the cultural and linguistic conditions articulated in the textual economy that I have described as the metonymic or the supplementary. The discourse of poststructuralism has largely been spelled out in an intriguing repetition of *a*, whether it is Lacan's *petit object a* or Derrida's *différance*. Observe, then, the agency of this postcolonial *a*.

There is something supplementary about *a* that makes it the initial letter of the Roman alphabet and, at the same time, the indefinite article. What is dramatized in this circulation of the *a* is a double scene on a double stage, to borrow a phrase from Derrida. The A – with which the verse begins – is the sign of a linguistic objectivity, inscribed in the Indo-European language tree, institutionalized in the cultural disciplines of empire; and yet as the Hindi vowel अ, which is the first letter of the Hindi alphabet and is pronounced as 'er', testifies, the object of linguistic science is always already in an enunciatory process of cultural translation, showing up the hybridity of any genealogical or systematic filiation.

Listen: 'An अ an er . . . a cough': in the same time, we hear the *a* repeated in translation, not as an object of linguistics, but in the *act* of the colonial enunciation of cultural contestation. This double scene articulates the ellipsis . . . which marks the *différance* between the Hindi sign अ and the demotic English signifier – 'er, a cough'. It is through the emptiness of ellipsis that the difference of colonial culture is articulated as a *hybridity* acknowledging that all cultural specificity is belated, *different unto itself* – अ . . . er . . . ugh! Cultures come to be represented by virtue of the processes of iteration and translation through which their meanings are very vicariously addressed to – *through* – an Other. This erases any essentialist claims for the inherent authenticity or purity of cultures which, when inscribed in the naturalistic sign of symbolic consciousness frequently become political arguments for the hierarchy and ascendancy of powerful cultures.[33] It is in this hybrid gap, which produces no relief, that the colonial subject *takes place*, its subaltern position inscribed in that space of iteration where अ *takes (the) place of 'er'*.

If this sounds like a schematic, poststructuralist joke – 'it's all words, words, words . . .' – then I must remind you of the linguistic insistence in Clifford Geertz's influential statement that the experience of understanding other cultures is 'more like grasping a proverb, catching an illusion, seeing a joke [or as I have suggested reading a poem] than it is like achieving communion.'[34] My insistence on locating the postcolonial subject *within* the play of the subaltern instance of writing is an attempt to develop Derrida's passing remark that the history of the decentred subject and its dislocation of European metaphysics is concurrent with the emergence of the problematic of cultural difference within ethnology.[35] He acknowledges the political nature of this moment but leaves it to us to specify it in the postcolonial text:

> 'Wiped out,' they say.
> Turn left or right,
> there's millions like you up here,
> picking their way through refuse,
> looking for words they lost.
> You're your country's lost property
> with no office to claim you back.
> You're polluting our sounds. You're so rude.
> 'Get back to your language,' they say.[36]

Embedded in these statements is a cultural politics of diaspora and paranoia, of migration and discrimination, of anxiety and appropriation, which is unthinkable without attention to those metonymic or subaltern moments that structure the subject of writing and meaning. Without the doubleness that I described in the postcolonial play of the 'a अ', it would be difficult to understand the anxiety provoked by the hybridizing of language, activated in the anguish associated with vacillating *boundaries* – psychic, cultural, territorial – of which these verses speak. Where do you draw the line between languages? between cultures? between disciplines? between peoples?

I have suggested here that a subversive political line is drawn in a certain poetics of 'invisibility', 'ellipsis', the evil eye and the missing person – all instances of the 'subaltern' in the Derridean sense, and near enough to the sense that Gramsci gives the concept: '[not simply an oppressed group] but lacking autonomy, subjected to the influence or hegemony of another social group, not possessing one's own hegemonic position.'[37] It is with this difference between the two usages that notions of autonomy and domination within the hegemonic would have to be carefully rethought, in the light of what I have said about the *proxy*-mate nature of any claim to *presence* or autonomy. However, what is implicit in both concepts of the subaltern, as I read it, is a strategy of ambivalence in the structure of identification that occurs precisely in the elliptical *in-between*, where the shadow of the other falls upon the self.

From that shadow (in which the postcolonial *a* plays) emerges cultural difference as an *enunciative* category; opposed to relativistic notions of cultural diversity, or the exoticism of the 'diversity' of cultures. It is the 'between' that is articulated in the camouflaged subversion of the 'evil eye' and the transgressive mimicry of the 'missing person'. The force of cultural difference is, as Barthes once said of the practice of metonymy, 'the violation of a signifying *limit of space*, it permits on the very level of discourse, a counter-division of objects, usages, meanings, spaces and properties' (my emphasis).[38]

It is by placing the violence of the poetic sign *within* the threat of political violation that we can understand the powers of language. Then, we can grasp the importance of the imposition of the imperial *a* as the cultural condition for the very movement of empire, its *logomotion* – the colonial creation of the Indian and African railways as the poet wrote. Now, we can begin to see why the threat of the (mis)translation of अ and 'er', among the displaced and diasporic peoples who pick through the refuse, is a constant reminder to the postimperial West, of the hybridity of its mother tongue, and the heterogeneity of its national space.

V

In his analytic mode Fanon explores such questions of the ambivalence of colonial inscription and identification. The state of emergency from which he writes demands insurgent answers, more immediate identifications. Fanon frequently attempts a close correspondence between the *mise-en-scène* of unconscious fantasy and the phantoms of racist fear and hate that stalk the colonial scene; he turns from the ambivalences of identification to the antagonistic identities of political alienation and cultural discrimination. There are times when he is too quick to name the Other, to personalize its presence in the language of colonial racism – 'the real Other for the white man is and will continue to be the black man. And conversely.'[39] Restoring the dream to its proper political time and cultural space can, at times, blunt the edge of Fanon's brilliant illustrations of the complexity of the psychic projections in the pathological colonial relation. Jean Veneuse, the Antillean *évolué*, desires not merely to be in the place of the white man but compulsively seeks to look back and down on himself from that position. Equally, the white racist cannot merely deny what he fears and desires by projecting it on 'them'. Fanon sometimes forgets that social paranoia does not indefinitely authorize its projections. The compulsive, fantasmatic identification with a persecutory 'they' is accompanied, even undermined, by an emptying, an evacuation of the racist 'I' who projects.

Fanon's sociodiagnostic psychiatry tends to explain away the ambivalent turns and returns of the subject of colonial desire, its masquerade of Western Man and the 'long' historical perspective. It is as if Fanon is fearful of his most radical insights: that the politics of race will not be entirely contained within the humanist myth of man or economic necessity or historical progress, for its psychic affects question such forms of determinism; that social sovereignty and human subjectivity are only realizable in the order of otherness. It is as if the question of desire that emerged from the traumatic tradition of the oppressed has to be modified, at the end of *Black Skin, White Masks*, to make way for an existentialist humanism that is as banal as it is beatific:

> Why not the quite simple attempt to touch the other, to feel the other, to explain the other to myself? . . . At the conclusion of this study, I want the world to recognize, with me, the open door of every consciousness.[40]

Despite Fanon's insight into the dark side of man, such a deep hunger for humanism must be an overcompensation for the closed consciousness or 'dual narcissism' to which he attributes the depersonalization of colonial man: 'There one lies body to body, with one's blackness or one's whiteness in full narcissistic cry, each sealed into his own particularity – with, it is true, now and then a flash or so.'[41] It is this flash of recognition – in its Hegelian sense with its transcendental, sublative spirit – that fails to ignite in the colonial relation where there is only narcissistic indifference: 'And yet the Negro knows there is a difference. He wants it. . . . The former slave needs a challenge to his humanity.'[42] In the absence of such a challenge, Fanon argues, the colonized can only imitate, a distinction nicely made by the psychoanalyst Annie Reich: 'It is imitation . . . when the child holds the newspaper *like* his father. It is identification when the child learns to read.'[43] In disavowing the culturally differentiated condition of the colonial world – in demanding 'Turn white or disappear' – the colonizer is himself caught in the ambivalence of paranoic identification, alternating between fantasies of megalomania and persecution.

However, Fanon's Hegelian dream for a human reality *in-itself-for-itself* is ironized, even mocked, by his view of the Manichaean structure of colonial consciousness and its non-dialectical division. What he says in *The Wretched of the Earth* of the demography of the colonial city reflects his view of the psychic structure of the colonial relation. The native and settler zones, like the juxtaposition of black and white bodies, are opposed, but not in the service of a higher unity. No conciliation is possible, he concludes, for of the two terms one is superfluous.

No, there can be no reconciliation, no Hegelian recognition, no simple, sentimental promise of a humanistic 'world of the You'. Can there be life without transcendence? Politics without the dream of perfectibility? Unlike Fanon, I think the *non-dialectical* moment of Manichaeanism suggests an answer. By following the trajectory of colonial desire – in the company of the bizarre colonial figure, the tethered shadow – it becomes possible to cross, even to shift the Manichaean boundaries. Where there is no human *nature*, hope can hardly spring eternal; but it emerges surely and surreptitiously in the strategic return of that difference that informs and deforms the image of identity, in the margin of otherness that displays identification. There may be no Hegelian negation, but Fanon must sometimes be reminded that the disavowal of the Other always exacerbates the edge of identification, reveals that dangerous place where identity and aggressivity are twinned. For denial is always a retroactive process; a half acknowledgement of that otherness has left its traumatic mark.

In that uncertainty lurks the white-masked black man; and from such ambivalent identification – black skin, white masks – it is possible, I believe, to redeem the pathos of cultural confusion into a strategy of political subversion. We cannot agree with Fanon that 'since the racial drama is played out in the open the black man has no time to make it unconscious,'[44] but that is a provocative thought. In occupying two places at once – or three in Fanon's case – the depersonalized, dislocated colonial subject can become an incalculable object, quite literally difficult to place. The demand of authority cannot unify its message nor simply identify its subjects. For the strategy of colonial desire is to stage the drama of identity at the point which the black man *slips* to reveal the white skin. At the edge, in-between the black body and the white body, there is a tension of meaning and being, or some would say demand and desire, which is the psychic counterpart to that muscular tension that inhabits the native body:

> The symbols of social order – the police, the bugle calls in the barracks, military parades and waving flags – are at one and the same time inhibitory and stimulating: for they do not convey the message 'Don't dare to budge'; rather, they cry out 'Get ready to attack.'[45]

It is from such tensions – both psychic and political – that a strategy of subversion emerges. It is a mode of negation that seeks not to unveil the fullness of Man but to manipulate his representation. It is a form of power that is exercised at the very limits of identity and authority, in the mocking spirit of mask and image; it is the lesson taught by the veiled Algerian woman in the course of the revolution as she crossed the Manichaean lines to claim her liberty. In Fanon's essay 'Algeria unveiled' the colonizer's attempt to unveil the Algerian woman does not simply turn the veil into a symbol of resistance; it becomes a technique of camouflage, a means of struggle – the veil conceals bombs. The veil that once secured the boundary of the home – the limits of woman – now masks the woman in her revolutionary activity, linking the Arab city and French quarter, transgressing the familial and colonial boundary. As the veil is liberated in the public sphere, circulation between and beyond cultural and social norms and spaces, it becomes the object of paranoid surveillance and interrogation. Every veiled woman, writes Fanon, became suspect. And when the veil is shed in order to penetrate deeper into the European quarter, the colonial police see everything and nothing. An Algerian woman is only, after all, a woman. But the Algerian *fidai* is an arsenal, and in her handbag she carries her hand grenades.

Remembering Fanon is a process of intense discovery and disorientation. Remembering is never a quiet act of introspection or retrospection. It is a painful remembering, a putting together of the dismembered past to make sense of the trauma of the present. It is such a memory of the history of race and racism, colonialism and the question of cultural identity, that Fanon reveals with greater profundity and poetry than any other writer. What he achieves, I believe, is something far greater: for in seeing the phobic image of the Negro, the native, the colonized, deeply woven into the psychic pattern of the West, he offers the master and slave a deeper reflection of their interpositions, as well as the hope of a difficult, even dangerous, freedom: 'It is through the effort to recapture the self and to scrutinize the self, it is through the lasting tension of their freedom that men will be able to create the ideal conditions of existence for a human world.'[46]

This leads to a meditation on the experience of dispossession and dislocation – psychic and social – which speaks to the condition of the marginalized, the alienated, those who have to live under the surveillance of a sign of identity and fantasy that denies their difference. In shifting the focus of cultural racism from the politics of nationalism to the politics of narcissism, Fanon opens up a margin of interrogation that causes a subversive slippage of identity and authority. Nowhere is this subaltern activity more visible than in his work itself, where a range of texts and traditions – from the classical repertoire to the quotidian, conversational culture of racism – vie to utter that last word that remains unspoken.

As a range of culturally and racially marginalized groups readily assume the mask of the black, or the position of the minority, not to deny their diversity, but audaciously to announce the important artifice of cultural identity and its difference, the need for Fanon becomes urgent. As political groups from different directions, refuse to homogenize their oppression, but make of it a common cause, a public image of the identity of otherness, the need for Fanon becomes urgent – urgent, in order to remind us of that crucial engagement between mask and identity, image and identification, from which comes the lasting tension of our freedom and the lasting impression of ourselves as others:

> In case of display. . . the play of combat in the form of intimidation, the being gives of himself, or receives from the other, something that is like a mask, a double, an envelope, a thrown-off skin, thrown off in order to cover the frame of a shield. It is through this separated form of himself that the being comes into play in his effects of life and death.[47]

The time has come to return to Fanon; as always, I believe, with a question: how can the human world live its difference; how can a human being live Other-wise?

VI

I have chosen to give poststructuralism a specifically postcolonial provenance in order to engage with an influential objection repeated by Terry Eagleton in his essay, 'The politics of subjectivity':

> We have as yet no political theory, or theory of the subject, which is capable in this dialectical way of grasping social transformation as at once diffusion and affirmation, the death and birth of the subject – or at least we have no such theories that are not vacuously apocalyptic.[48]

Taking my lead from the 'doubly inscribed' subaltern instance, I would argue that it is the *dialectical* hinge between the birth and death of the subject that needs to be interrogated. Perhaps the charge that a politics of the subject results in a vacuous apocalypse is itself a response to the poststructuralist probing of the notion of progressive negation – or sublation – in dialectical thinking. The subaltern or metonymic are *neither* empty nor full, *neither* part nor whole. Their compensatory and vicarious processes of signification are a spur to social translation, the production of something else *besides* which is not only the cut or gap of the subject but also the intercut across social sites and disciplines. This hybridity initiates the project of political thinking by continually facing it with the strategic and the contingent, with the countervailing thought of its own 'unthought'. It has to negotiate its goals through an acknowledgement of differential objects and discursive levels articulated not simply as contents but in their *address* as forms of textual or narrative subjections – be they governmental, judicial or artistic. Despite its firm commitments, the political must always pose as a problem, or a question, the *priority of the place from which it begins*, if its authority is not to become autocratic.

What must be left an open question is how we are to rethink ourselves once we have undermined the immediacy and autonomy of self-consciousness. It is not difficult to question the civil argument that the people are a conjugation of individuals, harmonious *under* the Law. We can dispute the political argument that the radical, vanguardist party and its masses represent a certain objectification in a historical process, or stage, of social transformation. What remains to be thought is the *repetitious* desire to recognize ourselves doubly, as, at once, decentred in the solidary processes of the political group, and yet, ourself as a consciously committed, even individuated, agent of change – the bearer of belief. What is this ethical pressure to 'account for ourselves' – but only *partially* – within a political theatre of agonism, bureaucratic obfuscation, violence and violation? Is this political desire for partial identification a beautifully human, even pathetic attempt to disavow the realization that, *betwixt and besides* the lofty dreams of political thinking, there exists an acknowledgement, somewhere between fact and fantasy, that the techniques and technologies of politics need not be *humanizing* at all, in no way endorsing of what we understand to be the human – humanist? – predicament. We may have to force the limits of the social as we know it to rediscover a sense of political and personal agency through the unthought within the civic and the psychic realms. This may be no place to end but it may be a place to begin.

NOTES

1   F. Fanon, *Black Skin, White Masks*, Introduction by H. K. Bhabha (London: Pluto, 1986), p. 231 (my emphasis).

2   Ibid., p. 218.

3   F. Fanon, *Toward the African Revolution* (Harmondsworth: Pelican, 1967), p. 63.

4   Fanon, *Black Skin, White Masks*, pp. 157–8.

5   W. Benjamin, 'Theses on the philosophy of history', in his *Illuminations* (New York: Schocken Books, 1968), p. 257.

6   Fanon, *Black Skin, White Masks*, pp. 110–12.

7   Ibid., p. 116.

8   F. Fanon, 'Concerning violence', in his *The Wretched of the Earth* (Harmondsworth: Penguin, 1969).

9   Ibid.

10 Fanon, *Black Skin, White Masks*, p. 16.

11 J. Rose, 'The imaginary', in Colin MacCabe (ed.) *The Talking Cure* (London: Macmillan, 1981).

12 Fanon, 'Concerning violence', p. 30.

13 A. Jussawalla, *Missing Person* (Clearing House, 1976), pp. 14–29.

14 M. Jin, 'Strangers on a Hostile Landscape', in R. Cobham and M. Collins (eds) *Watchers and Seekers* (London: The Women's Press, 1987), pp. 126–7.

15 E. Said, *Orientalism* (London: Routledge & Kegan Paul, 1978), pp. 26–7.

16 R. Barthes, 'The imagination of the sign', in his *Critical Essays* (Evanston, Ill.: Northwestern University Press, 1972), pp. 206–7.

17 J. Locke, *An Essay Concerning Human Understanding* (London: Fontana, 1969), pp. 212–13.

18 Barthes, 'Imagination of the sign', p. 207.

19   R. Rorty, 'Mirroring', in his *Philosophy and the Mirror of Nature* (Oxford: Blackwell, 1980), pp. 162–3.
20   Barthes, 'Imagination of the sign', p. 207.
21   Fanon, *Black Skin, White Masks*, p. 112.
22   Ibid.
23   J. Lacan, 'Seminar of 21 January 1975', in J. Mitchell and J. Rose (eds) *Feminine Sexuality* (London: Routledge & Kegan Paul, 1982), p. 164.
24   Barthes, 'Imagination of the sign', pp. 209–10.
25   J. Lacan, 'Alienation', in his *The Four Fundamental Concepts of Psychoanalysis* (London: The Hogarth Press, 1977), p. 206.
26   Derrida, 'The double session', in his *Dissemination*, B. Johnson (trans.) (Chicago: University of Chicago Press, 1981), p. 212.
27   Derrida, 'The double session', pp. 212–13.
28   J. Derrida, *Of Grammatology*, G. C. Spivak (trans.) (Baltimore, Md: Johns Hopkins University Press, 1976), p. 145.
29   Lacan, 'Alienation', p. 207.
30   M. Foucault, *The Archaeology of Knowledge*, A. H. Sheridan (trans.) (London: Tavistock, 1972), p. 111.
31   J.-F. Lyotard and J.-L. Thebaud, *Just Gaming*, W. Godzich (trans.) (Minneapolis: University of Minnesota Press, 1985), pp. 34 and 39.
32   Lacan, 'Alienation', p. 88.
33   See Chapters 1 and 6 [of *The Location of Culture*].
34   C. Geertz, 'Native's point of view: anthropological understanding', in his *Local Knowledge* (New York: Basic Books, 1983), p. 70.
35   J. Derrida, *Writing and Difference*, Alan Bass (trans.) (Chicago: University of Chicago Press, 1982), p. 282.
36   Jussawalla, *Missing Person*, p. 15.
37   A. Showstack Sassoon, *Approaches to Gramsci* (London: Writers and Readers, 1982), p. 16.
38   Barthes, 'Imagination of the sign', p. 246.
39   Fanon, *Black Skin, White Masks*, p. 161.
40   Ibid., pp. 231–2.
41   Ibid.
42   Ibid., p. 221.
43   A. Reich.
44   Fanon, *Black Skin, White Masks*, p. 150.
45   Ibid., p. 45.
46   Ibid., p. 231.
47   J. Lacan, *The Four Fundamental Concepts of Psychoanalysis*, Alan Sheridan (trans.) (New York: Norton, 1981), p. 107.
48   T. F. Eagleton, 'The politics of subjectivity', in L. Appignanesi (ed.) *Identity*, ICA Documents 6 (London: Institute of Contemporary Art, 1988).

15

Butler on Kristeva and Foucault

With her book *Gender Trouble* (1990) Judith Butler (1956–) emerged as a key figure in what became known as 'queer theory'. Queer theory works through an uneasy synthesis of feminism, psychoanalysis and post-structuralism. In ways comparable to postcolonial theory, queer theory subverts essentialist categories of identity, above all gender identities such as 'gay' and lesbian'. Butler's first book, *Subjects of Desire* (1986), discusses the way Hegel's conception of the subject has been appropriated by French thought. In *Gender Trouble*, as well as analysing Julia Kristeva (1941–) and Michel Foucault, she reassesses the thought of Simone de Beauvoir, Monique Wittig and Luce Irigaray. De Beauvoir's famous claim that one is not born but rather *becomes* a 'woman' is suggestive for Butler's analysis of gender as a process of subject-formation. As with Homi Bhabha's work, Butler works at the crossroads of different currents of post-structuralism, notably the work of Derrida and Foucault. The different theoretical currents on which Butler draws produce a similarly eclectic range of terms and concepts. Central to Butler's work, for example, is a 'performative' conception of identity, but it remains hard to specify what Butler means by 'performative'. Her use of the term owes something to Jacques Derrida's deconstruction of J. L. Austin's account of the 'performative' in *Limited Inc* (1988). The meaning of 'performative' is by no means stable in Austin's work, and the diffusion and destabilization of the term in Derrida's work resists summary or definition. For Butler, the codes of sex and gender work performatively through repeated citations of an always already unstable series of oppositions and differences. Butler's arguments for a Derridean understanding of 'gender' also draw on the work of Lacan and Foucault to suggest a reconfiguration of the way we conceive subject formation and the workings of power and discourse.

Aspects of Butler's thought can be understood, accordingly, as develop-
ments in post-structuralist and critical feminism, with affinities in the work of
Jacqueline Rose and Denise Riley, notably *Am I That Name? Feminism and the
Category of 'Women' in History* (1988) and *The Words of Selves: Identification,
Solidarity, Irony* (2000). There are also affinities with the work of Eve Kosofsky
Sedgwick. Butler's work shares in the feminist critique of 'identity' and identity
politics, preferring a performative and differential account of how sexual and
gender identity could be subverted. The turn to queer theory nevertheless
undermines key aspects of the collective identity formations associated with
feminist politics, suggesting instead a radical politicization of identity as such.
In the light of Butler's suggestions about subversive performance strategies,
such as parody and drag, there is a tendency for the reception of Butler's
work to confuse difference categories of play, performance and personal
style. This tendency often stumbles over a central difficulty in Butler's work,
the difference between particular performances and the discourses of power
that coerce existing identity formations. It is a moot point, for example,
whether gender performances in pantomime or drag transvestism act to
reinforce or subvert existing gender stereotypes. Her conception of performativity does not posit some prior identity or subjectivity for an agent or actor
who then performs, but rather seeks to describe the more diffuse conditions of
possibility necessary for the particular performances and processes of subject-
formation. In this sense, performativity does not presuppose the existence of a
subject. One mark of Butler's conception of performance and performativity is
the extent to which her often reflexively awkward style of writing *enacts* or
performs the theoretical difficulties under discussion. In *Subjects of Desire* Butler
suggests that Hegel's sentences *enact* the work of his argument, and while
Butler's work is less speculative or systematic than Hegel's, the emphasis on
rhetoric is critical. In the preface to the reissued edition of *Gender Trouble*,
Butler nevertheless concedes a number of difficulties in her account of performativity and performance. Some of the difficulties are reworked in *Bodies
That Matter*, which offers what might be called a Nietzschean genealogy of the
body, drawing on Derrida and Foucault. In subsequent works, notably in
Excitable Speech (1996), Butler has suggested some strategic and political consequences of her understanding of the performative. Theoretical aspects of
her project are further developed in *The Psychic Life of Power* (1997), while the
book *Contingency, Hegemony, Universality* collaboratively written with Ernesto
Laclau and Slavoj Žižek (see next chapter) reveals some of the more explicitly
political consequences of her thought. Butler has engaged in a number of such
dialogues, and many of these exchanges clarify difficult passages in her published
writing.

The extract from *Gender Trouble* entitled 'Subversive Bodily Acts' offers critical
readings of the work of Julia Kristeva and Michel Foucault. Julia Kristeva is a
prominent figure in psychoanalytic post-structuralism, whose work combines
insights from linguistics, semiotics and psychoanalysis. Her work offers alternative perspectives on theoretical interests associated with Lacan, Derrida and
Luce Irigaray. Kristeva's most important works include *Revolution in Poetic Lan-*

guage (1974), *Desire in Language* (1977–9) and *Powers of Horror* (1980). Butler seeks to dismantle residues of heterosexual essentialism in Kristeva's psychoanalytic understanding of the subject, and thus suggests a critique of influential strands in what has become known as French feminism. Butler's exposition of Kristeva is critical rather than sympathetic: her sympathies are more engaged by Foucault's work.

FURTHER READING

Primary works

Judith Butler, *Subjects of Desire: Hegelian Reflections in Twentieth-Century France*, revised edition with new preface (New York: Columbia University Press, 1999); *Gender Trouble*, Tenth Anniversary Edition, with new preface (New York: Routledge, 1999); *Bodies That Matter: On the Discursive Limits of 'Sex'* (New York: Routledge, 1993); *Excitable Speech: A Politics of the Performative* (London: Routledge, 1997); *The Psychic Life of Power: Theories in Subjection* (New York: Routledge, 1997); *Antigone's Claim: Kinship between Life and Death* (New York: Columbia University Press, 2000); 'What is Critique? An Essay on Foucault's Virtue', *The Political: Readings in Continental Philosophy*, ed. David Ingram (Oxford: Blackwell, 2001); Judith Butler and Joan W. Scott, eds., *Feminists Theorize the Political* (London: Routledge, 1992); Linda Singer, *Erotic Welfare: Sexual Theory and Politics in the Age of Epidemic*, eds. Judith P. Butler and Maureen MacGrogan (London: Routledge, 1993).

Secondary works

Seyla Benhabib, Judith Butler, Drucilla Cornell and Nancy Fraser, *Feminist Contentions: A Philosophical Exchange* (London: Routledge, 1994).

Jessica Benjamin, *The Bonds of Love: Psychoanalysis, Feminism, and the Problems of Domination* (London: Virago, 1988); *Like Subjects, Love Objects: Essays on Recognition and Sexual Difference* (New Haven: Yale University Press, 1995).

Sarah Cooper, *Relating to Queer Theory: Rereading Sexual Self-definition with Irigaray, Kristeva, Wittig and Cixous* (Bern and Oxford: Lang, 2000).

Jacques Derrida, *Limited Inc* (Evanston, IL: Northwestern University Press, 1988).

Diana Fuss, ed., *Inside Out: Lesbian Theories, Gay Theories* (London: Routledge, 1991).

Julia Kristeva, *Revolution in Poetic Language*, trans. Margaret Waller (New York: Columbia University Press, 1984); *Desire in Language*, trans. Thomas Gora, Alice Jardine and Leon S. Roudiez (Oxford: Blackwell, 1982); *Powers of Horror: An Essay on Abjection*, trans. Leon S. Roudiez (New York: Columbia University Press, 1982).

Lois McNay, 'Subject, Psyche and Agency: The Work of Judith Butler', *Theory, Culture and Society* 16(2) (1999): 175–93.

Toril Moi, *What Is a Woman? and Other Essays* (Oxford: Oxford University Press, 1999).

Toril Moi, ed., *The Kristeva Reader* (Oxford: Blackwell, 1986).

Peter Osborne and Lynne Segal, 'Gender as Performance: An Interview with Judith Butler', *Radical Philosophy* 67 (Summer, 1994): 32–9. (Also included in Peter Osborne, ed., *A Critical Sense: Interviews with Intellectuals* (London: Routledge, 1996).)

Denise Riley, *Am I That Name? Feminism and the Category of 'Women' in History* (Basingstoke: Macmillan, 1988); *The Words of Selves: Identification, Solidarity, Irony* (Stanford, CA: University of California Press, 2000).
Sarah Salih, *Judith Butler* (London: Routledge, 2002).
Eve Kosofsky Sedgwick, *Epistemologies of the Closet* (Harmondsworth: Penguin, 1990).
Alan Sinfield, 'Diaspora and Hybridity: Queer Identities and the Ethnicity Model', *Textual Practice* 10(2) (1996): 271–93.

Judith Butler, 'Subversive Bodily Acts', *Gender Trouble* (New York: Routledge, 1990), pp. 79–94.

The Body Politics of Julia Kristeva

Kristeva's theory of the semiotic dimension of language at first appears to engage Lacanian premises only to expose their limits and to offer a specifically feminine locus of subversion of the paternal law within language.[1] According to Lacan, the paternal law structures all linguistic signification, termed "the Symbolic," and so becomes a universal organizing principle of culture itself. This law creates the possibility of meaningful language and, hence, meaningful experience, through the repression of primary libidinal drives, including the radical dependency of the child on the maternal body. Hence, the Symbolic becomes possible by repudiating the primary relationship to the maternal body. The "subject" who emerges as a consequence of this repression becomes a bearer or proponent of this repressive law. The libidinal chaos characteristic of that early dependency is now fully constrained by a unitary agent whose language is structured by that law. This language, in turn, structures the world by suppressing multiple meanings (which always recall the libidinal multiplicity which characterized the primary relation to the maternal body) and instating univocal and discrete meanings in their place.

Kristeva challenges the Lacanian narrative which assumes cultural meaning requires the repression of that primary relationship to the maternal body. She argues that the "semiotic" is a dimension of language occasioned by that primary maternal body, which not only refutes Lacan's primary premise, but serves as a perpetual source of subversion within the Symbolic. For Kristeva, the semiotic expresses that original libidinal multiplicity within the very terms of culture, more precisely, within poetic language in which multiple meanings and semantic nonclosure prevail. In effect, poetic language is the recovery of the maternal body within the terms of language, one that has the potential to disrupt, subvert, and displace the paternal law.

Despite her critique of Lacan, however, Kristeva's strategy of subversion proves doubtful. Her theory appears to depend upon the stability and reproduction of precisely the paternal law that she seeks to displace. Although she effectively exposes the limits of Lacan's efforts to universalize the paternal law in language, she nevertheless concedes that the semiotic is invariably subordinate to the Symbolic, that it assumes its specificity within the terms of a hierarchy immune to challenge. If the semiotic promotes the possibility of the subversion, displacement, or disruption of the paternal law, what meanings can those terms have if the Symbolic always reasserts its hegemony?

The criticism of Kristeva which follows takes issue with several steps in Kristeva's argument in favor of the semiotic as a source of effective subversion. First, it is unclear whether the primary relationship to the maternal body which both Kristeva and Lacan appear to accept is a viable construct and whether it is even a knowable experience according to either of their linguistic theories. The multiple drives that characterize the semiotic constitute a prediscursive libidinal economy which occasionally makes itself known in language, but which maintains an ontological status prior to language itself. Manifest in language, in poetic language in particular, this prediscursive libidinal economy becomes a locus of cultural subversion. A second problem emerges when Kristeva argues that this libidinal source of subversion cannot be maintained within the terms of culture, that its sustained presence within culture leads to psychosis and to the breakdown of cultural life itself. Kristeva thus alternately posits and denies the semiotic as an emancipatory ideal. Though she tells us that it is a dimension of language regularly repressed, she also concedes that it is a kind of language which never can be consistently maintained.

In order to assess her seemingly self-defeating theory, we need to ask how this libidinal multiplicity becomes manifest in language, and what conditions its temporary lifespan there? Moreover, Kristeva describes the maternal body as bearing a set of meanings that are prior to culture itself. She thereby safeguards the notion of culture as a paternal structure and delimits maternity as an essentially precultural reality. Her naturalistic descriptions of the maternal body effectively reify motherhood and preclude an analysis of its cultural construction and variability. In asking whether a prediscursive libidinal multiplicity is possible, we will also consider whether what Kristeva claims to discover in the prediscursive maternal body is itself a production of a given historical discourse, an *effect* of culture rather than its secret and primary cause.

Even if we accept Kristeva's theory of primary drives, it is unclear that the subversive effects of such drives can serve, via the semiotic, as anything more than a temporary and futile disruption of the hegemony of the paternal law. I will try to show how the failure of her political strategy follows in part from her largely uncritical appropriation of drive theory. Moreover, upon careful scrutiny of her descriptions of the semiotic function within language, it appears that Kristeva reinstates the paternal law at the level of the semiotic itself. In the end, it seems that Kristeva offers us a strategy of subversion that can never become a sustained political practice.

[. . .]

Kristeva's description of the semiotic proceeds through a number of problematic steps. She assumes that drives have aims prior to their emergence into language, that language invariably represses or sublimates these drives, and that such drives are manifest only in those linguistic expressions which disobey, as it were, the univocal requirements of signification within the Symbolic domain. She claims further that the emergence of multiplicitous drives into language is evident in the semiotic, that domain of linguistic meaning distinct from the Symbolic, which is the maternal body manifest in poetic speech.

As early as *Revolution in Poetic Language* (1974), Kristeva argues for a necessary causal relation between the heterogeneity of drives and the plurivocal possibilities of poetic language. Differing from Lacan, she maintains that poetic language is not predicated upon a repression of primary drives. On the contrary, poetic language, she claims, is the linguistic occasion on which drives break apart the usual, univocal terms of language and reveal an irrepressible heterogeneity of multiple sounds and meanings. Kristeva thereby contests Lacan's equation of the Symbolic with all linguistic meaning by asserting that poetic language has its own modality of meaning which does not conform to the requirements of univocal designation.

In this same work, she subscribes to a notion of free or uncathected energy which makes itself known in language through the poetic function. She claims, for instance, that "in the intermingling of drives in language . . . we shall see the economy of poetic language" and that in this economy, "the unitary subject can no longer find his [sic] place."[2] This poetic function is a rejective or divisive linguistic function which tends to fracture and multiply meanings; it enacts the heterogeneity of drives through the proliferation and destruction of univocal signification. Hence, the urge toward a highly differentiated or plurivocal set of meanings appears as the revenge of drives against the rule of the Symbolic, which, in turn, is predicated upon their repression. Kristeva defines the semiotic as the multiplicity of drives manifest in language. With their insistent energy and heterogeneity, these drives disrupt the signifying function. Thus, in this early work, she defines the semiotic as "the signifying function . . . connected to the modality [of] primary process."[3]

In the essays that comprise *Desire in Language* (1977), Kristeva ground her definition of the semiotic more fully in psychoanalytic terms. The primary drives that the Symbolic represses and the semiotic obliquely indicates are now understood as *maternal drives*, not only those drives belonging to the mother, but those which characterize the dependency of the infant's body (of either sex) on the mother. In other words, "the maternal body" designates a relation of continuity rather than a discrete subject or object of desire; indeed, it designates that *jouissance* which precedes desire and the subject/object dichotomy that desire presupposes. While the Symbolic is predicated upon the rejection of the mother, the semiotic, through rhythm, assonance, intonations, sound play, and repetition, re-presents or recovers the maternal body in poetic speech. Even the "first echolalias of infants" and the "glossalalias in psychotic discourse" are manifestations of the continuity of the mother–infant relation, a heterogeneous field of impulse prior to the separation/individuation of infant and mother, alike effected by the imposition of the incest taboo.[4] The separation of the mother and infant effected by the taboo is expressed linguistically as the severing of sound from sense. In Kristeva's words, "a phoneme, as distinctive element of meaning, belongs to language as Symbolic. But this same phoneme is involved in rhythmic, intonational repetitions; it thereby tends toward autonomy from meaning so as to maintain itself in a semiotic disposition near the instinctual drive's body."[5]

The semiotic is described by Kristeva as destroying or eroding the Symbolic; it is said to be "before" meaning, as when a child begins to vocalize, or "after" meaning, as when a psychotic no longer uses words to signify. If the Symbolic and the semiotic are understood as two modalities of language, and if the semiotic is understood to be generally repressed by the Symbolic, then language for Kristeva is understood as a system in which the Symbolic remains hegemonic except when the semiotic disrupts its signifying process through elision, repetition, mere sound, and the multiplication of meaning through indefinitely signifying images and metaphors. In its Symbolic mode, language rests upon a severance of the relation of maternal dependency, whereby it becomes abstract (abstract*ed* from the materiality of language) and univocal; this is most apparent in quantitative or purely formal reasoning. In its semiotic mode, language is engaged in a poetic recovery of the maternal body, that diffuse materiality that resists all discrete and univocal signification. Kristeva writes:

> In any poetic language, not only do the rhythmic constraints, for example, go so far as to violate certain grammatical rules of a national language...but in recent texts, these semiotic constraints (rhythm, vocalic timbres in Symbolist work, but also graphic disposition on the page) are accompanied by nonrecoverable syntactic elisions; it is impossible to reconstitute the particular elided syntactic category (object or verb), which makes the meaning of the utterance decidable.[6]

For Kristeva, this undecidability is precisely the instinctual moment in language, its disruptive function. Poetic language thus suggests a dissolution of the coherent, signifying subject into the primary continuity which is the maternal body:

> Language as Symbolic function constitutes itself at the cost of repressing instinctual drive and continuous relation to the mother. On the contrary, the unsettled and questionable subject of poetic language (from whom the word is never uniquely sign) maintains itself at the cost of reactivating this repressed, instinctual, maternal element.[7]

Kristeva's references to the "subject" of poetic language are not wholly appropriate, for poetic language erodes and destroys the subject, where the subject is understood as a speaking being participating in the Symbolic. Following Lacan, she maintains that the prohibition against the incestuous union with the mother is the founding law of the subject, a foundation which severs or breaks the continuous relation of maternal dependency. In creating the subject, the prohibitive law creates the domain of the Symbolic or language as a system of univocally signifying signs. Hence, Kristeva concludes that "poetic language would be for its questionable subject-in-process the equivalent of incest."[8] The breaking of Symbolic language against its own founding law or, equivalently, the emergence of rupture into language from within its own interior instinctuality, is not merely the outburst of libidinal heterogeneity into language; it also signifies the somatic state of dependency on the maternal body prior to the individuation of the ego. Poetic language thus always indicates a return to the maternal terrain, where the maternal signifies both libidinal dependency and the heterogeneity of drives.

In "Motherhood According to Bellini," Kristeva suggests that, because the maternal body signifies the loss of coherent and discrete identity, poetic language verges on psychosis. And in the case of a woman's semiotic expressions in language, the return to the maternal signifies a prediscursive homosexuality that Kristeva also clearly associates with psychosis. Although Kristeva concedes that poetic language is sustained culturally through its participation in the Symbolic and, hence, in the norms of linguistic communicability, she fails to allow that homosexuality is capable of the same nonpsychotic social expression. The key to Kristeva's view of the psychotic nature of homosexuality is to be understood, I would suggest, in her acceptance of the structuralist assumption that heterosexuality is coextensive with the founding of the Symbolic. Hence, the cathexis of homosexual desire can be achieved, according to Kristeva, only through displacements that are sanctioned within the Symbolic, such as poetic language or the act of giving birth:

> By giving birth, the women enters into contact with her mother; she becomes, she is her own mother; they are the same continuity differentiating itself. She thus actualizes the homosexual facet of motherhood, through which a woman is simultaneously closer to her instinctual memory, more open to her psychosis, and consequently, more negatory of the social, symbolic bond.[9]

According to Kristeva, the act of giving birth does not successfully reestablish that continuous relation prior to individuation because the infant invariably suffers the prohibition on incest and is separated off as a discrete identity. In the case of the mother's separation from the girl-child, the result is melancholy for both, for the separation is never fully completed.

As opposed to grief or mourning, in which separation is recognized and the libido attached to the original object is successfully displaced onto a new substitute object, melancholy designates a failure to grieve in which the loss is simply internalized and, in that sense, *refused*. Instead of a negative attachment to the body, the maternal body is internalized as a negation, so that the girl's identity becomes itself a kind of loss, a characteristic privation or lack.

The alleged psychosis of homosexuality, then, consists in its thorough break with the paternal law and with the grounding of the female "ego," tenuous though it may be, in the melancholic response to separation from the maternal body. Hence, according to Kristeva, female homosexuality is the emergence of psychosis into culture:

> The homosexual-maternal facet is a whirl of words, a complete absence of meaning and seeing; it is feeling, displacement, rhythm, sound, flashes, and fantasied clinging to the maternal body as a screen against the plunge . . . for woman, a paradise lost but seemingly close at hand.[10]

For women, however, this homosexuality is manifest in poetic language which becomes, in fact, the only form of the semiotic, besides childbirth, which can be sustained within the terms of the Symbolic. For Kristeva, then, overt homosexuality cannot be a culturally sustainable activity, for it would constitute a breaking of the incest taboo in an unmediated way. And yet why is this the case?

Kristeva accepts the assumption that culture is equivalent to the Symbolic, that the Symbolic is fully subsumed under the "Law of the Father," and that the only modes of nonpsychotic activity are those which participate in the Symbolic to some extent. Her strategic task, then, is neither to replace the Symbolic with the semiotic nor to establish the semiotic as a rival cultural possibility, but rather to validate those experiences within the Symbolic that permit a manifestation of the borders which divide the Symbolic from the semiotic. Just as birth is understood to be a cathexis of instinctual drives for the purposes of a social teleology, so poetic production is conceived as the site in which the split between instinct and representation exists in culturally communicable form:

> The speaker reaches this limit, this requisite of sociality, only by virtue of a particular, discursive practice called "art." A woman also attains it (and in our society, *especially*) through the strange form of split symbolization (threshold of language and instinctual drive, of the "symbolic" and the "semiotic") of which the act of giving birth consists.[11]

Hence, for Kristeva, poetry and maternity represent privileged practices within paternally sanctioned culture which permit a nonpsychotic experience of that heterogeneity and dependency characteristic of the maternal terrain. These acts of *poesis* reveal an instinctual heterogeneity that subsequently exposes the repressed ground of the Symbolic, challenges the mastery of the univocal signifier, and diffuses the autonomy of the subject who postures as their necessary ground. The heterogeneity of drives operates culturally as a subversive strategy of displacement, one which dislodges the hegemony of the paternal law by releasing the repressed multiplicity interior to language itself. Precisely because that instinctual heterogeneity must be re-presented in and through the paternal law, it cannot defy the incest taboo altogether, but must remain within the most fragile regions of the Symbolic. Obedient, then, to syntactical requirements, the poetic-maternal practices of displacing the paternal law always remain tenuously tethered to that law. Hence, a full-scale refusal of the Symbolic is impossible, and a discourse of "emancipation," for Kristeva, is out of the question. At best, tactical subversions and displacements of the law challenge its self-grounding presumption. But, once again, Kristeva does not seriously challenge the structuralist assumption that the prohibitive paternal law is foundational to culture itself. Hence, the subversion of paternally sanctioned culture can not come from another version of culture, but only from within the repressed interior of culture itself, from the heterogeneity of drives that constitutes culture's concealed foundation.

This relation between heterogeneous drives and the paternal law produces an exceedingly problematic view of psychosis. On the one hand, it designates female homosexuality as a culturally unintelligible practice, inherently psychotic: on the other hand, it mandates maternity as a compulsory defense against libidinal chaos. Although Kristeva does not make either claim explicitly, both implications follow from her views on the law, language, and drives. Consider that for Kristeva poetic language breaks the incest taboo and, as such, verges always on psychosis. As a return to the maternal body and a concomitant de-individuation of the ego, poetic language becomes especially threatening when uttered by women. The poetic then contests not only the incest taboo, but the taboo against homosexuality as well. Poetic language is thus, for women, both displaced maternal dependency and, because that dependency is libidinal, displaced homosexuality.

For Kristeva, the unmediated cathexis of female homosexual desire leads unequivocally to psychosis. Hence, one can satisfy this drive only through a series of displacements: the incorporation of maternal identity — that is, by becoming a mother oneself — or through poetic language which manifests obliquely the heterogeneity of drives characteristic of maternal dependency. As the only socially sanctioned and, hence, nonpsychotic displacements for homosexual desire, both maternity and poetry constitute melancholic experiences for women appropriately acculturated into hetero-sexuality. The heterosexual poet–mother suffers interminably from the displacement of the homosexual cathexis. And yet, the consummation of this desire would lead to the psychotic unraveling of identity, according to Kristeva – the presumption being that, for women, heterosexuality and coherent selfhood are indissolubly linked.

How are we to understand this constitution of lesbian experience as the site of an irretrievable self-loss? Kristeva clearly takes heterosexuality to be prerequisite to kinship and to culture. Consequently, she identifies lesbian experience as the psychotic alterna-tive to the acceptance of paternally sanctioned laws. And yet why is lesbianism constituted as psychosis? From what cultural perspective is lesbianism constructed as a site of fusion, self-loss, and psychosis?

By projecting the lesbian as "Other" to culture, and characterizing lesbian speech as the psychotic "whirl-of-words," Kristeva constructs lesbian sexuality as intrinsically unintelligible. This tactical dismissal and reduction of lesbian experience performed in the name of the law positions Kristeva within the orbit of paternal-heterosexual privilege. The paternal law which protects her from this radical incoherence is pre-cisely the mechanism that produces the construct of lesbianism as a site of irration-ality. Significantly, this description of lesbian experience is effected from the outside and tells us more about the fantasies that a fearful heterosexual culture produces to defend against its own homosexual possibilities than about lesbian experience itself.

In claiming that lesbianism designates a loss of self, Kristeva appears to be delivering a psychoanalytic truth about the repression necessary for individuation. The fear of such a "regression" to homosexuality is, then, a fear of losing cultural sanction and privilege altogether. Although Kristeva claims that this loss designates a place *prior* to culture, there is no reason not to understand it as a new or unacknowledged cultural form. In other words, Kristeva prefers to explain lesbian experience as a regressive libidinal state prior to acculturation itself, rather than to take up the challenge that lesbianism offers to her restricted view of paternally sanctioned cultural laws. Is the fear encoded in the construction of the lesbian as psychotic the result of a developmentally necessitated repression, or is it, rather, the fear of losing cultural legitimacy and, hence, being cast, not outside or prior to culture, but outside cultural *legitimacy*, still within culture, but culturally "out-lawed"?

Kristeva describes both the maternal body and lesbian experience from a position of sanctioned heterosexuality that fails to acknowledge its own fear of losing that sanction. Her reification of the paternal law not only repudiates female homosexuality, but denies the varied meanings and possibilities of motherhood as a cultural practice. But *cultural subversion* is not really Kristeva's concern, for subversion, when it appears, emerges from beneath the surface of culture only inevitably to return there. Although the semiotic is a possibility of language that escapes the paternal law, it remains inevitably within or, indeed, beneath the territory of that law. Hence, poetic language and the pleasures of maternity constitute local displacements of the paternal law, temporary subversions which finally submit to that against which they initially rebel. By relegating the source of subversion to a site outside of culture itself, Kristeva appears to foreclose the possibility of subversion as an effective or realizable cultural practice. Pleasure beyond the paternal law can be imagined only together with its inevitable impossibility.

Kristeva's theory of thwarted subversion is premised on her problematic view of the relation among drives, language, and the law. Her postulation of a subversive multiplicity of drives raises a number of epistemological and political questions. In the first place, if these drives are manifest only in language or cultural forms already determined as Symbolic, then how is it that we can verify their pre-Symbolic ontological status? Kristeva argues that poetic language gives us access to these drives in their fundamental multiplicity, but this answer is not fully satisfactory. Since poetic language is said to depend upon the prior existence of these multiplicitous drives, we cannot, then, in circular fashion, justify the postulated existence of these drives through recourse to poetic language. If drives must first be repressed for language to exist, and if we can attribute meaning only to that which is representable in language, then to attribute meaning to drives prior to their emergence into language is impossible. Similarly, to attribute a causality to drives which facilitates their transformation into language and by which language itself is to be explained cannot reasonably be done within the confines of language itself. In other words, we know these drives as "causes" only in and through their effects, and, as such, we have no reason for not identifying drives with their effects. It follows that either (a) drives and their representations are coextensive or (b) representations preexist the drives themselves.

This last alternative is, I would argue, an important one to consider, for how do we know that the instinctual object of Kristeva's discourse is not a construction of the discourse itself? And what grounds do we have for positing this object, this multiplicitous field, as prior to signification? If poetic language must participate in the Symbolic in order to be culturally communicable, and if Kristeva's own theoretical texts are emblematic of the Symbolic, then where are we to find a convincing "outside" to this domain? Her postulation of a prediscursive corporeal multiplicity becomes all the more problematic when we discover that maternal drives are considered part of a "biological destiny" and are themselves manifestations of "a non-symbolic, non-paternal causality."[12] This pre-Symbolic, nonpaternal causality is, for Kristeva, a semiotic, *maternal* causality, or, more specifically, a teleological conception of maternal instincts:

> Material compulsion, spasm of a memory belonging to the species that either binds together or splits apart to perpetuate itself, series of markers with no other significance than the eternal return of the life-death biological cycle. How can we verbalize this prelinguistic, unrepresentable memory? Heraclitus' flux, Epicurus' atoms, the whirling dust of cabalic, Arab and Indian mystics, and the stippled drawings of psychedelics – all seem better metaphors than the theory of Being, the logos, and its laws.[13]

Here, the repressed maternal body is not only the locus of multiple drives, but the bearer of a biological teleology as well, one which, it seems, makes itself evident in the early stages of Western philosophy, in non-Western religious beliefs and practices, in aesthetic representations produced by psychotic or near-psychotic states, and even in avant-garde artistic practices. But why are we to assume that these various cultural expressions manifest the selfsame principle of maternal heterogeneity? Kristeva simply subordinates each of these cultural moments to the same principle. Consequently, the semiotic represents any cultural effort to displace the logos (which, curiously, she *contrasts* with Heraclitus' flux), where the logos represents the univocal signifier, the law of identity. Her opposition between the semiotic and the Symbolic reduces here to a metaphysical quarrel between the principle of multiplicity that escapes the charge of non-contradiction and a principle of identity based on the suppression of that multiplicity. Oddly, that very principle of multiplicity that Kristeva everywhere defends operates in much the same manner as a principle of identity. Note the way in which all manner of things "primitive" and "Oriental" are summarily subordinated to the principle of the maternal body. Surely, her description warrants not only the charge of Orientalism, but raises the very significant question of whether, ironically, multiplicity has become a univocal signifier.

Her ascription of a teleological aim to maternal drives prior to their constitution in language or culture raises a number of questions about Kristeva's political program. Although she clearly sees subversive and disruptive potential in those semiotic expressions that challenge the hegemony of the paternal law, it is less clear in what precisely this subversion consists. If the law is understood to rest on a constructed ground, beneath which lurks the repressed maternal terrain, what concrete cultural options emerge within the terms of culture as a consequence of this revelation? Ostensibly, the multiplicity associated with the maternal libidinal economy has the force to disperse the univocity of the paternal signifier and seemingly to create the possibility of other cultural expressions no longer tightly constrained by the law of non-contradiction. But is this disruptive activity the opening of a field of significations, or is it the manifestation of a biological archaism which operates according to a natural and "prepaternal" causality? If Kristeva believed the former were the case (and she does not), then she would be interested in a displacement of the paternal law in favor of a proliferating field of cultural possibilities. But instead, she prescribes a return to a principle of maternal heterogeneity which proves to be a closed concept, indeed, a heterogeneity confined by a teleology both unilinear and univocal.

Kristeva understands the desire to give birth as a species-desire, part of a collective and archaic female libidinal drive that constitutes an ever-recurring metaphysical reality. Here Kristeva reifies maternity and then promotes this reification as the disruptive potential of the semiotic. As a result, the paternal law, understood as the ground of univocal signification, is displaced by an equally univocal signifier, the principle of the maternal body which remains self-identical in its teleology regardless of its "multiplicitous" manifestations.

Insofar as Kristeva conceptualizes this maternal instinct as having an ontological status prior to the paternal law, she fails to consider the way in which that very law might well be the *cause* of the very desire it is said to *repress*. Rather than the manifestation of a prepaternal causality, these desires might attest to maternity as a social practice required and recapitulated by the exigencies of kinship. Kristeva accepts Lévi-Strauss' analysis of the exchange of women as prerequisite for the consolidation of kinship bonds. She understands this exchange, however, as the cultural moment in which the maternal body is repressed, rather than as a mechanism for the compulsory cultural construction of the female body *as* a maternal body. Indeed, we might understand the exchange of women as imposing a compulsory obligation on women's bodies to reproduce. According to Gayle Rubin's reading of Lévi-Strauss, kinship effects a "sculpting of . . . sexuality" such that the desire to give birth is the result of social practices which require and produce such desires in order to effect their reproductive ends.[14]

What grounds, then, does Kristeva have for imputing a maternal teleology to the female body prior to its emergence into culture? To pose the question in this way is already to question the distinction between the Symbolic and the semiotic on which her conception of the maternal body is premised. The maternal body in its originary signification is considered by Kristeva to be prior to signification itself; hence, it becomes impossible within her framework to consider the maternal itself as a significa-tion, open to cultural variability. Her argument makes clear that maternal drives constitute those primary processes that language invariably represses or sublimates. But perhaps her argument could be recast within an even more encompassing frame-work: What cultural configuration of language, indeed, of *discourse*, generates the trope of a prediscursive libidinal multiplicity, and for what purposes?

By restricting the paternal law to a prohibitive or repressive function, Kristeva fails to understand the paternal mechanisms by which affectivity itself is generated. The law that is said to repress the semiotic may well be the governing principle of the semiotic itself, with the result that what passes as "maternal instinct" may well be a culturally constructed desire which is interpreted through a naturalistic vocabulary. And if that desire is constructed according to a law of kinship which requires the heterosexual production and reproduction of desire, then the vocabulary of naturalistic affect effect-ively renders that "paternal law" invisible. What for Kristeva is a pre-paternal causality would then appear as a *paternal* causality under the guise of a natural or distinctively maternal causality.

Significantly, the figuration of the maternal body and the teleology of its instincts as a self-identical and insistent metaphysical principle – an archaism of a collective, sex-specific biological constitution – bases itself on a univocal conception of the female sex. And this sex, conceived as both origin and causality, poses as a principle of pure generativity. Indeed, for Kristeva, it is equated with *poesis* itself, that activity of making upheld in Plato's *Symposium* as an act of birth and poetic conception at once.[15] But is female generativity truly an uncaused cause, and does it begin the narrative that takes all of humanity under the force of the incest taboo and into language? Does the pre-paternal causality where of Kristeva speaks signify a primary female economy of pleasure and meaning? Can we reverse the very order of this causality and understand this semiotic economy as a production of a prior discourse?

In the final chapter of Foucault's first volume of *The History of Sexuality*, he cautions against using the category of sex as a "fictitious unity...[and] causal principle" and argues that the fictitious category of sex facilitates a reversal of causal relations such that "sex" is understood to cause the structure and meaning of desire:

> the notion of 'sex' made it possible to group together, in an artificial unity, anatomical elements, biological functions, conducts, sensations, and pleasures, and it enabled one to make use of this fictitious unity as a causal principle, an omnipresent meaning: sex was thus able to function as a unique signifier and as a universal signified.[16]

For Foucault, the body is not "sexed" in any significant sense prior to its determination within a discourse through which it becomes invested with an "idea" of natural or essential sex. The body gains meaning within discourse only in the context of power relations. Sexuality is an historically specific organization of power, discourse, bodies, and affectivity. As such, sexuality is understood by Foucault to produce "sex" as an artificial concept which effectively extends and disguises the power relations responsible for its genesis.

Foucault's framework suggests a way to solve some of the epistemological and political difficulties that follow from Kristeva's view of the female body. We can understand Kristeva's assertion of a "prepaternal causality" as fundamentally inverted. Whereas Kristeva posits a maternal body prior to discourse that exerts its own causal force in the structure of drives, Foucault would doubtless argue that the discursive production of the maternal body as prediscursive is a tactic in the self-amplification and concealment of those specific power relations by which the trope of the maternal body is produced. In these terms, the maternal body would no longer be understood as the hidden ground of all signification, the tacit cause of all culture. It would be understood, rather, as an effect or consequence of a system of sexuality in which the female body is required to assume maternity as the essence of its self and the law of its desire.

If we accept Foucault's framework, we are compelled to redescribe the maternal libidinal economy as a product of an historically specific organization of sexuality. Moreover, the discourse of sexuality, itself suffused by power relations, becomes the true ground of the trope of the prediscursive maternal body. Kristeva's formulation suffers a thoroughgoing reversal: The Symbolic and the semiotic are no longer interpreted as those dimensions of language which follow upon the repression or manifestation of the maternal libidinal economy. This very economy is understood instead as a reification that both extends and conceals the institution of motherhood as compulsory for women. Indeed, when the desires that maintain the institution of motherhood are transvaluated as pre-paternal and pre-cultural drives, then the institution gains a permanent legitimation in the invariant structures of the female body. Indeed, the clearly paternal law that sanctions and requires the female body to be characterized primarily in terms of its reproductive function is inscribed on that body as the law of its natural necessity. Kristeva, safeguarding that law of a biologically necessitated maternity as a subversive operation that pre-exists the paternal law itself, aids in the systematic production of its invisibility and, consequently, the illusion of its inevitability.

Because Kristeva restricts herself to an exclusively *prohibitive* conception of the paternal law, she is unable to account for the ways in which the paternal law *generates* certain desires in the form of natural drives. The female body that she seeks to express is itself a construct produced by the very law it is supposed to undermine. In no way do these criticisms of Kristeva's conception of the paternal law necessarily invalidate her general position that culture or the Symbolic is predicated upon a repudiation of women's bodies. I want to suggest, however, that any theory that asserts that signification is predicated upon the denial or repression of a female principle ought to consider whether that femaleness is really external to the cultural norms by which it is repressed. In other words, on my reading, the repression of the feminine does not require that the agency of repression and the object of repression be ontologically distinct. Indeed, repression may be understood to produce the object that it comes to deny. That production may well be an elaboration of the agency of repression itself. As Foucault makes clear, the culturally contradictory enterprise of the mechanism of repression is prohibitive and generative at once and makes the problematic of "liberation" especially acute. The female body that is freed from the shackles of the paternal law may well prove to be yet another incarnation of that law, posing as subversive but operating in the service of that law's self-amplification and proliferation. In order to avoid the emancipation of the oppressor in the name of the oppressed, it is necessary to take into account the full complexity and subtlety of the law and to cure ourselves of the illusion of a true body beyond the law. If subversion is possible, it will be a subversion from within the terms of the law, through the possibilities that emerge when the law turns against itself and spawns unexpected permutations of itself. The culturally constructed body will then be liberated, neither to its "natural" past, nor to its original pleasures, but to an open future of cultural possibilities.

[. . .]

Foucault's genealogical critique has provided a way to criticize those Lacanian and neo-Lacanian theories that cast culturally marginal forms of sexuality as culturally unintelligible. Writing within the terms of a disillusionment with the notion of a liberatory Eros, Foucault understands sexuality as saturated with power and offers a critical view of theories that lay claim to a sexuality before or after the law. When we consider, however, those textual occasions on which Foucault criticizes the categories of sex and the power regime of sexuality, it is clear that his own theory maintains an unacknowledged emancipatory ideal that proves increasingly difficult to maintain, even within the strictures of his own critical apparatus.

[. . .]

NOTES

1   This section, "The Body Politics of Julia Kristeva," was originally published in *Hypatia*, in the special issue on French Feminist Philosophy, Vol. 3, No. 3, Winter, 1989, pp. 104–118.

2   Julia Kristeva, *Revolution in Poetic Language*, trans. Margaret Waller, introduction by Leon Roudiez (New York: Columbia University Press, 1984), p. 132. The original text is *La Révolution du language poetique*, (Paris: Éditions du Seuil, 1974).

3   Ibid., p. 25.

4   Julia Kristeva, *Desire in Language, A Semiotic Approach to Literature and Art*, ed. Leon S. Roudiez, trans. Thomas Gora, Alice Jardine, and Leon S. Roudiez (New York: Columbia University Press, 1980), p. 135. This is a collection of essays compiled from two different sources: *Polylogue* (Paris: Editions du Seuil, 1977), and *Σημειωτιχή: Recherches pour une sémanalyse* (Paris: Edition du Seuil, 1969).

5   Ibid., p. 135.

6   Ibid., p. 134.

7   Ibid., p. 136.

8   Ibid.

9   Ibid., p. 239.

10   Ibid., pp. 239–240.

11   Ibid., p. 240. For an extremely interesting analysis of reproductive metaphors as descriptive of the process of poetic creativity, see Wendy Owen, "A Riddle in Nine Syllables: Female Creativity in the Poetry of Sylvia Plath," doctoral dissertation, Yale University, Department of English, 1985.

12   Kristeva, *Desire in Language*, p. 239.

13   Ibid., p. 239.

14   Gayle Rubin, "The Traffic in Women: Notes on the 'Political Economy' of Sex," in *Toward an Anthropology of Women*, Rayna R. Reiter, ed. (New York: Monthly Review Press, 1975), p. 182.

15 See Plato's *Symposium*, 209a: Of the "procreancy...of the spirit," he writes that it is the specific capacity of the poet. Hence, poetic creations are understood as sublimated reproductive desire.

16 Michel Foucault, *The History of Sexuality, Volume I: An Introduction*, trans. Robert Hurley (New York: Vintage, 1980), p. 154.

16
Žižek on Žižek

Slavoj Žižek emerged in the 1990s as a provocative, prolific and engagingly dissonant critical theorist. With an unusual Lacanian reading of Hegel at its core, his work cuts across currents in post-structuralism, Althusserian Marxism and psychoanalysis. Developed out of the collapse of Eastern European socialism, Žižek works through an implicit critique of the Yugoslavian reception of Western Marxism and the New Left. Although critical of the work of Adorno and Marcuse, there are similarities in the way in which Žižek uses motifs from psychoanalysis to diagnose the ideological substrates of contemporary society. In 1982 the group around Žižek in Slovenia founded 'The Society for Theoretical Psychoanalysis' and 'The Sigmund Freud School', but the turn to Lacanian psychoanalysis was less concerned with clinical practice than with intervening in cultural politics. If Adorno and Marcuse can be understood as unorthodox neo-Marxists, Žižek exemplifies the unstable terrain of post-Marxism. Žižek's use of Lacan's work needs to be distinguished, accordingly, from Althusserian cultural analysis and from feminist appropriations of Lacan.

Žižek's reputation was established by his first book in English, *The Sublime Object of Ideology* (1989), although he had already produced a number of books in French. He has gone on to produce a string of books, perhaps most notably *Tarrying with the Negative: Kant, Hegel, and the Critique of Ideology* (1993); *The Indivisible Remainder: An Essay on Schelling and Related Matters* (1996); and *The Ticklish Subject: The Absent Centre of Political Ontology* (1999). These books overlap and recirculate a constellation of ideas which use conceptual tools appropriated from Lacan to project ideas from the work of German idealists such as Kant, Schelling, and above all Hegel, into contemporary political problems. A further cluster of books, notably *Looking Awry: An Introduction to Jacques Lacan Through Popular Culture* (1991) and *Enjoy Your Symptom: Jacques Lacan in Hollywood and Out* (1993), foreground analogies between Lacanian theory and popular culture. Reference to popular culture in Žižek's work is not, however, a distinct area of analysis. Žižek specializes in perverse pronouncements and inversions, deploying a rhetoric of overstatement that works less by sustained formal argument than by a playful montage of theoretical propositions and cultural reference. The absence of a more systematic presentation of theory and critique tends to annoy those concerned to differentiate those aspects of his work relevant to philosophy, psychoanalysis or cultural studies. It is often difficult, for example, to determine whether Hitchcock is used to illustrate Lacan or whether Lacan is used to illuminate Hitchcock. Would a disagreement with one of Žižek's readings of a particular film have any theoretical consequences? Read sympathetically, Žižek politicizes the contemporary division of intellectual labour and suggests a new and imaginatively engaged role for critical thought, one which breaks down the barriers between theory and everyday life. Read less sympathetically, Žižek confuses disciplines, offering schematic readings which are opportunist in their use of distinct forms and contents.

Central to Žižek's work is his appropriation of the conception of the 'Real' developed in Lacan's later work. For Žižek, the 'Real' is not a way of describing reality, but an account of the conditions of possibility through which the human subject is constituted and thus through which reality is experienced, lived or spoken about. Put briefly, the 'Real' cannot be represented, remains resistant to all forms of symbolization and has no ontological consistency or underlying stability. The Real can nevertheless be construed retrospectively through the distortions and displacements of the symbolic structure. Ideology critique cannot hope to reveal the underlying truth of material interests, but can only trace antagonisms through the ideology effects and subject formations structured by the Real. Perhaps the most innovative and original way in which Žižek articulates this is by showing how the necessary failure of self-reflection in the formation of the subject is also at work in philosophy. Žižek finds this logic of reflection at work not just in ideology but in Hegel's *Logic*, though a number of critics have responded by showing how Žižek's reading of Hegel is reductive and schematic. A further series of objections to Žižek's Lacanian account of subject formation are sketched by Judith Butler and Ernesto Laclau in the collaborative exchanges which make up *Contingency, Hegemony, Universality*. Butler, for example, asks whether Žižek's recourse to the Lacanian conception of the subject is ahistorical and thus relies on a quasi-transcendental conception of the subject which is politically indeterminate. At issue is the extent to which Lacanian accounts of sexual difference provide political strategies for change rather than projecting a conception of sexuality which is itself ideological. The following essay by Žižek comes at the end of the exchanges which make up the book, and provides both a summary of some key criticisms of his work as well as an introduction to the ways in which Žižek currently seeks to defend his work. Of particular interest is the way Žižek dramatizes his differences from the post-Marxism of Ernesto Laclau, a turn towards conceptions of revolutionary politics also evident in Žižek's recent interest in Lukács and Lenin.

FURTHER READING

Primary works

Judith Butler, Ernesto Laclau and Slavoj Žižek, *Contingency, Hegemony, Universality: Contemporary Dialogues on the Left* (London: Verso, 2000); Slavoj Žižek, *The Sublime Object of Ideology* (London: Verso, 1989); *Tarrying with the Negative: Kant, Hegel, and the Critique of Ideology* (Durham, NC: Duke University Press, 1993); *The Indivisible Remainder: An Essay on Schelling and Related Matters* (London: Verso, 1996); *The Ticklish Subject: The Absent Centre of Political Ontology* (London: Verso, 1999); *Looking Awry: An Introduction to Jacques Lacan Through Popular Culture* (Cambridge, MA: MIT, 1991); *Enjoy Your Symptom: Jacques Lacan in Hollywood and Out*, 2nd edition (London: Routledge, 2001); *On Belief* (London: Routledge, 2001); Slavoj Žižek, ed., *Everything You Always Wanted to Know About Lacan (But Were Too Afraid to Ask Hitchcock)* (London: Verso, 1992); Slavoj Žižek, ed., *Mapping Ideology* (London: Verso, 1994).

Secondary works

Alain Badiou, *Ethics: An Essay on the Understanding of Evil*, trans. Peter Hallward (London: Verso, 2001).

Peter Dews, 'Slavoj Žižek's Lacanian Dialectics', *Limits of Disenchantment: Essays on Contemporary European Philosophy* (London: Verso, 1995), pp. 236–58.

Jacques Lacan, *The Ethics of Psychoanalysis, 1959–1960*, trans. Dennis Porter (London: Tavistock / Routledge, 1992).

Ernesto Laclau, *Emancipation(s)* (London: Verso, 1996).

Ernesto Laclau and Chantal Mouffe, *Hegemony and Socialist Strategy*, 2nd edition (London: Verso, 2001).

Sean Homer, 'It's the Political Economy, Stupid! On Žižek's Marxism', *Radical Philosophy* 108 (July–August, 2001): 7–16.

Dany Nobus, ed., *Key Concepts in Lacanian Psychoanalysis* (London: Rebus, 1998).

Jacob Torfing, *New Theories of Discourse: Laclau, Mouffe and Žižek* (Oxford: Blackwell, 1999).

Boris Vezjak, 'Hegelianism in Slovenia: A Short Introduction', *Bulletin of the Hegel Society of Great Britain* 34 (Autumn / Winter 1996): 1–12.

Elizabeth Wright and Edmond Wright, eds., *The Žižek Reader* (Oxford: Blackwell, 1999).

Alenka Zupancic, *Ethics of the Real: Kant and Lacan* (London: Verso, 2001).

Slavoj Žižek, 'Holding the Place', from Judith Butler, Ernesto Laclau and Slavoj Žižek, *Contingency, Hegemony, Universality: Contemporary Dialogues on the Left* (London: Verso, 2000), pp. 308–29.

Butler: The Real and Its Discontents

Perhaps the ultimate object of contention in our debate is the status of the (Lacanian) Real – so let me begin by reiterating what I perceive to be the core of the problem. Butler's critique relies on the opposition between the (hypostasized, proto-transcendental, pre-historical and pre-social) 'symbolic order', that is, the 'big Other', and 'society' as the field of contingent socio-symbolic struggles: all her main points against Laclau or me can be reduced to this matrix: to the basic criticism that we hypostasize some historically contingent formation (even if it is the Lack itself) into a proto-transcendental pre-social formal a priori. For example, when I write 'on the lack that inaugurates and defines, negatively, human social reality', I allegedly posit 'a transcultural structure to social reality that presupposes a sociality based in fictive and idealized kinship positions that presume the heterosexual family as constituting the defining social bond for all humans' (Judith Butler, in *Contingency, Hegemony, Universality* [hereafter JB], pp. 141–2). If we formulate the dilemma in these terms, then, of course,

> the disagreement seems inevitable. Do we want to affirm that there is an ideal big Other, or an ideal small other, which is more fundamental than any of its social formulations? Or do we want to question whether any ideality that pertains to sexual difference is ever not constituted by actively reproduced gender norms that pass their ideality off as essential to a pre-social and ineffable sexual difference? (JB, p. 144)

This critical line of reasoning, however, only works *if the (Lacanian) Real is silently reduced to a pre-historical a priori symbolic norm*, as is clear from the following formulation: 'The formal character of this originary, pre-social sexual difference in its ostensible emptiness is *accomplished* precisely through the reification by which a certain idealized and necessary dimorphism takes hold' (JB, p. 145). If, then, sexual difference is elevated into an ideal prescriptive norm – if all concrete variations of sexual life are 'constrained by this non-thematizable normative condition' (JB, p. 147), Butler's conclusion is, of course, inevitable: 'as a transcendental claim, sexual difference should be rigorously opposed by anyone who wants to guard against a theory that would prescribe in advance what kinds of sexual arrangements will and will not be permitted in intelligible culture' (JB, p. 148). Butler is, of course, aware how Lacan's *il n'y a pas de rapport sexuel* means that, precisely, any 'actual' sexual relationship is always tainted by failure; however, she interprets this failure as the failure of the contingent historical reality of sexual life fully to actualize the symbolic norm. Consequently, she can claim that, for Lacanians, 'sexual difference has a transcendental status *even when* sexed bodies emerge that do not fit squarely within ideal gender dimorphism'. In this way, I 'could nevertheless explain intersexuality by claiming that *the ideal is still there*, but the bodies in question – contingent, historically formed – do not conform to the ideal' (JB, p. 145; emphasis added).

I am tempted to say that, in order to get close to what Lacan aims at with his *il n'y a pas de rapport sexuel*, one should begin by replacing *even when* in the above quote with *because*: 'sexual difference has a transcendental status *because* sexed bodies emerge that do not fit squarely within ideal gender dimorphism'. That is to say: far from serving as an implicit symbolic norm that reality can never reach, sexual difference as real/impossible means precisely that *there is no such norm*: sexual difference is that 'rock of impossibility' on which every 'formalization' of sexual difference founders. In the sense in which Butler speaks of 'competing universalities', one can thus speak of *competing symbolizations/normativizations of sexual difference*: if sexual difference may be said to be 'formal', it is certainly a strange form – a form whose main result is precisely that it undermines every universal form which attempts to capture it. If one insists on referring to the opposition between the universal and the particular, between the transcendental and the contingent/pathological, then one should say that sexual difference is the paradox of the particular that is more universal than universality itself – a contingent difference, an indivisible remainder of the 'pathological' sphere (in the Kantian sense of the term) which always somehow derails, throws off balance, normative ideality itself. Far from being normative, sexual difference is therefore *pathological* in the most radical sense of the term: a contingent stain that all symbolic fictions of symmetrical kinship positions try in vain to obliterate. Far from constraining the variety of sexual arrangements in advance, the Real of sexual difference is the traumatic cause which sets their contingent proliferation in motion.[1]

This notion of the Real also enables me to answer Butler's criticism that Lacan hypostasizes the 'big Other' into a kind of pre-historical transcendental a priori: when Lacan emphatically asserts that 'there is no big Other [*il n'y a pas de grand Autre*]', his point is precisely that there is no a priori formal structural schema exempt from historical contingencies – there are only contingent, fragile, inconsistent configurations. (Furthermore, far from clinging to paternal symbolic authority, the 'Name-of-the-Father' is for Lacan a *fake*, a *semblance* which conceals this structural inconsistency.) In other words, the claim that the Real is inherent to the Symbolic is strictly equal to the claim that 'there is no big Other': the Lacanian Real is that traumatic 'bone in the throat' that *contaminates* every ideality of the symbolic, rendering it contingent and inconsistent. For this reason, far from being opposed to historicity, the Real is its very 'ahistorical' ground, the a priori of historicity *itself* (here I fully agree with Laclau). We can thus see how the entire *topology* changes from Butler's description of the Real and the 'big Other' as the pre-historical a priori to their actual functioning in Lacan's edifice: in her critical portrait, Butler describes an ideal 'big Other' which persists as a norm, although it is never fully actualized, although the contingencies of history thwart its full imposition; while Lacan's edifice is, rather, centred on the tension between some traumatic 'particular absolute', some kernel which resists symbolization, and the 'competing universalities' (to use Butler's appropriate term) that endeavour in vain to symbolize/normalize it.[2]

The gap between the symbolic a priori Form and history/sociality is utterly foreign to Lacan – that is to say, the 'duality' with which Lacan operates is not the duality of the a priori form/norm, the symbolic Order, and its imperfect historical realization: for Lacan, as well as for Butler, there is *nothing* outside contingent, partial, inconsistent symbolic practices, no 'big Other' that guarantees their ultimate consistency. In contrast to Butler and the historicists, however, Lacan grounds historicity in a different way: not in the simple empirical excess of 'society' over symbolic schemata (here Laclau is right in his criticism of Butler: her notion of society/history as opposed to 'the symbolic' is a direct empiricist reference to an ontologically unexplained positive wealth of reality), but in the resistant kernel *within* the symbolic process itself. The Lacanian Real is thus not simply a technical term for the neutral limit of conceptualization – here, one should be as precise as possible with regard to the relationship between the trauma as real and the domain of socio-symbolic historical practices: the Real is neither pre-social nor a social effect – the point is, rather, that the Social itself is *constituted* by the exclusion of some traumatic Real. What is 'outside the Social' is not some positive a priori symbolic form/norm, merely its negative founding gesture itself.[3]

As a result, when Butler criticizes my alleged inconsistencies, she gets entangled in the results of her own reductive reading of Lacan: she imposes on Lacan the network of classic oppositions (transcendental form versus contingent content; ideal versus material); then, when the object resists and, of course, does not fit this schema, she reads this as the criticized theory's inconsistency (*where*, for instance, do I 'alternately describe [the Real] as material and ideal' (JB, p. 152)?). In the same vein, Butler often uses the obvious fact of co-dependent tension between the two terms as the argument against their conceptual distinction. For example, while I endorse her claim that 'it would not be possible to postulate the social norm on the one side of the analysis, and the fantasy on the other, for the *modus operandi* of the norm is the fantasy, and the very syntax of the fantasy could not be read without an understanding of the lexicon of the social norm' (JB, p. 155), I none the less insist that the formal distinction between these two levels is to be maintained: the social norm (the set of symbolic rules) is sustained by fantasies; it can operate only through this phantasmic support, but the fantasy that sustains it had none the less to be *disavowed*, excluded from the public domain. It is on this level that I find Hannah Arendt's notion of the 'banality of Evil' problematic: to translate it somewhat crudely into Lacanese, Arendt's claim is that the ideal Nazi executor–subject (like Eichmann) was a pure subject of the signifier, an anonymous bureaucratic executor deprived of any passionate bestiality – he accomplished what was asked of or expected from him as a matter of pure routine, without any involvement. My counter-thesis is that, far from functioning in effect as a pure subject of the signifier with no idiosyncratic phantasmic investment, the ideal Nazi subject *did* rely on the passionate bestiality articulated in obscene phantasmic scenarios; these scenarios, however, were not directly subjectively assumed as part of his personal self-experience – they were externalized, materialized in the 'objective' Nazi state ideological apparatus and its functioning.[4]

Perhaps the best way to mark the theoretico-political distance that separates Butler from me is through what I consider her strongest and politically most engaged contribution to our debate: her argumentation apropos of the demand for the legal recognition of gay marriages. While she acknowledges the advantages involved in such a recognition (gay couples get all the entitlements that the 'straight' married couples get; they are integrated into the institution of marriage, and thus recognized as equal to 'straight' couples, etc.), she focuses on the traps of endorsing this demand: in doing so, gays break their alliance (or, to put it in Laclau's terms, exclude themselves from the chain of equivalences) with all those *not* included in the legal form of marriage marriage (single parents, non-monogamous subjects, etc.); furthermore, they strengthen state apparatuses by contributing to their increasing right to regulate private lives. The paradoxical result is thus that the gap between those whose status is legitimized and those who live a shadowy existence is widened: those who remain excluded are even more excluded. Butler's counter-proposal is that instead of endorsing legal form of marriage as the condition of entitlements (inheritance, parenthood, etc.), one should, rather, struggle to *dissociate* these entitlements from the form of marriage: to make them independent of it.

My first general point here is that, with regard to the way the notion of political universality is elaborated in recent French political philosophy (Rancière, Balibar, Badiou), I perceive the shadowy existence of those who are condemned to lead a spectral life outside the domain of the global order, blurred in the background, unmentionable, submerged in the formless mass of 'population', without even a proper particular place of their own, in a slightly different way from Butler. I am tempted to claim that this shadowy existence is *the very site of political universality*: in politics, universality is asserted when such an agent with no proper place, 'out of joint', posits itself as the direct embodiment of universality against all those who do have a place within the global order. And this gesture is at the same time that of subjectivization, since 'subject' designates by definition an entity that is *not 'substance'*: a dislocated entity, an entity which lacks its own place within the Whole.

While, of course, I fully support Butler's political aims, my main apprehension concerns the fact that she conceives state power in the Foucauldian mode, conceives state power as an agent of control and regulation, inclusion and exclusion; resistance to power is then, of course, located in the marginal spheres of those who are excluded or half-excluded from the official power network, leading a shadowy spectral half-existence, without a proper place within the social space, prevented from asserting their symbolic identity. Consequently, Butler locates emancipatory struggle primarily in these marginal agents' resistance against state regulatory mechanisms, which takes place within civil society. So what is my problem with this framework? What Butler leaves out of consideration is the way in which *state power itself is split from within and relies on its own obscene spectral underside*: public state apparatuses are always supplemented by their shadowy double, by a network of publicly disavowed rituals, unwritten rules, institutions, practices, and so on. Today, we should not forget that the series of publicly 'invisible' agents leading a spectral half-existence includes, among others, the entire white supremacist underground (fundamentalist Christian survivalists in Montana, neo-Nazis, the remnants of the Ku Klux Klan, etc.). So the problem is not simply the marginals who lead the spectral half-existence of those excluded by the hegemonic symbolic regime; the problem is that this regime itself, in order to survive, has to rely on a whole gamut of mechanisms whose status is spectral, disavowed, excluded from the public domain. Even the very opposition between state and civil society is thoroughly ambivalent today: no wonder the Moral Majority presents itself (and is in effect organized as) local civil society's resistance against the 'progressive' regulatory interventions of the liberal state.

Although Butler is well aware of the subversive potential of Hegel's notion of 'concrete universality', I am tempted to claim that it is her basic acceptance of the Foucauldian notion of power which explains her failure fully to develop the consequences of the notion of 'concrete universality' for the notion of power, and clearly to locate the split between 'official' universality and its spectral underside within the hegemonic power discourse itself, as its own obscene supplement. So when Butler notes critically that, in my work –

> sexual difference occupies a distinctive position within the chain of signifiers, one that both occasions the chain and is one link in the chain. How are we to think the vacillation between these two meanings, and are they always distinct, given that the transcendental is the ground, and occasions a sustaining condition for what is called the historical? (JB, p. 143)

– my answer is that I fully assume this paradox: it is the basic structural paradox of dialectics, and the *concept* that indicates 'how [we are] to think the vacillation between these two meanings' was proposed long ago by Hegel, and then applied by Marx; it is the concept of 'oppositional determination [*genensätzliche Bestimmung*]' which Hegel introduces in the subchapter on identity in his Greater Logic. In the course of the dialectical process, the universal genus encounters *itself* 'in its oppositional determination', that is, as one of its own species (which is why for Hegel, paradoxically, each genus has ultimately two species: itself and the Species as such). Marx refers to this concept twice: first in the Introduction to the *Grundrisse* manuscript, when he emphasizes the double structural role of production in the articulated totality of production, distribution, exchange, and consumption (production is simultaneously the encompassing universal element, the structuring principle of this totality, *and* one of its particular elements); then in *Capital*, when he posits that, among the multiple species of Capital, the universal genus of Capital 'encounters itself' in finance capital, the immediate embodiment of Capital in general as opposed to particular capitals. What Hegel does with this concept is thus, in my view, strictly analogous to Laclau's notion of antagonistic relationship: the key feature in both cases is that the external difference (constitutive of genus itself) coincides with the internal difference (between the species of the genus). Another way of making the same point is Marx's well-known insistence – again in the Introduction to the *Grundrisse* – that:

> [i]n all forms of society there is one specific kind of production which predominates over the rest, whose relations thus assign rank and influence to the others. It is a general illumination which bathes all the other colours and modifies their particularity. It is a particular ether which determines the specific gravity of every being which has materialized within it.[5]

This overdetermination of universality by part of its content, this short circuit between the universal and particular, is the key feature of Hegelian 'concrete universality', and I am in total agreement with Butler who, it seems to me, also aims at this legacy of 'concrete universality' in her central notion of 'competing universalities': in her insistence on how each particular position, in order to articulate itself, involves the (implicit or explicit) assertion of *its own mode of universality*, she develops a point which I also try repeatedly to make in my own work.

Take the example of religions: it is not enough to say that the genus Religion is divided into a multitude of species ('primitive' animism, pagan polytheism, monotheism, which is then further divided into Judaism, Christianity, Islam ...); the point, rather, is that *each of these particular species involves its own universal notion of what religion is 'as such', as well as its own view on (how it differs from) other religions.* Christianity is not simply different from Judaism and Islam; within its horizon, the very difference that separates it from the other two 'religions of the Book' appears in a way which is unacceptable for the other two. In other words, when a Christian debates with a Muslim, they do not simply disagree – they disagree about their very disagreement: about what makes the difference between their religions. (And, as I have repeatedly tried to argue, *mutatis mutandis* the same goes for the political difference between Left and Right: they do not simply disagree – the very political opposition between Left and Right appears in a different view perceived from the Left or from the Right.) *This* is Hegel's 'concrete universality': since each particularity involves *its own* universality, its own notion of the Whole and its own part within it, there is no 'neutral' universality that would serve as the medium for these particular positions. Thus Hegelian 'dialectical development' is not a deployment of a particular content within universality but the process by which, in the passage from one particularity to another, *the very universality that encompasses both also changes*: 'concrete universality' designates precisely this 'inner life' of universality itself, this process of passage in the course of which the very universality that aims at encompassing it is caught in it, submitted to transformations.

Laclau: Class, Hegemony, and the Contaminated Universal

This brings me to Laclau: in my view, all his critical remarks are ultimately grounded in what I have called his secret Kantianism, in his rejection of the Hegelian legacy of 'concrete universality'. So let me begin with Laclau's counter-argument: the Kantian regulative Idea involves a determinate *positive content* which is given in advance, while the open struggle for hegemony involves no such content. . . . Apart from the fact that the Kantian regulative idea ultimately also designates a purely formal notion of the full realization of Reason, I am tempted to argue that the main 'Kantian' dimension of Laclau lies in his acceptance of the unbridgeable gap between the enthusiasm for the impossible Goal of a political engagement and its more modest realizable content. Laclau himself evokes the example of the collapse of Socialism in Eastern Europe: it was experienced by many of its participants as the moment of sublime enthusiasm, as the promise of global panacea, as an event that would realize freedom and social solidarity, while the results are much more modest – capitalist democracy, with all its impasses, not to mention the rise of nationalist aspirations. My claim is that if we accept such a gap as the *ultimate* horizon of political engagement, does it not leave us with a choice apropos of such an engagement: either we must blind ourselves to the necessary ultimate failure of our endeavour – regress to naivety, and let ourselves be caught up in the enthusiasm – or we must adopt a stance of cynical distance, participating in the game while being fully aware that the result will be disappointing?[6] Laclau's Kantianism emerges at its purest when he deals with the relation between emancipation and power. Answering the criticism that if power is inherent to the emancipatory project, does this not contradict the idea that full emancipation involves the elimination of power, he argues:

the contamination of emancipation by power is not an unavoidable empirical imperfection to which we have to accommodate, but involves a higher human ideal than a universality representing a totally reconciled human essence, because a fully reconciled society, a transparent society, would be entirely free in the sense of self-determination, but that full realization of freedom would be equivalent to the death of freedom, for all possibility of dissent would have been eliminated from it. Social division, antagonism and its necessary consequence − power − are the true conditions of a freedom which does not eliminate particularity. (Ernesto Laclau, in *Contingency, Hegemony, Universality* [hereafter EL], p. 208)

Laclau's reasoning is as follows: the ultimate goal of our political engagement, full emancipation, will never be achieved; emancipation will remain forever contaminated by power; this contamination, however, is not due only to the fact that our imperfect social reality does not allow for full emancipation − that is, we are not dealing only with the gap between ideal and imperfect reality. The very full realization of emancipated society would mean the death of freedom, the establishment of a closed transparent social space with no opening for a free subjective intervention − the limitation of human freedom is at the same time its positive condition. ...Now, my claim is that this reasoning reproduces almost verbatim Kant's argumentation, from the *Critique of Practical Reason*, about the necessary limitation of human cognitive capacities: God, in his infinite wisdom, limited our cognitive capacities in order to make us free responsible agents, since, if we were to have direct access to the noumenal sphere, we would no longer be free, but would turn into blind automata. Human imperfection is thus, for Kant, the positive condition of freedom.[7] The hidden implication here is the reverse of Kant's 'You can, because you must!', the paradoxical logic of 'You cannot, because you must not!' − You cannot achieve full emancipation, because you must not achieve it, that is, because this would mean the end of freedom! I find a similar deadlock in Laclau's answer to my criticism that he does not account for the historical status of his own theory of hegemony. Basically I endorse his critical remarks about Butler's assertion of absolute historicity and context-dependency: Butler avoids the question of the conditions of context-dependency and historicity − had she asked this question explicitly:

> she would have been confronted with two alternatives which, [...] would have been equally unpalatable to her: either she would have had to assert that historicity as such is a contingent historical construct − and therefore that there are societies which are not historical and, as a result, fully transcendentally determined...; or she would have had to provide some ontology of historicity as such, as a result of which the transcendental-structural dimension would have had to be reintroduced into her analysis. (EL, pp. 183–4)

I am tempted to claim that this same criticism applies to Laclau himself − here is his answer to my critique that he does not account for the status of his theory of hegemony itself (is it a theory of today's specific contingent historical constellation, so that in Marx's time 'class essentialism' was adequate, while today we need the full assertion of contingency, or is it a theory describing a transcendental a priori of historicity?):

> Only in contemporary societies is there a generalization of the hegemonic form of politics, but for this reason we can interrogate the past, and find there inchoate forms of the same

processes that are fully visible today; and, when they did not occur, understand why things were different. (EL, p. 200)

What I find problematic in this solution is that it implicitly endorses the pseudo-Hegelian evolutionary point of view that I critically evoked in my first intervention in this debate: although sociopolitical life and its structure were always-already the outcome of hegemonic struggles, it is none the less only today, in our specific historical constellation – in the 'postmodern' universe of globalized contingency – that the radically contingent-hegemonic nature of political processes is finally allowed to 'come/return to itself', to free itself of 'essentialist' baggage. ... In other words, the real question is: what is the exact status of this 'generalization of the hegemonic form of politics' in contemporary societies? Is it in itself a contingent event, the result of hegemonic struggle, or is it the result of some underlying historical logic which is *not* itself determined by the hegemonic form of politics? My answer here is that this 'generalization of the hegemonic form of politics' is itself dependent on a certain socioeconomic process: it is contemporary global capitalism with its dynamics of 'deterritorialization', which has created the conditions for the demise of 'essentialist' politics and the proliferation of new multiple political subjectivities. So, again, to make myself clear: my point is *not* that the economy (the logic of Capital) is a kind of 'essentialist anchor' that somehow 'limits' hegemonic struggle – on the contrary, it is its *positive condition*; it creates the very background against which 'generalized hegemony' can thrive.[8]

It is along these lines that I am also tempted to address the relationship between 'class struggle' and identity politics. Laclau makes two points here. First: 'class antagonism is not inherent to capitalist relations of production, but [that] it takes place between those relations and the identity of the worker outside them' (EL, p. 202); it emerges only when workers as individuals, not as the mere embodiment of economic categories, for cultural and other reasons, experience their situation as 'unjust', and resist. Furthermore, even if and when workers resist, their demands are not intrinsically anti-capitalist, but can also aim at partial reformist goals that can be satisfied within the capitalist system. As such, 'class struggle is just one species of identity politics, and one which is becoming less and less important in the world in which we live' (EL, p. 203) – the workers' position does not give them any a priori privilege in the anti-systemic struggle.[9]

On the first point, I not only endorse Laclau's anti-objectivist stance; I even think that when he opposes 'objective' relations of production and 'subjective' struggle and resistance, he makes too much of a concession to objectivism. There are no 'objective' relations of production which can *then* involve or not involve the resistance of the individuals caught up in them: the very absence of struggle and resistance – the fact that both sides involved in relations accept them without resistance – *is already the index of the victory of one side in the struggle*. One should not forget that in spite of some occasional 'objectivist' formulations, the reduction of individuals to embodied economic categories (terms of the relations of production) is for Marx not a simple fact, but the result of the process of 'reification', that is, an aspect of the ideological 'mystification' inherent to capitalism. As for Laclau's second point about class struggle being 'just one species of identity politics, one which is becoming less and less important in the world in which we live', one should counter it by the already-mentioned paradox of 'oppositional determination', of the *part* of the chain that sustains its *horizon* itself: class antagonism certainly appears as one in the series of social antagonisms, but it is simultaneously the specific antagonism which 'predominates over the rest, whose relations thus assign rank and influence to the others. It is a general illumination which bathes all the other colours and modifies their particularity'. My example here is, again, the very proliferation of new political subjectivities: this proliferation, which seems to relegate 'class struggle' to a secondary role is the *result* of the 'class struggle' in the context of today's global capitalism, of the advance of so-called 'post-industrial' society. In more general terms, my point of contention with Laclau here is that I do not accept that all elements which enter into hegemonic struggle are in principle equal: in the series of struggles (economic, political, feminist, ecological, ethnic, etc.) there is always *one* which, while it is part of the chain, secretly overdetermines its very horizon.[10] This contamination of the universal by the particular is 'stronger' than the struggle for hegemony (i.e. for which particular content will hegemonize the universality in question): it structures in advance *the very terrain* on which the multitude of particular contents fight for hegemony. Here I agree with Butler: the question is not just which particular content will hegemonize the empty place of universality – the question is, also and above all, which secret privileging and inclusions/exclusions had to occur for this empty place as such to emerge in the first place.

Soyons Réalistes, Demandons l'Impossible!

This brings me, finally, to the Big Question of capitalism itself. Here is Laclau's answer to my claim that the proponents of postmodern politics accept capitalism as 'the only game in town', and renounce any attempt to overcome the existing liberal-capitalist regime:

> The difficulty with assertions like this is that they mean absolutely nothing. ... Should we understand that [Žižek] wants to impose the dictatorship of the proletariat? Or does he want to socialize the means of production and abolish market mechanisms? And what is his political strategy to achieve these rather peculiar aims? ... Without at least the beginning of an answer to these questions, [Žižek's] anti-capitalism is mere empty talk. (EL, p. 206)

First, let me emphasize what these lines mean: they mean, in effect, that *today, one cannot even imagine a viable alternative to global capitalism* – the only option for the Left is 'the introduction of state regulation and democratic control of the economy so that the worst effects of globalization are avoided' (EL, p. 206), that is, palliative measures which, while resigning themselves to the course of events, restrict themselves to limiting the damaging effects of the inevitable. Even if this *is* the case, I think one should at least *take note* of the fact that the much-praised postmodern 'proliferation of new political subjectivities', the demise of every 'essentialist' fixation, the assertion of full contingency, occur against the background of a certain silent *renunciation* and *acceptance*: the renunciation of the idea of a global change in the fundamental relations in our society (who still seriously questions capitalism, state and political democracy?) and, consequently, the acceptance of the liberal democratic capitalist framework which *remains the same*, the unquestioned background, in all the dynamic proliferation of the multitude of new subjectivities. In short, Laclau's claim about my anti-capitalism also holds for what he calls the 'democratic control of the economy', and, more generally, for the entire project of 'radical democracy': either it means palliative damage-control measures within the global capitalist framework, or it means *absolutely nothing*.

I am fully aware of what one should call, without any irony, the great achievements of liberal capitalism: probably, never in human history have so many people enjoyed such a degree of freedom and material standard of living as in today's developed Western countries. However, far from accepting the New World Order as an inexorable process which allows only for moderate palliative measures, I continue to think, in the old Marxist vein, that today's capitalism, in its very triumph, is breeding new 'contradictions' which are potentially even more explosive than those of standard industrial capitalism. A series of 'irrationalities' immediately comes to mind: the result of the breathtaking growth of productivity in the last few decades is rising unemployment, with the long-term perspective that developed societies will need only 20 per cent of their workforce to reproduce themselves, with the remaining 80 per cent reduced to the status of a surplus from a purely economic point of view; the result of decolonization is that multinationals treat even their own country of origin as just another colony; the result of globalization and the rise of the 'global village' is the ghettoization of whole strata of the population; the result of the much-praised 'disappearance of the working class' is the emergence of millions of manual workers labouring in the Third World sweatshops, out of our delicate Western sight . . . The capitalist system is thus approaching its inherent limit and self-cancellation: for the majority of the population, the dream of the virtual 'frictionless capitalism' (Bill Gates) is turning into a nightmare in which the fate of millions is decided in hyper-reflexive speculation on futures.

From the very beginning, capitalist globalization – the emergence of capitalism as the world system – involved its exact opposite: the split, within particular ethnic groups, between those who are included in this globalization and those who are excluded. Today, this split is more radical than ever. On the one hand, we have the so-called 'symbolic class': not only managers and bankers, but also academics, journalists, lawyers, and so on – all those whose domain of work is the virtual symbolic universe. On the other, there are the excluded in all their variations (the permanently unemployed, the homeless, underprivileged ethnic and religious minorities, and so on). In between, there is the notorious 'middle class', passionately attached to the traditional modes of production and ideology (say, a qualified manual worker whose job is threatened), and attacking both extremes, big business and academics as well as the excluded, as 'unpatriotic', 'rootless' deviations. As is always the case with social antagonisms, today's class *antagonism* functions as the intricate interplay between these *three* agents, with shifting strategic alliances: the 'politically correct' symbolic classes defending the excluded against the 'fundamentalist' middle class, and so forth. The split between them is becoming even more radical than traditional class divisions – one is tempted to claim that it is reaching almost ontological proportions, with each group evolving its own 'world-view', its own relation to reality: the 'symbolic class' is individualistic, ecologically sensitive and simultaneously 'postmodern', aware that reality itself is a contingent symbolic formation; the 'middle class' sticks to traditional stable ethics and a belief in 'real life', with which symbolic classes are 'losing touch'; the excluded oscillate between hedonistic nihilism and radical (religious or ethnic) fundamentalism. . . .

Are we not dealing again with the Lacanian triad of Symbolic, Imaginary and Real? Are the excluded not 'real' in the sense of the kernel which resists social integration, and is the 'middle class' not 'imaginary', clinging to the fantasy of society as a harmonious Whole corrupted through moral decay? The main point of this improvised description is that globalization *undermines its own roots*: one can already perceive on the horizon the conflict with the very principle of formal democracy, since, at a certain point, the 'symbolic class' will no longer be able 'democratically' to contain the resistance of the majority.[11] Which way out of this predicament will this class then resort to? Nothing is to be excluded, even up to genetic manipulation to render those who do not fit into globalization more docile . . .

How, then, are we to answer today's predominant consensus according to which the age of ideologies – of grand ideological projects like Socialism or Liberalism – is over, since we have entered the post-ideological era of rational negotiation and decision-making, based upon the neutral insight into economic, ecological, etc. necessities? This consensus can assume different guises, from the neoconservative or Socialist refusal to accept it and consummate the loss of grand ideological projects by means of a proper 'work of mourning' (different attempts to resuscitate global ideological projects) up to the neoliberal opinion according to which the passage from the age of ideologies to the post-ideological era is part of the sad but none the less inexorable process of the maturation of humanity – just as a young man has to learn to accept the loss of grand enthusiastic adolescent plans and enter the everyday adult life of realistic compromises, the collective subject has to learn to accept the withering-away of global utopian ideological projects and the entry into the post-utopian realist era. . . .

The first thing to note about this neoliberal cliché is that the neutral reference to the necessities of the market economy, usually invoked in order to categorize grand ideological projects as unrealistic utopias, is itself to be inserted into the series of great modern utopian projects. That is to say – as Fredric Jameson has pointed out – what characterizes utopia is not a belief in the essential goodness of human nature, or some similar naive notion, but, rather, belief in some global *mechanism* which, applied to the whole of society, will automatically bring about the balanced state of progress and happiness one is longing for – and, in this precise sense, is not *the market* precisely the name for such a mechanism which, properly applied, will bring about the optimal state of society? So, again, the first answer of the Left to those – Leftists themselves – who bemoan the loss of the utopian impetus in our societies should be that this impetus is alive and well – not only in the Rightist 'fundamentalist' populism which advocates the return to grass-roots democracy, but above all among the advocates of the market economy themselves.[12] The second answer should be a clear line of distinction between utopia and ideology: ideology is not only a utopian project of social transformation with no realistic chance of actualization; no less ideological is the *anti-utopian* stance of those who 'realistically' devalue every global project of social transformation as 'utopian', that is, as unrealistic dreaming and/or harbouring 'totalitarian' potential – *today's predominant form of ideological 'closure' takes the precise form of mental block which prevents us from imagining a fundamental social change, in the interests of an allegedly 'realistic' and 'mature' attitude.*

In his Seminar on the *Ethics of Psychoanalysis*,[13] Lacan developed an opposition between 'knave' and 'fool' as the two intellectual attitudes: the right-wing intellectual is a knave, a conformist who considers the mere existence of the given order as an argument for it, and mocks the Left for its 'utopian' plans, which necessarily lead to catastrophe; while the left-wing intellectual is a fool, a court jester who publicly displays the lie of the existing order, but in a way which suspends the performative efficiency of his speech. In the years immediately after the fall of Socialism, the knave was a neoconservative advocate of the free market who cruelly rejected all forms of social solidarity as counterproductive sentimentalism; while the fool was a deconstructionist cultural critic who, by means of his ludic procedures destined to 'subvert' the existing order, actually served as its supplement.

Today, however, the relationship between the couple knave–fool and the political opposition Right/Left is more and more the inversion of the standard figures of Rightist knave and Leftist fool: are not the Third Way theoreticians ultimately today's *knaves*, figures who preach cynical resignation, that is, the necessary failure of every attempt actually to change something in the basic functioning of global capitalism? And are not the conservative *fools* – those conservatives whose original modern model is Pascal and who as it were show the hidden cards of the ruling ideology, bringing to light its underlying mechanisms which, in order to remain operative, have to be repressed – far more attractive? Today, in the face of this Leftist knavery, it is more important than ever to *hold this utopian place of the global alternative open*, even if it remains empty, living on borrowed time, awaiting the content to fill it in.

I fully agree with Laclau that after the exhaustion of both the social democratic welfare state imaginary and the 'really-existing-Socialist' imaginary, the Left does need a new imaginary (a new mobilizing global vision). Today, however, the outdatedness of the welfare state and socialist imaginaries is a cliché – the real dilemma is what to do with – how the Left is to relate to – the predominant *liberal democratic* imaginary. It is my contention that Laclau's and Mouffe's 'radical democracy' comes all too close to merely 'radicalizing' this liberal democratic imaginary, while remaining within its horizon. Laclau, of course, would probably claim that the point is to treat the democratic imaginary as an 'empty signifier', and to engage in the hegemonic battle with the proponents of the global capitalist New World Order over what its content will be. Here, however, I think that Butler is right when she emphasizes that another way is also open: it is *not* 'necessary to occupy the dominant norm in order to produce an internal subversion of its terms. Sometimes it is important to refuse its terms, to let the term itself wither, to starve it of its strength' (JB, p. 177). This means that the Left has a choice today: either it accepts the predominant liberal democratic horizon (democracy, human rights and freedoms . . .), and engages in a hegemonic battle *within it, or it risks the opposite gesture of refusing its very terms, of flatly rejecting today's liberal blackmail that courting any prospect of radical change paves the way for totalitarianism*. It is my firm conviction, my politico-existential premiss, that the old '68 motto *Soyons réalistes, demandons l'impossible!* still holds: it is the advocates of changes and resignifications within the liberal-democratic horizon who are the true utopians in their belief that their efforts will amount to anything more than the cosmetic surgery that will give us capitalism with a human face.

In her second intervention, Butler superbly deploys the reversal that characterizes the Hegelian dialectical process: the aggravated 'contradiction' in which the very differential structure of meaning is collapsing, since every determination immediately turns into its opposite, this 'mad dance', is resolved by the sudden emergence of a new universal determination. The best illustration is provided by the passage from the 'world of self-alienated Spirit' to the Terror of the French Revolution in *The Phenomenology of Spirit*: the pre-Revolutionary 'madness of the musician "who heaped up and mixed together thirty arias, Italian, French, tragic, comic, of every sort; now with a deep bass he descended into hell, then, contracting his throat, he rent the vaults of heaven with a falsetto tone, frantic and soothed, imperious and mocking, by turns" (Diderot, *Nephew of Rameau*)',[14] suddenly turns into its radical opposite: the revolutionary stance pursuing its goal with an inexorable firmness. And my point, of course, is that today's 'mad dance', the dynamic proliferation of multiple shifting identities, also awaits its resolution in a new form of Terror. The only 'realistic' prospect is to ground a new political universality by opting for the *impossible*, fully assuming the place of the exception, with no taboos, no a priori norms ('human rights', 'democracy'), respect for which would prevent us also from 'resignifying' terror, the ruthless exercise of power, the spirit of sacrifice . . . if this radical choice is decried by some bleeding-heart liberals as *Links-faschismus* [left-wing fascism], so be it!

NOTES

1 Here, of course, I draw on Joan Copjec's path-breaking 'The Euthanasia of Reason', in *Read My Desire*, Cambridge, MA: MIT Press 1995. It is symptomatic that this essay, *the* essay on the philosophical foundations and consequences of the Lacanian notion of sexual difference, is silently passed over in numerous feminist attacks on Lacan.

2 Here, again, we can see how the key to the Lacanian notion of the Real is the overlapping of internal and external difference elaborated exemplarily by Laclau: 'reality' is the external domain that is delineated by the symbolic order, while the Real is an obstacle inherent to the Symbolic, blocking its actualization from within. Butler's standard argument against the Real (that the very line of separation between the Symbolic and the Real is a symbolic gesture *par excellence*) leaves out of consideration this overlapping, which renders the Symbolic inherently inconsistent and fragile.

3 Furthermore, as I have already emphasized in my previous two interventions, Lacan *has* a precise answer to the question of 'which specific content has to be excluded so that the very *empty form* of sexual difference emerges as a battlefield for hegemony': this 'specific content' is what Lacan calls *das Ding*, the impossible–real Thing, or, more specifically, in his *Seminar XI*, 'lamella', that is, libido itself as the undead object, the 'immortal life, or irrepressible life' that 'is subtracted from the living being by virtue of the fact that it is subject to the cycle of sexed reproduction' (Jacques Lacan, *The Four Fundamental Concepts of Psycho-Analysis*, New York: Norton 1977, p. 198).

4 The price Butler pays for this rejection of conceptual distinctions is that she over-simplifies a series of key psychoanalytic insights. For example, her claim that: '[a]lthough it might be inevitable that individuation requires a foreclosure that produces the unconscious, the remainder, it seems equally inevitable that the unconscious is not pre-social, but a certain mode in which the unspeakably social endures' blurs the distinction between the *foreclosure* that generates the traumatic Real and the straight *repression* of some content into the unconscious. What is foreclosed does not persist in the unconscious: the unconscious is the censored part of the subject's discourse; it is a signifying chain that insists on the 'Other Scene' and disturbs the flow of the subject's speech, while the foreclosed Real is an extimate kernel within the unconscious itself.

5 Karl Marx, *Grundrisse*, Harmondsworth: Penguin 1972, p. 107.

6 One should add here that, in historical experience, we often find the opposite gap: an agent introduced a modest measure that aimed merely at solving some particular problem, but then this measure triggered

a process of disintegration of the entire social edifice (like Gorbachev's *perestroika*, the aim of which was simply to make Socialism more efficient).

7   In the *Critique of Practical Reason*, Kant endeavoured to answer the question of what would happen to us if we were to gain access to the noumenal domain, to Things in themselves:

> instead of the conflict which now the moral disposition has to wage with inclinations and in which, after some defeats, moral strength of mind may be gradually won, God and eternity in their awful majesty would stand unceasingly before our eyes. . . . Thus most actions conforming to the law would be done from fear, few would be done from hope, none from duty. The moral worth of actions, on which alone the worth of the person and even of the world depends in the eyes of supreme wisdom, would not exist at all. The conduct of man, so long as his nature remained as it is now, would be changed into mere mechanism, where, as in a puppet show, everything would gesticulate well but no life would be found in the figures. (Immanuel Kant, *Critique of Practical Reason*, New York: Macmillan 1956, pp. 152–3)

So, for Kant, direct access to the noumenal domain would deprive us of the very 'spontaneity' which forms the kernel of transcendental freedom: it would turn us into lifeless automata, or – to put it in today's terms – into 'thinking machines'.

8   To avoid misunderstanding: I am fully aware of the autonomous logic of ideological struggle. According to Richard Dawkins, 'God's utility function' in living nature is the reproduction of genes; that is to say, genes (DNA) are not a means for the reproduction of living beings, but the other way round: living beings are the means for the self-reproduction of genes. The same question should be asked apropos of ideology: what is the 'utility function' of the Ideological State Apparatuses? The materialist answer is: neither the reproduction of ideology *qua* network of ideas, emotions, etc., nor the reproduction of social circumstances legitimized by this ideology, but *the self-reproduction of the ISA itself*. The 'same' ideology can accommodate to different social modes; it can change the content of its ideas, etc., just to 'survive' as an ISA. What I am claiming is that today's capitalism is a kind of global machine that enables a multitude of ideologies, from traditional religions to individualistic hedonism, to 'resignify' their logic so that they fit its frame – even the teachers of Zen Buddhism like to emphasize how the inner peace that comes with the achievement of *satori* enables you to function more efficiently in the market. . . .

9   Incidentally, my main criticism of identity politics is not its 'particularism' *per se* but, rather, its partisans' ubiquitous insistence that one's particular position of enunciation legitimizes or even guarantees the authenticity of one's speech: only gays can speak about homosexuality; only drug addicts about the drug experience, only women about feminism. . . . Here one should follow Deleuze, who wrote: 'one's own privileged experiences are bad and reactionary arguments' (*Negotiations*, New York: Columbia University Press 1995, p. 11): although it may play a limited progressive role in enabling the victims to assert their subjectivity against the patronizingly sympathetic liberal discourse *about* them, such 'authentication' by one's direct experience ultimately undermines the very foundations of emancipatory politics.

10 An example from cinema, again: the ultimate 'trauma' of *Paris Is Burning* – the film about a group of poor, black Americans who, as part of a parodic show, cross-dress as upper-class white ladies and mockingly imitate their rituals – is neither race nor gender identity, but *class*. The point of the film is that, in the three divides subverted by it (class, race and gender), the class divide, albeit the least 'natural' (i.e. the most 'artificial', contingent, socially conditioned, in contrast to the apparent 'biological' foundation of gender and race), is the most difficult to cross: the only way for the group to cross the class barrier, even in the parodic performance, is to subvert their gender and race identity. . . . (For this point I am indebted to Elisabeth Bronfen, Zurich University.)

11 As the model of an analysis of capitalism close to what I have in mind, see Michael Hardt and Antonio Negri's *Empire* (Cambridge, MA: Harvard University Press 2000), a book which tries to rewrite *The Communist Manifesto* for the twenty-first century. Hardt and Negri describe globalization as an ambiguous 'deterritorialization': triumphant global capitalism has penetrated all pores of social life, down to the most intimate spheres, introducing an unheard-off dynamics which no longer relies on patriarchal and other fixed hierarchical forms of domination, but generates fluid hybrid identities. However, this very dissolution of all substantial social links also lets the genie out of the bottle: it sets

free the centrifugal potentials that the capitalist system will no longer be able fully to contain. On account of its very global triumph, the capitalist system is thus more vulnerable than ever today – Marx's old formula still holds: capitalism generates its own gravediggers.

12 The paradox of the US administration's legal action against the monopoly of Microsoft is very pertinent here: does this action not demonstrate how, far from being simply opposed, state regulation and the market are mutually dependent? Left to itself, the market mechanism would lead to the full monopoly of Microsoft, and thus to the self-destruction of competition – it is only through direct state intervention (which, from time to time, orders overlarge companies to break up) that 'free' market competition can be maintained.

13 See Jacques Lacan, *The Ethics of Psychoanalysis*, London: Routledge 1992, pp. 182–3.

14 G. W. F. Hegel, *Phenomenology of Spirit*, Oxford: Oxford University Press 1977, p. 317.

Index

350 INDEX